Microsoft®
VISUAL BASIC® 2015

for Windows®, Web, Windows® Store, and Database Applications: Comprehensive

W9-AKV-593

Microsoft® VISUAL BASIC® 2015

for Windows®, Web, Windows® Store, and Database Applications: Comprehensive

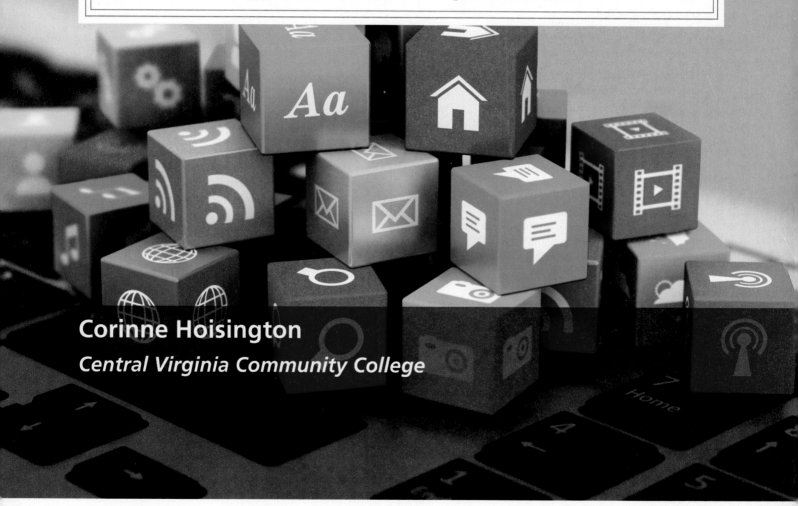

Corinne Hoisington

Central Virginia Community College

CENGAGE
Learning®

Australia • Brazil • Mexico • Singapore • United Kingdom • United States

Windows®, Web, Windows® Store, and Database Applications: Comprehensive
Corinne Hoisington

Product Director: Kathleen McMahon

Senior Product Manager: Jim Gish

Content Developer: Megan Chrisman

Senior Marketing Manager: Eric La Scola

Senior Content Project Manager:
  Matthew Hutchinson

Art Director: Heather Marshall, Lumina
  Datamatics, Inc.

Manufacturing Planner: Julio Esperas

Development Editor: Lisa Ruffolo

QA Manuscript Reviewer: Danielle Shaw

IP Analyst: Amber Hosea

Senior IP Project Manager: Kathryn Kucharek

Production Service: Lumina Datamatics, Inc.

Text Designer: Joel Sadagursky

Cover Designer: Lisa Kuhn, Curio Press, LLC

Cover Image: © Oleksiy Mark/shutterstock.com

Unless otherwise stated, all screenshots courtesy of Microsoft Corporation. Microsoft and the Office logo are either registered trademarks or trademarks of Microsoft Corporation in the United States and/or other countries. Cengage Learning is an independent entity from the Microsoft Corporation, and not affiliated with Microsoft in any manner.

> For product information and technology assistance, contact us at
> **Cengage Learning Customer & Sales Support, 1-800-354-9706**
>
> For permission to use material from this text or product,
> submit all requests online at **www.cengage.com/permissions.**
> Further permissions questions can be emailed to
> **permissionrequest@cengage.com.**

Library of Congress Control Number: 2015941674

Student Edition:

ISBN: 978-1-285-85689-6

Cengage Learning
20 Channel Center Street
Boston, MA 02210
USA

Cengage Learning is a leading provider of customized learning solutions with employees residing in nearly 40 different countries and sales in more than 125 countries around the world. Find your local representative at **www.cengage.com.**

Cengage Learning products are represented in Canada by Nelson Education, Ltd.

To learn more about Cengage Learning Solutions, visit **www.cengage.com.**

Purchase any of our products at your local college store or at our preferred online store **www.cengagebrain.com.**

Printed in the United States of America
Print Number: 01 Print Year: 2015

CONTENTS

CHAPTER 12 (ONLINE CHAPTER)
Windows Store Apps

This chapter describes Windows Store apps you can create for Windows 8.1 and Windows 10 devices using Visual Basic 2015. Because Windows 10 had not been released at the time of publication, this chapter is available free of charge online with the other resources for the book at CengageBrain.com.

PREFACE

The Shelly Cashman Series® offers the finest textbooks in computer education. This *Microsoft Visual Basic 2015* book utilizes an innovative step-by-step pedagogy, which integrates demonstrations of professional-quality programs with in-depth discussions of programming concepts and techniques and opportunities for hands-on practice and reinforcement. The new volume retains popular features and pedagogy from past editions, while emphasizing the changing development process in an increasingly mobile-oriented world. The popular Guided Program Development section supports students as they work independently to create useful, realistic, and appealing applications, building their confidence and skills while guiding them to select appropriate Visual Basic 2015 programming methods. Online Reinforcement boxes direct students to online videos that show how to perform a series of steps. Other marginal elements, such as In the Real World boxes, provide expert tips to add interest and depth to topics. A robust and varied collection of exercises, including a series of practical case-based programming projects, ensures students gain the knowledge and expertise they need to succeed when developing professional programs.

Visual Basic 2015 builds on the features of Visual Basic 2012, which emphasized coding once and deploying on multiple devices. Some of the major enhancements to Visual Basic 2015 include enhanced code editing, testing Web applications across cross browser platforms and smartphones, an improved interface that makes it easier to access frequently used files, and more efficient build management. Using Visual Basic 2015, you can design, create, and deploy Windows, Mobile, Web, Database, and Windows Store applications. Visual Studio 2015 includes several productivity enhancements such as debugging tools, mobile templates for both smartphones and tablet design, more powerful searching tools, Windows Store sample applications, and more.

Objectives of This Textbook

Microsoft Visual Basic 2015 for Windows, Web, Windows Store, and Database Applications: Comprehensive is intended for a year-long course that introduces students to the correct ways to design and write programs using Visual Basic 2015. The goal of this text is to provide a rigorous and comprehensive course in computer programming for students with little or no previous programming experience. The objectives of this book are as follows:

- To teach the fundamentals of the Microsoft Visual Basic 2015 programming language
- To understand and apply graphical user interface design principles
- To emphasize the development cycle when creating applications, which mirrors the same approach that professional developers use
- To illustrate well-written and readable programs using a disciplined coding style, including documentation and indentation standards

- To create Visual Basic applications that are deployed on multiple platforms such as mobile computers (smartphones and tablets), webpages, and Windows Store environments
- To demonstrate how to implement logic involving sequence, selection, and repetition using Visual Basic 2015
- To encourage the use of critical thinking skills in the application development process
- To write useful, well-designed programs for personal computers and mobile computers that solve practical business problems
- To create appealing, interactive Web applications that can be delivered and executed on the Internet on any device from scratch or using built-in templates
- To organize complex programs by using procedures and to anticipate and prevent errors by managing exceptions
- To produce sophisticated, professional programs by using arrays and files that handle data and to make programs more robust by defining classes and using the power of inheritance
- To encourage independent study and help those who are working on their own in a distance education environment

The Shelly Cashman Approach

Features of this *Microsoft Visual Basic 2015* book include the following:
- **Realistic, Up-to-Date Applications** Each programming chapter focuses on building a sample project, a complete, useful application that showcases Visual Basic 2015 features and the latest technology.
- **Guided Steps to Encourage Independence** After observing how a professional developer would build the chapter project and exploring related programming concepts and Visual Basic 2015 techniques, students create the sample application on their own in the Guided Program Development section. This step-by-step section provides enough guidance for students to work independently, with Hint Screens that verify students are performing the tasks correctly.
- **More Than Step-by-Step** Each chapter offers clear, thorough discussions of the programming concepts students need to understand to build the sample application. Important Visual Basic 2015 design and programming features are also highlighted, including time-saving techniques such as using IntelliSense, code snippets, and the Toolbox. As appropriate, students design and prepare for applications the way professional developers do — by creating or analyzing requirements documents, use case definitions, and event-planning documents.
- **Online Reinforcement Boxes** The Online Reinforcement boxes send students to the Student Companion site at CengageBrain.com to watch videos illustrating each step in the chapter project. Students can refer to the Online Reinforcement boxes when they work through or review the chapter, watching videos as they prepare to create the chapter application on their own.

- **Heads Up Boxes** Heads Up boxes appear in the margin to give advice for following best programming practices and tips about alternative ways of completing the same task.
- **In the Real World Boxes** This marginal feature provides insight into how developers use Visual Basic tools or programming techniques to save time or enhance professional development projects.
- **Watch Out For Boxes** These boxes explain how to avoid common pitfalls when using a particular command, programming structure, or technique.
- **Consider This Boxes** This element encourages independent problem solving by posing thought-provoking questions and providing answers related to programming and Visual Basic.
- **Critical Thinking Boxes** Critical thinking is an essential part of the programming process; developers need to be able to reason strategically and justify their decisions to craft an effective program. New to this edition, the Critical Thinking boxes encourage students to further explore the ideas in the chapters.

> **HEADS UP**
>
> Visual Basic 2015 can run on Windows 7, Windows 8, or Windows 10. In this book, the default operating system is Windows 8 with a screen resolution of 1366 × 768, but Windows applications such as the programs in these chapters work in all operating systems. Windows Store apps can only be written and executed using Windows 8 or 10.

Organization of This Textbook

Microsoft Visual Basic 2015 for Windows, Web, Windows Store, and Database Applications: Comprehensive provides detailed instructions on how to use Visual Basic 2015 to build authentic, effective, and appealing applications for Microsoft Windows personal computers and mobile devices. The material is divided into 11 chapters with an additional online chapter for Windows Store app development and three appendices as follows:

Chapter 1 — Introduction to Visual Basic 2015 Programming
Chapter 1 provides an overview of programming with Visual Basic 2015. The chapter defines a computer program, describes the role of a developer in creating computer programs, and discusses event-driven programs that have a graphical user interface (GUI). The chapter also explains the roles of input, processing, output, and data when running a program on a computer; examines the basic arithmetic and logical operations a program can perform; and explores the use of databases and computer programming languages in general. Finally, the chapter introduces Visual Studio 2015 and the .NET 5 Framework, including the .NET class libraries and related features, and surveys the types of Visual Basic 2015 applications.

Chapter 2 — Program and Graphical User Interface Design
Chapter 2 introduces students to the major elements of the Visual Studio 2015 integrated development environment (IDE) while designing a graphical user interface mock-up. Topics include opening Visual Studio 2015, creating a Windows Forms Application project, adding objects to a Windows form, assigning properties to objects, aligning objects on the Windows form, and saving Visual Basic projects. The chapter also discusses how to apply GUI design principles and examines the first two phases of the program development life cycle (PDLC).

Chapter 3 — Program Design and Coding Chapter 3 provides students with the skills and knowledge necessary to complete phases 2, 3, and 4 of the PDLC by enhancing a GUI mock-up, designing program processing objects, and coding a program. Topics include using IntelliSense when writing code and enhancing a Visual Basic 2015 form by changing the BackColor property of an object and displaying images. This chapter also explains how to enter Visual Basic 2015 code, correct errors, and run a completed program. Finally, the chapter discusses the value of creating an event-planning document.

Chapter 4 — Variables and Arithmetic Operations Chapter 4 introduces variables and arithmetic operations used in the coding of a Visual Basic application. The chapter provides in-depth coverage of declaring variables, gathering input for an application, differentiating data types, performing mathematical calculations, and understanding the proper scope of variables. The chapter also shows how to use various types of TextBox objects.

Chapter 5 — Decision Structures Chapter 5 explains how to create a Visual Basic 2015 Windows application that uses decision structures to take different actions depending on the user's input. Topics include using If...Then statements, If...Then... Else statements, nested If statements, logical operators, and Case statements. The chapter also explores how to use the GroupBox object, place RadioButton objects, display a message box, insert code snippets, and test input to ensure it is valid.

Chapter 6 — Loop Structures Chapter 6 presents another type of fundamental programming structure — the repetition structure, including Do While, Do Until, For...Next, For Each...Next, and While...End While loops. Topics include repeating a process using the For...Next and Do loops; priming a loop; creating a nested loop; selecting the best type of loop; avoiding infinite loops; validating data; and understanding compound operators, counters, and accumulators. The chapter also shows how to insert a MenuStrip object, use the InputBox function, display data using the ListBox object, debug programs using DataTips at breakpoints, and publish a finished application using ClickOnce technology.

Chapter 7 — Using Procedures and Exception Handling Chapter 7 focuses on using procedures to organize complex programs and handling exceptions to prevent errors. The chapter begins by demonstrating how to create a splash screen that is displayed as a program loads. It then explores how to organize long, complex programs into procedures, including Sub and Function procedures, and shows how to pass an argument to a procedure by value and by reference, how to code a Function procedure to return a value, and how to create a class-level variable. The chapter concludes by discussing exception handling and using Try-Catch blocks to detect errors and take corrective actions.

Chapter 8 — Using Arrays and File Handling Chapter 8 explains how to develop applications that maintain data for later processing, including sorting, calculating, and displaying the data. The chapter project demonstrates an application that reads data from a file, displays the data in a ComboBox object, and then uses the data in calculations. This chapter also shows how to create a Windows application that uses more than one form.

Chapter 9 — Creating Web Applications Chapter 9 explains how to create a Web application by building an interactive web form, a page displayed in a browser that requests data from users. The chapter examines ASP.NET 5 technology and explores tools that help to create appealing, useful Web applications, including web form properties, CheckBox, DropDownList, and Calendar objects and custom tables. The chapter also explains how to validate data on web forms and format text using the HTML <br> tag and the string manipulation properties and procedures in the Visual Basic String class.

Chapter 10 — Incorporating Databases with ADO.NET Chapter 10 examines databases and explores the ADO.NET 5 technology. The chapter discusses how to take advantage of the data access technology of ADO.NET 5 to connect to databases and update, add, and delete data and retrieve database information for viewing and decision making. The chapter project demonstrates how to create a professional application that connects to a Microsoft Access database, temporarily stores data from the database, and lets users add, select, and delete records.

Chapter 11 — Multiple Classes and Inheritance Chapter 11 explores the advanced topics of defining classes, using inheritance, and designing a three-tier structure for a program. The chapter begins by introducing the three-tier program structure and thoroughly defining classes and the object-oriented programming concepts related to classes. The chapter project shows how to create a class, instantiate an object, write a class constructor, call a procedure in a separate class, and use inheritance to code a base class and a subclass. Other topics include calling procedures in a base and subclass, writing overridable and overrides procedures, and creating and writing a comma-delimited text file.

Chapter 12 (online) — Windows Store Apps Chapter 12 explains how to design a touch-first app as required for the Windows Store, the online marketplace for programs created for Windows 8 and 10. The chapter outlines the Windows Store application life cycle and explains how to obtain a free Windows developer license. After demonstrating how to create a Windows Store app that includes a customized splash screen (required for the Windows Store), appealing images, and a TextBlock object, the chapter guides readers through running the app in a simulator and then packaging, certifying, and publishing the app. This chapter has been posted online at CengageBrain.com to provide students with the latest updates for Windows 10.

Appendices This book concludes with three appendices. Appendix A explains the purpose of Unicode and provides a table listing Unicode characters and their equivalents. Appendix B examines the My namespace element of Visual Basic 2015 in detail. Appendix C lists the common data types used in Visual Basic 2015, including the recommended naming convention for the three-character prefix preceding variable names.

End-of-Chapter Activities

A notable strength of this Microsoft Visual Basic 2015 book is the extensive student activities at the end of each chapter. Well-structured student activities can make the difference between students merely participating in a class and retaining the information they learn. These end-of-chapter activities include the following:

- **Learn Online** The Learn Online section directs students to reinforcement activities and resources to augment concepts, key terms, techniques, and other material in the chapter.
- **Knowledge Check** The Knowledge Check section includes short exercises and review questions that reinforce concepts and provide opportunities to practice skills.
- **Debugging Exercises** In these exercises, students examine short code samples to identify errors and solve programming problems.
- **Program Analysis** The Program Analysis exercises let students apply their knowledge of Visual Basic 2015 and programming techniques. In some exercises, students write programming statements that meet a practical goal or solve a problem. In other exercises, students analyze code samples and identify the output.
- **Case Programming Assignments** Nine programming assignments for each chapter challenge students to create applications using the skills learned in the chapter. Each assignment presents a realistic business scenario and requires students to create programs of varying difficulty.
  - ● Easiest: The first three assignments provide most of the program design information, such as a requirements document and use case definition, for a business application. Students design an application, create an event-planning document, and write the code for the application.
  - ●● Intermediate: The next three assignments provide some of the program design information, such as a requirements document. Students create other design documents, such as a use case definition and event-planning document and then build the user interface and code the application.
  - ●●● Challenging: The final three assignments provide only a description of a business problem, and students create all the design documents, design the user interface, and code the application.

To the Instructor

Each chapter in this book focuses on a realistic, appealing Visual Basic 2015 application. A chapter begins with a completed application, which you can run to demonstrate how it works, the tasks it performs, and the problems it solves. The chapter introduction also identifies the application's users and their requirements, such as running the program on a mobile computer or validating input data.

The steps in the next section of a chapter show how to create the user interface for the application. You can perform these steps in class — each step clearly explains an action, describes the results, and includes a figure showing the results, with callouts directing your attention to key elements on the screen. Some marginal features, such as the Heads Up boxes, provide additional tips for completing the steps. The Online Reinforcement boxes direct students to videos that replay the steps, which is especially helpful for review and for distance learning students.

This section also explains the Visual Basic 2015 tools and properties needed to understand and create the user interface. For example, while placing a text box in an application, the chapter describes the purpose of a text box and why you should set its maximum and minimum size. You can discuss these ideas and strategies and then continue your demonstration to show students how to apply them to the chapter application.

After completing the user interface, the chapter explores the programming concepts students should understand to create the application, such as proper syntax, variables, data types, conditional statements, and loops. This section uses the same types of steps, figures, and marginal features to demonstrate how to enter code to complete and test the application.

To prepare students for building the application on their own, the chapter next considers the program design and logic by examining planning documents:

- *Requirements document* — The requirements document identifies the purpose, procedures, and calculations of the program and specifies details such as the application title, restrictions, and comments that help to explain the program.
- *Use case definition* — The use case definition describes what the user does and how the program responds to each action.
- *Event-planning document* — The event-planning document lists each object in the user interface that causes an event, the action the user takes to trigger the event, and the event processing that must occur.

You can discuss these documents in class and encourage students to review them as they create a program, reinforcing how professional developers create applications in the modern workplace.

In the innovative Guided Program Development section, students work on their own to create the chapter application. They complete the tasks within each numbered step, referring to Hint Screens when they need a reminder about how to perform a step or which method to use. Many tasks reference figures are shown earlier in the chapter. Students can refer to these figures for further help — they show exactly how to use a particular technique for completing a task. Steps end with a results figure, which illustrates how the application should look if students performed the tasks correctly. To reinforce how students learned the chapter material, the Guided Program Development section also focuses first on designing the user interface and then on coding the application. A complete program listing appears at the end of this section, which students can use to check their work.

At the end of each chapter, you'll find plenty of activities that provide review, practice, and challenge for your students, including a summary table that lists skills and corresponding figures and videos, descriptions of online learning opportunities, and exercises ranging from short, focused review questions to assignments requiring complete programs and related planning documents. You can assign the Knowledge

Check, Debugging Exercises, and Program Analysis activities as necessary to reinforce and assess learning. Depending on the expertise of your class, you can assign the Case Programming assignments as independent projects, selecting one from each level of difficulty (easiest, intermediate, and challenging) or concentrating on the level that is most appropriate for your class.

INSTRUCTOR RESOURCES

The following resources are available through www.cengage.com to instructors who have adopted this book. Search for this title by ISBN, title, author, or keyword. From the Product Overview page, select the Instructor's Companion Site to access your complementary resources.

- **Instructor's Manual** The Instructor's Manual consists of Microsoft Word files, which include chapter objectives, lecture notes, teaching tips, classroom activities, lab activities, quick quizzes, figures and boxed elements summarized in the chapters, and a glossary page.

- **Syllabus** Sample syllabi, which can be customized easily to a course, cover policies, assignments, exams, and procedural information.

- **Figure Files** Illustrations for every figure in the textbook are available in electronic form. Figures are provided both with and without callouts.

- **PowerPoint Presentation** PowerPoint is a multimedia lecture presentation system that provides slides for each chapter. Presentations are based on chapter objectives. Use this presentation system to present well-organized lectures that are both interesting and knowledge based. PowerPoint presentations provide consistent coverage at schools that use multiple lecturers.

- **Solutions to Exercises** Solutions are included for all end-of-chapter and chapter reinforcement exercises.

- **Test Bank and Test Engine** Test Banks include a wide range of questions for every chapter, featuring objective-based and critical-thinking question types, and include page number references and figure references, when appropriate. The test engine, Cognero, is a flexible, online system that allows you to author, edit, and manage test bank content from multiple Cengage Learning solutions; create multiple test versions in an instant; and deliver tests from your LMS, your classroom, or wherever you want.

- **Printed Test Bank** A printable Rich Text File (.rtf) version of the test bank is also included.

- **Data Files for Students** Includes all the files that are required by students to complete the exercises.

- **Additional Activities for Students** These additional activities consist of Chapter Reinforcement Exercises, which are true/false, multiple-choice, and short answer questions that help students gain confidence in the material learned.

To the Student

Getting the Most Out of Your Book

Welcome to *Microsoft Visual Basic 2015 for Windows, Web, Windows Store, and Database Applications: Comprehensive*. To save yourself time and gain a better understanding of the elements in this text, spend a few minutes reviewing the descriptions and figures in this section.

Introduction and Initial Chapter Figures Each chapter presents a programming project and shows the solution in the first figure of the chapter. The introduction and initial chapter figure let you see firsthand how your finished product will look and illustrate your programming goals.

Eric Audras/Getty Images

Guided Program Development After reading through the chapter and observing how to create the chapter application, the Guided Program Development section takes you through building the chapter project step by step. As you perform each task, you can refer to Hint Screens that remind you how to complete a step or use a particular technique. If you need further help, some steps include references to figures shown earlier in the chapter — you can revisit these figures to review exactly how to perform a task. Each step ends with a results figure, so you can make sure your application is on the right track. A complete program listing also appears at the end of the Guided Program Development section, which you can use to check your work.

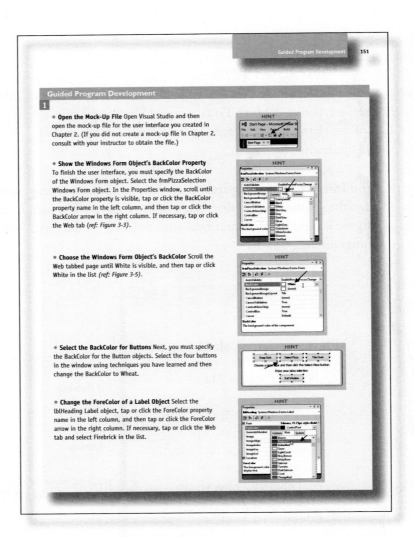

Visual Basic 2015 Online Reinforcement Videos The first of their kind, the Shelly Cashman Companion Site provides video reenactments of every new Visual Basic process that is introduced in each chapter. These animated tutorials provide a web-based visual instruction on how to complete a Visual Basic task. You can watch these videos to learn how to perform the steps shown in the book or to review the steps and techniques.

To access the Online Reinforcement videos, you need only a computer with an Internet connection. Use your web browser to visit *cengagebrain.com*, navigate to the resources for this title, tap or click the "Videos" link, and then follow the directions onscreen to play a video.

Marginal Boxes Marginal elements include Heads Up boxes, which offer tips and programming advice, In the Real World boxes, which indicate how professional developers use Visual Basic 2015 tools, Watch Out For boxes, which identify common errors and explain how to avoid them, and Critical Thinking boxes, which help you go beyond the reading to think critically about the development process.

HEADS UP

Unlike some programming languages, the capitalization of object names, properties, property values, and other values is not important in Visual Basic. Therefore, the object name picDeepDish is equivalent to the object name picdeepdish. Capitalization is used within the object name to make the name easier to read.

IN THE REAL WORLD

Some developers use the AutoSize property for a Button object to ensure that the button always is large enough for the text. By setting the AutoSize property for a Button object to True in the Properties window, the Button object will expand or contract when you change the text so it fits precisely in the button.

WATCH OUT FOR

When you tap or click an object to select it, you might double-tap or double-click it accidentally. If you do, a tabbed page with programming code opens. To return to the form and continue developing the user interface, tap or click the [Design] tab for your form, such as the frmPizzaSelection.vb [Design] tab.

CRITICAL THINKING

When a program displays an error and a line number, is it possible that the error is on another line?
Yes. When an error is detected, review the line of code before the statement in error.

Learn Online Reinforcing what you're learning is a snap with the Chapter Reinforcement exercises. Visit cengagebrain.com to access these exercises.

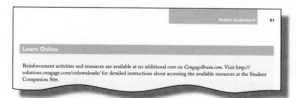

Knowledge Check To verify you've learned the essential information in the chapter, you can work through the Knowledge Check exercises. Use these short exercises to test your knowledge of concepts and tools and to prepare for longer programming assignments.

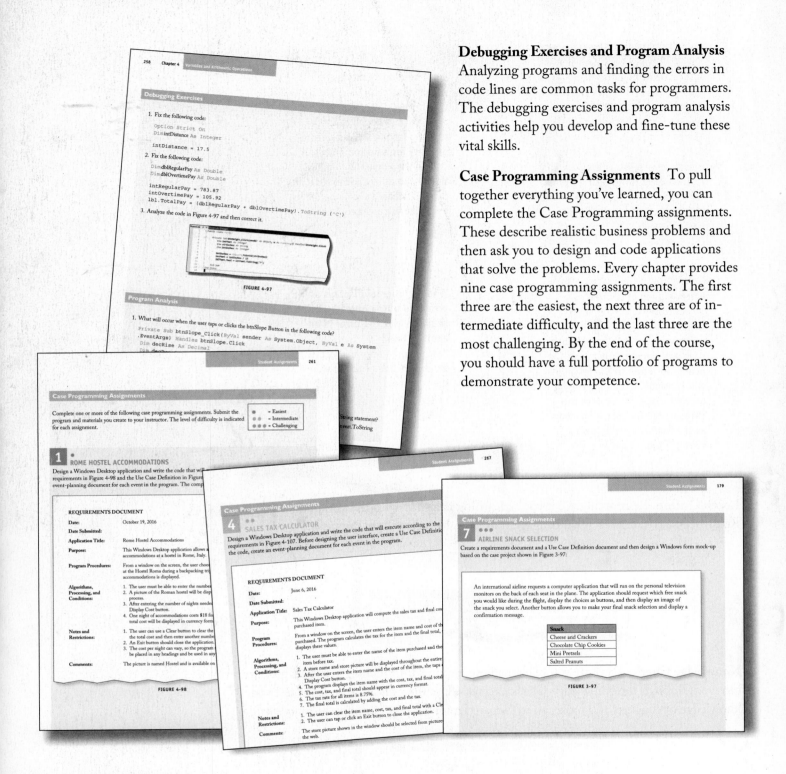

Debugging Exercises and Program Analysis
Analyzing programs and finding the errors in code lines are common tasks for programmers. The debugging exercises and program analysis activities help you develop and fine-tune these vital skills.

Case Programming Assignments To pull together everything you've learned, you can complete the Case Programming assignments. These describe realistic business problems and then ask you to design and code applications that solve the problems. Every chapter provides nine case programming assignments. The first three are the easiest, the next three are of intermediate difficulty, and the last three are the most challenging. By the end of the course, you should have a full portfolio of programs to demonstrate your competence.

Acknowledgments

To Tim, my husband, for sharing this wonderful world filled with snowflakes falling in Latvia. To Liam and Lochlan, my grandsons, without whose loving attention this book would have been finished in half the time. To my six children Timothy, Brittany, Ryan, Daniel, Bre, and Eric, who are no longer children but my dear friends. To Lisa Ruffolo, my editor, for being the motivating master of her detailed craft. And lastly, to Thomas Cashman, in memory of his kindness and wisdom that changed the technology world today.

—Corinne Hoisington

CHAPTER 1

Introduction to Visual Basic 2015 Programming

OBJECTIVES

You will have mastered the material in this chapter when you can:

- Understand software and computer programs

- State the role of a developer in creating computer programs

- Specify the use of a graphical user interface and describe an event-driven program

- Specify the roles of input, processing, output, and data when running a program on a computer

- Describe the arithmetic operations a computer program can perform

- Explain the logical operations a computer program can perform

- Define and describe the use of a database

- Identify the use of a computer programming language in general and Visual Basic 2015 in particular

- Explain the use of Visual Studio 2015 when developing Visual Basic 2015 programs

- Specify the programming languages available for use with Visual Studio 2015

- Explain .NET Framework 4.6

- Explain RAD

- Describe classes, objects, and the .NET Framework class libraries

- Explain ADO.NET, ASP.NET, MSIL, and CLR

- Specify the types of Visual Basic 2015 applications

Introduction

A computer is an electronic device that completes tasks under the direction of a sequence of instructions to produce useful results for people. Computers include desktop models, laptops, tablets, and smartphones. The set of instructions that directs a computer to perform tasks is called **computer software**, or a **computer program**. A computer program on a mobile device or on a Windows 8 or Windows 10 computer is also called an **app**.

When controlled by programs, computers and mobile devices can accomplish a wide variety of activities. For example, computers can interpret and display a webpage, compute and write payroll checks for millions of employees, display video and play audio from the web, post to a social network on a smartphone, and run a game for users to play (Figure 1-1).

FIGURE 1-1

Internal hard drive
(storage)

On-screen keyboard
(input device)

Monitor
(output device)

System unit
(processing)

Mobile devices

Keyboard
(input device)

Mouse
(input device)

Speakers
(output device)

RAM
(storage)

Printer
(output device)

Scanner
(input device)

Digital camera
(input device)

FIGURE 1-2

Two vital components of a computer must interact with each other for any activity to be performed. These components are computer hardware and computer software. **Computer hardware** is the physical equipment associated with a computer. It includes the keyboard (traditional or on-screen), mouse, touch screen or monitor, central processing unit (CPU), random access memory (RAM), and hard disk (Figure 1-2). A **mobile device** is portable computer hardware such as a smartphone, tablet computer, or wearable device such as a smart watch or glasses.

A computer program, or app, is a set of electronic instructions that directs the hardware to perform tasks such as displaying a character on the screen when a key is pressed on the keyboard, adding an employee's regular pay and overtime pay to calculate the employee's total pay, or displaying a picture from an attached digital camera. Computer hardware cannot perform any activity unless an instruction directs that hardware to act. In most cases, the instruction is part of a computer program a developer has created to carry out the desired activity. A third component required is data. **Data** includes words, numbers, videos, graphics, and sound that programs manipulate, display, and otherwise process. The basic function of many programs is to accept some form of data (sometimes called **input data**), manipulate the data in some manner

FIGURE 1-3

(sometimes called **processing**), and create some form of data that is usable by people or other computers (sometimes called **output data**, or **information**) (Figure 1-3). In short, many computer programs perform the following general steps: accept input data, process the data, and create output data. The data that acts as input to a program, the processing that occurs, and the output that is created vary with the requirements of the program.

In order for the computer to execute a program, both the program and the data must be placed in the computer's **random access memory (RAM)** (Figure 1-4). Once the program is stored in RAM, the computer's **central processing unit (CPU)** can access the program instructions and the data in RAM to perform activities as directed by the program.

Another activity that hardware and software typically carry out is saving both the data and other software. **Saving**, or **storing**, data refers to placing the data or software electronically on a storage medium such as a hard disk or a Universal Serial Bus (USB) drive or saving to a cloud storage server. The software and data are stored so they can be accessed and retrieved at a later time. Stored local data is said to be **persistent** because it remains available even after the computer power is turned off.

FIGURE 1-4

© iStock.com/Asergieiev

Computer Programmers and Developers

A computer program is designed and developed by people known as **computer programmers**, or developers. **Developers** are people skilled in designing computer programs and creating them using programming languages. Some computer programs are small and relatively simple, but often a problem to be solved on a computer requires more than one program. Thus, developers speak of developing an **application**, which can mean several computer programs working together to solve a problem.

When designing a program, developers analyze the problem and determine how to solve it. Once a computer program or an application is designed, the developer must create it so it can be executed on a computer. In most cases, the developer creates the program by writing its code using a **programming language**, which is a set of words and symbols that can be interpreted by special computer software and eventually executed as instructions by a computer. In this book, you will learn the skills required both to design and to create computer programs and apps using the Visual Basic 2015 programming language (Figure 1-5).

```vb
frmDownloads.vb  ⊅ ×
    8
    9   ⊟Public Class frmDownloads
   10
   11       ' Cost per download - used in multiple procedures
   12       Const _cdecPricePerDownload As Decimal = 0.99D
   13
   14   ⊟  Private Sub btnCalculate_Click(ByVal sender As System.Object, ByVal e As System.EventArgs) Handles btnCalculate.Click
   15           ' This event handler is executed when the user clicks the
   16           ' Calculate button. It calculates and displays the cost
   17           ' of music downloads (number of downloads times the cost per download).
   18
   19           Dim strNumberOfSongs As String
   20           Dim intNumberOfSongs As Integer
   21           Dim decTotalCostOfDownloads As Decimal
   22
   23           strNumberOfSongs = txtNumberOfDownloads.Text
   24           intNumberOfSongs = Convert.ToInt32(strNumberOfSongs)
   25           decTotalCostOfDownloads = intNumberOfSongs * _cdecPricePerDownload
   26           lblTotalCost.Text = decTotalCostOfDownloads.ToString("C")
   27
   28       End Sub
   29
   30   ⊟  Private Sub btnClear_Click(ByVal sender As System.Object, ByVal e As System.EventArgs) Handles btnClear.Click
   31           ' This event handler is executed when the user clicks the
   32           ' Clear button. It clears the number of songs text box
   33           ' and the Text property of the Total Cost of Downloads label.
   34           ' Then, it sets the focus on the txtNumberOfSongs Textbox object.
   35
   36           txtNumberOfDownloads.Clear()
   37           lblTotalCost.Text = ""
   38           txtNumberOfDownloads.Focus()
   39
   40       End Sub
```

FIGURE 1-5

CONSIDER THIS

Will I be able to find a job in computer programming?

According to Robert Half Technology, the following positions are in highest demand in 2015:

- Mobile applications developers

- Software developers

- Business intelligence analysts

(www.roberthalf.com/technology/it-salary-center)

Event-Driven Computer Programs with a Graphical User Interface

Most Visual Basic 2015 programs are **event-driven programs** that communicate with the user through a **graphical user interface (GUI)**. The GUI usually consists of a window that contains a variety of objects and that can be displayed on various devices such as a computer monitor or a smartphone screen. Users employ GUI objects to select options, enter data, and cause events to occur. An **event** means the user has initiated an action that causes the program to perform a type of processing in response. For example, a user might enter data into the program, and then tap or click a button. The button action triggers an event, resulting in the program performing the appropriate processing in response.

To illustrate the process of entering data when using a GUI and then triggering an event, consider the window shown in Figure 1-6.

FIGURE 1-6

This window is part of a banking application. When it is displayed, the teller at the bank or a user on the web can enter an account number. Next, the user can tap or click the Display Account Balance button (which triggers an event) and the program displays the account balance. The following steps illustrate the dynamics of the interaction with the program:

STEP 1   The user enters the account number in the Account Number box.

The account number the user entered is displayed in the Account Number text box (Figure 1-7). The Account Balance label displays no information.

FIGURE 1-7

STEP 2   The user taps or clicks the Display Account Balance button.

The account balance is displayed in the Account Balance label (Figure 1-8). Tapping or clicking the Display Account Balance button triggered the event that caused the program to determine and display the account balance based on data that the program accessed.

FIGURE 1-8

STEP 3   The user taps or clicks the Reset Window button to clear the text box and the label, and prepare the user interface for the next account number.

Tapping or clicking the Reset Window button triggers another event. The text box and the label are cleared and the insertion point is placed in the Account Number text box (Figure 1-9). The user now can enter a new account number to determine the account balance.

FIGURE 1-9

The events in the previous example consist of tapping or clicking the Display Account Balance button and tapping or clicking the Reset Window button. The program reacts to the events by performing specific actions (showing the account balance and resetting the text box and label). This is an example of an event-driven program. The Visual Basic developer designs the user interface and writes the program code that performs these event-triggered actions.

Basic Program Operations

All programs, regardless of their size and complexity, execute only a few fundamental operations: input, output, basic arithmetic operations, and logical operations. These operations can be combined in countless different ways to accomplish the tasks required of the program. The following pages describe these basic program operations.

Input Operation

As noted previously, a fundamental operation in most computer programs involves a user who enters data. For instance, in Figure 1-7, the user entered the account number. The steps that occurred when the user typed the account number are shown in Figure 1-10.

Step 1:
User types the account number on the keyboard.

Step 2:
The data is stored in RAM.

Step 3:
Data is displayed on the computer screen.

FIGURE 1-10

In Figure 1-10, the banking computer program that processes the user's request is stored in RAM. The data entered by the user also is stored in RAM. Depending on the input device, the entered data might also be displayed on the computer screen. The input device used to enter data depends on the application. In Figure 1-10, the user typed the account number on a traditional keyboard or mobile device keyboard. Other applications might allow data to be entered with a scanner, touch screen, digital camera, video camera, mouse, or other device. In each instance, the data is stored in the computer's RAM. When the data is in RAM, instructions in the program can operate on the data.

Output Operation

The second basic program operation is creating output, or information. As you learned previously, a major goal of most computer programs is to create output data, or information, that is useful to people. In Figure 1-8 on page 7, the information requested of the program is the account balance. The process of creating output is shown in Figure 1-11.

$13,422.85

$13,422.85
Account Balance

Account Balance

Account Number   73-0529

Account Balance   **$13,422.85**

Display Account Balance

Reset Window

FIGURE 1-11

© iStock.com/Tpopova

As always, the program must be stored in RAM to control the operations of the computer. In the example, the program sets the text of the Account Balance label equal to the account balance, and then displays it on the screen.

As with input operations, a variety of devices can present output. In addition to computer monitors, common output devices include printers, gaming console screens, and smartphone screens (Figure 1-12).

Smartphones

Printer

FIGURE 1-12

© iStock.com/Torian Dixon/MrIncredible; © iStock.com/Gergana Valcheva/gerisima; © iStock.com/scorpion26

Input and output operations are basic to all computers and most computer programs. The ability to enter data, process it in some manner, and create output in the form of useful information is what makes a computer valuable. Understanding input/output operations is essential because they provide the foundation for many of the programs you will write in this text.

Basic Arithmetic Operations

After data is stored in main computer memory as a result of an input operation, the program can process it in some manner. In many programs, arithmetic operations (addition, subtraction, multiplication, and division) are performed on numeric data to produce useful output.

Prior to performing arithmetic operations, the numeric data used in calculations must be stored in RAM. Then, program instructions that also are stored in RAM can

Program: (Test 1 Score + Test 2 Score + Test 3 Score) / 3 = Average Test Score

Data: (90 + 83 + 94) / 3 = 89

FIGURE 1-13

© iStock.com/Tpopova

direct the computer to add, subtract, multiply, or divide the numbers. The answers from arithmetic operations can be used in additional calculations and processing, stored for future use, and used as output from the program.

The example in Figure 1-13 illustrates the steps an application performs to calculate an average test score. The average score is calculated from the three test scores a user enters.

In the example in Figure 1-13, the program adds the three test scores the user enters, and then divides the total by 3 to obtain the average score. As always, both the program and the data required to calculate the average test score must be stored in the computer's RAM. As you can see, when the user enters data in a text box, the data is stored in RAM and is available for arithmetic and other operations.

This example demonstrates the three fundamental operations of input (entering the three test scores), processing (calculating the average test score), and output (displaying the average test score). Although most applications are more complex than the one illustrated, they use input, process, and output operations; arithmetic operations are commonly part of the processing step.

Logical Operations

The ability of a computer to perform logical operations separates it from other types of calculating devices. Computers, through the use of programs, can compare numbers, letters of the alphabet, and special characters. Based on the result of these comparisons, the program can perform one processing task if the tested condition is true and another processing task if the condition is not true. Using a program to compare data and perform alternative operations allows the computer to complete sophisticated tasks such as predicting weather, formatting and altering digital photographs, editing digital video, and running high-speed games.

A program can perform the following types of logical operations:

- Comparing to determine if two values are equal
- Comparing to determine if one value is greater than another value
- Comparing to determine if one value is less than another value

Based on the results of these comparisons, the program can direct the computer to take alternative actions.

Comparing — Equal Condition

A program can compare two values stored in RAM to determine whether they are equal. If the values are equal, one set of instructions will be executed; if they are not equal, another set of instructions will be executed.

When a program determines whether two values are equal, it must compare one value to another. In an application for calculating student tuition, different rates might apply based on the student's residence. If the school is located in Texas and the student resides in Texas, the tuition per unit is one value; if the student does not reside in Texas, the tuition per unit is another value (Figure 1-14).

BEFORE:

State of Residence is equal to TX

AFTER:

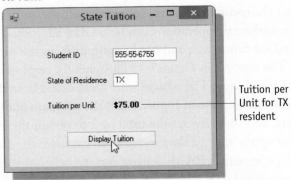

Tuition per Unit for TX resident

BEFORE:

State of Residence is equal to NY

AFTER:

Tuition per Unit for non-TX resident

FIGURE 1-14

When the Display Tuition button is tapped or clicked and the state is equal to TX, the program displays the in-state tuition per unit. If the state is not equal to TX, the program displays the out-of-state tuition per unit.

Comparing can be used to determine if a condition is selected. For example, in Figure 1-15, the Campus Parking Fees window contains a Student Name text box that provides space for the student's name and On-Campus Housing and Off-Campus Housing option buttons, or radio buttons, that allow the user to select either on-campus housing or off-campus housing. When the user taps or clicks the Calculate Parking Fees button, the program displays the appropriate parking fee.

In Example 1, the On-Campus Housing option button is selected. When the user taps or clicks the Calculate Parking Fees button, the program performs a comparison and determines that the On-Campus Housing button is selected. Because it is selected, the result of the comparison is true and the program displays the parking fee for on-campus housing. In Example 2, the Off-Campus Housing button is selected, so the program displays the parking fee for off-campus housing.

FIGURE 1-15

Comparing — Less Than Condition

A second type of comparison a computer program can perform is to determine if one value is less than another value. If it is, one set of instructions will be executed; if it is not, another set of instructions will be executed. For example, in the Student Dorm Assignment program in Figure 1-16, the user taps or clicks the Submit Application button and the program makes a comparison to determine if the person registering for a dorm room is less than 18 years old. If so, the person is considered a minor and a parent's signature is required. If not, no signature is required. An instruction is performed in the program to place a check in the Parent Signature Required check box if the age is less than 18, and the instruction is not executed if the age is 18 or more.

BEFORE:

AFTER:

parent signature is required because Student Age is less than 18

BEFORE:

Student Age is not less than 18

AFTER:

parent signature is not required because Student Age is greater than 18

FIGURE 1-16

Comparing — Greater Than Condition

The other condition a computer program can determine is whether one value is greater than another value. For example, in a payroll application, the hours worked by an employee can be compared to the value 40. If the hours worked are greater than 40, then overtime pay (1.5 times the hourly rate) is calculated for the hours over 40. If the employee worked 40 hours or less, no overtime pay is calculated. This comparing operation is shown in Figure 1-17.

In Figure 1-17a, the Hours Worked box contains 42, so the program calculates overtime pay for employee Lisa Hueve. In Figure 1-17b, Mia Ortega worked 30 hours, so no overtime pay is calculated. If the Hours Worked value is greater than 40, the program executes one set of instructions; if the Hours Worked value is not greater than 40, the program executes another set of instructions.

FIGURE 1-17a

FIGURE 1-17b

Logical Operations Summary

While the logical operations shown in the previous examples might seem simple, the ability of a computer running under program control to perform millions of these comparisons in a single second demonstrates the computer's processing power. For example, if you are participating in a road race computer game, the game program uses comparisons to determine where your car is located on the screen, which graphic road elements should be displayed, whether your car has collided with your competitor, and so on. All of the many decisions that are required to display your game on the screen and respond to your actions are based on comparisons to determine if one value is equal to, greater than, or less than another value. As you can imagine, millions of these decisions must be made every second for your high-speed game to provide an enjoyable experience.

Saving Software and Data

When you develop and write a program, the code you write and other features, such as the GUI, must be saved on disk. Then, when you want the program to run, you can have the program loaded into RAM and executed. By saving the program on disk, you can execute the same program many times without rewriting it each time you want to run it.

The program you write, however, also can save data. This data, which can be generated from the processing in the program, can be saved on disk for future use. For example, in a banking application, a customer might open an account. The computer program that is used to open the account saves the customer's information, such as name, address, account number, and account balance, to a local file on the device or in the cloud on a remote server. Later, when the customer makes a deposit or withdrawal, the customer information will be retrieved and modified to reflect the deposit or withdrawal.

In most cases, data such as a customer's name and address is saved in a database. A **database** is a collection of data organized in a manner that allows access, retrieval, and use of that data. Once the data is saved in the database, any programs with permission can reference the data. You will learn more about databases and their use when programming using Visual Basic 2015 later in this textbook.

Visual Basic 2015 and Visual Studio 2015

To write a computer program, a developer uses a programming language. As you learned previously, a programming language is a set of written words, symbols, and codes, following a strict set of usage rules called the language **syntax**, that a developer uses to communicate instructions to a computer. An example of code statements in the Visual Basic 2015 programming language is shown in Figure 1-18.

Each program statement causes the computer to perform one or more operations. When written, these instructions must conform to the rules of the Visual Basic 2015 language. Coding a program is a precise skill. The developer must follow the syntax, or **programming rules**, of the programming language precisely. Even a single coding error can cause a program to execute improperly. Therefore, the developer must pay strict attention to coding an error-free program.

When writing Visual Basic 2015 programs, most developers use a tool called Visual Studio 2015. **Visual Studio 2015** is a software application that allows you to develop Visual Basic 2015 programs using the code you write, code prewritten by others that can be incorporated into your program, and sophisticated tools that speed up the programming process significantly while building better executing and more reliable programs. In this book, you will use Visual Studio 2015 to write Visual Basic 2015 programs.

FIGURE 1-18

Visual Studio 2015 is a type of **integrated development environment (IDE)**, which provides services and tools that enable a developer to code, test, and implement a single program, or sometimes a series of programs that comprise an application. Visual Studio 2015, which was developed by Microsoft Corporation, works specifically with Visual Basic 2015 as well as other programming languages to develop program code.

Visual Basic, part of Visual Studio, can be installed on a computer running Windows 7 with service pack 1, Windows 8, Windows 10, Windows Server 2008, or Windows Server 2015. Visual Studio 2015 can be installed on a 32-bit or 64-bit computer. Students, educators, and academic institutions can access a free copy of Visual Studio 2015 at *www.dreamspark.com*. DreamSpark (Figure 1-19) is a Microsoft program that supports technical education by providing access to Microsoft software for learning, teaching, and research purposes. This text uses the Microsoft Visual Studio 2015 Professional version to present the programming topics.

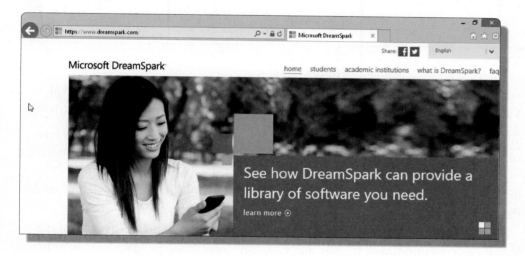

FIGURE 1-19

After you start the Visual Studio 2015 application, the Visual Studio 2015 window is displayed. In this window, you can develop and write your Visual Basic 2015 program, as shown in Figure 1-20.

The following elements help you use the Visual Studio 2015 window. In subsequent chapters, you will learn to use each of the elements found in this window.

Title bar: The title bar identifies the window and the application open in the window. In Figure 1-20, the open application is named Payroll Program.

Menu bar: The menu bar displays the Visual Studio 2015 menu names. The menus contain lists of commands that allow you to create, edit, save, print, test, and run a Visual Basic program, and to perform other functions that are critical to developing Visual Basic programs.

Standard toolbar: The Standard toolbar contains buttons that execute frequently used commands such as Open Project, New Project, Save, Cut, Copy, Paste, and Undo.

title bar

Microsoft account sign in to sync settings

menu bar
Standard
toolbar

Solution
Explorer

Toolbox

Properties
window

main work area

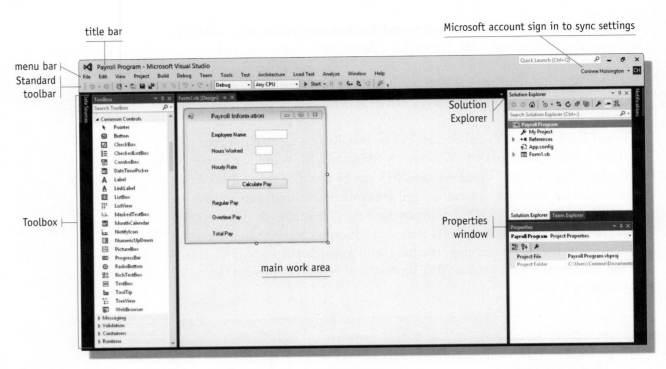

FIGURE 1-20

Toolbox: The Toolbox contains **.NET components** that help you develop the GUI for your program. For example, you can use the Toolbox to place buttons, picture boxes, labels, radio buttons, and other Windows GUI objects in the windows of your program.

Main work area: The main work area contains the item you are currently developing. In Figure 1-20, this area contains the Payroll Information window of the Payroll program.

Solution Explorer: The Solution Explorer window displays the elements of the Visual Basic **solution**, which is the name for the Visual Basic program and other items generated by Visual Studio to help the program execute properly. You will learn about these items and how to use the Solution Explorer window throughout this book.

Properties window: An item that is a visible part of a GUI, such as the Calculate Pay button in Figure 1-20, is called an **object** or **control**. Each object in a Visual Basic program has a set of characteristics called the **properties** of the object. These properties, such as the size of the button and the text displayed within the button, can be set in the Properties window within Visual Studio. You will learn about the properties of many objects throughout this book.

To code a Visual Basic program, the developer starts the Visual Studio program, identifies the kind of program to be developed, and then uses the tools and features of Visual Studio to create the program.

CONSIDER THIS

Does Visual Studio Express contain the same developer tools as Visual Studio Professional?
Microsoft Visual Studio Express is a free software IDE developed by Microsoft with multiple products that include lightweight versions of the Microsoft Visual Studio product line. The Visual Studio Express product line includes a subset of the full Visual Studio Professional product. Express 2015 products include Express for Web, Express for Windows Store Apps, Express for Windows Desktop, Express for Windows Phone, and Team Foundation Server Express.

Programming Languages

Several thousand programming languages exist today. Each language has its own rules and syntax for writing instructions. Languages often are designed for specific purposes, such as scientific applications, business solutions, or webpage development.

Visual Studio can be used to write programs in five languages: Visual Basic, Visual C++ (pronounced see plus plus and called C++ for short), Visual C# (pronounced see sharp and called C# for short), JavaScript, and Visual F# (pronounced eff sharp and called F# for short). You can develop a Windows Store app for Windows 8/10 or a Windows smartphone coded with Visual Basic, C++, or C#. Each of these languages is described in the following sections.

Visual Basic

Visual Basic is a programming language that allows developers to easily build complex Windows and web programs, as well as other software tools. Visual Basic 2015 is based on the Visual Basic programming language that Microsoft developed in the early 1990s. Visual Basic was created from the BASIC (Beginner's All-purpose Symbolic Instructional Code) language, which was developed in the 1960s.

Visual Basic's popularity evolved from the wide range of productivity features that enabled developers to quickly generate high-quality software applications for Windows. Today, Visual Basic is one of the most widely used programming languages in the world because it is English-like and is considered one of the easier enterprise-level programming languages to learn. Visual Basic is the only language in Visual Studio that is not case sensitive, which makes it easy for entry-level programmers. It is as powerful as the other programming languages in the Visual Studio suite, such as C++ or C#. An example of Visual Basic 2015 code is shown in Figure 1-18 on page 16.

In this book, you will learn to become a proficient Visual Basic developer.

Visual C++

C++ is a derivative of the programming language C, which originally was developed at Bell Labs in the 1970s. It gives developers exacting control of their applications through optimized code and access to system-provided services. It contains powerful language constructs, though at the price of added complexity. C++ provides unrivaled performance and precision for applications that require a high degree of control.

Visual C#

Introduced in 2001 by Microsoft, Visual C# offers a synthesis of the elegance and syntax of C++ with many of the productivity benefits enjoyed in Visual Basic. Visual C# can be used to create both Windows and Web applications, as well as other types of software tools. Microsoft designed Visual C# to overcome some of the limitations of C++ while still providing the depth of control that C++ developers demand. The language includes aspects of several other programming languages, such as C++, Java, and Delphi, with a strong emphasis on code simplification.

JavaScript

Fully included in the Visual Studio 2015 version, JavaScript (JS) is an open-source client-side scripting language that enhances web browser user interfaces and dynamic websites. Visual Studio 2015 provides complete IntelliSense and debugging support for all the JavaScript objects and its methods.

Visual F#

A Microsoft .NET object-oriented language that debuted with Visual Studio 2010 is called F#. A multipurpose language similar to Visual Basic and C#, the F# language is known for its math-intensive focus, making it perfect for heavy-duty scientific programming applications. The language is relatively new and is just beginning to gain popularity in the business and science environments.

.NET Framework 4.6

In the year 2000, Microsoft announced a set of software technologies and products under the umbrella name of .NET. The .NET technologies and products were designed to work together to allow businesses to connect information, people, systems, and devices through software. Much of this connection occurs over the Internet.

The software environment in which programs and applications can be developed for .NET is called the **.NET Framework**, which provides tools and processes developers can use to produce and run programs. The .NET Framework is a development platform for building apps for Windows, Windows Phone, Windows Server, and Windows Azure (the Microsoft professional cloud computing platform). The most recent version is called **.NET Framework 4.6**. Visual Studio 2015 provides the development environment for the developer to have access to the .NET Framework 4.6 tools and processes.

Major features of .NET Framework 4.6 include the .NET class library, ADO.NET (provides the ability to read and write data in databases), ASP.NET 5 (provides the ability to develop web applications across desktop, tablet, and mobile browsers), Windows Presentation Foundation (WPF), Windows services, and the Common Language Runtime (CLR; allows programs to run on different computers under different operating systems). Each of these features is explained in the following sections.

.NET Class Library

As you have learned, most programs written using Visual Basic 2015 are event-driven programs in which a user performs an action, such as tapping or clicking a button, and the program executes the appropriate instructions. The instructions a program executes when a user taps or clicks a button are normally written by the Visual Basic developer and are unique to the processing required by the program. For example, when a user taps or clicks a button in one program, the overtime pay is calculated for an employee, whereas in another program parking fees are calculated. Each program responds to the events triggered by users with unique processing based on the requirements of the program.

In many programs, however, much of the programming code that must be developed is common for all the programs. For example, in all the programs you have seen in this chapter, a button was used to trigger an event in the program. The button appears in a window on a screen and senses when it has been clicked through the use of program instructions.

When code is common to multiple programs, the best approach is to write the code once and then reuse it when appropriate. For example, when a button is required in the GUI of a program, it is more efficient to use common programming code to insert the button than to require a developer to write all the code for a button each time one is required. When a common task must be performed or a new object such as a button is required, a developer can write the code once and save it as a class. That class can then be referenced by all other programs when the task or object is required.

In short, the coding required for a button can be placed in a class. A **class** is a named group of program code. Once the class is coded, it can be stored in a **class library**, which makes the class available to all developers who need to use it. For example, when you as a developer need to place a button in the user interface, you can use the Button class stored in a class library to create the button without writing all the programming code associated with the button (Figure 1-21).

A button created from a class is called an **object**, or sometimes an **instance** of a class. In programming terminology, the process of creating a Button object from the Button class is called **instantiation**. In other words, a class acts as a general template, while an object is a specific item that is generated based on the class template. Thus, all buttons can be generated, or instantiated, from the Button class. The Display Account Balance button in Figure 1-21 is a specific Button object instantiated from the Button class.

To create a Button object from the Button class in Visual Studio 2015, you only need to drag the Button .NET component from the Toolbox to a Windows Form object, as you will learn in Chapter 2.

A button in a GUI is only a single example of using classes and class libraries. The .NET Framework 4.6 class library contains thousands of classes and many class libraries for Visual Basic developers who use Visual Studio to create programs.

FIGURE 1-21

With so many classes available in .NET Framework 4.6, developers use a method of program development called rapid application development. **Rapid application development (RAD)** refers to the process of using prebuilt classes to make application development faster, easier, and more reliable. Throughout this book, you will gain a further understanding of classes and their use in modern computer programming, and will see how the classes in the .NET Framework 4.6 class libraries can be used for RAD.

ADO.NET

Often, programs you write must access data stored in a database. A set of prewritten classes called ADO.NET (ADO stands for ActiveX Data Objects) provides the functionality for a program to perform the four primary tasks required when working with a database: getting the data, examining the data, editing the data, and updating the data.

Getting the data refers to retrieving it from the database and making it available to the program. Once the data is retrieved from the database, ADO.NET 4.6 provides the tools for the program to examine the data and determine how to use it. For example, a program might retrieve data from a database to create a printed report. The program can examine the data to determine its use for the report.

In other applications, the program might examine the data to determine if it is appropriate to display for a user. Thus, in a banking application, such as in Figure 1-22, the program might require the user to enter a special value, such as her mother's maiden name, to verify her identity before displaying the requested information. The program, using ADO.NET classes, can compare the special value to the data retrieved from the database to determine if the user is permitted to access the data.

A third facility provided by ADO.NET is the ability to edit the data, which means to make changes to it. For example, if you change your address or telephone number, those values should be changed in your account database information. ADO.NET supports the ability to make those changes.

FIGURE 1-22

Finally, once changes have been made to data, ADO.NET enables a program to update the database with the new information by writing the data into the database.

ADO.NET is a powerful and necessary part of .NET Framework 4.6. Developers use Visual Studio 2015 to access the ADO.NET 4.6 classes.

ASP.NET 5

The Internet and the web are integral technological resources. Modern websites provide services from selling products to sharing the latest medical research on any known disease. The development and maintenance of these websites is a constant requirement and consumes many developer hours.

Recognizing the importance of the web, Microsoft developed .NET Framework 4.6 to include a programming framework called ASP.NET 5. Developers can use this framework through Visual Studio 2015 to build powerful and sophisticated web applications on a web server. Using ASP.NET 5 classes, Visual Basic 2015 programmers can create websites that perform any function available on the web today. In addition to traditional websites, you can automatically adapt web applications to target mobile devices with enhanced ASP.NET support for mobile browsers. ASP.NET 5 is designed for cloud technologies and server-side applications. **Cloud computing** is the connection of remote servers hosted on the Internet to store and process data, instead of storing the information locally on a personal computer or device.

ASP.NET 5 offers several advantages for developers. First, almost all the objects available in the .NET framework, such as buttons, text boxes, and picture boxes, are available in ASP.NET 5. So, developers can use the same techniques to create a web application that they use to create Windows applications such as those shown in this chapter. In addition, ASP.NET 5 is dedicated to mobile-first and cloud-first development. The code footprint for mobile webpages have been slimmed down to load quickly within mobile browsers. The ASP.NET 5 within Visual Studio provides tools to develop interactive HTML5 web applications easily and efficiently with JavaScript and jQuery. Instead of coding separate webpages for each type of mobile device, a single programming model is available for designing webpages and services.

Important web requirements such as performance and security are enhanced and maximized through use of the tools offered with ASP.NET 5. In short, ASP.NET 5 offers a complete solution for developing modern web applications and cloud services for computers, tablets, and smartphones.

Microsoft Intermediate Language and Common Language Runtime

After a developer writes a program in a programming language such as Visual Basic 2015 using Visual Studio 2015, the programming statements must be translated into a collection of instructions that eventually can be understood by the electronics of the computer. These electronic instructions then are executed by the computer to carry out the tasks of the program. This process of translation is called **program compilation**.

Program compilation for a Visual Basic 2015 program creates a set of electronic code expressed in an intermediate language called the **Microsoft Intermediate**

Language (MSIL). When the program is executed, a portion of .NET 4.6 called the **Common Language Runtime (CLR)** reads the MSIL and causes the instructions within the program to be executed (Figure 1-23).

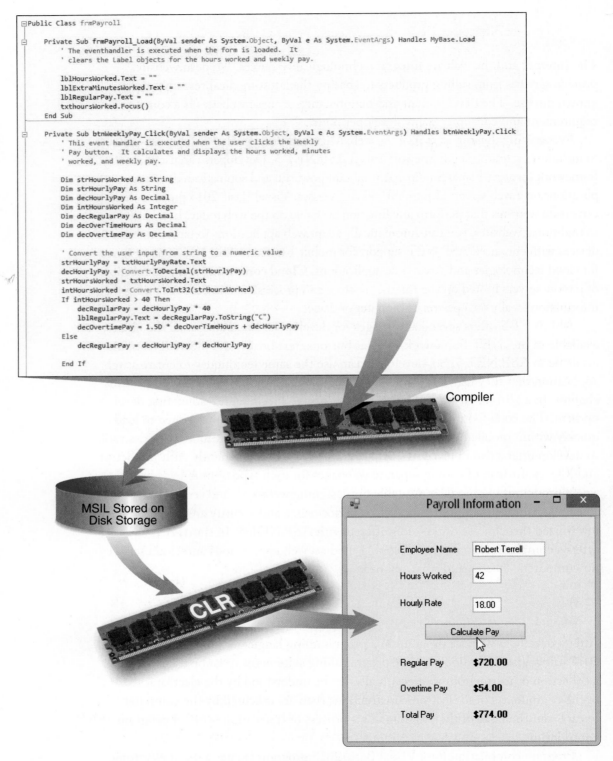

```
Public Class frmPayroll

    Private Sub frmPayroll_Load(ByVal sender As System.Object, ByVal e As System.EventArgs) Handles MyBase.Load
        ' The eventhandler is executed when the form is loaded.  It
        ' clears the Label objects for the hours worked and weekly pay.

        lblHoursWorked.Text = ""
        lblExtraMinutesWorked.Text = ""
        lblRegularPay.Text = ""
        txthoursWorked.Focus()
    End Sub

    Private Sub btnWeeklyPay_Click(ByVal sender As System.Object, ByVal e As System.EventArgs) Handles btnWeeklyPay.Click
        ' This event handler is executed when the user clicks the Weekly
        ' Pay button.  It calculates and displays the hours worked, minutes
        ' worked, and weekly pay.

        Dim strHoursWorked As String
        Dim strHourlyPay As String
        Dim decHourlyPay As Decimal
        Dim intHoursWorked As Integer
        Dim decRegularPay As Decimal
        Dim decOverTimeHours As Decimal
        Dim decOvertimePay As Decimal

        ' Convert the user input from string to a numeric value
        strHourlyPay = txtHourlyPayRate.Text
        decHourlyPay = Convert.ToDecimal(strHourlyPay)
        strHoursWorked = txtHoursWorked.Text
        intHoursWorked = Convert.ToInt32(strHoursWorked)
        If intHoursWorked > 40 Then
            decRegularPay = decHourlyPay * 40
            lblRegularPay.Text = decRegularPay.ToString("C")
            decOvertimePay = 1.5D * decOverTimeHours + decHourlyPay
        Else
            decRegularPay = decHourlyPay * decHourlyPay

        End If
```

Compiler

MSIL Stored on Disk Storage

CLR

Payroll Information

Employee Name   Robert Terrell

Hours Worked   42

Hourly Rate   18.00

Calculate Pay

Regular Pay   **$720.00**

Overtime Pay   **$54.00**

Total Pay   **$774.00**

FIGURE 1-23

In Figure 1-23, the Visual Basic program written by a developer is compiled, which translates the human-readable statements in Visual Basic into MSIL, the set of electronic code that forms the input to CLR. Then, when the program is ready for execution, the CLR reads the MSIL in RAM in a form that allows the computer's CPU to execute the instructions in the program.

The use of MSIL and CLR offers multiple benefits that provide speed and flexibility for both the development and execution environments of a program. Utmost among these benefits is that a program written using Visual Studio 2015 and compiled into MSIL can be executed on any computer using any operating system, as long as .NET Framework 4.6 is available on the computer. So, with no changes to a program you write, the program could be executed on a Dell computer running Windows 10, a mobile smartphone, an older operating system, or an IBM computer using the Linux operating system. This ability to execute programs on different computers running different operating systems is a primary benefit of using .NET Framework 4.6.

Types of Visual Basic 2015 Applications

When you begin creating a new Visual Basic 2015 program in Visual Studio 2015, you must choose the type of application you will be developing. Based on your choice, Visual Studio 2015 provides the classes, tools, and features required for that type of application.

Five major types of applications are Windows Desktop applications, Windows Store apps, Web/Cloud applications, Office/SharePoint applications, and database applications. A **Windows Desktop application** means the program will run on a computer or other device that supports the Windows GUI. You can run Windows Desktop applications on a variety of computers.

You can also create **Windows Store apps** that are designed to run on Windows 8 or Windows 10 computers and mobile devices such as smartphones and tablets. Windows Store apps have a new look and feel; run on a variety of devices such as a desktop, Windows tablet, or Windows phone; and can be sold in the Windows Store. Unlike traditional desktop apps, a Windows Store app has a single, chromeless window that fills the entire screen by default. (Chromeless windows have few or no user interface features such as tools displayed in toolbars.) To develop a Windows Store app, you must have Visual Studio 2015 installed on a Windows 8 or Windows 10 computer. You cannot develop Windows Store apps on Windows 7 or Windows Server products. You must obtain a free developer license to develop and test Windows Store apps before the Windows Store can certify them. The free developer license is provided on a per-machine basis and for a fixed amount of time using a Microsoft account.

When you open Visual Studio 2015 to create any type of application, you can sign in to Visual Studio with a Microsoft account to enable features such as synchronized settings that roam with you to your other Visual Studio devices (Figure 1-24). If you do not have a Microsoft account, Visual Studio provides the opportunity to sign up for an account for free.

FIGURE 1-24

You create a **Web application** using ASP.NET 5. The application runs on a web server. It produces HTML5 code that is downloaded to the client computer, where the browser interprets the HTML and displays the contents of a webpage in a traditional or mobile browser. In a web application, the developer can include items such as security and forms processing to provide all the cloud and local services required of a modern website on a computer or mobile device.

An **Office/SharePoint application** includes writing Visual Basic 2015 code to automate and manipulate documents created using Microsoft Office 2010 or Office 2013 and SharePoint. **SharePoint** is a Microsoft product that provides cloud-based services to store, access, and organize information throughout an organization.

A **database application** is written using ADO.NET 4.6 to reference, access, display, and update data stored in a database. The Visual Basic 2015 developer writes the code to process the data.

Other types of applications Visual Basic 2015 developers can create include console applications, classes for class libraries, certain controls to use in Windows applications, reporting applications, LightSwitch business applications using Silverlight, and device-specific applications.

Summary

In this chapter, you have learned the fundamentals of computer programming and have been introduced to the Visual Studio 2015 and Visual Basic 2015 program development environments. In subsequent chapters, you will learn to use Visual Studio 2015 and Visual Basic 2015 to create Windows Desktop applications, Windows Store apps, Office/SharePoint applications, database applications, and Web/Cloud applications for computer and mobile devices.

Knowledge Check

1. The basic functions of many programs are: a. _____; b. _____;
   c. _____.

2. Explain the differences between computer hardware and computer software.

3. Match the following terms and their definitions:

   a. Developer

   b. Persistent data

   c. Programming language

   d. Graphical user interface

   e. Database

   f. Class library

   g. Rapid application development (RAD)

   h. Cloud computing

   1. A collection of classes that are available for use in programs

   2. Someone skilled in designing computer programs and implementing them in programming languages

   3. A window with a variety of objects that can be displayed on a variety of devices

   4. Data that is stored on a storage medium

   5. The process of using prebuilt classes to make application development faster, easier, and more reliable

   6. A collection of data organized in a manner that allows access, retrieval, and use of that data

   7. The connection of remote servers hosted on the Internet to store and process data instead of storing the information locally on a personal computer or device

   8. A set of words and symbols that can be interpreted by special computer software and eventually can be executed as instructions by a computer

4. Explain what an event is in the context of event-driven programs. Give two examples.

5. Give examples of the differences between an input operation and an output operation.

6. What are the four primary arithmetic operations a computer program can perform? Give an example of each.

7. In the following examples, identify the condition a program would detect (the first exercise is solved for you):

   a. 4 is _____ 3   a. greater than

   b. 9 is _____ 9   b. _____

   c. 17 is _____ 17.8   c. _____

   d. 102 is _____ 65   d. _____

   e. "Twitter" is _____ "Twitter"   e. _____

8. Describe three different databases where you think information about yourself might be stored.

9. What is programming language syntax? Why is it important?

10. What is a Toolbox in Visual Studio 2015? Why is it valuable?

11. Name two properties that a Button object can possess.

12. What are the five programming languages you can use with Visual Studio 2015?

(continues)

13. Where can you sell the Windows Store apps that you develop?

14. State three reasons that Visual Basic is one of the most widely used programming languages in the world.

15. Name two purposes of creating a Microsoft account for use in Visual Studio 2015.

16. Why is a class developed? How are classes organized and stored?

17. Differentiate between a class and an object. Give three examples each of classes and objects.

18. What is the primary use of ADO.NET?

19. What do you call the process of translating statements written by a developer? What is the result of this process?

20. What are five types of applications you can create in Visual Basic 2015?

CHAPTER 2

Program and Graphical User Interface Design

OBJECTIVES

You will have mastered the material in this chapter when you can:

- Open and close Visual Studio 2015

- Create a Visual Basic 2015 Windows Desktop application project

- Name and set the title bar text in a Windows Form object and resize a Windows Form object

- Add a Label object to a Windows Form object, name the Label object, set the text in the Label object, and change the

Font properties of the text in the Label object

- Add a PictureBox object to the Windows Form object, name the PictureBox object, and resize the PictureBox object

- Add a Button object to the Windows Form object, name the Button object, set the text in the Button object, and change the Button object's size

- Align objects on the Windows Form object

- Save and open Visual Basic projects

- Understand and implement design principles of the graphical user interface

- Understand and implement the first two phases of the program development life cycle

Introduction

Before a program can be coded using Visual Basic 2015, it must be designed. Designing a program can be compared to constructing a building. Before cement slabs are poured, steel beams are put in place and walls are built. Architects and engineers must design a building to ensure it will perform as required and be safe and reliable. The same holds true for a computer program or app. Once the program is designed, it can be implemented through the Visual Basic 2015 programming language to perform its intended functions.

To illustrate the process of creating a computer program in Visual Basic 2015 using **Visual Studio 2015** as the integrated development environment, you will design and implement the application shown in Figure 2-1 throughout this chapter and Chapter 3.

The application in Figure 2-1 could be part of a larger menu application used to select your pizza order. The program that creates the window in Figure 2-1 will run on a personal computer using the Windows operating system. Similar design principles for desktop computers and mobile devices taught in this chapter assist with graphic and text layout on any user interface to deliver a consistent experience across

FIGURE 2-1a

FIGURE 2-1b

touch screens or desktop's keyboard and mouse interaction. The program will allow customers to select their favorite pizza type between the two options of Chicago deep-dish pizza and New York thin-crust pizza.

In Figure 2-1a, the program begins by displaying the Pizza Selection window. The program provides instructions for the user to choose the pizza type by tapping or clicking the Deep Dish or Thin Crust button, and then to complete the selection by tapping or clicking the Select Pizza button. If the user taps or clicks the Deep Dish button, a picture of a deep-dish pizza is displayed (Figure 2-1b). If the user taps or clicks the Thin Crust button, a picture of a thin-crust pizza is displayed (Figure 2-1c). After choosing a pizza type, the user can tap or click the Select Pizza button and the program informs the user that a pizza has been selected (Figure 2-1d). To close the window and exit the program, the user can tap or click the Exit Window button after making a pizza selection.

By the end of Chapter 3, you will have completed the design and implementation of this program.

FIGURE 2-1c

FIGURE 2-1d

Brand X Pictures/Getty Images

Using Visual Studio 2015

When designing an event-driven program that uses a graphical user interface (GUI), such as the program in this chapter, one of the first steps after defining the purpose for the program is to design the user interface itself. Recall that the user interface is the window that appears on the screen when the program is running. The user interface includes a variety of objects such as buttons that are displayed in the window. Before beginning to design the user interface, however, the developer should know how to use Visual Studio and Visual Basic **rapid application development** (**RAD**) tools in the design process. For example, you use the Visual Studio tools to place a button on the window. Before starting the design of the program shown in Figure 2-1, you should know how to accomplish the Visual Studio tasks described on the following pages. In this text, you can complete steps by tapping if you are using a touch screen or by clicking if you are using a mouse or touchpad.

CONSIDER THIS

Can I store code and other files in the Visual Studio Cloud?

Microsoft provides an online storage cloud for the Visual Studio 2015 community. This optional storage space allows you to store your code, collaborate with team server members, test your code in the cloud, and sync your personal settings such as themes or keyboard shortcuts across various computers. The first time Visual Studio 2015 is launched, your Microsoft account sign-in and password information is requested. If you do not have a Microsoft account, you can create one for free at outlook. com. Signing into your Microsoft account is optional for Windows Desktop applications, but is necessary for creating a Windows Store app. After signing into your Microsoft account, Visual Studio 2015 requests the user interface settings and color theme. These options can be changed at a later time in the Options menu of Visual Studio. To confirm that you are connected to your Microsoft account, check the profile name in the upper-right corner of Visual Studio.

Open Visual Studio 2015

To design a user interface using Visual Studio, the developer opens Visual Studio 2015 and then uses the tools the program provides. To open Visual Studio 2015, you can complete the following steps:

STEP 1   In Windows 8, tap or click the Visual Studio 2015 tile on the Start screen. In Windows 10, tap or click the Start button on the Windows taskbar, tap or click All Apps on the Start menu, and then tap or click Visual Studio 2015 on the All Apps submenu. Tap or click Visual Studio 2015, and then tap or click the Sign in button.

A Visual Studio splash screen appears briefly, and then the Microsoft Visual Studio 2015 sign-in screen opens (Figure 2-2).

FIGURE 2-2

STEP 2 Type your Microsoft account name and password in the Microsoft account and Password text boxes. (If you do not have a Microsoft account, you can sign up for one for free.) Tap or click the Sign in button.

A Visual Studio window opens where you can select development settings (Figure 2-3).

FIGURE 2-3

STEP 3 Tap or click the Development Settings arrow and select Visual Basic. Tap or click the Start Visual Studio button.

Microsoft Visual Studio 2015 opens (Figure 2-4). The title of the window is Start Page - Microsoft Visual Studio. The menu bar and the Standard toolbar are displayed at the top of the window. The Start Page contains information about Visual Studio. To close the Start Page, tap or click the Close button on the Start Page title bar. Your Microsoft account name appears in the upper-right corner. You will learn the other elements of this window as you progress through this book.

FIGURE 2-4

CRITICAL THINKING

What else can I do with a Microsoft Cloud Account, also called OneDrive?

You can store and share any type of file such as images, music, college papers, spreadsheets, and databases from your cloud.

Create a New Visual Basic 2015 Windows Desktop Project

A **project** is equivalent to a single program created using Visual Studio. A **Windows Desktop project** is a program that includes a user interface whose windows are created using the Windows operating system. When the program is executed, the user interacts with the program by using its windows and components (the user interface).

To create a new project using Visual Studio, you must specify the programming language you want to use and the type of program or application you will create. To create a new Visual Basic Windows Desktop project, you can complete the following steps:

STEP 1 Tap or click the New Project button on the Standard toolbar.

Visual Studio opens the New Project window (Figure 2-5). The New Project window on your computer might be displayed differently, depending on selections made when Visual Studio was installed on your computer. For example, if you are using Windows 7, you will not see the Windows Store templates listed because you need Windows 8 or Windows 10 to develop a Windows Store app. The left pane contains the programming languages and other types of templates available in Visual Studio. The middle pane contains the types of applications you can create within each programming language. The right pane displays a description of the selected application. At this point, you want to create a Windows Desktop project using Visual Basic.

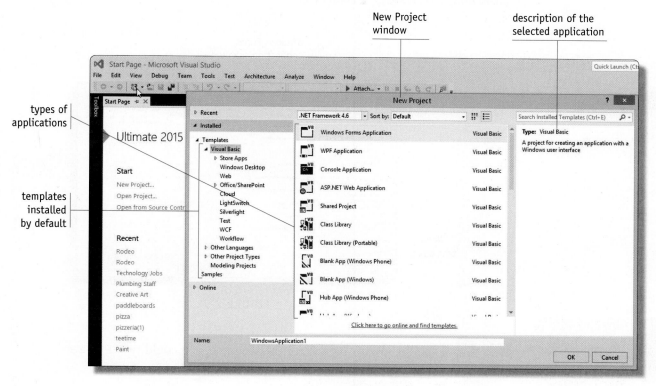

FIGURE 2-5

STEP 2   If necessary, tap or click Windows Desktop in the left pane so it is selected.

Windows Desktop is highlighted in the left pane and the types of Windows Desktop projects you can create using Visual Basic are listed in the middle pane (Figure 2-6).

FIGURE 2-6

STEP 3   If necessary, tap or click Windows Forms Application in the middle pane.

Windows Forms Application is selected in the middle pane (Figure 2-7). By making this selection, you specify you are creating a program that runs under the Windows operating system using the Windows Desktop GUI.

Windows Forms
Application selected

Name
text box

FIGURE 2-7

STEP 4   Type the project name. For this example, you could type `Pizza Selection` as the name.

The project name appears in the Name text box (Figure 2-8).

OK
button

project
name

FIGURE 2-8

STEP 5 Tap or click the OK button in the New Project window.

Visual Studio creates a new project (Figure 2-9). The project name is displayed in the title bar of the window.

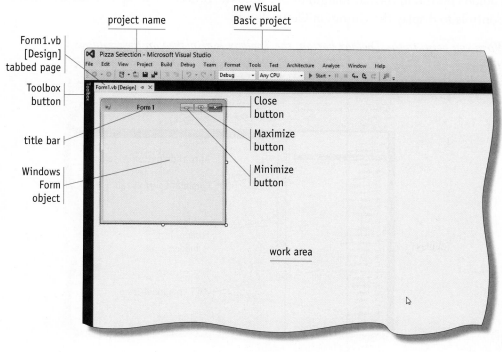

FIGURE 2-9

The Visual Studio window contains several important features you should know. First, in the portion of the window known as the **work area**, a tabbed page named Form1.vb [Design] contains a Windows Form object called Form1. A **Windows Form object** is the window you will use to build the program and then display it on your screen when you execute the program. The Windows Form object is the fundamental object in the GUI you will create using Visual Studio tools. Notice in Figure 2-9 that the Windows Form object contains a title bar, a window title (Form1), a Minimize button, a Maximize button, and a Close button.

A second important element is displayed on the left side of the window. Depending on the settings in Visual Studio, the left portion of the window will appear as shown in Figure 2-9 or Figure 2-10. In Figure 2-9, the left margin contains the Toolbox button. The Toolbox button also appears on the Standard toolbar.

Display the Toolbox

You can use the **Toolbox button** to display the Toolbox. The **Toolbox** is the primary tool you use to place objects such as buttons on the Windows Form object. Items in the Toolbox are grouped into sections called **tabs**. To display the Toolbox, you can complete the following steps:

STEP 1   If the window does not already display the Toolbox, tap or click the Toolbox button in the left margin of the window. If necessary, tap or click Common Controls to display the Common Controls tab.

When you point to the Toolbox button, the Toolbox is displayed on the window (Figure 2-10). Notice that the Toolbox hides the Form1 Windows Form object.

FIGURE 2-10

Among other things, the Toolbox contains many graphical elements called **controls** that you can place on the Windows Form object as GUI objects. For example, the Toolbox contains buttons that can be placed on the Windows Form object. You will learn how to perform this activity in the next section of this chapter.

Permanently Display the Toolbox

When you tap or click outside the Toolbox, it no longer is displayed. When you are designing the GUI, normally it helps to display the Toolbox at all times. To always display the Toolbox, you can complete the following step:

STEP 1   If necessary, tap or click the Toolbox button in the left margin of the window to display the Toolbox. Then, tap or click the Auto Hide button (Pushpin icon) on the Toolbox title bar.

When you tap or click the Auto Hide button, the Pushpin icon on the button changes from being horizontal, which indicates Auto Hide, to vertical, which indicates the Toolbox has been pinned to the window and will remain there (Figure 2-11). Form1 is moved to the right so you can see both the Toolbox and all of Form1.

Pushpin icon on
Auto Hide button
is vertical

Toolbox
displayed at
all times

Form1 moved
to right

FIGURE 2-11

ONLINE REINFORCEMENT

To view a video of the process in the previous step, visit CengageBrain.com and navigate to the resources for this title. Tap or click the link for Chapter 2 and then navigate to Video 2-5.

When the Pushpin icon is vertical, the Toolbox is said to be in Dockable mode, which means it can be dragged around and placed anywhere within the Visual Studio window. In most applications, it should remain on the left side of the window, as shown in Figure 2-11. Later, you can change the Toolbox back to Auto Hide mode by tapping or clicking the Auto Hide button again.

View Object Properties

Every object you create in the user interface, including the Windows Form object, has properties. **Properties** can describe a multitude of characteristics about the object, including its color, size, name, and position on the screen. You will learn about the properties of all the objects you create using the Toolbox.

HEADS UP

If the Solution Explorer window is not displayed on your screen, you can display the window by completing the following steps:

1. Tap or click View on the menu bar.
2. Tap or click Solution Explorer on the View menu. The Solution Explorer window will be displayed in the location shown in Figure 2-12.

To view the properties for an object in Visual Studio, you use the Properties window. By default, the Properties window is displayed in the right section of the Visual Studio window (Figure 2-12). Your window might display the Solution Explorer window above the Properties window.

FIGURE 2-12

<table>
</table>

HEADS UP

If you want to reset your Visual Basic window to its original installed layout, you can complete the following steps:

1. Tap or click Window on the menu bar.
2. Tap or click Reset Window Layout on the Window menu.

In the **Properties window** shown in Figure 2-12, the property names in the left list appear in Alphabetical view. Many developers find the Alphabetical view the easiest to use when searching for properties. Some developers, however, prefer the Categorized view, in which properties are organized according to type. You can change the order of the properties to Categorized if you tap or click the Categorized button on the Properties window toolbar (see Figure 2-12). In this book, the properties are shown in Alphabetical view, which you select by tapping or clicking the Alphabetical button on the Properties window toolbar.

Name the Windows Form Object

Visual Studio assigns a default name to every object in a Visual Basic GUI. For example, the first Windows Form object in a project is named Form1. In virtually every instance, a developer should assign a meaningful name to an object so the program can reference it if required. The name of an object should reflect the object's use. For example, a good name for the Pizza Selection window might be frmPizzaSelection. Notice in the name that each word is capitalized and the remaining letters are lowercase. You should always follow this naming method when naming objects.

No spaces or other special characters are allowed in the object name. Also, by convention, each object name should begin with a prefix that identifies the type of object. For Windows Form objects, the prefix is frm. Therefore, the complete name for the Windows Form object would be frmPizzaSelection. The form name should be changed from Form1 to a more descriptive name in the Solution Explorer.

To give the name frmPizzaSelection to the form using the Solution Explorer in Figure 2-12, you can complete the following steps:

STEP 1 Tap or click anywhere in the Windows Form object to select it and then tap or click View on the menu bar.

When you tap or click within any object, including a Windows Form object, it is selected (Figure 2-13). Sizing handles and a heavier border surround the selected object. In addition, the Properties window displays the properties of the selected object. When you tap or click View on the menu bar, the View menu is displayed (Figure 2-13).

FIGURE 2-13

STEP 2 If necessary, tap or click Solution Explorer on the View menu to display the Solution Explorer. In the Solution Explorer window, press and hold or right-click the Form1.vb file name to display a shortcut menu with the Rename command.

The shortcut menu for the Form1.vb file appears in the Solution Explorer (Figure 2-14).

FIGURE 2-14

STEP 3   Tap or click Rename. Type `frmPizzaSelection.vb` and press the ENTER key.

The Form1.vb form file is given the new name frmPizzaSelection.vb in the Solution Explorer window (Figure 2-15).

FIGURE 2-15

CONSIDER THIS

Why should you name the Form object?
Later in this text, you add multiple Form objects. It can become confusing if you do not have unique identifying names for each of the Form objects within the project.

Set the Title Bar Text in a Windows Form Object

After you name the Windows Form object, often the next step in GUI design is to change the title bar text to reflect the function of the program. In this example, the name used is Pizza Selection. The **Text property** in the Properties window for the Windows Form object contains the value displayed in the title bar of the window. You can set the Text property using the following steps:

STEP 1   Tap or click the Windows Form object and then scroll in the Properties window as necessary until you find the Text property. (Remember that the properties are in alphabetical order.) Then, double-tap or double-click the Text property in the right column.

The text, Form1, is selected in the Properties window (Figure 2-16). Form1 is the default text value for the first Windows Form object created in a project. Whenever a property is selected, you can change it.

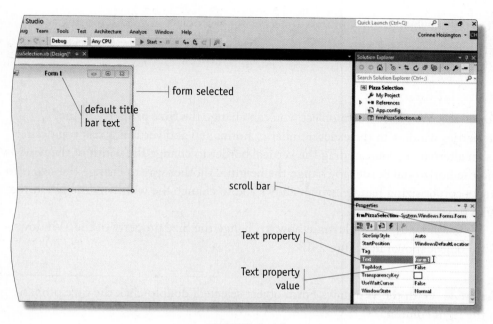

FIGURE 2-16

STEP 2 Type `Pizza Selection` and then press the ENTER key.

The value Pizza Selection is displayed for the Text property in the Properties window and is partially displayed in the title bar of the Windows Form object (Figure 2–17). You can enter any value you like for the Text property of the Windows Form object.

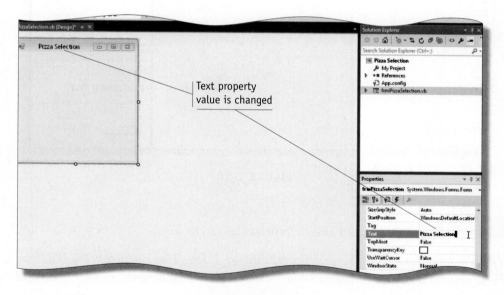

FIGURE 2-17

ONLINE REINFORCEMENT

To view a video of the process in the previous steps, visit CengageBrain.com and navigate to the resources for this title. Tap or click the link for Chapter 2 and then navigate to Video 2-7.

You can change many of the properties for any object in the GUI using the techniques just illustrated.

Resize a Form

To resize a Windows Form object, you can change the **Size property** in the Properties window to the exact number of horizontal and vertical pixels you desire. As an alternative, you can drag the vertical border to change the width of the window and the horizontal border to change the height. Another way to change the size is to drag a corner sizing handle, which allows you to change the width and height at the same time.

The following steps illustrate how to change the Size property of the Windows Form object shown in Figure 2-18:

STEP 1   With the Windows Form object selected, double-click the Size property in the right column.

The Size property is selected in the Properties window (Figure 2-18).

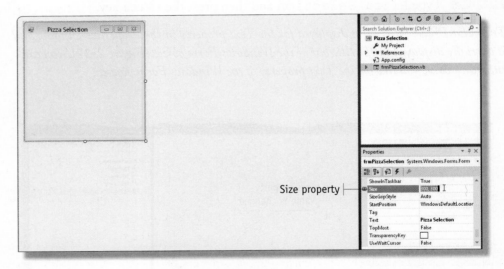

FIGURE 2-18

STEP 2   Type 430, 395 and then press the ENTER key.

The Windows Form object has been resized (Figure 2-19). The exact size of the Windows Form object is shown on the status bar as (number of horizontal pixels, number of vertical pixels). In Figure 2-19, the size of the Windows Form object is 430 pixels horizontally by 395 pixels vertically.

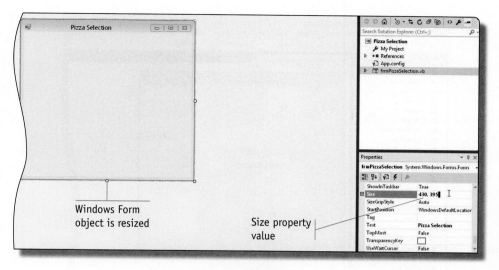

FIGURE 2-19

Adding GUI Objects

After setting up the Windows Form object as necessary for a project, you continue working on the user interface design by adding GUI objects to the form, such as labels, picture boxes, and buttons. Format and position the objects to make the form appealing and easy to use.

Add a Label Object

After sizing the Windows Form object, you can use the Toolbox to add other GUI objects as required. For example, a GUI often displays a message or labels an item in the window. To accomplish this, you can use the **Label .NET component** in the Toolbox to place a **Label object** on the Windows Form object. To add a Label object to a Windows Form object, you can complete the following steps:

> **STEP 1** Drag the Label .NET component from the Common Controls tab in the Toolbox over the Windows Form object to the approximate location where you want to place the Label object.

The pointer changes to a crosshair and small rectangle when you place it over the Windows Form object (Figure 2-20). The Label object will be placed on the form at the location of the small rectangle in the pointer.

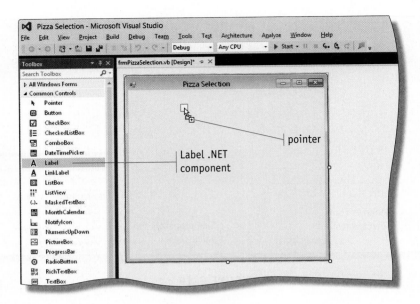

FIGURE 2-20

STEP 2   When the Label object is in the correct location, release the left mouse button.

The Label object is placed on the Windows Form object at the location you selected (Figure 2–21). The label is selected, as identified by the dotted border surrounding it. The default text within the label is Label1. In virtually all cases, you must change the label text to reflect the needs of the interface.

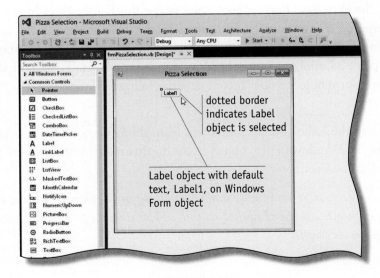

FIGURE 2-21

Name the Label Object

As with most objects you place on the Windows Form object, the first step after creating the object should be to name it. To give the Label object the name Heading with the Label prefix lbl, complete the following steps:

STEP 1 With the Label object selected, scroll in the Properties window until you find the (Name) property. Then, double-tap or double-click the (Name) property in the right column.

The default name, Label1, is selected (Figure 2-22). When a property is selected, you can change it.

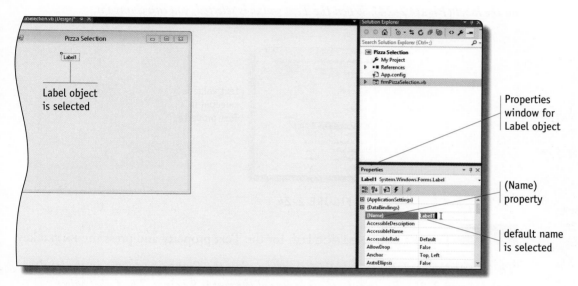

Label object is selected

Properties window for Label object

(Name) property

default name is selected

FIGURE 2-22

STEP 2 Type the new name as `lblHeading` and then press the ENTER key.

The name you entered is displayed in the (Name) property in the Properties window (Figure 2-23). You now can reference the Label object by its name in other parts of the program.

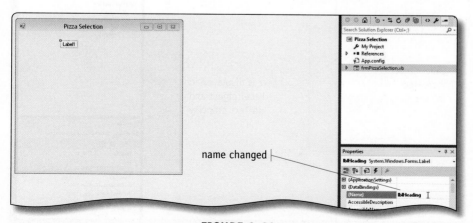

name changed

FIGURE 2-23

WATCH OUT FOR

If you make an error while typing a property value, such as the name, you can press the BACKSPACE key to erase your mistake and then type the correct data. You also can double-tap or double-click the property you want to change and start over.

ONLINE REINFORCEMENT

To view a video of the process in the previous steps, visit CengageBrain.com and navigate to the resources for this title. Tap or click the link for Chapter 2 and then navigate to Video 2-10.

Change the Text in a Label Object

The default text in a Label object, Label1, normally is not the text you want to display in the label. Therefore, you should change the Text property for the Label object to the value you want. To change the text on the label in Figure 2-21 to Pizza Selection, you can complete the following steps:

STEP 1 With the Label object selected, scroll in the Properties window until you find the Text property. Then, double-tap or double-click the value for the Text property in the right column.

The text value is selected in the right column of the Text property. The same text is displayed on the label (Figure 2-24). When the Text value is selected, you can change it.

FIGURE 2-24

STEP 2 Type `Pizza Selection` for the Text property and press the ENTER key.

The text you entered, Pizza Selection, is displayed in the Text property and in the label itself (Figure 2-25). By default, the font size of the text is 8 points. The Label object automatically expanded horizontally to accommodate the text you typed. By default, Label objects change to be the right size for the text in the Text property.

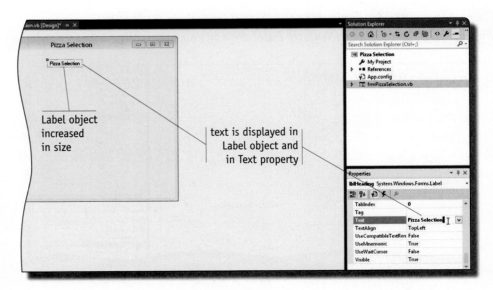

FIGURE 2-25

ONLINE REINFORCEMENT

To view a video of the process in the previous steps, visit CengageBrain.com and navigate to the resources for this title. Tap or click the link for Chapter 2 and then navigate to Video 2-11.

The text in a Label object can span multiple lines. To enter multiple lines for a Label object, you can complete the following steps:

STEP 1 With the Label object selected, tap or click the Text property name in the left column of the Properties window. Then, tap or click the arrow in the right column of the Text property.

A box opens in which you can enter multiple lines (Figure 2-26). As you type, you can move the insertion point to the next line by pressing the ENTER key. To accept the text for the label, press CTRL+ENTER. (In other words, hold down the CTRL key, press the ENTER key, and then release both keys.)

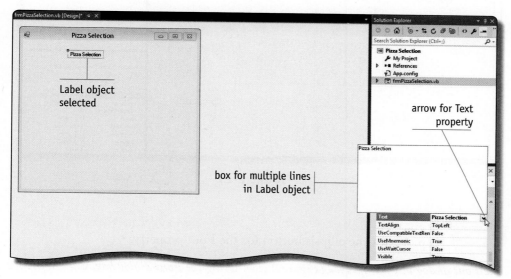

FIGURE 2-26

Change the Label Font, Font Style, and Font Size

The default font, font style, and font size of the text in a Label object often must be changed to reflect the purpose of the label. For example, in a label used as a heading for a window, the text should be larger than the default 8-point font size used for Label objects, and it should be bold to stand out as a heading. To change the font, font style, and font size of a label, you can select the label and then use the **Font property** to make the changes. To change the text in the lblHeading label to Tahoma font, make the font bold, and increase the font size to 16 points, you can complete the following steps:

STEP 1 Tap or click the Label object to select it. Scroll until you find the Font property in the Properties window. Tap or click the Font property in the left column of the Properties window.

The Label object is selected, as shown by the dotted border surrounding it (Figure 2-27). When you tap or click the Font property in the Properties window, a button with an ellipsis (three dots) is displayed in the right column. In the Properties window, an ellipsis button indicates that multiple choices for the property will be made available when you tap or click the button.

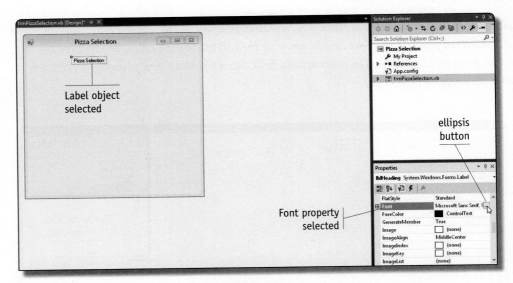

FIGURE 2-27

STEP 2   Tap or click the ellipsis button for the Font property.

The Font dialog box is displayed (Figure 2-28). Using the Font dialog box, you can change the font, font style, and size of the text in the Label object.

FIGURE 2-28

STEP 3   In the Font dialog box, scroll in the Font list until you find Tahoma and then tap or click it. Tap or click Bold in the Font style list. Tap or click 16 in the Size list.

The selections are highlighted in the Font dialog box (Figure 2-29).

Tahoma selected

Bold selected

OK button

16 points selected

FIGURE 2-29

STEP 4   Tap or click the OK button.

The font, font style, and font size in the Label object are changed as specified in the Font dialog box (Figure 2-30). The Label object automatically expands to accommodate the changed font. The changes also are made for the Font property in the Properties window.

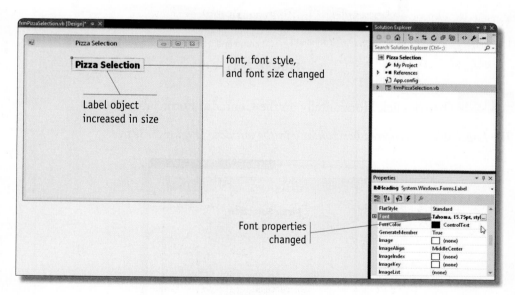

font, font style, and font size changed

Label object increased in size

Font properties changed

FIGURE 2-30

ONLINE REINFORCEMENT

To view a video of the process in the previous steps, visit CengageBrain.com and navigate to the resources for this title. Tap or click the link for Chapter 2 and then navigate to Video 2-13.

Center a Label Object in the Windows Form Object

When you place an object on the Windows Form object, your object may not be located in precisely the correct position. So you must align the object in the window. A single label often is centered horizontally in the window; that is, the distance from the left frame of the window to the beginning of the text should be the same as the distance from the end of the text to the right frame of the window. To horizontally center the label that contains the heading, you can complete the following steps:

STEP 1   With the Label object selected, tap or click Format on the menu bar and then point to Center in Form on the Format menu.

The Format menu is displayed and the pointer is located on the Center in Form command (Figure 2-31). The Center in Form submenu also is displayed. The two choices on the Center in Form submenu are Horizontally and Vertically. Horizontally means the label will be centered between the left and the right edge of the window. Vertically means the label will be centered between the top edge and the bottom edge of the window.

FIGURE 2-31

STEP 2   Tap or click Horizontally on the Center in Form submenu.

The Label object is centered horizontally in the window (Figure 2-32).

FIGURE 2-32

Aligning objects is an important aspect of user interface design because it makes objects and the interface easy to use. Centering within the Windows Form object is the first of several alignments you will make in this chapter.

Delete GUI Objects

In some instances, you might add an object to the Windows Form object and later discover you do not need the object in the user interface. When this occurs, you should delete the object from the Windows Form object. Visual Studio provides two primary ways to delete an object from the Windows Form object: the keyboard and a shortcut menu. To delete an object using the keyboard, perform the following steps:

STEP 1 Select the object to delete by tapping or clicking it.

When you tap or click an object, such as the label in Figure 2-33, the object is selected. When a label is selected, it is surrounded by a dotted border. As you saw with the Windows Form object (Figure 2-13), other objects are surrounded by a heavier border and sizing handles.

FIGURE 2-33

STEP 2 Press the DELETE key.

Visual Studio removes the object from the screen (Figure 2-34).

FIGURE 2-34

A second way to delete an object is to use a shortcut menu. To do so, press and hold or right-click the object to be deleted and then select Delete on the shortcut menu.

Use the Undo Button on the Standard Toolbar

As you work in Visual Studio to create a GUI, you might delete an object or perform another activity that you realize was an error. You can undo an action you just performed by tapping or clicking the Undo button on the Standard toolbar. To undo the action of deleting the heading label, you can perform the following step:

STEP 1 Tap or click the Undo button on the Standard toolbar.

When you tap or click the Undo button, the last action performed in Visual Studio is reversed. In Figure 2-35, the action that deleted the label (Figure 2-34) is reversed and the Label object now appears on the Windows Form object again.

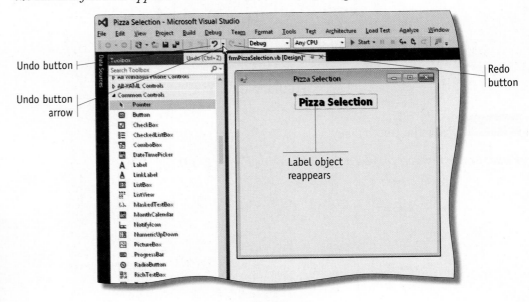

FIGURE 2-35

You can use the Undo button to undo more than just the last action performed. If you tap or click the Undo button arrow (Figure 2-35), many of the previous activities are shown in a list. You can undo any displayed activity by tapping or clicking it in the list.

When you use the Undo button, you might undo something you do not want to undo. You can tap or click the Redo button on the Standard toolbar to redo an action.

Learning to use the Undo and Redo buttons on the Standard toolbar means you can add or delete items in the GUI with the assurance that any error you make can be corrected immediately.

Add a PictureBox Object

When you want to display a picture in a window, such as the pizza pictures shown in Figure 2-1b and Figure 2-1c on pages 30 and 31, you must place a PictureBox object on the Windows Form object. Then, you place the picture in the PictureBox object. In this section, you will learn to add a PictureBox object to the Windows Form object. In Chapter 3, you will learn how to place a picture in the PictureBox object.

A **PictureBox** is an object much like a label. To add a PictureBox object to the window, you can use the Toolbox, as shown in the following steps:

STEP 1   With the Toolbox visible, drag the PictureBox .NET component on the Toolbox over the Windows Form object to the approximate location where you want the PictureBox object to be displayed.

The pointer changes when you place it over the Windows Form object (Figure 2-36). The upper-left corner of the PictureBox object will be placed on the form at the location of the small square in the pointer.

FIGURE 2-36

STEP 2 When the pointer is in the correct location, release the left mouse button.

A PictureBox object is placed on the Windows Form object in the default size (Figure 2-37). The PictureBox object is selected, as indicated by the sizing handles and the heavier border. Notice that when the pointer is inside the PictureBox object, it changes to a crosshair with four arrowheads. This indicates you can drag the PictureBox object anywhere on the Windows Form object.

FIGURE 2-37

As you can see, placing a PictureBox object on the Windows Form object is similar to placing a Label object on the Windows Form object. You can use the same technique for most objects within the Toolbox.

Name a PictureBox Object

When you add an object to the Windows Form object, your next action should be to name the object. The technique for naming a PictureBox object is identical to that for a Label object, except that the prefix for a PictureBox object is pic. For example, to give the name picDeepDish to the PictureBox object just added to the form, you can complete the following steps:

Step 1: Select the PictureBox object.
Step 2: Locate the (Name) property in the Properties window for the PictureBox object.
Step 3: Double-tap or double-click the value in the right column for the (Name) property, type picDeepDish as the name, and then press the ENTER key.

Resize a PictureBox Object

When you place a PictureBox object on the Windows Form object, it often is not the size required for the application. You can resize a PictureBox object using the same technique you used to resize the Windows Form object. Complete the following step to resize the PictureBox object:

STEP 1   Double-tap or double-click to the right of the Size property of the PictureBox object, type 185, 150, and then press the ENTER key.

When you change the Size property, the width and height of the PictureBox object are changed. In Figure 2-38, the width and height of the PictureBox object are increased. The actual size of the PictureBox object in pixels (185 horizontal pixels, 150 vertical pixels) is shown on the status bar.

HEADS UP

The Size property will change to the new size in the Properties window. If you know the exact size you want, you can enter it directly in the Size property for that object.

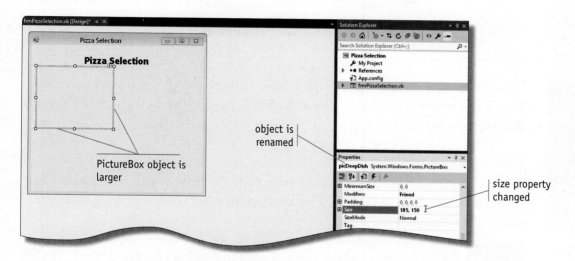

FIGURE 2-38

Add a Second PictureBox Object

You can add a second PictureBox object to the Windows Form object by performing the same technique you used previously, as in the following step:

STEP 1   Drag the PictureBox .NET component in the Toolbox to any location in the Windows Form object, and then release the left mouse button.

The PictureBox object is placed on the Windows Form object (Figure 2-39). Notice that the PictureBox objects in Figure 2-39 are different sizes. If you see a blue line as you drag the PictureBox object onto the Windows Form object, ignore it. You will learn about these lines later in this chapter.

ONLINE REINFORCEMENT

To view a video of the process in the previous step, visit CengageBrain.com and navigate to the resources for this title. Tap or click the link for Chapter 2 and then navigate to Video 2-18.

FIGURE 2-39

PictureBox .NET component

As with all objects you add to the Windows Form object, you should name the PictureBox object immediately after adding it. A good name for the second Picture-Box object is picThinCrust.

Make Objects the Same Size

Often you will want picture boxes and other GUI elements in your user interface to be the same size. You can use the Format menu to make GUI objects the same size, as shown in the following steps:

STEP 1 Select the object whose size you want to duplicate (in this example, the left PictureBox object in the window), hold down the CTRL key, and then tap or click the object you want to resize (the right PictureBox object in the window).

The left and right PictureBox objects are selected (Figure 2–40). The left PictureBox object is surrounded by white sizing handles and the right PictureBox object is surrounded by black sizing handles, which indicates the left PictureBox object is the controlling *object when sizing or alignment commands are executed. The first object selected always is the controlling object.*

FIGURE 2-40

STEP 2 Tap or click Format on the menu bar and then point to the Make Same Size command on the Format menu.

The Format menu and the Make Same Size submenu are displayed (Figure 2-41). The Make Same Size submenu provides commands to make the width, height, or both dimensions the same as the controlling object.

FIGURE 2-41

STEP 3 Tap or click Both on the Make Same Size submenu.

Visual Studio changes the size of the right PictureBox object to match the size of the left PictureBox object (Figure 2-42). Both the width and the height of the right PictureBox object are changed.

FIGURE 2-42

ONLINE REINFORCEMENT

To view a video of the process in the previous steps, visit CengageBrain.com and navigate to the resources for this title. Tap or click the link for Chapter 2 and then navigate to Video 2-20.

Align the PictureBox Objects

Notice in Figure 2-42 that the left PictureBox object is higher in the form than the right PictureBox object. When designing a GUI, you should consider aligning the elements to create a clean, uncluttered look for the user. **Alignment** means one element in the GUI is lined up horizontally (left and right) or vertically (up and down) with another element in the window. For example, in Figure 2-42 the GUI would look better if the PictureBox objects were aligned horizontally so their tops and bottoms were even across the window.

When you want to align objects that are already on the Windows Form object, select the objects to align and then specify the alignment you want. As you saw when changing the object size, the first object selected is the controlling object; when aligning, this means the other selected objects will be aligned with the first object selected. To horizontally align the two PictureBox objects in Figure 2-42, you can perform the following steps:

STEP 1 With the left and right PictureBox objects selected, as shown in Figure 2-42, tap or click Format on the menu bar and then point to Align on the Format menu.

The Format menu and the Align submenu are displayed (Figure 2-43). The left PictureBox object is the controlling object, as indicated by the white sizing handles, so the right Picture-Box object will be aligned horizontally with the left PictureBox object.

FIGURE 2-43

STEP 2 Tap or click Bottoms on the Align submenu.

The bottom of the right PictureBox object is aligned horizontally with the bottom of the left PictureBox object (Figure 2-44). Because the PictureBox objects are the same size, the tops also are aligned.

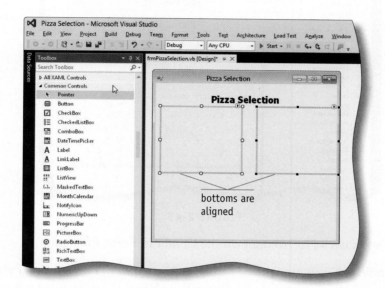

FIGURE 2-44

Notice on the Align submenu in Figure 2-43 that Visual Studio offers seven choices for alignment. When you are aligning objects horizontally, you should choose from the Tops, Middles, and Bottoms group. When you are aligning objects vertically, you should choose from the Lefts, Centers, and Rights group. You will learn how to align to a grid later in this book.

Center Multiple Objects Horizontally in the Window

From Figure 2-44, you can see that the PictureBox objects are not centered horizontally in the Windows Form object. As you learned, you can center one or more objects horizontally within the Windows Form object by using a command from the Format menu. To center the two PictureBox objects as a unit, you can complete the following steps:

STEP 1 With both PictureBox objects selected, tap or click Format on the menu bar and then point to the Center in Form command.

The Format menu is displayed (Figure 2-45). The Center in Form submenu also is displayed.

Format on
menu bar

FIGURE 2-45

STEP 2   Tap or click Horizontally on the Center in Form submenu.

The two PictureBox objects are centered horizontally as a unit in the Windows Form object (Figure 2-46). The left border of the left PictureBox object is the same distance from the window frame as the right border of the right PictureBox object.

FIGURE 2-46

ONLINE REINFORCEMENT

To view a video of the process in the previous steps, visit CengageBrain.com and navigate to the resources for this title. Tap or click the link for Chapter 2 and then navigate to Video 2-22.

Adding an object, naming it, sizing it, and aligning it are basic to GUI design.

Add a Button Object

A **Button object** is commonly used in a GUI. For example, you probably are familiar with the OK button used in many applications. Generally, when the program is executing, buttons are used to cause an event to occur. To place a Button object on the Windows Form object, you use the Toolbox. To create a Button object, you can complete the following steps:

STEP 1 With the Toolbox displayed in the Visual Studio window, drag the Button control in the Toolbox over the Windows Form object to the position where you want to place the button below the first PictureBox object.

When you drag the button over the Windows Form object, the pointer changes (Figure 2–47). The upper-left corner of the Button object will be placed at the lower-left corner of the rectangle.

Button .NET component

control pointer

FIGURE 2-47

STEP 2 When the pointer is positioned properly, release the left mouse button.

A standard-sized Button object is added to the Windows Form object (Figure 2–48). The text on the button is the default, Button1. The button is selected, as indicated by the heavier border and sizing handles.

default text

Button object is selected

Button object added

FIGURE 2-48

ONLINE REINFORCEMENT

To view a video of the process in the previous steps, visit CengageBrain.com and navigate to the resources for this title. Tap or click the link for Chapter 2 and then navigate to Video 2-23.

Name and Set Text for a Button Object

As with other objects you add to the Windows Form object, the first step after adding the Button object is to name it. A Button object name should begin with the prefix btn. For example, the name for the button you just added could be btnDeepDish.

In most cases, you also will change the text that appears on the Button object. To change the text on the btnDeepDish button, you can do the following:

STEP 1 With the Button object selected, scroll in the Properties window until you find the Text property. Double-tap or double-click the Text value in the right column, type Deep Dish, and then press the ENTER key.

The text for the Deep Dish button is changed on the button and in the Properties window (Figure 2-49).

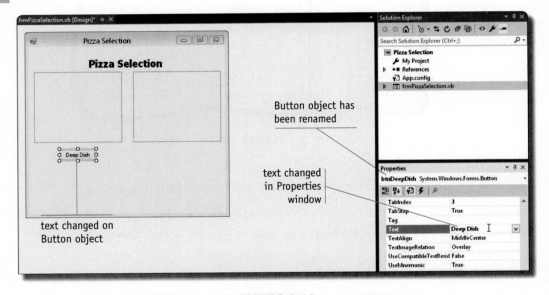

FIGURE 2-49

Change a Button Object's Size

Sometimes, the designer of the form may desire a large button or the button may not be big enough to display the button text. To change a Button object's size to a larger width, you can perform the following steps:

STEP 1 Place the pointer over the right edge of the Button object until the pointer changes to a double-headed arrow.

The pointer changes to a double-headed arrow, which indicates you can drag the border of the button to increase or decrease its size (Figure 2-50).

FIGURE 2-50

STEP 2 Drag the pointer to the right to increase the button's width, and then release the left mouse button.

As you drag the pointer to the right, the button becomes bigger (Figure 2-51).

FIGURE 2-51

To move a Button object, first place the pointer on the button; when the pointer changes to a crosshair with four arrowheads, drag the button to any location on the Windows Form object. You can move other objects on the Windows Form object using the same technique.

Add and Align a Second Button

Often, a window requires more than one button. When a second button is added to the window, a normal requirement is to align the buttons. As with PictureBox objects, you can align Button objects horizontally or vertically.

With the PictureBox objects, you saw that you can align objects after placing them on the Windows Form object. You also can align objects when you place them on the Windows Form object. To add a second button to the Windows Form object in Figure 2-51 and align it horizontally at the same time, you can complete the following steps:

STEP 1   Drag the Button .NET component from the Toolbox to the right of the Deep Dish button on the Windows Form object. Align the top of the rectangle in the pointer to the top of the Deep Dish button until a red line appears under the text of the buttons.

*The red line, called a **snap line**, indicates the text on the Deep Dish button is aligned with the text on the Button object being added to the Windows Form object (Figure 2-52). You can drag the Button object left or right to obtain the desired spacing between the buttons. If the red line disappears while you are dragging, move the pointer up or down until the red line reappears, signaling the objects are aligned horizontally.*

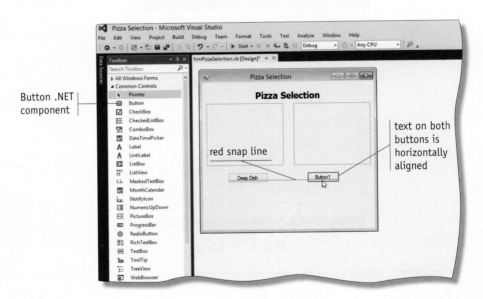

FIGURE 2-52

STEP 2   When the buttons are aligned and spaced as you like, release the left mouse button.

The Button2 object is aligned horizontally with the Deep Dish button (Figure 2-53). The text of each button is on the same line.

Button objects are
aligned horizontally
by their text

FIGURE 2-53

After adding the second Button object, you should name it, change the text as needed, and size the Button object if necessary. Assume you have named the second Button object btnThinCrust, changed the button text to Thin Crust, and made the two buttons the same size. Recall that you can make the Thin Crust button the same size as the Deep Dish button by completing the following steps:

Step 1: Tap or click the Deep Dish button and then, while holding down the CTRL key, tap or click the Thin Crust button.

Step 2: Tap or click Format on the menu bar, point to Make Same Size on the Format menu, and then tap or click Both on the Make Same Size submenu.

Step 3: To deselect the Button objects, tap or click anywhere on the Windows Form object except on another object.

Align Objects Vertically

The buttons in Figure 2-53 are aligned horizontally, but they also can be aligned vertically. To illustrate this point and to use snap lines to align objects that are already on the Windows Form object, assume that the Deep Dish and Thin Crust buttons are aligned vertically on the left side of the Windows Form object, with the Deep Dish button above the Thin Crust button. To align the Button objects vertically, you can complete the following steps:

STEP 1   If necessary, tap or click anywhere in the Windows Form object to deselect any other objects. Then, slowly drag the Thin Crust button below the Deep Dish button until vertical blue snap lines are displayed.

*As you drag, **blue snap lines** indicate when the sides of the objects are aligned vertically. In Figure 2-54, the buttons are the same size, so when the left side of the Deep Dish button is aligned with the left side of the Thin Crust button, the right sides are aligned as well. As a result, two blue vertical lines are displayed. If you drag the button a little more to the left or right, the buttons will not be aligned and the blue lines will disappear.*

FIGURE 2-54

STEP 2   When the blue lines appear, indicating the buttons are aligned vertically, drag the Thin Crust button up or down to create the proper spacing between the buttons, and then release the left mouse button.

The proper vertical distance between the buttons is a judgment call based on the needs of the application, the size of the Windows Form object, and the number of other elements in the window (Figure 2-55). As with many aspects of GUI design, the eye of the developer is critical when placing objects in the window.

FIGURE 2-55

The use of red and blue snap lines allows you to align objects on the Windows Form object by dragging instead of selecting the objects and using the Format menu.

Visual Studio offers a variety of tools to create and align elements in the GUI, and to make the user interface as effective and useful as possible.

Saving, Closing, and Opening a Visual Basic Project

As you are working on a Visual Basic project, you must save your work on a regular basis. Some developers save every 10 to 15 minutes, while others might wait for a natural break to save their work. Regardless, it is important to develop the habit of regularly saving your work.

To save the work you have completed, you can tap or click the Save All button on the Standard toolbar. The first time you save a project, the Save Project dialog box is displayed (Figure 2-56).

FIGURE 2-56

Select the location where you want to store your program. You might use a USB drive, the hard drive on your computer, or a network drive. If you have questions about where to store your program, check with your instructor or network administrator.

After you save the program the first time, tap or click the Save All button on the Standard toolbar to save your program in the same location with the same name.

Close Visual Studio 2015

To close Visual Studio, you can tap or click the Close button to the right of the title bar in the Visual Studio window. If you try to close Visual Studio but you have never saved your program, Visual Studio displays the Close Project dialog box (Figure 2-57).

FIGURE 2-57

You can choose to save your program or discard it. If you tap or click the Save button, the Save Project dialog box will be displayed (Figure 2-56) and you can save the program. If you tap or click the Discard button, your program will be discarded and not saved.

If you try to close Visual Studio but you have done more work since last saving your project, Visual Studio will ask if you want to save your recent work. In most cases, you should choose Yes.

Open a Visual Basic Project

After you save a project and close Visual Studio, you often will want to open the project and work on it again. To open a saved project, you can use one of several methods:

Method 1: Double-tap or double-click the solution file in the folder where it is stored. This method opens the solution and allows you to continue your work.

Method 2: With Visual Studio open, tap or click the Open File button on the Standard toolbar, locate the solution file, and open it in the same manner you do for most Windows programs.

Method 3: With Visual Studio open, tap or click File on the menu bar and then point to Recent Projects and Solutions on the File menu. A list of recent projects is displayed. Tap or click the name of the project you want to open. This method might not work well if you are not using your own computer because other projects might be listed.

After using one of these methods, you can continue working on your project.

Program Development Life Cycle

Now that you have learned the necessary skills to design a user interface in Visual Studio and Visual Basic, you are ready to learn about the program development life cycle. The **program development life cycle** is a set of phases and steps that developers follow to design, create, and maintain a computer program. The phases of the program development life cycle are as follows:

1. **Gather and Analyze the Program Requirements** — The developer must obtain information that identifies the program requirements and then document these requirements.
2. **Design the User Interface** — After the developer understands the program requirements, the next step is to design the user interface. The user interface provides the framework for the processing that will occur within the program.
3. **Design the Program Processing Objects** — A computer program consists of one or more processing objects that perform the tasks required by the program. The developer must determine what processing objects are required and then determine the requirements of each object.

4. **Code the Program** — After a processing object has been designed, the object must be implemented in program code. **Program code** is the set of instructions, written using a programming language such as Visual Basic 2015, that a computer executes.

5. **Test the Program** — As the program is being coded, and after the coding is completed, the developer should test the program code to ensure it is executing properly. The testing process is ongoing and includes a variety of stages.

6. **Document the Program/System** — As a program is being designed and coded, and after the process is completed, the developer should document the program. **Documenting a program** means using a prescribed method to write down the instructions for using the program, the way the program performs its tasks, and other items that users, developers, and management might require.

7. **Maintain the Program/System** — After a program is put into use, it probably will have to be modified in the future. For example, if a third type of pizza is added to the Pizza Selection program, it must be changed to reflect the new pizza type. The process of changing and updating programs is called **program and system maintenance**.

The program development life cycle rarely is accomplished in a linear fashion, with one phase completed before the next phase starts. Rather, programs are developed iteratively, which means phases and steps within phases might have to be repeated several times before the program is completed. For example, the requirements for a program might change after the developer has begun coding the program. If so, the developer must return to Phase 1 and gather and document the new requirements. Then, changes might be needed to the user interface or other parts of the program to accommodate the updated requirements. This process of moving back and forth within the program development cycle is normal when developing a computer program.

The next sections in this chapter explain Phase 1 and Phase 2 of the program development life cycle in more detail. The remaining phases are explained in Chapter 3.

Phase 1: Gather and Analyze the Program Requirements

An old programming adage states, "If you don't understand the problem to be solved, you will never develop a solution." While this seems self-evident, too often a program does not perform as desired because the designer did not understand the problem to be solved. Before beginning the user interface design, it is mandatory that the developer understand the problem.

In many programming projects, the developer is responsible for gathering program requirements by interviewing users, reviewing current procedures, and completing other fact-gathering tasks. The emphasis in this book is on learning to program using the Visual Basic 2015 language, so the process of gathering program requirements is beyond the scope of the book. You will be given the program requirements for each program in this book.

When the requirements have been determined, they must be documented so the developers can proceed to design and implement the program. The exact form of the requirements documentation can vary significantly. The format and amount of documentation might be dictated by the application itself or by the documentation standards of the organization for which the program is being developed. For Windows Desktop applications in this book, two types of requirements documentation will be provided for you. The first is the requirements document.

A **requirements document** identifies the purpose of the program being developed, the application title, the procedures to be followed when using the program, any equations and calculations required by the program, any conditions within the program that must be tested, notes and restrictions that the program must follow, and any other comments that would be helpful to understanding the problem.

Recall that the program being developed in this chapter and Chapter 3 is the Pizza Selection program (see Figure 2-1 on pages 30 and 31). The requirements document for the Pizza Selection program is shown in Figure 2-58.

REQUIREMENTS DOCUMENT

Date Submitted:	January 23, 2017
Application Title:	Pizza Selection
Purpose:	The Pizza Selection program will allow a user to select a type of pizza.
Program Procedures:	From a window on the screen, the user should view two different pizza types and then make a pizza selection.
Algorithms, Processing, and Conditions:	1. The user must be able to view choices for a deep-dish and thin-crust pizza until the user selects a pizza type. 2. When the user chooses a pizza type, a picture of the selected type should appear in the window. 3. Only one picture should be displayed at a time, so if a user chooses deep-dish pizza, only its picture should be displayed. If a user then chooses thin-crust pizza, its picture should be displayed instead of deep-dish pizza. 4. When the user makes a pizza selection, a confirming message should be displayed. In addition, the user should be prevented from identifying a pizza type after making the pizza selection. 5. After the user makes a pizza selection, the only allowable action is to exit the window.
Notes and Restrictions:	The user should be able to make a pizza selection only after choosing a pizza type.
Comments:	The pictures shown in the window should be selected from pictures available on the web.

FIGURE 2-58

The requirements document contains all the information a developer needs to design the program. In an event-driven program such as the Pizza Selection program, however, one additional document often is needed to clarify for the developer what should occur in the program. This document is the Use Case Definition.

A **use case** is a sequence of actions a user will perform when using the program. The **Use Case Definition** specifies each of these sequences by describing what the user will do and how the program will respond. The Use Case Definition for the Pizza Selection program is shown in Figure 2-59.

USE CASE DEFINITION

1. User taps or clicks Deep Dish or Thin Crust button.
2. Program displays a picture of the pizza chosen by the user and enables the pizza selection button.
3. User taps or clicks pizza type buttons to view the types of pizza as desired. Program displays the picture of the chosen pizza type.
4. User taps or clicks the Select Pizza button.
5. Program displays a pizza selection confirmation message, and disables both pizza type buttons and the Select Pizza button. The Exit Window button becomes active.
6. User terminates the program by tapping or clicking the Exit Window button.

FIGURE 2-59

As you can see, the Use Case Definition specifies the actions that the user performs and the actions the program must take in response.

The Use Case Definition is an important part of the requirements documentation for two reasons: (1) It defines for the developer exactly what will occur as the user operates the program. (2) It allows users to review the requirements documentation and ensure that the specifications are correct before the developer begins designing the program.

When gathering and documenting the program requirements, it is critical that users be involved. After all, the program is being developed for their use. When the users concur that the requirements documentation is correct, the developer can move forward into the design phases of the program with confidence that it will fulfill users' needs.

For the programs you will design in this book, the program requirements, including the requirements document and the Use Case Definition, will be provided to you. However, be aware that in many cases in the industry, an experienced developer must gather the requirements as well as implement them in a program.

Phase 2: Design the User Interface

Virtually all programs developed for a GUI are driven by the user's actions within the interface. These actions dictate the processing that the program should execute. Therefore, by designing the user interface, the developer will obtain a foundation for designing the rest of the program. By designing the user interface early in the design process, the developer also can interact with users and ensure that the interface will fulfill their requirements.

Expert program developers recognize the importance of the GUI. These developers spend 25 to 40 percent of program design on the user interface, which sometimes is called the **presentation layer** of the program because it is so critical to the program's success. Mobile devices use small screens, so an easy-to-follow user interface assists in clear navigation that relies on fingers instead of keyboard input.

In the past, developers would draw the user interface on paper and present the drawings to users for their approval. When using Visual Studio 2015, however, the developer should use the program's rapid application development tools to create the user interface. The interface is created with no functionality; that is, none of the buttons or other GUI elements will cause processing to occur. Often, these interface designs are called **mock-ups** because they are provided only for approval of the design. When the users or others approve the interface design, the developer can design the program elements required to implement the functions of the program.

An additional benefit of using Visual Studio to design the user interface is that you can use the completed design in the actual program; you do not have to re-create the design using other software.

CONSIDER THIS

My boss at my programming job asked me to design a prototype for the layout of the user interface. What is a prototype?

A prototype is a model of a software product or information system built for customer approval. It is similar to a mock-up of a user interface.

Principles of User Interface Design

Because the presentation layer of the program is so important, a number of principles and guidelines have been developed over the years for user interface design. While the intent of this book is not to create experts in user interface design, you should understand some of the principles so you can develop programs that are useful and usable. The following are some **design principles** you should incorporate into your user interface designs:

1. The most important principle to remember is that the user's ability to operate the program effectively depends on the design of the interface. If the GUI is easy to use and follow, the user will have a productive and enjoyable experience. On the other hand, if the user struggles to figure out how to enter data or which button to tap or click, the user interface design is defeating the purpose of the program.

2. If the user interface is not easy to use, the user will not be satisfied with the application regardless of how well it works.

3. The user interface includes the windows, graphics, and text shown on the screen, as well as the methods that interact with your program and cause operations to occur. Four primary means of interacting with a user interface are the keyboard, a pointing device such as a mouse, a touch interface, and voice input. The correct use of these tools significantly increases the probability of success for a traditional or touch-based user interface.

4. Using the interface should feel natural and normal. The developer must be aware of who the user is and how the user is accustomed to working. For example, the interface for a banking program in which a teller enters account information will be different from that of a graphic arts program that allows manipulation of graphics and photographs. Each must reflect the needs of the user.

5. Visual Studio contains a wide variety of objects, many of which can be used for similar purposes in the GUI. A good user interface provides the most appropriate object for each requirement. You will learn about all these objects and their correct use throughout this text.

6. Once an object is used for a particular purpose in the user interface, such as a button that causes a particular action, the object should be used for the same purpose throughout the program interface.

7. Objects must be arranged in the sequence in which they are used so the user can move from item to item on the screen in a logical, straightforward manner. Following this principle helps create an interface that is clean and easy to use. Again, the developer must understand the needs of the user. When this principle is not followed, a confusing interface can result.

8. The interface should be kept as simple as possible while containing all required functionality. Generally, the simpler the interface is, the more effective it will be. Consider using colors that are easy on the eyes to prevent eye fatigue.

9. When implemented, the user interface should be intuitive, which means the user should be able to use it with little or no instruction. In fact, the user should feel that no other interface could have been designed because the one they are using is the most natural.

By following these principles, you will create user interfaces that assist the user. The success of your program can depend on the user interface you design.

Sample Program

As you learned earlier, the Pizza Selection program is the sample program for this chapter and Chapter 3 (see Figure 2-1 on pages 30 and 31). The requirements document for this program is shown in Figure 2-58 on page 72, and the Use Case Definition is shown in Figure 2-59 on page 73. With these documents in hand, the first phase of the program development cycle is complete.

Sample Program — Phase 2: Design the User Interface

When beginning the design of the user interface, the primary sources of reference are the requirements document and the Use Case Definition for the program. Using these documents, the developer must analyze the program requirements and determine which elements are required in the user interface.

On a line-for-line basis, the analysis of the requirements document in Figure 2-58 on page 72 could proceed as follows:

1. The application will be presented in a window on the screen, so a Windows Forms Application using a Windows Form object is the appropriate means for creating the program.

2. The user will review the choices — a deep-dish or a thin-crust pizza — and then make a selection. When a pizza is selected, a picture of the pizza should be displayed. To choose each pizza, the program uses a Button object, a common tool that is familiar to users. When a user taps or clicks a button, the user has made a choice and the program responds appropriately. In this application, a good design decision is to use buttons so the user can decide between pizza types and then make a pizza selection. When the user taps or clicks the Deep Dish button, a picture of deep-dish pizza will be displayed. When the user taps or clicks the Thin Crust button, a picture of thin-crust pizza will be displayed. The user then taps or clicks the Select Pizza button to make the selection.

3. Two pictures must be displayed in the user interface — a deep-dish picture and a thin-crust picture. Although it is possible to display two different pictures in a single PictureBox object depending on the user's choice, you can develop a simpler and more easily understood user interface if a PictureBox object and a button work together. In other words, when the user taps or clicks the Deep Dish button, the deep-dish picture is displayed in the Deep Dish PictureBox object; when the user taps or clicks the Thin Crust button, the thin-crust picture is displayed in the Thin Crust PictureBox object. In this way, the user can associate a button with a picture box location and the user interface is intuitive and easy to use.

4. When the user makes a pizza selection by tapping or clicking the Select Pizza button, a message must be displayed to confirm the pizza selection. Therefore, a Label object must be included for the confirmation message.

5. After the user makes a pizza selection, the only action available to the user is to exit the window, so an Exit Window button is required.

6. In addition to the requirements in the program requirements document, standard procedure usually dictates that a heading should appear in the program window. Also, it is common practice to include simple instructions in the window so the user is not confused while using the interface. The heading and instructions can be included as Label objects.

7. As a result of this analysis, the user interface should include the following items: a Windows Form object that will contain all the other objects, two PictureBox objects to contain pictures of deep-dish and thin-crust pizzas, four Button objects (Deep Dish button, Thin Crust button, Select Pizza button, and Exit Window button), and three Label objects (Heading, Instructions, and Pizza Selection Confirmation).

After determining the elements required for the user interface, the developer can use Visual Studio 2015 to create a mock-up of the user interface. The exact placement of objects in the window is a creative process, and is guided by the principles of user interface design you have learned. Usually, no right answer exists because each developer will see a slightly different solution, but you must adhere to the principles of a good user interface design. Figure 2-60 shows the mock-up created for the Pizza Selection program.

FIGURE 2-60

Guided Program Development

This section on guided program development takes you step by step through the process of creating the sample program in this chapter. To create the mock-up shown in Figure 2-60, complete the steps on the following pages.

Guided Program Development

1

● **Open Visual Studio 2015**
Open Visual Studio and sign
in to your Microsoft account
(ref: Figure 2-2). If necessary,
change your Development
settings to Visual Basic, maximize
the Visual Studio window, and
close the Start page.

● **Create a New Visual Basic Windows Forms
Application** Create a new Visual Basic Windows
Forms Application project by tapping or
clicking the New Project button, selecting
Windows Desktop in the left pane, selecting
Windows Forms Application in the middle pane,
naming the project Pizza Selection, and then
tapping or clicking the OK button in the New
Project window *(ref: Figure 2-5)*.

● **Keep the Toolbox Visible** If necessary,
tap or click the Auto Hide button to keep the
Toolbox visible *(ref: Figure 2-11)*.

*The Visual Studio application
opens and a new project is
displayed in the window
(Figure 2-61). The Toolbox
remains visible regardless of the
location of the pointer.*

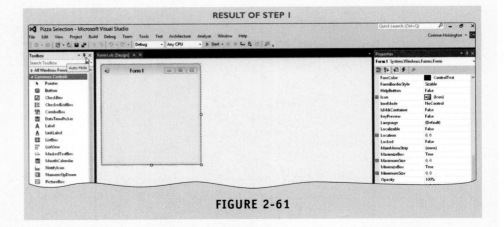

RESULT OF STEP I

FIGURE 2-61

● **Name the Windows Form Object** Tap or click View on the menu bar and select Solution Explorer to display the Solution Explorer. In the Solution Explorer window, press and hold or right-click Form1.vb. On the shortcut menu, tap or click Rename. Name the form `frmPizzaSelection` *(ref: Figure 2-15)*.

● **Change the Windows Form Object Text Property** With the Windows Form object selected, double-tap or double-click the text value for the Windows Form object in the Text property of the Properties window. Change the title bar text for the Windows Form object to `Pizza Selection` *(ref: Figure 2-17)*.

The text in the title bar of the Windows Form object has been changed to Pizza Selection (Figure 2-62). In addition, the name of the object has been changed to frmPizzaSelection.

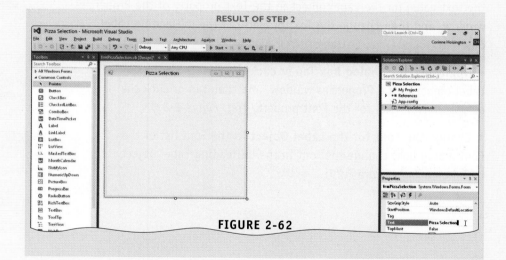

FIGURE 2-62

(continues)

Guided Program Development *continued*

3

- **Resize the Windows Form Object** Resize the Windows Form object to the approximate size shown in Figure 2-60 (430 × 395) by changing the Size property in the Properties window to `430, 395` *(ref: Figure 2-18)*.

4

- **Add a Label Object** Add a Label object by dragging the Label .NET component from the Toolbox to the Windows Form object. Place the label near the center and top of the Windows Form object *(ref: Figure 2-20)*.

- **Name the Label Object** Change the name of the Label object to `lblHeading` by using the (Name) property in the Properties window for the Label object *(ref: Figure 2-23)*.

- **Change the Label Object Text Property** Double-tap or double-click the text value for the Label object in the Text property of the Properties window, and then change the Text property of the lblHeading Label object to `Pizza Selection` *(ref: Figure 2-25)*.

- **Open the Font Dialog Box** Tap or click the Font property for the Label object in the Properties window, and then tap or click the ellipsis button (...) for the Font property *(ref: Figure 2-27)*.

- **Change the Font for the Label Object** In the Font list of the Font dialog box, change the font in the lblHeading Label object to Tahoma *(ref: Figure 2-29)*.

- **Change the Font Style for the Label Object** Using the Font style list in the Font dialog box, change the font style in the lblHeading Label object to Bold *(ref: Figure 2-29)*.

- **Change the Size for the Label Object** Using the Size list in the Font dialog box, change the font size in the lblHeading Label object to 16 points *(ref: Figure 2-29)*.

HINT

- **Center the Heading Horizontally** If necessary, select the lblHeading Label object. Using the Center in Form command on the Format menu, tap or click the Horizontally command on the Center in Form submenu to center the lblHeading Label object horizontally on the Windows Form object *(ref: Figure 2-31)*.

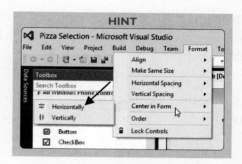

The lblHeading Label object text has been changed and the label object is centered horizontally on the Windows Form object (Figure 2-63). The vertical placement of the label (that is, the distance from the top of the window frame) depends on the eye of the developer, the size of the Windows Form object, and the other objects in the GUI. Although your label might be a little higher or lower, your window should closely resemble the one in Figure 2-63.

RESULT OF STEPS 3 AND 4

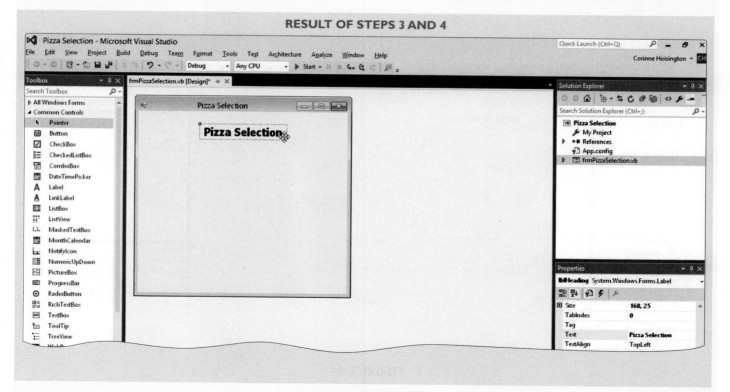

FIGURE 2-63

(continues)

Guided Program Development   *continued*

5

● **Add a PictureBox Object** Add a PictureBox object to the
Windows Form object by dragging a PictureBox .NET component
from the Toolbox to the Windows Form object. Place the PictureBox
object below and to the left of the heading label, as shown in
Figure 2-64 *(ref: Figure 2-36)*.

● **Name the PictureBox Object** Using the (Name) property in the
PictureBox Properties window, name the PictureBox object
picDeepDish.

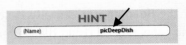

● **Resize the PictureBox Object** Resize the PictureBox object by
changing its Size property to 185, 150 *(ref: Figure 2-38)*.

*A properly sized PictureBox object is displayed in the Windows Form object (Figure 2-64). This PictureBox object will
display a picture of a deep-dish pizza when the program is completed in Chapter 3.*

RESULT OF STEP 5

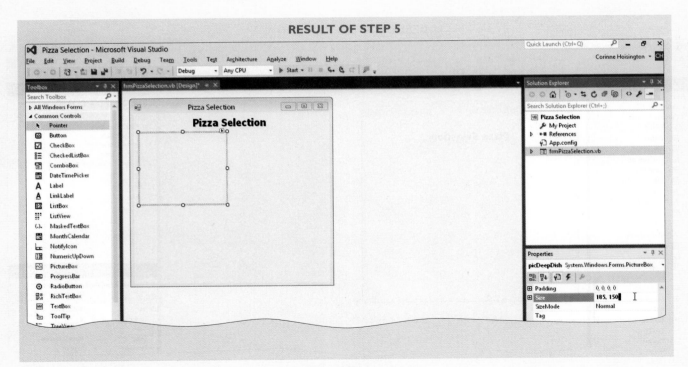

FIGURE 2-64

● **Add a PictureBox Object** Add a second PictureBox object to the Windows Form object by dragging a PictureBox .NET component from the Toolbox to the Windows Form object. Place it to the right of the first PictureBox object in the Windows Form object *(ref: Figure 2-39)*.

● **Name the PictureBox Object** Using the (Name) property in the PictureBox Properties window, name the PictureBox object `picThinCrust`.

● **Size the PictureBox Object** Make the second PictureBox object on the Windows Form object the same size as the first by using the Both command on the Make Same Size submenu of the Format menu *(ref: Figure 2-41)*.

● **Align the PictureBox Objects Horizontally** Align the bottoms of the two PictureBox objects horizontally by using the Bottoms command on the Align submenu of the Format menu *(ref: Figure 2-43)*.

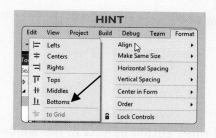

● **Set the Distance Between the PictureBox Objects** If necessary, adjust the distance between the two PictureBox objects to the approximate distance shown in Figure 2-65. First, tap or click the Windows Form object to deselect the two PictureBox objects. Then, place the pointer in the right PictureBox object and drag the object left or right to set the correct distance. As you drag, red snap lines should indicate the PictureBox objects still are aligned horizontally. When the PictureBox objects are the correct distance apart, release the object.

● **Center the PictureBox Objects in the Windows Form Object** Center the PictureBox objects horizontally as a unit within the Windows Form object by selecting both PictureBox objects, displaying the Center in Form command on the Format menu, pointing to the Center in Form command, and then tapping or clicking Horizontally on the Center in Form submenu *(ref: Figure 2-45)*.

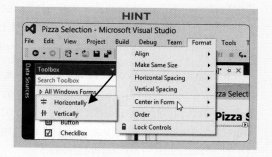

(continues)

Guided Program Development *continued*

The PictureBox objects are sized and located properly within the Windows Form object (Figure 2-65).

RESULT OF STEP 6

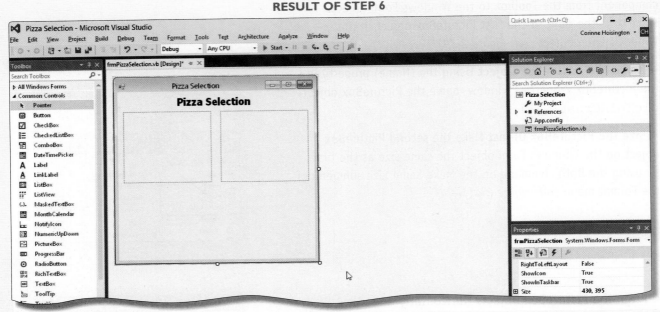

FIGURE 2-65

7

• **Add Three Button Objects to the Windows Form Object** Add three Button objects by dragging them onto the Windows Form object. Align them horizontally below the PictureBox objects at about the same locations shown in Figure 2-60 on page 77. Use red snap lines to align horizontally the buttons on the Windows Form object as you drag them onto the form *(ref: Figures 2-47 and 2-52)*.

• **Name the Three Button Objects** Using the (Name) property in the Properties window, name the left Button object `btnDeepDish`, the center Button object `btnSelectPizza`, and the right Button object `btnThinCrust`.

• **Change the Text Property for the Three Button Objects** Using the Text property in the Properties window, change the text for the left Button object to `Deep Dish`, the text for the middle Button object to `Select Pizza`, and the text for the right Button object to `Thin Crust` *(ref: Figure 2-49)*.

HINT

HINT

- **Change the Button Object Size** Change the size of the Select Pizza button to accommodate the Select Pizza with extra room on each side of the text *(ref: Figure 2-50)*.

- **Resize the Button Objects** Using the same technique you used for sizing the PictureBox objects, make all three Button objects the same size as the Select Pizza Button object.

- **Align the btnDeepDish Button Object** Center the Deep Dish Button object under the Deep Dish PictureBox object. First, select the Deep Dish PictureBox object and then select the Deep Dish Button object, either by using the ctrl key or by tapping or clicking *(ref: Figure 2-40)*. With the Deep Dish PictureBox object as the controlling object, use the Centers command on the Align submenu of the Format menu to align the PictureBox object and the Deep Dish Button object *(ref: Figure 2-43)*.

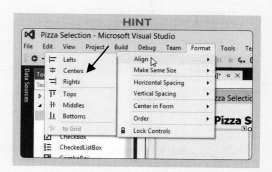

- **Align the btnThinCrust Button Object** Using the same technique, center the Thin Crust Button object below the Thin Crust PictureBox object.

- **Center the btnSelectPizza Button Object** Center the Select Pizza Button object horizontally within the Windows Form object by selecting the Select Pizza Button object and then using the Horizontally command on the Center in Form submenu of the Format menu *(ref: Figure 2-31)*.

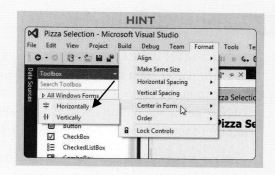

(continues)

The Button objects are sized and placed properly within the Windows Form object (Figure 2-66). All three buttons are the same size. The Deep Dish and Thin Crust buttons are centered under their respective PictureBox objects, and the Select Pizza button is centered in the Windows Form object.

RESULT OF STEP 7

FIGURE 2-66

8

- **Add a Label Object** Add the instructions Label object to the Windows Form object by dragging a Label .NET object from the Toolbox to the Windows Form object. Place it below the Button objects at the approximate location shown in Figure 2-60 on page 77 *(ref: Figure 2-19)*.

- **Name a Label Object** Using the techniques you have learned, name the Label object `lblInstructions`.

- **Change the Label Object Text Property** Using the techniques you have learned, change the text in the lblInstructions Label object to `Choose a pizza type and then click the Select Pizza button`.

HINT

A   Label

● **Change the Label Object Font** Using the techniques you have learned, change the font for the lblInstructions Label object to Tahoma, change the font style to Regular, and change the size to 9 points.

● **Center the Label Object** Using the techniques you have learned, center the lblInstructions Label object horizontally within the Windows Form object.

● **Add a Label Object** Using the techniques you have learned, add the final message Label object to the Windows Form object. The text of the label should read Enjoy your pizza selection. Place the Label object in the location shown in Figure 2-67. Name it lblConfirmation. Change the font to Tahoma, the font style to Regular, and the size to 9 points. Center the Label object within the Windows Form object.

The two Label objects contain the correct text and are centered horizontally in the Windows Form object (Figure 2-67).

RESULT OF STEP 8

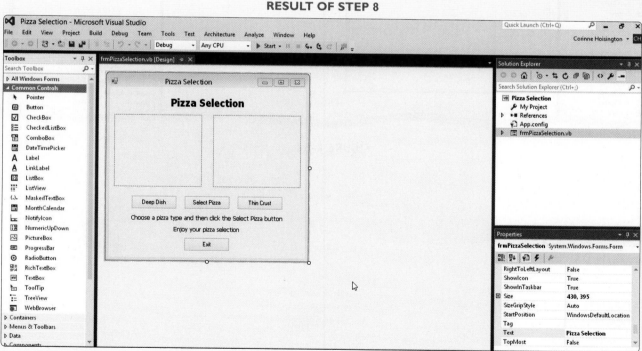

FIGURE 2-67

9

- **Add a Button Object** Add the Exit Window Button object by dragging a Button control onto the Windows Form object. Place it in the approximate location shown in Figure 2-68. Then, using the techniques you have learned, give the name `btnExit` to the Button object, change its text to `Exit Window`, make the Exit Window Button object the same size as the other Button objects in the window, and center the Exit Window Button object horizontally in the window.

The user interface mock-up is complete (Figure 2-68).

RESULT OF STEP 9

FIGURE 2-68

After completing the user interface mock-up, the designers will distribute the design to the users and others for approval. In many cases, the developers must implement changes the users request. Then they will resubmit the design for approval.

Summary

You have completed the steps to create the GUI mock-up for the Pizza Selection program. As you can see, many of the required steps are somewhat repetitive; the same technique is used repeatedly to accomplish similar tasks. When you master these techniques and other principles of user interface design, you will be able to design user interfaces for a variety of programs.

The items listed in the following table include all the new Visual Studio and Visual Basic skills you have learned in this chapter.

Visual Basic Skills		
Skill	**Figure Number**	**Video Number**
Run the completed program	Figure 2-1	Video 2-1
Open Visual Studio 2015	Figure 2-2	Video 2-2
Create a New Visual Basic 2015 Windows Desktop application	Figure 2-4	Video 2-3
Display the Toolbox	Figure 2-9	Video 2-4
Permanently Display the Toolbox	Figure 2-10	Video 2-5
Name the Windows Form Object	Figure 2-14	Video 2-6
Set the Title Bar Text in a Windows Form Object	Figure 2-16	Video 2-7
Resize a Form	Figure 2-18	Video 2-8
Add a Label Object	Figure 2-20	Video 2-9
Name a Label Object	Figure 2-22	Video 2-10
Change the Text in a Label Object	Figure 2-24	Video 2-11
Enter Multiple Lines for a Label Object	Figure 2-26	Video 2-12
Change the Label Font, Font Style, and Font Size	Figure 2-27	Video 2-13
Center a Label Object in the Windows Form Object	Figure 2-31	Video 2-14
Delete GUI Objects	Figure 2-33	Video 2-15
Use the Undo Button on the Standard Toolbar	Figure 2-35	Video 2-16
Add a PictureBox Object	Figure 2-36	Video 2-17
Resize a PictureBox Object	Figure 2-37	Video 2-18
Add a Second PictureBox Object	Figure 2-39	Video 2-19
Make Objects the Same Size	Figure 2-40	Video 2-20

Visual Basic Skills *(continued)*

Skill	Figure Number	Video Number
Align PictureBox Objects	Figure 2-43	Video 2-21
Center Multiple Objects Horizontally	Figure 2-45	Video 2-22
Add a Button Object	Figure 2-47	Video 2-23
Set Text for a Button Object	Figure 2-48	Video 2-24
Change the Button Object's Size	Figure 2-50	Video 2-25
Add a Button with Alignment (Use Snap Lines)	Figure 2-52	Video 2-26
Align Objects Vertically	Figure 2-54	Video 2-27
Save and Close a Visual Basic Project	Figure 2-56 and 2-57	
Open a Visual Basic Project	Page 70	

FIGURE 2-69

Learn Online

Reinforcement activities and resources are available at no additional cost on *CengageBrain.com*. Visit http://solutions.cengage.com/ctdownloads/ for detailed instructions about accessing the available resources at the Student Companion Site.

Knowledge Check

1–5. Label the following parts of the window:

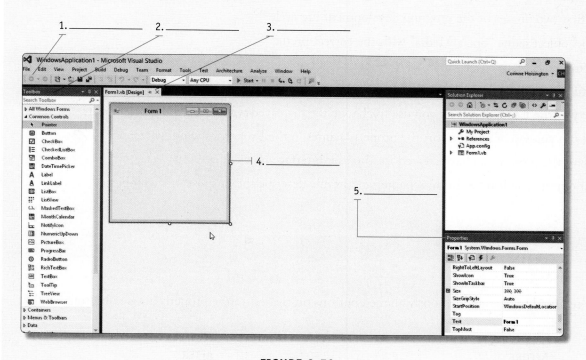

FIGURE 2-70

(continues)

Knowledge Check *continued*

6. What is the address of the website that allows you to sign up for a free Microsoft account?

7. What does RAD stand for?

8. What is the difference between red and blue snap lines?

9. What is the prefix of the Form object?

10. A Button, a Label, and a PictureBox are all _____.

11. How do you select four Button objects on the Windows Form object at the same time for alignment purposes?

12. What is the purpose of a mock-up?

13. What are the first two phases of the program development life cycle?

14. Write the Label object name "SocialMedia" with the correct prefix.

15. Write the Button object name "Report" with the correct prefix.

16. Write the PictureBox object name "Selfie" with the correct prefix.

17. Which property of the Label object do you use to change the displayed writing on the Form object?

18. Which button can you tap or click to sort the property names in the Properties window from A to Z?

19. How do you save the project you have created for the user interface mock-up?

20. Name the four objects you learned in this chapter and briefly describe the purpose of each object.

Debugging Exercises

1. List the steps required to change the poorly aligned buttons on the left to the properly aligned buttons on the right.

BEFORE   **AFTER**

FIGURE 2-71a   FIGURE 2-71b

Debugging Exercises *continued*

2. Change the order of the numbered Use Case Definition steps to correspond to the following problem definition: A college provides every incoming freshman with a gift card for a choice of two types of coffee from the cafeteria. Students should select the type of coffee they want. A program opens a window that displays each coffee type one picture at a time when a student taps or clicks the corresponding button. After making a decision, the student should tap or click the Place Order button. After selecting a type of coffee, the student should exit the application.

USE CASE DEFINITION

1. User taps or clicks the Place Order button.
2. User taps or clicks the Coffee button or Frappuccino button.
3. User taps or clicks the button not selected in Step 2.
4. User terminates the program by tapping or clicking the Close button.
5. Program displays an order confirmation message and disables both order buttons. The Close button becomes active.
6. Program displays a picture of the coffee order selected by the user and enables the Place Order button.
7. Program displays a picture of the coffee order selected by the user.

Program Analysis

1. After you have placed objects on the Windows Form object (Figure 2-72), list the steps you would follow to change the font for the Save the Polar Bears label to Tahoma font, Bold style, 18 points.

2. List the steps you would perform to center the Save the Polar Bears label horizontally.

3. List the steps you would perform to center the PictureBox object horizontally on the Windows Form object in Figure 2-72.

4. List the steps you would perform to change the font for the Donate Now button in Figure 2-72 to Tahoma, 10 points.

5. List the steps you would perform to align the two Button objects horizontally by the tops of the buttons.

6. List the steps you would perform to make the Donate Now button the same size as the Close Window button.

7. In the real world, why is it important to have a user interface mock-up approved before proceeding with the rest of the project?

FIGURE 2-72

Case Programming Assignments

Complete one or more of the following case programming assignments. Submit the program and materials you create to your instructor. The level of difficulty is indicated for each assignment.

●   = Easiest
●●   = Intermediate
●●●   = Challenging

1 ●
TECH JOB FAIR

Create a Windows form mock-up for the requirements document shown in Figure 2-73 and the Use Case Definition shown in Figure 2-74 on page 95. The Windows Form object and the other objects in the user interface are shown in Figure 2-75 on page 95.

REQUIREMENTS DOCUMENT	
Date:	October 13, 2015
Date Submitted:	
Application Title:	Tech Job Fair
Purpose:	This Windows Desktop application displays a welcome screen for the Tech Job Fair. The user can choose an option to view the date and location.
Program Procedures:	From a window on the screen, the user makes a request to see the fair's date and location.
Algorithms, Processing, and Conditions:	1. The user first views a Tech Job Fair window that displays the job fair name (Tech Job Fair), a job fair picture, and a phrase that states all students are welcome. 2. When the user chooses to view the date and location, the following information is displayed: May 2, 2016 Located in Lochlan Hall Room 101 3. After the user views the job fair information, the only allowable action is to exit the window.
Notes and Restrictions:	n/a
Comments:	The picture shown in the window can be found on CengageBrain.com. The name of the picture is Fair. Images will be added Chapter 3.

FIGURE 2-73

Tech Job Fair (continued)

USE CASE DEFINITION

1. The window opens, displaying the name of the event and a message stating that all students are welcome. All buttons are enabled.
2. User taps or clicks the View Job Fair Details button.
3. Program displays the tech job fair date and location between the buttons. The View Job Fair Details button is disabled.
4. User taps or clicks the Exit Window button to terminate the application.

FIGURE 2-74

Tahoma font, 22 points, bold

no text in title bar

Tech Job Fair

All Students are Welcome

View Job Fair Details

May 2, 2016

Tahoma font, 11 points

Located in Lochlan Hall

Room 101

Exit Window

FIGURE 2-75

2 • VEGETARIAN SPECIALS

Create a Windows Form mock-up for the requirements document in Figure 2-76 and the Use Case Definition shown in Figure 2-77 on page 97. The Windows Form object and the other objects in the user interface are shown in Figure 2-78 on page 97.

REQUIREMENTS DOCUMENT

Date:	January 10, 2017
Date Submitted:	
Application Title:	Vegetarian Specials
Purpose:	This Windows Desktop application displays the vegetarian specials for a restaurant named Plant. The user can select one of two specials: falafel or veggie burger.
Program Procedures:	From a window on the screen, the user orders one of two vegetarian special dishes and confirms the order with a message.
Algorithms, Processing, and Conditions:	1. The user must be able to identify the falafel or veggie burger special name as many times as necessary until making a decision.
	2. When the user identifies the vegetarian special, a picture of that meal appears in the window.
	3. Only one picture should be displayed at a time.
	4. When the user selects falafel, a message should be displayed to confirm the selection of the vegetarian dish. In addition, the user should be prevented from identifying another meal after selecting a dish.
	5. After the user selects a meal, the only allowable action is to exit the window.
Notes and Restrictions:	A user can select a meal only after viewing one of the images of the meals.
Comments:	1. The picture shown in the window can be found on cengagebrain.com.
	2. The names of the pictures are Falafel and Veggie. Images will be added Chapter 3.

FIGURE 2-76

Vegetarian Specials (continued)

USE CASE DEFINITION

1. User taps or clicks Falafel button or Veggie Burger button.
2. Program displays a picture of the meal identified by the user and enables the meal selection button.
3. User taps or clicks meal buttons to view meals as desired. Program displays the picture of the identified vegetarian meal.
4. User taps or clicks the Select Meal button.
5. Program displays a meal confirmation message and disables both meal buttons and the Select Meal button.
6. The Exit Window button becomes active. User terminates the program by tapping or clicking the Exit Window button.

FIGURE 2-77

FIGURE 2-78

3 ● VOTE FOR THE BEST CAMPUS SELFIE

Create a Windows Form mock-up for the requirements document shown in Figure 2-79 and the Use Case Definition shown in Figure 2-80 on page 99. The Windows Form object and the other objects in the user interface are shown in Figure 2-81 on page 99.

REQUIREMENTS DOCUMENT

Date:	August 16, 2016
Date Submitted:	
Application Title:	Selfies
Purpose:	This Windows Desktop application displays the two finalists for the best campus selfie photos. The user can select one of two selfies.
Program Procedures:	From a window on the screen, the user selects one of two selfie finalists and confirms the vote with a message.
Algorithms, Processing, and Conditions:	1. The user must be able to identify the first finalist selfie entitled "Cheer" or the second finalist entitled "Connect" as many times as necessary until making a decision. 2. When the user taps or clicks the button to view a selfie, a picture of that finalist appears in the window. 3. Only one picture should be displayed at a time. 4. When the user selects the first selfie, a message should be displayed to thank the user for voting. In addition, the user should be prevented from identifying the other selfie picture after voting. 5. After the user selects a selfie, the only allowable action is to exit the window.
Notes and Restrictions:	A user can select a selfie only after viewing one of the images.
Comments:	1. The picture shown in the window can be found on CengageBrain.com. 2. The names of the pictures are Selfie1 and Selfie2. Images will be added in Chapter 3.

FIGURE 2-79

Vote for the Best Campus Selfie (*continued*)

USE CASE DEFINITION

1. User taps or clicks Selfie "Cheer" button or Selfie "Connect" button.
2. Program displays a selfie identified by the user and enables the Select Selfie button.
3. User taps or clicks selfie buttons to view finalist pictures as desired. Program displays the picture of the identified selfie.
4. User taps or clicks the Select Selfie button.
5. Program displays a vote confirmation message and disables both selfie buttons and the Select Selfie button.
6. The Exit Window button becomes active. User terminates the program by tapping or clicking the Exit Window button.

FIGURE 2-80

FIGURE 2-81

4 ●●
FALL MARATHON

Create a Use Case Definition document and design a Windows form mock-up based on the requirements document in Figure 2-82.

REQUIREMENTS DOCUMENT

Date:	October 13, 2016
Date Submitted:	
Application Title:	Fall Marathon
Purpose:	This Windows Desktop application displays a welcome screen to market the Fall Marathon. The user can choose an option to view the date, start location, and details.
Program Procedures:	From a window on the screen, the user makes a request to see the marathon's date, start location, and details.
Algorithms, Processing, and Conditions:	1. The user first views a Fall Marathon window that displays the title (Fall Marathon), a marathon picture, and a phrase that states that full and half marathon runners are welcome.
	2. When the user chooses to view the date, start location, and details, the following information is displayed:
	May 30, 2017
	Ryan Park
	Start Time: 8:00 AM
	For more information, view the Fall Marathon Facebook page 3.
	After the user views the marathon information, the only allowable action is to exit the window.
Notes and Restrictions:	Design your own layout.
Comments:	1. The picture shown in the window can be found on cengagebrain.com.
	2. The name of the picture is Marathon. Images will be added in Chapter 3.

FIGURE 2-82

5 ●● GUITAR STORE

Create a Use Case Definition document and design a Windows Form mock-up based on the requirements document in Figure 2-83.

REQUIREMENTS DOCUMENT

Date:	March 21, 2017
Date Submitted:	
Application Title:	Guitar Store
Purpose:	A local guitar store has set special prices on three guitars this week. A customer can choose one of three guitar types. The program must display each of the guitars upon request. The customer can then select a guitar for purchase.
Program Procedures:	From a window on the screen, the user selects one of three guitars. A picture of the selected guitar is displayed in the window. The user then can choose a guitar for purchase.
Algorithms, Processing, and Conditions:	1. The user selects a guitar. Then, a picture of the guitar is displayed in the window. 2. The user can select any of the three guitars. Only the picture of the selected guitar should be displayed. 3. The user can select guitars as many times as necessary and display the pictures of the guitars. 4. The user finds a guitar, chooses it for purchase, and taps or clicks the Purchase button. 5. After the user chooses a guitar, a message stating "Enjoy your guitar!" should be displayed. 6. After the user chooses a guitar, the only allowable action is to exit the window.
Notes and Restrictions:	The user should not be able to choose a guitar until viewing at least one guitar image.
Comments:	1. The available guitars are classical acoustic, steel string acoustic, and electric guitar. 2. The pictures shown in the window can be found on cengagebrain.com. The names of the pictures are Classical, Electric, and Steel. Images will be added in Chapter 3.

FIGURE 2-83

6 ●●
FACEBOOK MOVIE VOTING

Create a Use Case Definition document and design a Windows Form mock-up based on the requirements document in Figure 2-84.

REQUIREMENTS DOCUMENT

Date:	October 16, 2016
Date Submitted:	
Application Title:	Movie Voting
Purpose:	Facebook wants you to select your favorite movie of the year and allows the user to vote for his or her overall favorite. The user should be able to select one of three movies and then be able to vote for that movie as his or her overall favorite.
Program Procedures:	From a window on the screen, the user selects one of three movies. The names of the three top movies are displayed together with a picture of each movie. Then, the user can vote for the movie as his or her overall favorite.
Algorithms, Processing, and Conditions:	1. The user selects each movie and a picture of the movie is displayed in the window.
	2. The user can select any of three movie titles. Only the name of the movie and picture for the selected movie should be displayed.
	3. The user can select different movies back and forth to make a decision for their favorite movie.
	4. After the user selects a movie, the user should be able to vote for their favorite movie. The user cannot select their favorite movie until viewing at least one movie picture.
	5. After the user votes, a message stating that their favorite movie vote has been received.
	6. After the user votes, the only acceptable action is to tap or click the Exit Window button.
Notes and Restrictions:	The user should be able to vote until he or she has selected their favorite movie.
Comments:	1. You (the developer) should select three movie titles from this year and select three online pictures to represent those movies.
	2. You can download the pictures from a site such as www.google.com/images. Images will be added in Chapter 3.

FIGURE 2-84

7 ● ● ●
AIRLINE SNACK SELECTION

Create a requirements document and a Use Case Definition document and then design a Windows Form mock-up based on the case project shown in Figure 2-85.

An international airline requests a computer application that will run on the personal television monitors on the back of each seat in the plane. The application should request which free snack you would like during the flight, display the choices as buttons, and then display an image of the snack you select. Another button allows you to make your final snack selection and display a confirmation message.

Snack
Cheese and Crackers
Chocolate Chip Cookies
Mini Pretzels
Salted Peanuts

FIGURE 2-85

8 ••• TRAVEL SPECIALS

Create a requirements document and a Use Case Definition document and then design a Windows Form mock-up based on the case project shown in Figure 2-86.

Your local travel agent requests a computer application that advertises the travel specials of the week from your city. This week's flight specials are as follows:

Destination	Price
New York City	$399 round trip
Las Vegas	$419 round trip
Miami	$520 round trip
St. Thomas	$619 round trip
Hawaii	$828 round trip

Write an application that allows the user to select any of the five vacation destinations. When the user selects a vacation destination, the corresponding flight price and a picture of the destination should be displayed. Clear each prior price and picture when the user selects a different vacation destination. In addition to a picture of the destination, include a webpage address that features the selected location. After selecting a destination, the user should be able to book the flight and then exit the window.

FIGURE 2-86

9 ●●●
LACROSSE TICKETS

Create a requirements document and a Use Case Definition document and then design a Windows Form mock-up based on the case project shown in Figure 2-87.

Your favorite university lacrosse team has asked you to develop a Windows application that allows the user to see the four types of game tickets offered, one at a time. Then, the user should be able to reserve a single game ticket for the selected seat type. The four types of stadium seating and their base prices are as follows:

Name of Ticket	Minimum Price
Upper Endline Seating	$15.00
Lower Endline Seating	$25.00
Sideline Seating	$30.00
Club Seats	$50.00

For each type of seating, your program should display the base price and a picture depicting an example of the seating type. Clear each price and picture when the user selects a different seating type. After selecting a ticket, the user should be able to purchase the ticket and then exit the window.

FIGURE 2-87

Program Design and Coding

OBJECTIVES

You will have mastered the material in this chapter when you can:

- Change the color properties of an object

- Add images to a PictureBox object

- Locate and save an image from the web

- Import an image into the Program Resources folder

- Size an image

- Set the Visible property in the Properties window

- Set the Enabled property in the Properties window

- Run a Visual Basic 2015 program

- Enter Visual Basic 2015 code

- Understand Visual Basic 2015 code statement formats

- Use IntelliSense to enter Visual Basic 2015 code statements

- Use code to set the Visible property of an object

- Use code to set the Enabled property of an object

- Enter comments in Visual Basic 2015 code

- Correct errors in Visual Basic 2015 code

- Write code to use the Close() procedure

- Print code

- Prepare an event-planning document

Introduction

In Chapter 2 you completed the design of a graphical user interface (GUI) mock-up. While users and others can approve the mock-up as being functional, the developer normally must make a variety of changes to the GUI to prepare it for the actual production version of the program. Among these changes are the following:

- Adding color to the interface to make it more visually appealing
- Acquiring and including images that are required for the program
- Setting interface object properties in accordance with the needs of the program

Once these tasks have been completed, Phase 2 of the program development life cycle (PDLC) is complete.

The next two phases of the PDLC are as follows:

- Phase 3: Design the program processing objects
- Phase 4: Code the program

This chapter will provide the skills and knowledge necessary to complete Phase 2 of the PDLC and then complete Phases 3 and 4.

Sample Program

You will recall that the sample program for Chapter 2 and this chapter is the Pizza Selection program. Windows for the program are shown in Figure 3-1.

PictureBox objects are not visible

Select Pizza button is dimmed

confirmation message is not visible

Exit Window button is dimmed

FIGURE 3-1a

picture of thin-crust pizza is displayed

Select Pizza button is enabled

Thin Crust button is clicked

Exit Window button is dimmed

FIGURE 3-1b

Brand X Pictures/Getty Images

Select Pizza
button is
clicked

instructions are
not displayed

confirmation message
indicates pizza has
been selected

Exit Window
button is enabled

FIGURE 3-1c

Brand X Pictures/Getty Images

In the opening window (Figure 3-1a), no images appear in the PictureBox
objects, and the Select Pizza button and Exit Window button are dimmed, which
means they are disabled (visible, but not available for selection) when the program
begins. In Figure 3-1b, the user tapped or clicked the Thin Crust button, so the
picture is displayed. In addition, the Select Pizza button is enabled. The Exit
Window button still is dimmed. In Figure 3-1c, the user has selected a type of pizza,
so the pizza selection confirmation message is displayed. The Deep Dish, Select
Pizza, and Thin Crust buttons are dimmed and the Exit Window button is enabled.
When the program runs, each of these changes occurs through the use of Visual
Basic code you enter into the program, as you will discover later in this chapter.

Fine-Tune the User Interface

You learned about some properties of Visual Basic objects in Chapter 2, including
the Name property and the Text property. As you probably noted while viewing the
Properties window in Chapter 2, more properties are available for each of the objects
in a GUI. In many cases, you set these properties to fine-tune the user interface and
make it more usable. In the sample program, the BackColor and ForeColor properties make the user interface more attractive and effective.

BackColor and ForeColor Properties

The **BackColor** of an object is the color displayed in its background. For example, in
Figure 3-1 on pages 108 and 109 the BackColor of the Windows Form object is white
instead of the default gray color, and the BackColor of the Button objects is a wheat
shade. You can select the BackColor of an object by using the **BackColor property** in
the Properties window. The **ForeColor** of an object is the color displayed in the text
of the object. The heading Label object that displays the Pizza Selection text uses a
text color called Firebrick. To change the BackColor of a Windows Form object from
its default color of Control (gray) to White, you can complete the following steps:

STEP 1   Tap or click the Windows Form object to select it. (Do not tap or click any of the objects on the Windows Form object.)

The Windows Form object is selected, as indicated by the thick border and the sizing handles (Figure 3-2).

Windows Form object is selected

FIGURE 3-2

STEP 2   If necessary, scroll in the Properties window until the BackColor property is displayed, and then tap or click the right column of the BackColor property.

The BackColor property is selected, and the BackColor arrow is displayed (Figure 3-3).

BackColor arrow

BackColor property is selected

FIGURE 3-3

STEP 3   Tap or click the BackColor arrow. Then, tap or click the Web tab to display the Web tabbed page.

The color window opens within the Properties window (Figure 3-4). The Web tabbed page contains more than 100 named colors you can display as the BackColor for the selected object, which in this case is the Windows Form object.

FIGURE 3-4

STEP 4 If necessary, scroll until White is displayed in the list of colors.

The name and a sample of the White color are displayed (Figure 3-5).

FIGURE 3-5

STEP 5 Tap or click White on the color list.

The background color in the Windows Form object is changed to White (Figure 3-6).

FIGURE 3-6

You can use the same technique to change the BackColor or ForeColor of any object that contains the BackColor or ForeColor properties, including Button and Label objects.

Add Images to a PictureBox Object

PictureBox objects are used to display a graphic image. The sample program can display a picture of a deep-dish pizza and a thin-crust pizza. You must specify the image that will be displayed in a particular PictureBox object. Before specifying the image, however, you must locate the image and then place it in the Resources folder that is linked to the application. The general steps for displaying an image in a PictureBox object are as follows:

1. Locate the image to be displayed in the PictureBox object. You might locate this image on the web, in which case you must store the image in a folder on your computer, or the image might already be stored on your computer or a local network.
2. Import the image into the **Resources folder**. This step makes the image available for display within the PictureBox object. Multiple images can be placed in the Resources folder.
3. Specify the image to be displayed within the PictureBox object.

Each of these steps will be explained on the following pages.

Locate and Save an Image from the Web

Images are available from a multitude of sources, from your own digital camera to millions of publicly available images on the web. If you work for a company, it might have photos and graphic logo images that can be used in company applications.

In this book, you can use the Student Companion Site to retrieve an image. For example, to retrieve the DeepDish image from this site, you can complete the following steps:

STEP 1   Open your web browser. (This example uses Internet Explorer; steps for other browsers might vary slightly.) Enter www.cengagebrain.com in the Address box, and then press the ENTER key. Enter 9781285856896 (the book's ISBN) in the Search text box, and then tap or click the Search button. Select the Free Materials tab, and then tap or click the Access Now button to display your student resources.

The browser window opens and the Student Companion Site for this book is displayed (Figure 3-7).

HEADS UP

While many websites offer images you can select, three sites are particularly useful: bing.com/images, www.google.com/images, and www.webshots.com. When you visit sites, not all images are available for free download. In some cases, the images are copyrighted and you must acquire rights to use them. In addition, some sites require a fee before the image can be used. Therefore, you should download only images for which you have paid and acquired the rights to use or that are free of copyright restrictions and available to everyone.

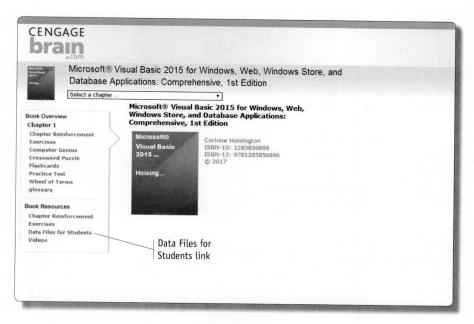

FIGURE 3-7

STEP 2   In the left pane, tap or click Data Files for Students.

The file available for download is displayed in the browser window (Figure 3-8).

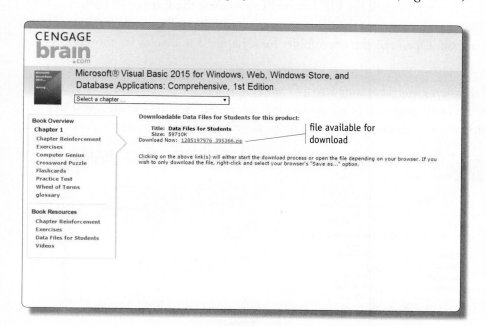

FIGURE 3-8

STEP 3   Tap or click the Download Now link, tap or click Save as, and then navigate to the location on your computer where you store downloaded files.

In the Save As dialog box (Figure 3-9), you must identify the drive and folder in which you want to store the zipped files containing the Data Files for Students. The location depends on your computer and drives.

Save As
dialog box

location for saving
downloaded files

zipped file containing
Data Files for Students

FIGURE 3-9

STEP 4 Tap or click the Save button to save the zipped file. Navigate to the
location of the downloaded file, and then double-click the file. Tap or click
the Browse button, navigate to the folder where you want to store files for this
book, and then tap or click the OK button. Tap or click the Extract all button
on the Extract tab to extract the files to the selected folder. Tap or click the
Extract button. Open the extracted folder for Chapter 3 to display its contents.

*The image files for Chapter 3 are displayed in a folder window (Figure 3-10). Remember
where you save the images because later you must locate and import them into the Resources
folder for use in the program. In all sample programs in this book, images are stored on a
USB drive that is designated as drive E. Image file names should not contain spaces.*

files are
on drive E:

image files
for Chapter 3

ONLINE REINFORCEMENT

To view a video of the process
in the preceding steps, visit
CengageBrain.com and navigate
to the resources for this title.
Tap or click the link for Chapter 3
and then navigate to Video 3-3.

FIGURE 3-10

Import the Image into the Program Resources Folder

After you have saved an image on a storage device that is available to your computer, you should import the image into the program's Resources folder so the image is available for use. To import the DeepDish image into the Resources folder, you can complete the following steps:

STEP 1 If necessary, open Visual Studio 2015 and the Pizza Selection Visual Basic program. Select the picDeepDish PictureBox object by tapping or clicking it. Scroll in the PictureBox Properties window until the Image property is visible. Tap or click the Image property name in the left list of the Properties window.

*With the PictureBox object selected, the Properties window displays all the properties of the object (Figure 3-11). The **Image property** specifies the image that should be displayed in the selected PictureBox object. The Image property is selected in the Properties window. The Image property's ellipsis button is displayed in the right column of the Image property.*

FIGURE 3-11

STEP 2 Tap or click the ellipsis button in the right column of the Image property.

*The **Select Resource dialog box** opens (Figure 3-12) and displays the resources that have been imported for the program. In Figure 3-12, no resources have been imported.*

Select Resource
dialog box

no resources
imported

Import button

FIGURE 3-12

STEP 3 Tap or click the Import button in the Select Resource dialog box. Use the features of the Open dialog box to locate the file you want to import into the program. In this case, you want to import the DeepDish.jpg file stored on drive E, which is a USB drive.

The Open dialog box opens when you tap or click the Import button (Figure 3–13). The DeepDish.jpg file is stored on drive E.

Open dialog
box

Chapter 3 folder on
REMOVABLE (E:)

DeepDish picture

Open button

FIGURE 3-13

STEP 4   Select DeepDish.jpg. Tap or click the Open button in the Open dialog box.

The Select Resource dialog box is displayed again, but now the DeepDish image is identified in the Project resource file list (Figure 3-14). The image appears in the preview window. This means the image is now part of the resources for the program. You no longer need to locate the image on the USB drive to include the image in a Picture Box object.

Select Resource
dialog box

DeepDish image
is selected

DeepDish image in
preview window

FIGURE 3-14
Brand X Pictures/Getty Images

STEP 5   With the DeepDish file name selected in the Project resource file list, tap or click the OK button in the Select Resource dialog box.

The DeepDish image is displayed in the picDeepDish PictureBox object (Figure 3-15). In addition, the Resources folder is added to the Solution Explorer window, indicating the Resources folder now is part of the program.

Resources
folder

DeepDish image
in picDeepDish
PictureBox object

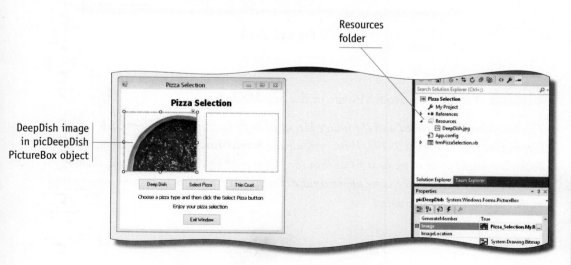

FIGURE 3-15

Brand X Pictures/Getty Images

ONLINE REINFORCEMENT

To view a video of the process in the preceding steps, visit CengageBrain.com and navigate to the resources for this title. Tap or click the link for Chapter 3 and then navigate to Video 3-4.

HEADS UP

In the example, StretchImage is selected in the SizeMode list in the Properties window for PictureBox objects (see Figure 3-16). The other choices and their actions are as follows:

- **Normal** — No changes are made to the image size or the size of the PictureBox object. Visual Studio places the image in the PictureBox object and aligns the upper-left corner of the image with the upper-left corner of the PictureBox object.

- **AutoSize** — Visual Studio increases or decreases the size of the PictureBox object to accommodate the size of the image. The entire image is visible and fits precisely in the PictureBox object.

- **CenterImage** — No changes are made to the image size or the size of the PictureBox object. Visual Studio places the image in the PictureBox object and aligns the center of the image with the center of the PictureBox object.

- **Zoom** — The image size is either reduced or enlarged to fit in the PictureBox object. The fit can be left and right or up and down, depending on the dimensions of the image and the PictureBox object. If the image and PictureBox object are not exactly proportional to each other, the image will not fill out the entire PictureBox object.

Size an Image

In most cases, when you import an image into a program, the image will not fit in the PictureBox object perfectly because the two items have different sizes or dimensions. The developer must adjust the size of the image to fit in the PictureBox object or adjust the size of the PictureBox object to accommodate the image.

By comparing the images in Figures 3-14 and 3-15, you can see that the image is larger than the PictureBox object. Because the PictureBox object must remain its current size, the image must be adjusted using the **SizeMode property**. To adjust an image's size to fit in a PictureBox object, you can complete the following steps:

STEP 1 Select the PictureBox object that contains the DeepDish image, and then scroll in the picDeepDish Properties window until you see the SizeMode property. Tap or click the SizeMode property name in the left column, and then tap or click the SizeMode arrow in the right column of the SizeMode property.

The SizeMode property list is displayed (Figure 3-16). The list contains five choices you can use to change either the size of the image or the size of the PictureBox object. Normal is selected because it is the default value.

Brand X Pictures/Getty Images

FIGURE 3-16

STEP 2 Tap or click StretchImage in the SizeMode list.

*The SizeMode list is closed and the image is resized to fit within the picDeepDish PictureBox object (Figure 3-17). When you use the **StretchImage option**, some image distortion might occur to make it fit within the PictureBox object. Therefore, you should select an image that has the same approximate dimensions (or at least the same aspect ratio) as the selected PictureBox object.*

image is resized

StretchImage is selected

FIGURE 3-17

Brand X Pictures/Getty Images

Set the Visible Property

As you have learned, when the Pizza Selection program begins, neither of the two pizza types is pictured in the window. When the user taps or clicks the Deep Dish button, the program displays the appropriate picture in the Deep Dish PictureBox object. When the user taps or clicks the Thin Crust button, the program displays the appropriate picture in the other PictureBox object.

The **Visible property** controls whether an object is displayed on the Windows Form object. By default, the Visible property is set to True so that any object you place on the Windows Form object is displayed when the program runs. If you do not want an object to be displayed, you must set the Visible property to False. To set the Visible property to False for the picDeepDish PictureBox object, you can complete the following steps:

STEP 1 If necessary, select the picDeepDish PictureBox object. Scroll in the Properties window until the Visible property is displayed. Tap or click the Visible property name in the left column, and then tap or click the Visible arrow in the right column of the Visible property.

When you tap or click the Visible arrow, the list displays the options True and False (Figure 3-18). To make the object visible when the program starts, select True. If you do not want the object to be visible when the program starts, select False.

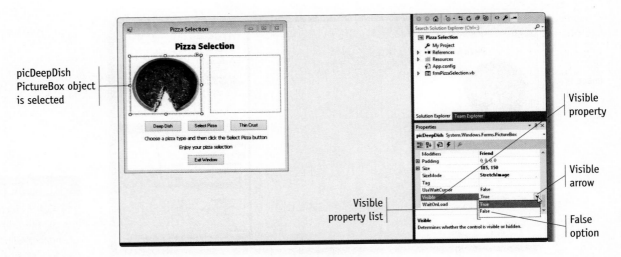

picDeepDish
PictureBox object
is selected

Visible
property

Visible
arrow

Visible
property list

False
option

FIGURE 3-18

Brand X Pictures/Getty Images

STEP 2   Tap or click False in the Visible property list.

The Visible property is set to False (Figure 3-19). When the program begins, the DeepDish picture will not be displayed on the Windows Form object. Note that the image and object are displayed on the frmPizzaSelection.vb [Design] tabbed page regardless of the Visible property setting.

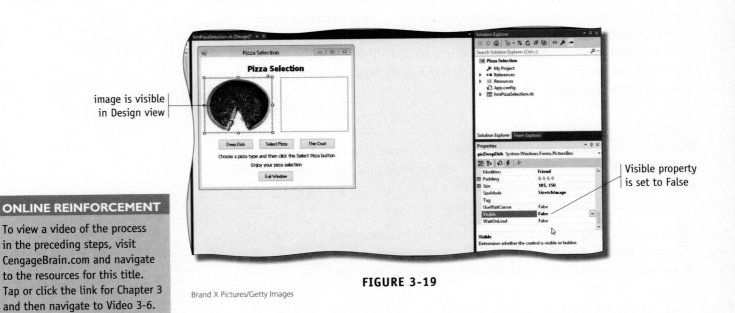

image is visible
in Design view

Visible property
is set to False

ONLINE REINFORCEMENT

To view a video of the process in the preceding steps, visit CengageBrain.com and navigate to the resources for this title. Tap or click the link for Chapter 3 and then navigate to Video 3-6.

FIGURE 3-19

Brand X Pictures/Getty Images

Once you have set an object's Visible property to False, the only way to display the object on the Windows Form object while the program is running is to set the Visible property to True. You can do this by writing code, as you will see later in this chapter.

Set the Enabled Property

In an event-driven program, objects such as Button objects can be used to make events occur. For example, when you tap or click the Deep Dish button, a picture of a deep-dish pizza is displayed in the PictureBox object. In addition, the Select Pizza Button object becomes **enabled**, which means it can be tapped or clicked to make an event occur. When the program begins, however, the Select Pizza button is **disabled**, which means nothing will happen when you tap or click the button. A disabled button is displayed as dimmed (see Figure 3-1a on page 108).

The **Enabled property** controls when a Button object is enabled. The property also controls when a Button object is not enabled, which means tapping or clicking the button causes no action. The default selection for the Enabled property is True, which means the associated Button object is enabled. To set the Enabled property to False for the Select Pizza button, you can complete the following steps:

STEP 1 Select the btnSelectPizza object. Scroll in the Properties window until the Enabled property is displayed. Tap or click the Enabled property name in the left column, and then tap or click the Enabled arrow in the right column of the Enabled property.

When you tap or click the Enabled arrow, the list contains the words True and False (Figure 3-20). To make the object enabled when the program starts, select True. If you do not want the object to be enabled when the program starts, select False.

FIGURE 3-20

Brand X Pictures/Getty Images

STEP 2   Tap or click False in the Enabled property list.

The Enabled property is set to False (Figure 3-21). When the program begins, the btnSelectPizza Button object will not be enabled on the Windows Form object.

Enabled property is set to False

Brand X Pictures/Getty Images

FIGURE 3-21

Once you have set the Enabled property to False, the only way to enable a Button object on the Windows Form object while the program is running is to set the Enabled property to True. You can do this by writing code, as you will see later in this chapter.

Run a Program

When you set some object properties, the effect of their changes might not be evident until you run the program. For example, you have set the Visible property to False for the picDeepDish PictureBox object, and you have set the Enabled property to False for the btnSelectPizza Button object. Neither change is evident, however, when you view the Pizza Selection Windows Form object on the frmPizzaSelection.vb [Design] tabbed page in Visual Studio. These settings are applied only when you actually run the program.

To ensure the settings are correct for the user interface, you must run the program. **Running the program** means it is compiled, or translated, from the instructions you have written or generated in Visual Basic into a form of instructions that the computer can execute. These instructions are saved and then executed as a program.

To run the program you have created, you can tap or click the Start Debugging button on the Standard toolbar, as shown in the following steps:

STEP 1   Point to the Start Debugging button on the Standard toolbar.

The pointer appears over the Start Debugging button (Figure 3-22).

FIGURE 3-22

Brand X Pictures/Getty Images

STEP 2   Tap or click the Start Debugging button on the Standard toolbar.

The program is compiled and saved, and then it runs on the computer. When the program runs, the Pizza Selection window is displayed on the screen (Figure 3-23). Notice that the DeepDish image is not displayed in the window because the Visible property was set to False for the picDeepDish PictureBox object (see Figure 3-19 on page 120). Notice also that the Select Pizza button is dimmed, which indicates its Enabled property is set to False.

FIGURE 3-23

ONLINE REINFORCEMENT

To view a video of the process in the preceding steps, visit CengageBrain.com and navigate to the resources for this title. Tap or click the link for Chapter 3 and then navigate to Video 3-8.

Once you start running the program, it continues to run until you close it. To close a program, tap or click the Close button on the right side of the window title bar (see Figure 3-23).

After you set all the properties for the objects in the user interface, the design of the user interface is complete. You now are ready to move to the next phase of the PDLC — designing the program processing objects.

Visual Basic Program Coding

Before beginning to design the program processing objects, the developer must understand certain program coding principles and techniques. **Program code** is the set of instructions written by the developer that direct the program to carry out its required processing. The following sections explain the Visual Basic 2015 code required for the Pizza Selection program.

Enter Visual Basic Code for Event Handling

As you have learned, most processing in an event-driven program occurs when the user triggers an event. For example, when a user taps or clicks a button on the GUI, the activity can trigger an event and the program performs the required processing. The developer writes program code to carry out the processing. This code is placed in a section of the program called an **event handler** — it *handles* the event that the user action triggers by executing code that performs the required processing.

To write the code for an event handler, the developer first must identify the GUI object that will be used to trigger the event. For example, when the Deep Dish button is tapped or clicked in the sample program, the DeepDish picture should appear in the picDeepDish PictureBox object. To write the code that will display the DeepDish picture, the developer must inform Visual Studio that the Deep Dish button is the object for which the code is being written and that an event handler must be created for the tap or click event. You can create the event handler using the following steps:

STEP 1   If necessary, open Visual Studio 2015 and the Pizza Selection program and make the frmPizzaSelection.vb [Design] tabbed window visible. Point to the Deep Dish Button object in the Windows Form object.

The pointer appears over the Deep Dish Button object (Figure 3-24). The four-headed arrow pointer indicates you can drag the Button object to another location in the window.

FIGURE 3-24

Brand X Pictures/Getty Images

STEP 2 Double-tap or double-click the Deep Dish Button object.

The code window is displayed on the frmPizzaSelection.vb* tabbed page (Figure 3-25). The code in the window is generated by Visual Studio. This code identifies an event handler, which is the code that executes when an event is triggered. When the Deep Dish button is tapped or clicked, the program will execute the code in this event handler. The list box in the upper-left corner of the tabbed page identifies the object for which the event handler will execute — in this case, the btnDeepDish object. The list box in the upper-right corner of the tabbed page identifies the event that must occur to execute the code in the event handler. The event identified in Figure 3-25 is "Click." When the user taps or clicks the Deep Dish button, the program executes the code between the Private Sub statement and the End Sub statement. In Figure 3-25, no code has been entered other than the event handler identification code generated by Visual Studio. The insertion point is located where the developer should begin entering the code that executes when the user taps or clicks the btnDeepDish Button object.

FIGURE 3-25

ONLINE REINFORCEMENT

To view a video of the process in the preceding steps, visit CengageBrain.com and navigate to the resources for this title. Tap or click the link for Chapter 3 and then navigate to Video 3-9.

Visual Basic 2015 Coding Statements

A Visual Basic 2015 coding statement contains instructions that the computer eventually executes. Visual Basic has a set of rules, or **syntax**, that specifies how each statement must be written.

When the user taps or clicks the Deep Dish button while the Pizza Selection program is running, the DeepDish image should be displayed in the picDeepDish PictureBox object. Figure 3-26 shows a Visual Basic coding statement that sets the Visible property to True for the picDeepDish PictureBox object so the image is displayed in the picture box after the statement executes.

FIGURE 3-26

The first part of the statement, picDeepDish, identifies the object that contains the property to set. The name of the object is followed by the dot operator (period) with no intervening spaces. The dot operator separates the name of the object from the next entry in the statement and is required.

Following the dot operator is the name of the property to set. In Figure 3-26 on page 126, the name of the property is Visible. You will recall that the Visible property determines whether an image is displayed in the PictureBox object when the program is running. In Figure 3-19 on page 120, the Visible property was set to False for the picDeepDish PictureBox object so the image would not be displayed when the program started. This statement sets the Visible property to True so the image will be displayed.

The property name is followed by a space and then an equal sign. The space is not required, but good coding practice dictates that elements within a statement should be separated by a space so the statement is easier to read. One or more spaces can be used, but most developers use only one space. The equal sign is required because it indicates that the value to be used for setting the property follows. A space follows the equal sign for readability.

The word *True* follows the space. The value True in the Visible property indicates that the image should be displayed in the PictureBox object. When the program is running and the Visible property is set to True, the image appears in the picture box.

Each entry within the program statement must be correct or the program will not compile. This means the object name must be spelled properly, the dot operator must be placed in the correct location, the name of the property must be spelled properly, the equal sign must be present, and a valid entry for the property must follow the equal sign. For the Visible property, the only valid entries are True and False.

General Format of a Visual Basic Statement

The general format of the Visual Basic statement shown in Figure 3-26 appears in Figure 3-27.

General Format: Property Value Assignment Statement

```
objectname.property = propertyvalue
```

EXAMPLE	*RESULT*
picDeepDish.Visible = True	Picture is visible
btnSelectPizza.Enabled = False	Button is dimmed

FIGURE 3-27

In the general format, the object name always is the first item in the Visual Basic statement. The object name is the name you specified in the (Name) property of the Properties window. In Figure 3-26 on page 126, the object name is picDeepDish because that name was given to the Deep Dish PictureBox object.

The dot operator (period) is required. It follows the object name with no space between them. Immediately following the dot operator is the name of the property that will be set by the statement. The property name must be spelled correctly and must be a valid property for the object named in the statement. Valid properties that can be specified in the statement are identified in the Properties window associated with the object.

The equal sign must follow the property name in the statement. Visual Basic statements do not require spaces, nor is there a limit to how many spaces you can place between elements in the statement. The equal sign identifies the statement as an **assignment statement**, which means the value on the right side of the equal sign is assigned to the element on the left side of the equal sign. When setting properties, the element on the left side of the equal sign is the property.

The property value specified in the assignment statement must be a valid value for the property identified on the left side of the equal sign. You can see the valid values for a given property by looking in the Properties window for the object whose property you are setting.

After you have entered the property value, the Visual Basic statement is complete. Because correct programming protocol dictates that only one statement should appear on a line, the next step is to press the ENTER key to move the insertion point to the next line in the code window.

The general statement format shown in Figure 3-27 is used for all statements in which the code sets the value of an object property.

IN THE REAL WORLD

Microsoft created IntelliSense in response to the demands of rapid application development so statements can be entered accurately and easily. Most developers use IntelliSense; it is the standard within the software industry.

IntelliSense

In Figure 3-25 on page 125, the insertion point is located in the code window. To enter the statement shown in Figure 3-26 into the program using the code window, you can type the entire statement. Visual Studio, however, provides help so that you will be less prone to make a typing error when entering the statement. This help feature is called IntelliSense.

IntelliSense displays all allowable entries you can make in a Visual Basic statement each time a dot (period), an equal sign, or another special character is required for the statement. When you type the prefix pic as shown in Figure 3-28, an IntelliSense window opens with all the objects that begin with the prefix. Instead of possibly misspelling the object name, you can select it from the IntelliSense list. The complete Visual Basic statement is shown in Figure 3-28.

```
picDeepDish.Visible = True
```

FIGURE 3-28

When you type the first few letters of the object name, IntelliSense displays a list of all the objects and other entries that can be specified in the statement.

Enter a Visual Basic Statement

To enter the Visual Basic statement in Figure 3-28 using IntelliSense, you can complete the following steps:

STEP 1   Tap or click the Close button to close the Toolbox. With the code window open and the insertion point positioned as shown in Figure 3-25 on page 125, type pic.

The characters "pic" are displayed in the code window (Figure 3-29). IntelliSense displays a list of all the entries that can follow the prefix in the statement. Sometimes the selected entry is correct for the statement you are entering, but often it is not. Therefore, you must identify the correct statement in the list before entering it.

characters *pic* typed

IntelliSense list

FIGURE 3-29

STEP 2 To identify the correct entry, type its next letter until the entry is selected. In this case, type d.

As you type, IntelliSense highlights an entry in the list that begins with the letters you enter (Figure 3-30). When you enter picd, IntelliSense highlights the only term in the list that begins with picd, which is picDeepDish. This is the object name you want to enter into the Visual Basic statement.

picd typed

picDeepDish is highlighted

FIGURE 3-30

STEP 3 When IntelliSense highlights the correct object name, press the key corresponding to the entry that follows the object name. In this case, press the PERIOD key.

IntelliSense automatically enters the entire object name into the Visual Basic statement and the period you typed following the object name (Figure 3-31). In addition, IntelliSense realizes that the dot you entered means more information is required in the statement, so it displays a list of the allowable entries following the dot.

period entered

entire object name entered

IntelliSense list of allowable entries

FIGURE 3-31

STEP 4 As with the object name in Step 2, the next step is to enter one or more characters until IntelliSense highlights the desired property in the list. Type the letter v for the Visible property.

IntelliSense highlights the properties in the list that begin with the letter v (Visible) or that contain the letter v, such as ProductVersion (Figure 3-32). Because the Visible property is highlighted, no further action is required to select it. The red curly line below the code indicates that the line of code is not complete.

FIGURE 3-32

STEP 5   Press the key for the character that follows the property name. In this case, press the SPACEBAR.

IntelliSense enters the highlighted property name (Visible) followed by the space you typed (Figure 3-33). The space indicates to Visual Basic that the object name and property name entry is complete. Notice also that the IntelliSense tip specifies what the statement will do. In Figure 3-33, the statement gets or sets a value indicating whether the control is displayed. This means the Visible property indicates whether the picDeepDish PictureBox object is displayed.

FIGURE 3-33

STEP 6   Press the EQUAL SIGN key and then press the SPACEBAR and the letter t.

The equal sign and a space are displayed and then IntelliSense displays a list of the entries you can make (Figure 3-34). For the Visible property, the correct entries following the equal sign are False and True. An entry of False indicates the PictureBox object should not be visible; True indicates the opposite.

FIGURE 3-34

STEP 7 Type t for True.

IntelliSense highlights the True entry (Figure 3-35).

t typed

FIGURE 3-35

STEP 8 Press the key for the character that follows the True entry. In this case, press the ENTER key.

Because you pressed the ENTER key, IntelliSense enters True into the statement and then Visual Studio moves the indented insertion point to the next line (Figure 3-36). The Visual Basic statement now is entered completely.

True is entered
in statement

FIGURE 3-36

Can I turn on line numbers to receive assistance while creating my program?

Line numbers help identify each line of code in the code window. They do not appear by default, however, so you must instruct Visual Studio to display the line numbers. If line numbers do not appear in the code window on your computer, you can display them by completing the following steps:

1. Tap or click Tools on the menu bar.
2. Tap or click Options on the Tools menu.
3. If necessary, tap or click the triangle next to Text Editor in the Options dialog box.
4. If necessary, tap or click the triangle next to Basic in the list below Text Editor.
5. Tap or click General in the list below Basic.
6. Place a check mark in the Line numbers check box.
7. Tap or click the OK button in the Options dialog box.

CONSIDER THIS

Visual Studio and IntelliSense automatically create the indentations in the program statements in Figure 3-36 on page 131 because indentations make the statements easier to read and understand. As programs become more complex, proper indentation of program statements can be an important factor in developing error-free programs.

The following general steps summarize the procedure for using IntelliSense to enter a Visual Basic statement that sets a property:

1. In the IntelliSense list, type the first letter(s) of the name of the object whose property will be set.
2. When the object name is selected in the list, press the PERIOD key.
3. Type the first letter(s) of the name of the property to be set until the name is highlighted in the IntelliSense list.
3. Press the SPACEBAR to complete the first portion of the statement.
4. Press the EQUAL SIGN key.
5. Press the SPACEBAR.
6. Press the first letter(s) of the entry you want to select in the list until the entry is highlighted. If IntelliSense does not display a list, type the value for the property.
7. Press the ENTER key.

Using IntelliSense to enter a Visual Basic statement provides two significant advantages. First, it is faster to enter a statement using IntelliSense than it is to type the statement. Second, using IntelliSense drastically reduces the number of errors when entering statements. By using only the entries in the IntelliSense lists, the developer seldom will make an invalid entry. In addition, because the entry is chosen from a list, it cannot possibly be misspelled or mistyped.

Entering a programming statement is a fundamental skill for a Visual Basic programmer. You should thoroughly understand how to enter a programming statement using IntelliSense.

Set the Visible Property to False

In Figure 3-36 on page 131, the programming statement set the Visible property to True for the picDeepDish PictureBox object, which will display the image in the picture box when the statement is executed. The statement will execute when the user taps or clicks the Deep Dish button because the statement is part of the btnDeepDish_Click event handler.

When the user taps or clicks the Deep Dish button, the Visible property also must be set to False for the picThinCrust PictureBox so the ThinCrust picture is not displayed alongside the DeepDish picture. To set the Visible property to False for the picThinCrust PictureBox object, you can complete the following steps:

STEP 1   With the insertion point on the next line of the code window for the Deep Dish button click event, type pic.

The letters you typed are displayed in the code window and the IntelliSense list shows the valid entries you can choose (Figure 3-37). The entry picDeepDish is highlighted because it is the last entry that was selected from this list.

pic typed

IntelliSense
list

picDeepDish is
highlighted

FIGURE 3-37

STEP 2 Type t to highlight the picThinCrust entry in the IntelliSense list.

*IntelliSense highlights picThinCrust in the list because it is the only entry that starts with
the characters "pict" (Figure 3-38).*

pict typed

picThinCrust is
highlighted

FIGURE 3-38

STEP 3 Press the key for the character that follows the object name. In this case,
press the PERIOD key.

*The picThinCrust entry is placed in the statement followed by the dot operator (period) you
typed (Figure 3-39). In addition, IntelliSense displays the list of allowable entries. The
Visible entry is highlighted in the list because it was selected the last time the list was used.
If Visible was not highlighted, you could type the letter v to highlight Visible in the list.*

picThinCrust entered
in statement

period entered

Visible

FIGURE 3-39

STEP 4   Press the SPACEBAR, press the EQUAL SIGN key, and then press the SPACEBAR.

IntelliSense places the Visible entry in the statement (Figure 3-40). Next, the space you typed appears, followed by the equal sign and the second space you typed. When you typed the equal sign, IntelliSense displayed the list of allowable entries following the equal sign.

FIGURE 3-40

STEP 5   Type f and then press the ENTER key.

When you type the letter f, IntelliSense highlights False in the list. When you press the ENTER key, IntelliSense inserts False at the insertion point (Figure 3-41).

FIGURE 3-41

Again, using IntelliSense to enter a Visual Basic programming statement results in a correct statement entered in minimal time with a reduced chance of errors.

Set the Enabled Property

You learned earlier that if the Enabled property is True for a Button object, the tap or click event code will be executed for the button when the user taps or clicks it. If the Enabled property is False for a Button object, the event code for the button will not be executed. In Figure 3-21 on page 122, the Enabled property was set to False for the Select Pizza button so that the button is not active when the program begins. When the user taps or clicks a picture button such as the Deep Dish button, however, the Enabled property must be set to True so the Select Pizza button is active. To set the Enabled property to True, the developer must enter a coding statement for the btnSelectPizza Button object. To enter the coding statement into the btnDeepDish_Click event handler, you can complete the following steps:

STEP 1 Type btn to display the IntelliSense list (Figure 3-42).

FIGURE 3-42

STEP 2 Type s (or more characters if necessary) until IntelliSense highlights the btnSelectPizza entry in the list.

IntelliSense highlights btnSelectPizza, the only entry that starts with the characters "btns" (Figure 3-43). Sometimes, the correct entry will be highlighted before you type all the distinguishing characters. If so, you need not type more characters.

FIGURE 3-43

STEP 3 Type a period, type e, press the SPACEBAR, press the EQUAL SIGN key, press the SPACEBAR again, and then type true to select True in the IntelliSense list.

IntelliSense places the highlighted entry (btnSelectPizza) in the statement and displays a list of the next allowable entries. When you typed e, Enabled was selected in the list. Pressing the SPACEBAR caused IntelliSense to place Enabled and then the space in the statement. When you typed the equal sign and second space, IntelliSense inserted both and displayed the list of entries that can follow the equal sign (Figure 3-44).

space, equal
sign, space

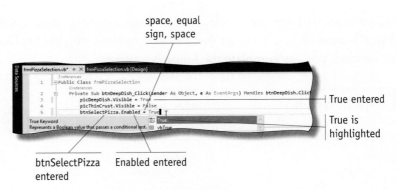

True entered

True is
highlighted

btnSelectPizza
entered

Enabled entered

FIGURE 3-44

STEP 4 Press the ENTER key to enter the completed statement and place the
insertion point on the next line.

*IntelliSense enters True in the statement (Figure 3-45). Pressing the ENTER key completes
the statement and moves the indented insertion point to the next line.*

indented
insertion point

True entered

FIGURE 3-45

Learning how to enter program statements using IntelliSense is fundamental to
writing programs using the Visual Basic 2015 language.

Comments in Program Statements

A well-written Visual Basic 2015 program normally contains **comment statements**
within the code itself to document what the code is doing. The general purpose of
comments is to help code readers understand the code and how it accomplishes its
tasks. An example of comment statements used in code is shown in Figure 3-46.

apostrophe
indicates
comment

comments are
displayed in
green

FIGURE 3-46

A comment is preceded by an apostrophe. Whenever the Visual Basic compiler encounters an apostrophe in the code, it ignores the remaining characters on the line. To the compiler, it's as if the comments do not exist.

The comments in the code are displayed in green text and describe the processing that will occur in the code that follows. Because comments are ignored by the Visual Basic compiler, developers must not include programming language syntax in the comments. Any letters or characters are allowed within comments.

To enter comments, first type an apostrophe in the code. All characters following the apostrophe on a line of code are considered a comment. To enter the comment code shown in Figure 3-46, you can complete the following steps:

STEP 1   To insert a blank line following the event code generated by Visual Studio that begins with the word Private, tap or click anywhere in that line and then press the END key.

Visual Studio positions the insertion point at the end of the line that you tapped or clicked (Figure 3-47).

insertion point at end of line

code generated by Visual Studio

FIGURE 3-47

STEP 2   Press the ENTER key.

Visual Studio inserts a blank line in the code and then moves the insertion point to the blank line (Figure 3-48). The comments can be inserted on the blank line.

Visual Studio inserts blank line

insertion point moved to next line

FIGURE 3-48

STEP 3   Type the first line of the comments, beginning with an apostrophe as shown in Figure 3-46 on page 136, and then press the ENTER key.

The apostrophe identifies the rest of the line as a comment (Figure 3-49). The comment line is displayed in green text. When you press the ENTER key, Visual Studio creates a new blank line and places the indented insertion point on that line.

apostrophe indicates comment line

indented insertion point

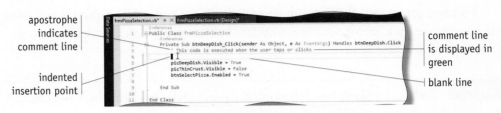

comment line is displayed in green

blank line

FIGURE 3-49

You can continue to enter lines of comments by typing an apostrophe and the comment and then pressing the ENTER key until all comments are completed.

Same-Line Comments

Because the Visual Basic compiler treats all characters following an apostrophe as comments, it is possible to place a comment on the same line as executable code. In Figure 3-50, a comment is shown on the same line as the statement that sets the btnSelectPizza Enabled property to True.

apostrophe identifies comment

FIGURE 3-50

In Figure 3-50, the apostrophe specifies that subsequent characters on the line are to be treated as comments. Therefore, the Enable button text is displayed in green and is treated as a comment. To enter a comment on any line, enter an apostrophe and then type the comment. Remember that all characters after an apostrophe are treated as comments on a line of code.

Introductory Comments

Every program should begin with comments that state the name of the program, the developer's name, the date, and the purpose of the program. These introductory comments should precede all code in the program — even the code generated by Visual Studio (Figure 3-51).

introductory comments

FIGURE 3-51

To enter introductory comments, you can complete the following steps:

STEP 1 Tap or click to the left of the word Public on line 1 of the program to place the insertion point on that line.

The insertion point is positioned at the beginning of line 1 in the code (Figure 3-52).

insertion point positioned on line 1

FIGURE 3-52

STEP 2 Press the ENTER key and then press the UP ARROW key.

When you press the ENTER key, Visual Studio inserts a blank line on line 1 of the code and moves the line that begins with the words Public Class down to line 2 (Figure 3-53). Visual Studio also moves the insertion point to line 2 when you press the ENTER key. When you press the UP ARROW key, the insertion point moves to the first line, which is blank.

insertion point

Public Class line now on line 2

FIGURE 3-53

STEP 3 Type an apostrophe, a space, the text `Program Name:`, and then press the TAB key.

The apostrophe identifies all characters and words that follow as comments, so those characters are displayed in green (Figure 3-54). The first line of introductory comments normally specifies the name of the program. Pressing the TAB key moves the insertion point to the right.

comment

insertion
point

FIGURE 3-54

STEP 4 Type Pizza Selection as the name of the program, and then press
the ENTER key.

*The program name appears in the first line of comments and the insertion point is moved to
line 2 (Figure 3-55).*

insertion
point

program name

FIGURE 3-55

You can enter the remaining comments using the same techniques. Press the TAB
key one or more times to vertically align the paragraphs on the right so they appear as
shown in Figure 3-51 on page 139.

CONSIDER THIS

What do the yellow and green lines to the left of the code represent?
The yellow lines indicate lines of code that have not been saved. The green lines indicate the changes in code that have been
saved. The yellow and green lines are a method of tracking your most recent changes in code.

Correct Errors in Code

Using IntelliSense to help you enter code reduces the likelihood of coding errors
considerably. Nevertheless, because you could create errors when entering code, you
should understand what to do when a coding error occurs.

One possible error would be to forget an apostrophe in a comment statement. In
Figure 3-56, a comment was entered without a leading apostrophe.

apostrophe omitted

comment appears in black text

FIGURE 3-56

In Figure 3-56, the comment words are displayed in black and red text, which indicates an error because comment characters normally are displayed in green text. Visual Studio gives no other indication that an error has occurred.

From this point where the error occurred, the developer might take any course of action. For example, she might immediately run the program. Or she might tap or click anywhere in the window to move the insertion point, or press the ENTER key to insert a blank line. If the program in Figure 3-56 is executed immediately by tapping or clicking the Start Debugging button on the Standard toolbar, the window shown in Figure 3-57 will be displayed.

build errors message

No button

FIGURE 3-57

The **build errors message** means the Visual Basic compiler detected a coding error in the program. An absolute requirement when creating Visual Basic programs is that when you see the build errors message, you *always tap or click the No button.* Under no circumstances should you tap or click the Yes button in the dialog box. When you tap or click the No button, you can perform the following steps to make corrections in your program:

STEP 1   Tap or click the No button in the Microsoft Visual Studio dialog box that informs you of a build error (Figure 3-57 on page 141).

*When you tap or click the No button, Visual Studio displays the program code and the Error List window (Figure 3-58). The **Error List window** identifies the number of errors that occurred and displays descriptions of the errors. For example, the Syntax error in Figure 3-58 means Visual Studio expected to find a different type of statement. The window also contains the file name in which the error occurred (frmPizzaSelection.vb), the line number of the statement in error (5), and the vertical column within the statement where the error was detected (17). In the code window, the location of the error is noted by a red squiggly line.*

FIGURE 3-58

STEP 2   Double-tap or double-click anywhere on the error line.

Visual Studio highlights the error with a red squiggly line. The developer can type and replace the highlighted text with the correct code (Figure 3-59). With the error highlighted, the developer must examine the statement to determine the error. By looking at line 5, column 17, where the left parenthesis is highlighted, it is clear that the developer created a line that was intended to be a comment. Further examination reveals the required apostrophe is missing.

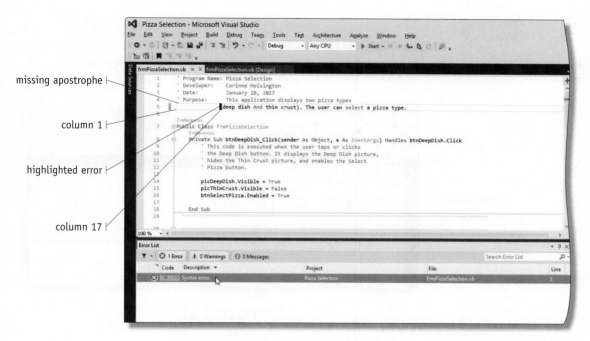

missing apostrophe

column 1

highlighted error

column 17

FIGURE 3-59

STEP 3 Tap or click in the far left column on line 5 to place the insertion point there.

The insertion point is placed in the far left column on line 5 of the program (Figure 3-60).

insertion point
in first column
of line 5

FIGURE 3-60

STEP 4   Type an apostrophe.

The apostrophe is placed in the first column on line 5 of the program (Figure 3-61).

apostrophe in
column 1, line 5

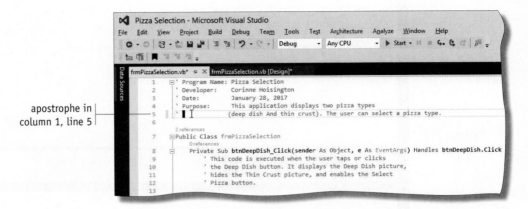

FIGURE 3-61

STEP 5   Tap or click anywhere in the code window.

When you tap or click anywhere in the window, the insertion point moves to that location (Figure 3-62). If the statement has been corrected, the error line is removed from the Error List window, and the number of errors is reduced by one. In Figure 3-62, the number of errors now is zero because the one error found in the program has been corrected. Multiple errors can be detected when the program is compiled.

comment in green
and no red
squiggly line

insertion point

0 errors in
program

Close button for
Error List window

error message
removed

FIGURE 3-62

ONLINE REINFORCEMENT

To view a video of the process in the preceding steps, visit CengageBrain.com and navigate to the resources for this title. Tap or click the link for Chapter 3 and then navigate to Video 3-15.

You can close the Error List window by tapping or clicking its Close button (see Figure 3-62 on page 144).

In Figure 3-57 on page 141, the example assumed that the developer made an error and then immediately ran the program. If the developer moved the insertion point to another part of the program or tapped or clicked any other element in the window before running the program, then Visual Studio would provide a visual cue that an error occurred by displaying a red squiggly line under the error (Figure 3-58 on page 142). You do not have to run the program to find coding errors. If a red squiggly line appears, you must correct the error.

CRITICAL THINKING

When a program displays an error and a line number, is it possible that the error is on another line?
Yes. When an error is detected, review the line of code before the statement in error.

Additional Tap or Click Events

In the sample program in this chapter, multiple buttons can trigger events. For example, when the user taps or clicks the Exit Window button, the program window should close and the program should terminate. To indicate that tapping or clicking the Exit Window button will trigger an event, and to prepare to write the code for the event, complete the same steps for the Exit Window button that you learned for the Deep Dish button, as shown in the following example:

STEP 1 On the frmPizzaSelection.vb [Design] tabbed page, double-tap or double-click the Exit Window Button object.

Visual Studio opens the code window and displays the frmPizzaSelection.vb tabbed page (Figure 3-63). Visual Studio also inserts the event handler code for the tap or click event on the btnExit object. Two horizontal lines separate the event handler code for the btnExit object from code for other event handlers that might be in the program. The developer must write the code that will be executed when the tap or click event occurs. The insertion point is located in the proper place to begin writing code.

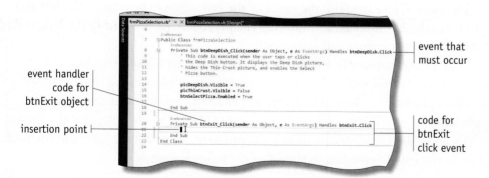

FIGURE 3-63

ONLINE REINFORCEMENT

To view a video of the process in the preceding steps, visit CengageBrain.com and navigate to the resources for this title. Tap or click the link for Chapter 3 and then navigate to Video 3-16.

Enter Comments

As you have learned, you can enter code in the code window using the IntelliSense tools. The first code written for an event, however, should be comment code that identifies the event and the processing that will occur. The comment code for the Exit Window event handler is shown in Figure 3-64.

comments for btnExit event handler

FIGURE 3-64

Close Procedure

The Visual Basic statement to close the window and terminate the program calls a procedure that performs the actual processing. A **procedure** is a set of prewritten code that can be called by a statement in the Visual Basic program. When the procedure is called, the program processes the code. The procedure used to close a window and terminate a program is the Close procedure.

You can use the statement in Figure 3-65 to call the Close procedure.

procedure name

FIGURE 3-65

The word Close specifies the name of the procedure to be called. The left and right parentheses immediately following the procedure name identify the Visual Basic statement as a **procedure call statement**.

When the statement in Figure 3-65 is executed, the Close procedure will be called and control will be given to the prewritten programming statements in the Close procedure. These statements will close the window and terminate the application.

To enter the Close statement into the program, you can type "clo" and then select Close in the IntelliSense list, as shown in the following steps:

STEP 1   With the insertion point positioned as shown in Figure 3-64 on page 146, type `clo` to highlight Close in the IntelliSense list.

When you type the letters "clo," IntelliSense highlights the word Close in the IntelliSense list (Figure 3-66).

FIGURE 3-66

STEP 2   Press the ENTER key.

IntelliSense enters Close in the statement and, because it knows Close is a procedure call, automatically appends the open and closed parentheses to the statement (Figure 3-67). Then, Visual Studio returns the insertion point to the next line.

FIGURE 3-67

Prewritten procedures are an important element when using rapid application development in Visual Basic and Visual Studio because the developer is not required to write the procedure code. The developer merely writes a single statement to call the procedure. You will use many procedures in this book for a variety of reasons.

Print Code

In some instances, you will need to print the code in the program. While reviewing code, you might find it easier to read and understand the code on a printed page rather than on your computer screen. In other cases, you might want to share the code with another developer; the printed page often is a better tool for sharing than a monitor screen. To print the code in a program, you can complete the following steps:

1. Tap or click File on the menu bar to display the File menu.
2. Tap or click Print on the File menu to display the Print dialog box.
3. Ensure that a check mark appears in the Include line numbers check box if you want to include line numbers on your printout. Most developers prefer line numbers on printouts.
4. Make any other needed selections in the Print dialog box.
5. Tap or click the OK button in the Print dialog box to print the code.

If you have a color printer, the code will be printed with correct color. Otherwise, shades of gray will represent the colors shown in the code window. If a line of code extends beyond one printed line, an arrow will appear at the end of the first line to indicate it continues to the next printed line.

Coding Summary

Writing code is the essence of programming in Visual Basic 2015. Much of the emphasis in this book will be on writing the code required to implement applications of all kinds.

Once you understand coding and the statements shown in this chapter, you are ready to continue the process of designing and implementing the Pizza Selection program.

Phase 3 — Design the Program Processing Objects

The next phase in the PDLC requires determining the processing objects for the program and creating the event-planning document. In the Pizza Selection program and programs of similar complexity, the designer need not be concerned about determining the processing objects. The only processing object required for the program is the Windows Form object. In more complex programs, determining processing objects will become important.

For the Pizza Selection program, the next task is to design the event-planning document.

Event-Planning Document

As you have learned, programs written using a GUI normally are event-driven programs. An **event** means the user has initiated an action that causes the program to perform the appropriate type of processing in response. Once the mock-up has been created for the user interface, the developer must document the events that can occur based on the user interface.

The **event-planning document** is a table that specifies objects in the user interface that will cause events, the actions taken by the user to trigger the events, and the event processing that must occur. The event-planning document for the Pizza Selection program is shown in Figure 3-68.

EVENT PLANNING DOCUMENT

Program Name:	Developer:	Object:	Date:
Pizza Selection	Corinne Hoisington	frmPizzaSelection	January 28, 2017

Object	Event Trigger	Event Processing
btnDeepDish	Tap or click	Display the DeepDish picture Hide the ThinCrust picture Enable the Select Pizza button
btnSelectPizza	Tap or click	Disable the Deep Dish button Disable the Select Pizza button Disable the Thin Crust button Hide the Instructions label Display the Confirmation Message label Enable the Exit Window button
btnThinCrust	Tap or click	Display the ThinCrust picture Hide the DeepDish picture Enable the Select Pizza button
btnExit	Tap or click	Close the window and terminate the program

FIGURE 3-68

The left column in the event-planning document identifies the object in the GUI that can trigger an event. In the Pizza Selection program, each of the four Button objects can be used to trigger an event, so each must be included in the event-planning document. Notice each Button object is identified by its name. Using this technique ensures that the documentation is precise and provides little room for error when the developer creates the code to implement these events.

The middle column identifies the event trigger, which is the action a user takes to cause the event. In all four event cases in Figure 3-68, tapping or clicking a button triggers the event. As you will learn in this book, users can perform a variety of acts to trigger an event. For example, a user might point to an object, press or right-click the object, or double-tap or double-click the object. Each event trigger could trigger a different event.

The right column in the event-planning document specifies the event processing that the program must perform when the event occurs. This list of tasks for each event is a critical element in the program design. It must be precise and accurate. No processing step that must occur should be left out of the event-processing column. The tasks should be listed in the same sequence as they will be performed in the program.

For example, the first task for the btnDeepDish_Click event is to display the DeepDish picture. This is the primary task for the Deep Dish button. However, several other tasks must be completed. When the program begins, the Thin-Crust picture is not visible, but if the user taps or clicks the Thin Crust button, then the picture is displayed. When the user taps or clicks the Deep Dish button, however, the ThinCrust picture should not be visible. Therefore, each time the user taps or clicks the Deep Dish button, the processing must hide the ThinCrust picture.

You also will recall that when the program begins, the Select Pizza button is dimmed (disabled). After the user taps or clicks a pizza-type button, the Select Pizza button must be enabled. For example, each time the user taps or clicks the Deep Dish button, the Select Pizza button must be enabled.

As you review the event-planning document in Figure 3-68, be sure you understand the processing that must occur for each event.

You should note that the event-processing tasks in the right column identify *what* processing must be done when the event occurs. *How* these tasks will be accomplished is not identified specifically, although the information in the event-planning document must be precise enough that the developer can easily write the code to implement the specified tasks.

Phase 4 — Code the Program

After the events and tasks within the events have been identified, the developer is ready to code the program. As you have learned in this chapter, coding the program means entering Visual Basic statements to accomplish the tasks specified in the event-planning document. As the developer enters the code, she also will implement the logic to carry out the required processing.

Guided Program Development

To fine-tune the user interface in the Pizza Selection program and enter the code required to process each event in the program, complete the following steps to create the program shown in Figure 3-1 on pages 108 and 109.

NOTE TO THE LEARNER

In the following activity, you should complete the tasks within the specified steps. Each of the tasks is accompanied by a Hint Screen. The purpose of the Hint Screen is to indicate where you should perform the activity in the Visual Studio window and to remind you which method to use. If you need further help completing a step, refer to the figure identified by *ref:*.

● **Open the Mock-Up File** Open Visual Studio and then open the mock-up file for the user interface you created in Chapter 2. (If you did not create a mock-up file in Chapter 2, consult with your instructor to obtain the file.)

HINT

● **Show the Windows Form Object's BackColor Property** To finish the user interface, you must specify the BackColor of the Windows Form object. Select the frmPizzaSelection Windows Form object. In the Properties window, scroll until the BackColor property is visible, tap or click the BackColor property name in the left column, and then tap or click the BackColor arrow in the right column. If necessary, tap or click the Web tab (ref: Figure 3-3).

HINT

● **Choose the Windows Form Object's BackColor** Scroll the Web tabbed page until White is visible, and then tap or click White in the list (ref: Figure 3-5).

HINT

● **Select the BackColor for Buttons** Next, you must specify the BackColor for the Button objects. Select the four buttons in the window using techniques you have learned and then change the BackColor to Wheat.

HINT

● **Change the ForeColor of a Label Object** Select the lblHeading Label object, tap or click the ForeColor property name in the left column, and then tap or click the ForeColor arrow in the right column. If necessary, tap or click the Web tab and select Firebrick in the list.

HINT

Guided Program Development   *continued*

1

The BackColor for
the Windows Form
object is changed
to White, the
ForeColor of the
heading is changed
to Firebrick, and
the BackColor for
the buttons in the
window is changed
to Wheat
(Figure 3-69).

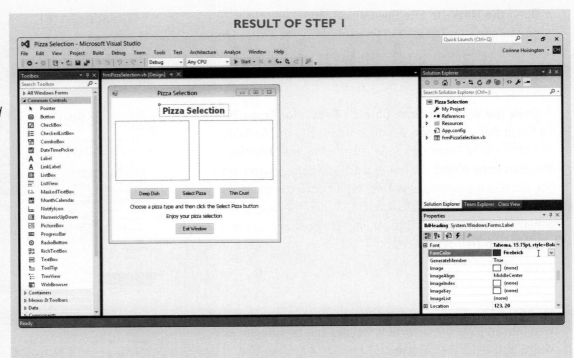

FIGURE 3-69

2

● **Download the DeepDish Image** To display the pictures
in the PictureBox object, you might need to use your web
browser to download the pictures from the book's webpage
at CengageBrain.com and store them on your computer. After
downloading the files for Chapter 3, save the DeepDish image
on a USB drive or other available storage media on your computer *(ref: Figure 3-7)*.

● **Download the ThinCrust Image** Save the ThinCrust image
on a USB drive or other storage media on your computer
(ref: Figure 3-9).

• **Display the Select Resource Dialog Box** After acquiring the pictures, you must import them into the Resources folder and specify the PictureBox object where they will be displayed. Select the picDeepDish PictureBox object. In the Properties window, tap or click Image and then tap or click the ellipsis button in the right column (*ref: Figure 3-11*).

• **Import the DeepDish Image** In the Select Resource dialog box, tap or click the Import button, import the DeepDish image from its saved location, and then tap or click the OK button (*ref: Figure 3-12*).

Brand X Pictures/Getty Images

• **Import the ThinCrust Image** Using the same technique, specify the ThinCrust image as the image for the picThinCrust PictureBox object.

Brand X Pictures/Getty Images

(continues)

● **Set the SizeMode Property to StretchImage for the DeepDish Image** When you import a picture, normally you must resize it or the PictureBox object so the picture is displayed properly. To resize the DeepDish image, select the picDeepDish PictureBox object. In the Properties window for the picDeepDish PictureBox object, tap or click the SizeMode property name, tap or click the SizeMode arrow, and then set the property to StretchImage *(ref: Figure 3-16).*

● **Set the SizeMode Property to StretchImage for the ThinCrust Image** Using the same technique, set the SizeMode property to StretchImage for the picThinCrust PictureBox object.

The images are displayed in the correct PictureBox objects (Figure 3-70).

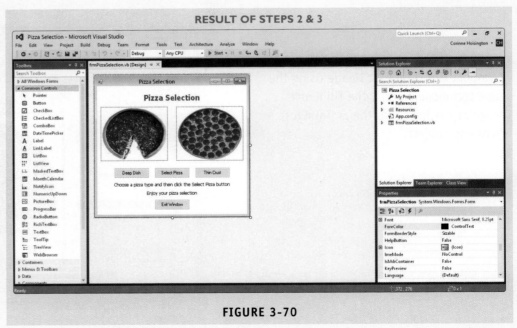

FIGURE 3-70

Brand X Pictures/Getty Images

● **Set the Visible Property to False for the DeepDish Image**
When the program begins, the pictures are not displayed in
the window, so you must set their Visible property to False.
In the Properties window for the picDeepDish PictureBox
object, tap or click the Visible property name in the left
column, tap or click the Visible arrow for the Visible property,
and then set the Visible property to False for the picDeepDish
PictureBox object *(ref: Figure 3-18)*.

● **Set the Visible Property to False for the ThinCrust
Image** Using the same technique, set the Visible
property to False for the picThinCrust PictureBox object
(ref: Figure 3-18).

● **Set the Visible Property to False for the Confirmation
Message** The confirmation message is not displayed when the
program begins, so you must set its Visible property to False.
In the Properties window, set the Visible property to False for
the lblConfirmation Label object *(ref: Figure 3-18)*.

● **Run the Program** After you make changes to a program,
you should run it to ensure your changes work properly and
are correct *(ref: Figure 3-22)*.

(continues)

Guided Program Development   *continued*

In Figure 3-71, the pizza-type pictures are not displayed. In addition, the confirmation message is not displayed.

FIGURE 3-71

5

● **Set the Select Pizza Button's Enabled Property to False**
Initially, the Select Pizza button and the Exit Window button must be dimmed. In the Properties window for the btnSelect-Pizza object, tap or click the Enabled property name, tap or click the Enabled arrow, and then set the Enabled property to False for the btnSelectPizza Button object *(ref: Figure 3-20)*.

● **Set the Exit Window Button's Enabled Property to False**
Using the same technique, set the Enabled property to False for the btnExit Button object *(ref: Figure 3-20)*.

● **Run the Program** Again, after you make changes, always ensure the changes are correct. Run the program.

Both the Select Pizza button and the Exit Window button are dimmed, indicating the Enabled property for both buttons is False (Figure 3-72).

FIGURE 3-72

6

● **Open the Code Window for the btnDeepDish Event Handler** The user interface now is complete, so you should begin writing the code for the program. To write code, you must open the code window. Double-tap or double-click the Deep Dish button to open the code window for the btnDeepDish_Click event *(ref: Figure 3-24).*

● **Position the Insertion Point** Close the Toolbox window. When you begin writing the code for a program, the first step is to write the introductory comments. Tap or click in the far left position of the first line of code (Public Class) *(ref: Figure 3-52).*

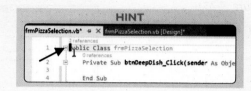

● **Create a Blank Line and Position the Insertion Point** Press the ENTER key and then press the UP ARROW key *(ref: Figure 3-53).*

● **Enter the First Line of the Introductory Comments** The introductory comments provide the code reader with important information about the program. The first line normally specifies the name of the program. Type an apostrophe, press the SPACEBAR, type `Program Name:`, press TAB, type `Pizza Selection`, and then press the ENTER key and the BACKSPACE key to return to the left position *(ref: Figure 3-55).*

● **Enter the Developer Identification Comment Line** Type an apostrophe, press the SPACEBAR, type `Developer:`, press TAB, type your name, and then press the ENTER key.

● **Enter the Date Comment Line** Type an apostrophe, press the SPACEBAR, type `Date:`, press TAB three times, enter the current date, and then press the ENTER key.

● **Enter the First Program Purpose Comment Line** Type an apostrophe, press the SPACEBAR, type `Purpose:`, press TAB two times, enter the first line of your own comments about the program, and then press the ENTER key.

(continues)

● **Enter the Remaining Program Purpose Comment Lines**
Insert additional lines of comments about the purpose of the
program as you see fit.

*The comments appear at
the top of the program
code (Figure 3-73).*

RESULT OF STEP 6

FIGURE 3-73

7

● **Position the Insertion Point Inside
the Click Event Handler** With the insertion
point located on the line above the line of
code that begins with Public Class (see
Figure 3-73), press the DOWN ARROW key
three times and then press TAB two times to
position the insertion point in the btnDeepDish_Click
event handler (*ref: Figure 3-48*).

HINT

● **Enter the First Line of the Event Handler
Comments** Each event handler should begin
with comments describing what the event
handler accomplishes. Type an apostrophe,
press the SPACEBAR, and then enter the first
line of comments for the btnDeepDish_Click
event handler. Press the ENTER key (*ref: Figure 3-49*).

HINT

```
7    Public Class frmPizzaSelection
8         Private Sub btnDeepDish_Click(sender As Object, e As EventArgs) Handles btnDeepDish.Click
9             ' This code is executed when the user taps or clicks
10
11        End Sub
12    End Class
13
```

● **Enter the Remaining Event Handler
Comments** Enter the remaining comments
for the btnDeepDish_Click event handler.

HINT

● **Make the Deep Dish PictureBox Object Visible** The first executable line of code in the Deep Dish Button object click event handler must make the Deep Dish PictureBox object visible. Using IntelliSense, enter the Visual Basic code statement to set the Visible property to True for the picDeepDish PictureBox object *(ref: Figure 3-32)*.

● **Make Sure the Thin Crust PictureBox Object is Not Visible** As documented in the event-planning document, the next task is to make sure the ThinCrust picture is not visible in the window. Using IntelliSense, enter the Visual Basic code statement to set the Visible property to False for the picThinCrust PictureBox object *(ref: Figure 3-40)*.

● **Enable the Select Pizza Button Object** The last task for the btnDeepDish_Click event handler is to enable the Select Pizza button. Using IntelliSense, enter the Visual Basic code statement to set the Enabled property to True for the btnSelectPizza Button object *(ref: Figure 3-44)*.

The lines of code are entered in the Deep Dish Button object's click event handler (Figure 3-74). The code will set the Visible property to True for the picDeepDish PictureBox object, set the Visible property to False for the picThinCrust PictureBox object, and set the Enabled property to True for the btnSelectPizza Button object.

FIGURE 3-74

(continues)

Guided Program Development *continued*

8

• **Run the Program** When the code for an event handler is complete, good practice dictates that you should run the program to ensure the event handler code works properly. Run the program. Tap or click the Deep Dish button.

When you tap or click the Deep Dish button, the DeepDish picture is displayed, the ThinCrust picture is not displayed, and the Select Pizza button is enabled (Figure 3-75). These are the correct results. Note that if you tap or click any of the other buttons in the window, nothing happens because you have not yet written the event handler code for these objects.

RESULT OF STEP 8

FIGURE 3-75

Brand X Pictures/Getty Images

9

• **Display the Design Window** When the code for an event handler is completed, the next task is often to write the code for another event handler. To do so, you must go to the Design tabbed page and indicate the object for which the code will be written. Tap or click the frmPizzaSelection.vb [Design] tab to return to the Design tabbed page.

HINT

• **Open the Code Window for the btnSelectPizza Event Handler** You must open the code window for the btnSelectPizza Button object to enter code for the event handler. Double-tap or double-click the Select Pizza button to open the code window for the btnSelectPizza_Click event *(ref: Figure 3-24).*

HINT

```
20        Private Sub btnSelectPizza_Click(sender As Object, e As EventArgs) Handles btnSelectPizza.Click
21    
22        End Sub
23    End Class
```

• **Enter Event Handler Comments** When beginning the code for an event handler, the first step is to enter the event handler comments. Enter the comments that describe the processing in the btnSelectPizza_Click event handler.

HINT

```
20        Private Sub btnSelectPizza_Click(sender As Object, e As EventArgs)
21        ' This code is executed when the user taps or clicks the
22        ' Select Pizza button. It disables the Deep Dish button, the
23        ' Select Pizza button, and the Thin Crust button.
24        ' It hides the Instructions label, displays the
25        ' Confirmation label, and enables the Exit Window button.
26    
27    
28        End Sub
29    End Class
30
```

● **Disable the btnDeepDish Button Object** According to the event-planning document (Figure 3-68 on page 149), the next task is to disable the Deep Dish button. Using IntelliSense, enter the Visual Basic code statement to set the Enabled property to False for the btnDeepDish Button object (*ref: Figure 3-42*).

● **Disable the btnSelectPizza Button Object** The next task is to disable the Select Pizza button. Using IntelliSense, enter the Visual Basic code statement to set the Enabled property to False for the btnSelectPizza Button object (*ref: Figure 3-42*).

● **Disable the btnThinCrust Button Object** Using IntelliSense, enter the Visual Basic code statement to set the Enabled property to False for the btnThinCrust Button object (*ref: Figure 3-42*).

● **Hide the Instructions Label Object** When the Select Pizza button is tapped or clicked, the instructions should not be displayed. Using IntelliSense, enter the Visual Basic code statement to set the Visible property to False for the lblInstructions Label object (*ref: Figure 3-32*).

● **Display the Confirmation Message** The confirmation message must be displayed when the user taps or clicks the Select Pizza button. Using IntelliSense, enter the Visual Basic code statement to set the Visible property to True for the lblConfirmation Label object *(ref: Figure 3-35)*.

● **Enable the Exit Window Button** After the user taps or clicks the Select Pizza button, the only allowable action is to tap or click the Exit Window button and close the application. Therefore, the Exit Window button must be enabled. Using IntelliSense, enter the Visual Basic code statement to set the Enabled property to True for the btnExit Button object (*ref: Figure 3-42*).

● **Run the Program** Save and then run the program to ensure that it works correctly. Tap or click the Deep Dish button and then tap or click the Select Pizza button.

(continues)

After tapping or clicking the two buttons, the DeepDish picture is displayed; the Deep Dish, Select Pizza, and Thin Crust buttons are disabled; the Instructions label is not displayed; the Confirmation Message label is displayed; and the Exit Window button is enabled (Figure 3-76).

FIGURE 3-76

Brand X Pictures/Getty Images

10

● **Display the Design Window** The next task is to write the code for the btnThinCrust event handler. To return to the Design tabbed page so you can select the Thin Crust button, tap or click the frmPizzaSelection.vb [Design] tab.

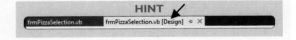

● **Open the Code Window for the btnThinCrust Event Handler** Double-tap or double-click the Thin Crust button to open the code window for the btnThinCrust_Click event (*ref: Figure 3-24*).

● **Enter the Event Handler Comments** Using the techniques you have learned, enter the comments that describe the processing in the btnThinCrust_Click event handler.

● **Make the ThinCrust PictureBox Object Visible** According to the event-planning document, the next task is to make the ThinCrust picture visible. Using IntelliSense, enter the Visual Basic code statement to set the Visible property to True for the picThinCrust PictureBox object (*ref: Figure 3-35*).

● **Make Sure the DeepDish Picture Is Not Visible** Using IntelliSense, enter the Visual Basic code statement to set the Visible property to False for the picDeepDish PictureBox object (*ref: Figure 3-41*).

- **Enable the Select Pizza Button** Using IntelliSense, enter the Visual Basic code statement to set the Enabled property to True for the btnSelectPizza Button object (*ref: Figure 3-44*).

- **Run the Program** Run the program and then tap or click the Thin Crust button to ensure your code works correctly.

The completed code for the Select Pizza button event handler and the Thin Crust button event handler is shown in Figure 3-77.

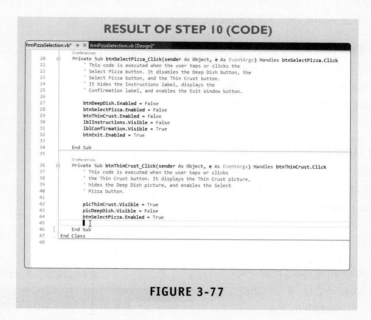

RESULT OF STEP 10 (CODE)

```
frmPizzaSelection.vb*    frmPizzaSelection.vb [Design]*
                    0 references
20          Private Sub btnSelectPizza_Click(sender As Object, e As EventArgs) Handles btnSelectPizza.Click
21              ' This code is executed when the user taps or clicks the
22              ' Select Pizza button. It disables the Deep Dish button, the
23              ' Select Pizza button, and the Thin Crust button.
24              ' It hides the Instructions label, displays the
25              ' Confirmation label, and enables the Exit Window button.
26
27              btnDeepDish.Enabled = False
28              btnSelectPizza.Enabled = False
29              btnThinCrust.Enabled = False
30              lblInstructions.Visible = False
31              lblConfirmation.Visible = True
32              btnExit.Enabled = True
33
34          End Sub
35
                    0 references
36          Private Sub btnThinCrust_Click(sender As Object, e As EventArgs) Handles btnThinCrust.Click
37              ' This code is executed when the user taps or clicks
38              ' the Thin Crust button. It displays the Thin Crust picture,
39              ' hides the Deep Dish picture, and enables the Select
40              ' Pizza button.
41
42              picThinCrust.Visible = True
43              picDeepDish.Visible = False
44              btnSelectPizza.Enabled = True
45              |
46          End Sub
47      End Class
48
```

FIGURE 3-77

When you tap or click the Thin Crust button, the ThinCrust picture is displayed, the DeepDish picture is not displayed, and the Select Pizza button is enabled (Figure 3-78). The program is working properly.

RESULT OF STEP 10 (PROGRAM EXECUTION)

FIGURE 3-78
Brand X Pictures/Getty Images

(continues)

Guided Program Development *continued*

11

- **Display the Design Window** Tap or click the frmPizzaSelection.vb [Design] tab to return to the Design tabbed page.

HINT

`frmPizzaSelection.vb*` ⊸ ✕ `frmPizzaSelection.vb [Design]*`

- **Open the Code Window for the btnExit Event Handler** Double-tap or double-click the Exit Window button to open the code window for the btnExit_Click event (*ref: Figure 3-24*).

- **Enter the Event Handler Comments** Using the techniques you have learned, enter the comments that describe the processing in the btnExit_Click event handler.

```
48        Private Sub btnExit_Click(sender As Object, e As EventArgs) Handles btnExit.Click
49            ' This code is executed when the user taps or clicks the Exit Window
50            ' button. It closes the window and terminates the program execution.
51
52        End Sub
53    End Class
54
```

- **Enter the Close() Procedure Call** Using IntelliSense, enter the Visual Basic code statement to close the window and terminate the program (*ref: Figure 3-66*).

```
0 references
        Private Sub btnExit_Click(sender As Object, e As EventArgs) Handles btnExit.Click
            ' This code is executed when the user taps or clicks the Exit Window
            ' button. It closes the window and terminates the program execution.

            Close()

        End Sub
    End Class
```

The Close() procedure call statement is entered (Figure 3-79). When the procedure call is executed, the application will be closed.

RESULT OF STEP 11

Pizza Selection - frmPizzaSelection.vb*

frmPizzaSelection.vb* ⊸ ✕

```
     0 references
20        Private Sub btnSelectPizza_Click(sender As Object, e As EventArgs) Handles btnSelectPizza.Click
21            ' This code is executed when the user taps or clicks the
22            ' Select Pizza button. It disables the Deep Dish button, the
23            ' Select Pizza button, and the Thin Crust button.
24            ' It hides the Instructions label, displays the
25            ' Confirmation label, and enables the Exit Window button.
26
27            btnDeepDish.Enabled = False
28            btnSelectPizza.Enabled = False
29            btnThinCrust.Enabled = False
30            lblInstructions.Visible = False
31            lblConfirmation.Visible = True
32            btnExit.Enabled = True
33
34        End Sub
35
     0 references
36        Private Sub btnThinCrust_Click(sender As Object, e As EventArgs) Handles btnThinCrust.Click
37            ' This code is executed when the user taps or clicks
38            ' the Thin Crust button. It displays the Thin Crust picture,
39            ' hides the Deep Dish picture, and enables the Select
40            ' Pizza button.
41
42            picThinCrust.Visible = True
43            picDeepDish.Visible = False
44            btnSelectPizza.Enabled = True
45
46        End Sub
47
     0 references
48        Private Sub btnExit_Click(sender As Object, e As EventArgs) Handles btnExit.Click
49            ' This code is executed when the user taps or clicks the Exit Window
50            ' button. It closes the window and terminates the program execution.
51
52            Close()
53
54        End Sub
55    End Class
56
```

FIGURE 3-79

12

- **Run the Program** Run the program to ensure that it works correctly. Tap or click the Deep Dish button, the Thin Crust button, the Select Pizza button, and the Exit Window button.

Code Listing

The complete code for the sample program is shown in Figure 3-80.

```vbnet
1    ' Program Name: Pizza Selection
2    ' Developer:     Corinne Hoisington
3    ' Date:          January 28, 2017
4    ' Purpose:       This application displays two pizza types
5    '                (deep dish And thin crust). The user can select a pizza type.
6
7    Public Class frmPizzaSelection
8        Private Sub btnDeepDish_Click(sender As Object, e As EventArgs) Handles btnDeepDish.Click
9            ' This code is executed when the user taps or clicks
10           ' the Deep Dish button. It displays the Deep Dish picture,
11           ' hides the Thin Crust picture, and enables the Select
12           ' Pizza button.
13
14           picDeepDish.Visible = True
15           picThinCrust.Visible = False
16           btnSelectPizza.Enabled = True
17
18       End Sub
19
20       Private Sub btnSelectPizza_Click(sender As Object, e As EventArgs) Handles btnSelectPizza.Click
21           ' This code is executed when the user taps or clicks the
22           ' Select Pizza button. It disables the Deep Dish button, the
23           ' Select Pizza button, and the Thin Crust button.
24           ' It hides the Instructions label, displays the
25           ' Confirmation label, and enables the Exit Window button.
26
27           btnDeepDish.Enabled = False
28           btnSelectPizza.Enabled = False
29           btnThinCrust.Enabled = False
30           lblInstructions.Visible = False
31           lblConfirmation.Visible = True
32           btnExit.Enabled = True
33
34       End Sub
35
36       Private Sub btnThinCrust_Click(sender As Object, e As EventArgs) Handles btnThinCrust.Click
37           ' This code is executed when the user taps or clicks
38           ' the Thin Crust button. It displays the Thin Crust picture,
39           ' hides the Deep Dish picture, and enables the Select
40           ' Pizza button.
41
42           picThinCrust.Visible = True
43           picDeepDish.Visible = False
44           btnSelectPizza.Enabled = True
45
46       End Sub
47
48       Private Sub btnExit_Click(sender As Object, e As EventArgs) Handles btnExit.Click
49           ' This code is executed when the user taps or clicks the Exit Window
50           ' button. It closes the window and terminates the program execution.
51
52           Close()
53
54       End Sub
55   End Class
56
```

FIGURE 3-80

Summary

In this chapter you have learned to fine-tune a GUI to maximize its usefulness and to enter code for object event handlers.

The items listed in Figure 3-81 include all the new Visual Studio and Visual Basic skills you have learned in this chapter. Video 3-1 demonstrates the complete program execution.

Visual Basic Skills

Skill	Figure Number	Video Number
Run the completed program	Figure 3-1	Video 3-1
Set the BackColor Property	Figure 3-2	Video 3-2
Locate and Save an Image from the Web	Figure 3-7	Video 3-3
Import an Image into the Program Resources Folder	Figure 3-11	Video 3-4
Size an Image	Figure 3-16	Video 3-5
Set the Visible Property in the Properties Window	Figure 3-18	Video 3-6
Set the Enabled Property in the Properties Window	Figure 3-20	Video 3-7
Run a Visual Basic 2015 Program	Figure 3-22	Video 3-8
Enter Visual Basic 2015 Code for Event Handling	Figure 3-24	Video 3-9
Enter a Visual Basic 2015 Statement Using IntelliSense	Figure 3-29	Video 3-10
Enter a Visual Basic 2015 Statement to Set the Visible Property to True	Figure 3-29	Video 3-10
Enter a Visual Basic 2015 Statement to Set the Visible Property to False	Figure 3-37	Video 3-11
Enter a Visual Basic 2015 Statement to Set the Enabled Property to True	Figure 3-42	Video 3-12
Enter Comments in Visual Basic 2015 Code	Figure 3-47	Video 3-13
Enter Introductory Comments in Visual Basic Code	Figure 3-52	Video 3-14
Correct Errors in a Visual Basic 2015 Program	Figure 3-58	Video 3-15
Enter Additional Tap or Click Events	Figure 3-63	Video 3-16
Enter a Close() Statement into Visual Basic 2015 Code	Figure 3-66	Video 3-17
Print Code	Page 148	

FIGURE 3-81

Learn Online

Reinforcement activities and resources are available at no additional cost on *www.CengageBrain.com*. Visit *http://solutions.cengage.com/ctdownloads/* for detailed instructions about accessing the available resources at the Student Companion Site.

Knowledge Check

1. When the Pizza Selection program was executed, was the Visible property of the PictureBox objects set to True or False?

2. Which property controls the background color of the Form object?

3. Which property controls the text color of a Label object?

4. Which color palette is guaranteed to be displayed properly on every computer?

5. When a PictureBox object is placed on the form, what is the default SizeMode property setting?

6. When you place a PictureBox object on a Windows form, in which project folder is the image stored in the Solution Explorer?

7. In which property of the PictureBox object do you tap or click the ellipsis button to select the correct picture?

8. Which option should be selected in the SizeMode property to make the image fit within the PictureBox object?

9. Which property has been set to False if a Button object is dimmed in a window when the program begins?

10. Which property has been set to False if a PictureBox object is not displayed when you run the application?

11. What two options can you select for the Visible property in the Properties window?

12. Write a line of code that would set the Visible property to False for a PictureBox object shown in Figure 3-82.

FIGURE 3-82

13. Write a line of code that would set the Enabled property to True for a Button object named btnHarvard.

14. Write a line of code that would set the Visible property to True for a PictureBox object named picBirthday.

15. Write a comment line of code that states, "This code displays the birthday image."

16. What color is used to display comments in the code window of Visual Basic 2015?

17. Write a line of code that will close an application window and terminate the application.

18. What does a red squiggly line mean in the code window?

19. Which symbol is associated with the assignment statement?

20. Why is it best to use IntelliSense when you enter code in the code window? List two reasons.

Debugging Exercises

1. Fix the following line of code to set the Enabled property to False for the btnDisplayCartoon Button object.

   ```
   btnCartoon.Enable.False
   ```

2. Fix the following line of code to change the visibility of the btnExitProgram Button object so that you can view it when the program runs.

   ```
   btnExitProgram.Visibilty = Yes
   ```

3. Fix the following line of code to set the Visible property to False for the lblDirections Label object.

   ```
   lblDirections.Visible = ' False
   ```

4. Fix the following comment line of code.

   ```
   The ' following line of code makes the college logo visible
   ```

5. Fix the following line of code.

   ```
   Close
   ```

6. Examine the code window and the Error List window in Figure 3-83. Then, write a line of code to replace the erroneous line.

FIGURE 3-83

Program Analysis

1. For the hiking application shown in Figure 3-84, write the Visual Basic 2015 coding statement to view the picture when the user taps or clicks the btnView button, assuming the Visible property had been set to False for the picHike PictureBox object in the Properties window.

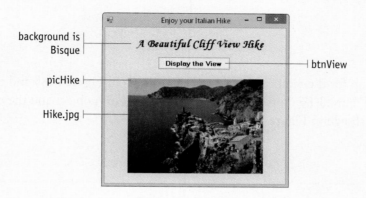

background is
Bisque

picHike

Hike.jpg

btnView

FIGURE 3-84

Photo courtesy of Corinne Hoisington

2. Which property in the Properties window controls whether the picHike image is displayed when the program begins? Which option for the property would you select to make the button dimmed when the program begins?

3. When you import the picture into the Resources folder and select the image to use in the picHike PictureBox object, which SizeMode property option would you select to view the complete picture?

4. Write the Visual Basic 2015 coding statement for the btnView click event that would cause the image to be displayed.

5. To change the window background color to Bisque as shown in Figure 3-84, what property should you modify?

6. What property is used to display the text "Enjoy your Italian Hike" in the window title bar?

Case Programming Assignments

Complete one or more of the following case programming assignments. Submit the program and materials you create to your instructor. The level of difficulty is indicated for each assignment.

● = Easiest
●● = Intermediate
●●● = Challenging

1 ●

TECH JOB FAIR

Create a Windows form mock-up for the requirements document shown in Figure 3-85 and the Use Case Definition shown in Figure 3-86 on page 171. The Windows Form object and the other objects in the user interface are shown in Figure 3-87 on page 171.

REQUIREMENTS DOCUMENT

Date:	October 13, 2015
Date Submitted:	
Application Title:	Tech Job Fair
Purpose:	This Windows Desktop application displays a welcome screen for the Tech Job Fair. The user can choose an option to view the date and location.
Program Procedures:	From a window on the screen, the user makes a request to see the fair's date and location.
Algorithms, Processing, and Conditions:	1. The user first views a Tech Job Fair window that displays the job fair name (Tech Job Fair), a job fair picture, and a phrase that states all students are welcome.
	2. When the user chooses to view the date and location, the following Information is displayed:
	May 2, 2016
	Located in Lochlan Hall - Room 101
	3. After the user views the job fair information, the only allowable action is to exit the window.
Notes and Restrictions:	N/A
Comments:	The picture shown in the window can be found on CengageBrain.com. The name of the picture is Fair.

FIGURE 3-85

Tech Job Fair (continued)

USE CASE DEFINITION

1. The window opens, displaying the name of the event and a message stating that all students are welcome. All buttons are enabled.
2. User taps or clicks the View Job Fair Details button.
3. Program displays the tech job fair date and location between the buttons. The View Job Fair Details button is disabled.
4. User tap or clicks the Exit Window button to terminate the application.

© 2014 Cengage Learning

FIGURE 3-86

In Figure 3-87a, no button has been tapped or clicked. In Figure 3-87b, the user has tapped or clicked the View Job Fair Details button.

background color is BlanchedAlmond

button background color is Honeydew

FIGURE 3-87a

© iStock.com / fstop123

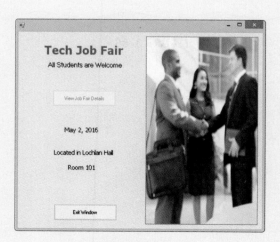

FIGURE 3-87b

© iStock.com / fstop123

2   VEGETARIAN SPECIALS

Create a Windows form mock-up for the requirements document shown in Figure 3-88 and the Use Case Definition shown in Figure 3-89 on page 173. The Windows Form object and the other objects in the user interface are shown in Figure 3-90 on page 173.

REQUIREMENTS DOCUMENT

Date:	January 10, 2017
Date Submitted:	
Application Title:	Vegetarian Specials
Purpose:	This Windows Desktop application displays the vegetarian specials for a restaurant named Plant. The user can select one of two specials: falafel or veggie burger.
Program Procedures:	From a window on the screen, the user orders one of two vegetarian special dishes and confirms the order with a message.
Algorithms, Processing, and Conditions:	1. The user must be able to identify the falafel or veggie burger special name as many times as necessary until making a decision.
	2. When the user identifies the vegetarian special, a picture of that meal appears in the window.
	3. Only one picture should be displayed at a time.
	4. When the user selects falafel, a message should be displayed to confirm the selection of the vegetarian dish. In addition, the user should be prevented from identifying another meal after selecting a dish.
	5. After the user selects a meal, the only allowable action is to exit the window.
Notes and Restrictions:	A user can select a meal only after viewing one of the images of the meals.
Comments:	1. The picture shown in the window can be found on CengageBrain.com.
	2. The names of the pictures are Falafel and Veggie.

FIGURE 3-88

Vegetarian Specials (continued)

USE CASE DEFINITION

1. User taps or clicks Falafel button or Veggie Burger button.
2. Program displays a picture of the meal identified by the user and enables the meal selection button.
3. User taps or clicks meal buttons to view meals as desired. Program displays the picture of the identified vegetarian meal.
4. User taps or clicks the Select Meal button.
5. Program displays a meal confirmation message and disables both meal buttons and the Select Meal button.
6. The Exit Window button becomes active. User terminates the program by tapping or clicking the Exit Window button.

FIGURE 3-89

In Figure 3-90a, no button has been tapped or clicked. In Figure 3-90b, the user has tapped or clicked the Falafel button. In Figure 3-90c, the user has tapped or clicked the Select Meal button.

FIGURE 3-90a

FIGURE 3-90b

© iStock.com / TheCrimsonMonkey

FIGURE 3-90c

© iStock.com / TheCrimsonMonkey

3

VOTE FOR THE BEST CAMPUS SELFIE

Create a Windows form mock-up for the requirements document shown in Figure 3-91 and the Use Case Definition shown in Figure 3-92 on page 175. The Windows Form object and the other objects in the user interface are shown in Figure 3-93 on page 175.

REQUIREMENTS DOCUMENT

Date:	August 16, 2016
Date Submitted:	
Application Title:	Selfies
Purpose:	This Windows Desktop application displays the two finalists for the best campus selfie photos. The user can select one of two selfies.
Program Procedures:	From a window on the screen, the user selects one of two selfie finalists and confirms the vote with a message.
Algorithms, Processing, and Conditions:	1. The user must be able to identify the first finalist selfie entitled "Cheer" or the second finalist entitled "Connect" as many times as necessary until making a decision.
	2. When the user taps or clicks the button to view a selfie, a picture of the finalist appears in the window.
	3. Only one picture should be displayed at a time.
	4. When the user selects the first selfie, a message should be displayed to thank the user for voting. In addition, the user should be prevented from identifying the other selfie picture after voting.
	5. After the user selects a selfie, the only allowable action is to exit the window.
Notes and Restrictions:	A user can select a selfie only after viewing one of the images.
Comments:	1. The picture shown in the window can be found on CengageBrain.com.
	2. The names of the pictures are Selfie1 and Selfie2.

FIGURE 3-91

Vote for the Best Campus Selfie *(continued)*

USE CASE DEFINITION

1. User taps or clicks Selfie "Cheer" button or Selfie "Connect" button.
2. Program displays a selfie identified by the user and enables the Select Selfie button.
3. User taps or clicks selfie buttons to view finalist pictures as desired. Program displays the picture of the identified selfie.
4. User taps or clicks the Select Selfie button.
5. Program displays a vote confirmation message and disables both selfie buttons and the Select Selfie button.
6. The Exit Window button becomes active. User terminates the program by tapping or clicking the Exit Window button.

FIGURE 3-92

In Figure 3-93a, no button has been tapped or clicked. In Figure 3-93b, the user has tapped or clicked the Finalist "Cheer" button. In Figure 3-93c, the user has tapped or clicked the Select Selfie button.

FIGURE 3-93a

FIGURE 3-93b

© iStock.com / RapidEye

FIGURE 3-93c

Case Programming Assignments

4 ●● FALL MARATHON

Create a Use Case Definition document and design a Windows form mock-up based on the requirements document in Figure 3-94.

REQUIREMENTS DOCUMENT

Date:	October 13, 2016
Date Submitted:	
Application Title:	Fall Marathon
Purpose:	This Windows Desktop application displays a welcome screen to market the Fall Marathon. The user can choose an option to view the date, start location, and details.
Program Procedures:	From a window on the screen, the user makes a request to see the marathon's date, start location, and details.
Algorithms, Processing, and Conditions:	1. The user first views a Fall Marathon window that displays the title (Fall Marathon), a marathon picture, and a phrase that states that full- and half-marathon runners are welcome. 2. When the user chooses to view the date, start location, and details, the following information is displayed: May 30, 2017 Ryan Park Start Time: 8:00 AM For more information, view the Fall Marathon Facebook page. After the user views the marathon information, the only allowable action is to exit the window.
Notes and Restrictions:	Design your own layout.
Comments:	1. The picture shown in the window can be found on CengageBrain.com. 2. The name of the picture is Marathon.

FIGURE 3-94

5 •• GUITAR STORE

Create a Use Case Definition document and design a Windows form mock-up based on the requirements document in Figure 3-95.

REQUIREMENTS DOCUMENT

Date:	March 21, 2017
Date Submitted:	
Application Title:	Guitar Store
Purpose:	A local guitar store has three guitars on special this week. A customer can choose one of three guitar types. The program must display each of the guitars upon request. The customer can then select a guitar for purchase.
Program Procedures:	From a window on the screen, the user selects one of three guitars. A picture of the selected guitar is displayed in the window. The user then can choose a guitar for purchase.
Algorithms, Processing, and Conditions:	1. The user selects a guitar. Then, a picture of the guitar is displayed in the window. 2. The user can select any of the three guitars. Only the picture of the selected guitar should be displayed. 3. The user can select guitars as many times as necessary and display the pictures of the guitars. 4. The user finds a guitar, chooses it for purchase, and taps or clicks the Purchase button. 5. After the user chooses a guitar, a message stating "Enjoy your guitar!" should be displayed. 6. After the user chooses a guitar, the only allowable action is to exit the window.
Notes and Restrictions:	The user should not be able to choose a guitar until viewing at least one guitar image.
Comments:	1. The available guitars are classical acoustic, steel-string acoustic, and electric. 2. You can download appropriate pictures from a site such as www.google.com/images.

FIGURE 3-95

Case Programming Assignments

6

FACEBOOK MOVIE VOTING

Create a Use Case Definition document and design a Windows form mock-up based on the requirements document shown in Figure 3-96.

REQUIREMENTS DOCUMENT

Date:	October 16, 2016
Date Submitted:	
Application Title:	Movie Voting
Purpose:	Facebook wants you to select your favorite movie of the year and allows the user to vote for his or her overall favorite. The user should be able to select one of three movies and then be able to vote for that movie as his or her overall favorite.
Program Procedures:	From a window on the screen, the user selects one of three movies. The names of the three top movies are displayed together with a picture of each movie. Then, the user can vote for the movie as his or her overall favorite.
Algorithms, Processing, and Conditions:	1. The user selects each movie and a picture of the movie is displayed in the window.
	2. The user can select any of three movie titles. Only the name of the movie and the picture for the selected movie should be displayed.
	3. The user can select different movies back and forth to make a decision for their favorite movie.
	4. After the user selects a movie, the user should be able to vote for their favorite movie. The user cannot select their favorite movie until viewing at least one movie picture.
	5. After the user votes, a message stating that their favorite movie vote has been received.
	6. After the user votes, the only acceptable action is to tap or click the Exit Window button.
Notes and Restrictions:	The user should be able to vote until he or she has selected their favorite movie.
Comments:	1. You (the developer) should select three movie titles from this year and select three online pictures to represent those movies.
	2. You can download the pictures from a site such as www.google.com/images.

FIGURE 3-96

7

• • •

AIRLINE SNACK SELECTION

Create a requirements document and a Use Case Definition document and then design a Windows form mock-up based on the case project shown in Figure 3-97:

An international airline requests a computer application that will run on the personal television monitors on the back of each seat in the plane. The application should request which free snack you would like during the flight, display the choices as buttons, and then display an image of the snack you select. Another button allows you to make your final snack selection and display a confirmation message.

Snack
Cheese and Crackers
Chocolate Chip Cookies
Mini Pretzels
Salted Peanuts

FIGURE 3-97

8 ●●●
TRAVEL SPECIALS

Create a requirements document and a Use Case Definition document and then design a Windows form mock-up based on the case project shown in Figure 3-98:

Your local travel agent requests a computer application that advertises the travel specials of the week from your city. This week's flight specials are:

Destination	Price
New York City	$399 round trip
Las Vegas	$419 round trip
Miami	$520 round trip
St. Thomas	$619 round trip
Hawaii	$828 round trip

Write an application that allows the user to select any of the five vacation destinations. When the user selects a vacation destination, the corresponding flight price and a picture of the destination should be displayed. Clear each prior price and picture when the user selects a different vacation destination. In addition to a picture of the destination, include a webpage address that features the selected location. After selecting a destination, the user should be able to book the flight and then exit the window.

FIGURE 3-98

9 ●●●
LACROSSE TICKETS

Create a requirements document and a Use Case Definition document and then design a Windows form mock-up based on the case project shown in Figure 3-99.

Your favorite university lacrosse team has asked you to develop a Windows application that allows the user to see the four types of game tickets offered, one at a time. Then, the user should be able to reserve a single game ticket for the selected seat type. The four types of stadium seating and their base prices are as follows:

Name of Ticket	Minimum Price
Upper Endline Seating	$15.00
Lower Endline Seating	$25.00
Sideline Seating	$30.00
Club Seats	$50.00

For each type of seating, your program should display the base price and a picture depicting an example of the seating type. Clear each price and picture when the user selects a different seating type. After selecting a ticket, the user should be able to purchase the ticket and then exit the window.

FIGURE 3-99

CHAPTER 4

Variables and Arithmetic Operations

OBJECTIVES

You will have mastered the material in this chapter when you can:

- Create, modify, and program a TextBox object

- Use code to place data in the Text property of a Label object

- Use the AcceptButton and CancelButton properties

- Understand and declare String and Numeric variables

- Use assignment statements to place data in variables

- Use literals and constants in coding statements

- Understand scope rules for variables

- Convert string and numeric data

- Understand and use arithmetic operators and arithmetic operations

- Format and display numeric data as a string

- Create a form load event

- Create a concatenated string

- Debug a program

Introduction

In the Pizza Selection program you developed in Chapter 2 and Chapter 3, you tapped or clicked buttons in the user interface to trigger events, but you did not enter data. In many applications, users must enter data that the program then uses in its processing.

When processing data entered by a user, a common requirement is to perform arithmetic operations on the data to generate useful output. Arithmetic operations include adding, subtracting, multiplying, and dividing numeric data.

To illustrate user data input and arithmetic operations, the application in this chapter allows the user to specify a number of bikes to rent from a city bike rental program. The application then calculates the total cost of renting the bikes. The user interface for the program is shown in Figure 4-1.

© iStock.com/phototropic

FIGURE 4-1

In Figure 4-1, the user entered 4 as the number of city bikes to rent for the day. The maximum time rental is 24 hours. If the user wants to rent for multiple days, he or she must bring the bike back to a bike kiosk rental station and pay for individual day rentals. When the user taps or clicks the Calculate Cost button, the program multiplies 4 by the cost per bike rental for a 24-hour period ($9.95) and then displays the result as the total cost of the city bike rental for a group. When the user taps or clicks the Clear button, the values for the number of bikes and the total cost of the bike rental are cleared so the next user can enter a value. Tapping or clicking the Exit button closes the window and terminates the program.

To create this application, the developer must understand how to perform the following processes, among others:

1. Define a text box for data entry
2. Define a label to hold the results of arithmetic operations
3. Convert data in a text box to data that can be used for arithmetic operations
4. Perform arithmetic operations on data entered by a user

The following pages describe the tools and techniques required to create the program shown in Figure 4-1.

Design the User Interface

As you have learned in Chapter 2 and Chapter 3, the next step after completing the program requirements document for an application is to define the graphical user interface. In this chapter, three new elements are introduced:

- TextBox objects
- Labels intended for variable text property values
- Accept buttons

Each of these elements is described in the following sections.

TextBox Objects

A **TextBox object** allows users to enter data into a program. In Figure 4-2, the user can enter a value into the text box.

FIGURE 4-2

In Figure 4-2, the TextBox object is placed on the Windows Form object. A TextBox object automatically allows the user to enter data in the text box. To place a TextBox object on the Windows Form object, you can complete the following steps. (Note that the examples in this chapter illustrate new objects in the user interface. Portions of the user interface have already been completed for you. You should not expect to *tap or click along* with these examples unless you create all the elements or follow the steps using an unformatted user interface.)

STEP 1   With Visual Studio open, the City Bike Rentals Windows Desktop application created, and the frmBikes.vb [Design] tabbed page visible, point to the TextBox .NET component in the Toolbox.

The TextBox .NET component is highlighted in the Toolbox (Figure 4-3).

© iStock.com/phototropic

FIGURE 4-3

STEP 2   Drag the TextBox .NET component onto the Windows Form object at the desired location.

While you drag, the pointer changes to indicate a TextBox object will be placed on the Windows Form object (Figure 4-4). Snap lines indicate where the TextBox object aligns with other objects on the Windows Form object. In Figure 4-4, the bottom of the TextBox object aligns with the bottom of the Label object. When adding a TextBox object to the Windows Form object, bottom alignment often provides a good beginning position.

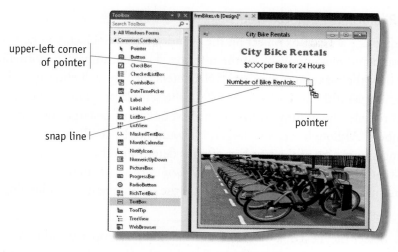

upper-left corner
of pointer

snap line

pointer

FIGURE 4-4

© iStock.com/phototropic

STEP 3   When the upper-left corner of the pointer is located where you want to place the TextBox object's upper-left corner, release the TextBox object.

Visual Studio places the TextBox object at the location identified by the pointer (Figure 4-5). The default size of the TextBox object is 100 pixels wide by 22 pixels high. Notice that by default the TextBox object contains no text. You can change that by entering text in the Text property of the TextBox object.

TextBox object placed on
Windows Form object

TextBox object
contains no text

FIGURE 4-5

© iStock.com/phototropic

ONLINE REINFORCEMENT

To view a video of the process in the preceding steps, visit CengageBrain.com and navigate to the resources for this title. Tap or click the link for Chapter 4 and then navigate to Video 4-2.

As you have learned, whenever you place an object on the Windows Form object, you must name the object. When naming a TextBox object, the prefix should be txt. Therefore, the name of the TextBox object in Figure 4-5 could be txtNumberOfBikes.

Size and Position a TextBox Object

To properly place a TextBox object on the Windows Form object, you need to know the minimum and maximum size of the text box. The minimum size normally is determined by the maximum number of characters the user will enter into the text box. For example, if the user can enter 999 in the sample program as the maximum number of rentals, the minimum size of the text box must be large enough to display three numbers. Although it can be larger, it should not be smaller.

The maximum size of the text box often is determined by the design of the user interface; that is, the size should *look and feel good* in the user interface. To determine the minimum size of the text box, you can use the technique in the following steps:

STEP 1 Select the TextBox object. Select the (Name) property and name the TextBox object `txtNumberOfBikes`. Scroll in the Properties window until the Text property is visible and then tap or click the right column for the Text property.

The TextBox object is selected, as shown by the thick border and sizing handles (Figure 4-6). The TextBox object is named txtNumberOfBikes. The Text property for the TextBox object is highlighted and the insertion point indicates you can enter text for the Text property.

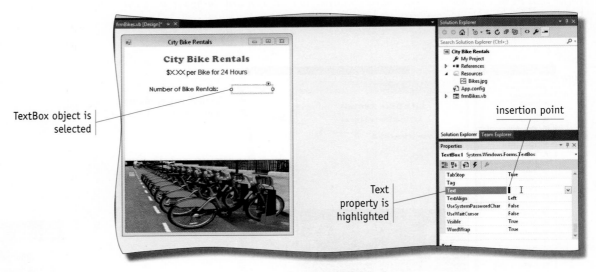

© iStock.com/phototropic

FIGURE 4-6

STEP 2 Type the maximum number of characters the user normally will enter into the text box and then press the ENTER key. Programmers often use the digit 8 in this situation because it is wider than other digits. This example uses the value 888 because three digits is the maximum number the user normally will enter.

When the value is entered in the Text property of the TextBox object, the value is displayed in the TextBox object (Figure 4-7).

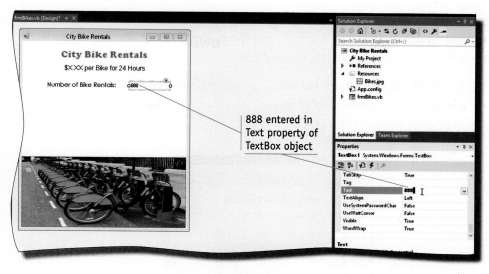

FIGURE 4-7

STEP 3   Using the Properties window, change the Font property to the correct font and font size. For this application, change the font to Century Gothic and change the font size to 11. Then, drag the right edge of the TextBox object and resize it to be slightly wider than the 888 entry.

As you drag, the size of the TextBox object changes (Figure 4–8). When you release the TextBox object, the text box will be resized. When the font size is changed, the horizontal alignment of the text will change.

FIGURE 4-8

STEP 4 To horizontally align the text in the label and the text in the text box, drag the text box up until a red snap line indicates the bottoms of the text are aligned (Figure 4-9). Then, release the left mouse button.

As you drag the TextBox object, the red snap line indicates when the bottoms of the text in the label and the text box are aligned (Figure 4-9). When you release the TextBox object, it will be placed so the bottoms of the text are aligned.

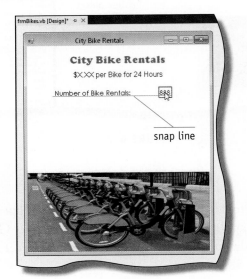

snap line

FIGURE 4-9

© iStock.com/phototropic

CONSIDER THIS

Are details such as alignment important in design and programming?
The user interface is more important than ever with Windows application and mobile design. Many colleges teach entire courses on interface design. Remember, your users respond to consistency in your design layout. Language is another interface element that should be consistent. A consistent interface enables your users to have a better understanding of how the application works and increases their efficiency.

Align Text in a TextBox Object

In Figure 4-9, the numbers are left-aligned in the text box. Often, the user interface will be more useful if the value the user enters is centered in the text box. To align the text in a TextBox object, you can use the following method:

STEP 1 Select the TextBox object. In the Properties window, scroll until the TextAlign property is visible, tap or click the TextAlign property in the left column, and then tap or click the list arrow in the right column of the TextAlign property.

The TextAlign property list contains the values Left, Right, and Center (Figure 4-10).

text in TextBox
object is left-aligned

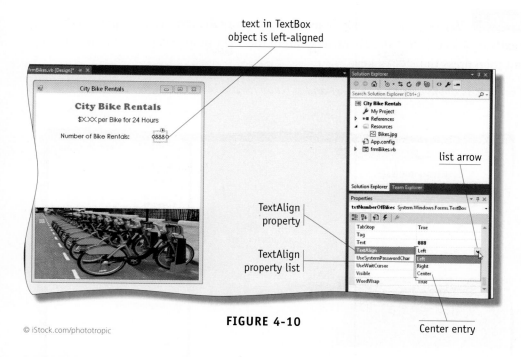

list arrow

TextAlign
property

TextAlign
property list

Center entry

FIGURE 4-10

© iStock.com/phototropic

STEP 2 Tap or click Center in the TextAlign property list.

The text in the TextBox object is centered (Figure 4–11). When a user enters data in the text box, the data also will be centered.

text is centered
in the text box

FIGURE 4-11

© iStock.com/phototropic

STEP 3 Because the TextBox object is sized properly, remove the digits in the TextBox object. Select the characters 888 in the Text property, press the DELETE key, and then press the ENTER key.

The TextBox object contains no text and is ready for use in the user interface (Figure 4-12).

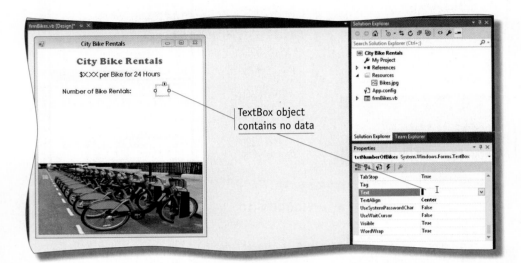

FIGURE 4-12

© iStock.com/phototropic

ONLINE REINFORCEMENT

To view a video of the process in the preceding steps, visit CengageBrain.com and navigate to the resources for this title. Tap or click the link for Chapter 4 and then navigate to Video 4-4.

Enter Data in a TextBox Object

When the program is executed, the user can enter data in the text box. Users can enter letters, numbers, and other characters. If the user enters more characters than the text box can display, the characters that have already been entered scroll to the left and no longer are visible. A text box does not contain a scroll bar, so if a user enters more characters than the text box can display, the user must move the insertion point left or right with the arrow keys on the keyboard to view the data in the text box. In most situations, a user should not enter more characters than are expected, and the text box should be designed to display all expected characters.

In a default text box, only a single line of text can be entered regardless of the number of characters in the line. However, programmers can select a special option for a text box to allow the user to enter multiple lines of text. Additionally, the MaskedTextBox object can be used to control the format of data that a user enters. These types of text boxes are explained in the following sections.

Create a MultiLine Text Box

A MultiLine text box allows the user to enter multiple lines in the text box. The TextBox object must be resized vertically to display the multiple lines. To create a TextBox object that can accept multiple lines, you can complete the following steps:

STEP 1 Select the TextBox object, tap or click the Action tag, and then point to the MultiLine check box.

The TextBox Tasks list is displayed with the MultiLine check box (Figure 4-13). When you tap or click the MultiLine check box, the TextBox object will be able to accept multiple lines.

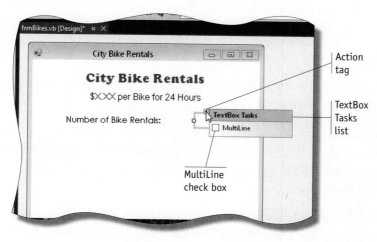

FIGURE 4-13

© iStock.com/phototropic

STEP 2 Tap or click the MultiLine check box.

The text box is enabled to accept multiple lines.

In addition to enabling multiple lines, you should increase the vertical size of the TextBox object so the multiple lines will be visible when the user enters them.

Create a MaskedTextBox Object

The MaskedTextBox object allows you to specify the data format of the value typed into the text box. Using the MaskedTextBox object removes confusion about which format should be used for data the user enters. The term *mask* refers to a predefined layout for the data. Figure 4-14 shows three examples of the MaskedTextBox used for the Short date input mask, the Phone number input mask, and the Social Security number input mask.

ONLINE REINFORCEMENT

To view a video of the process in the preceding steps, visit CengageBrain.com and navigate to the resources for this title. Tap or click the link for Chapter 4 and then navigate to Video 4-5.

Prior to Data Entry

After Data Entry

FIGURE 4-14

In Figure 4-14, before the user enters data, the mask demonstrates the format of the data to be entered. To enter data, the user selects the text box and then types data into it. The user need not enter punctuation or spacing. To enter the date in the Order Date text box, the user typed 09302017 with no spaces, punctuation, or other keystrokes. Similarly, for the phone number, the user typed 9455553281, again with no spaces or other keystrokes. For the Social Security number, the user typed 999999999.

To place a MaskedTextBox object on the Windows Form object, you can complete the following steps:

STEP 1   Drag a MaskedTextBox .NET component from the Toolbox to the Windows Form object. Then, tap or click the Action tag on the TextBox object and point to the Set Mask command.

The MaskedTextBox object is placed on the Windows Form object (Figure 4-15). When the Action tag is tapped or clicked, the MaskedTextBox Tasks list is displayed. The Set Mask command is the only command in the list.

FIGURE 4-15

STEP 2   Tap or click Set Mask on the MaskedTextBox Tasks list and then tap or click the Short date mask description in the Input Mask dialog box.

Visual Studio displays the Input Mask dialog box (Figure 4-16). The Mask Description column contains all the masks that can be used for the MaskedTextBox object. The Short date mask description is highlighted. In the Preview box, you can type data to see how the mask will perform when it is used in the MaskedTextBox object. The Use Validating Type check box is selected to verify that the user entered valid numeric data.

Input Mask
dialog box

Phone number
mask description

Short date mask
description is
highlighted

Social security
number mask
description

mask

type here to see
preview

Use ValidatingType
check box

FIGURE 4-16

STEP 3 Tap or click the OK button in the Input Mask dialog box and then tap or
click anywhere in the Windows Form object.

The mask is placed in the MaskedTextBox object (Figure 4-17).

Short date mask in
MaskedTextBox
object

FIGURE 4-17

ONLINE REINFORCEMENT

To view a video of the process
in the preceding steps, visit
CengageBrain.com and navigate
to the resources for this title.
Tap or click the link for Chapter 4
and then navigate to Video 4-7.

You can use the same technique to place the phone number and Social Security number in the MaskedTextBox.

Label Objects

In the sample program, a Label object is used to display the total cost of bike rentals (see Figure 4-1 on page 184). The developer must accomplish two tasks to prepare the label for this purpose: place the label on the Windows Form object in the correct location, and then ensure that when the Label object contains its maximum value, its location will work within the user interface design.

To accomplish these two tasks, you can complete the following steps:

STEP 1   Drag a Label object onto the Windows Form object to the correct location. Name the label `lblTotalCost`. Change the label to the appropriate font and size (Century Gothic, 11 points). In the Text property for the Label object, enter the maximum number of characters ($888.88) that will appear in the label during execution of the program.

The properly sized characters appear in the label (Figure 4-18). The label is aligned vertically, but should be moved up to align horizontally with the Total Cost of Bikes Rented label.

FIGURE 4-18

© iStock.com/phototropic

STEP 2   Drag the Label object up until the red snap line appears (Figure 4-19). Then release the Label object.

The label is aligned (Figure 4-19).

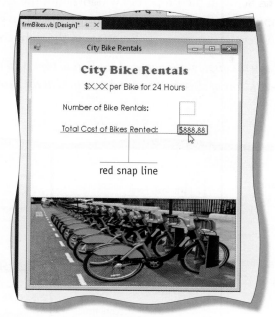

FIGURE 4-19

© iStock.com/phototropic

When program execution begins, the label that will contain the total cost of the bike rental should be blank. In Figure 4-19, however, it contains the value in the Text property of the Label object ($888.88). If the Text property in a Label object is set to hold no content, it will not be displayed in the Windows Form object during the design phase, which makes the Label object difficult to work with in Design mode. Therefore, most designers place a value in the Text property of the Label object and leave it there during user interface design. Then, when the program begins, the label Text property will be set to blank. You will learn to perform this task later in the chapter.

Accept Button in Form Properties

Computer users often press the ENTER key to enter data in a text box and cause processing to occur. For instance, in the sample program for this chapter, users might prefer to type the number of bikes and press the ENTER key instead of typing the number and tapping or clicking the Calculate Cost button.

You can assign a button to be an Accept button in the user interface, which means the program will carry out the event handler processing associated with the button if the user taps or clicks it or presses the ENTER key. To assign the Calculate Cost button as the Accept button, you can complete the following steps:

STEP 1　After the Button objects are added, tap or click a blank area in the Windows Form object to select it. Scroll in the Properties window until the AcceptButton property is visible. Tap or click the AcceptButton property name in the left column and then tap or click the AcceptButton property list arrow in the right column.

The AcceptButton property list displays the names of the Button objects on the selected Windows Form object (Figure 4-20). Any of these buttons can be specified as the Accept button.

© iStock.com/phototropic

FIGURE 4-20

STEP 2　Tap or click btnCalculate in the AcceptButton property list.

The btnCalculate Button object is designated as the Accept button. When the program is running, the user can press the ENTER key after entering data to execute the event handler processing for the Calculate Cost button. Notice the border of the Calculate Cost button displays a blue edge to identify that the AcceptButton property is set.

Cancel Button in Form Properties

In the same manner as the Accept button, you can designate a Cancel button for the Windows Form object. When the user presses the esc key, the event handler processing will be executed for the button identified as the Cancel button. In the sample program, the Cancel button will be used to clear the text box and the total cost of bikes rented and to place the insertion point in the text box. Thus, it performs the same activity that occurs when the user taps or clicks the Clear button. To specify the Cancel button for the sample program, you complete the following steps:

Step 1: Tap or click a blank area in the Windows Form object to select it.

Step 2: Tap or click the CancelButton property name in the left column of the Properties window for the Windows Form object, and then tap or click the CancelButton list arrow.

Step 3: Tap or click the button name (btnClear) in the CancelButton property list.

When the program is executed, the user can press the ESC key to perform the same processing as when the Clear button is tapped or clicked.

Visual Studio Preparation for Code Entry

When you are designing and creating the user interface, the Toolbox in Visual Studio 2015 provides the objects that you can place in the interface. When you write the code in the code window, however, the Toolbox is of little use. Therefore, many developers close the Toolbox when writing code to increase the space used for coding. To close the Toolbox, you can complete the following step:

STEP 1 With the Toolbox visible (Figure 4-21), tap or click the Toolbox Close button. The Toolbox closes and the work area expands in size. To display the Toolbox after it has been closed, tap or click the View menu and then tap or click Toolbox.

Figure 4-21 illustrates the screen before the Toolbox is closed. The Toolbox Close button is visible.

Toolbox Close button

© iStock.com/phototropic

FIGURE 4-21

CRITICAL THINKING

Why does a developer have to test every possible input and action that a user may perform while running an application? Users do not always follow the *expected path*. They enter data incorrectly. They decide they need to go back and change something they have already entered. They discover they need to learn more about what the application is asking of them and require more detailed assistance. By adding properties such as the AcceptButton and others, you will eliminate any actions that may crash the program.

ONLINE REINFORCEMENT

To view a video of the process in the preceding step, visit CengageBrain.com and navigate to the resources for this title. Tap or click the link for Chapter 4 and then navigate to Video 4-10.

In the following sections, the Toolbox has been closed in the windows that show code.

Introduction to Data Entry and Data Types

As you have seen, the user can enter data into the program by using the TextBox object. When the user enters data, it becomes the value stored in the Text property of the object. For example, if the user enters 15 as the number of bikes, the Text property for the txtNumberOfBikes TextBox object will contain the value 15.

String Data Type

When data is stored in RAM, it is stored as a particular data type. Each data type allows data to be used in a specific manner. For example, to add two values together, the values must be stored in one of the numeric data types. The **String** data type is used for values that the user enters in a TextBox object and that are stored in the Text property of the TextBox object. A String data type can store any character available on the computer.

When the user enters data into a TextBox object, it is good programming style to copy the entered value from the Text property of the TextBox object to a String variable. A **variable** is a named location in RAM where data is stored. A **String variable** is a named location in RAM that can store a string value. Thus, a person's name, a dollar amount, a telephone number, or the number of bikes rented can be stored in a String variable.

The programmer defines a variable during the coding of the program. The statement in Figure 4-22 defines a string.

FIGURE 4-22

To begin the statement, the keyword Dim is required. This keyword stands for *variable dimension*. It indicates to the Visual Basic compiler that the entries after Dim are defining a variable.

The next entry is the variable name. Every variable must have a name so it can be referenced in other statements within the program. By convention, every String variable name begins with the letters str followed by a descriptive name. The name in Figure 4-22 (strNumberOfBikes) indicates a String variable that will contain the number of bikes entered by the user.

The keyword As must follow the name of the variable, as shown in Figure 4-22. If it is not included, a compilation error will occur. Following the word As is the declaration for the variable's data type. In Figure 4-22, the data type is specified as String.

As a result of the statement in Figure 4-22, when the program is compiled, the Visual Basic compiler will allocate an area in RAM that is reserved to contain the value in the string.

The general format to define a variable is shown in Figure 4-23.

General Format: Define a Variable

Dim VariableName As DataType

EXAMPLE	RESULT
Dim strNumberOfBikes	String variable
Dim intNumberOfBikes	Integer variable
decTotalCost As Decimal	Decimal variable

FIGURE 4-23

The Integer and Decimal variables defined as examples in Figure 4-23 are numeric variables. You will learn about numeric variables shortly.

Assignment Statements

When a variable is defined as shown in Figure 4-22, the variable does not contain any data. One method used to place data in the variable is an **assignment statement**. The assignment statement shown in Figure 4-24 will copy the data from the Text property of the txtNumberOfBikes TextBox object into the strNumberOfBikes String variable.

FIGURE 4-24

The variable name to the left of the assignment statement (strNumberOfBikes) identifies the variable to which a value will be copied. The equal sign indicates to the Visual Basic compiler that the statement is an assignment statement. The equal sign is required.

The value to the right of the equal sign will be copied to the variable to the left of the equal sign. In Figure 4-24, the value in the Text property of the txtNumberOfBikes TextBox object will be copied to the strNumberOfBikes variable.

To enter the definition of the strNumberOfBikes variable and then enter the assignment statement in Figure 4-24 using IntelliSense, you can complete the following steps:

STEP 1 With Visual Studio open to the code window and the insertion point located in the desired column, type `Dim` followed by a space. Then, type the name of the String variable you want to define, `strNumberOfBikes`.

The Dim keyword and the String name you typed are displayed in the code window (Figure 4-25). Notice that Dim is blue to indicate it is a keyword. The green curly line indicates that the keyword has not been assigned a value in the program.

FIGURE 4-25

STEP 2 Press the SPACEBAR, type the word `As`, and then press the SPACEBAR again.

The letters you typed are entered. When you typed the space following the word As, IntelliSense displayed a list (Figure 4-26). The list contains all the allowable entries that can follow the As keyword. To define a String variable, the correct entry is String.

FIGURE 4-26

STEP 3 Because the correct entry is String, type `str`.

IntelliSense highlights String in the list (Figure 4-27).

FIGURE 4-27

STEP 4 Press the ENTER key.

The Dim statement is entered (Figure 4-28). The green squiggly underline indicates the variable is not referenced within the program. Visual Studio will remove the underline when the variable is used in an assignment statement or other statement.

FIGURE 4-28

STEP 5 To begin the assignment statement, type `strn`. IntelliSense displays the only variable name that starts with the letters strn, which is the String variable strNumberOfBikes.

IntelliSense displays a list of allowable entries for the statement (Figure 4-29). Whenever you want to reference a variable name in a statement, you can type the first few letters of the name to have IntelliSense display a list of allowable entries. The variable name strNumberOfBikes is highlighted because you typed strn.

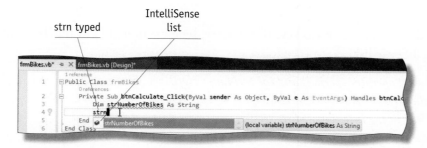

FIGURE 4-29

STEP 6   Press the SPACEBAR, press the EQUAL SIGN key, and then press the SPACEBAR.

IntelliSense enters the highlighted variable name, the spaces, and the equal sign you typed (Figure 4-30). The spaces are not required in Visual Basic but should be included in the statement for ease of reading. An IntelliSense list automatically appears and displays the possible valid entries.

FIGURE 4-30

STEP 7   Type txt to display the IntelliSense list of Form objects, and then type n to identify the txtNumberOfBikes TextBox object in the IntelliSense list.

The IntelliSense list contains the valid entries for the statement; in this case, only one object has the prefix of txt. The TextBox object txtNumberOfBikes is highlighted in the list (Figure 4-31).

FIGURE 4-31

STEP 8   Press the PERIOD key. If necessary, type te to highlight the Text entry in the IntelliSense list.

After the dot operator (period) and the txtNumberOfBikes object name are entered, Visual Studio displays the IntelliSense list (Figure 4-32). When you typed te, the Text entry was highlighted in the IntelliSense list.

dot operator   te typed

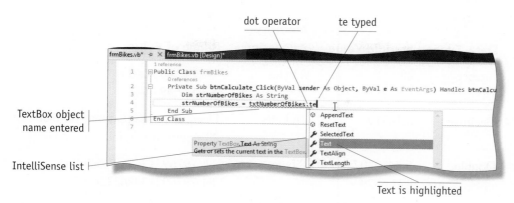

TextBox object
name entered

IntelliSense list

Text is highlighted

FIGURE 4-32

STEP 9 Press the ENTER key.

The assignment statement is entered (Figure 4-33). When the statement is executed, the value in the Text property of the txtNumberOfBikes TextBox object will be copied to the location in memory identified by the strNumberOfBikes variable name. Notice also that the green squiggly lines in the Dim statement are removed because the variable now is referenced in a statement.

For any variable you define within a program, you can use the method shown in the previous steps to declare a variable name and include it in assignment statements. IntelliSense works the same with each variable name, regardless of the variable type.

completed
assignment   IntelliSense
statement   entered Text

no green
squiggly line

FIGURE 4-33

Numeric Data Types

As you will recall, the String data type can contain any character that can be entered or stored on a computer. String data types, however, cannot be used in arithmetic operations. A **numeric data type** must be used in arithmetic operations. To multiply two values, for example, the values must be stored in one of the numeric data types.

Visual Basic allows a variety of numeric data types depending on the need of the application. Each numeric data type requires a different amount of RAM to store the numeric value, and each data type can contain a different form of numeric data and a different maximum range of values. The table in Figure 4-34 lists three widely used numeric data types. These data types are explained in the following sections.

Data Type	Sample Value	Memory Allocation	Range of Values
Integer	48	4 bytes	−2,147,483,648 to +2,147,483,647
Decimal	3.14519	16 bytes	Decimal values that may have up to 28 significant digits
Double	5.3452307 or 673.6529	8 bytes	−1.79769313486232e308 to +1.79769313486232e308

FIGURE 4-34

Integer Data Type

An **Integer data type** holds a nondecimal whole number in Visual Basic. As you can see from Figure 4-34, an Integer data type can store a value that is greater or less than 2 billion. Examples of integers include the number of bikes to be rented, the number of credit hours you are taking in a semester, and the number of points your favorite football team scored. Notice that each of these examples is a whole number.

Normally, an Integer data type is stored in an Integer variable. An **Integer variable** identifies a location in RAM where an integer value is stored. To define an Integer variable and place a value in the variable, you can use the Dim statement and the assignment statement, as shown in Figure 4-35.

```
6        Dim intNumberOfBikes As Integer
7        intNumberOfBikes = 34
```

FIGURE 4-35

The Dim statement in Figure 4-35 is similar to the Dim statement used to define the String variable (Figure 4-28 on page 203), except that the variable name begins with the prefix int and the word Integer follows the word As. Four bytes of RAM will be reserved for any value that is stored in the intNumberOfBikes Integer variable as a result of the Dim statement in Figure 4-35.

The definition in Figure 4-35 will not place a value in the intNumberOfBikes variable. To place a value in the variable, you can use an assignment statement. Enter the intNumberOfBikes variable that will hold the value on the left side of the equal sign, and enter the value to be placed in the variable (34) on the right side of the equal sign. When the statement is executed, the value 34 will be copied to the RAM location identified by the variable name intNumberOfBikes.

You also can place an initial value in the variable. For example, to define an Integer variable to hold the number of credit hours you are taking and to place the value 12 in that variable, you could write the Dim statement in Figure 4-36.

value placed in
intCreditHours
Integer variable

```
9        Dim intCreditHours As Integer = 12
```

FIGURE 4-36

The statement in Figure 4-36 defines the Integer variable named intCreditHours. The equal sign after the word *Integer* indicates to the Visual Basic compiler that the value to the right of the equal sign should be placed in the variable. The value 12 will be placed in the intCreditHours Integer variable when the program is compiled.

Decimal Data Type

A **Decimal data type** accurately represents large or very precise decimal numbers. It is ideal for use in the accounting and scientific fields to ensure that numbers keep their precision and are not subject to rounding errors. The Decimal data type can be accurate to 28 significant digits. (Significant digits are those that contribute to the precision of a number.) Often, Decimal data types are used to store dollar amounts. For example, to define the Decimal variable for the total cost of the bike rental in the sample program, you can use the statement in Figure 4-37.

```
22        Dim decTotalCost As Decimal
```

FIGURE 4-37

The Dim statement is used to define the Decimal variable. The dec prefix is used for all Decimal variable names. When the compiler processes the statement in Figure 4-37, 16 bytes of RAM will be reserved for a value to be placed in the decTotalCost variable. Initially, no value will be present in the variable unless you specify a value, as shown in Figure 4-36. You can use an assignment statement to place data into the decTotalCost variable.

Double Data Type

A **Double data type** can represent huge positive numbers and very small negative numbers that can include values to the right of the decimal point. Sometimes, a Double data type is said to represent floating-point numbers, which means the decimal point can be anywhere within the number. The Dim statement in Figure 4-38 declares a Double variable that could be used in a tax application.

```
13              Dim dblTaxRate As Double
14              dblTaxRate = 0.07875
```

FIGURE 4-38

In Figure 4-38, the dblTaxRate Double variable is declared and then the assignment statement places the value 0.07875 in the memory location identified by the variable name. Note that a Double variable begins with the dbl prefix.

Other Data Types

Visual Basic supports other data types that are used for more specialized situations. Two widely used data types are Char and Boolean (Figure 4-39).

Data Type	Sample Value	Memory Allocation	Range of Values
Char	A single character such as ? or M	2 bytes	Any single character
Boolean	True or False	2 bytes	True or False

FIGURE 4-39

Char Data Type

The **Char data type** represents a single keystroke such as a letter of the alphabet, a punctuation mark, or a symbol. The prefix for a Char variable name is chr. When you assign a value to a Char variable, you must place quotation marks around the value. For example, in Figure 4-40, the value A is assigned to the chrTopGrade Char variable.

```
16              Dim chrTopGrade As Char
17              chrTopGrade = "A"
```

FIGURE 4-40

The value A in the assignment statement has quotation marks around it. In addition, Visual Studio displays the letter and the quotation marks in red text, indicating they are not Visual Basic keywords, variable names, or object names. In fact, the value is called a literal. You will learn more about literals shortly.

Visual Studio allows 65,534 different characters in a program. These characters consist of numbers, letters, and punctuation symbols. In addition, a wide variety of technical characters, mathematical symbols, and worldwide textual characters are available, which allows developers to work in almost every known language, including Korean (Figure 4-41). These characters are represented by a coding system called Unicode. To learn more about Unicode, visit www.unicode.org.

유니코드에 대해 ?

어떤 플랫폼,
어떤 프로그램,
어떤 언어에도 상관없이
유니코드는 모든 문자에 대해 고유 번호를 제공합니다.

FIGURE 4-41

Even though you can assign a number to a Char variable, it cannot be used in arithmetic operations. A number to be used in an arithmetic operation must be assigned a numeric variable.

Boolean Data Type

A Boolean data variable can contain a value that Visual Basic interprets as either true or false. A Boolean variable name begins with the bln prefix. If a variable in your program should represent whether a condition is true or not true, then the variable should be Boolean. In Figure 4-42, a Boolean variable called blnFullTimeStudent is declared and then the assignment statement sets the Boolean variable to True.

```
19      Dim blnFullTimeStudent As Boolean
20      blnFullTimeStudent = True
```

FIGURE 4-42

In Figure 4-42, the Dim statement is used to declare the blnFullTimeStudent Boolean variable. The assignment statement sets the Boolean variable to True. This variable can be checked in the program to determine whether it is true or false, and appropriate processing can occur as a result.

Miscellaneous Data Types

Visual Basic has several other data types that are used less often than the ones you have seen so far. These data types are summarized in the table in Figure 4-43.

Data Type	Sample Value	Memory Allocation	Range of Values
Byte	A whole number such as 7	1 bytes	0 to 255
Date	April 22, 2014	8 bytes	Dates and times
Long	A whole number such as 342,534,538	8 bytes	−9,223,372,036,854,775,808 through +9,223,372,036,854,775,807
Object	Holds a reference	4 bytes	A memory address
Short	A whole number such as 16,546	2 bytes	−32,786 through 32,767
Single	A number such as 312,672.3274	4 bytes	$-3.4028235E+38$ through $1.401298E-45$ for negative values; and from $1.401298E-45$ through $3.4028235E+38$ for positive values

FIGURE 4-43

As a review, the prefixes for each of the data type variable names are shown in Figure 4-44.

Data Type	Prefix
String	str
Integer	int
Decimal	dec
Double	dbl
Char	chr
Boolean	bln
Byte	byt
Date	dtm
Long	lng
Short	shr
Single	sng

FIGURE 4-44

Literals

When an assignment statement includes a value like the one in Figure 4-38 on page 208 or Figure 4-40 on page 208, the value is called a **literal** because it literally is the value required by the assignment statement. It is not a variable. The Visual Basic compiler determines the data type of the value you use for a literal based on the value itself. For example, if you type *Chicago*, the compiler treats the literal as a String data type, and if you type 49.327, the compiler treats the literal as a Double data type. The table in Figure 4-45 displays the default literal types as determined by the Visual Basic compiler.

Standard Literal Form	Default Data Type	Example
Numeric, no fractional part	Integer	104
Numeric, no fractional part, too large for Integer data type	Long	3987925494
Numeric, fractional part	Double	0.99 8.625
Enclosed within double quotes	String	"Bre Pauley"
Enclosed within number signs	Date	#3/17/2017 3:30 PM#

FIGURE 4-45

Forced Literal Types

Sometimes you might want a literal to be a different data type than the Visual Basic default type. For example, you may want to assign the number 9.95 to a Decimal data variable to take advantage of the precision of the Decimal data type. As you can see in Figure 4-45, Visual Basic will consider the value 9.95 a Double data type by default. To define the literal as a Decimal literal, you must use a special character to force Visual Basic to use a data type other than the default. Specifically, you place the literal-type character at the end of the literal value. The table in Figure 4-46 shows the available literal-type characters and examples of their use.

Literal-Type Character	Data Type	Example
S	Short	Dim shoAge As Short shoAge = 40S
I	Integer	Dim intHeight as Integer intHeight = 76I
D	Decimal	Dim decPricePerSong As Decimal decPricePerSong = 0.99D
R	Double	Dim dblWeight As Double dblWeight = 8491R
C	Char	Dim chrNumberOfDays As Char chrNumberOfDays = "7"C

FIGURE 4-46

In the first example, the value 40 will be processed by Visual Basic as a Short data type literal, even though the value would be considered an Integer value by default. In the second example, the literal-type character confirms that the value should be treated as an Integer data type. In the third example, the value 9.95 will be processed as a Decimal data type, even though it would be considered a Double data type by default. In the next example, the value 8491 would be considered an Integer data value by default, but because the R literal-type character is used, Visual Basic will treat it as a Double data type. In the final example, the value 7 will be treated as a Char data type.

Constants

Recall that a variable identifies a location in memory where a value can be stored. By its nature, the value in a variable can be changed by statements within the program. For instance, in the sample program in this chapter, one user might request 4 bike rentals and another user might request 12 bike rentals for a large group; the value in the strNumberOfBikes variable can change based on the user's needs. In some instances, however, you might not want the value to be changed. For example, the price per bike rented in the sample program is $9.95 per day. This value will not change, regardless of how many bikes were rented.

When a value will remain the same throughout the execution of the program, you should assign a meaningful name to a value. A **constant** contains one permanent value throughout the execution of the program. It cannot be changed by any statement within the program. To define a constant value, you can use the code in Figure 4-47.

```
12      Const _cdecPricePerBike As Decimal = 9.95D
```

FIGURE 4-47

The following rules apply to a constant:

1. The declaration of a constant begins with the letters Const, not the letters Dim.
2. You must assign the value to be contained in the constant on the same line as its definition. In Figure 4-47, the value 9.95D is assigned to the constant on the same line as the Const definition.
3. You cannot attempt to change the value of the constant anywhere in the program. If you do, you will produce a compiler error.
4. The letter c often is placed before the constant name to identify it throughout the program as a variable that cannot be changed.
5. Other than the letter c, constant names are formed using the same rules and techniques as other variable names.

Using a named constant instead of a literal provides significant advantages:

6. The program becomes easier to read because the value is identified by the name. For example, instead of using the value 9.95D in a literal, you can use it in a constant called cdecPricePerBike. This variable name describes the use of the value 9.95D and makes the program easier to read.
7. If you discover that a value must be changed in the code, it is much easier and more reliable to change the value one time in the constant as opposed to changing every occurrence of the value in a literal.

Reference a Variable

You learned earlier that when a variable is declared, it is underlined with a green squiggly line until it is referenced in a statement. This feature of Visual Basic is intended to ensure that you do not declare a variable and then forget to use it. It also helps ensure that you do not waste memory by declaring an unnecessary variable.

When using a variable in a program, it is mandatory that you define the variable before using the variable name in a statement. For example, the statements in Figure 4-48 *will cause an error* because the variable is used in an assignment statement before it is declared.

```
25      strNumberOfBikes = txtNumberOfBikes.Text
26      Dim strNumberOfBikes As String
```

FIGURE 4-48

In the code in Figure 4-48, the variable strNumberOfBikes is referenced in an assignment statement (line 25) before it is defined (line 26). This creates a compile error, as indicated by the blue squiggly line beneath the variable name strNumberOfBikes on line 25. If you attempt to compile the statements on lines 25 and 26, you will receive a build error. Always define a variable before it is used in a statement.

Scope of Variables

When you declare a variable in Visual Basic, you not only declare the data type of the variable but also implicitly define its scope. The **scope of a variable** specifies where the variable can be referenced in a Visual Basic statement within the program. In larger programs with multiple classes and forms, scope becomes critical, but it is important that you understand the concept at this point.

You declare a variable in a region within a program. For instance, in the sample program in this chapter, you can declare a variable in the click event handler for the Calculate Cost button. You could declare another variable in the click event handler for the Clear button. Scope determines where each of these variables can be referenced and used in the Visual Basic program. *The rule is: A variable can be referenced only within the region of the program where it is defined.* A region in the programs you have seen thus far in the book is the code between the Sub statement and the End Sub statement in the event handlers. The code between the Sub statement and the End Sub statement is a **procedure**.

Therefore, if you declare a variable within the click event handler for the Calculate Cost button, that variable cannot be referenced in the click event handler for the Clear button, and vice versa. A variable that can be referenced only within the region of the program where it is defined is called a **local variable**. This variable is defined in one region of the program and cannot be changed by a statement in another region of the program.

In addition, when a variable is defined in a procedure and the procedure ends, the values of the local variables within the procedure are destroyed. Thus, local variables have a certain **lifetime** in the program. They are only *alive* from the time the procedure begins until it ends. If the procedure is executed again, the value the variable once contained no longer is present. One execution of the procedure is a variable's lifetime. Therefore, if a user taps or clicks the Calculate Cost button, the values in the variables are valid until the tap or click event is completed. When the user taps or clicks the Calculate Cost button again, all values from the first tap or click are gone.

You can also define variables that can be used in multiple regions of a Visual Basic program. These variables are called **global variables**. In most programs, local variables should be used because they cause fewer errors than global variables.

Understanding the scope of a variable is important when developing a program. You will learn more about the scope of variables later in this chapter and throughout this book.

Convert Variable Data

Variables used in arithmetic statements in a Visual Basic program must be numeric. String variables cannot be used in an arithmetic statement. If you attempt to use them, you will create a compilation error.

A user often enters data in a text box. Data in the Text property of a TextBox object is treated as String data. Because String data cannot be used in an arithmetic statement, the String data entered by a user must be converted to numeric data before it can be used in an arithmetic statement.

For instance, in the sample program in this chapter, the user enters the number of bikes to rent. Before this number can be used in an arithmetic statement to determine the total cost of bike rentals, the value must be converted to an Integer data type.

Visual Basic includes several procedures that allow you to convert one data type to another data type. You will recall that a procedure is a prewritten set of code that can be called by a statement in the Visual Basic program. When the procedure is called, it performs a particular task. In this case, the task is to convert the String value the user entered into an Integer data type that can be used in an arithmetic operation. One procedure that converts a String data type to an Integer data type is named ToInt32. The number 32 in the procedure name identifies that the representation of the integer will require 32 bits or 4 bytes, which is the amount of memory required for the Integer data type. The procedure is in the Convert class, which is available in a Visual Studio 2015 class library.

Use a Procedure

When you need to use a procedure to accomplish a task in your program, you must understand what the procedure does and how to code the procedure call in a program statement. A procedure can operate in one of two ways: It can perform its task and return a value, or it can perform its task without returning a value. You will recall in the Chapter 3 sample program that the Close() procedure closed the window and terminated the program. The procedure performed its task but did not return a value. A procedure of this type is called a **Sub procedure**.

In the City Bike Rentals program in this chapter, the requirement is to convert the String value for the number of bikes the user enters into an Integer data type. Then, it can be used in an arithmetic operation. Therefore, the procedure must return a value (the Integer value for the number of bikes). A procedure that returns a value is called a **Function procedure**, or a **function**.

In addition, a procedure might require data to be passed to it when called in order to carry out its processing. In the sample program in this chapter, the Function procedure to convert a String variable to an Integer variable first must be able to access the String variable. Therefore, in the statement that calls the Function procedure, the variable name for the String variable to be converted must be passed to the procedure. A value is passed to a procedure through the use of an argument.

An **argument** identifies a value required by a procedure. To pass the argument to the procedure, include its name within parentheses following the name of the procedure in the calling statement. For example, to pass the value stored in the strNumberOfBikes variable to the ToInt32 procedure, you could use the statement in Figure 4-49.

```
...ToInt32(strNumberOfBikes)
```

argument

name of
procedure

FIGURE 4-49

The name of the procedure is ToInt32. The argument is strNumberOfBikes, which is the String variable that contains the value to be converted to an Integer data type by the ToInt32 procedure. Notice that the argument is enclosed within parentheses.

Every procedure is part of a class in Visual Basic. You will recall from Chapter 1 that a **class** is a named grouping of program code. When the calling statement must call a procedure, it first must identify the class that contains the procedure.

Thus, in Figure 4-49 the calling statement is incomplete because the class name is not included. The class that contains the ToInt32 procedure is the Convert class. To complete the procedure call statement, the class must be added, as shown in Figure 4-50.

procedure name   argument

```
Convert.ToInt32(strNumberOfBikes)
```

class name

FIGURE 4-50

In Figure 4-50, the class name Convert begins the procedure call. A dot operator separates the class name from the procedure name (ToInt32). The argument (strNumberOfBikes) within the parentheses completes the procedure call.

When a Function procedure returns a value, such as the ToInt32 procedure that returns an integer value, the returned value essentially replaces the Function procedure call in the assignment statement. So, in Figure 4-51, you can see that when the processing is completed within the Function procedure, the integer value is substituted for the procedure call in the assignment statement.

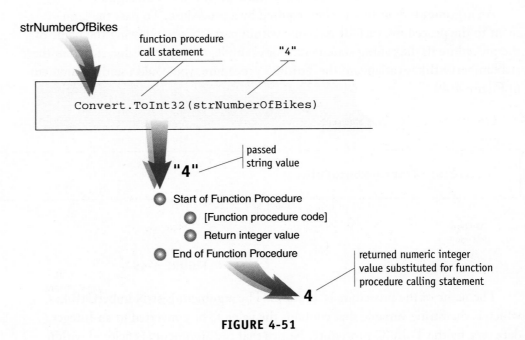

strNumberOfBikes

function procedure
call statement   "4"

```
Convert.ToInt32(strNumberOfBikes)
```

"4"   passed
       string value

● Start of Function Procedure
  ● [Function procedure code]
  ● Return integer value
● End of Function Procedure   returned numeric integer
                                     value substituted for function
                              4   procedure calling statement

FIGURE 4-51

Figure 4-52 shows the complete assignment statement to convert the String data type in the strNumberOfBikes variable to an Integer data type and place it in the intNumberOfBikes variable.

FIGURE 4-52

The intNumberOfBikes variable name to the left of the equal sign identifies the Integer variable where the converted value will be copied. The equal sign in the assignment statement is required. As a result of the assignment statement in Figure 4-52, the ToInt32 Function procedure in the Convert class will convert the value in the strNumberOfBikes String variable to an integer value. The assignment statement will place that integer value in the intNumberOfBikes variable.

The use of Function procedures and arguments with procedure calls is common when programming in Visual Basic. You will encounter many examples of Function procedure calls throughout this book.

Option Strict On

In the previous section, you saw an example of how to explicitly change a value from one data type to another. By default, Visual Basic will automatically convert data types if the one on the right side of the equal sign in an assignment statement is different from the one on the left side of the equal sign. Quite often, however, the automatic conversion can introduce errors and produce an incorrect converted value. Therefore, allowing automatic conversion typically is not a good programming style.

To prevent automatic conversion of values, the developer must insert the Option Strict On statement in the program prior to any event handler code. In Figure 4-53, the Option Strict On statement is shown just after the introductory comments in the sample program for this chapter.

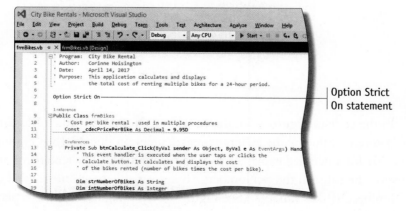

FIGURE 4-53

The Option Strict On statement explicitly prevents any default data type conversions that would cause data loss and prevents any conversion between numeric types and strings. Therefore, you must write explicit conversion statements to convert from one data type to another. This approach minimizes potential errors that can occur from data conversion.

Arithmetic Operations

The ability to perform arithmetic operations on numeric data is fundamental to computer programs. Many programs require arithmetic operations to add, subtract, multiply, and divide numeric data. For example, in the City Bike Rentals program in this chapter, the price per bike rented must be multiplied by the cost of each bike rental for a 24-hour period to calculate the total cost. The formula is shown in Figure 4-54.

Total Cost of Bikes = Number of Bikes times Price per Bike

FIGURE 4-54

An assignment statement is used in Visual Basic 2015 to perform the arithmetic operation shown in Figure 4-54. The statements used in the sample program and a depiction of the operation are shown in Figure 4-55.

```
20        Dim strNumberOfBikes As String
21        Dim intNumberOfBikes As Integer
22        Dim decTotalCost As Decimal
23        Const _cdecPricePerBike As Decimal = 9.95D
24
25        strNumberOfBikes = txtNumberOfBikes.Text
26        intNumberOfBikes = Convert.ToInt32(strNumberOfBikes)
27        decTotalCost = intNumberOfBikes * _cdecPricePerBike
28        lblTotalCost.Text = decTotalCost.ToString("C")
```

decTotalCost = intNumberOfBikes * _cdecPricePerBike

FIGURE 4-55

© iStock.com/Tpopova

In the code in Figure 4-55, the variable strNumberOfBikes is assigned the user's entered value by the assignment statement on line 25. (See Figure 4-24 on page 201 for a detailed explanation of this statement.) The statement on line 26 converts the value in the strNumberOfBikes variable to an integer and copies it to the intNumberOfBikes variable. (See Figure 4-52 on page 216 for an explanation of this statement.)

The statement on line 27 multiplies the integer value in the intNumberOfBikes variable by the constant value in the _cdecPricePerBike variable, and then copies the result to the decTotalCost variable. For example, if the user enters 4 as the number of bikes rented, the value 4 is multiplied by 9.95 (the value in the _cdecPricePerBike variable), and the result (39.80) is copied to the decTotalCost variable.

Arithmetic Operators

The asterisk (*) is an important element on the right side of the equal sign in the assignment statement on line 26. This asterisk is the multiplication **arithmetic operator**. Whenever the compiler encounters this operator, the value to the left of the operator is multiplied by the value to the right of the operator, and these values are replaced in the assignment statement by the product of the two numbers. Thus, in Figure 4-55 on page 218, the arithmetic expression intNumberOfBikes * _cdecPricePerBike is replaced by the value 39.80. Then, the assignment statement places the value 39.80 in the decTotalCost variable.

The multiplication arithmetic operator is only one of the arithmetic operators available in Visual Basic 2015. The table in Figure 4-56 lists the arithmetic operators in Visual Basic 2015, describes their use, and provides an example of their use.

Arithmetic Operator	Use	Assignment Statement Showing Use
+	Addition	decTotal = decPrice + decTax
−	Subtraction	decCost = decRegularPrice − decDiscount
*	Multiplication	decTax = decItemPrice * decTaxRate
/	Division	decClassAverage = decTotalScores / intNumberOfStudents
^	Exponentiation	intSquareArea = intSquareSide ^ 2
\	Integer Division	intResult = 13 \ 5
Mod	Modulus Arithmetic (remainder)	intRemainder = 13 Mod 5

FIGURE 4-56

The arithmetic operators shown in Figure 4-56 are explained in the following paragraphs:

Addition

The **addition arithmetic operator** (+) adds the numeric values immediately to the left and right of the operator and replaces the arithmetic expression in the assignment statement. For example, in Figure 4-57, the value in the decPrice variable is added to the value in the decTax variable.

arithmetic expression

```
40          decTotal = decPrice + decTax
```

decTotal   decPrice   decTax

FIGURE 4-57

© iStock.com/Tpopova

In Figure 4-57, the arithmetic expression (decPrice + decTax) is evaluated, and then the assignment statement copies the sum to the decTotal variable in RAM.

An arithmetic expression that uses the addition operator can contain more than two numeric values to be added. For example, in Figure 4-58, three variables are used in the arithmetic expression.

```
47          decTotalPay = decRegularPay + decOvertimePay + decBonusPay
```

FIGURE 4-58

In Figure 4-58, the value in decRegularPay is added to the value in decOvertimePay. The result then is added to decBonusPay, and that sum is copied to the decTotalPay variable. Visual Basic imposes no limit on the number of variables in an arithmetic expression.

In addition to variables, arithmetic expressions can contain literals. The assignment statement in Figure 4-59 uses a literal.

```
53          decTicketCost = decInternetTicketCost + 10.25
```

FIGURE 4-59

In Figure 4-59, the value 10.25 is added to the value in the decInternetTicketCost variable, and that sum is placed in the decTicketCost variable. Generally, literals should not be used in arithmetic expressions unless you know that the value will not change. For example, if the extra cost for the ticket could change in the future, good program design would dictate that the value be placed in a variable (perhaps even a constant).

Subtraction

To subtract one value from another in an assignment statement, Visual Basic 2015 uses the **subtraction arithmetic operator** (–), as shown in Figure 4-60.

```
59          decNetProfit = decRevenue - decCosts
```

FIGURE 4-60

In Figure 4-60, the value in the decCosts variable is subtracted from the value in the decRevenue variable. The result then is copied into the decNetProfit variable. If the value in decCosts is greater than the value in decRevenue, the value placed in the decNetProfit variable will be negative.

Use Arithmetic Results

After an arithmetic operation has been performed using an assignment statement, the values used in the operation and the resulting answer can be used in subsequent arithmetic operations or for other purposes within the program. For example, the result of one operation can be used in a subsequent calculation (Figure 4-61).

```
67          decComputerCost = decMonitorCost + decSystemUnitCost
68          decNetComputerCost = decComputerCost - decSystemDiscount
```

FIGURE 4-61

In Figure 4-61, the statement on line 67 determines the computer cost by adding the costs of the monitor and the system unit. The statement on line 68 calculates the net computer cost by subtracting the system discount from the computer cost calculated on line 67. Whenever a value is stored in a variable, it can be used in other statements within the program.

Multiplication

Multiplication is accomplished through the use of an assignment statement and the multiplication operator (*), as shown in Figure 4-62.

```
74          intLandPlotArea = intLandPlotLength * intLandPlotWidth
```

FIGURE 4-62

In Figure 4-62, the value in the intLandPlotLength variable is multiplied by the value in the intLandPlotWidth variable. The product of the multiplication is placed in the intLandPlotArea variable.

If two positive numbers are multiplied, the answer is positive. If two negative numbers are multiplied, the answer is positive. If one positive number and one negative number are multiplied, the answer is negative.

When two numbers are multiplied, you must be aware of the size of the result. The largest number of digits that can appear as a result of multiplication is the sum of the number of digits in the values being multiplied. If the product is greater than the value that can be stored in the variable to the left of the assignment statement, an overflow error can occur and the program will be terminated.

CONSIDER THIS

How should I test my program to make sure it works properly?
When you allow user input, be sure to test every possible entry by the user. If a decimal value is input instead of an expected integer value, your program may stop functioning. As you learn more about coding in the next chapters, error validation will become an important part of developing your program.

Division

Visual Basic 2015 provides three arithmetic operators for division and related calculations: the slash (/), the backslash (\), and the MOD operator.

You use the slash for normal division. For example, in Figure 4-63, the value in the decTestScores variable is divided by 3 to obtain the average test score.

```
79          decAverageTestScore = decTestScores / 3
```

FIGURE 4-63

WATCH OUT FOR

The divisor is the number to the right of the division operator. Make sure the divisor is not zero. If you attempt to divide by zero, your program will be terminated with an error.

You use the backslash (\) for integer division. With integer division, the quotient returned from the division operation is an integer. If the division operation produces a quotient with a remainder, the remainder is dropped, or truncated. The examples in Figure 4-64 illustrate the use of the integer division arithmetic operator.

Division Operation	Result
12\5	2
25\4	6
30\7	4

FIGURE 4-64

Notice in each example in Figure 4-64 that the result is a whole number with the remainder truncated.

The MOD operator divides the number to the left of the operator by the number to the right of the operator and returns an integer value that is the remainder of the division operation. Integer division and the MOD operator often are used together, as shown in Figure 4-65.

```
86              intHours = intTotalNumberOfMinutes \ 60
87              intMinutes = intTotalNumberOfMinutes Mod 60
```

FIGURE 4-65

In Figure 4-65, the operation on line 86 will return only the integer value of the division. For example, if the intTotalNumberOfMinutes variable contains 150, a result of 2 (2 = 150\60) will be placed in the intHours variable. The operation on line 87 will place the remainder in the intMinutes variable. The remainder in the example is 30; 150 divided by 60 is 2, with a remainder of 30.

Exponentiation

Exponentiation means raising a number to a power. It is accomplished in Visual Basic 15 using the exponentiation arithmetic operator (^), as shown in Figure 4-66.

exponentiation
arithmetic operator

```
92              intCubeArea = intLengthOfCubeSide ^ 3
```

FIGURE 4-66

In Figure 4-66, the arithmetic expression is the same as intLengthOfCubeSide * intLengthOfCubeSide* intLengthOfCubeSide. Therefore, the value is cubed and copied to the intCubeArea variable.

The exponent used in the operation can be a fraction. If so, the root is taken (Figure 4-67).

```
94              intLengthOfCubeSide = intCubeArea ^ (1 / 3)
```

FIGURE 4-67

In Figure 4-67, the cube root of the value in the intCubeArea variable is calculated and the result is copied to the intLengthOfCubeSide variable. Thus, if the area of the cube is 64, the value calculated for the length of the cube side would be 4 (4 * 4 * 4 = 64). The fractional exponent can never be negative, and it must be placed within parentheses.

Multiple Operations

A single assignment statement can contain multiple arithmetic operations. In Figure 4-68, the addition and subtraction operators are used to calculate the new balance in a savings account by adding the deposits to the old balance and subtracting withdrawals.

```
101         decNewBalance = decOldBalance + decDeposits - decWithdrawals
```

FIGURE 4-68

When the assignment statement is executed in Figure 4-68, the value in the decOldBalance variable is added to the value in the decDeposits variable. Then, the value in the decWithdrawals variable is subtracted from that sum and the result is copied to the decNewBalance variable.

Notice in Figure 4-68 that the calculations proceed from left to right in the arithmetic expression.

Hierarchy of Operations

When multiple operations are included in a single assignment statement, the sequence for performing the calculations is determined by the following rules:

1. Exponentiation (^) is performed first.
2. Multiplication (*) and division (/) are performed next.
3. Integer division (\) is next.
4. MOD then occurs.
5. Addition (+) and subtraction (−) are performed last.
6. Within each of the preceding five steps, calculations are performed from left to right.

As a result of this predetermined sequence, an arithmetic expression such as decBonus + decHours * decHourlyRate would result in the product of decHours * decHourlyRate being added to decBonus.

An arithmetic expression such as decGrade1 + decGrade2 / 2 would cause the value in the decGrade2 variable to be divided by 2 and then the quotient to be added to the value in decGrade1 because division is performed before addition. However, this calculation probably was not intended. Instead, the intent probably was to add the values in decGrade1 and decGrade2 and then divide the sum by 2. To force certain operations to be performed before others, you can use parentheses. Any arithmetic expression within parentheses is evaluated before expressions outside the parentheses, as shown in Figure 4-69.

```
108          decAverageGrade = (decGrade1 + decGrade2) / 2
```

FIGURE 4-69

In Figure 4-69, the addition operation is inside the parentheses, so it will be completed before the division operation. Therefore, the result of the arithmetic expression is that the value in decGrade1 is added to the value in decGrade2. That sum then is divided by 2 and the quotient is copied to the decAverageGrade variable.

If you want to make the sequence of operations explicitly clear, you can use parentheses around multiple arithmetic operations in an arithmetic expression even if the predetermined sequence of operations will produce the correct answer.

Display Numeric Output Data

As you have learned, the result of an arithmetic expression is a numeric value that typically is stored in a numeric variable. To display the numeric data as information in a graphical user interface, usually the data must be placed in the Text property of a Label object or a TextBox object. The Text property of these objects, however, requires that the data be a String data type. Therefore, to display a numeric value in a label or a text box, the numeric data must be converted to a String data type.

Each of the numeric data types provides a function called ToString that converts data from a numeric data type to the String data type. The general format of the function call for a Decimal numeric variable is shown in Figure 4-70.

General Format: ToString Function

```
decimalvariable.ToString()
```

FIGURE 4-70

The statement shown in Figure 4-70 consists of the name of the Decimal variable that contains data to be converted, the dot operator (.), and the name of the function (ToString). Notice that the function name is followed immediately by closed parentheses, which indicates to the Visual Basic compiler that ToString is a procedure name. When the function call is executed, the value returned by the ToString function replaces the call.

The function call normally is contained within an assignment statement to assign the returned string value to the Text property of a Label or TextBox object. The example in Figure 4-71 shows the assignment statement to convert the numeric value in the decTemperature variable to a String value that then is placed in the Text property of the lblTemperature Label object.

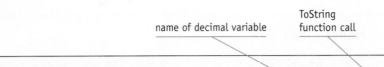

```
118         lblTemperature.Text = decTemperature.ToString()
```

FIGURE 4-71

In Figure 4-71, the name of the Decimal variable (decTemperature) is followed by the dot operator and then the name of the function (ToString) with the required parentheses. When the statement on line 118 is executed, the ToString function is called. It converts the numeric value in the decTemperature variable to a String data type and returns the String data. The assignment statement then copies the returned String data to the Text property of the Temperature Label object.

Format Specifications for the ToString Function

In the example in Figure 4-71, the conversion from numeric value to String value is a straight conversion, which means the value is returned but not formatted in any manner. For example, if the numeric value in the Decimal variable was 47.235, then the same value was returned as a String value.

The ToString function, however, can convert numeric data to String data using a specified format. For example, the value 2317.49 could be returned as $2,317.49. The returned value is in the form of dollars and cents, or currency. To identify the format for the numeric data to be returned by the ToString function, the **format specifier** must be included as an argument in the parentheses following the ToString function name. The table in Figure 4-72 on page 227 identifies the commonly used format specifiers; in the examples, the value in the numeric field is 8976.43561.

HEADS UP

Rounding is an important consideration when determining the formatting of a number. When using the ToString function, all values are rounded based on the digit after the last digit to be displayed. For example, if the value 729.837 is being converted to a Currency string from a numeric format, the returned result will be rounded up ($729.84). If the value to be converted is 575.371, the returned result will be rounded down ($575.37). Rounding also is used with the precision specifier.

Format Specifier	Format	Description	Output from the Function
General(G)	ToString("G")	Displays the numbers as is	8976.43561
Currency(C)	ToString("C")	Displays the number with a dollar sign, a thousands separator (comma), 2 digits to the right of the decimal and negative numbers in parentheses	$8,976.44
Fixed(F)	ToString("F")	Displays the number with 2 digits to the right of the decimal and a minus sign for negative numbers	8976.44
Number(N)	ToString("N")	Displays a number with a thousands separator, 2 digits to the right of the decimal and a minus sign for negative numbers	8,976.44
Percent(P)	ToString("P")	Displays the number multiplied by 100 with a % sign, a thousands separator, 2 digits to the right of the decimal and a minus sign for negative numbers	897,643.56%
Scientific(E)	ToString("E")	Displays the number in E-notation and a minus sign for negative numbers	8.976436E+03

FIGURE 4-72

In Figure 4-72, each format specifier is used as an argument within parentheses. The argument must be included in the quotation marks on each side of the format specifier, as shown. The letter for the format specifier can be uppercase or lowercase.

Precision Specifier

Each format specifier has a default number of digits that will be returned to the right of the decimal point. You can use a precision specifier, however, to override this default number. The **precision specifier** is a number included within the quotation marks in the function call that identifies the number of positions that should be returned to the right of the decimal point. The examples in Figure 4-73 illustrate the use of the precision specifier; assume that the value in the decNumericValue variable is 8976.43561.

Statement	Copied to Text Property of lblOutput Label Object
lblOutput = decNumericValue.ToString("C2")	$8,976.44
lblOutput = decNumericValue.ToString("C3")	$8,976.436
lblOutput = decNumericValue.ToString("F1")	8976.4
lblOutput = decNumericValue.ToString("N4")	8,976.4356
lblOutput = decNumericValue.ToString("P0")	897,644%

FIGURE 4-73

As you can see, the precision specifier identifies the number of digits that should be displayed to the right of the decimal point in the string returned from the ToString function. Notice that if the precision specifier is 0, no digits are returned to the right of the decimal point.

As with all conversions, when the number of positions to the right of the decimal point in the returned string is less than the number of digits to the right of the decimal point in the numeric value being converted, the returned value is rounded to the specified number of decimal places.

Clear the Form — Clear Procedure and Focus Procedure

Earlier in this chapter, you learned that when the user taps or clicks the Clear button in the City Bike Rentals program (see Figure 4-1 on page 184), the event handler for the Clear button must clear the results from the window and allow the user to enter the next number of bikes rented. To clear the results, the Clear button event handler must complete the following tasks:

1. Clear the Text property of the TextBox object
2. Clear the Text property of the Label object that displays the total cost of the bikes rented
3. Set the focus on the TextBox object, which means placing the insertion point in the text box

You will learn to accomplish these tasks in the following sections.

Clear Procedure

The Clear procedure clears any data in the Text property of a TextBox object. The general format of the Clear procedure is shown in Figure 4-74.

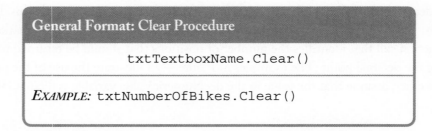

General Format: Clear Procedure

```
txtTextboxName.Clear()
```

EXAMPLE: `txtNumberOfBikes.Clear()`

FIGURE 4-74

When the Clear procedure is executed, the Text property is cleared of data. As with every procedure call, the name of the procedure must be followed by parentheses.

Clear the Text Property of a Label

The Clear procedure cannot be used with a Label object. Instead, to clear the Text property of a Label object, you must write an assignment statement that assigns a null length string to the Text property. A null length string has no length, which means it is a string with no characters. A null length string is represented by two quotation marks with no character between them (""). To assign a null length string to the Text property, you can use the statement shown in Figure 4-75.

```
39                lblTotalCost.Text = ""
```

FIGURE 4-75

In Figure 4-75, the null length string represented by the two empty quotation marks is assigned to the Text property of the lblTotalCost Label object. As a result of the assignment statement, the Text property is cleared.

Set the Focus

When the focus is on a TextBox object, the insertion point is located in the text box (Figure 4-76).

insertion point in text box

FIGURE 4-76

© iStock.com/phototropic

When the user taps or clicks a button or other item in the graphical user interface, the focus shifts to that item. Therefore, to place the focus on a text box, the user can tap or click it. However, the programmer can use the Focus procedure to place the focus on a text box automatically without requiring the user to tap or click it first, thus making it easier for the user to enter data in the text box (Figure 4-77).

object name   Focus procedure name

```
52                txtNumberOfBikes.Focus()
```

FIGURE 4-77

As with most procedure calls, the name of the object begins the statement, followed immediately by the dot operator (period). The name of the procedure (Focus) follows the dot operator. When the statement on line 52 is executed, the focus is placed on the txt-NumberOfBikes TextBox object, which means the insertion point is placed in the text box.

Form Load Event

In the sample programs in Chapter 3 and this chapter, you have seen that an event can occur when the user taps or clicks a button. The user's action triggers the code to execute in the event handler for the button tap or click. For example, in the City Bike Rentals program in this chapter, the user taps or clicks the Calculate Cost button and the event handler code responds by multiplying the number of bikes rented by the price per 24-hour period and displaying the result (see Figure 4-1 on page 184).

Tapping or clicking a button is not the only action that can trigger an event. For example, a form load event occurs each time a program is started and the Windows Form object is loaded into computer memory. For the program in this chapter, a form load event occurs when the program starts and the City Bike Rentals form is loaded. In some programs, an event handler is not written for this particular event and no processing occurs. In the City Bike Rentals program, however, a form loading event handler is required. This event handler completes the following tasks:

1. Displays the cost per day per bike heading
2. Clears the placeholder from the lblTotalCost Text property
3. Sets the focus on the txtNumberOfBikes text box

Concatenation

In the City Bike Rentals program, the lblCostHeading Label object displays the cost per day (see Figure 4-1 on page 184). In the user interface design, the lblCostHeading Label contains placeholder information for the label, but does not contain the actual cost per 24-hour rental period (Figure 4-78).

FIGURE 4-78
© iStock.com/phototropic

In Figure 4-78, the programmer had two reasons for not placing the actual rental cost in the label during the design phase. First, in the original implementation of the program, the cost per 24-hour rental period is $9.95 per bike. In the future, however, the cost might change. Generally, data that might change should be placed in the Text property of a Label object during execution time, not at design time. Therefore, the cost per bike should be placed in the label by the form load event handler when the form opens. Second, the cost per bike is used in two places in the program — in the label and when the actual calculation is performed to determine the total cost (see Figure 4-55 on page 218). Instead of using the numeric value of 9.95 several times within the program, the value should be assigned to a variable. If the value must be changed in the future, only one change to the variable is necessary. For example, if the price per daily bike rental changes to $12.95, the price can be changed in the price per bike rented variable and then it will be correct for all uses of the variable. To illustrate, the variable for the price per bike rented is shown in Figure 4-79.

```
12      Const _cdecPricePerBike As Decimal = 0.99D
```

FIGURE 4-79

As you can see, the price per bike rented is declared as a constant that cannot be changed during program execution. If the price changes in the future, the developer can make one change to this declaration and all elements of the program that use the value will be correct.

To create the heading for the City Bike Rentals program, the value in the variable declared in Figure 4-79 must be combined with the words *Per Day* and the result must be placed in the Text property of the lblCostHeading Label object. The process of joining two different values into a single string is called **concatenation**. When you use concatenation, the values being concatenated must be String data types. Note in Figure 4-79 that the _cdecPricePerBike variable is a Decimal data type. Therefore, it must be changed to a String data type before being joined with the words in the heading.

The statement in Figure 4-80 converts the Decimal data type to a String data type, concatenates (or joins) the two strings together, and then places the result in the Text property of the lblCostHeading Label object.

FIGURE 4-80

Can I connect string text together with a plus sign as well?

Yes, for example the following two statements are allowed in Visual Basic:

```
Dim x As String =
"Con" & "caten" &
"ation"

Dim y As String =
"Con" + "caten" +
"ation"
```

In Figure 4-80, the string generated to the right of the equal sign will be placed in the Text property of the lblCostHeading Label object. The first entry to the right of the equal sign is the price variable name (see Figure 4-79). Following the dot operator is the ToString procedure name, followed by the currency argument within parentheses. Remember that the ToString procedure converts a numeric value to a String data type. When the currency argument ("C") is used, the String value returned is in a currency format. (See Figure 4-72 on page 227 for a detailed explanation.)

Following the conversion statement is the **concatenation operator (&)**. When the Visual Basic compiler encounters this operator, the string to the left of the operator is joined with the String data to the right of the operator to create a single concatenated string. The resulting string then is placed in the Text property of the lblCostHeading Label object.

The process that occurs to the right of the equal sign is illustrated in Figure 4-81.

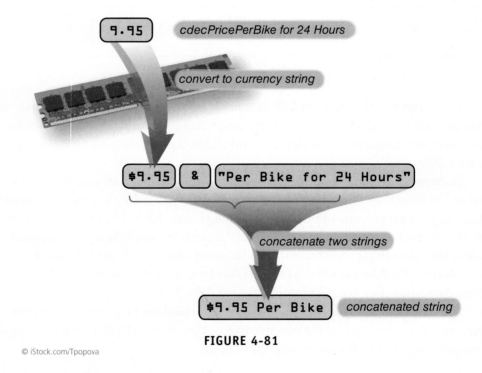

FIGURE 4-81

© iStock.com/Tpopova

In Figure 4-81 you can see that to obtain the concatenated string, the Decimal value in the cdecPricePerBike Decimal variable is converted to a currency String data type. Then, that value is combined with the string literal to create the concatenated string. In the assignment statement in Figure 4-80 on page 231, the concatenated string is assigned to the Text property of the lblCostHeading Label object.

Class Scope

Remember that when you declare a variable, you also define its scope. The scope of a variable identifies where within the program the variable can be referenced.

For example, if a variable is declared within an event handler procedure, the variable can be referenced only within that procedure.

Sometimes, a variable must be referenced in multiple event handlers. In the City Bike Rentals program, the value in the _cdecPricePerBike variable is referenced in the Calculate Cost button event handler when the total cost is calculated (see Figure 4-55 on page 218). The value also is referenced in the form load event when the heading is displayed (see Figure 4-80 on page 231). Because the variable is referenced in two different event-handling procedures, it must be defined at the class level instead of the procedure (event handler) level. This means that the variable must be declared in the code before the first procedure in the program. As you can see in Figure 4-82, the declaration of the _cdecPricePerBike variable follows the class definition statement but appears before the first event handler procedure.

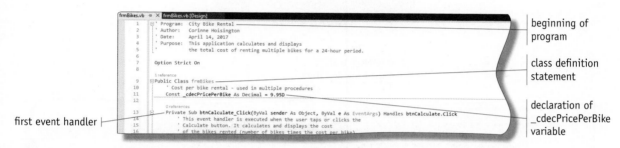

FIGURE 4-82

As a result of the code in Figure 4-82, the scope of the _cdecPricePerBike variable will be all procedures within the class; that is, code in any event handler procedure within the class can reference the variable. Because the variable is declared a constant, the value in the variable cannot be changed by code within the class; however, the value in the class can be referenced to calculate the total cost and to create the cost heading.

Debug Your Program

When your program processes numeric data entered by a user, you should be aware of several errors that can occur when the user enters data the program does not expect. The three errors that occur most often are Format Exceptions, Overflow Exceptions, and Divide By Zero Exceptions.

A **Format Exception** occurs when the user enters data that a statement within the program cannot process properly. In the City Bike Rentals program, the user must enter a numeric value for the number of bikes that he or she would like to rent. When the user taps or clicks the Calculate Cost button, the program converts the entered value to an integer and then uses the numeric value in the calculation (see Figure 4-52 on page 217). If the user enters a nonnumeric value, such as ab (Figure 4-83a), the conversion process cannot take place because the argument passed to the Convert class is not a numeric value. In this situation, a Format Exception error is recognized and the error box in Figure 4-83b is displayed.

FIGURE 4-83a

© iStock.com/phototropic

statement that
caused the exception

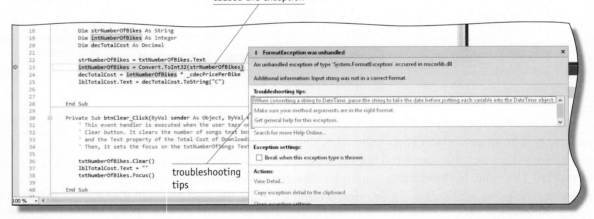

troubleshooting
tips

FIGURE 4-83b

In Figure 4-83a, the user entered the value ab and then tapped or clicked the Calculate Cost button. When control was passed to the ToInt32 procedure to convert the String value in the text box to an integer, the Format Exception was triggered because the value in the strNumberOfBikes variable was not numeric. When an exception occurs, the execution of the program is terminated. With Visual Studio running, tap or click the Stop Debugging button on the Standard toolbar.

An **Overflow Exception** occurs when the user enters a value greater than the maximum value the statement can process. For example, in the City Bike Rentals program, if the user enters a value in the text box that is too large for the ToInt32 procedure to convert, an Overflow Exception occurs.

An Overflow Exception also can occur when a calculation creates a value larger than a procedure can process. For example, if two large but valid numbers are multiplied, the product of the multiplication might be too large to process.

The third type of common error is the **Divide By Zero Exception**. It is not possible to divide by zero, so if your program contains a division operation and the divisor is zero, the Divide By Zero Exception will occur.

Whenever an exception occurs, a window similar to that in Figure 4-83b will be displayed.

To avoid exceptions, which should always be your goal, you can use certain techniques for editing the data and ensuring that the user has entered valid data. In Chapter 5 and Chapter 6, you will learn how to write code that checks user input to ensure that exceptions do not occur.

Program Design

As you have learned, the requirements document identifies the purpose of the program being developed, the application title, the procedures to be followed when using the program, any required equations and calculations, any conditions within the program that must be tested, notes and restrictions that must be followed by the program, and any other comments that would be helpful to understanding the problem. The requirements document for the City Bike Rentals application is shown in Figure 4-84 on page 235.

REQUIREMENTS DOCUMENT

Date: April 14, 2017

Date Submitted:

Application Title: City Bike Rentals

Purpose: The City Bike Rentals program allows the user to enter the number of bikes to be rented. The program calculates the total cost of the bike rentals based on a price of $9.95 per 24-hour rental period.

Program Procedures: In a Windows Desktop application, the user enters the number of bikes she wants to rent for one day. The program calculates the total cost of bikes rented. The user can clear the values on the screen and enter a new value for the number of bikes.

Algorithms, Processing, and Conditions:
1. The user must be able to enter the number of bikes to be rented.
2. The user can initiate the calculation and display the total cost of the bikes rented.
3. The application computes the total cost by multiplying the number of bikes by the cost per bike per day ($9.95).
4. The total cost of bikes rented is displayed as a currency value.
5. The user should be able to clear the value entered for the number of bikes and the total cost of bike rental.
6. The user should be provided with a button to exit the program.

Notes and Restrictions: n/a

Comments: A graphic should depict a bike rental image. A graphic named Bikes is available on CengageBrain.com.

FIGURE 4-84

The Use Case Definition for the City Bike Rentals program is shown in Figure 4-85.

USE CASE DEFINITION

1. The Windows Desktop application opens with a text box in which the user can enter the number of bikes being rented over a 24-hour period. The user interface includes the text box, an area to display the total cost of the bike rental, a Calculate Cost button, a Clear button, and an Exit button.
2. The user enters the number of bikes rented.
3. The user taps or clicks the Calculate Cost button.
4. The program displays the total cost of the bike rental.
5. The user taps or clicks the Clear button to clear the Number of Bike Rentals text box and erase the Total Cost of Bikes Rented amount.
6. The user can repeat Steps 2 through 5.
7. The user taps or clicks the Exit button to terminate the application.

FIGURE 4-85

Event-Planning Document

You will recall that the event-planning document is a table that specifies which objects in the user interface will cause events, the action taken by the user to trigger each event, and the event processing that must occur. The event-planning document for the City Bike Rentals program is shown in Figure 4-86.

EVENT-PLANNING DOCUMENT

Program Name: City Bike Rentals	Developer: Corinne Hoisington	Object: frmBikes	Date: April 14, 2017
OBJECT	**EVENT TRIGGER**	**EVENT PROCESSING**	
btnCalculate	Tap or click	Assign data entered in text box to a String variable Convert entered data to numeric integer Calculate total cost of bike rental (number of bikes* price per bike rental) Display total cost of bikes rented	
btnClear	Tap or click	Clear Number of Bike Rentals text box Clear Total Cost of Bikes Rented label text Set focus on Number of Bike Rentals text box	
btnExit	Tap or click	Close the window and terminate the program	
frmBikes	Load	Display heading with price per bike rental Clear the placement digits for Total Cost of Bikes Rented Label object Set focus on Number of Bike Rentals text box	

FIGURE 4-86

Code the Program

You are now ready to code the program by entering Visual Basic statements to accomplish the tasks specified in the event-planning document. You also will implement the logic to carry out the required processing.

Guided Program Development

To design the user interface for the City Bike Rentals program and enter the code required to process each event in the program, complete the following steps:

NOTE TO THE LEARNER

In the following activity, you should complete the tasks within the specified steps. Each of the tasks is accompanied by a Hint Screen. The purpose of the Hint Screen is to indicate where you should perform the activity in the Visual Studio window and to remind you which method to use. If you need further help completing a step, refer to the figure identified by *ref:*.

Guided Program Development

Phase 1: Create the User Interface Mockup

1

● **Create a Windows Desktop Application** Open Visual Studio using the Search charm (Windows 8) or the Start button on the Windows taskbar and the All Programs submenu (Windows 7). Close the Start page by tapping or clicking the Close button. To create a Windows Desktop application, tap or click the New Project button on the Standard toolbar. If necessary, tap or click Windows in the Installed Templates pane, tap or click

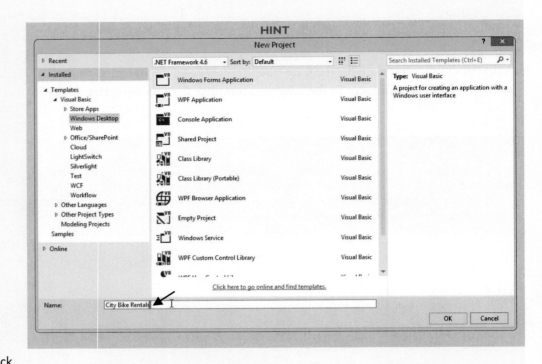

Windows Forms Application in the center pane, and then type `City Bike Rentals`. Tap or click the OK button in the New Project window.

● **Display the Toolbox** Ensure that the Toolbox is displayed in the Visual Studio window. If it is not, tap or click View on the menu bar and then tap or click Toolbox. If necessary, tap or click the triangle next to the Common Controls category name in the Toolbox and tap or click the Auto Hide button to display the tools.

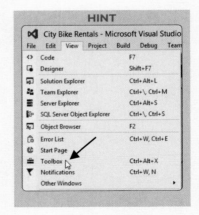

● **Name the Windows Form Object** In the Solution Explorer window, press and hold or right-click the Form1.vb form file name and select Rename. Type `frmBikes.vb` and then press the ENTER key.

● **Change the Title on the Title Bar** To change the title on the Windows Form object, tap or click the form, scroll in the Properties window until the Text property is displayed, double-tap or double-click in the right column of the Text property, type City Bike Rentals, and then press the ENTER key.

● **Resize the Windows Form Object** Change the Size property of the form to 425, 500.

● **Add a PictureBox Object** Add a PictureBox object to the Windows Form object by dragging the PictureBox .NET component onto the Windows Form object. Place the object in the bottom of the Windows Form object.

● **Name the PictureBox Object** With the PictureBox object selected, scroll in the Properties window until the (Name) property is visible. Double-tap or double-click in the right column of the (Name) property, type picBikes, and then press the ENTER key.

● **Resize the PictureBox Object** To resize the picBikes PictureBox object, first select it if necessary. Tap or click to the right of the Size property and change it to 407, 175.

(continues)

- **Add a Heading Label** To insert the City Bike Rentals heading label, drag the Label .NET component from the Toolbox to the Windows Form object. Position the Label object as shown in Figure 4-87.

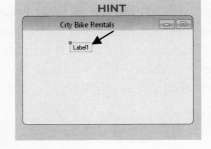

- **Name the Label Object** Name the Label object `lblHeading` by scrolling to the (Name) property in the Properties window, double-tapping or double-clicking the (Name) property in the right column, typing `lblHeading`, and then pressing the ENTER key.

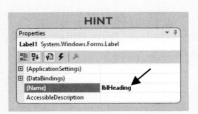

- **Change the Text of the Label Object** To change the text displayed in the Label object, scroll until the Text property is visible, double-tap or double-click in the right column of the Text property, type `City Bike Rentals`, and then press the ENTER key.

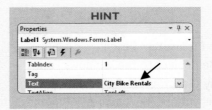

- **Change the Heading Font, Font Style, and Size** To make the heading stand out on the Windows form, its font should be larger and more prominent. To change the font to Cooper, its style to Black, and its size to 18, select the Label object and then scroll in the Properties window until the Font property is visible. Tap or click the Font property in the right column, and then tap or click the ellipsis button. In the Font dialog box, scroll if necessary, tap or click Cooper (or a similar font) in the Font list, tap or click Black in the Font style list, and then tap or click 18 in the Size list. Tap or click the OK button in the Font dialog box.

- **Horizontally Center the Label Object** The Label object should be centered horizontally in the form. Tap or click Format on the menu bar, point to Center in Form on the Format menu, and then tap or click Horizontally on the Center in Form submenu.

The PictureBox object and the Label object are placed on the resized Windows Form object (Figure 4-87). The font and font size for the Label object are appropriate for a heading in the window.

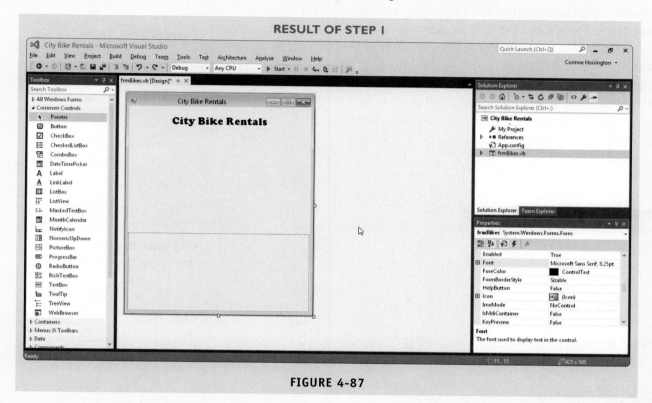

FIGURE 4-87

2

● **Add a Second Heading Label** To add the second heading label required for the window, drag a Label .NET component from the Toolbox to the Windows Form object. Place the second Label object below the lblHeading object.

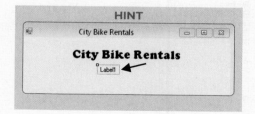

● **Name the Label Object** Give the name `lblCostHeading` to the Label object you just placed on the Windows Form object.

(continues)

● **Change the Text in the Label Object** Change the text in the lblCostHeading object to $X.XX per Bike for 24 Hours. This text is a placeholder so that the Label object can be properly aligned and will be visible when it is not selected.

● **Set the Font, Font Style, and Size of the Font** Use the Font property and ellipsis button in the Properties window to display the Font dialog box, and then change the font to Microsoft Sans Serif, the style to Regular, and the size to 12 points.

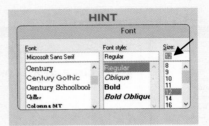

● **Center-Align the Label Object** Select the label, tap or click Format on the menu bar, point to Center in Form, and then tap or click Horizontally.

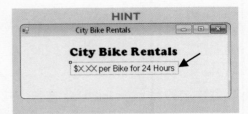

The PictureBox object and the Label objects are properly aligned in the Windows Form object (Figure 4-88).

RESULT OF STEP 2

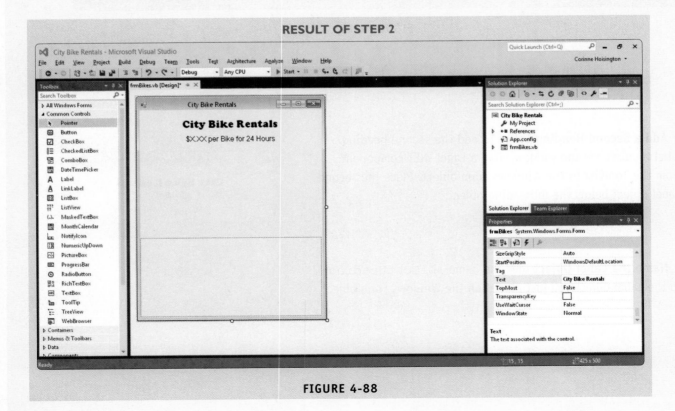

FIGURE 4-88

3

● **Add a Label for the Number of Bike Rentals**
Add the Label object for the number of bikes
rented by dragging it from the Toolbox. Place
it below the two other Label objects.

HINT

● **Change the Name, Enter Text, and Change the Font for
the Number of Bike Rentals Label** Using techniques you have
learned previously, change the name of the Label object to
`lblNumberOfBikes`. In the Text property, enter `Number
of Bike Rentals:`. Using the Font property in the Properties
window, change the font to Century Gothic, Regular style, and
11-point size.

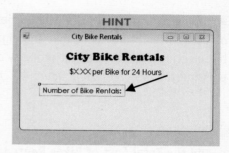
HINT

● **Add a TextBox Object for the Number of Bike Rentals**
Drag a TextBox object to the Windows Form object. Name
the TextBox object `txtNumberOfBikes` *(ref: Figure 4-3)*.

HINT

● **Enter Data into the Text Property** As you learned in this
chapter, even though the TextBox object will not contain text when
the program begins, it still is necessary to enter text in the Text
property of the TextBox object to size it properly. To enter text into
the TextBox, select the TextBox object. In the Properties window,
change the Text property to `888` *(ref: Figure 4-6)*.

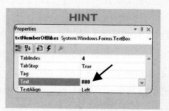
HINT

● **Change the Font and Size of the TextBox Object** Using the
Properties window, change the font for the TextBox object to
Century Gothic, Regular style, and 11-point size. Drag the right
border of the TextBox object so the numbers fit properly in the
text box *(ref: Figure 4-8)*.

HINT

● **Align the Resized TextBox Object** To realign the resized TextBox
object, drag it up until the red snap line indicates the text in the
TextBox object is bottom-aligned with the label *(ref: Figure 4-9)*.

HINT

(continues)

- **Center-Align Text in the TextBox Object** To center-align the text in the TextBox object, select the TextBox object, scroll in the Properties window until the TextAlign property is visible, tap or click the list arrow in the right column of the TextAlign property, and then tap or click Center in the TextAlign property list *(ref: Figure 4-10)*.

- **Remove Text from the TextBox Object** Because the TextBox object is sized properly, remove the digits from the TextBox object by selecting them in the Text property of the object and then pressing the DELETE key *(ref: Figure 4-12)*.

- **Add the Total Cost of Bikes Rented Label Objects** A label that reports the total cost of the bikes rented must be displayed as the Text property of a Label object. A second label actually identifies the total cost. Drag two labels onto the Windows Form object and place them on the same horizontal line using the blue snap lines. Vertically align the left side of the left label with the label above it. Vertically align the left side of the right label with the text box above it. Name the Label object on the left `lblTotalCostLabel`. Name the label on the right `lblTotalCost` *(ref: Figure 4-18)*.

- **Enter Text for the Labels and Change the Font** Select the lblTotalCostLabel Label object and then double-tap or double-click the right column of the Text property for the label. Type `Total Cost of Bikes Rented:` and then press the ENTER key. Select the lblTotalCost Label object and then double-tap or double-click the right column of the Text property for the label. Enter the value `$888.88` to represent the widest expected value for the label. With the right label selected, hold down the CTRL key and then tap or click the left label. With both labels selected, change the font to Century Gothic, Regular style, 11-point size. Select lblNumberOfBikes, txtNumberOfBikes, lblTotalCostLabel, and lblTotalCost and Center in Form horizontally (Format menu) to center the four objects across the form.

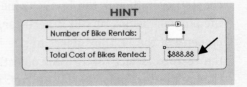

● **Add Buttons** Three buttons are required for the user interface: the Calculate Cost button, the Clear button, and the Exit button. Drag three buttons onto the Windows Form object below the labels. Use blue snap lines to horizontally align the tops of the buttons. Using the (Name) property for each button, name the first button `btnCalculate`, the second button `btnClear`, and the third button `btnExit`.

● **Change the Button Text and the Font Style** Using the Text property for each button, change the text for the btnCalculate Button object to `Calculate Cost` and the text for the btnClear button to `Clear`. Change the text for the btnExit button to `Exit`. Select all three buttons by tapping or clicking the Calculate Cost button, holding down the CTRL key, and then tapping or clicking the other two buttons. Next, tap or click the Font property, tap or click the ellipsis button in the right column of the Font property, and then change the font style to Bold and size 9 in the Font dialog box.

● **Change Button Size** The btnCalculate button does not display the entire Text property, so it must be enlarged. Drag the right border of the btnCalculate button until the entire Text property is visible.

● **Change the Size of the Other Buttons** Tap or click the btnCalculate button first, and then hold down the CTRL key and tap or click the other two buttons to select all three buttons. Make these buttons the same size by tapping or clicking Format on the menu bar, pointing to Make Same Size on the Format menu, and tapping or clicking Both on the Make Same Size submenu.

● **Space and Center the Buttons** With all three buttons selected, display the Format menu, point to Horizontal Spacing on the Format menu, and then tap or click Make Equal on the Horizontal Spacing submenu. Display the Format menu, point to Center in Form on the Format menu, and then tap or click Horizontally on the Center in Form submenu to center all three buttons horizontally in the Windows Form object.

(continues)

The mockup for the user interface is complete (Figure 4-89).

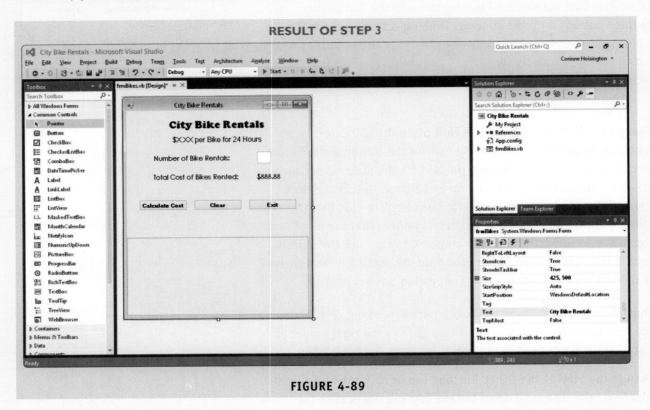

RESULT OF STEP 3

FIGURE 4-89

Phase 2: Fine-Tune the User Interface

4

● **Set the BackColor Property for the Windows Form Object** The user interface must be finished by setting the colors, adding images, and preparing for program execution. To set the BackColor property to White for the user interface, select the Windows Form object. In the Properties window, tap or click the BackColor property, and then tap or click the BackColor arrow in the right column of the BackColor property. If necessary, tap or click the Web tab. Scroll as required and then tap or click White in the BackColor list.

● **Set the ForeColor for the Button Objects and Label Object** To set the ForeColor to RoyalBlue for the button objects and the first Label object, select all three buttons and the lblHeading object. Tap or click the ForeColor property in the Properties window, and then tap or click the ForeColor arrow in the right column of the ForeColor property. Tap or click the Web tab, if necessary. Scroll as required and then tap or click RoyalBlue in the ForeColor list.

● **Set the Calculate Cost Button Object as the Accept Button** When the user enters the number of bikes rented, she should be able to calculate the total cost by tapping or clicking the Calculate Cost button or by pressing the ENTER key. To assign the Calculate Cost button as the Accept button, first select the Windows Form object by tapping or clicking anywhere in the window except on another object. Scroll in the Properties window until the AcceptButton property is visible, tap or click the AcceptButton property, tap or click the AcceptButton property arrow, and then tap or click btnCalculate *(ref: Figure 4-20)*.

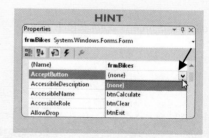

● **Set the Clear Button Object as the Cancel Button** By pressing the ESC key, the user should cause the same action as tapping or clicking the Clear button. To set the Clear button as the Cancel button, tap or click the Windows Form object, tap or click the CancelButton property in the Properties window, tap or click the CancelButton arrow, and then tap or click btnClear *(ref: page 199)*.

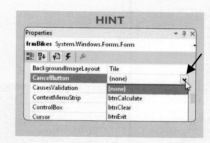

● **Insert the Bikes Image into the picBikes PictureBox Object** The last step to ready the user interface for execution is to insert the image into the PictureBox object. If necessary, download and save the Bikes image from the Student Companion Site. Then, with the picture box selected, tap or click the ellipsis button for the Image property in the Properties window, tap or click the Import button in the Select Resource dialog box, locate the Bikes image, and then import the image into the Resource folder. Tap or click the OK button in the Select Resource dialog box.

© iStock.com/phototropic

(continues)

Guided Program Development   *continued*

• **Resize the Image** To resize the Bikes image, change the SizeMode property. With the picBikes PictureBox object selected, tap or click the SizeMode property in the Properties window, tap or click the SizeMode arrow in the right column, and then tap or click StretchImage.

The user interface is complete (Figure 4-90).

RESULT OF STEP 4

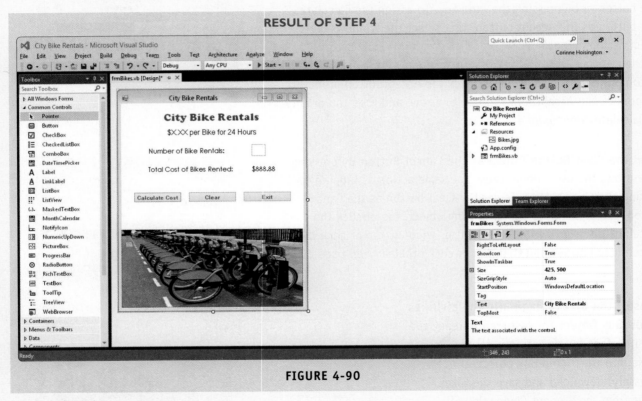

FIGURE 4-90

Phase 3: Code the Application

5

- **Code the Comments** Double-click the btnCalculate Button object on the frmBikes Windows Form object to open the code window and create the btnCalculate_Click event handler. Tap or click the Close button on the Toolbox title bar to close the Toolbox. Tap or click in front of the first words, Public Class frmBikes, and press the ENTER key to create a blank line. Press the UP ARROW key and then insert the first four standard comments. Insert the Option Strict On command at the beginning of the code to turn on strict type checking *(ref: Figure 4-53)*.

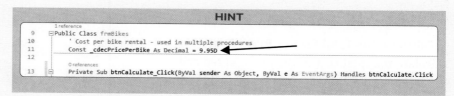

- **Enter the _cdecPricePer Bike Class Variable** The next step is to enter the class variable that is referenced in more than one event handler in this program. This variable contains the price per bike and is referenced in the heading and to calculate the total cost. To enter this variable, press the DOWN ARROW key until the insertion point is on the blank line following the Public Class command (line 9). Press the ENTER key to add a blank line, and then type the comment that identifies the variable. Press the ENTER key and then write the declaration for the _cdecPricePerBike variable. The constant Decimal variable should contain the value 9.95. The underline character (_) in the name indicates a class variable that is referenced in multiple procedures within the class *(ref: Figure 4-47)*.

- **Comment the btnCalculate Tap or Click Event Handler** Following the Private statement for the btnCalculate_Click event handler, enter a comment to describe the purpose of the btnCalculate_Click event.

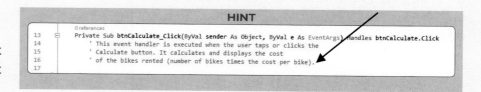

(continues)

- **Declare and Initialize the Variables** This event handler requires three variables: (1) strNumberOfBikes, which holds the number of bike rentals entered by the user; (2) intNumberOfBikes, which holds the integer value for the number of bike rentals entered by the user; and (3) decTotalCost, which holds the calculated total cost of bikes rented. Declare these three variables *(ref: Figure 4-22, Figure 4-35, Figure 4-37).*

HINT

```
17
18        Dim strNumberOfBikes As String
19        Dim intNumberOfBikes As Integer
20        Dim decTotalCost As Decimal
21
```

- **Write the Statements to Place the Number of Bikes Rented in a Variable and Convert the Value to an Integer** The first steps in the event handler are to move the number of bikes value from the Text property of the txtNumberOfBikes TextBox object to a String variable and then convert that value to an Integer value. Using IntelliSense, write the code to complete these steps *(ref: Figure 4-29, Figure 4-52).*

HINT

```
22        strNumberOfBikes = txtNumberOfBikes.Text
23        intNumberOfBikes = Convert.ToInt32(strNumberOfBikes)
```

- **Calculate the Total Cost of Bikes Rented** To calculate the total cost of the bikes rented and place the result in the decTotalCost variable, the number of bikes is multiplied by the price per bike. Using IntelliSense, write the statement to perform this calculation *(ref: Figure 4-55).*

HINT

```
24        decTotalCost = intNumberOfBikes * _cdecPricePerBike
```

- **Convert the Decimal Total Cost of Bikes Rented to a String Currency Value and Place It in the Text Property of the lblTotalCost Label Object** After calculating the total cost of bikes rented, the result must be converted from a Decimal value to a currency String value so it can be displayed as the value in the Text property of a Label object. Write the statement to perform this conversion and place the converted value in the Text property of the lblTotalCost Label object.

HINT

```
25        lblTotalCost.Text = decTotalCost.ToString("C")
```

The coding for the btnCalculate_Click event handler is complete (Figure 4-91).

RESULT OF STEP 5

```
12
      0 references
13    Private Sub btnCalculate_Click(ByVal sender As Object, ByVal e As EventArgs) Handles btnCalculate.Click
14        ' This event handler is executed when the user taps or clicks the
15        ' Calculate button. It calculates and displays the cost
16        ' of the bikes rented (number of bikes times the cost per bike).
17
18        Dim strNumberOfBikes As String
19        Dim intNumberOfBikes As Integer
20        Dim decTotalCost As Decimal
21
22        strNumberOfBikes = txtNumberOfBikes.Text
23        intNumberOfBikes = Convert.ToInt32(strNumberOfBikes)
24        decTotalCost = intNumberOfBikes * _cdecPricePerBike
25        lblTotalCost.Text = decTotalCost.ToString("C")
26
27    End Sub
28
```

FIGURE 4-91

6

• **Run the Application** After you enter code, you should
run the application to ensure it is working properly. Run the
City Bike Rentals application by tapping or clicking the Start
Debugging button on the Standard toolbar. Enter 2 for the
Number of Bike Rentals and then tap or click the Calculate
Cost button. The Total Cost of Bikes Rented should be $19.90.
Enter 10 for the Number of Bike Rentals and then press the
ENTER key.

When the number of bikes rented is 10, the
total cost of the city bike rental is $99.50
(Figure 4-92).

RESULT OF STEP 6

City Bike Rentals

City Bike Rentals

$9.95 Per Bike for 24 Hours

Number of Bike Rentals: 10

Total Cost of Bikes Rented: $99.50

Calculate Cost   Clear   Exit

FIGURE 4-92

(continues)

7

- **Write the Code for the Clear Button Event Handler** Tap or click the frmBikes.vb [Design] tab in the code window to return to the design window. Double-tap or double-click the Clear button to create the event handler for the Clear button. The Clear button event handler must accomplish the following tasks: Clear the txtNumberOfBikes text box; clear the value in the Text property of the lblTotalCost Label object; and set the focus to the txtNumberOfBikes text box. Write the comments for the event handler and then use IntelliSense to write the code for the event handler *(ref: Figure 4-74, Figure 4-75, Figure 4-77).*

```
28
29   Private Sub btnClear_Click(ByVal sender As Object, ByVal e As EventArgs) Hand
30        ' This event handler is executed when the user taps or clicks the
31        ' Clear button. It clears the number of bikes text box
32        ' and the Text property of the Total Cost label.
33        ' Then, it sets the focus on the txtNumberOfBikes Textbox object.
34
35        txtNumberOfBikes.Clear()
36        lblTotalCost.Text = ""
37        txtNumberOfBikes.Focus()
38
39   End Sub
```

- **Write the Code for the Form Load Event Handler** Tap or click the frmBikes.vb [Design] tab in the code window to return to the design window. Double-tap or double-click the Windows Form object to create the event handler for the Form Load event. The Form Load event handler must accomplish the following tasks: Using concatenation, create and display the Price Per Bike heading in the Text property of the lblCostHeading Label object; clear the Text property of the lblTotalCost Label object; and set the focus to the txtNumberOfBikes TextBox object. Write the comments for the event handler and then use IntelliSense to write the code for the event handler *(ref: Figure 4-75, Figure 4-77, Figure 4-80).*

```
40
41   Private Sub frmDigitalDownloads_Load(ByVal sender As Object, ByVal e As EventArgs) Handles MyBase.Load
42        ' This event handler is executed when the form is loaded.
43        ' It displays the cost heading, clears the Text property of the
44        ' Total Cost label, and sets the focus on
45        ' the txtNumberOfBikes Textbox object.
46
47        lblCostHeading.Text = _cdecPricePerBike.ToString("C") & " Per Bike for 24 Hours"
48        lblTotalCost.Text = ""
49        txtNumberOfBikes.Focus()
50
51   End Sub
```

- **Write the Code for the Exit Button Event Handler** Tap or click the frmBikes.vb [Design] tab in the code window to return to the design window. Double-tap or double-click the Exit button to create its event handler. The Exit button event handler must close the window and terminate the application. Write the comments and code for this event handler.

```
52
53   Private Sub btnExit_Click(ByVal sender As Object, ByVal e As EventArgs) Handles btnExit.Click
54        ' Close the window and terminate the application
55
56        Close()
57
58   End Sub
```

The coding is complete for the Clear button event handler, the Form load event handler, and the Exit button event handler (Figure 4-93).

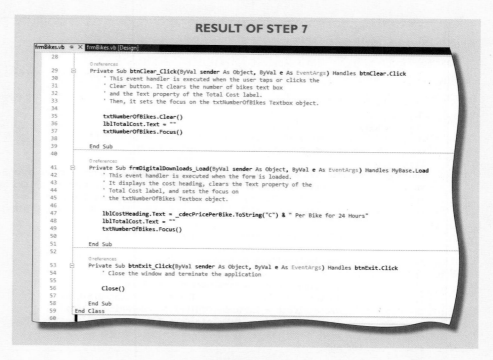

RESULT OF STEP 7

```
frmBikes.vb  ↔ ✕  frmBikes.vb [Design]
28
          0 references
29        Private Sub btnClear_Click(ByVal sender As Object, ByVal e As EventArgs) Handles btnClear.Click
30            ' This event handler is executed when the user taps or clicks the
31            ' Clear button. It clears the number of bikes text box
32            ' and the Text property of the Total Cost label.
33            ' Then, it sets the focus on the txtNumberOfBikes Textbox object.
34
35            txtNumberOfBikes.Clear()
36            lblTotalCost.Text = ""
37            txtNumberOfBikes.Focus()
38
39        End Sub
40
          0 references
41        Private Sub frmDigitalDownloads_Load(ByVal sender As Object, ByVal e As EventArgs) Handles MyBase.Load
42            ' This event handler is executed when the form is loaded.
43            ' It displays the cost heading, clears the Text property of the
44            ' Total Cost label, and sets the focus on
45            ' the txtNumberOfBikes Textbox object.
46
47            lblCostHeading.Text = _cdecPricePerBike.ToString("C") & " Per Bike for 24 Hours"
48            lblTotalCost.Text = ""
49            txtNumberOfBikes.Focus()
50
51        End Sub
52
          0 references
53        Private Sub btnExit_Click(ByVal sender As Object, ByVal e As EventArgs) Handles btnExit.Click
54            ' Close the window and terminate the application
55
56            Close()
57
58        End Sub
59    End Class
60
```

FIGURE 4-93

8

• **Test the Program** After finishing the coding, you should test the program to ensure it works properly. Run the City Bike Rentals application by tapping or clicking the Start Debugging button on the Standard toolbar. Enter 2 for the Number of Bike Rentals and then tap or click the Calculate Cost button. The Total Cost of Bikes Rented should be $19.90. Tap or click the Clear button to clear the text box and the label that contains the total cost of the bikes rented. Enter 5 for the Number of Bike Rentals and then press the ENTER key. The Total Cost of Bikes Rented should be $49.75. Press the ESC key to clear the text box and the label that contains the total cost of bikes rented. Enter other values to test the program completely.

The program runs properly (Figure 4-94).

RESULT OF STEP 8

FIGURE 4-94

Code Listing

The complete code for the sample program is shown in Figure 4-95.

```vbnet
1   ' Program:  City Bike Rental
2   ' Author:   Corinne Hoisington
3   ' Date:     April 14, 2017
4   ' Purpose:  This application calculates and displays
5   '           the total cost of renting multiple bikes for a 24-hour period.
6
7   Option Strict On
8
9   Public Class frmBikes
10      ' Cost per bike rental - used in multiple procedures
11      Const _cdecPricePerBike As Decimal = 9.95D
12
13      Private Sub btnCalculate_Click(ByVal sender As Object, ByVal e As EventArgs) Handles btnCalculate.Click
14          ' This event handler is executed when the user taps or clicks the
15          ' Calculate button. It calculates and displays the cost
16          ' of the bikes rented (number of bikes times the cost per bike).
17
18          Dim strNumberOfBikes As String
19          Dim intNumberOfBikes As Integer
20          Dim decTotalCost As Decimal
21
22          strNumberOfBikes = txtNumberOfBikes.Text
23          intNumberOfBikes = Convert.ToInt32(strNumberOfBikes)
24          decTotalCost = intNumberOfBikes * _cdecPricePerBike
25          lblTotalCost.Text = decTotalCost.ToString("C")
26
27      End Sub
28
29      Private Sub btnClear_Click(ByVal sender As Object, ByVal e As EventArgs) Handles btnClear.Click
30          ' This event handler is executed when the user taps or clicks the
31          ' Clear button. It clears the number of bikes text box
32          ' and the Text property of the Total Cost label.
33          ' Then, it sets the focus on the txtNumberOfBikes Textbox object.
34
35          txtNumberOfBikes.Clear()
36          lblTotalCost.Text = ""
37          txtNumberOfBikes.Focus()
38
39      End Sub
40
41      Private Sub frmDigitalDownloads_Load(ByVal sender As Object, ByVal e As EventArgs) Handles MyBase.Load
42          ' This event handler is executed when the form is loaded.
43          ' It displays the cost heading, clears the Text property of the
44          ' Total Cost label, and sets the focus on
45          ' the txtNumberOfBikes Textbox object.
46
47          lblCostHeading.Text = _cdecPricePerBike.ToString("C") & " Per Bike for 24 Hours"
48          lblTotalCost.Text = ""
49          txtNumberOfBikes.Focus()
50
51      End Sub
52
53      Private Sub btnExit_Click(ByVal sender As Object, ByVal e As EventArgs) Handles btnExit.Click
54          ' Close the window and terminate the application
55
56          Close()
57
58      End Sub
59   End Class
60
```

FIGURE 4-95

Summary

In this chapter you have learned to declare variables and write arithmetic operations. The items listed in the table in Figure 4-96 include all the new Visual Studio and Visual Basic skills you have learned in this chapter.

Visual Basic Skills

Skill	Figure Number	Video Number
Place a TextBox Object on the Windows Form Object	Figure 4-3	Video 4-2
Size and Position a TextBox Object	Figure 4-6	Video 4-3
Align Text in a TextBox Object	Figure 4-10	Video 4-4
Create a MultiLine TextBox Object	Figure 4-13	Video 4-5
Create a Masked TextBox Object	Figure 4-14	Video 4-6
Place a Masked TextBox Object on the Windows Form Object	Figure 4-15	Video 4-7
Place and Size a Label object on the Windows Form Object	Figure 4-18	Video 4-8
Assign a Button Object as the Accept Button	Figure 4-20	Video 4-9
Assign a Button Object as the Cancel Button	Page 199	
Close the Toolbox	Figure 4-21	Video 4-10
Define a String Variable	Figure 4-22	
Write an Assignment Statement	Figure 4-24	
Use IntelliSense to Enter a Variable and an Assignment Statement	Figure 4-25	Video 4-11
Declare an Integer Data Type	Figure 4-35	
Declare a Decimal Data Type	Figure 4-37	
Declare a Char Data Type	Figure 4-40	
Declare a Boolean Data Type	Figure 4-42	
Declare a Constant	Figure 4-47	
Use an Argument in a Procedure Call Statement	Figure 4-49	
Write a Procedure Call Statement for the ToInt32 Procedure in the Convert Class	Figure 4-52	
Enter the Option Strict On Statement	Figure 4-53	
Perform Arithmetic Operations Using Arithmetic Operators	Figure 4-56	
Display Numeric Output Data	Figure 4-70	
Write a Procedure Call for the Clear Procedure	Figure 4-74	
Write a Procedure Call for the Focus Procedure	Figure 4-76	
Write a String Concatenation Statement	Figure 4-80	
Write a Variable with Class Scope	Figure 4-82	
Understand a Format Exception	Figure 4-83	

FIGURE 4-96

Learn Online

Reinforcement activities and resources are available at no additional cost on www.CengageBrain.com. Visit http://solutions.cengage.com/ctdownloads/ for detailed instructions about accessing the resources available at the Student Companion Site.

Knowledge Check

1. Which data type should a hash tag (#) symbol be assigned?

2. Write a Dim statement for each of the following variables using the variable type and variable name that would be best for each value.

   a. The number of students at Harvard

   b. Your weekly pay

   c. The smallest data type you can use for your age

   d. A constant for the first initial of your first name

   e. The minimum wage

   f. The name of the street where you live

   g. The answer to a true/false question

3. Determine whether each of the following variable names is valid or invalid. Explain the error in each invalid variable name.

   a. _cdecPi

   b. PercentOfSales%

   c. first_Input_Value

   d. Orange-is-new-black

   e. 3CPO

   f. Close

   g. Name Of Cortana

4. List the steps that specify how you would perfectly align a group of TextBox objects along their left edges.

5. Which data type is best for currency amounts?

6. Explain the hierarchy in for the order of operations.

7. What is the solution to each of the following arithmetic expressions?

   a. $3 + 4 * 2 + 9$

   b. $48 / 6 * 4 - 3$

   c. $40 - 6 \wedge 2 / 3$

   d. 71 Mod 9

   e. $9 \setminus 4 + 3$

   f. $2 \wedge 3 + (8 - 5)$

   g. $(15$ Mod $2) - 1 + 4 * (16 \setminus 5)$

8. What is the difference between a method and a procedure?

9. What is the difference between a variable and a literal?

10. Correct the following statements:

```
a. Dim itSize As Integr

b. Dim dblDiscountRate As Dbl

c. Constant cstrCollege As String = "CVCC"

d. Dim strLastName As Number

e. strLastName = 'J Starks'

f. 2.0 * decHourlyPay = decOverTimePayRate
```

11. Write a statement that sets the focus on the txtSoup TextBox object.

12. Write a statement that removes the contents of the txtLuggage TextBox object.

13. Write a statement that blanks the Text property of the lblEligibilityAge Label object.

14. Write a statement to convert the value in the String variable strWaistSize to an integer value and place the integer value in a variable named intWaistSize.

15. Write a statement to convert the value in the String variable strHourlyPay to a Decimal value and place the Decimal value in a variable named decWage.

16. Write a statement to close a form that currently is open.

17. Write a statement that declares a constant named decInsuranceDeductible as a Decimal data type and set its value to 250.00.

18. Which Windows Form property allows the user to press the ENTER key while the form is active and activate a button's event handler?

19. What is a local variable? How does its scope differ from that of a global variable?

20. When the following statements are executed, what would be displayed in the lblHourlyWage Label object?

```
decHourlyWage = 13.637
lblHourlyWage.Text = decHourlyWage.ToString("C")
```

Debugging Exercises

1. Fix the following code:

```
Option Strict On
Dim intDistance As Integer

intDistance = 17.5
```

2. Fix the following code:

```
Dim dblRegularPay As Double
Dim dblOvertimePay As Double

intRegularPay = 783.87
intOvertimePay = 105.92
lbl.TotalPay = (dblRegularPay + dblOvertimePay).ToString ('C')
```

3. Analyze the code in Figure 4-97 and then correct it.

```
Form1.vb  ⊕ X  Form1.vb [Design]
   1   ☐Public Class Form1
   2
   3   ☐    Private Sub btnHeight_Click(sender As Object, e As EventArgs) Handles btnHeight.Click
   4            Dim intFeet As Integer
   5            Dim strInches As String
   6            Dim intInches As Integer
   7
   8            intInches = Convert.ToInt32(strInches)
   9            intFeet = intInches / 12
  10            lblFeet.Text = intFeet.ToString("P")
  11
  12        End Sub
  13   End Class
  14
```

FIGURE 4-97

Program Analysis

1. What will occur when the user taps or clicks the btnSlope Button in the following code?

```
Private Sub btnSlope_Click(ByVal sender As System.Object, ByVal e As System
.EventArgs) Handles btnSlope.Click
  Dim decRise As Decimal
  Dim decRun As Decimal
  Dim decSlope As Decimal
  decRise = 12.3D
  decRun = 2.1D
  decSlope = decRise / decRun
  lblSlope.Text = "The Line Slope is" & decSlope.ToString("F3")
End Sub
```

2. How would the number .0256 be displayed if the format specifier ("P") is used in a Convert.ToString statement?

3. How would the number 3746.35555 be displayed if the format specifier ("F3") is used in a Convert.ToString statement?

Program Analysis *continued*

4. If you want the user to enter her telephone number with the area code, which .NET component would be best to use on the Windows Form object?

5. Using the format specifier with the ToString procedure, write the statement that would display:

   a. The value in the decDvdCost variable with a dollar sign and two places to the right of the decimal point in a label named lblDvd

   b. The value in the decWithholdingTaxRate variable with a percent sign and one place to the right of the decimal point in a label named lblWithholdingTaxRate

   c. The value in the decOilRevenue variable with commas as needed, two places to the right of the decimal point, and no dollar sign in a label called lblOilRevenue

6. Write a single line of code to declare a variable decWindSpeed as a Decimal data type and assign it the value 25.47. Use a forced literal to ensure that the compiler views this number as a Decimal data type.

7. What would the values of these variables be at the end of the code that follows?

   a. intParts

   b. intBoxes

   c. intLeftovers

```
Dim intParts As Integer
Dim intBoxes As Integer
Dim intLeftovers As Integer

intParts = 77
intPartsPerBox = 9

intBoxes = intParts \ intPartsPerBox
intLeftovers = intParts Mod intBoxes
```

8. Are the following statements written correctly? If not, how should they be written?

```
Dim dblPay as Double
lblPay.Text = dblPay.ToString("C2")
```

9. For a Button object named btnCalories, write the tap or click event handler to implement the following requirements and calculate the number of calories burned during a run:

   a. Declare variables named strMilesRan, decCaloriesConsumed, and decMilesRan.

   b. Declare a constant named cdecCaloriesBurnedPerHour and assign it the value 700. (Assume you burn 700 calories for every mile you run.)

   c. Allow the user to enter the number of miles she ran today.

   d. Convert the number of miles to a Decimal data type.

   e. Calculate the number of calories the user burned during her run.

   f. Display the result rounded to zero decimal places in a label named lblCaloriesBurned.

10. What would the output be when the user taps or clicks the btnDrivingAge Button?

```
Private Sub btnDrivingAge_Click(ByVal sender As System.Object, ByVal e As
System.EventArgs) Handles btnDrivingAge.Click
  Dim intPresentAge As Integer
  Const cintDrivingAge As Integer = 16
  Dim intYearsToDrive As Integer

  intPresentAge = 13
  intYearsToDrive = cintDrivingAge - intPresentAge
  lblYearsLeft.Text = intYearsToDrive.ToString() & " year(s) until you can
  drive."
End Sub
```

Case Programming Assignments

Complete one or more of the following case programming assignments. Submit the program and materials you create to your instructor. The level of difficulty is indicated for each assignment.

● = Easiest
● ● = Intermediate
● ● ● = Challenging

1 ● ROME HOSTEL ACCOMMODATIONS

Design a Windows Desktop application and write the code that will execute according to the program requirements in Figure 4-98 and the Use Case Definition in Figure 4-99. Before writing the code, create an event-planning document for each event in the program. The completed program is shown in Figure 4-100.

REQUIREMENTS DOCUMENT

Date:	October 19, 2016
Date Submitted:	
Application Title:	Rome Hostel Accommodations
Purpose:	This Windows Desktop application allows a user to calculate the cost of accommodations at a hostel in Rome, Italy.
Program Procedures:	From a window on the screen, the user chooses the number of nights to stay at the Hostel Roma during a backpacking trip in Italy; the total cost of the accommodations is displayed.
Algorithms, Processing, and Conditions:	1. The user must be able to enter the number of nights. 2. A picture of the Roman hostel will be displayed throughout the entire process. 3. After entering the number of nights needed, the user taps or clicks the Display Cost button. 4. One night of accommodations costs $18 for a bunk in the dorm room; the total cost will be displayed in currency format.
Notes and Restrictions:	1. The user can use a Clear button to clear the number of nights entered and the total cost and then enter another number of nights. 2. An Exit button should close the application. 3. The cost per night can vary, so the program should allow a different price to be placed in any headings and be used in any calculations.
Comments:	The picture is named Hostel and is available on CengageBrain.com.

FIGURE 4-98

(continues)

Rome Hostel Accommodations (continued)

USE CASE DEFINITION

1. The Windows Desktop application opens.
2. The user enters the number of nights.
3. The user taps or clicks the Display Cost button.
4. The program displays the total cost for the stay.
5. The user can tap or click the Clear button and repeat Steps 2 through 4.
6. The user terminates the program by tapping or clicking the Exit button.

FIGURE 4-99

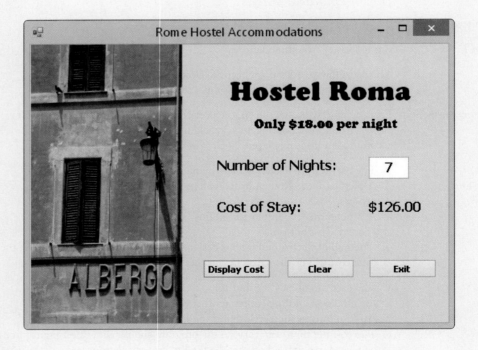

© iStock.com / jemorse

FIGURE 4-100

2   BOSTON WALKING TOUR

Design a Windows Desktop application and write the code that will execute according to the program requirements in Figure 4-101 and the Use Case Definition in Figure 4-102. Before writing the code, create an event-planning document for each event in the program. The completed program is shown in Figure 4-103.

REQUIREMENTS DOCUMENT

Date:	February 19, 2016
Date Submitted:	
Application Title:	Boston Walking Tour
Purpose:	This Windows Desktop application computes the cost of a Boston walking tour.
Program Procedures:	From a window on the screen, the user enters the number of tickets needed for a three-hour walking tour of the city of Boston. The program calculates and displays the cost of the tickets.
Algorithms, Processing, and Conditions:	1. The user must be able to enter the number of tickets for the Boston Walking Tour. 2. The title of the program and an image of Boston's Faneuil Hall will be displayed throughout the entire process. 3. After entering the number of tickets, the user taps or clicks the Display Cost button. 4. Each tour ticket is $14.99. 5. The program displays the cost in currency format.
Notes and Restrictions:	1. The user can clear the number of tickets and make another entry. 2. An Exit button should close the application.
Comments:	The Boston image is named Boston and is available on CengageBrain.com.

FIGURE 4-101

(continues)

Case Programming Assignments

Boston Walking Tour (continued)

USE CASE DEFINITION

1. The Windows Desktop application opens.
2. The user enters the number of tour tickets needed.
3. The user taps or clicks the Display Cost button.
4. The program displays the total cost of the Boston walking tour tickets.
5. The user can tap or click the Clear button and repeat Steps 2 through 4.
6. The user terminates the program by tapping or clicking the Exit button.

FIGURE 4-102

FIGURE 4-103

3
SMART CAR RENTAL

Design a Windows Desktop application and write the code that will execute according to the program requirements in Figure 4-104 and the Use Case Definition in Figure 4-105. Before writing the code, create an event-planning document for each event in the program. The completed program is shown in Figure 4-106.

REQUIREMENTS DOCUMENT

Date:	October 20, 2016
Date Submitted:	
Application Title:	Smart Car Rental
Purpose:	This Windows Desktop application calculates the cost of renting a smart car.
Program Procedures:	From a window on the screen, a user enters the number of days she rented a smart car and the number of miles she drove. The program displays the flat rate per day, the flat rate per mile, and the total cost of the car rental.
Algorithms, Processing, and Conditions:	1. The user must be able to enter the number of days she rented a smart car and the number of miles she drove the car.
	2. A picture of a car rental sign will be displayed throughout the entire process.
	3. After entering the number of days and the number of miles driven, the user taps or clicks the Display Fare button.
	4. The cost per day is $29.99 to rent a smart car plus $0.39 per mile driven.
	5. The total cost for the rental is displayed using the currency format.
Notes and Restrictions:	1. The user can clear the days and miles entered by tapping or clicking a Clear button. The user can then can enter another rental period and mileage.
	2. An Exit button should close the application.
Comments:	The car rental picture is named Car Rental and is available on CengageBrain.com.

FIGURE 4-104

(continues)

Case Programming Assignments

Smart Car Rental (continued)

USE CASE DEFINITION

1. The Windows Desktop application opens.
2. The user enters the number of days and the total miles driven.
3. The user taps or clicks the Display Fare button.
4. The program displays the total cost of the rental.
5. The user can tap or click the Clear button and then repeat Steps 2 through 4.
6. The user terminates the program by tapping or clicking the Exit button.

FIGURE 4-105

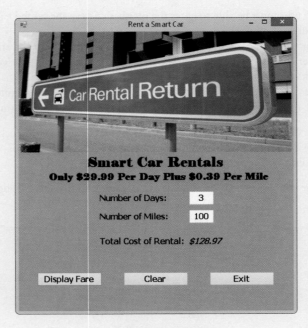

FIGURE 4-106

© iStock.com / ollo

Case Programming Assignments

4 ●●
SALES TAX CALCULATOR

Design a Windows Desktop application and write the code that will execute according to the program requirements in Figure 4-107. Before designing the user interface, create a Use Case Definition. Before writing the code, create an event-planning document for each event in the program.

REQUIREMENTS DOCUMENT

Date: June 6, 2016

Date Submitted:

Application Title: Sales Tax Calculator

Purpose: This Windows Desktop application will compute the sales tax and final cost of a purchased item.

Program Procedures: From a window on the screen, the user enters the item name and cost of the item purchased. The program calculates the tax for the item and the final total, and then displays these values.

Algorithms, Processing, and Conditions:
1. The user must be able to enter the name of the item purchased and the cost of the item before tax.
2. A store name and store picture will be displayed throughout the entire process.
3. After the user enters the item name and the cost of the item, she taps or clicks the Display Cost button.
4. The program displays the item name with the cost, tax, and final total.
5. The cost, tax, and final total should appear in currency format.
6. The tax rate for all items is 8.75%.
7. The final total is calculated by adding the cost and the tax.

Notes and Restrictions:
1. The user can clear the item name, cost, tax, and final total with a Clear button.
2. The user can tap or click an Exit button to close the application.

Comments: The store picture shown in the window should be selected from pictures available on the web.

FIGURE 4-107

5 ●● INCOME TAX CALCULATOR

Design a Windows Desktop application and write the code that will execute according to the program requirements in Figure 4-108. Before designing the user interface, create a Use Case Definition. Before writing the code, create an event-planning document for each event in the program.

REQUIREMENTS DOCUMENT

Date:	January 4, 2016
Date Submitted:	
Application Title:	Income Tax Calculator
Purpose:	This Windows Desktop application will compute and display the FICA tax, federal tax, and state tax for one year based on your income.
Program Procedures:	From a window on the screen, the user enters her yearly income. The program estimates the FICA tax, federal tax, and state tax for one year based on the user's income.
Algorithms, Processing, and Conditions:	1. Users must be able to enter their annual income. 2. The FICA tax (7.65%), federal tax (22%), and state income tax (3%) are computed. 3. The tax amounts should be displayed on separate lines and in currency format, two places past the decimal point. 4. The net pay should be displayed after the tax amounts have been deducted.
Notes and Restrictions:	1. The user can clear the income and taxes and then enter new data. 2. The user can use an Exit button to close the application.
Comments:	The designer should design the user interface, including all graphics and words displayed.

FIGURE 4-108

Case Programming Assignments

6 •• CURRENCY CONVERSION

Design a Windows Desktop application and write the code that will execute according to the program requirements in Figure 4-109. Before designing the user interface, create a Use Case Definition. Before writing the code, create an event-planning document for each event in the program.

REQUIREMENTS DOCUMENT

Date:	November 4, 2016
Date Submitted:	
Application Title:	Currency Conversion
Purpose:	This Windows Desktop application will display the value of U.S. dollars in euros, Canadian dollars, and Mexican pesos.
Program Procedures:	From a window on the screen, the user should enter the number of U.S. dollars to be converted. The program will display the equivalent value in euros, Canadian dollars, and Japanese yen.
Algorithms, Processing, and Conditions:	1. The user must be able to enter the number of U.S. dollars to be converted.
	2. After entering a number of U.S. dollars, the user taps or clicks the Convert Currency button.
	3. The program converts the number of U.S. dollars entered into the equivalent number of euros, Canadian dollars, and Japanese yen. The program displays all three currency amounts with the amount in U.S. dollars.
	4. To find the conversion rates, the developer must consult appropriate websites. A possible site is *www.xe.com*.
	5. Because currency rates change dynamically, the user should enter the date and time that the conversion rates were applied. The date and time should be displayed in U.S. format.
	6. The user should be able to clear the date and time, the number of U.S. dollars entered, and the results of the calculations, and then enter new values.
Notes and Restrictions:	The user should be able to tap or click an Exit button to close the application.
Comments:	The designer must determine the design of the user interface and the words and graphics used in it.

FIGURE 4-109

7 ●●●
MULCH CALCULATOR

Create a requirements document and a Use Case Definition document and then design a Windows application based on the case project shown in Figure 4-110. Before writing the code, create an event-planning document for each event in the program.

A local landscaping design business requests a Windows application that allows you to compute how much rubber mulch you need to fill a playground. The rubber mulch is designed for safety and costs $9.87 per cubic foot. In addition, the mulch supplier charges a one-time delivery fee of $25. The Windows application should request the playground's length, width, and average depth (for example, 0.25 of a foot equals a mulch depth of 3 inches). The program then determines the volume of the playground in cubic feet (volume = length * width * depth) and displays the final cost of landscaping the playground, including the delivery fee. Allow the user to enter values with decimal places. The user should be able to clear all entries and then reenter data. To close the program, the user should be able to tap or click a button.

FIGURE 4-110

8 ●●●
HOT TUB AREA AND CIRCUMFERENCE

Create a requirements document and a Use Case Definition document and then design a Windows application based on the case project shown in Figure 4-111. Before writing the code, create an event-planning document for each event in the program.

You are interested in purchasing a hot tub. The listings on the Internet describe hot tubs that have a perfectly round shape. Each ad states the diameter of the hot tub. Create a Windows application that computes the area and circumference of a hot tub after the user enters the diameter in feet and inches (for example, 8 feet and 4 inches). The area and circumference results should display two decimal places. You should be able to clear the entry, enter a new diameter, and exit the form.

FIGURE 4-111

9 ●●●
EXERCISE FOR A LIFETIME

Create a requirements document and a Use Case Definition document and then design a Windows application based on the case project shown in Figure 4-112. Before writing the code, create an event-planning document for each event in the program.

The YMCA has asked you to write a Windows application that its members can use to determine the total number of hours they have exercised during their lifetimes, assuming they exercise an average of 3 hours per week. All users should enter their first name, their birth date, and the current date. For both dates, ask for the month, day, and year separately in numeric form. To calculate the number of hours exercised, assume 365 days per year and 30 days per month. The program must display the user's name and the number of hours the user has exercised in his or her lifetime. The user can tap or click a Clear button to clear all entries and results. An Exit button must be available to close the application.

FIGURE 4-112

CHAPTER 5

Decision Structures

OBJECTIVES

You will have mastered the material in this chapter when you can:

- Use the GroupBox object

- Place RadioButton objects in applications

- Display a message box

- Make decisions using If . . . Then statements

- Make decisions using If . . . Then . . . Else statements

- Make decisions using nested If statements

- Make decisions using logical operators

- Make decisions using Case statements

- Insert code snippets

- Test input to ensure a value is numeric

Introduction

Developers can code Visual Basic applications to make decisions based on the input of users or other conditions that occur. Decision making is one of the fundamental activities of a computer program. In this chapter, you will learn to write decision-making statements in Visual Basic 2015.

Visual Basic allows you to test conditions and perform different operations depending on the results. You can test whether a condition is true or false and change the flow of what happens in a program based on the user's input.

The sample program in this chapter is called the Flooring Cost Calculator application. It is written for homeowners and flooring contractors who want to compare the costs of three different flooring options for materials. The application compares the cost of midrange tile, carpet, and hardwood flooring.

The application asks the user to enter the number of square feet of the room size for the flooring required and the desired flooring material. The application then computes the cost of the flooring based on a rate of $4.49 per square foot for tile, $4.99 per square foot for carpet, and $7.49 per square foot for hardwood. Figure 5-1 shows the user interface for the application.

FIGURE 5-1

Eric Audras/Getty Images

In Figure 5-1, the Flooring Cost Calculator Windows application displays the text "Flooring Cost Calculator" in the title bar. The square footage that the user enters in the TextBox object includes all flooring materials for the job. The user chooses the flooring type by selecting one of the following radio buttons: Tile, Carpet, or Hardwood. After the user enters the number of square feet of flooring and selects a type of flooring, the user taps or clicks the Calculate button to obtain the cost estimate. The calculation is the square feet multiplied by the cost of the selected flooring. The cost estimate is displayed in currency format. In the example in Figure 5-1, the user entered 120 square footage of flooring and selected Hardwood. After the user tapped or clicked the Calculate button, the application displayed a cost of $898.80 (120 × $7.49).

Tapping or clicking the Clear button clears the square footage; resets the radio button selection to Tile, which is the least expensive flooring type; and clears the calculation result.

Checking the validity of data the user entered is a requirement of the sample program in this chapter. In Chapter 4, you learned that if you enter nonnumeric data and attempt to use it in a calculation, the program will be terminated. To check for invalid data, the Flooring Cost Calculator application ensures that the user enters a numeric value greater than zero in the Square Footage TextBox object. A warning appears if the user leaves the TextBox blank or does not enter a valid number. Figure 5-2 displays the Input Error dialog box, called a Message Box, which directs the user to enter the square footage for the flooring.

user did not enter square feet

warning message in Message Box

FIGURE 5-2

Checking input data for validity is an important task in Visual Basic programs. You will learn several data validation techniques in this chapter.

User Interface Design

The user interface for the Flooring Cost Calculator application includes three new objects: a GroupBox, RadioButtons, and Message Boxes. The Message Boxes appear when the user enters a negative number or a nonnumeric value.

Use the GroupBox Object

The Flooring Cost Calculator Form object requires a GroupBox object and RadioButton objects (Figure 5-3).

FIGURE 5-3

Eric Audras/Getty Images

A **GroupBox** object associates items as a group, allowing the user to select one item from the group. It also includes caption text. RadioButton objects allow the user to make choices. In Figure 5-3, the GroupBox object groups the radio buttons for selecting the flooring type. When RadioButton objects are contained in a group box, the user can select only one radio button. For example, in Figure 5-3 the Tile radio button is selected. If the user taps or clicks the Carpet radio button, it becomes selected, and the Tile radio button is automatically deselected.

The GroupBox object shown in Figure 5-3 is displayed with the Text property of FloorType as the caption text. The prefix for the GroupBox object (Name) property is grp. To place a GroupBox object on the Form object, you can complete the following steps:

STEP 1   Drag the GroupBox object from the Containers category of the Toolbox to the approximate location where you want to place the GroupBox object on the Form object.

The pointer changes when you place it over the Form object (Figure 5-4). The GroupBox object will be placed on the form at the location of the outline in the pointer.

FIGURE 5-4

Eric Audras/Getty Images

STEP 2 When the pointer is in the correct location, release the object. With the GroupBox object selected, scroll in the Properties window to the (Name) property. Double-tap or double-click in the right column of the (Name) property and then enter the name `grpFloorType`. Double-tap or double-click in the right column of the Text property to change the caption of the GroupBox object. Enter the text `Flooring Type`. Tap or click the right column of the Size property for the GroupBox object and enter `175, 105` as the size.

The name you entered is displayed in the (Name) property in the Properties window, the caption Flooring Type is displayed, and the object is resized (Figure 5-5).

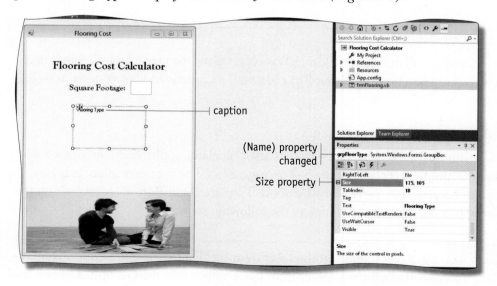

FIGURE 5-5

Eric Audras/Getty Images

STEP 3   Change the Font property to Goudy Old Style, Regular, 12 points. Change the BackColor property to White.

If you want to move the GroupBox to another location on the form, place the pointer over the drag box on the border of the GroupBox object and then drag it to the desired location. The Font property is set to Goudy Old Style, and the BackColor is White (Figure 5-6).

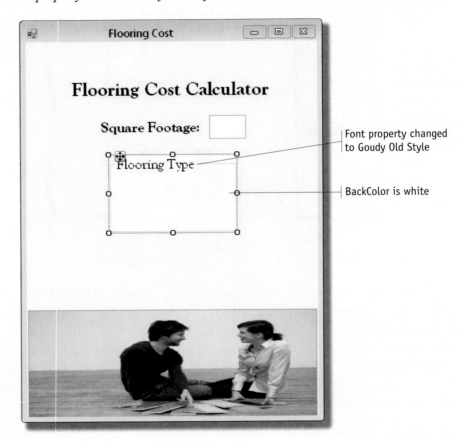

Font property changed to Goudy Old Style

BackColor is white

Eric Audras/Getty Images

FIGURE 5-6

ONLINE REINFORCEMENT

To view a video of the process in the preceding steps, visit CengageBrain.com and navigate to the resources for this title. Tap or click the link for Chapter 5 and then navigate to Video 5-2.

Grouping all options in a GroupBox object gives the user a logical visual cue. Also, when you move the GroupBox object, all its contained objects move as well.

Add the RadioButton Objects

The GroupBox object in the Flooring Cost Calculator application contains a set of RadioButton objects (see Figure 5-3 on page 276). The user may select only one type of flooring: tile, carpet, or hardwood. To place RadioButton objects within the GroupBox object, you can complete the following steps:

STEP 1   Drag one RadioButton object from the Toolbox to the GroupBox object. Drag a second RadioButton object from the Toolbox into the GroupBox object, and use blue snap lines to align and separate the RadioButton objects vertically.

The second RadioButton object is aligned vertically with a blue snap line, which separates it vertically from the first RadioButton object (Figure 5-7).

snap line

RadioButton .NET
component

RadioButton
object on form

pointer

FIGURE 5-7

Eric Audras/Getty Images

STEP 2   Release the RadioButton object to place it within the GroupBox object. Using the same technique, add a third RadioButton object.

Three RadioButton objects are placed on the form and aligned within the GroupBox object (Figure 5-8).

three RadioButton
objects

FIGURE 5-8

STEP 3   Name the RadioButton objects by selecting them one at a time, double-tapping or double-clicking in the right column of the (Name) property in the Properties window, and entering the name. The names for the radio buttons, from top to bottom, should be `radTile`, `radCarpet`, and `radHardwood`.

The (Name) property is selected. The names radTile, radCarpet, and radHardwood are entered (Figure 5-9).

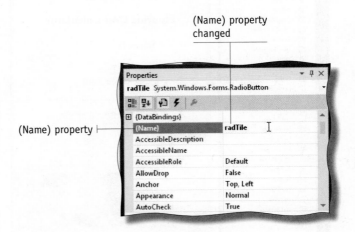

FIGURE 5-9

STEP 4   Change the Text property for each RadioButton object by double-tapping or double-clicking the right column of the Text property and typing `Tile` for the first RadioButton, `Carpet` for the second RadioButton, and `Hardwood` for the third RadioButton.

The Text property is changed to the types of flooring available: Tile, Carpet, and Hardwood (Figure 5-10).

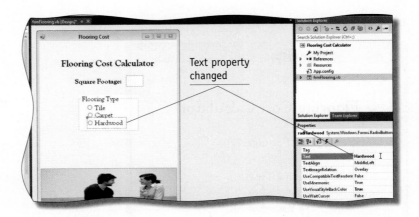

Eric Audras/Getty Images

FIGURE 5-10

A RadioButton object is best used when you have only one selection per group. What type of object would you use to select more than one option?
CheckBox objects are used with lists of options in which the user may select any number of choices. In other words, each CheckBox object is independent of all other CheckBox objects in the list, so checking one box does not uncheck the others.

Use the Checked Property of RadioButton Objects

The RadioButton objects in the Flooring Cost Calculator application allow the user to select one flooring type. When the user selects Hardwood, as shown in Figure 5-11, the radio button is selected, and the small circle in the radio button is shaded. When the Hardwood radio button is selected, its Checked property changes from False (unselected) to True (selected).

Hardwood is selected

FIGURE 5-11
Eric Audras/Getty Images

During design time, you usually set the Checked property to True for the most commonly selected radio button to save the user from having to select it. In the Flooring Cost Calculator application, homeowners select Tile most often due to the reduced cost. To cause the radTile RadioButton object to appear selected (shaded) when the program begins, you change the Checked property for the radTile RadioButton object from False to True (Figure 5-12).

Checked property is True

FIGURE 5-12

Windows Application Container Objects

The Panel object in a Windows application works like a GroupBox object. For Windows applications, Visual Basic provides four additional container objects: FlowLayoutPanel, SplitContainer, TabControl, and TableLayoutPanel. The GroupBox object is used most often; it provides several options that are not available with the Panel object. Figure 5-13 shows the differences between the GroupBox and the Panel objects.

Option	GroupBox Object	Panel Object
Have a caption	Yes	No
Have scroll bars	Yes	No
Display a labeled border	Yes	No

FIGURE 5-13

Figure 5-14 shows the Visual Basic Toolbox and a GroupBox object and Panel object in a Windows Form. Notice in the Toolbox that the GroupBox and Panel objects are in a category called Containers.

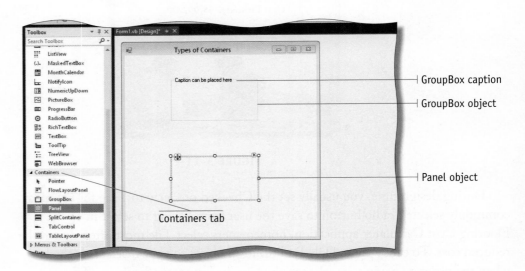

FIGURE 5-14

GroupBox and Panel objects have the same purpose of grouping RadioButtons and other objects, but they differ in their appearance. The GroupBox object in Figure 5-14 displays a border around its edges, with a text area in the upper-left portion for a caption. The Panel object has a black dashed border that does not appear when the application is executed.

Related sets of RadioButtons should be placed in separate container objects so that the user can select one radio button from each group. Always place the container object on the form first, and then drag the RadioButton objects into the container object.

The Course Sign-Up example in Figure 5-15 displays a Windows application that allows the user to sign up for a technology course. Notice the two separate groups of RadioButton objects. In the Choose Course Level GroupBox object, the user should select a course level. In the Choose Semester GroupBox object, the user should identify the semester for the course. As you can see, the user selects one radio button from the left group and one radio button from the right group.

FIGURE 5-15

Display a Message Box

In the Flooring Cost Calculator application, a message box, also called a dialog box, opens if the user does not enter the square footage of the flooring correctly. The dialog box displays an error message if the user omits the square footage or enters nonnumeric data (Figure 5-16).

FIGURE 5-16

Eric Audras/Getty Images

If the user enters a negative number for the square footage of the flooring, a message box appears and indicates that a positive number is necessary (Figure 5-17).

user entered a negative number

error message

FIGURE 5-17

Eric Audras/Getty Images

This message box reminds the user to enter the square footage of the flooring as a positive number. A message box must be closed before the application can continue. The user can continue the application by tapping or clicking the OK button in the message box.

In Visual Basic, the message in a message box window is displayed using a procedure named Show, which is found in the MessageBox class. The syntax for the statement that displays a message in a message box is shown in Figure 5-18.

General Format: Message Box Statement
MsgBox ("Message")

EXAMPLE	*RESULT*
Windows Application: MsgBox("Enter the Square Footage of Flooring")	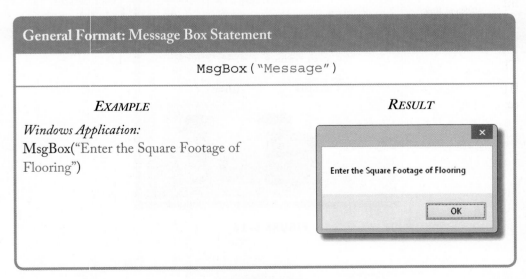

FIGURE 5-18

The string message shown in the parentheses will appear in the message box when the code is executed. The string message is considered an argument of the procedure. You will recall that an argument is a value passed to a procedure. The first argument for the MsgBox command contains the message to be printed in the message box window during execution.

The example in Figure 5-19 illustrates the code that could be used in the Calculate button click event handler. This code could be executed if the user taps or clicks the Calculate button without entering a numeric value in the Square Footage text box (Figure 5-16 on page 283).

notice the two
commas
between the
two arguments

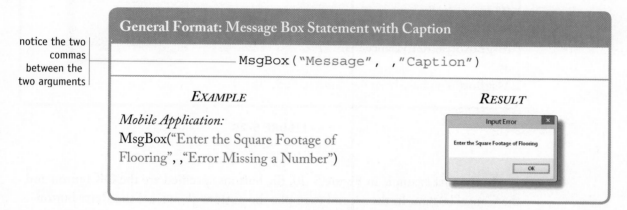

FIGURE 5-19

Display Message Box Captions

A message box can be displayed during execution with a variety of arguments. For example, by using the syntax shown in Figure 5-19, a message box can display a message and a caption in the title bar (two arguments with two commas between the arguments).

The title bar in the example in Figure 5-19 displays a caption and the message box displays a message. In many applications, the caption is used to give further information to the user.

Message Box Buttons

The general format for changing the button command from OK to another button type is shown in Figure 5-20. The button entry can be a command or a value representing a command.

General Format: Message Box Statement with Caption and Button

MsgBox("Message", Button Entry, "Caption")

EXAMPLE

Windows Application:
MsgBox("User name is missing", MsgBoxStyle.OKCancel, "Entry Error")
or
MsgBox("User name is missing", 1, "Entry Error")

Windows Application:
MsgBox("You have been disconnected", MsgBoxStyle.RetryCancel, "ISP")
or
MsgBox("You have been disconnected", 5, "ISP")

RESULT

FIGURE 5-20

In the first example in Figure 5-20, the buttons specified are the OK button and the Cancel button. In the second example, the buttons shown are the Retry button and the Cancel button.

Figure 5-21 shows all the possible entries that can be placed in the Button Entry portion of the argument passed to the Show procedure.

MsgBoxButtons Arguments	Value	Use
MsgBoxStyle.OKOnly	0	Displays an OK button — default setting
MsgBoxStyle.OKCancel	1	Displays an OK and Cancel button
MsgBoxStyle.AbortRetryIgnore	2	After a failing situation, the user can choose to Abort, Retry, or Ignore
MsgBoxStyle.YesNoCancel	3	Displays Yes, No, and Cancel buttons
MsgBoxStyle.YesNo	4	Displays Yes and No buttons
MsgBoxStyle.RetryCancel	5	After an error occurs, the user can choose to Retry or Cancel

FIGURE 5-21

Message Box Icons

In the button entry portion of the argument (the second argument), you can add a message box icon (Figure 5-22). The word "or" connects the button entry to the icon entry.

General Format: Message Box Statement with Button and Icon

```
MsgBox("Message", Button Entry or Icon Picture, "Caption")
```

EXAMPLE   *RESULT*

Windows Application:
MsgBox("User name is missing", MsgBoxStyle.
OKCancel or MsgBoxStyle.Critical, "User Name Error")
or
MsgBox("User name is missing", 1 Or 16, "User Name Error")

Windows Application:
MsgBox("You have been disconnected",
MsgBoxStyle.RetryCancel or MsgBoxStyle.Question, "ISP")
or
MsgBox("You have been disconnected", 5 Or 32, "ISP")

FIGURE 5-22

The picture icon represents the MsgBoxStyle that can be displayed as a graphic icon in the message box. Both examples in Figure 5-22 show an icon added to the message box.

The picture icon in the second argument can contain any of the entries shown in Figure 5-23.

MsgBoxStyle Icons	Value	Icon	Use
MsgBoxStyle.Critical	16		Alerts the user to an error
MsgBoxStyle.Question	32		Displays a question mark
MsgBoxStyle.Exclamation	48		Alerts the user to a possible problem
MsgBoxStyle.Information	64		Displays an information icon

FIGURE 5-23

In the general formats shown for a message box, you must follow the syntax of the statements exactly, which means the commas, quotation marks, and parentheses must be placed in the statement as shown.

You can also add values to display both the buttons and a picture icon. In Figure 5-24, the value of the message button type AbortRetryIgnore is 2 and the value of the critical icon is 16. If you add 16 plus 2, the result is 18.

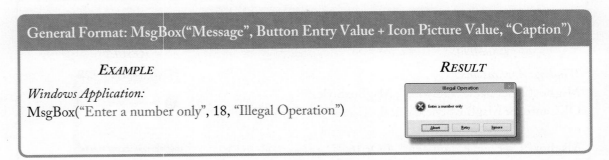

General Format: MsgBox("Message", Button Entry Value + Icon Picture Value, "Caption")

EXAMPLE	RESULT
Windows Application: MsgBox("Enter a number only", 18, "Illegal Operation")	

FIGURE 5-24

Message Box IntelliSense

When you enter the code for a message box, IntelliSense can assist you. For example, the message box you create in the following steps contains a message, caption, and buttons. To use IntelliSense to enter the code, you can complete the following steps:

STEP 1　In the code window, inside the event handler you are coding, type msg to display MsgBox in the IntelliSense list.

IntelliSense displays a list of the allowable entries (Figure 5-25). When you type msg, MsgBox is selected in the IntelliSense list.

FIGURE 5-25

STEP 2 Press the TAB key to select MsgBox in the IntelliSense list. Type the following
text: ("You have been disconnected from the Internet", m)

*The first argument for the message box is entered (Figure 5-26). IntelliSense displays a list
of allowable entries for the second argument.*

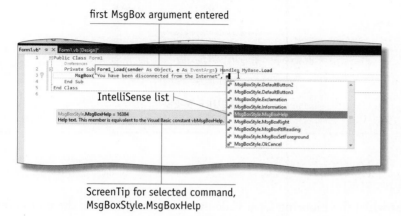

first MsgBox argument entered

IntelliSense list

ScreenTip for selected command,
MsgBoxStyle.MsgBoxHelp

FIGURE 5-26

STEP 3 Select the MsgBoxStyle.AbortRetryIgnore argument by pressing the UP
ARROW until the correct argument is highlighted. Type a comma. Then type "ISP"
and a right parenthesis.

*The MsgBoxStyle.AbortRetryIgnore argument is selected. Next, the comma and the caption
"ISP" are entered with a right parenthesis (Figure 5-27).*

Start Debugging button

statement is entered   caption is entered

FIGURE 5-27

STEP 4 Tap or click the Start Debugging button on the Standard toolbar.

The application runs, displaying the message box that shows the message, buttons, and caption (Figure 5-28).

FIGURE 5-28

String Concatenation

Recall that when the Flooring Cost Calculator application runs, the user enters the square footage of the flooring. If the user enters a number that is not greater than zero, such as –6, a message box displays "You entered –6. Enter a Positive Number", as shown in Figure 5-29.

To create the message in the message box, you can use concatenation, which you learned about in Chapter 4. In Figure 5-29, the string message is constructed by joining a string ("You entered"), a variable named decFeet that contains the entered square footage (which must be converted to a string), and a string for the final part of the message (". Enter a Positive Number"). The code in Figure 5-30 creates the message box.

message box with error message

message created using concatenation

FIGURE 5-29

Eric Audras/Getty Images

You will recall that the operator to concatenate strings is the ampersand (&). When the statement is executed, the three string elements are joined together (concatenated) to form the one string that is displayed in the message box.

```
44        MsgBox("You entered " & decFootage.ToString() & ". Enter a Positive Number", , "Input Error")
```

FIGURE 5-30

Make Decisions with Conditional Statements

In the Flooring Cost Calculator application, users can select one of three types of flooring: tile, carpet, or hardwood. The price per square foot is based on the user's choice of flooring. To select the flooring type, the user must tap or click one of three radio buttons titled Tile, Carpet, and Hardwood. Then, based on the choice, the application uses a different flooring cost.

Visual Basic uses decision structures to deal with the different conditions that occur based on the values entered into an application. A **decision structure** is one of the three fundamental control structures used in computer programming. For example, if the user taps or clicks the Carpet radio button, the flooring cost is set to $4.99 per square foot. The statement that tests the radio button is called a **conditional statement**. The condition to check is whether the Carpet radio button is selected. If so, the flooring cost is set to $4.99.

When a condition is tested in a Visual Basic program, the condition is either true or false. For example, when checking to determine if the Carpet radio button is selected, the condition can be either true (the button is checked) or false (is not checked). All conditional statements result in the tested condition being either true or false.

To implement a conditional statement and the statements that are executed when a condition is true or false, Visual Basic uses the If statement and its variety of formats. You will learn about the If statement in the following sections.

Use the If . . . Then Statement

In the sample program, an If . . . Then statement is used to determine the cost of the flooring. The simplest form of the If . . . Then statement is shown in Figure 5-31.

```
5        If condition Then
6            Statement(s) executed when condition is true
7        End If
8
```

FIGURE 5-31

In Figure 5-31, when the condition tested in the If statement on line 5 is true, the statement(s) between the If and the End If keywords will be executed. If the condition is not true, no statements between the If and End If keywords will be executed, and program execution will continue with the statement(s) after the End If statement.

Visual Basic automatically indents statements to be executed when a condition is true or not true to indicate which lines of code are within the conditional If . . . Then structure. This is why the statement on line 6 in Figure 5-31 on the previous page is indented. The End If keywords terminate the If . . . Then block of code. After executing the If . . . Then block, execution continues with any statements that follow the closing End If statement.

Relational Operators

In Figure 5-31, the condition portion of the If . . . Then statement means a condition is tested to determine if it is true or false. The conditions that can be tested are as follows:

1. Is one value equal to another value?
2. Is one value not equal to another value?
3. Is one value greater than another value?
4. Is one value less than another value?
5. Is one value greater than or equal to another value?
6. Is one value less than or equal to another value?

To test these conditions, Visual Basic provides relational operators that are used within the conditional statement to express the relationship being tested. Figure 5-32 shows these relational operators.

Relational Operator		Meaning	Example	Resulting Condition
1	=	Equal to	8 = 8	True
2	<>	Not equal to	6 <> 6	False
3	>	Greater than	7 > 9	False
4	<	Less than	4 < 6	True
5	> =	Greater than or equal to	3 > = 3	True
6	< =	Less than or equal to	7 < = 5	False

FIGURE 5-32

A condition tested using a relational operator is evaluated as true or false. Example 1 tests whether 8 is equal to 8. Because they are equal, the resulting condition is true. Example 2 tests whether 6 is not equal to 6. Because they are equal, the resulting condition is false. Similarly, Example 5 tests whether 3 is greater than or equal to 3. Because they are equal, the resulting condition is true.

As an example of using a conditional operator, consider the following problem, in which an If statement is used to determine if someone is old enough to vote. If the value in the intAge variable is greater than or equal to 18, then the person is old enough to vote. If not, the person is not old enough to vote. The If . . . Then statement to test this condition is shown in Figure 5-33.

```
8        If intAge >= 18 Then
9                lblVotingEligibility.Text = "You are old enough to vote"
10       End If
```

FIGURE 5-33

In Figure 5-33, if the value in the intAge variable is greater than or equal to 18, the string value "You are old enough to vote" is assigned to the Text property of the lblVotingEligibility Label object. If not, then no processing occurs based on the conditional statement, and any statement(s) following the End If keywords will be executed.

You can see in Figure 5-33 that several keywords are required in an If . . . Then statement. The word If must be the first item. Next, the condition(s) to be tested are stated, followed by the word Then. This keyword is required in an If statement.

The End If keywords follow the statements to be executed when the condition is true. This entry is also required. It signals to the Visual Basic compiler that the statements following it must be executed regardless of the result of the conditional statement; that is, the End If keywords are the last element within the If block, and no subsequent statements depend on the If block for execution.

To enter the If . . . Then statement shown in Figure 5-33, you can complete the following steps:

STEP 1   With the insertion point in the correct location in the code, type if and then press the SPACEBAR.

The statement begins with the word If (Figure 5-34). The If command is displayed in blue because it is a Visual Basic keyword. You can type uppercase or lowercase letters.

If is entered

FIGURE 5-34

STEP 2 Type `inta` to select the variable named intAge in the IntelliSense list. Type `>=18` as the condition to be tested. Press the ENTER key.

The If . . . Then statement is entered in the code window (Figure 5-35). When the ENTER key is pressed, Visual Basic adds the keyword Then to the end of the If statement line of code and inserts spaces between the elements of the statement for ease of reading. In addition, Visual Basic inserts the End If keywords following a blank line. Notice the keywords Then and End If are capitalized and displayed in blue.

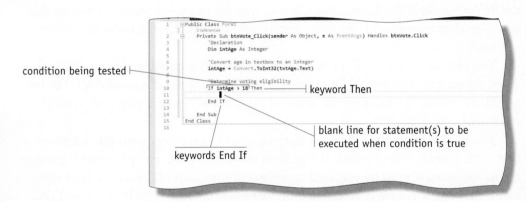

condition being tested

keyword Then

blank line for statement(s) to be executed when condition is true

keywords End If

FIGURE 5-35

STEP 3 On the blank line (line 11 in Figure 5-35), enter the statement that should be executed when the condition is true. To place the message "You are old enough to vote" in the Text property of the lblVotingEligibility Label object, insert the code shown in Figure 5-33 on the previous page. Remember to use IntelliSense to reference the lblVotingEligibility Label object.

The resulting statement is entered between the If and End If keywords (Figure 5-36). Notice that Visual Basic automatically indents the line for ease of reading. The blank line allows you to enter more statements. If you have no further statements, you can press the DELETE key to delete the blank line in the If . . . Then statement.

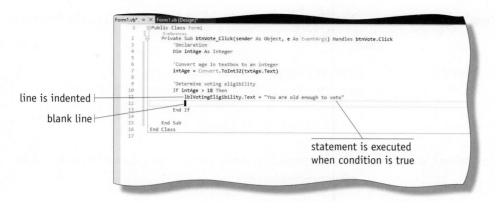

line is indented

blank line

statement is executed when condition is true

FIGURE 5-36

Compare Strings

You also can write an If . . . Then statement to compare string values using the relational operators shown in Figure 5-32 on page 292. A string value comparison compares each character in two strings, starting with the first character in each string. For example, in the two strings in Figure 5-37, the comparison begins with the first character (a) in each string. Because the characters are equal, the comparison continues with the second character in each string, which is b. Because these characters are equal, the comparison continues with the third character in each string, c. Because all three characters are equal, the strings are considered equal, and the resulting condition from the If statement is true.

```
13      Dim String1 As String = "abc"
14      Dim String2 As String = "abc"
15
16      If String1 = String2 Then
17          lblStringTest.Text = "Equal"
18      End If
```

FIGURE 5-37

All characters found in strings, including letters, numbers, and special characters, are in a sequence based on how the characters are coded internally on the computer. In Visual Studio 2015, characters are stored and sequenced in Unicode, which is a coding methodology that can accommodate more than 60,000 characters. Appendix A shows the Unicode sequence for the standard keyboard characters. You will find that numbers have lower Unicode values than uppercase letters and uppercase letters have lower values than lowercase letters.

Using the If . . . Then statement, the following comparisons produce the following resulting conditions:

Example 1:

```
Dim String1 As String = "Powder"
Dim String2 As String = "Power"

If String1 < String2 Then
```

Resulting Condition: True because in the fourth character position, the letter d is less than the letter e.

Example 2:
```
Dim String1 As String = "6"
Dim String2 As String = "T"

If String1 < String2 Then
```

Resulting Condition: True because in a string comparison, a number is less than an uppercase letter.

Example 3:
```
Dim String1 As String = "12"
Dim String2 As String = "9"

If String1 < String2 Then
```

Resulting Condition: True because in a string comparison, the characters in the first position of the string are compared first. Because the value 1 in String1 is less than the value 9 in String2, the entire value in String1 is considered less than the value in String2.

Example 4:
```
Dim String1 As String = "anchor"
Dim String2 As String = "Anchorline"

If String1 > String2 Then
```

Resulting Condition: True because a lowercase letter (the a in the first position of String1) is considered greater than an uppercase letter (the A in the first position of String2).

Compare Different Data Types

Every type of data available in Visual Basic can be compared. Different numeric types can be compared to each other using an If statement. A single string character can be compared to a Char data type. The following examples illustrate some of the allowable comparisons.

Example 1: Decimal compared to Double

```
If decQuarterlySales > dblSalesQuota Then
```

If decQuarterlySales = 110,324.54 and dblSalesQuota = 112,435.54, the condition is false.

Example 2: *Decimal compared to Integer*

```
If decTirePressureReading > intTirePressureMaximum Then
```

If decTirePressureReading = 30.21 and intTirePressureMaximum = 30, the condition is true.

Example 3: *Double compared to Integer*

```
If dblCurrentTemperature >= intHeatDanger Then
```

If dblCurrentTemperature = 94.543 and intHeatDanger = 98, the condition is false.

Example 4: *String compared to Char*

```
If strChemistryGrade < chrPassingGrade Then
```

If strChemistryGrade = "B" and chrPassingGrade = "C", the condition is true.

Visual Basic allows comparisons between most data types. If you are unsure whether a comparison can be made, write an If statement to ensure that the comparison is working properly.

Use the If . . . Then . . . Else Statement

An If . . . Then statement executes a set of instructions if a condition is true. If the condition is false, the instructions between the If statement and the End If statement are not executed and program execution continues with the statement(s) following the End If statement.

In many applications, the logic requires one set of instructions to be executed if a condition is true and another set of instructions to be executed if a condition is false. For example, a program requirement could specify that if a student's test score is 70 or greater, the message "You passed the examination" should be displayed, while if the test score is less than 70, the message "You failed the examination" should be displayed.

To execute one set of instructions if a condition is true and another set of instructions if the condition is false, you can use the If . . . Then . . . Else statement. Figure 5-38 illustrates the syntax of the If . . . Then . . . Else statement.

```
16        If condition Then
17             Statement(s) executed if condition is true
18        Else
19             Statement(s) executed if condition is false
20        End If
```

FIGURE 5-38

If the condition tested by the If statement is true, the statement(s) between the Then keyword and the Else keyword will be executed. If the condition tested is false, the statement(s) between the Else keyword and the End If keywords will be executed.

The example in Figure 5-39 shows the use of the If . . . Then . . . Else statement to calculate student fees by testing the student's status.

statement is executed if
student is a graduate

```
27          If strStudentStatus = "Graduate" Then
28              decStudentFees = decGraduateFee * intNumberOfUnits
29          Else
30              decStudentFees = decUndergraduateFee * intNumberOfUnits
31          End If
```

statement is executed if
student is not a graduate

FIGURE 5-39

HEADS UP

A condition cannot be true and false at the same time, so both statements for a true condition and statements for a false condition cannot be executed based on a single comparison.

If the student is in graduate school, the student fees are calculated by multiplying the graduate fee by the number of units. If the student is not a graduate student, the student fees are calculated by multiplying the undergraduate fee by the number of units. Notice that a student cannot be both an undergraduate and a graduate student, so either the statement following the Then keyword will be executed or the statement following the Else keyword will be executed.

Compare to an Arithmetic Expression

An If statement can compare an arithmetic expression to a constant or other data type. For example, in Figure 5-40, the withdrawals from a bank account are compared to the value obtained by adding the current balance to deposits and then subtracting account charges.

```
41          If decWithdrawals > decCurrentBalance + decDeposits - decAccountCharges Then
42              lblAccountStatus.Text = "Overdrawn"
43          Else
44              lblAccountStatus.Text = "Balance is Positive"
45          End If
```

FIGURE 5-40

In Figure 5-40, if the value in the decWithdrawals variable is greater than the current balance plus the deposits minus the account charges, the Text property of the lblAccountStatus Label object is set to Overdrawn. If the value in decWithdrawals is less than or equal to the value from the arithmetic expression, the message "Balance is Positive" is placed in the Text property of the lblAccountStatus Label object. Notice that the arithmetic expression is evaluated prior to the comparison. If the condition is true, the statement between the Then and Else keywords is executed. If the condition is false, the statement between the Else and End If keywords is executed.

Complex logic problems might require a more complex structure than the If . . . Then . . . Else logic structure. For example, consider the following logical problem that must be solved in a computer program:

An online store charges a shipping fee based on the dollar amount of the order being shipped. The rules are as follows:

1. If the order amount is above $500, the shipping cost is $30.
2. If the order amount is more than $400 and not greater than $500, the shipping cost is $25.
3. If the order amount is more than $200 and not greater than $400, the shipping cost is $20.
4. If the order amount is equal to or less than $200, the shipping cost is $15.

When one of the conditions is found to be true, the rest of the conditions are not tested because the correct condition has been found. To solve this problem, you should think this way:

1. If the order amount is greater than $500.00, then the shipping cost is $30.00, and no more processing is needed to determine the shipping cost.
2. If, however, the order amount is not greater than $500.00, you must check further to see if it is greater than $400.00 (400.01 through 500.00). If so, the shipping cost is $25.00.
3. If the order amount is not greater than $400.00, the next step is to check whether it is greater than $200.00. In other words, check within the range of $201.00 to $400.00. If this is true, the shipping cost is $20.00.
4. If none of the above is true, then the order amount must be less than or equal to $200. In this case, the shipping cost is $15.00.

As you can see, a simple If . . . Then . . . Else statement could not solve this logic problem because the structure tests only a single condition and specifies the processing based on whether the condition is true or false. For a problem in which multiple conditions must be tested, the If . . . Then . . . ElseIf statement might be appropriate. The general format of the If . . . Then . . . ElseIf statement is shown in Figure 5-41.

```
105        If decOrderAmount > 500D Then
106            Statement(s) executed if condition is true
107        ElseIf decOrderAmount > 400D Then
108            Statement(s) executed if condition is true
109        ElseIf decOrderAmount > 200D Then
110            Statement(s) executed if condition is true
111        ElseIf decOrderAmount > 0D Then
112            Statement(s) executed if condition is true
113        End If
```

FIGURE 5-41

HEADS UP

When testing conditions like those in the example in Figure 5-41, make sure that you do not leave a number out of the range of numbers being tested. For example, if one ElseIf statement tests decOrderAmount > 400.00 and the next ElseIf statement tests < 400.00, the value 400.00 has not been tested and the program will not properly process the value 400.00.

Once a condition is true in the code in Figure 5-41 on the previous page, Visual Basic bypasses the rest of the ElseIf statements. For example, assume the order amount is $455. The first condition tests whether the order amount is greater than 500. The first condition would test false because 455 is not greater than 500.

Next, the ElseIf entry will test whether 455 is greater than 400. Because the value 455 is greater than 400, the condition is true and the statement(s) on line 108 will be executed. The remaining ElseIf statements will not be evaluated because the true condition has been found.

Separate If . . . Then statements are not used in the example in Figure 5-41 because each condition would have to be tested even though a condition had already been found to be true. When using an If . . . Then . . . ElseIf statement, any remaining conditions are not tested after a condition is found to be true, making the process faster and more efficient.

Trailing Else Statements

You may want to include a trailing Else statement at the end of an If . . . Then . . . ElseIf conditional statement to handle a condition that does not meet any of the previous conditions tested. In the example in Figure 5-42, the code is determining whether the user is eligible for Social Security benefits. If the user's age is greater than or equal to 65, the user receives full benefits. If the user's age is between 0 and 65, the user is not eligible for benefits.

```
115        If intAge >= 65 Then
116            lblSocialSecurity.Text = "Full Benefits"
117        ElseIf intAge > 0 Then
118            lblSocialSecurity.Text = "Not Eligible for Benefits"
119        Else
120            lblSocialSecurity.Text = "Invalid Age"
121        End If
```

FIGURE 5-42

In Figure 5-42, the statement on line 120 that follows the trailing Else statement on line 119 is executed if the number in the intAge variable does not meet the conditions stated in the previous If statements. For example, if the intAge variable contains a negative value such as −12, the Text property of the lblSocialSecurity Label object will be set to "Invalid Age."

Nested If Statements

At times, more than one decision has to be made to determine what processing must occur. For example, if one condition is true, a second condition may need to be tested before the correct code is executed. To test a second condition only after determining that a first condition is true (or false), you must place an If statement within another If statement. When you place one If statement within another one, the inner If statement is said to be nested within the outer If Statement. The syntax of a nested If statement is shown in Figure 5-43.

nested If
statement –
(first inner
If statement)

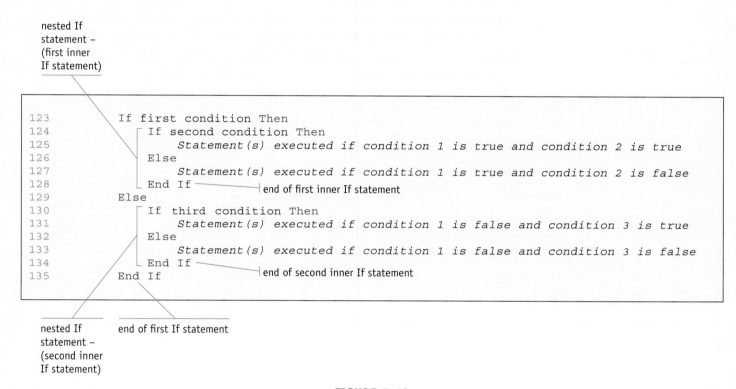

```
123        If first condition Then
124            If second condition Then
125                Statement(s) executed if condition 1 is true and condition 2 is true
126            Else
127                Statement(s) executed if condition 1 is true and condition 2 is false
128            End If              end of first inner If statement
129        Else
130            If third condition Then
131                Statement(s) executed if condition 1 is false and condition 3 is true
132            Else
133                Statement(s) executed if condition 1 is false and condition 3 is false
134            End If              end of second inner If statement
135        End If
```

nested If   end of first If statement
statement –
(second inner
If statement)

FIGURE 5-43

In Figure 5-43, if the first condition tested is true, the statements following the keyword Then are executed. The statement to be executed when the first condition is true is another If statement (line 124) that tests the second condition. This second If statement is said to be a nested If statement or an inner If statement. If the second condition is true, the program executes the statement(s) on line 125 following the keyword Then for the first inner If statement. If the second condition is not true, the program executes the statement(s) on line 127 following the keyword Else for the first inner If statement. The End If entry (line 128) follows the first inner If statement, indicating the end of the effect of the first inner If statement.

If the first condition is not true, then the program executes the statements following the keyword Else on line 129 for the first If statement. The statement to be executed when the first condition is not true is an If statement that tests the third condition (line 130). If the third condition is true, the program executes the statement(s) on line 131 following the Then keyword of the second inner If statement. Finally, if the second inner If statement that tests the third condition is false, the statements on line 133 are executed.

To illustrate a nested If statement, assume a college has the following admissions policy: If an applying student has a GPA (grade point average) greater than 3.5 and a score greater than 1000 on the SAT college entrance exam, then that student is granted admission. If an applying student has a GPA greater than 3.5 but an SAT score of 1000 or lower, the student is advised to retake the SAT exam. If an applying student has a GPA of 3.5 or lower but an SAT score greater than 1200, the student is granted probationary admission, which means she must achieve a 2.5 GPA in the first semester of college. If an applying student has a GPA lower than 3.5 and an SAT score of 1200 or lower, the student is denied admission. The nested If statement to process this admission policy is shown in Figure 5-44.

```
140        If decGPA > 3.5D Then
141            If intSatScore > 1000 Then
142                lblAdmissionStatus.Text = "You have earned admission"
143            Else
144                lblAdmissionStatus.Text = "Retake the SAT exam"
145            End If
146        Else
147            If intSatScore > 1200 Then
148                lblAdmissionStatus.Text = "You have earned probationary admission"
149            Else
150                lblAdmissionStatus.Text = "You have been denied admission"
151            End If
152        End If
```

FIGURE 5-44

Notice in Figure 5-44 that the test for greater than 1000 on the SAT (line 141) must take place only after the test for a GPA greater than 3.5 (line 140), because the test for greater than 1000 is required only after the program determines that the GPA is greater than 3.5. Therefore, a nested If statement is required. In addition, the test for greater than 1200 (line 147) should occur only after the program determines that the GPA is less than 3.5. As you can see, you should use a nested If statement when a condition must be tested only after another condition has been tested.

Other Nested If Configurations

You can use nested If statements in a variety of forms. Assume, for example, that a school's admissions policy is as follows: If an applying student has a GPA greater than 3.5 and an SAT score greater than 1100, then that student is granted admission. If an applying student has a GPA greater than 3.5 but an SAT score of 1100 or lower, the student is advised to retake the SAT exam. If an applying student has a GPA of 3.5 or lower, the student is denied admission. The nested If statement in Figure 5-45 solves this logic problem.

```
154            If decGPA > 3.5D Then
155                If intSatScore > 1100 Then
156                    lblAdmissionStatus.Text = "You have earned admission"
157                Else
158                    lblAdmissionStatus.Text = "Retake the SAT exam"
159                End If
160            Else
161                lblAdmissionStatus.Text = "You have been denied admission"
162            End If
```

FIGURE 5-45

In Figure 5-45, if the GPA is greater than 3.5, then the first inner If statement on line 155 is executed to determine if the SAT score is greater than 1100. If so, the person has earned admission. If not, the person is advised to retake the SAT exam. If the GPA is not greater than 3.5, the student is denied admission. Notice that an If statement does not follow the Else keyword on line 160. An inner If statement need not follow both the If and the Else keywords.

Sometimes, after a condition is found to be true, a statement must be executed before the inner If statement is executed. For example, assume that if a student's GPA is greater than 3.5, then the student should be informed that her GPA is acceptable for admission. The code in Figure 5-46 implements this condition.

```
164            If decGPA > 3.5D Then
165                lblGPAStatus.Text = "Your GPA is acceptable"
166                If intSatScore > 1100 Then
167                    lblAdmissionStatus.Text = "You have earned admission"
168                Else
169                    lblAdmissionStatus.Text = "Retake the SAT exam"
170                End If
171            Else
172                lblGPAStatus.Text = "Your GPA is not acceptable"
173                lblAdmissionStatus.Text = "You have been denied admission"
174            End If
```

FIGURE 5-46

On line 165 in Figure 5-46, the message "Your GPA is acceptable" is assigned to the Text property of the lblGPAStatus Label object before checking the SAT score. As you can see, after the first condition has been tested, one or more statements can be executed prior to executing the inner If statement. This holds true for the Else portion of the If statement as well.

Match If, Else, and End If Entries

When you write a nested If statement, the inner If statement must be fully contained within the outer If statement. To accomplish this, you must ensure that each Else entry has a corresponding If entry, and an inner If statement must be terminated with an End If entry before either the Else entry or the End If entry for the outer If statement. If you code the nested If statement incorrectly, one or more of its entries will be shown with a blue squiggly line, indicating an error in the structure of the statement.

You also must place the correct executing statements with the If and Else statements within the nested If statement. For example, in Figure 5-47, the code is incorrect because the statements following the Else statements have been switched.

```
164        If decGPA > 3.5D Then
165            lblGPAStatus.Text = "Your GPA is acceptable"
166            If intSatScore > 1100 Then
167                lblAdmissionStatus.Text = "You have earned admission"
168            Else
169                lblAdmissionStatus.Text = "You have been denied admission"
170            End If
171        Else
172            lblGPAStatus Text = "Your GPA is not acceptable"          incorrect
173            lblAdmissionStatus.Text = "Retake the SAT exam"            statements
174        End If
```

FIGURE 5-47

You must be precise when placing the executing statements in the nested If statement. It is easy to miscode a nested If statement.

Nest Three or More Levels of If Statements

If statements are not limited to two levels of nesting. Three or more levels can be included in a nested If statement, although the statement can become difficult to understand and code. If more than two levels are required to solve a logic problem, great care must be taken to prevent errors such as the one shown in Figure 5-47.

Test the Status of a RadioButton Object in Code

In the Flooring Cost Calculator application, the user selects one RadioButton in the GroupBox object to select the flooring type. The code must check each RadioButton to determine if it has been selected by the user. When the user selects a radio button, its Checked property is changed from False to True. In addition, the Checked property for other RadioButton objects in the GroupBox object is set to False. This Checked property can be tested in an If statement to determine if the RadioButton object has been selected.

To test the status of the Checked property for the radTile RadioButton object, a programmer can write the general statement shown in Figure 5-48.

```
237          If radTile.Checked Then
238              Statement(s) to be executed if radio button is checked
239          End If
```

FIGURE 5-48

Notice in Figure 5-48 that the RadioButton property is not compared using a relational operator. Instead, when a program tests a property that can contain only True or False, only the property must be specified in the If statement. When the property contains True, then the If statement is considered true, and when the property contains False, then the If statement is considered false.

Test Radio Buttons with the If . . . Then . . . ElseIf Statement

When a program contains multiple RadioButton objects in a Panel object or a GroupBox object, only one of the radio buttons can be selected. The If . . . Then . . . ElseIf statement is used to check multiple radio buttons because once the checked radio button is detected, checking the remaining radio buttons is unnecessary.

In the Flooring Cost Calculator application, the user taps or clicks one of three radio buttons (Tile, Carpet, or Hardwood) to select the type of flooring used for flooring. When using an If . . . Then . . . ElseIf statement to check the status of the radio buttons, the most likely choice should be checked first. Thus, the fewest number of tests are performed. Therefore, the first If statement should test the status of the Tile radio button (radTile). If the radTile button is checked, the Cost Per Square Foot should be set to the value in the decTileCost variable, which is 4.49. No further testing should be done (Figure 5-49).

```
31              If radTile.Checked Then
32                  decCostPerSquareFoot = decTileCost
33              ElseIf radCarpet.Checked Then
34                  decCostPerSquareFoot = decCarpetCost
35              ElseIf radHardwood.Checked Then
36                  decCostPerSquareFoot = decHardwoodCost
37              End If
```

FIGURE 5-49

If the radTile button is not checked, then the radCarpet button should be tested. If radCarpet is checked, the Cost Per Square Foot should be set to the value in the decCarpetCost variable (4.99), and no further testing should be done. If the radCarpet button is not checked, then the radHardwood button should be tested. If the other two buttons are not checked, then the radHardwood button must be checked because one of the three must be checked. The Cost Per Foot will be set to the value in the decHardwoodCost variable (7.49).

As you learned earlier, during design time you can set the Checked property to True for the most frequently selected RadioButton to save the user from having to select it. In the Flooring Cost Calculator application, after the Cost Per Square Foot has been determined and the Cost Estimate has been calculated, the user can tap or click the Clear button to clear the Square Footage text box, clear the Cost Estimate, and reset the radio buttons so that the Tile button is selected. The code to reset the radio buttons is shown in Figure 5-50.

```
62          radTile.Checked = True
63          radCarpet.Checked = False
64          radHardwood.Checked = False
```

FIGURE 5-50

In Figure 5-50, the Checked property for the radTile RadioButton object is set to True using the same method you have seen in previous chapters for setting an object property. Similarly, the Checked property for the other two RadioButton objects is set to False. As a result of these statements, the Tile radio button will be selected in the user interface, and the Carpet and Hardwood radio buttons will not be selected.

Block-Level Scope

In Chapter 4, you learned that the scope of a variable is defined by where it is declared within a program. For example, if a variable is declared within an event handler, then only code within that event handler can reference the variable. Code in one event handler within a program cannot reference a variable declared in another event handler.

Within an event handler, an If . . . Then . . . Else statement is considered a block of code. To review, this statement is the code beginning with the If keyword and ending with the corresponding Else keyword or the code beginning with the Else keyword and ending with the End If keywords. Variables can be declared within the block of code, but they can be referenced only within the block of code where they are declared. For example, variables defined within an If . . . Then block of code fall out of scope (cannot be referenced) outside that block of code. To illustrate this concept, the code in Figure 5-51 shows a variable named intYears declared within an If . . . Then block of code.

```
11          If intAge < 18 Then
12              Dim intYears As Integer
13              intYears = 18 - intAge
14              lblMessage.Text = "You can vote in " & intYears & " years(s)."
15          Else
16              lblMessage.Text = "You can vote!"
17          End If
```

FIGURE 5-51

On line 12 in Figure 5-51, the variable intYears is declared as an Integer variable. On line 13, the variable is used in an arithmetic statement to receive the result of the calculation 18 − intAge, which determines the number of years less than 18 that is stored in intAge. The result in intYears is concatenated with literals in the statement on line 14. The intYears variable can be referenced in any statement between the If keyword and the Else keyword. It cannot be referenced anywhere else in the program, not even in the Else portion of the If statement. When a statement referencing the intYears variable is written outside the area between the If keyword and the Else keyword, a compilation error will occur and the program will not compile and execute.

Although the scope of the intYears variable in Figure 5-51 is between the If keyword on line 11 and the Else keyword on line 15, you should realize that the variable itself perseveres during the execution of the event handler procedure. Therefore, if the If statement in Figure 5-51 is executed a second time, the value in the intYears variable will be the same as when the If statement was completed the first time. To avoid unexpected results when the If statement is executed the second time, you should initialize block variables at the beginning of the block. In Figure 5-51, the statement on line 13 sets the value in the intYears variable immediately after it is declared, which is good programming technique.

Use Logical Operators

The If statements you have seen thus far test a single condition. In many cases, more than one condition must be true or one of several conditions must be true to execute the statements in the Then portion of the If . . . Then . . . Else statement. When more than one condition is included in an If . . . Then . . . Else statement, the conditions are called a **compound condition**. For example, consider the following business traveling rule: "If the flight costs less than $300 and the hotel is less than $120.00 per night, the business trip is approved." In this case, both conditions—flight less than $300 *and* hotel less than $120.00 per night—must be true for the trip to be approved. If either condition is not true, then the business trip is not approved.

To create an If statement that processes the business traveling rule, you must use a **logical operator**. The most common set of logical operators are listed in Figure 5-52.

Logical Operator	Meaning
And	All conditions tested in the If statement must be true
Or	One condition tested in the If statement must be true
Not	Negates a condition

FIGURE 5-52

For the business traveling rule, you should use the And logical operator.

Use the And Logical Operator

The **And logical operator** allows you to combine two or more conditions into a compound condition that can be tested with an If statement. If any of the conditions stated in the compound condition is false, the compound condition is considered false, and the statements following the Else portion of the If statement will be executed. The code in Figure 5-53 uses the And logical operator to implement the business traveling rule.

```
137        If decFlightCost < 300D And decHotelCost < 120D Then
138            lblTripMessage.Text = "Your business trip is approved"
139        Else
140            lblTripMessage.Text = "Your business trip is denied"
141        End If
```

FIGURE 5-53

In Figure 5-53, both conditions in the compound condition (flight cost less than 300 and hotel cost less than 120) must be true for the business trip to be approved. If one of the conditions is false, then the compound condition is considered false and the If statement would return a false indication. For example, if the flight cost is 300 or more, the trip will not be approved regardless of the hotel cost. Similarly, if the hotel cost is 120 or more, the trip will not be approved regardless of the flight cost. This process is illustrated in Figure 5-54.

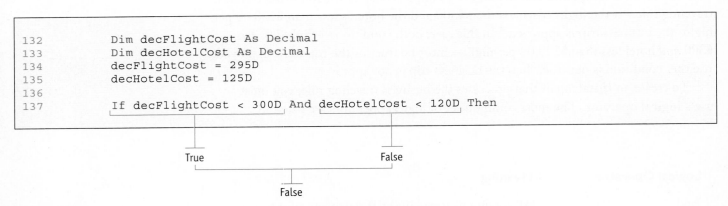

FIGURE 5-54

In Figure 5-54, the flight cost is 295, so it is less than 300 and the first part of the compound condition is true. Following the And logical operator, the hotel cost (125) is not less than 120. Therefore, the second part of the compound condition is false. When either condition is false with the And logical operator, the If statement considers the compound condition to be false. The result of the If statement in Figure 5-54 is that the compound condition is considered to be false.

Use the Or Logical Operator

When the **Or logical operator** is used to connect two or more conditions, the compound condition is true if any tested condition is true. Even if four conditional statements are included in the compound condition, only one conditional statement in the compound condition must be true for the entire statement to be considered true.

As an example, assume a college requires each student to have either at least a 3.5 GPA or at least a 1080 score on the SAT exam to be accepted for enrollment. If the student meets one or both conditions, the student is accepted. The If statement in Figure 5-55, which uses the Or logical operator, will solve this problem.

```
147         If decGPA >= 3.5D Or intSATScore >= 1080 Then
148             lblAcceptance.Text = "You have been accepted"
149         Else
150             lblAcceptance.Text = "You are not accepted"
151         End If
```

FIGURE 5-55

In Figure 5-55, if the decGPA is 3.2 but the intSATScore is 1130, the compound condition would be considered true because at least one of its conditions (intSATScore >= 1080) is true (Figure 5-56).

FIGURE 5-56

Use the Not Logical Operator

The **Not logical operator** allows you to state conditions that are best expressed in a negative way. In essence, the Not logical operator reverses the logical value of a condition on which it operates. For example, if a shoe store sells shoes under size 14 from its showroom but requires special orders for larger sizes, the code could use the Not logical operator shown in Figure 5-57 to negate the condition in the statement.

```
155          If Not decShoeSize >= 14 Then
156              lblOrderPolicy.Text = "Showroom shoe style available"
157          Else
158              lblOrderPolicy.Text = "Special order needed"
159          End If
```

FIGURE 5-57

The statement in Figure 5-57 works, but the use of the Not logical operator makes the If statement somewhat difficult to understand. Generally, a statement that avoids using the Not logical operator is more easily understood. For example, the code in Figure 5-58 accomplishes the same task as the code in Figure 5-57 and is easier to understand.

```
162          If decShoeSize < 14 Then
163              lblOrderPolicy.Text = "Showroom shoe style available"
164          Else
165              lblOrderPolicy.Text = "Special order needed"
166          End If
```

FIGURE 5-58

Other Logical Operators

The Visual Basic programming language provides three other logical operators, as shown in Figure 5-59.

Logical Operator	Meaning
Xor	When one condition in the compound condition is true, but not both, the compound condition is true
AndAlso	As soon as a condition is found to be false, no further conditions are tested and the compound condition is false
OrElse	As soon as a condition is found to be true, no further conditions are tested and the compound condition is true

FIGURE 5-59

Order of Operations for Logical Operators

You can combine more than one logical operator in the same If . . . Then statement. In an If statement, arithmetic operators are evaluated first, relational operators are evaluated next, and logical operators are evaluated last. The order of operations for logical operators is shown in Figure 5-60.

Logical Operator	Order
Not	Highest Precedence
And, AndAlso	Next Precedence
Or, OrElse, Xor	Last Precedence

FIGURE 5-60

In most cases, if a developer uses multiple relational or logical operators in an If statement, the order of precedence should be established through the use of parentheses to clarify the sequence of evaluation. As in arithmetic expressions, conditional expressions within parentheses are evaluated before conditional expressions outside parentheses.

Select Case Statement

In some programming applications, different operations can occur based on the value in a single field. For example, in Figure 5-61, the user enters the number of the day in the week and the program displays the name of the day. The program must evaluate the number of the day value and display the name of the correct day.

FIGURE 5-61

In Figure 5-61, if the number of the day is 1, then the value Monday should be displayed. If the number of the day is 2, then the value Tuesday should be displayed, and so on. If the number of the day is 6 or 7, then the value Weekend should be displayed. If the user does not enter a value of 1 through 7, the user should be prompted to do so.

To solve this problem, a series of If . . . Then . . . ElseIf statements could be used, but an easier and clearer way to solve the problem is to use the Select Case statement.

When using a Select Case statement, the value in a single field, such as the day number, is evaluated. Based on the value in the field, a distinct action is taken. In this case, the name of the day is displayed.

A general example of the Select Case statement is shown in Figure 5-62.

```
168        Select Case Test Expression
169            Case First Expression
170                Statement(s) for First Case
171            Case Second Expression
172                Statement(s) for Second Case
173            Case Third Expression
174                Statement(s) for Third Case
175            Case Else
176                Statement(s) for when the Case Conditions do not match the
177                    test expressions above
178        End Select
```

FIGURE 5-62

The code for the Determine Day of Week application is shown in Figure 5-63.

```
13        Select Case intDayNumber
14            Case 1
15                lblDayOfWeek.Text = "Monday"
16            Case 2
17                lblDayOfWeek.Text = "Tuesday"
18            Case 3
19                lblDayOfWeek.Text = "Wednesday"
20            Case 4
21                lblDayOfWeek.Text = "Thursday"
22            Case 5
23                lblDayOfWeek.Text = "Friday"
24            Case 6
25                lblDayOfWeek.Text = "Weekend"
26            Case 7
27                lblDayOfWeek.Text = "Weekend"
28            Case Else
29                lblDayOfWeek.Text = "Enter 1 through 7"
30        End Select
```

FIGURE 5-63

The Select Case statement begins with the Select Case command. The test expression specifies the value or variable to be tested in the Select Case statement. In Figure 5-63, the variable is intDayNumber. So, when the Select Case statement is executed, each of the cases will be compared to the value in the intDayNumber variable.

Each Case statement specifies the value for which the test expression is checked. For example, the first Case statement on line 14 in Figure 5-63 specifies the value 1. If the value in the variable intDayNumber is equal to 1, the program executes the statement following the first Case statement up to the second Case statement (line 16). In Figure 5-63, the assignment statement on line 15 that sets the Text property of lblDayOfWeek to Monday is executed if the value in intDayNumber is equal to 1. More than one statement can follow a Case statement.

If the expression following the first Case statement is not true, then the next Case statement is evaluated. In Figure 5-63, the Case statement on line 16 checks if the value in intDayNumber is equal to 2. If so, the Text property of lblDayOfWeek is set to Tuesday. This process continues through the remainder of the Case statements.

The Case Else statement on line 28 is an optional entry that includes all conditions not specifically tested in the other Case statements. In Figure 5-63, if the value in the intDayNumber variable is not equal to 1 through 7, then the statement following the Case Else statement is executed. While not required, good programming practice dictates that the Case Else statement should be used so that all cases are accounted for and the program performs a specific action regardless of the value found in the test expression.

The End Select statement is required to end the Select Case statement. When you enter the Select Case statement in Visual Studio 2015, IntelliSense automatically includes the End Select statement.

Select Case Test Expressions

The example in Figure 5-63 on the previous page used an integer as the test expression value, but a value of any data type can be used in the test expression. For example, the test expression in Figure 5-64 uses the Text property of the txtStudentMajor TextBox object as a string value.

```
217        Select Case txtStudentMajor.Text
218            Case "Accounting"
219                lblDepartment.Text = "Business"
220            Case "Marketing"
221                lblDepartment.Text = "Business"
222            Case "Electrical Engineering"
223                lblDepartment.Text = "Engineering"
224            Case "Biochemistry"
225                lblDepartment.Text = "Chemistry"
226            Case "Shakespearean Literature"
227                lblDepartment.Text = "English"
228            Case "Web Design and E-Commerce"
229                lblDepartment.Text = "CIS"
230            Case Else
231                lblDepartment.Text = "Other"
232        End Select
```

FIGURE 5-64

In Figure 5-64, the Select Case statement is used to test the value in the Text property of the txtStudentMajor TextBox object and move the corresponding department name to the Text property of the lblDepartment object. The Case statements specify the values to be tested in the text box. The use of a string for the Select Case statement works in the same manner as other data types.

HEADS UP

If you forget to type the Is keyword in the Case Is statement, Visual Studio will insert it for you.

Use Relational Operators in a Select Case Statement

You can use relational operators in a Select Case statement, but you must use the keyword Is with the relational operator. For example, in Figure 5-41 on page 299, an If . . . Then . . . ElseIf statement was used to determine the shipping cost. That same processing could be accomplished using a Select Case statement, as shown in Figure 5-65.

```
191        Select Case decOrderAmount
192            Case Is > 500D
193                decShippingCost = 30D
194            Case Is > 400D
195                decShippingCost = 25D
196            Case Is > 200D
197                decShippingCost = 20D
198            Case Is > 0D
199                decShippingCost = 15D
200            Case Else
201                decShippingCost = 0D
202        End Select
203
```

FIGURE 5-65

Use Ranges in Select Case Statements

Another way to specify values in a Select Case statement is to use ranges. In Figure 5-66, the Case statements illustrate testing for six different conditions.

```
224        Select Case intGradeLevel
225            Case 1 To 3
226                lblGradeLevelExam.Text = "Early elementary"
227            Case 4 To 6
228                lblGradeLevelExam.Text = "Late elementary"
229            Case 7 To 8
230                lblGradeLevelExam.Text = "Middle school"
231            Case 9 To 10
232                lblGradeLevelExam.Text = "Early high school"
233            Case 11
234                lblGradeLevelExam.Text = "Late high school"
235            Case 12
236                lblGradeLevelExam.Text = "Final exam"
237            Case Else
238                lblGradeLevelExam.Text = "Invalid grade level"
239        End Select
```

FIGURE 5-66

As you can see, a range of values is specified in a Case statement by stating the beginning value, the word To, and then the ending value in the range. The Case statements will test the value in the intGradeLevel variable, and the appropriate statements will be executed.

You also can write Case statements so that more than one distinct value is tested. In Figure 5-67, the Case statement tests the individual values of 1, 3, 8, 11, and 17 against the value specified in the intDepartmentNumber variable.

```
230          Select Case intDepartmentNumber
231              Case 1, 3, 8, 11, 17
232
```

FIGURE 5-67

Notice in Figure 5-67 that each value in the Case statement is separated by a comma. The code in Figure 5-68 shows a combination of the two techniques, using both commas and a To statement.

```
234          Select Case intDepartmentNumber
235              Case 2, 4, 7, 12 To 16, 22
```

FIGURE 5-68

Select Which Decision Structure to Use

In some instances, you might need to determine if you should use the Select Case statement or the If . . . Then . . . ElseIf statement to solve a problem. Generally, the Select Case statement is most useful when more than two or three values must be tested for a given variable. For example, in Figure 5-64 on page 313, six different values are checked in the Text property of the txtStudentMajor TextBox object. This is a perfect example of when to use the Select Case statement.

The If . . . Then . . . ElseIf statement is more flexible because more than one variable can be used in the comparison. Programmers can also use compound conditions with the And, Or, and Not logical operators.

Use Code Snippets

Visual Basic includes a library of almost 500 pieces of code, called IntelliSense **code snippets** that you can insert into an application. Each snippet consists of a complete programming task such as an If . . . Then . . . Else decision structure, sending an email message, or drawing a circle. Inserting these commonly used pieces of code is an effective way to enhance productivity. You also can create your own snippets and add them to the library.

In addition to inserting snippets in your program, you can display a code snippet to ensure that you understand the syntax and requirements for a given type of statement. To insert and display a code snippet for the If . . . Then . . . Else statement, you can complete the following steps:

STEP 1   Press and hold or right-click the line in the code window where you want to insert the snippet.

Visual Studio displays a shortcut menu (Figure 5-69). It is important to press and hold or right-click the code window in the exact location where you want the code snippet to appear. If you press and hold or right-click outside this location, the shortcut menu might list customized choices for the wrong area of code. In addition, if you tap or click in the wrong place, the snippet will be positioned in the incorrect location in your program.

Insert Snippet command

shortcut menu

FIGURE 5-69

STEP 2   Tap or click Insert Snippet on the shortcut menu.

Visual Studio displays a menu of folders that contain snippets (Figure 5-70). The code snippets in each folder correspond to their folder titles.

snippet menu of folders

Code Patterns folder

FIGURE 5-70

STEP 3   Double-tap or double-click the folder named Code Patterns - If, For Each,
Try Catch, Property, etc, which contains commonly used code such as the If . . .
Then . . . Else statement.

Visual Studio displays a menu of folders for code patterns (Figure 5-71).

FIGURE 5-71

STEP 4   Double-tap or double-click the Conditionals and Loops folder because an
If . . . Then . . . Else statement is a conditional statement.

*Visual Studio displays the list of Conditionals and Loops code snippets (Figure 5-72). Some
of these statements will be unfamiliar until you complete Chapter 6, but you can see that the
list of code snippets includes several different types of If statements.*

FIGURE 5-72

STEP 5   Double-tap or double-click the If . . . Else . . . End If Statement code
snippet.

*The If . . . Else . . . End If Statement code snippet is inserted into the code on the line
selected in Step 1 (Figure 5-73). The highlighted text must be replaced by the condition(s)
to be tested in the If statement. The programmer must add the code to be executed when the
condition is true and the code to be executed when the condition is false.*

FIGURE 5-73

You must modify the code snippet shown in Figure 5-73 for the code to work properly. You may find that modifying a complicated code snippet is more work than using IntelliSense to enter the statement.

Code snippets are also helpful for learning or reviewing the format and syntax of a statement. For example, if you want to review the syntax of an If . . . Then . . . ElseIf statement, you could insert the statement into the code window and examine it. You could then either tap or click the Undo button to remove the statement, or you could comment out the snippet code and keep it for your review. In many cases when checking syntax, reviewing a snippet is faster and clearer than consulting Visual Basic help.

Validate Data

Since the first days of computers, the phrase "garbage in, garbage out" has described the fact that allowing incorrect input data into a program produces incorrect output. Developers should anticipate that users will enter invalid data. Therefore, they must write code that prevents the invalid data from being used in the program to produce invalid output.

For example, in the Flooring Cost Calculator application, the user is asked to enter the number of square footage for the flooring. If the user enters a negative number or a letter or even leaves the text box blank, the program should inform the user of the input error and allow the user to reenter a proper value. If the program attempts to process invalid data, unexpected errors can occur, which is not the way a program should respond to invalid input data.

To properly check the square footage value entered by the user, two tests must be performed. First, the program must check the value to ensure it is numeric. Second, the numeric value entered by the user must be checked to ensure it is greater than zero. These tests are explained in the following sections.

Test Input to Determine If the Value Is Numeric

In the Flooring Cost Calculator application, if no check is performed on the input data and the user accidentally enters a nonnumeric character such as an "a" or does not enter a value at all, the program will fail when Visual Basic attempts to convert that value to a number. An exception (error) screen will open, and the program will be terminated. Therefore, the program must check the value entered by the user to ensure it is numeric. In addition, if the user enters a nonnumeric value, the program should inform the user of the error and request a valid numeric value.

The Visual Basic **IsNumeric function** can check the input value to determine if it can be converted into a numeric value such as an Integer or Decimal data type. If so, it returns a True Boolean value. If the value is not recognized as a numeric value, the IsNumeric function returns a False Boolean value.

For example, the IsNumeric function can check the value in the Text property of the Square Footage text box. If the user enters a letter such as "a" in the text box, the IsNumeric function will return a False Boolean value because the letter "a" is not numeric.

Because the IsNumeric function returns a Boolean value (True or False), it can be placed within an If statement as the condition to be tested. If the returned value is True, the condition in the If statement is considered true. If the returned value is False, the condition in the If statement is considered false. The code in Figure 5-74 uses an If statement to determine if the Text property of the txtFootage TextBox object is numeric.

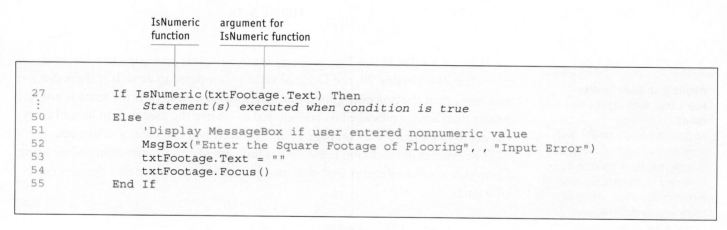

```
               IsNumeric    argument for
               function     IsNumeric function

27       If IsNumeric(txtFootage.Text) Then
 :              Statement(s) executed when condition is true
50       Else
51              'Display MessageBox if user entered nonnumeric value
52              MsgBox("Enter the Square Footage of Flooring", , "Input Error")
53              txtFootage.Text = ""
54              txtFootage.Focus()
55       End If
```

FIGURE 5-74

In Figure 5-74, the If statement on line 27 calls the IsNumeric function. The Text property of the txtFootage TextBox object is the argument for the IsNumeric function. As a result of this specification, the IsNumeric function will analyze the data in the Text property of the txtFootage TextBox object. If the data can be converted to a numeric data type, then the function will return a Boolean value of True. If the data cannot be converted to a numeric data type, the function will return a Boolean value of False.

Once the function has returned a Boolean value, the If statement tests the Boolean value. If it is true, the value in the Text property of the txtFootage TextBox object is numeric, and the appropriate statements are executed. If the condition is false, meaning the value is not numeric, the statements on lines 52–54 are executed. The statement on line 52 displays a message box telling the user to enter the square footage of the flooring (see Figure 5-2 on page 275). The caption of the message box is "Input Error". The statement on line 53 clears the Text property. The statement on line 54 sets the focus on the text box so the user can reenter the value.

Check for a Positive Number

If the condition in Figure 5-74 on the previous page is true, the value in the Text property must be converted to a Decimal data type. Then, the program checks to ensure that the entered value is greater than zero. These statements are shown in Figure 5-75.

```
24                              eric value?
25      If IsNumeric(txtFootage.Text) Then
26          decFootage = Convert.ToDecimal(txtFootage.Text)
27
28          ' Is Square Footage greater than zero
29          If decFootage > 0 Then
30              ' Determine cost per square foot
31              If radTile.Checked Then
32                  decCostPerSquareFoot = decTileCost
33              ElseIf radCarpet.Checked Then
34                  decCostPerSquareFoot = decCarpetCost
35              ElseIf radHardwood.Checked Then
36                  decCostPerSquareFoot = decHardwoodCost
37              End If
38
39              ' Calculate and display the cost estimate
40              decCostEstimate = decFootage * decCostPerSquareFoot
41              lblCostEstimate.Text = decCostEstimate.ToString("C")
42          Else
43              ' Display error message if user entered a negative value
44              MsgBox("You entered " & decFootage.ToString() & ". Enter a Positive Number", , "Input Error")
45              txtFootage.Text = ""
46              txtFootage.Focus()
47          End If
48
```

FIGURE 5-75

Why is it so important to check that each input value is valid?
As devices become smaller and more mobile, data validation is more important because it is so easy to accidentally enter incorrect characters with your touch keyboard. Developers cannot have their programs and apps crash each time someone makes an erroneous keystroke. Keep in mind that your instructor will test each of your programs with all kinds of keyboard input to verify that your program will not fail.

When the value in the Text property is numeric, it is converted to a Decimal value (line 26). On line 29, the Decimal value is compared to zero. If it is greater than zero, then the processing for a true statement is executed. If the value is not greater than zero, a message box is displayed to inform the user that an invalid entry was made (see Figure 5-29 on page 290). The user then can enter a valid value.

The process of validating input data is fundamental to programming when using a graphical user interface. A well-designed program must ensure that the user enters valid data.

Program Design

As you have learned, the requirements document identifies the purpose of the program being developed, the application title, the procedures to be followed when using the program, any required equations and calculations, any conditions that must be tested, notes and restrictions that must be followed by the program, and any other comments that would be helpful to understanding the problem. The requirements document for the Flooring Cost Calculator application is shown in Figure 5-76. The Use Case Definition document is shown in Figure 5-77.

REQUIREMENTS DOCUMENT

Date:	January 29, 2017
Date Submitted:	
Application Title:	Flooring Cost Calculator
Purpose:	This application calculates the estimated cost of flooring for a job bid or homeowner installation.
Program Procedures:	The user should enter the square footage of flooring needed and select the type of flooring. The estimated cost for the flooring job will be displayed.
Algorithms, Processing, and Conditions:	1. The user must be able to enter the number of square footage of flooring. 2. The user must be able to select one of three flooring types: tile, carpet, or hardwood. 3. The user can initiate the calculation and display the cost estimate for the flooring. 4. The application computes the cost estimate of the flooring based on the number of square feet and the cost of the flooring. Tile costs $4.49 per square foot of flooring, carpet costs $4.99 per square foot, and hardwood costs $7.49 per square foot. 5. The estimate calculation is square footage $\times$ cost per square foot. 6. The cost estimate is displayed in currency format. 7. The user should be able to clear the square footage entered, reset the flooring type to tile, and clear the cost estimate.
Notes and Restrictions:	1. If the user enters a nonnumeric value for the square footage or leaves the TextBox object empty, the user should be advised and asked for a valid entry. 2. If the user enters a negative number for the square footage, the user should be advised and asked for a valid entry.
Comments:	The title of the Windows Form should be Flooring Cost Calculator.

FIGURE 5-76

USE CASE DEFINITION

1. The window opens and displays the Flooring Cost Calculator, a text box requesting the number of square footage for the flooring, radio buttons to select the flooring type, and two buttons labeled Calculate and Clear.
2. The user enters the square footage and selects one of the flooring types.
3. The user taps or clicks the Calculate button.
4. The user will be warned if a nonnumeric value is entered, the text box is left empty, or a negative number is entered.
5. The program displays the cost estimate for the flooring materials cost.
6. The user taps or clicks the Clear button to clear the Square Footage text box, set the flooring choice to Tile, and erase the cost estimate.
7. The user taps or clicks the Close button to exit the application.

FIGURE 5-77

Event Planning Document

You will recall that the event-planning document is a table that specifies which objects in the user interface will cause events, the action taken by the user to trigger each event, and the event processing that must occur. The event-planning document for the Flooring Cost Calculator application is shown in Figure 5-78.

EVENT-PLANNING DOCUMENT

Program Name: Flooring Cost Calculator	Developer: Corinne Hoisington	Object: frmFlooring	Date: January 29, 2017
OBJECT	**EVENT TRIGGER**	**EVENT PROCESSING**	
btnCalculate	Click	Ensure data entered is numeric Display error message if data is not numeric or text box is empty Convert data entered to numeric Ensure data entered is greater than zero Display error message if data is not greater than zero Assign flooring cost per foot based on type of flooring selection Calculate cost (square footage × cost per foot) Display cost	
btnClear	Click	Clear input text box Clear cost estimate Set the Tile radio button to checked Clear the Carpet radio button Clear the Hardwood radio button Set focus on input text box	
frmFlooring	Load	Set focus on input text box Clear the placement zeros for cost	

FIGURE 5-78

Design and Code the Program

After identifying the events and tasks within the events, the developer is ready to create the program. As you have learned, creating the program means designing the user interface and then entering Visual Basic statements to accomplish the tasks specified in the event planning document. As the developer enters the code, she also will implement the logic to carry out the required processing.

NOTE TO THE LEARNER

In the following activity, you should complete the tasks within the specified steps. Each of the tasks is accompanied by a Hint Screen. The purpose of the Hint Screen is to indicate where you should perform the activity in the Visual Studio window and to remind you which method to use. If you need further help completing a step, refer to the figure identified by *ref:*.

To design the user interface for the Flooring Cost Calculator application and enter the code required to process each event in the program, complete the steps on the next page.

Guided Program Development

Phase 1: Design the Form

1

- **Create a Windows Application** Open Visual Studio using the Search charm (Windows 8) or the Start button on the Windows taskbar and the All Programs submenu (Windows 7). Create a new Visual Basic Windows Application project by completing the following: Tap or click the New Project button on the Standard toolbar; tap or click Windows Desktop in the left pane; select Windows Forms Application; name the project by entering `Flooring Cost Calculator` in the Name text box; then tap or click the OK button in the New Project window.

HINT

- **Name the Form** In the Solution Explorer pane, press and hold or right-click Form1.vb and then tap or click Rename. Type `frmFlooring.vb` and then press the ENTER key. Tap or click the Yes button to automatically change the form (Name) in the Properties window.

HINT

- **Change the Size Property** In the Properties window, change the Size property to `420, 560`.

- **Change the BackColor Property** In the Properties window, change the BackColor property to `Ivory`.

- **Change the Text on the Title Bar** To change the text on the title bar, tap or click the form, scroll down the Properties window until the Text property is displayed, double-tap or double-click the right column of the Text property, type `Flooring Cost`, and then press the ENTER key.

HINT

- **Add a Heading Title** Drag a label onto the form and name the label `lblHeading`. Set the Text property for the Label object to `Flooring Cost Calculator`. Set the font to Goudy Old Style, Bold, 20 points. Position the label horizontally in the center of the form.

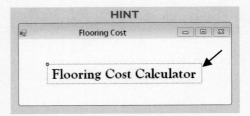

HINT

- **Add a Label** Drag a second label onto the frmFlooring Form object and name the label `lblSquareFeet`. Set the Text property of the Label object to `Square Footage:`. Set the font to Goudy Old Style, Bold, 16 points. Position the label to resemble the one shown in Figure 5-79.

- **Add a TextBox Object** Drag a TextBox object onto the form. Using snap lines, align the top of the TextBox object with the top of the second Label object. Name the TextBox object `txtFootage`. Change the TextAlign property to Center. Change the font to Goudy Old Style, Bold, 14 points. Reduce the width of the TextBox object to closely resemble the one in Figure 5-79. Center the Label object and the TextBox object horizontally in the frmFlooring Form object.

A title Label object is displayed on the first line of the form. A Label object and TextBox object occupy the second line of the frmFlooring Form object (Figure 5-79). They are centered horizontally in the form.

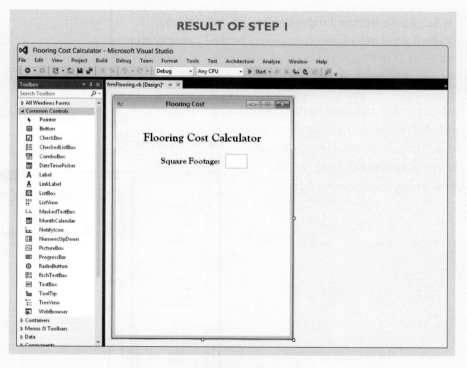

FIGURE 5-79

(continues)

Guided Program Development   *continued*

2

- **Add a GroupBox** Drag a GroupBox object from the Container category of the Toolbox to the frmFlooring Form object. Name the GroupBox `grpFloorType`. Change the Text property to `Flooring Type`. Set the size of the GroupBox object to `175, 105`. Change the BackColor of the GroupBox object to White. Center the GroupBox object horizontally in the frmFlooring Form object, and change the font to Goudy Old Style, Regular, 14 points *(ref: Figure 5-4)*.

HINT

Flooring Type

- **Add Radio Buttons** Place three RadioButton objects on the GroupBox object. Name the first RadioButton `radTile` and change its Text property to `Tile`. Name the second RadioButton `radCarpet` and change its Text property to `Carpet`. Name the third RadioButton `radHardwood` and change its Text property to `Hardwood`. If necessary, select the three RadioButtons and change the font to Goudy Old Style, Regular, 14 points *(ref: Figure 5-7)*.

HINT

Flooring Type
- ○ Tile
- ○ Carpet
- ○ Hardwood

- **Set Radio Button Properties** Tap or click the radTile RadioButton object and change its Checked property from False to True. Tile is the flooring most commonly used by homeowners *(ref: Figure 5-11)*.

The group box and radio buttons are included on the frmFlooring Form object (Figure 5-80). The radTile radio button is selected because it is the most widely used flooring type.

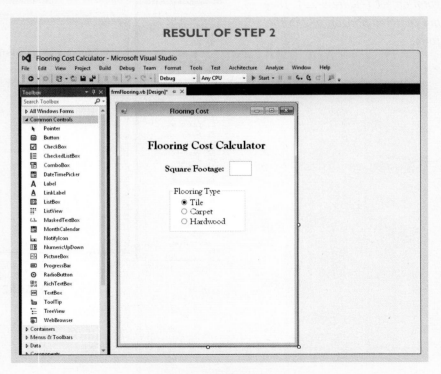

RESULT OF STEP 2

FIGURE 5-80

3

• **Add Estimate and Cost Labels** Drag two more Label objects onto the form below the GroupBox object. Align these labels by their tops using snap lines. Name the first label `lblCost`, change its Text property to `Cost Estimate:`, and resize the Label object to view the text. Name the second label `lblCostEstimate` and set its Text property to `$0000.00`. These placement zeros allow you to view the Label object when it is not selected. The placement zeros will be cleared using code when the form is loaded. Change the font for both Label objects to Goudy Old Style, Bold, 16 points. Horizontally center the labels as a unit on the frmFlooring Form object.

• **Add Calculate and Clear Buttons** Drag two Button objects onto the form. Align the tops of the Button objects using snap lines. Name the left Button object `btnCalculate` and change its Text property to `Calculate`. Name the right Button object btnClear and change its Text property to `Clear`. Change the font for these two buttons to Goudy Old Style, Bold, 14 points. Change the size of each button to `116, 30`. Change the BackColor property for each button to White.

• **Add a Picture to the Windows Form** Download the Flooring.jpg picture by visiting CengageBrain.com and accessing the resources for this chapter. Drag a PictureBox object to the bottom of the Windows Form. Name the picture `picFlooring`. Change the Size property of the PictureBox object to `400, 150`. Change the SizeMode property to StretchImage.

Guided Program Development *continued*

The user interface is complete (Figure 5-81).

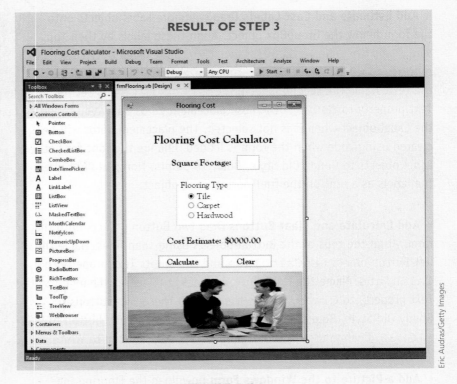

FIGURE 5-81

Phase 2: Code the Application

4

● **Code the Comments** Double-tap or double-click the btnCalculate Button object on the frmFlooring Form object to open the code window and create the btnCalculate_Click event handler. Close the Toolbox. Tap or click in front of the first words, Public Class frmFlooring, and then press the ENTER key to create a blank line. Insert the first four standard comments. Insert the Option Strict On command at the beginning of the code to turn on strict-type checking.

```
HINT
frmFlooring.vb   ⊣ ₱ ✕  frmFlooring.vb [Design]
  1  ⊟ ' Program Name:  Flooring Cost Calculator Application
  2    ' Author:        Corinne Hoisington
  3    ' Date:          January 29, 2017
  4    ' Purpose:       This Windows application computes the estimated cost
  5    '                of flooring based on the number of square feet and the
  6    '                following cost per square foot: Tile - $4.49 per square foot;
  7    '                Carpet - $4.99 per square foot; Hardwood - $7.49 per square foot.
  8
  9      Option Strict On
```

● **Add Comments to the btnCalculate_ Click Event Handler** Enter a comment to describe the purpose of the btnCalculate_ Click event.

```
HINT
 12    Private Sub btnCalculate_Click(sender As Object, e As EventArgs) Handles btnCalculate.Click
 13      ' The btnCalculate event handler calculates the estimated cost of
 14      ' flooring based on the square footage and the flooring type.
 15
```

● **Declare and Initialize the Variables** This application requires six Decimal variables: (1) decFootage: Holds the estimated square footage of the flooring; (2) decCostPerSquareFoot: Holds the cost per square foot based on the flooring type; (3) decCost Estimate: Is assigned the calculated final estimated cost; (4) decTileCost: Is assigned the value 4.49; (5) decCarpetCost: Is assigned the value 4.99; (6) decHardwoodCost: Is assigned the value 7.49. Declare and initialize these six variables.

```
HINT
 16      ' Declaration Section
 17      Dim decFootage As Decimal
 18      Dim decCostPerSquareFoot As Decimal
 19      Dim decCostEstimate As Decimal
 20      Dim decTileCost As Decimal = 4.49D
 21      Dim decCarpetCost As Decimal = 4.99D
 22      Dim decHardwoodCost As Decimal = 7.49D
```

● **Write the If Statement to Test for Numeric Data** When the user taps or clicks the Calculate button, the program must first ensure that the user entered a valid numeric value in the txtFootage TextBox object. If the user has entered a valid numeric value, the value must be converted from a string value into a Decimal data type. Write the If statement and conversion statement required for this process *(ref: Figure 5-74)*.

```
HINT
 23
 24      ' Did user enter a numeric value?
 25      If IsNumeric(txtFootage.Text) Then
 26          decFootage = Convert.ToDecimal(txtFootage.Text)
```

(continues)

Guided Program Development *continued*

● **Write the If Statement to Test for a Positive Number** If the value in the txtFootage TextBox object is numeric, then the converted numeric value must be checked to ensure that it is a positive number. Write the If statement to check whether the converted numeric value is greater than zero *(ref: Figure 5-75)*.

HINT

```
28              ' Is Square Footage greater than zero
29              If decFootage > 0 Then
30
```

● **Write the If Statement to Determine the Cost Per Square Foot** When the value is greater than zero, the cost per square foot is determined by checking the status of the RadioButton objects and placing the appropriate cost per square foot in the decCostPerSquareFoot variable. Using the If . . . Then . . . ElseIf structure, write the statements to identify the checked radio button and place the appropriate cost in the decCostPerSquareFoot variable *(ref: Figure 5-49)*.

HINT

```
30              ' Determine cost per square foot
31              If radTile.Checked Then
32                  decCostPerSquareFoot = decTileCost
33              ElseIf radCarpet.Checked Then
34                  decCostPerSquareFoot = decCarpetCost
35              ElseIf radHardwood.Checked Then
36                  decCostPerSquareFoot = decHardwoodCost
37              End If
38
39          End If
```

● **Calculate and Display the Cost Estimate** The next step is to calculate the cost estimate by multiplying the value in the decCostPerSquareFoot variable by the square footage. Next, display the cost estimate in the cost estimate label. Write the statements to calculate and display the cost estimate in the currency format.

HINT

```
39              ' Calculate and display the cost estimate
40              decCostEstimate = decFootage * decCostPerSquareFoot
41              lblCostEstimate.Text = decCostEstimate.ToString("C")
```

● **Display a Message Box If the Value Entered Is Not Greater Than Zero** After the processing is finished for the true portion of the If statements, the Else portion of the If statements must be written. Write the code to display the message box that contains the error message when the user enters a value that is not greater than zero *(ref: Figure 5-24)*.

HINT

```
42          Else
43              ' Display error message if user entered a negative value
44              MsgBox("You entered " & decFootage.ToString() & ". Enter a Positive Number", , "Input Error")
45              txtFootage.Text = ""
46              txtFootage.Focus()
47          End If
48
49      End If
```

● **Display an Error Message If the Value Entered Is Not Numeric** Write the Else portion of the If statement to display an error message if the value entered by the user is not numeric *(ref: Figure 5-24)*.

HINT

```
42          Else
43              ' Display error message if user entered a negative value
44              MsgBox("You entered " & decFootage.ToString() & ". Enter a Positive Number", , "Input Error")
45              txtFootage.Text = ""
46              txtFootage.Focus()
47          End If
48      Else
49          ' Display error message if user entered a nonnumeric value
```

Guided Program Development *continued*

The code for the click event of the Calculate button is completed (Figure 5-82).

RESULT OF STEP 4

```vb
 1  ' Program Name: Flooring Cost Calculator Application
 2  ' Author:        Corinne Hoisington
 3  ' Date:          January 29, 2017
 4  ' Purpose:       This Windows application computes the estimated cost
 5  '                of flooring based on the number of square feet and the
 6  '                following cost per square foot: Tile - $4.49 per square foot;
 7  '                Carpet - $4.99 per square foot; Hardwood - $7.49 per square foot.
 8
 9  Option Strict On
10
    1 reference
11  Public Class frmFlooring
      0 references
12      Private Sub btnCalculate_Click(sender As Object, e As EventArgs) Handles btnCalculate.Click
13          ' The btnCalculate event handler calculates the estimated cost of
14          ' flooring based on the square footage and the flooring type.
15
16          ' Declaration Section
17          Dim decFootage As Decimal
18          Dim decCostPerSquareFoot As Decimal
19          Dim decCostEstimate As Decimal
20          Dim decTileCost As Decimal = 4.49D
21          Dim decCarpetCost As Decimal = 4.99D
22          Dim decHardwoodCost As Decimal = 7.49D
23
24          ' Did user enter a numeric value?
25          If IsNumeric(txtFootage.Text) Then
26              decFootage = Convert.ToDecimal(txtFootage.Text)
27
28              ' Is Square Footage greater than zero
29              If decFootage > 0 Then
30                  ' Determine cost per square foot
31                  If radTile.Checked Then
32                      decCostPerSquareFoot = decTileCost
33                  ElseIf radCarpet.Checked Then
34                      decCostPerSquareFoot = decCarpetCost
35                  ElseIf radHardwood.Checked Then
36                      decCostPerSquareFoot = decHardwoodCost
37                  End If
38
39                  ' Calculate and display the cost estimate
40                  decCostEstimate = decFootage * decCostPerSquareFoot
41                  lblCostEstimate.Text = decCostEstimate.ToString("C")
42              Else
43                  ' Display error message if user entered a negative value
44                  MsgBox("You entered " & decFootage.ToString() & ". Enter a Positive Number", , "Input Error")
45                  txtFootage.Text = ""
46                  txtFootage.Focus()
47              End If
48          Else
49              ' Display error message if user entered a nonnumeric value
50              MsgBox("Enter the Square Footage of Flooring", , "Input Error")
51              txtFootage.Text = ""
52              txtFootage.Focus()
53          End If
54      End Sub
55
```

FIGURE 5-82

(continues)

Guided Program Development   *continued*

5

● **Create the Clear Button Click Event Handler** The Clear Button click event includes the following processing: (1) clear the txtFootage Text property; (2) clear the lblCostEstimate Text property; (3) set the radTile Checked property to True; (4) set the radCarpet and radHardwood Checked properties to False; (5) set the focus in the txtFootage text box. To enter this code, tap or click the frmFlooring. vb [Design] tab and then double-tap or double-click the Clear button. Using IntelliSense, enter the required code.

HINT

```
55
56    Private Sub btnClear_Click(sender As Object, e As EventArgs) Handles btnClear.Click
57        ' This event handler is executed when the user taps or clicks the Clear button. It
58        ' clears the square footage text box and the cost estimate label, resets the radio
59        ' buttons with Tile selected, and sets the focus to the square footage text box.
60
61        txtFootage.Clear()
62        lblCostEstimate.Text = ""
63        radTile.Checked = True
64        radCarpet.Checked = False
65        radHardwood.Checked = False
66        txtFootage.Focus()
67    End Sub
```

● **Create the Form Load Event Handler** When the frmFlooring Form object loads, the following processing should occur: (1) the focus is in the txtFootage text box; (2) the lblCostEstimate Text property is set to null. Tap or click the frmFlooring.vb [Design] tab to return to Design view and then double-tap or double-click the form. Enter the code for the form load event handler.

HINT

```
68
69    Private Sub frmFlooring_Load(sender As Object, e As EventArgs) Handles MyBase.Load
70        ' This event handler is executed when the form is loaded at the start of
71        ' the program. It sets the focus to the square footage text box and
72        ' clears the cost estimate label.
73
74        txtFootage.Focus()
75        lblCostEstimate.Text = ""
76    End Sub
77    End Class
78
```

6

● **Run the Application** After you have completed the code, you should run the application to ensure that it works properly.

● **Test the Application** Test the application with the following data: (1) square footage 250, flooring type Tile; (2) square footage 210, flooring type Hardwood; (3) square footage 170, flooring type Carpet; (4) square footage Fifteen (use this word), flooring type Hardwood; (5) square footage -800, flooring type Tile; (6) use other values to thoroughly test the program. After each test, tap or click the Clear button before entering new data.

● **Close the Program** After testing the application, close the window by tapping or clicking the Close button in the title bar of the window.

HINT

(continues)

Code Listing

The complete code for the sample program is shown in Figure 5-83.

```vbnet
1    ⊟' Program Name: Flooring Cost Calculator Application
2     ' Author:        Corinne Hoisington
3     ' Date:          January 29, 2017
4     ' Purpose:       This Windows application computes the estimated cost
5     '                of flooring based on the number of square feet and the
6     '                following cost per square foot: Tile - $4.49 per square foot;
7     '                Carpet - $4.99 per square foot; Hardwood - $7.49 per square foot.
8
9      Option Strict On
10
       1 reference
11   ⊟Public Class frmFlooring
           0 references
12   ⊟      Private Sub btnCalculate_Click(sender As Object, e As EventArgs) Handles btnCalculate.Click
13             ' The btnCalculate event handler calculates the estimated cost of
14             ' flooring based on the square footage and the flooring type.
15
16             ' Declaration Section
17             Dim decFootage As Decimal
18             Dim decCostPerSquareFoot As Decimal
19             Dim decCostEstimate As Decimal
20             Dim decTileCost As Decimal = 4.49D
21             Dim decCarpetCost As Decimal = 4.99D
22             Dim decHardwoodCost As Decimal = 7.49D
23
24             ' Did user enter a numeric value?
25             If IsNumeric(txtFootage.Text) Then
26                 decFootage = Convert.ToDecimal(txtFootage.Text)
27
28                 ' Is Square Footage greater than zero
29                 If decFootage > 0 Then
30                     ' Determine cost per square foot
31                     If radTile.Checked Then
32                         decCostPerSquareFoot = decTileCost
33                     ElseIf radCarpet.Checked Then
34                         decCostPerSquareFoot = decCarpetCost
35                     ElseIf radHardwood.Checked Then
36                         decCostPerSquareFoot = decHardwoodCost
37                     End If
38
39                     ' Calculate and display the cost estimate
40                     decCostEstimate = decFootage * decCostPerSquareFoot
41                     lblCostEstimate.Text = decCostEstimate.ToString("C")
42                 Else
43                     ' Display error message if user entered a negative value
44                     MsgBox("You entered " & decFootage.ToString() & ". Enter a Positive Number", , "Input Error")
45                     txtFootage.Text = ""
46                     txtFootage.Focus()
47                 End If
48             Else
49                 ' Display error message if user entered a nonnumeric value
50                 MsgBox("Enter the Square Footage of Flooring", , "Input Error")
51                 txtFootage.Text = ""
52                 txtFootage.Focus()
53             End If
54         End Sub
```

FIGURE 5-83 (continues)

```
55
      0 references
56 ⊟  Private Sub btnClear_Click(sender As Object, e As EventArgs) Handles btnClear.Click
57          ' This event handler is executed when the user taps or clicks the Clear button. It
58          ' clears the square Footage text box and the cost estimate label, resets the radio
59          ' buttons with Tile selected, and sets the focus to the square footage text box.
60
61          txtFootage.Clear()
62          lblCostEstimate.Text = ""
63          radTile.Checked = True
64          radCarpet.Checked = False
65          radHardwood.Checked = False
66          txtFootage.Focus()
67      End Sub
68
      0 references
69 ⊟  Private Sub frmFlooring_Load(sender As Object, e As EventArgs) Handles MyBase.Load
70          ' This event handler is executed when the form is loaded at the start of
71          ' the program. It sets the focus to the square footage text box and
72          ' clears the cost estimate label.
73
74          txtFootage.Focus()
75          lblCostEstimate.Text = ""
76      End Sub
77  End Class
78
```

FIGURE 5-83 (continued)

Summary

In this chapter, you have learned to make decisions based on the user's input.

The items listed in Figure 5-84 on the next page include all the new Visual Studio and Visual Basic skills you have learned in this chapter.

Visual Basic Skills		
Skill	**Figure Number**	**Video Number**
Explore the Flooring Cost Calculator Application	Figure 5-1	Video 5-1
Use a GroupBox Object	Figure 5-4	Video 5-2
Add RadioButton Objects	Figure 5-7	Video 5-3
Use Windows Application Container Objects	Figure 5-14	
Display a Message Box	Figure 5-16	Video 5-4
Concatenate Strings	Figure 5-29	
Code an If . . . Then Statement	Figure 5-31	
Turn on Pretty Listing for Indentation	Page 292	
Use Relational Operators	Figure 5-32	
Enter an If . . . Then Statement	Figure 5-34	Video 5-5
Compare Strings	Figure 5-37	
Code If . . . Then . . . Else Statements	Figure 5-38	
Compare Values Using an Arithmetic Expression	Figure 5-40	
Code an If . . . Then . . . ElseIf Statement	Figure 5-41	
Code a Nested If Statement	Figure 5-43	
Test the Status of a RadioButton Object in Code	Figure 5-48	
Understand Block-Level Scope	Figure 5-51	
Code Logical Operators	Figure 5-52	
Code Select Case Statements	Figure 5-62	
Insert Code Snippets	Figure 5-69	Video 5-6
Validate Input Data	Figure 5-74	

FIGURE 5-84

Reinforcement activities and resources are available at no additional cost on *www.cengagebrain.com*. Visit http://solutions.cengage.com/ctdownloads/ for detailed instructions about accessing the available resources at the Student Companion Site.

Knowledge Check

1. Write an If . . . Then statement that tests whether the value in the variable decGPA is between 3.5 and 4.0. If the number is in that range, set the Text property for the lblHonor Label object to "Dean's List."

2. If a form opens and the first of three RadioButtons is checked within a GroupBox object, what happens to the first RadioButton object when you tap or click the second RadioButton object?

3. Name the six relational operators and state the purpose of each operator.

4. Write an If . . . Then . . . Else statement that assigns 65 to a variable named intSpeed if strHighway is equal to "405 Highway." Otherwise, assign 50 to intSpeed.

5. List the three most common logical operators and explain their meaning.

6. Rewrite the following line of code without a Not logical operator but keep the same logical processing:

   ```
   If Not decXBox <= 139.99 Then
   ```

7. The intent of the following statement is to check whether the radSingleTaxStatus RadioButton object is checked. What is the error in the statement? Rewrite the statement so it is correct.

   ```
   If radSingleTaxStatus = Checked Then
   ```

8. The intent of the following statement is to check whether the value in the intGrade variable is less than 0 or greater than 100. What is the error in the statement? Rewrite the statement so it is correct.

   ```
   If intGrade < 0 And intGrade > 100 Then
   ```

9. What is the most commonly used container object?

10. Fix this statement.

    ```
    If decMinWage > 7.25 and < 15.25 Then
    ```

11. Why do most developers indent the code within a decision structure?

12. Write a statement that creates the dialog box shown in Figure 5-85 in a Windows application. Use a single numerical value to create the button.

13. What is the difference between a Panel object and a GroupBox object?

14. What is the difference between the Or logical operator and the Xor logical operator?

15. Write a data validation statement that would check to ensure that the value in the intAge variable is between 1 and 120. If the age is not valid, display an error message box that states the age is invalid.

FIGURE 5-85

(continues)

16. How many radio buttons in a group can be selected at one time?

17. Using the concatenation operator (&), write a statement that would create the compound word "reunion" from the following two strings: strTerm1 = "re" and strTerm2= "union." Assign the compound word to the strCompound string variable.

18. Write a statement that would clear the radio button named radKatyPerry.

19. Write a Select Case statement using the fewest Case statements possible to display the number of days in each month. The user enters the number of the month, such as 8, which is converted to an integer and assigned to the intMonth variable. The Select Case statement should display a message box that states the number of days in the month, such as "31 Days."

20. Which logical operator has the highest precedence in the order of operations?

Debugging Exercises

1. Explain how the two statements shown in Figure 5-86 are evaluated.

```
If strAirline = "Jet Green" AndAlso strHotel = "Homeland Suites" Then

    If strAirline = "Jet Green" And strHotel = "Homeland Suites" Then
```

FIGURE 5-86

2. Identify the error in the code shown in Figure 5-87 and explain how to correct the code.

```
If dblCommission >= 2500 Then
    Dim intBonus As Integer
    intBonus = 500
Else
    intBonus = 0
End If
```

FIGURE 5-87

Debugging Exercises

3. The Select Case statement shown in Figure 5-88 contains one or more errors. Identify the error(s) and rewrite the statements correctly.

```
Select Case intNumberOfSeats
    Case > 5000
        strVenueType = "Stadium"
    Case > 2000
        strVenueType = "Amphitheater"
    Case > 1000
        strVenueType = "Auditorium"
    Case > 200
        strVenueType = "Theater"
    Case > 0
        strVenueType = "Club"
    Else Case
        strVenueType = "Error"
Select End
```

FIGURE 5-88

4. The Select Case statement shown in Figure 5-89 contains one or more errors. Identify the error(s) and rewrite the statements correctly.

```
Select Case charFlightCode
    Case 'F', 'A'
            lblFare.Text = 'First Class'
    Case 'B', 'Q'
            lblFare.Text = 'Business Class'
    Case 'Y', 'S', 'M'
            lblFare.Text = 'Full Fare Economy'
    Case 'K', 'C'
            lblFare.Text = 'Preferred Economy'
    Case 'U', 'J', 'P', 'G'
            lblFare.Text = 'Economy'
    Else
            lblFare.Text = 'Unknown'
End Select
```

FIGURE 5-89

(continues)

5. The If . . . Then . . . Else statement shown in Figure 5-90 contains one or more errors. Identify the error(s) and rewrite the statements correctly.

```
If strShippingMethod = "Overnite" Then
    If strDeliveryTime = "Morning"
        decDeliveryCost = 29.00D
    Else
        decDeliveryCost = 24.00D
Else
    If strShippingMethod = "Two Days" Then
        decDeliveryCost = 14.00D
    Else
        decDeliveryCost = 4.00D
End If
```

FIGURE 5-90

Program Analysis

1. Write an If . . . Then decision structure to compare the two numbers in the decDeveloperPay and dec WebDesignerPay variables. Display a message box that states decDeveloperPay is greater than decWebDesignerPay.

2. Write an If statement that displays the message box "Sleet is possible" if the value in the variable decTemp is within the range from 30 to 35.

3. Write an If . . . Then . . . Else statement that checks the value in the variable chrGender for the value M (Male) or F (Female) and assigns the information shown in Figure 5-91 to lblCollegeExpectation.Text based on the gender. If the variable chrGender contains a value other than M or F, assign the message "Invalid Gender" to lblCollegeExpectation.Text.

Gender	College Expectation
Male	75% plan to graduate from college
Female	85% plan to graduate from college

FIGURE 5-91

Program Analysis *continued*

4. Write a Select Case statement that tests the user's age in a variable named intAge and assigns the generation name of that age group to the variable strGeneration, according to the information shown in Figure 5-92.

Age Group	Generation Name
50 and above	Baby Boomers
39–49	Generation X
18–38	Generation Y
Below 18	Millennials

FIGURE 5-92

5. Rewrite the Select Case statement shown in Figure 5-93 as an If . . . Then . . . Else statement.

```
Select Case chrDepartment
    Case "B", "b"
        strDept = "Baby / Infant Clothing"
    Case "T", "t"
        strDept = "Technology"
End Select
```

FIGURE 5-93

6. Rewrite the If . . . Then . . . Else statement shown in Figure 5-94 as a Select Case statement.

```
If intGrade >= 9 And intGrade <= 12 Then
    lblSchool.Text = "High School"
ElseIf intGrade >= 7 Then
    lblSchool.Text = "Middle School"
ElseIf intGrade >= 1 Then
    lblSchool.Text = "Elementary School"
Else
    lblSchool.Text = "Invalid Grade"
End If
```

FIGURE 5-94

(continues)

7. What is the output of the code shown in Figure 5-95 if the word Black is entered in the txtSkiSlope text box?

```
Select Case Me.txtSkiSlope.Text
    Case "Green"
        MsgBox("Beginner Slope")
    Case "Blue"
        MsgBox("Intermediate Slope")
    Case "Black"
        MsgBox("Expert Slope")
    Case Else
        MsgBox("Invalid Entry")
End Select
```

FIGURE 5-95

8. After the execution of the Select Case structure in Figure 5-96, what value will be found in the Text property of lblFemaleHeight if the user enters the number 74 into the txtEnterHeight text box? If the number 81 is entered? If the number 59 is entered?

```
Dim intHeightInches As Integer
intHeightInches = Convert.ToInt32(txtEnterHeight.Text)
Select Case intHeightInches
    Case Is < 61
        lblFemaleHeight.Text = "Petite"
    Case 61 To 69
        lblFemaleHeight.Text = "Average"
    Case 70 To 80
        lblFemaleHeight.Text = "Tall"
    Case 80 To 120
        lblFemaleHeight.Text = "Towering"
    Case Else
        lblFemaleHeight.Text = "Not Possible"
End Select
```

FIGURE 5-96

Program Analysis *continued*

9. In each of the following examples, is the condition True or False?

    a. "CVCC" >= "GRCC"

    b. "G" >= "g"

    c. "Nerdy" < "Nerd"

    d. "Cool" <> "cool"

    e. "50" >= "Fifty"

    f. ("Paris" < "Barcelona") And ("Amsterdam" <= "Prague")

    g. ("Ford" > "Chevrolet") Or ("Toyota" < "Honda")

    h. 3 ^ 2 <= 3 * 4

    i. Not ("CNN" >= "ABC")

    j. Not ("Tim" > "Tom") And Not ("Great" <> "great")

Complete one or more of the following case programming assignments. Submit the program and materials you create to your instructor. The level of difficulty is indicated for each assignment.

● = Easiest
●● = Intermediate
●●● = Challenging

1
●
METRO CITY COMMUTE

Design a Windows Desktop application and write the code that will execute according to the program requirements in Figure 5-97. Before writing the code, create a Use Case Definition, as shown in Figure 5-98. Before writing the code, create an event-planning document for each event in the program. The completed Form object and other objects in the user interface are shown in Figure 5-99 on the next page.

REQUIREMENTS DOCUMENT

Date:	May 6, 2017
Date Submitted:	
Application Title:	Metro City Commute Application
Purpose:	This Windows Desktop application calculates the cost of commuting to New York City using the metro.
Program Procedures:	The user selects the number of tickets and the type of ticket (single ride, 7-day, or 30-day). The user then requests that the program calculate and display the cost of the metro tickets for the subway.
Algorithms, Processing, and Conditions:	1. The user selects the number of metro tickets. 2. Metro tickets can be purchased for a single ride ($2.75), 7 days ($30), or 30 days ($112). 3. The user must be able to initiate the calculation of the metro tickets. 4. The user should be able to clear the number of tickets and the type of ticket.
Notes and Restrictions:	Negative and invalid numbers are not accepted.
Comments:	Obtain an image for this program from CengageBrain.com. The name of the image file is Metro.

FIGURE 5-97

Metro City Commute (continued)

USE CASE DEFINITION

1. The Windows Desktop application window opens.
2. The user enters the number of tickets to be purchased and selects the type of metro ticket.
3. The user taps or clicks the Buy Tickets button to display the cost of the ticket(s).
4. The user clears the input and the result by tapping or clicking the Clear button.
5. If desired, the user repeats the process.

FIGURE 5-98

FIGURE 5-99

(continues)

2

MEDICAL WEIGHT CONVERSION CALCULATOR

Design a Windows Desktop application and write the code that will execute according to the program requirements in Figure 5-100 and the Use Case Definition in Figure 5-101 on the next page. Before writing the code, create an event-planning document for each event in the program. The completed Form object and other objects in the user interface are shown in Figure 5-102 on the next page.

REQUIREMENTS DOCUMENT

Date:	October 7, 2017
Date Submitted:	
Application Title:	Medical Weight Conversion Calculator
Purpose:	This Windows Desktop application converts a patient's weight into pounds or kilograms for medication purposes.
Program Procedures:	The medical staff enters the patient's weight and selects either Pounds to Kilograms or Kilograms to Pounds. The application will determine the user's weight in pounds or kilograms. Many medications are prescribed based on patient weight in kilograms.
Algorithms, Processing, and Conditions:	1. The medical staff must be able to enter the patient's weight and indicate whether it should be converted from pounds to kilograms or kilograms to pounds. 2. To convert pounds to kilograms – divide the number of pounds by 2.2046. To convert kilograms to pounds – multiply the number of kilograms by 2.2046. 3. The medical staff must be able to initiate the calculation and display the converted weight. 4. The medical staff must be able to clear their input and the results.
Notes and Restrictions:	1. If the patient's weight entry is blank or nonnumeric, the medical staff should be advised and asked for a valid entry. 2. The results should be displayed three places past the decimal point.
Comments:	The image in this application is named Scale and is available on CengageBrain.com.

FIGURE 5-100

Case Programming Assignments

Medical Weight Conversion Calculator (continued)

USE CASE DEFINITION

1. The Windows Desktop application window opens.
2. The medical staff enters the weight for the patient and select Pounds to Kilograms or Kilogram to Pounds.
3. The user taps or clicks the Display Weight button.
4. The program displays the converted weight with the appropriate units to three decimal places.
5. A MsgBox appears and displays a warning if the user enters a negative number for the weight value.
6. A MsgBox appears and displays a warning if the user enters a nonnumeric value for the weight value or does not enter a value.
7. The user can clear the input and the results by tapping or clicking the Clear button.

FIGURE 5-101

FIGURE 5-102

(continues)

3

COMIC CHARACTER CONVENTION

Design a Windows Desktop application and write the code that will execute according to the program requirements in Figure 5-103 and the Use Case Definition in Figure 5-104 on the next page. Before writing the code, create an event-planning document for each event in the program. The completed Form object and other objects in the user interface are shown in Figure 5-105 on the next page.

REQUIREMENTS DOCUMENT

Date:	May 11, 2017
Date Submitted:	
Application Title:	Comic Character Convention
Purpose:	This Windows Desktop application computes the registration cost of attending a Comic Character Convention.
Program Procedures:	The user enters the size of the group attending the Comic Character Convention. The application computes the registration cost for the group based on badge type and attendance at the optional preview night.

Algorithms, Processing, and Conditions:

1. A user must be able to enter the size of the group and select the desired badge type. The user can select the follow badge types:
   - Convention + Superhero Experience ($330)
   - Convention + Autographs ($255)
   - Convention ($199)
2. The user can select an optional preview night for $59, which is added to their convention badge registration fee.
3. The user must be able to initiate the registration calculation and the display of the registration cost.
4. The user must be able to clear the entries and results.

Notes and Restrictions:

1. If the user enters a nonnumeric value for the group size or does not enter a group size, the user should be advised and asked for a valid entry.
2. If the user enters a negative group size, the user should be advised and asked for a valid entry.
3. If the value entered is greater than 20, the user should be advised and asked for a valid entry.
4. The default conference badge type is Convention + Superhero experience.
5. The registration cost should be displayed in currency format.

Comments:

Obtain an image for this program from CengageBrain.com. The name of the image file is Comic.

FIGURE 5-103

Case Programming Assignments

Comic Character Convention (continued)

USE CASE DEFINITION

1. The Windows Desktop application window opens.
2. The user enters the size of the group.
3. The user selects the badge type for the group.
4. The user selects whether they are attending the optional preview night.
5. The user taps or clicks the Calculate button to display the registration cost.
6. The user clears the input and the result by tapping or clicking the Clear button.
7. If desired, the user repeats the process.

FIGURE 5-104

FIGURE 5-105

4

XBOX GAMING GROUP

Design a Windows Desktop application and write the code that will execute according to the program requirements in Figure 5-106. Before designing the user interface, create a Use Case Definition. Before writing the code, create an event-planning document for each event in the program.

REQUIREMENTS DOCUMENT

Date:	April 22, 2016
Date Submitted:	
Application Title:	XBox Gaming Group
Purpose:	This Windows Desktop application calculates the payment amount for a monthly XBox subscription.
Program Procedures:	The user should enter the name of the new member, the number of months the new member would like to prepay, and the type of membership. The gaming prepayment cost will be computed and displayed for the entered number of months. The monthly costs for the three types of membership are as follows: • Single Subscription: $7 per month • Family Subscription (up to 4 members): $12 per month • XBox Developer Subscription: $3 per month
Algorithms, Processing, and Conditions:	1. The user must enter the name of the new member, the type of membership, and the number of months to prepay. 2. Based on the type of subscription, the prepayment cost is calculated using the following formula: number of prepaid months × cost per month. 3. The user must be able to initiate the calculation and display the prepaid amount for the XBox subscription, which covers the costs of unlimited gaming usage. 4. The user should be able to clear the name of the new member, the number of prepaid months, the type of membership, and the prepaid amount for the new member.
Notes and Restrictions:	1. If the user enters a nonnumeric value for the number of months, the user should be advised and asked for a valid entry. 2. If the user enters a negative number of months or does not enter a number, the user should be advised and asked for a valid entry. 3. If the user does not enter a member name, the user should be advised and asked for a valid entry. 4. The default subscription type is single membership.
Comments:	n/a

FIGURE 5-106

5 ●●
WEIGHT ON THE MOON AND MARS

Design a Windows Desktop application and write the code that will execute according to the program requirements in Figure 5-107. Before designing the user interface, create a Use Case Definition. Before writing the code, create an event-planning document for each event in the program.

REQUIREMENTS DOCUMENT

Date:	May 6, 2017
Date Submitted:	
Application Title:	Weight on the Moon and Mars
Purpose:	This Windows Desktop application calculates a user's weight in pounds and kilograms on the Moon or on Mars.
Program Procedures:	The user enters her weight in pounds and selects either the Moon or Mars. The application will determine the user's weight on the Moon or Mars in pounds and kilograms.
Algorithms, Processing, and Conditions:	1. The user must be able to enter her weight in pounds and indicate that she wants to see her equivalent weight on the Moon or Mars. 2. One pound on the Moon is equivalent to 0.166 pounds. One pound on Mars is equivalent to 0.377 pounds. 3. One pound is equivalent to 0.454 kilograms. 4. The user must be able to initiate the calculation and the display of her weight on the Moon or Mars. 5. The user must be able to clear her input and the results.
Notes and Restrictions:	1. If the user's weight entry is blank or nonnumeric, the user should be advised and asked for a valid entry. 2. The results should be displayed one place past the decimal point.
Comments:	n/a

FIGURE 5-107

6 RETRO CLOTHING PAYROLL CALCULATOR

Design a Windows Desktop and write the code that will execute according to the program requirements in Figure 5-108. Before designing the user interface, create a Use Case Definition. Before writing the code, create an event planning document for each event in the program.

REQUIREMENTS DOCUMENT

Date:	May 11, 2017
Date Submitted:	
Application Title:	Retro Clothing Payroll Calculator
Purpose:	This Windows Desktop application calculates the payroll for employees of a retro clothing store.
Program Procedures:	The user enters an employee's name, number of hours worked, and pay per hour. If the employee works more than 40 hours per week, the store pays time and a half for overtime. The tax rate can be a single rate (22%) or a family rate (19.8%). The application should compute and display the gross pay, the tax based on the single or family rate, and the net pay.
Algorithms, Processing, and Conditions:	1. The user must be able to enter the employee's name, hours worked, and pay per hour.
	2. The user must be able to indicate whether the tax rate is the single rate (22%) or the family rate (19.8%).
	3. The user must be able to initiate the calculation and display of the gross pay, the tax amount based on the single or family rate, and the net pay.
	4. A Clear button will clear the user's input and final results.
Notes and Restrictions:	1. If the employee name, hours worked, or pay per hour is left blank, the user should be advised and asked for a valid entry.
	2. If the hours worked or pay per hour is nonnumeric, the user should be advised and asked for a valid entry.
	3. The minimum value for hours worked is 8. The maximum for hours worked is 60. If the user enters a value that is not within the valid range, the user should be advised and asked for a valid entry.
	4. The minimum pay per hour is $7.25. The maximum pay per hour is $40.00. If the user enters a value that is not within the valid range, the user should be advised and asked for a valid entry.
	5. The user must be able to clear the employee's name, the hours worked, the pay per hour, and the other pay information.
Comments:	n/a

FIGURE 5-108

7 ●●●
APP DEVELOPER'S CONFERENCE REGISTRATION

Based on the case project shown in Figure 5-109, create a requirements document and a Use Case Definition document and then design a Windows application. Before writing the code, create an event-planning document for each event in the program.

App developers can update their skills by attending developers' conferences. To encourage companies to send multiple employees to the conference, the cost per attendee is determined based on the number of attending developers from a given company. The following table specifies the cost per attendee. Write this program using Case statements for the number of conference registrations.

Number of Conference Registrations per Company	Cost per Attendee
1	$795
2–4	$645
5–7	$475
8–16	$385

The App Developer's Conference has asked you to develop a Windows application that can determine and display the total cost per company for developers attending the conference. The conference has a policy that if any company member has attended a previous conference, the company receives a 15% discount for the total cost of the conference. The policy also states that no more than 16 people from a single company can attend the conference. The conference has asked you to design the program so that the user must enter valid data.

FIGURE 5-109

Case Programming Assignments

8   ● ● ●
OFFICE 365 SUBSCRIPTION PLANS

Based on the case project shown in Figure 5-110, create a requirements document and a Use Case Definition document and then design a Windows application. Before writing the code, create an event-planning document for each event in the program.

Your school has asked that you create a Windows application to determine how much it would cost a university student, an entire family, or a small business to use Microsoft Office 365 subscription plans over several months. The user can enter the number of months and a price comparison can be made. The user also can select one of three plan options; you can research the cost of these plans at *office365.com*. After the user selects a plan, its total cost for the entered amount of months is displayed to compare the prices of the plans. Do not accept negative numbers of months or nonnumeric values.

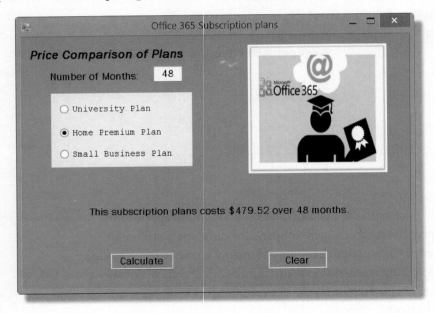

FIGURE 5-110

9 ●●●
HUMMUS RESTAURANT

Based on the case project shown in Figure 5-111, create a requirements document and a Use Case Definition document and then design a Windows application. Before writing the code, create an event-planning document for each event in the program.

A local restaurant offers hummus platters made to order. The hummus restaurant has asked you to create a Windows application that allows customers to enter their orders on a flat-screen computer. Create an application that allows the user to select one of five hummus platters. Create and display a list of platters, along with a display of prices for each platter, three types of pita bread choices at no additional cost, and two toppings at no additional cost. The hummus restaurant has a loyalty program that deducts 5% of the total order cost for every 10 points a customer has earned. Allow users to enter their total number of loyalty points and compute the cost of their order. Customers cannot receive money back if their loyalty points exceed the full cost of their order.

FIGURE 5-111

CHAPTER 6

Loop Structures

OBJECTIVES

You will have mastered the material in this chapter when you can:

- Add a MenuStrip object
- Use the InputBox function
- Display data using the ListBox object
- Add a Background Image
- Understand the use of counters and accumulators

- Understand the use of compound operators
- Repeat a process using a For... Next loop
- Repeat a process using a Do loop
- Avoid infinite loops
- Prime a loop

- Validate data
- Create a nested loop
- Select the best type of loop
- Debug using DataTips at breakpoints
- Publish a finished application using ClickOnce technology

Introduction

In Chapter 5, you learned about the decision structure, one of the major control structures used in computer programming. In this chapter, you will learn another major structure called the **looping structure**, or the **iteration structure**.

A fundamental process in a computer program is to repeat a series of instructions either while a condition is true (or not true) or until a condition is true (or not true). For example, if a company is processing electronic paychecks for 5,000 employees, it can use the same set of instructions to post an electronic deposit for each employee, varying only the name of the employee and amount paid for each check. This process would continue until all checks are deposited. Unique check deposit instructions for each employee in the company are not required.

The process of repeating a set of instructions while a condition is true or until a condition is true is called **looping**. When the program is executing those instructions, it is said to be in a loop. Another term for looping is **iteration**.

The programming project in this chapter uses a loop to obtain input data and produce output information. A large company challenged groups of eight employees to form weight loss fitness teams. The Human Resource department requested a Windows application that determines the average weight loss for each team. This application, called the Fitness Challenge application, computes the average weight loss for up to eight team members who enter the total number of pounds they lost during their weight loss challenge. The application uses a loop to request and display the weight loss amounts of the team members. The application then displays the average weight loss by the fitness team (Figure 6-1).

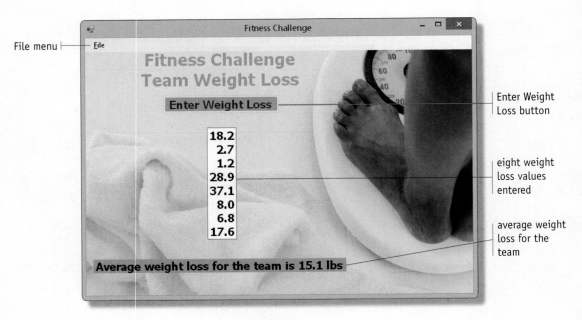

File menu

Enter Weight Loss button

eight weight loss values entered

average weight loss for the team

FIGURE 6-1

JGI/Blend Images/Getty Images

Figure 6-1 shows eight values the user entered in a list. After the user enters the weight loss values, the application calculates the average weight loss of the entire team.

When the Fitness Challenge application begins, the main window shows no weight loss values (Figure 6-2).

no weight losses entered

JGI/Blend Images/Getty Images

FIGURE 6-2

When the user taps or clicks the Enter Weight Loss button, the Weight Loss dialog box opens (Figure 6-3), allowing the user to enter the weight loss of the first team member. This dialog box is called an **input box**.

user enters weight loss here

FIGURE 6-3

After entering the first weight loss value, the user taps or clicks the OK button in the Weight Loss dialog box. The application lists the weight loss value in the main window and then displays the input box again, requesting the next team member's weight loss. This process repeats for up to eight team members and is implemented using a loop in the program. When the user is entering weight loss values, the program is said to be in a loop. The loop is terminated when the user enters the weight loss for the eighth team member or taps or clicks the Cancel button in the Weight

Loss dialog box. After the loop is terminated, the Fitness Challenge application displays the average weight loss for the team, as shown in Figure 6-1 on page 358.

The Fitness Challenge application has several other features. Figure 6-1 shows a menu bar containing the File menu at the top of the window. The File menu contains the Clear command, which clears the list and the average weight loss, and the Exit command, which closes the window and terminates the application. In this chapter, you will learn to design and code a menu.

In addition, the application contains input validation. For example, if a user enters a nonnumeric or negative value for the weight loss, the application requests the weight loss amount again, until the user enters a reasonable value.

Finally, the application displays the average weight loss to one decimal place, such as 9.2 lbs.

User Interface Design

The user interface for the Fitness Challenge application includes three new elements: a menu, an input box, and a list for the weight loss values. The menu and the list of team member weight loss values are objects placed on the Windows Form object. The input box is created through the use of a function call in the program code. Each of these items is explained in the following sections.

Insert a MenuStrip Object

A **menu bar** is a strip across the top of a window that contains one or more menu names. A **menu** is a group of commands, or items, presented in a list. In the sample program, a File menu is created in the application window (Figure 6-4).

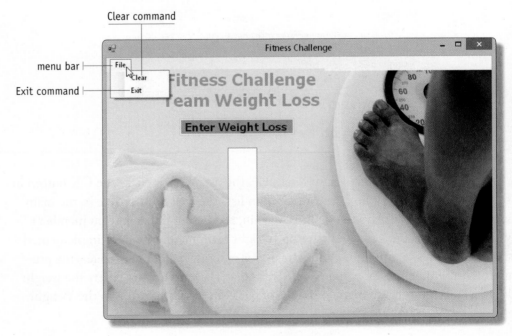

FIGURE 6-4

When the user taps or clicks File on the menu bar during program execution, a menu appears with two commands: Clear and Exit. The user taps or clicks the Clear menu command to clear the entered weight values and the results. Tapping or clicking the Exit menu command closes the application. An advantage of a menu is that it conserves space instead of cluttering the form with objects such as buttons.

Using Visual Studio 2015, you can place menus at the top of a Windows Form using the MenuStrip object. To place a MenuStrip object on a Windows Form, you can complete the following steps:

STEP 1   With a Windows Form object open in the Visual Studio window, scroll in the Toolbox to display the Menus & Toolbars category. If the category is not open, tap or click the expand icon (the right-pointing triangle) next to the Menus & Toolbars category name. Drag the MenuStrip .NET component to the Windows Form object.

The pointer changes when you place it over the Windows Form object (Figure 6-5).

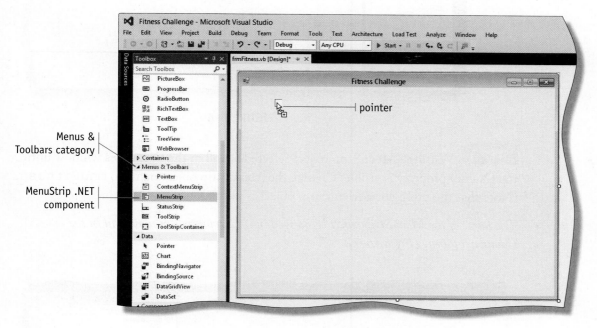

FIGURE 6-5

STEP 2 Release the object.

Visual Studio places the MenuStrip object at the top of the form regardless of where you released the object (Figure 6-6). The Component Tray, which is displayed below the form, organizes nongraphical Toolbox objects. It displays the MenuStrip1 object name.

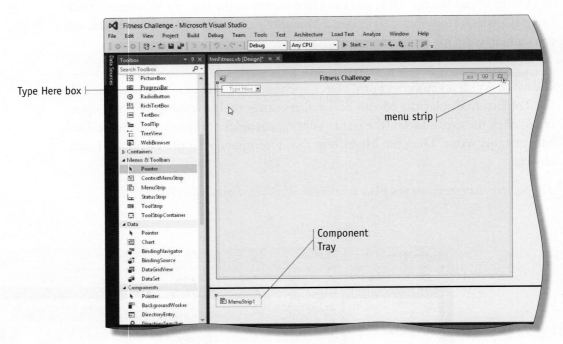

FIGURE 6-6

STEP 3 With the MenuStrip object selected, scroll in the Properties window until the (Name) property is visible. Change the MenuStrip object name to mnuFitness. (Note that the prefix for a MenuStrip object is mnu).

The name of the MenuStrip object is changed in the Properties window and in the Component Tray (Figure 6-7).

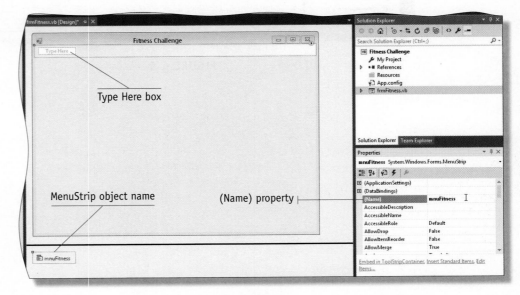

FIGURE 6-7

STEP 4 Tap or click the Type Here box on the menu bar. Type `&File` to identify the File menu, and then press the ENTER key.

The menu name File is displayed in the upper-left corner of the MenuStrip object and new Type Here boxes are available to create other menu items (Figure 6-8). The ampersand (&) you entered preceding the F indicates that F is a hot key. A hot key provides a keyboard short-cut for opening the menu. Instead of tapping or clicking File to open the menu, the user can press and hold the ALT key and then press the designated hot key, such as ALT+F. After you enter the menu name, the character following the ampersand is underlined to indicate it is the hot key.

HEADS UP

Instead of typing the menu name on a MenuStrip object, you can choose to add a menu item, combo box, or text box to the menu bar. To do so, point to the Type Here box, tap or click its list arrow, and then tap or click MenuItem, ComboBox, or TextBox.

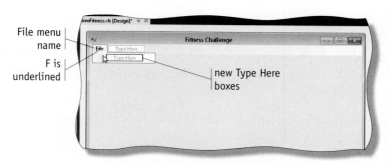

FIGURE 6-8

STEP 5 Tap or click File in the MenuStrip object to select it, scroll in the Properties window to the (Name) property, and then change the name to `mnuFile`.

The name of the File menu is displayed in the (Name) property in the Properties window (Figure 6-9).

FIGURE 6-9

STEP 6 To add a menu item to the File menu, tap or click the Type Here box below the File menu name. Type `&Clear` and then press ENTER to create a new menu item named Clear with c as the hot key.

The Clear menu item is displayed below the File menu (Figure 6-10). After you press the ENTER key, the character following the ampersand is underlined to indicate it is the hot key.

Clear menu item

C is underlined

FIGURE 6-10

STEP 7 On the File menu, tap or click Clear to select it, scroll in the Properties window until the (Name) property is visible, and then change the name to mnuClear.

The mnuClear name is displayed in the (Name) property in the Properties window (Figure 6-11).

(Name) property

FIGURE 6-11

The letter representing a hot key appears underlined in the menu name, as shown in Figure 6-10. The first letter often is used for the hot key, but not always. For example, in the chapter project, the File menu includes the Exit item (see Figure 6-4 on page 356). The hot key typically used for the Exit item is the letter x. When entering the Exit menu item on the File menu, the developer can type E&xit, which assigns the letter following the & (x) as the hot key.

When assigning menu item hot keys, you should be aware that they are not case-sensitive. Therefore, you should not assign "T" to one menu item and "t" to another.

Event Handlers for Menu Items

Recall that the design of the user interface occurs before you write the code for event handlers. When you are ready to write code, however, you must write an event handler for each menu item because tapping or clicking it or using its hot key triggers an event. Writing a menu item event handler is the same as writing an event handler for a button tap or click.

To code the event handler for the Exit menu item, you can complete the following steps:

STEP 1   In Design view, double-tap or double-click the Exit menu item to open the code window.

The code window is displayed and the insertion point is located within the Exit item click event handler (Figure 6-12). When the user taps or clicks the Exit item on the File menu, the code in the event handler will be executed.

FIGURE 6-12

STEP 2   Using IntelliSense, enter the Close procedure call to close the window and terminate the application.

When executed, the Close procedure will close the window and terminate the program (Figure 6-13).

FIGURE 6-13

Insert Standard Items for a Menu

Developers often customize the MenuStrip object for the specific needs of an application. In addition, Visual Basic 2015 contains an **Action Tag** that allows you to create a full standard menu bar commonly provided in Windows programs, with File, Edit, Tools, and Help menus. In Visual Basic 2015, an Action Tag appears in the upper-right corner of many objects, including a MenuStrip. Action Tags provide a way for you to specify a set of actions, called **smart actions**, for an object as you design a form. For example, to insert a full standard menu, you can complete the following steps:

STEP 1   With a new Windows Form object open, drag the MenuStrip .NET component onto the Windows Form object. Tap or click the Action Tag on the MenuStrip object.

The MenuStrip Tasks menu opens (Figure 6-14).

FIGURE 6-14

STEP 2   Tap or click Insert Standard Items on the MenuStrip Tasks menu.

The MenuStrip object contains four menu names: File, Edit, Tools, and Help (Figure 6-15). These are the standard menus found in many Windows applications. Each menu contains the items typically listed on the menus.

FIGURE 6-15

STEP 3   Tap or click File on the menu bar to view the individual menu items, their associated icons, and their shortcut keys.

The standard File menu items (New, Open, Save, Save As, Print, Print Preview, and Exit) are displayed with their associated icons and shortcut keys (Figure 6-16). The other menus also contain standard items. You can code an event handler for each menu item by double-tapping or double-clicking the item.

standard File menu

FIGURE 6-16

Use the InputBox Function

To calculate a team's weight loss, the Fitness Challenge application uses an InputBox object in which users enter the weight loss of each team member. The InputBox object is a dialog box that prompts the user to enter a value. You can use the InputBox function instead of a TextBox object to obtain input. Similar to coding a MessageBox object, you use the InputBox function to specify when the InputBox object appears. The InputBox function displays a dialog box that consists of a message asking for input, an input area, a title, an OK button, and a Cancel button (see Figure 6-3 on page 359). When the user enters the text and taps or clicks the OK button, the InputBox function returns the text as a string. If the user taps or clicks the Cancel button, the function returns a null string (""). Figure 6-17 shows the syntax of the InputBox function:

General Format: InputBox Function

```
strVariableName = InputBox("Question to Prompt User",
                  "Title Bar")
```

FIGURE 6-17

For example, the code in Figure 6-18 creates a dialog box that requests the user's age for a driver's license application. The string returned by the InputBox function is assigned to the strAge variable.

```
5        Dim strAge As String
6
7        strAge = InputBox("Please enter your age", "Driver's License Agency")
```

FIGURE 6-18

When the application is executed, the InputBox object in Figure 6-19 opens, requesting that the user enter his or her age.

assigned to
strAge

FIGURE 6-19

The InputBox object returns all data entered as a string, which then can be converted to the appropriate data type.

Display a Default Value in an InputBox Object

The InputBox object can be assigned a default value. For example, if a college application for admission requests the student's home state and the college or university is located in Virginia, the most likely state, Virginia, can be the default value in the InputBox, as shown in Figure 6-20.

default value

FIGURE 6-20

The code to produce this input box is shown in Figure 6-21.

```
9        Dim strState As String
10
11       strState = InputBox("Please enter the state in which you reside:", _
12           "College Application", "Virginia")
```

FIGURE 6-21

As you can see, the third argument for the InputBox function call is the default value that is placed in the input box. It must be a String value and follow the syntax shown in Figure 6-21.

Create the InputBox Object for Fitness Challenge Application

The Fitness Challenge application uses an InputBox object that requests the weight loss amounts of team members numbered 1–8, as shown in Figure 6-22.

FIGURE 6-22

The code for the Weight Loss InputBox is shown in Figure 6-23. Notice that the prompt message for the user is assigned to the strInputMessage variable, and the title bar text (Weight Loss) is assigned to the strInputHeading variable.

```
15          Dim strWeightLoss As String
16          Dim strInputMessage As String = "Enter the weight loss for team member #"
17          Dim strInputHeading As String = "Weight Loss"
18          Dim intNumberOfEntries As Integer = 1
19
20          strWeightLoss = InputBox(strInputMessage & intNumberOfEntries, strInputHeading, " ")
21
```

FIGURE 6-23

The variable intNumberOfEntries identifies the team member's number. It is included in the prompt message through the use of concatenation. The variable intNumberOfEntries is incremented later in the code so that it refers to the correct team member each time the InputBox function call is executed.

In Figure 6-23, the default value is specified as a space (" "). When the input box is displayed, a space will be selected in the input area. This space is required so that if a user taps or clicks the OK button without entering any data, the InputBox will not return a null character (" "), which indicates the user tapped or clicked the Cancel button. This normally is a good programming practice.

When the user taps or clicks the Cancel button in an input box and the InputBox function returns a null character, the program can test for the null character to determine further processing.

Display Data Using the ListBox Object

In the Fitness Challenge application, the user enters weight loss values into the InputBox object, and the application displays the weight loss values in a list box (see Figure 6-1 on page 358). To create such a list, you use the ListBox object provided in the Visual Basic Toolbox. A ListBox object displays a group of values, called items, with one item per line. To add a ListBox object to a Windows Form object, you can complete the following steps:

STEP 1   Drag the ListBox object from the Toolbox to where you want to place the ListBox object on the Windows Form object. When the pointer is in the correct location, release the object.

The ListBox object is placed on the form (Figure 6-24).

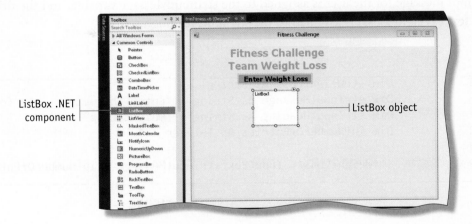

ListBox .NET component

ListBox object

FIGURE 6-24

ONLINE REINFORCEMENT

To view a video of the process in the previous steps, visit CengageBrain.com and navigate to the resources for this title. Tap or click the link for Chapter 6 and then navigate to Video 6-5.

STEP 2   With the ListBox object selected, scroll in the Properties window to the (Name) property. Name the ListBox object `lstWeightLoss`.

The name you entered is displayed in the (Name) property in the Properties window (Figure 6-25). Notice a ListBox object name begins with lst (be sure to use a lowercase letter l, not the number one).

FIGURE 6-25

After placing a ListBox object on the Windows Form object, you can adjust the size by dragging the size handles. Be sure to resize the ListBox so that it is large enough to hold the application data. The ListBox object for the Fitness Challenge application is designed to be wide enough to hold three digits and a decimal point and long enough to hold eight numbers (Figure 6-26).

FIGURE 6-26

JGI/Blend Images/Getty Images

To display the weight loss of each team member in the list box, you must write code to add each item to the ListBox object. After an item is added, it is displayed in the list box. The general format of the statement to add an item to a ListBox object is shown in Figure 6-27.

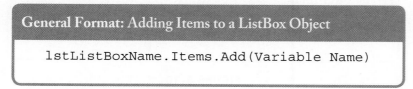

General Format: Adding Items to a ListBox Object

```
lstListBoxName.Items.Add(Variable Name)
```

FIGURE 6-27

In Figure 6-27, the Add procedure will add the item contained in the variable identified by the Variable Name entry. The syntax for the statement must be followed precisely.

Figure 6-28 shows the code to add the team member weight loss values to the lstWeightLoss ListBox object and then display the weight loss of each team member (decWeightLoss) in the ListBox object.

```
45 |          lstWeightLoss.Items.Add(decWeightLoss)
```

FIGURE 6-28

If the number of items exceeds the number that can be displayed in the designated length of the ListBox object, a scroll bar automatically is added to the ListBox object, as shown in Figure 6-29.

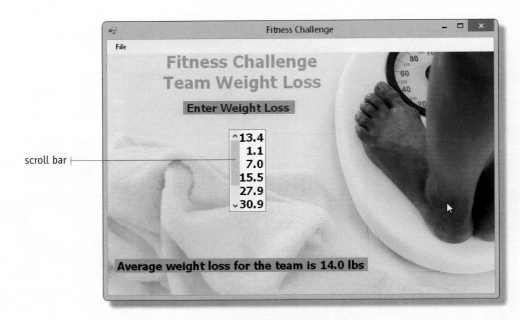

FIGURE 6-29

JGI/Blend Images/Getty Images

To clear the items in a ListBox object, the Clear method works as it does for the TextBox object. The syntax of the statement to clear the ListBox is shown in Figure 6-30.

General Format: Clear the ListBox Object

```
lstListBoxName.Items.Clear()
```

FIGURE 6-30

In the Fitness Challenge application, the user can select the Clear menu item to clear the form. The code in Figure 6-31 removes the items from the lstWeightLoss ListBox.

```
81          lstWeightLoss.Items.Clear()
```

FIGURE 6-31

Can I control where the InputBox appears on the screen?
To control the position of the InputBox, you can add an optional X position and Y position representing the upper-left edge of the dialog box. The syntax of the InputBox with sample X and Y positions is as follows:
myValue = InputBox(message, title, defaultValue, 150, 100)
The 150 pixels represents the X position (horizontal) and the 100 pixels represents the Y position (vertical).

Add ListBox Items during Design

The Fitness Challenge application allows the user to add items to the ListBox object during program execution, but you can also add items to a ListBox object while designing the form. Adding items to the ListBox object during the design phase allows the user to select an item from the ListBox object during execution. For example, in an application to select a favorite clothing store, you can add items to a ListBox object named lstStores during the form design by completing the following steps:

STEP 1   Assume the lstStores ListBox object already has been placed and named on the Windows Form object. Select the ListBox object on the Windows Form object and then tap or click the Items property in the Properties window.

The Items property in the Properties window is selected. An ellipsis button appears to the right of the (Collection) entry (Figure 6-32).

FIGURE 6-32

STEP 2   Tap or click the ellipsis button in the right column of the Items property.

The String Collection Editor window opens, allowing you to enter items that will be displayed in the lstStores ListBox object (Figure 6-33).

String Collection
Editor window

enter items to
be placed in the
ListBox object

FIGURE 6-33

STEP 3   Tap or click the String Collection Editor window. Type the following items to represent popular retail stores, and then press ENTER at the end of each line:

```
Abercrombie & Fitch
Anthropologie
Express
H & M
Urban Outfitters
```

The items representing favorite retail stores appear in the String Collection Editor window on separate lines (Figure 6-34).

items entered for
the ListBox object

OK button

FIGURE 6-34

ONLINE REINFORCEMENT

To view a video of the process
in the previous steps, visit
CengageBrain.com and navigate
to the resources for this title.
Tap or click the link for Chapter 6
and then navigate to Video 6-6.

STEP 4   Tap or click the OK button.

The Windows Form object displays the stores in the lstStores ListBox object (Figure 6-35). The user can select one of the items in the ListBox object during execution.

FIGURE 6-35

Use the SelectedItem Property

The SelectedItem property identifies which item in the ListBox is selected. An assignment statement assigns that property to a variable, as shown in Figure 6-36.

> **General Format: Assign the Selected Item in a ListBox Object**
>
> ```
> StrVariableName = lstListBoxName.selectedItem
> ```

FIGURE 6-36

Figure 6-37 shows the code to display the user's selection of his or her favorite store from the lstStores ListBox object in a message box.

```
5          MsgBox("Your favorite store is "_
6          &lstStores.SelectedItem & ".")
```

FIGURE 6-37

Add a Background Image

In addition to using background colors to design the Windows Form object, you may want to place a background image on the form itself. Background images are commonly displayed in your Facebook header and in mobile apps such as clouds in the background of the Weather Channel app. The **BackgroundImage** property of the Form object can set the background image to an imported image. The **Background ImageLayout** property can be used to control the appearance of the image on the form. By default the background image repeats the same picture in a tile pattern, but the Background ImageLayout property can be changed to Center, Stretch, or Zoom.

To change the background image on the form, you can complete the following steps, which assumes that you have downloaded the Scale image file from the CengageBrain site.

STEP 1   Tap or click the Form object. In the Properties window, tap or click the ellipsis button of the BackgroundImage property. Tap or click the Import button and open the file location of the Scale image file. Tap or click Scale.jpg and tap or click the Open button.

The Select Resource window displays the imported background image file named Scale.jpg (Figure 6-38).

FIGURE 6-38

STEP 2   Tap or click the OK button.

The background image Scale.jpg is displayed in the frmFitness form (Figure 6-39).

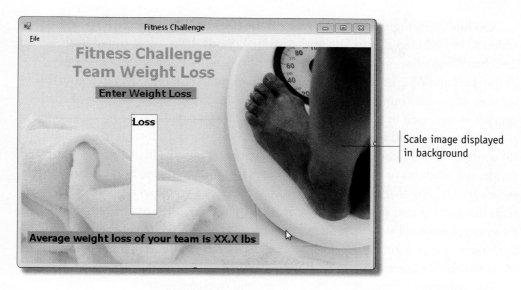

Scale image displayed
in background

FIGURE 6-39

JGI/Blend Images/Getty Images

Use Accumulators, Counters, and Compound Operators

After the user enters the weight loss values of up to eight team members, the Fitness Challenge application calculates the average weight loss (see Figure 6-1 on page 358). The formula to calculate the average weight loss is: (total of all weight loss values entered) / (number of team members). For example, if the total of all the weight loss values entered is 145.2 and weight loss values were entered for eight team members, the average weight loss is 18.2 pounds.

To calculate the average, the program must add the weight loss of each team member to a variable. The variable that contains an accumulated value such as the total of all the weight loss values is called an **accumulator**.

To compute the average weight loss, the program must also keep track of how many weight loss values have been entered. The variable that keeps track of this value is called a **counter**. A counter always is incremented with a constant value. This value can be positive or negative. In the Fitness Challenge application, the counter is incremented by 1 each time the user enters a weight loss number for a team member. Only positive values that indicate how many pounds were lost are accepted; for example, 8.3 represents 8.3 pounds lost.

You can use one of two techniques to add a value to a variable and then update the value in the variable, as with an accumulator or a counter. The first technique is shown in Figure 6-40.

```
26        decTotalWeightLoss = decTotalWeightLoss + decWeightLoss
27        intNumberOfEntries = intNumberOfEntries + 1
```

FIGURE 6-40

On line 26 in Figure 6-40, the value in the decTotalWeightLoss variable is added to the value in the decWeightLoss variable and the result is stored in the decTotalWeightLoss variable. This statement accumulates the weight loss values in the decTotalWeightLoss accumulator. The statement in line 27 increments the number of entries counter by 1. The effect is that the value in the number of entries counter is increased by 1 each time the statement is executed.

A second method for accomplishing this task is to use a shortcut mathematical operator called a **compound operator** that allows you to add, subtract, multiply, divide, use modulus or exponents, or concatenate strings, storing the result in the same variable. An assignment statement that includes a compound operator begins with the variable that will contain the accumulated value, such as an accumulator or a counter, followed by the compound operator. A compound operator consists of an arithmetic operator and an equal sign. The last element in the assignment statement is the variable or literal containing the value to be used in the calculation.

An assignment statement using a compound operator such as:

```
intNumberOfEntries += 1
```

is the same as:

```
intNumberOfEntries = intNumberOfEntries + 1
```

The += compound operator adds the value of the right operand to the value of the left operand and stores the result in the left operand's variable. Similarly, the statement:

```
decTotalWeightLoss += decWeightLoss
```

is the same as:

```
decTotalWeightLoss = decTotalWeightLoss + decWeightLoss
```

The table in Figure 6-41 shows an example of compound operators used in code. Assume that intResult = 24, decResult = 24, and strSample = "tree".

Operation	Example with Single Operators	Example with Compound Operator	Result
Addition	intResult = intResult + 1	intResult + = 1	intResult = 25
Subtraction	intResult = intResult − 3	intResult − = 3	intResult = 21
Multiplication	intResult = intResult * 2	intResult * = 2	intResult = 48
Decimal Division	decResult = decResult / 5	decResult / = 5	decResult = 4.8
Integer Division	intResult = intResult \ 5	intResult \ = 5	intResult = 4
Exponents	intResult = intResult ^ 2	intResult ^ = 2	intResult = 576
Concatenate	strSample = strSample & "house"	strSample & = "house"	strSample = "tree house"

FIGURE 6-41

Developers often use compound operators in Visual Basic coding. The coding example in Figure 6-42 uses several compound operators and a MsgBox object. When the following code is executed, the result shown in the MsgBox object is "Final Result = 2."

```
30          Dim intTotal As Integer
31          intTotal = 7
32          intTotal += 6
33          intTotal *= 2
34          intTotal /= 13
35          MsgBox("Final Result = " & intTotal.ToString(), , "Compound Operators")
```

FIGURE 6-42

Compound operators can also be used to connect two strings with the concatenation operator (&). The code in Figure 6-43 creates the phrase "To err is human!" in a MsgBox object by using compound operators to concatenate the strPhrase variable. Each compound operator joins another word to the end of the phrase assigned to the strPhrase variable.

HEADS UP

The compound operators +=, −=, *=, /=, \=, ^=, and &= run faster than their regular longer equation counterparts because the statement is more compact.

```
30          Dim strPhrase As String
31          strPhrase = "To err"
32          strPhrase &= " is "
33          strPhrase &= "human!"
34          MsgBox(strPhrase, , "Compound Operators")
```

FIGURE 6-43

Use Loops to Perform Repetitive Tasks

In the Fitness Challenge application, the user enters weight loss values in an InputBox for up to eight team members. The repetitive process of entering eight weight loss values can be coded within a loop to simplify the task with fewer lines of code. Unlike If...Then statements that execute only once, loops repeat multiple times. Each repetition of the loop is called an iteration. An iteration is a single execution of a set of instructions that are to be repeated.

Loops are powerful structures that repeat a section of code a certain number of times or until a particular condition is met. Visual Basic has two main types of loops: For...Next loops and Do loops.

Repeat a Process Using the For...Next Loop

You can use a For...Next loop when a section of code should be executed an exact number of times. The syntax of a For...Next loop is shown in Figure 6-44.

```
General Format: For...Next loop

For Control Variable = Beginning Numeric Value To Ending
                       Numeric Value

   ' Body of the Loop

Next
```

FIGURE 6-44

In Figure 6-44, the For...Next loop begins with the keyword For. Following this keyword is the control variable, which is the numeric variable that keeps track of the number of iterations the loop completes. To begin the loop, the For statement places the beginning numeric value in the control variable. The program then executes the code between the For and Next statements, which is called the body of the loop.

Upon reaching the Next statement, the program returns to the For statement and increments the value of the control variable. This process continues until the value in the control variable is greater than the ending numeric value. The program then executes the statement(s) that follows the Next command.

Figure 6-45 shows a For...Next loop designed to execute four times. The control value is a variable named intNumber.

FIGURE 6-45

The first line in Figure 6-45 specifies that the control variable (intNumber) is assigned the value 1 because the literal 1 is the beginning value. Then the program executes the body of the loop. When the program encounters the Next statement, control returns to the For statement where, by default, the value 1 is added to the control variable. The code in the body of the loop is executed again. This process continues until the value in the control variable is greater than the ending value, which is 4 in this example. Then the program executes the statement(s) that follow the Next command. A loop never exits in the middle of the loop. The comparison is made to the upper limit of the For statement and when the value exceeds the upper limit, loop terminates. The table in Figure 6-46 illustrates the looping process.

Loop Iteration	Value of intNumber	Process
1	intNumber = 1	Executes the code inside the loop
2	intNumber = 2	Executes the code inside the loop
3	intNumber = 3	Executes the code inside the loop
4	intNumber = 4	Executes the code inside the loop
5 (exits the loop)	intNumber = 5	The control variable value exceeds the ending value, so the application exits the For...Next loop. This means the statement(s) following the Next command are executed.

FIGURE 6-46

Include a Step Value in a For...Next Loop

A Step value is the value in a For...Next loop that is added to or subtracted from the beginning value on each iteration of the loop. If you do not include a Step value in the For statement, as shown in Figure 6-47, by default the value in the control variable is incremented by 1 after each iteration of the loop.

Step value

```
49          For intNumber = 1 To 99 Step 2
50              ' Body of loop
51          Next
```

FIGURE 6-47

In Figure 6-47, a Step value of 2 has been added to the For statement. The control variable intNumber is set to the initial value of 1, and the lines of code in the body of the loop are executed. After the first iteration of the loop, the Step value is added to the control variable, changing the value in the control variable to 3 (1 + 2 = 3). The For loop will continue until the value in intNumber is greater than 99.

The Step value can be negative. If so, the value in the control variable is decreased on each iteration of the loop. To exit the loop, you must specify an ending value that is less than the beginning value, as shown in Figure 6-48.

negative
Step value

```
55          For intCount = 25 To -10 Step -5
56              ' Body of loop
57          Next
```

FIGURE 6-48

In the first iteration of the For...Next loop in Figure 6-48, the control variable value is 25. The value in the intCount control variable is decreased by 5 each time the loop repeats. This repetition continues until the value in intCount is less than −10. Then the loop ends.

You can also assign decimal values to the control variable in a For...Next loop. For example, the For loop in Figure 6-49 has a starting value of 3.1. The loop ends when the value in the control variable is greater than 4.5. The Step value is 0.1, which means the value in decNumber increments by 0.1 on each pass through the loop.

decimal
Step value

```
61          For decNumber = 3.1 To 4.5 Step 0.1
62              ' Body of loop
63          Next
```

FIGURE 6-49

A For...Next loop can also include variables and mathematical expressions, as shown in Figure 6-50.

```
69          For intNumber = intBegin To (intEnd * 2) Step intIncrement
70              'Body of loop
71          Next
```

FIGURE 6-50

In Figure 6-50, the intNumber control variable is initialized with the value in the intBegin variable. Each time the Next statement is encountered and control is returned to the For statement, the value in intNumber is incremented by the value in the intIncrement variable. The loop continues until the value in intNumber is greater than the product of the value in intEnd times 2.

Use IntelliSense to Enter the For...Next Loop Code

Suppose an application is designed to have a list box that displays the population growth for Alaska during the next six years. Assume that the current population of Alaska is 675,000 people and is expected to grow at 5 percent per year for the next six years. The code in Figure 6-51 accomplishes this processing.

```
4          Dim intAlaskaPopulation As Integer = 675000
5          Dim intYears As Integer
6
7          For intYears = 1 To 6
8              intAlaskaPopulation += (intAlaskaPopulation * 0.05)
9              lstGrowth.Items.Add("Year " & intYears & " Population " & intAlaskaPopulation)
10
11         Next
```

FIGURE 6-51

To use IntelliSense to enter the code shown in Figure 6-51, you can complete the following steps, which assume a lstGrowth ListBox object has been defined on a Windows Form object.

STEP 1 In the code window, type `Dim intAlaskaPopulation As Integer = 675000` and then press the ENTER key. Type `Dim intYears As Integer` and then press the ENTER key two times. Type `for` and a space to open an IntelliSense list.

When you press the SPACEBAR, For is capitalized because it is a reserved word (Figure 6-52).

variables declared

For command entered

IntelliSense list

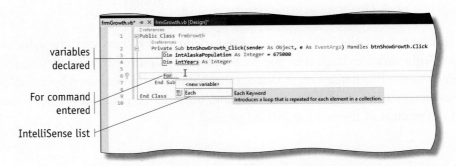

FIGURE 6-52

STEP 2 Type the first four letters of the intYears variable name (`intY`) to select intYears in the IntelliSense list. Type `= 1 to 6` and then press the ENTER key to specify the beginning value and ending value for the loop.

Visual Basic automatically inserts the Next statement in the code (Figure 6-53). For, To, and Next are blue to indicate they are keywords.

For statement entered

line indented

Next statement entered automatically

FIGURE 6-53

STEP 3 Use IntelliSense to select the appropriate variables. Enter the two new lines shown in Figure 6-54.

statements in
body of loop

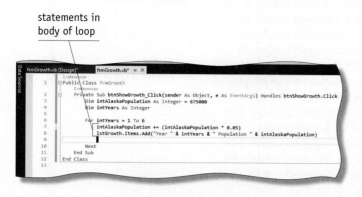

```
        2 references
 1   ⊟Public Class frmGrowth
        0 references
 2         Private Sub btnShowGrowth_Click(sender As Object, e As EventArgs) Handles btnShowGrowth.Click
 3             Dim intAlaskaPopulation As Integer = 675000
 4             Dim intYears As Integer
 5
 6             For intYears = 1 To 6
 7                 intAlaskaPopulation += (intAlaskaPopulation * 0.05)
 8                 lstGrowth.Items.Add("Year " & intYears & " Population " & intAlaskaPopulation)
 9
10             Next
11         End Sub
12     End Class
13
```

FIGURE 6-54

Each line of code automatically is indented between the For and Next statements (Figure 6-54).

STEP 4 Run the program to see the results of the loop.

The loop calculates and displays the Alaskan population growth for six years based on 5 percent growth per year (Figure 6-55).

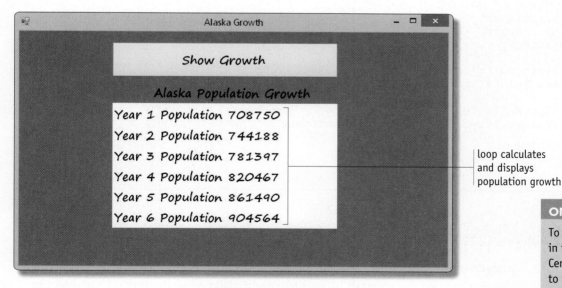

loop calculates
and displays
population growth

FIGURE 6-55

Handle User Input in a For...Next Loop

The beginning, ending, and Step values used in a For...Next loop can vary based on user input. For example, the Squared Values application shown in Figure 6-56 displays the squared values of a range of numbers the user enters. The user enters the beginning (minimum) and ending (maximum) range of values and then taps or clicks the Calculate Values button to view the squares of the numbers in the range.

FIGURE 6-56

The code for the Squared Values application is shown in Figure 6-57.

```
5     Dim intCount As Integer
6     Dim intBegin As Integer
7     Dim intEnd As Integer
8
9     intBegin = Convert.ToInt32(txtMinimumNumber.Text)
10    intEnd = Convert.ToInt32(txtMaximumNumber.Text)
11
12    For intCount = intBegin To intEnd
13        lstSquaredValues.Items.Add("Number: " & intCount & " Squared Value: " & (intCount ^ 2))
14    Next
15
16    End Sub
```

FIGURE 6-57

On line 9 in Figure 6-57, the minimum value the user entered is converted to an integer and placed in the intBegin variable. Similarly, on line 10, the maximum value the user entered is converted to an integer and assigned to the intEnd variable. On line 12, the value in intBegin is used as the beginning value in the For...Next loop, and the value in intEnd is used as the ending value. As you can see, the number of iterations for the loop is determined by values the user entered.

Within the loop, the value in intCount begins with the value in intBegin and is incremented by the default value of 1 each time through the loop. The application calculates the squared value from the number in intCount. As a result, the application calculates the squared values for all numbers beginning with the minimum number and ending with the maximum number.

Repeat a Process Using a Do Loop

You use a For...Next loop to repeat a process an exact number of times. In many applications, however, a loop should be repeated until a certain condition changes. For example, in the Fitness Challenge application, the user repeats the process of entering a weight loss value eight times, and then stops entering values by tapping or clicking the Cancel button. The loop in the Fitness Challenge application continues until one of two conditions becomes true: either the count of the weight loss values entered reaches 8 or the user taps or clicks the Cancel button on the InputBox object.

In a **Do loop**, the body of the loop is executed while or until a condition is true or false. The Do loop uses a condition similar to an If...Then decision structure to determine whether it should continue looping. In this way, you can use a Do loop to execute a body of statements an indefinite number of times. In the Fitness Challenge application, a Do loop can run an indefinite number of times because the user can end the loop at any time by tapping or clicking the Cancel button.

Visual Basic 2015 provides two types of Do loops: the Do While loop and the Do Until loop. Both Do loops execute statements repeatedly until a specified condition becomes true or false. Each loop examines a condition to determine whether the condition is true. The **Do While loop** executes as long as the condition is true. It is stated as, "Do the loop processing while the condition is true."

The **Do Until loop** executes until the condition becomes true. It is stated as, "Do the loop processing until a condition is true."

Do loops are either top-controlled or bottom-controlled, depending on whether the condition is tested before the loop begins or after the body of the loop has executed one time. A **top-controlled loop** is tested before the loop is entered. A top-controlled loop is also called a pre-test. The body of a top-controlled loop might not be executed at all because the condition being tested might be true before any processing in the loop occurs.

Bottom-controlled loops test the condition at the bottom of the loop, also called a post test, so the body of a bottom-controlled loop is executed at least once. Visual Basic provides top-controlled and bottom-controlled Do While and Do Until loops, meaning it can execute four types of Do loops.

Top-Controlled Do While Loops

You use a top-controlled Do While loop if you want the body of the loop to repeat as long as a condition remains true. Figure 6-58 shows the syntax of a top-controlled Do While loop.

General Format: Do While Loop (Top-Controlled)

```
Do While condition
    ' Body of loop
Loop
```

FIGURE 6-58

A top-controlled Do While loop begins with the keywords Do While. Next, the condition is specified. The condition is expressed using the same relational operators that are available with the If statements that you learned in Chapter 5. Any condition that can be specified in an If statement can be specified in a Do While condition. The condition can compare numeric values or string values.

The body of the loop contains the instructions that are executed as long as the condition is true. The Loop keyword indicates the end of the loop. Visual Basic inserts it automatically when you enter the Do While keywords.

A statement within the body of the Do While loop must cause the condition to change at some point so the loop ends. For example, consider the following statement:

```
Do While strColor = "Red"
```

The loop continues to process as long as the value in the strColor variable remains Red. Based on the processing in the body of the loop, at some point the value in the strColor variable must be changed from Red. If not, the loop will not end. A loop that does not end is called an **infinite loop**.

The code in Figure 6-59 is an example of a top-controlled Do While loop. It continues to add 1 to the variable intScore while intScore is less than 5. It is considered a top-controlled loop because the condition is checked at the top of the loop.

```
17        Dim intScore As Integer = 0
18        Do While intScore < 5
19            intScore += 1
20        Loop
```

FIGURE 6-59

The loop in Figure 6-59 begins by testing whether intScore is less than 5. Because intScore starts with the value 0, the condition tested is true: 0 is less than 5. Next, the variable intScore is incremented by 1, and the loop repeats. The table in Figure 6-60 displays the values that are assigned to intScore each time the condition is checked in the code in Figure 6-59.

Loop Iteration	Value of intScore	Result of Condition Tested
1	intScore = 0	True
2	intScore = 1	True
3	intScore = 2	True
4	intScore = 3	True
5	intScore = 4	True
6	intScore = 5	False

FIGURE 6-60

The loop in Figure 6-59 is executed five times because intScore is less than 5 during five iterations of the loop. As shown in Figure 6-59, if the value in the variable intScore is 5 or greater when the Do While statement is first executed, the body of the loop never will be executed because the condition is not true prior to the first iteration of the loop.

Enter a Do Loop Using IntelliSense

To use IntelliSense to enter the Do While loop shown in Figure 6-59, you can complete the following steps:

STEP 1   In the code window, enter the intScore variable declaration and then press the ENTER key. Type Do While and a space to display an IntelliSense list. Type ints to highlight intScore in the list.

The words Do While appear in blue because they are Visual Basic keywords (Figure 6-61). The IntelliSense list contains the valid entries and the intScore variable name is highlighted.

FIGURE 6-61

STEP 2   Type < 5 and then press the ENTER key.

Visual Basic automatically inserts the intScore variable name and the characters you typed (Figure 6-62). The keyword Loop is also inserted and the insertion point is located inside the loop, ready to enter the body of the loop.

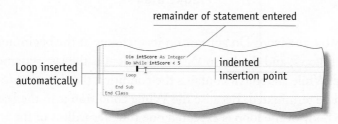

FIGURE 6-62

STEP 3   Type ints to highlight the intScore variable. Complete the statement by typing += 1 and then pressing the ENTER key. Press the DELETE key to delete the blank line.

The statement automatically is indented between the Do While and Loop statements (Figure 6-63). The intScore +=1 statement uses a compound operator to increment the intScore variable.

FIGURE 6-63

Bottom-Controlled Do While Loops

You can write a Do While loop in which the condition is tested at the bottom of the loop. A bottom-controlled loop works the same way as the top-controlled Do While loop except that the body of the loop is executed before the condition is checked the first time, guaranteeing that at least one iteration of a loop will be completed. The bottom-controlled Do While loop has the syntax shown in Figure 6-64.

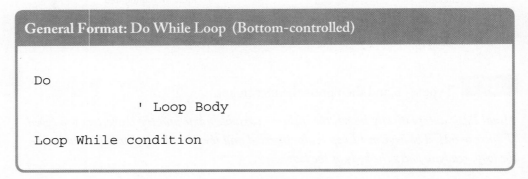

FIGURE 6-64

In Figure 6-64, the word Do appears on its own line at the beginning of the loop. The loop body follows, and the Loop While statement is the last statement in the loop. The Loop While statement contains the condition that is tested to determine if the loop should be terminated. Because the While condition is in the last statement of the loop, the body of the loop is executed one time regardless of the status of the condition.

The code in Figure 6-65 is an example of a bottom-controlled Do While loop.

```
22          Dim intScore As Integer = 0
23          Do
24              intScore = intScore + 1
25          Loop While intScore < 5
```

FIGURE 6-65

The body of the Do loop in Figure 6-65 is executed one time before the condition in the Loop While statement is checked. The variable intScore begins with the initial value of 0 and is incremented in the body of the loop, changing the value to 1. The condition is then tested and found to be true because 1 < 5. The loop repeats and the value of intScore increases, as shown in Figure 6-66.

Loop Iteration	Value of intScore at Start of the Loop	Value of intScore When Checked	Result of Condition Tested
1	intScore = 0	intScore = 1	True
2	intScore = 1	intScore = 2	True
3	intScore = 2	intScore = 3	True
4	intScore = 3	intScore = 4	True
5	intScore = 4	intScore = 5	False

FIGURE 6-66

The body of the loop in Figure 6-65 is executed four times because intScore is less than 5 during five iterations of the loop.

Use Do Until Loops

A loop similar to a Do While loop is called a Do Until loop. The Do Until loop allows you to specify that an action repeats until a condition becomes true. When the condition in a Do Until loop becomes true, the loop ends.

Top-Controlled Do Until Loops

A Do Until loop can be both top-controlled and bottom-controlled. The syntax of the top-controlled Do Until loop is shown in Figure 6-67.

General Format: Do UntilLoop (Top-Controlled)

```
Do Until condition
                ' Loop Body

Loop
```

FIGURE 6-67

A top-controlled Do Until loop begins with the keywords Do Until. Next, as with the Do While top-controlled loop, the condition is specified. The condition is expressed using the same relational operators that are available with If statements. Any condition that can be specified in an If statement can be specified in a Do Until condition. The condition can compare numeric values or string values.

The Do Until loop example shown in Figure 6-68 displays a parking meter application that computes the number of minutes a user can purchase based on the cost of 25 cents for each 15 minutes of parking. If the user only has 88 cents in pocket change, for example, the application computes how many minutes of parking time 88 cents will purchase.

```
4        Dim decAmount As Decimal = 0.88
5        Dim intQuarters As Integer = 0
6        Dim intTime As Integer = 15
7        Dim intParkingTime As Integer
8
9        Do Until decAmount < 0.25
10           intQuarters += 1
11           decAmount -= 0.25
12       Loop
13       intParkingTime = intQuarters * intTime
14       lblParkingTime.Text = "Parking Time: " &
15                       intParkingTime.ToString() & " minutes"
```

FIGURE 6-68

In the code example in Figure 6-68, the application checks the Do Until loop condition before executing the body of the loop. The first time the condition is tested, the expression decAmount < 0.25 is false because the decAmount variable contains 0.88. The body of the loop is executed because the Do Until statement specifies that the loop continues until the value in decAmount is less than 0.25. When the body of the loop is executed, it adds 1 to intQuarters to count the number of quarters the user has for the parking meter, and then subtracts 0.25 from decAmount because a quarter is worth 25 cents. Because decAmount is first assigned the value 0.88, the loop executes three times (decAmount = 0.88, decAmount = 0.63, and decAmount = 0.38) and stops when decAmount becomes less than 0.25. The lblParkingTime Label object displays the text "Parking Time: 45 minutes."

Bottom-Controlled Do Until Loops

The last of the four Do loops is the bottom-controlled Do Until loop. This Do Until loop checks the condition after the body of the loop is executed. The loop continues until the condition becomes true. The syntax of the bottom-controlled Do Until loop is shown in Figure 6-69.

```
General Format: Do UntilLoop (Botttom-Controlled)

Do

            ' Loop Body

Loop Until condition
```

FIGURE 6-69

In Figure 6-69, the bottom-controlled Do Until loop begins with the word Do. The body of the loop is executed one time regardless of the condition being tested. The Loop Until statement checks the condition. The loop will be repeated until the condition is true.

Other Loop Considerations

Other considerations when using loops are creating user input loops, avoiding infinite loops, priming a loop, validating data with a loop, creating a nested loop, and selecting the best type of loop.

User Input Loops

Do loops often are written to end when the user enters a certain value or performs a certain action such as tapping or clicking the Cancel button in an input box. The developer determines the value or action. For example, the Do Until loop in Figure 6-68 accumulates the total of all the entered test scores until the user taps or clicks the Cancel button in the input box. If the user taps or clicks the Cancel button, the InputBox function returns a null string that is assigned to the strTestGrade variable. The Do Until statement tests the string. If it contains a null character, the loop is terminated.

Avoid Infinite Loops

Recall that an infinite loop is a loop that never ends. It happens when the condition specified to end the loop never occurs. If the loop does not end, it repeats until the program is interrupted. Figure 6-70 shows an example of an infinite loop.

```
22        Dim intProblem = 0
23        Do While intProblem <= 5
24            Box.Show("This loop will not end", "Infinite Loop")
25        Loop
```

FIGURE 6-70

The Do While loop in Figure 6-70 never ends because the value in the variable intProblem is never changed from its initial value of zero. Because the value in intProblem never exceeds 5, the condition in the Do While loop (intProblem <= 5) never becomes false. The processing in a loop eventually must change the condition being tested in the Do While loop so the loop will terminate. When working in Visual Basic 2015, you can interrupt an infinite loop by tapping or clicking the Stop Debugging button on the Standard toolbar.

CONSIDER THIS

How do I know which type of loop to use?
All loops have the same basic function of repeating certain lines of a program. Some loops are best suited under certain conditions. For example, if you want to check the condition before the loop is run, use a top-controlled loop. Often the type of loop you use is just programmer preference.

Prime the Loop

As you have learned, a top-controlled loop tests a condition prior to beginning the loop. In most cases, the value to test must be set before the condition is tested the first time in the Do While or Do Until statement. Starting a loop with a preset value in the variable(s) tested in the condition is called **priming the loop**. You have seen this in previous examples, such as in Figure 6-68 on page 392, where the value in decAmount is set before the condition is tested the first time.

In some applications, the loop is primed with a value the user enters or an action the user takes. For example, in the Fitness Challenge application, the user enters the weight loss value for each team member (up to eight values) or taps or clicks the Cancel button in the input box. Prior to executing the Do Until statement the first time in the Do Until loop that processes the data the user enters, the InputBox function must be executed to obtain an initial value. Then, the Do Until statement can test the action taken by the user (enter a value and tap or click the Cancel button). The coding to implement this processing is shown in Figure 6-71.

```
30              Dim strCancelClicked As String = ""
31              Dim intMaxNumberOfEntries As Integer = 8
32              Dim intNumberOfEntries As Integer = 1
⋮
38              strWeightLoss = InputBox(strInputMessage & intNumberOfEntries, strInputHeading, " ")
39
40              Do Until intNumberOfEntries > intMaxNumberOfEntries Or strWeightLoss = strCancelClicked
⋮
47                      intNumberOfEntries += 1
⋮
56                  If intNumberOfEntries <= intMaxNumberOfEntries Then
57                      strWeightLoss = InputBox(strInputMessage & intNumberOfEntries, strInputHeading, " ")
58                  End If
59
60              Loop
```

FIGURE 6-71

In the Do Until loop shown in Figure 6-71, the Do Until statement on line 40 tests two conditions: Is the value in the intNumberOfEntries variable greater than the value in the intMaxNumberOfEntries variable, or is the value in the strWeightLoss variable equal to the value in the strCancelClicked variable, which is a null character (see line 30)? If either condition is true, the body of the loop is not executed.

The Do Until loop must have two primed variables: the intNumberOfEntries variable and the strWeightLoss variable. The intNumberOfEntries variable is initialized to 1 on line 33. The strWeightLoss variable is initialized by the InputBox function call on line 39. In this function call, either the user entered a value or tapped or clicked the Cancel button. If the user tapped or clicked the Cancel button, the body of the loop should not be entered.

To continue the loop, the processing within the body of the loop eventually must change one of the conditions being tested in the Do Until statement or the loop never terminates. In the sample program, the conditions being tested are whether the user entered eight weight loss values or tapped or clicked the Cancel button. Therefore, within the loop, the variable containing intNumberOfEntries must be incremented when the user enters a valid weight loss value. The user then must be able to enter more weight loss values or tap or click the Cancel button. On line 48 in Figure 6-71, the value in intNumberOfEntries is incremented by 1 each time the user enters a valid weight loss value. In addition, the statement on line 58 displays an input box that allows the user to enter a new value or tap or click the Cancel button as long as the number of valid entries is not greater than the maximum number of entries.

Validate Data

As you learned in Chapter 5, you must test the data a user enters to ensure it is accurate and that its use in other programming statements, such as converting string data to numeric data, will not cause a program exception. When using an input box, the data should be checked using the IsNumeric function and If statements, as discussed in Chapter 5. If the data is not valid, the user must be notified of the error and an input box displayed to allow the user to enter valid data.

For example, if the user enters nonnumeric data, the input box in Figure 6-72 should be displayed.

FIGURE 6-72

Similarly, if the user enters a negative number, the message in Figure 6-73 should be displayed in an input box.

FIGURE 6-73

When error checking is performed within a loop and the user is asked to enter data in an input box, the body of the loop must be executed each time the user enters data, regardless of whether the data is valid or invalid. If the user enters valid data, then the data is processed according to the needs of the program.

If the user enters invalid data, an error message is displayed and the user is given the opportunity to enter valid data in the input box. The coding for the Fitness Challenge application that accomplishes these tasks is shown in Figure 6-74.

```
38          strWeightLoss = InputBox(strInputMessage & intNumberOfEntries, strInputHeading, " ")
39
40          Do Until intNumberOfEntries > intMaxNumberOfEntries Or strWeightLoss = strCancelClicked
41
42              If IsNumeric(strWeightLoss) Then
43                  decWeightLoss = Convert.ToDecimal(strWeightLoss)
44                  If decWeightLoss > 0 Then
45                      lstWeightLoss.Items.Add(decWeightLoss)
46                      decTotalWeightLoss += decWeightLoss
47                      intNumberOfEntries += 1
48                      strInputMessage = strNormalMessage
49                  Else
50                      strInputMessage = strNegativeError
51                  End If
52              Else
53                  strInputMessage = strNonNumericError
54              End If
55
56              If intNumberOfEntries <= intMaxNumberOfEntries Then
57                  strWeightLoss = InputBox(strInputMessage & intNumberOfEntries, strInputHeading, " ")
58              End If
59
60          Loop
```

FIGURE 6-74

In Figure 6-74, the loop is primed by the InputBox function call on line 39. The Do Until statement on line 41 checks the two conditions—if the value in the intNumberOfEntries counter is greater than the maximum number of entries, or if the user taps or clicks the Cancel button. In either case, the body of the loop is not executed.

When the body of the loop is executed, the application checks the data the user entered to verify it is numeric. If it is numeric, the value is converted to a Decimal data type and then is checked to ensure it is greater than zero (line 45). If it is greater than zero, it is added to the lstWeightLoss ListBox object, the decTotalWeightLoss accumulator is incremented by the weight loss value the user entered, the intNumberOfEntries counter is incremented by 1, and the normal message is moved to the strInputMessage variable. This variable contains the message that is displayed in the input box (see line 39).

If the value the user entered is not greater than zero, the statement following the Else statement on line 50 moves the value in the strNegativeError variable to the strInputMessage variable so that the next time the InputBox function is called, the message will indicate an error, as shown in Figure 6-73.

If the value the user entered was not numeric (as tested by the statement on line 43), the statement on line 54 moves the value in the strNonNumericError variable to the strInputMessage variable so that the next time the InputBox function is called, the message will indicate a nonnumeric error, as shown in Figure 6-72.

On lines 57 and 58, as long as the number of entries is not greater than the maximum number of entries, the InputBox function is called. The message that is displayed in the input box depends on whether an error occurred. The Do Until statement on line 41 is executed and the process begins again.

Create a Nested Loop

In the last chapter, you learned to nest If...Then...Else statements within each other. Loops can also be nested. You can place any type of loop within any other type of loop under the following conditions: Interior loops must be completely contained inside the outer loop and must have a different control variable. The example in Figure 6-75 uses a nested For loop to display a list of the weeks in the first quarter of the year (13 weeks) along with the days in each week. The outer For...Next loop counts from 1 to 13 for the 13 weeks, and the inner For...Next loop counts from 1 to 7 for the days in each of the 13 weeks.

The code in Figure 6-75 displays the output shown in Figure 6-76.

```
 6          Dim intOuterCount As Integer ' Counts the first 13 weeks in a quarter
 7          Dim intInnerCount As Integer ' Counts the 7 days in a week
 8          For intOuterCount = 1 To 13 ' For weeks in the 1st quarter of the year
 9              For intInnerCount = 1 To 7 ' For the 7 days in a week
10                  lstDays.Items.Add("Week: " & intOuterCount.ToString() _
11                                    & " Day: " & intInnerCount.ToString())
12              Next
13          Next
```

FIGURE 6-75

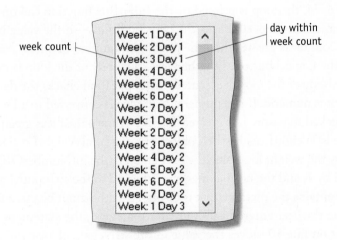

FIGURE 6-76

Select the Best Loop

When writing a program, you might have to make a decision regarding which loop structure to use. For...Next loops are best when the number of repetitions is fixed. Do loops are best when the condition to enter or exit the loop needs to be re-evaluated continually. When deciding which loop to use, keep the following considerations in mind:

1. Use a Do loop if the number of repetitions is unknown and is based on a condition changing; a For...Next loop is best if the exact number of repetitions is fixed.
2. If a loop condition must be tested before the body of the loop is executed, use a top-controlled Do While or Do Until loop. If the instructions within a loop must be executed one time regardless of the status of a condition, use a bottom-controlled Do While or Do Until loop.
3. Use the keyword While if you want to continue execution of the loop while the condition is true. Use the keyword Until if you want to continue execution until the condition is true.

Use a DataTip with Breakpoints

As programs become longer and more complex, the likelihood of errors increases, and you need to carefully find and remove these errors. Resolving defects in code is called **debugging**. When you debug a program, you collect information and find out what is wrong with the code in the program. You then fix that code.

A good way to collect information is to pause the execution of the code where a possible error could occur. One way to pause execution is to use breakpoints. **Breakpoints** are stop points placed in the code to tell the Visual Studio 2015 debugger where and when to pause the execution of the application. During this pause, the program is in break mode. While in break mode, you can examine the values in all variables that are within the scope of execution through the use of **DataTips**. In the Fitness Challenge application, you can insert a breakpoint in the assignment statement that increments the decTotalWeightLoss accumulator to view its value after each iteration of the loop as the user enters each weight loss value. To set a breakpoint in your code and then check the data at the breakpoint using DataTips, you can complete the following steps:

STEP 1   With the Fitness Challenge application open in the code window, press and hold or right-click line 46, which contains the code where you want to set a breakpoint, and then point to Breakpoint on the shortcut menu.

A shortcut menu opens that contains the Breakpoint command (Figure 6-77). The Breakpoint submenu contains the Insert Breakpoint command. Setting a breakpoint on line 46 means that the program will pause at that line during execution so that the values in variables within the scope of execution can be examined.

set breakpoint
on line 46

shortcut menu

Breakpoint
submenu

Breakpoint
command

FIGURE 6-77

STEP 2   Tap or click Insert Breakpoint on the submenu.

A breakpoint is set on line 46, which is the line in the Do Until loop that adds the weight loss value the user entered to the weight loss accumulator — decTotalWeightLoss (Figure 6-78). The breakpoint is identified by the bullet to the left of the line numbers and the highlight effect on the code.

breakpoint set

FIGURE 6-78

STEP 3   To run and test the program with the breakpoint, tap or click the Start Debugging button on the Standard toolbar.

The program starts and the Fitness Challenge window opens (Figure 6-79).

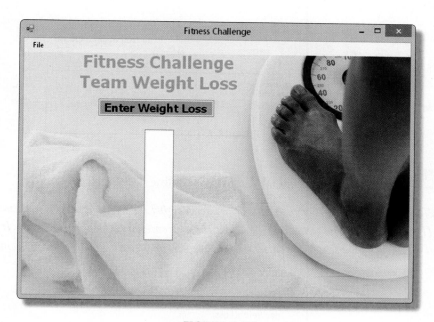

FIGURE 6-79

JGI/Blend Images/Getty Images

STEP 4 Tap or click the Enter Weight Loss button. Type 3 . 4 as the weight loss amount of the first team member.

The Weight Loss input box contains 3.4 as the weight loss amount of the first team member (Figure 6-80).

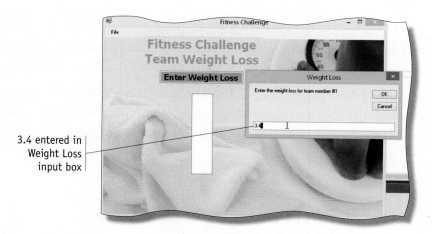

3.4 entered in Weight Loss input box

FIGURE 6-80

STEP 5 Tap or click the OK button in the input box.

The program executes the lines of code in the event handler until reaching the breakpoint, where it pauses execution on the accumulator line (Figure 6-81). The application is now in break mode. Notice the breakpoint line is highlighted in yellow.

program execution
paused at breakpoint

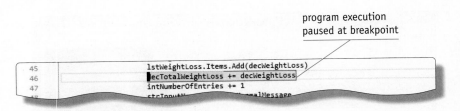

FIGURE 6-81

STEP 6 Point to the variable decWeightLoss on line 46.

A DataTip appears, displaying the value of the decWeightLoss variable when execution was paused (Figure 6-82). The value is 3.4 because the user entered this value in Step 4. It is a Decimal value (3.4D) because the statement in line 43 converted the value the user entered to a Decimal value.

pointer on
decWeightLoss
variable

DataTip displays
the value in the
decWeightLoss
variable

FIGURE 6-82

STEP 7 You can view the value in any other variable within execution scope by pointing to that variable. To illustrate, point to the variable decTotalWeightLoss on line 46.

The value in the decTotalWeightLoss variable is displayed (Figure 6-83). The value is zero, which means the assignment statement on line 46 has not yet been executed. When a break-point is set, the program pauses before executing the statement that contains the breakpoint.

pointer on
decTotalWeightLoss
variable

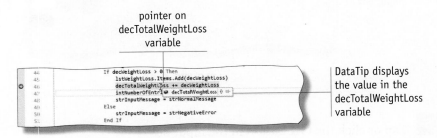

DataTip displays
the value in the
decTotalWeightLoss
variable

FIGURE 6-83

STEP 8   Continue the program by tapping or clicking the Continue button on the Standard toolbar. Notice that the Continue button is the same as the Start Debugging button.

The program continues by opening the next InputBox function, where the user can enter the weight loss value for the next team member. The program runs until it again reaches the breakpoint, where it pauses so you can point to any variable to view its present value in a DataTip (Figure 6-84).

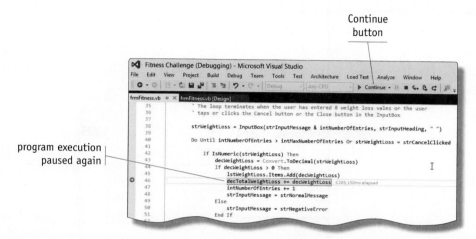

FIGURE 6-84

STEP 9   Point to the decTotalWeightLoss variable.

The updated value in the decTotalWeightLoss variable is displayed (Figure 6-85). The value 3.4D is in the variable as a result of the processing in the first iteration of the loop. You can also examine the values in other variables by pointing to the variable name.

ONLINE REINFORCEMENT

To view a video of the process in the previous steps, visit CengageBrain.com and navigate to the resources for this title. Tap or click the link for Chapter 6 and then navigate to Video 6-9.

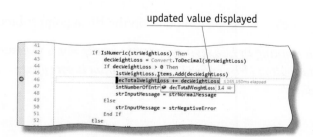

FIGURE 6-85

The preceding example illustrated the use of one breakpoint, but you can include multiple breakpoints in a program if they will be useful. Sometimes, breakpoints before and after an instruction that you suspect is in error can pinpoint the problem.

To remove a breakpoint, you can complete the following steps:

STEP 1 Press and hold or right-click the statement containing the breakpoint, and then point to Breakpoint on the shortcut menu.

The shortcut menu is displayed, the pointer is located on the Breakpoint entry, and the Breakpoint submenu is displayed (Figure 6-86). You can press and hold or right-click the statement containing the breakpoint either when the program is running in Debugging mode or when the program is not running.

FIGURE 6-86

STEP 2 Tap or click Delete Breakpoint on the Breakpoint submenu.

If the program is running in Debugging mode, the breakpoint is removed when you tap or click the Continue button (Figure 6-87). If the program is not running, the breakpoint is removed immediately.

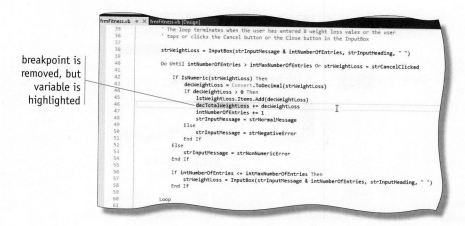

breakpoint is removed, but variable is highlighted

```
frmFitness.vb ⊕ ✕  frmFitness.vb [Design]
35        ' The loop terminates when the user has entered 8 weight loss vales or the user
36        ' taps or clicks the Cancel button or the Close button in the InputBox
37
38        strWeightLoss = InputBox(strInputMessage & intNumberOfEntries, strInputHeading, " ")
39
40        Do Until intNumberOfEntries > intMaxNumberOfEntries Or strWeightLoss = strCancelClicked
41
42            If IsNumeric(strWeightLoss) Then
43                decWeightLoss = Convert.ToDecimal(strWeightLoss)
44                If decWeightLoss > 0 Then
45                    lstWeightLoss.Items.Add(decWeightLoss)
46                    decTotalWeightLoss += decWeightLoss
47                    intNumberOfEntries += 1
48                    strInputMessage = strNormalMessage
49                Else
50                    strInputMessage = strNegativeError
51                End If
52            Else
53                strInputMessage = strNonNumericError
54            End If
55
56            If intNumberOfEntries <= intMaxNumberOfEntries Then
57                strWeightLoss = InputBox(strInputMessage & intNumberOfEntries, strInputHeading, " ")
58            End If
59
60        Loop
61
```

FIGURE 6-87

Using breakpoints and DataTips allows you to examine any variables during the execution of the program. By moving step by step through the program, normally you can identify any errors that might occur in the program.

Publish an Application with ClickOnce Deployment

After an application is completely debugged and working properly, you can deploy the project. Deploying a project means placing an executable version of the program on your hard disk (which then can be placed on CD, DVD, or in the cloud), on a web server, or on a network server.

You probably have purchased software on a CD or DVD or downloaded software from a cloud-based site. To install the application on your computer, you insert the CD or DVD into your computer and then follow the setup instructions. The version of the program you receive on the CD or DVD is the deployed version of the program.

When programming using Visual Basic 2015, you can create a deployed program by using **ClickOnce Deployment**. The deployed version of the program you create can be installed and executed on any computer that has the .NET framework installed. The computer does not need Visual Studio 2015 installed to run the program.

To publish the Fitness Challenge application using ClickOnce Deployment, you can complete the following steps:

STEP 1 With the Fitness Challenge application open, tap or click Build on the menu bar.

The Build menu is displayed (Figure 6–88).

Publish Fitness
Challenge command

Build menu

FIGURE 6-88

STEP 2   Tap or click Publish Fitness Challenge on the Build menu.

The Publish Wizard starts (Figure 6-89). The first Publish Wizard dialog box asks where you want to publish the application. The application can be published to a web server, a network, or as a setup file on a hard disk or USB drive for burning on a CD or DVD. This dialog box includes publish\ as the default location, which you can change to a file location.

Publish Wizard

wizard
message

default location

FIGURE 6-89

STEP 3   Change the default location from publish\ to a file location. To publish to a USB drive, type the drive letter. In this example, enter E: for a USB drive. Tap or click the Next button.

The Publish Wizard dialog box requests where you want to publish the application. The Fitness Challenge application will be saved to the USB drive, which is drive E: in this example (Figure 6-90).

From a CD-ROM or
DVD-ROM selected

FIGURE 6-90

STEP 4   If necessary, tap or click the From a CD-ROM or DVD-ROM radio
button, and then tap or click the Next button.

*Visual Basic displays a Publish Wizard dialog box that asks, "Where will the application
check for updates?" (Figure 6-91). You can select and enter a location or indicate that the
application will not check for updates. Generally, when an application will be deployed to
a CD or DVD, the application will not check for updates. If the application is deployed to
a web server or network server, then it might check for updates before being executed on the
user's computer.*

application will
not check for
updates

FIGURE 6-91

STEP 5 If necessary, tap or click the "The application will not check for updates" radio button, and then tap or click the Next button.

The Ready to Publish! window is displayed (Figure 6-92). Notice the message in this window—when the program is installed on the user's machine, a shortcut for the program will be added to the user's computer, and the program can be deleted using the Add/Remove Programs function in the Control Panel.

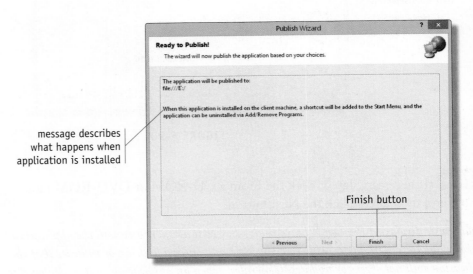

message describes
what happens when
application is installed

Finish button

FIGURE 6-92

STEP 6 Tap or click the Finish button.

The Visual Basic window displays several messages indicating that the application is being published. The last message is "Publish succeeded" (Figure 6-93).

Publish succeeded
message

FIGURE 6-93

STEP 7 To view the finished result, minimize the Visual Studio window and then open the Search charm. Type `Computer` in the Search box. Double-tap or double-click the USB drive icon to view the published installation folder.

Installation files are placed on the USB drive (Figure 6-94). If all of these files are copied to a computer with the .NET framework, the user can double-tap or double-click the setup file to begin the installation.

installation files → ← double-tap or double-click setup to install the application

FIGURE 6-94

STEP 8   To install the application, double-tap or double-click the setup file.

After the user double-taps or double-clicks the setup file, the application is installed on the local computer. During installation, Windows might display the dialog box shown in Figure 6-95. This dialog box is intended to protect you from installing programs that might harm your computer. Because you know the source of this program, you can tap or click the Install button to continue installing the program.

Application Install – Security Warning dialog box |

Install button

FIGURE 6-95

STEP 9   After installation, the program runs. To run the installed application again, open the Search charm, type `Fitness`, and then click the Fitness Challenge icon.

Program Design

As you have learned, the requirements document identifies the purpose of the program being developed, the application title, the procedures to be followed when using the program, any required equations and calculations, any conditions that must be tested, notes and restrictions that must be followed by the program, and any other comments that would be helpful to understanding the problem. The requirements document for the Fitness Challenge application is shown in Figure 6-96.

REQUIREMENTS DOCUMENT

Date:	September 30, 2016
Date Submitted:	
Application Title:	Fitness Challenge Application
Purpose:	This application finds the average weight loss of a team of eight employees.
Program Procedures:	In a Windows Desktop application, the user enters the weight loss amounts of eight employees as positive numbers to compute the average weight loss for the entire team.

Algorithms, Processing, and Conditions:

1. The user must be able to enter each of eight weight loss values in pounds after tapping or clicking the Enter Weight Loss button.
2. Each weight loss value is validated to confirm it is numeric and greater than zero.
3. Each weight loss value is displayed in a ListBox object.
4. After the user enters eight weight loss values or taps or clicks the Cancel button in an input box, the program calculates and displays the average weight loss for the team.
5. A menu bar includes the File menu, which contains Clear and Exit items. The Clear menu item clears the result and the weight loss values. The Exit menu item closes the application.

Notes and Restrictions:

1. If a nonnumeric or negative value is entered for the weight loss, the program should display an error message and ask the user to re-enter the value.
2. If the user taps or clicks the Cancel button before entering any weight loss values, a message should indicate no weight loss values were entered. An average is not calculated when no weight loss values are entered.

Comments:

1. The picture shown in the window can be found on CengageBrain.com. The name of the picture is Weight.
2. The average weight loss should be formatted as a Decimal value with one decimal place.

FIGURE 6-96

The Use Case Definition shown in Figure 6-97 specifies the procedures the user will follow to use this application.

USE CASE DEFINITION

1. The Windows application opens, displaying the Fitness Challenge title, a ListBox object to hold the numeric entries, and a Button object that allows the user to begin entering up to eight weight loss values.
2. A menu bar displays the File menu, which has two menu items: Clear and Exit.
3. In an InputBox object, the user enters up to eight values representing the number of pounds lost, such as 3.2 pounds.
4. The program asks the user for the weight loss value again if a value is nonnumeric or negative.
5. The user terminates data entry by entering eight values or by tapping or clicking the Cancel button in the InputBox object.
6. The program calculates the average weight loss for the values the user entered.
7. In a Label object, the program displays the average weight loss as a Decimal value with one decimal place.
8. The user can clear the input and the results by tapping or clicking the Clear menu item, and can then repeat Steps 3 through 7.
9. The user taps or clicks Exit on the File menu to close the application.

FIGURE 6-97

Event Planning Document

You will recall that the event planning document is a table that specifies which objects in the user interface will cause events, the action taken by the user to trigger each event, and the event processing that must occur. The event planning document for the Fitness Challenge application is shown in Figure 6-98.

EVENT PLANNING DOCUMENT

Program Name: Fitness Challenge Application	Developer: Corinne Hoisington	Object: frmFitness	Date: September 30, 2016
OBJECT	**EVENT TRIGGER**	**EVENT PROCESSING**	
btnWeightLoss	Tap or click	Display an InputBox object to obtain each team member's weight loss up to eight times or until the user taps or clicks the Cancel button	
		Check if strWeightLoss is numeric	
		If the weight loss value is numeric, convert strWeightLoss to a Decimal value	
		If strWeightLoss is numeric, check whether the value is positive	
		If the weight loss value is positive:	
		Display the value in lstWeightLoss	
		Accumulate the total of the weight loss values in decTotalWeightLoss	
		Update the number of entries	
		Set the InputBox message to the normal message	
		If the value entered is not numeric, display an error message in the input box	
		If the value entered is not positive, display an error message in the input box	
		After all weight loss values are entered, change the Visible property of lblAverageLoss to true	
		If one or more weight loss values are entered: Calculate the average weight loss in decAverageLoss Display the average weight loss in lblAverageLoss	
		If no values are entered: Display the text "No weight loss value entered" Disable the btnWeightLoss Button	
mnuClear	Tap or click	Clear the lstWeightLoss ListBox	
		Change the Visible property of lblAverageLoss to False	
		Enable the btnWeightLoss Button	
mnuExit	Tap or click	Exit the application	

FIGURE 6-98

Design and Code the Program

After identifying the events and tasks within the events, the developer is ready to create the program. As you have learned, creating the program means designing the user interface and then entering Visual Basic statements to accomplish the tasks specified in the event planning document. As the developer enters the code, she will also implement the logic to carry out the required processing.

Guided Program Development

To design the user interface for the Fitness Challenge application and enter the code required to process each event in the program, complete the steps on the following pages:

Guided Program Development

Phase 1: Design the Form

1

- **Create a Windows Application** Open Visual Studio and then close the Start page. Create a new Visual Basic Windows Forms Application project by tapping or clicking the New Project button on the Standard toolbar, selecting Windows Desktop as the project type, selecting Windows Forms Application in the center pane, naming the project Fitness Challenge in the Name text box, and then tapping or clicking the OK button in the New Project window.

HINT

- **Display the Toolbox** Ensure that the Toolbox is displayed in the Visual Studio window and that the Common Controls are accessible.

HINT

- **Name the Windows Form Object** In the Solution Explorer window, press and hold or right-click Form1.vb, tap or click Rename, and then rename the form frmFitness.

- **Change the Text on the Title Bar for the Windows Form Object** Change the title bar text of the Windows Form object to Fitness Challenge.

HINT

- **Change the Size of the Form Object** Resize the Form object by changing the Size property to 675, 475.

HINT

● **Add the MenuStrip Object** Drag a MenuStrip object from the Menus & Toolbars category of the Toolbox to the Windows Form object. The MenuStrip snaps into place below the title bar. Name the MenuStrip object `mnuFitness` in the Properties window. Tap or click the Type Here box on the MenuStrip object, type `&File`, and then press the ENTER key. The ampersand creates a hot key for the letter F. Name the File menu item `mnuFile` (*ref: Figure 6-5*).

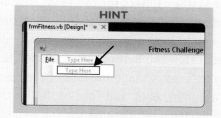
HINT

● **Add Menu Items** The next step is to add two menu items to the File menu. Tap or click the Type Here box below the word File, and then enter `&Clear`. Name the Clear menu item `mnuClear`. Tap or click the Type Here box below the Clear menu item, and then enter `E&xit` to make the "x" in Exit the hot key. Name the Exit menu item `mnuExit` (*ref: Figure 6-10*).

HINT

● **Add the Title Label Object** Drag a Label .NET component onto the Windows Form object. Name the label `lblTitle`. Enter the text for this label as `Fitness Challenge Team Weight Loss` on two lines. (*Hint*: Tap or click the Text property list arrow in the Properties window to enter a label with multiple lines. Press the ENTER key to move to a new line.) Change the FontColor to Goldenrod. Choose Tahoma as the font, Bold as the font style, and 22 points as the size. Change the TextAlign property to MiddleCenter by tapping or clicking the TextAlign list arrow and then tapping or clicking the Center block. Change the Location property of the lblTitle Label object to `90, 20`.

HINT

● **Add the Enter Weight Loss Button Object** Drag a Button object onto the Windows Form object below the title label. Name the Button `btnWeightLoss`. Change the text of the button to `Enter Weight Loss`. Change the font to 14-point, Bold, and Tahoma. Change the BackColor property to Goldenrod. Resize the Button object to view the complete text. Align the centers of the Button object with the title Label object.

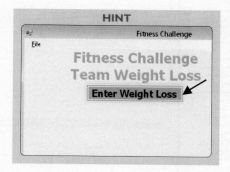
HINT

(continues)

● **Add the ListBox Object for the Team Members' Weight
Loss** To add the ListBox object that displays the team
members' weight loss, drag a ListBox object onto the Windows
Form object below the Button object. Name the ListBox
`lstWeightLoss`. Change the font of the text in the ListBox
object to 14-point, Bold, and Tahoma. Resize the ListBox to the
width of four characters because the top weight loss of a team
member could reach an amount such as 46.3 pounds. Lengthen
the ListBox object to display eight numbers. The Size property
for the ListBox object in the sample program is 50, 188. Change
the RightToLeft property to No to right-align the numeric
values. Align the centers of the ListBox object with the Button
object (*ref: Figure 6-24*).

● **Add the Result Label** To add the label where the average
weight loss message is displayed, drag a Label object
onto the Windows Form object. Name the Label object
`lblAverageLoss`. Change the text to `Average weight
loss of your team is XX.X lbs`. Change the
font to Tahoma, Bold, and 14-point. Change the BackColor
to Goldenrod. Align the centers of the Label object with the
ListBox object.

The user interface mockup is complete (Figure 6-99).

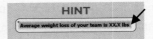

HINT

**Fitness Challenge
Team Weight Loss**

Enter Weight Loss

tLoss

HINT

Average weight loss of your team is XX.X lbs

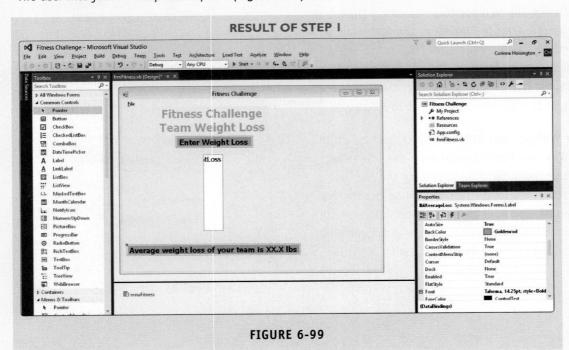

RESULT OF STEP I

FIGURE 6-99

Phase 2: Fine-Tune the User Interface

2

- **Change the BackgroundImage Property of the Windows Form Object** Select the Windows Form object and then tap or click the ellipsis button on the BackgroundImage property. Tap or click the Import button and navigate to the Scale image. Tap or click the OK button.

- **Change the Visible Property for the Average Weight Loss Label** Select the lblAverageLoss Label object and change its Visible property to False because the Label object is not displayed until the average weight loss is calculated.

- **Make the Enter Weight Loss Button the Accept Button** Tap or click the background of the Windows Form object to select it. In the Properties window, tap or click the AcceptButton list arrow to display the buttons in the user interface. Tap or click btnWeightLoss in the list. During program execution, when the user presses the ENTER key, the event handler for btnWeightLoss executes.

HEADS UP

As you work on your program, do not forget to save it from time to time. You can save the work you have done by tapping or clicking the Save All button on the Standard toolbar.

The user interface design is complete (Figure 6-100).

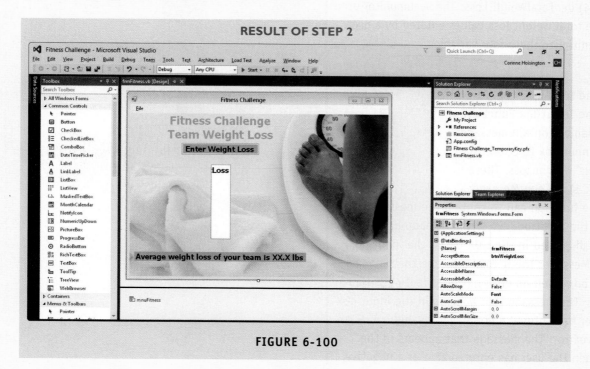

FIGURE 6-100

(continues)

Phase 3: Code the Program

3

- **Enter the Comments for the Enter Weight Loss Button Event Handler** Double-tap or double-click the btnWeightLoss Button object on the Windows Form object to open the button event handler. Insert the first four standard comments at the top of the code window. Insert the command Option Strict On at the beginning of the code to turn on strict type checking.

HINT

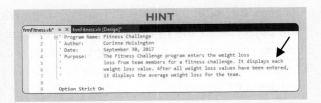

- **Comment on the btnWeightLoss_Click Event Handler** Enter a comment to describe the purpose of the btnWeightLoss_Click event handler.

HINT

- **Declare and Initialize the Variables to Calculate the Average Weight Loss** Four variables are used to calculate the average weight loss (besides the team member count). These variables are: 1) strWeightLoss: Is assigned the value from the InputBox function call; 2) decWeightLoss: Is assigned the converted team member weight loss; 3) decAverageLoss: Contains the calculated average weight loss; 4) decTotalWeightLoss: The accumulator used to collect the total weight loss values entered by a user. Declare and initialize these four variables.

HINT

- **Declare and Initialize the Variables Used with the InputBox Function Call** Five variables contain messages used in the input box to obtain the team members' weight loss. These variables are: 1) strInputMessage: Is used in the function call to contain the message displayed in the input box; 2) strInputHeading: Contains the message displayed in the title bar of the input box; 3) strNormalMessage: The normal message that appears in the input box when no error has occurred; 4) strNon-NumericError: The message that appears in the input box when the user has entered a nonnumeric value; 5) strNegativeError: The message that appears in the input box when the user has entered zero or a negative number. Declare and initialize these five variables.

HINT

● **Declare and Initialize Variables Used in the Loop Processing** Three variables are used for processing the loop in the program. These variables are: 1) strCancelClicked: This variable contains a null string and is used to determine if the user tapped or clicked the Cancel button in the input box; 2) intMaxNumberOfEntries: Contains the maximum number of entries for team member weight losses (program requirements state the maximum number is eight); 3) intNumberOfEntries: The counter for the valid number of team member weight loss values entered by the user. This variable is used to determine when the maximum number of entries has been made and to act as the divisor when calculating the average weight loss per team member.

```
28              'Declare and initialize loop variables
29
30              Dim strCancelClicked As String = ""
31              Dim intMaxNumberOfEntries As Integer = 8
32              Dim intNumberOfEntries As Integer = 1
33
```

● **Write Comments for the Do Until Loop and Write the Priming InputBox Function Call** You often can use comments to document a loop or other set of major processing statements. The comments here alert the reader to the role of the Do Until loop. The priming InputBox function call obtains the first team members' weight loss or allows the user to tap or click the Cancel button. The normal message is displayed. The space at the end of the argument list places a space in the input box so if the user taps or clicks the OK button without entering any data, the command will not be treated the same as tapping or clicking the Cancel button *(ref: Figure 6-72).*

```
34        ' This loop allows the user to enter the weight loss of up to 8 team members.
35        ' The loop terminates when the user has entered 8 weight loss vales or the user
36        ' taps or clicks the Cancel button or the Close button in the InputBox
37
38        strWeightLoss = InputBox(strInputMessage & intNumberOfEntries, strInputHeading, " ")
39
```

● **Code the Do Until Loop** Because the application requests the weight loss values of up to eight team members, the Do Until loop should continue until eight weight losses are entered or until the user taps or clicks the Cancel or Close button in the input box. Enter the Do Until loop using IntelliSense *(ref: Figure 6-65, Figure 6-72).*

```
40        Do Until intNumberOfEntries > intMaxNumberOfEntries Or strWeightLoss = strCancelClicked
41
42        Loop
```

(continues)

● **Validate That the Entry Is a Number** The first process in the Do Until loop is to validate that the team member weight loss entered by the user is a numeric value. Enter the If...Then statement to test if the value in the strWeightLoss variable is numeric.

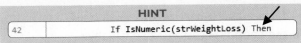

```
HINT
42        If IsNumeric(strWeightLoss) Then
```

● **Convert the Value Entered from a String to the Decimal Data Type** If the user entered a numeric value, the next step is to convert the string value the user entered to a Decimal data type. Using IntelliSense, enter the code to convert the value in the strWeightLoss variable from the String to the Decimal data type and place the result in the decWeightLoss variable.

```
HINT
43        decWeightLoss = Convert.ToDecimal(strWeightLoss)
```

● **Validate That the Entered Value Is a Positive Number** After the value is converted, the program must validate that the number is positive. Write the If...Then statement to test whether the value in the decWeightLoss variable is greater than zero.

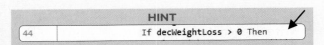

```
HINT
44        If decWeightLoss > 0 Then
```

● **Perform the Processing When the User Enters a Valid Weight Loss** After ensuring the weight loss entered by the user is valid, the next steps are to perform the processing for valid weight loss. Four steps are required: 1) Add the weight loss as an item to the lstWeightLoss ListBox object (*ref: Figure 6-28*); 2) Add the weight loss the user entered to the decTotalWeightLoss accumulator (*ref: Figure 6-38*). The accumulated weight loss is used to calculate the average weight loss; 3) Increment the intNumberOfEntries counter by 1 because the user entered a valid weight loss (*ref: Figure 6-38*). This value is used as the divisor to determine the average weight loss, and as one of the indicators that the loop should be terminated; 4) Because the user entered a valid weight loss, the normal message should appear the next time the input box is displayed. Therefore, the normal message should be moved to the strInputMessage variable. Using IntelliSense, enter the code for these four activities.

```
HINT
44        If decWeightLoss > 0 Then
45            lstWeightLoss.Items.Add(decWeightLoss)
46            decTotalWeightLoss += decWeightLoss
47            intNumberOfEntries += 1
48            strInputMessage = strNormalMessage
```

- **Assign an Error Message If the User Entered a Negative Weight Loss** If the user entered a negative weight loss, the next input box should display the negative number error message *(ref: Figure 6-75)*. Following the Else statement for the If statement that checks for a number greater than zero, enter the assignment statement that places the value in the strNegativeError variable in the strInputMessage variable.

```
HINT
49          Else
50              strInputMessage = strNegativeError
51          End If
```

- **Assign an Error Message If the User Enters a Nonnumeric Weight Loss** If the user enters a nonnumeric weight loss, the next input box should show the nonnumeric error message *(ref: Figure 6-75)*. Following the Else Statement for the If statement that checks for numeric data, enter the assignment statement that places the value in the strNonNumericError variable in the strInput-Message variable.

```
HINT
52          Else
53              strInputMessage = strNonNumericError
54          End If
```

- **Code the InputBox Function Call** The first InputBox function call was placed before the Do Until loop to prime the loop. To

```
HINT
55
56          If intNumberOfEntries <= intMaxNumberOfEntries Then
57              strWeightLoss = InputBox(strInputMessage & intNumberOfEntries, strInputHeading, " ")
58          End If
59
60      Loop
61
```

continue the process after the first value is entered, another In-putBox function is needed as the last statement inside the loop to request subsequent values. This statement should be executed only if the maximum number of entries has not been exceeded. So, an If structure is required to determine if the maximum number of entries has been reached. If not, the InputBox function call is executed *(ref: Figure 6-73)*.

The coding for the variables and Do Until loop that processes the data in the program is complete (Figure 6-101). It is important that you examine the code in Figure 6-101 and understand the loop processing. The priming of the loop, by both setting the value in the intNumberOfEntries variable (line 32) and calling the InputBox function (line 38), is critical for proper execution of the loop. Increasing the loop counter when a valid entry is made (line 46) also is fundamental in the loop processing because testing this counter is one way the Do Until loop can be terminated. Also, using variables for messages instead of literals in the actual code demonstrates how professional programs are coded. You should follow these examples in your programming.

(continues)

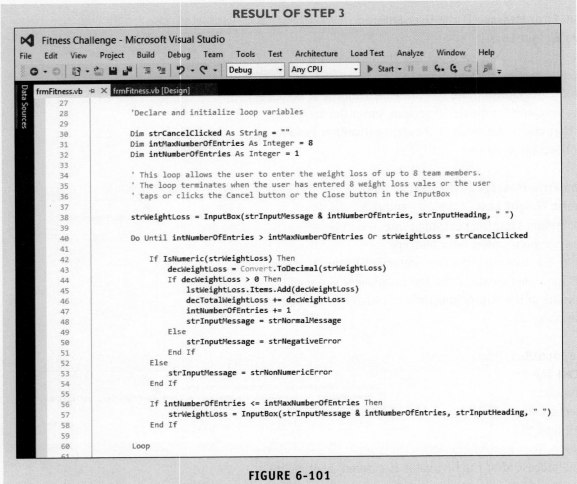

RESULT OF STEP 3

FIGURE 6-101

4

● **Set the Result Label's Visible
Property** When you finish the Do
Until loop, you must complete three
tasks to finish the Enter Weight Loss
button click event handler: 1) Make the label that will
contain the average weight loss visible; 2) Calculate and
display the average weight loss; 3) Disable the Enter
Weight Loss button. If at least one weight loss value has
been entered using IntelliSense, write the code to create the If statement and make the lblAverageLoss label
visible.

HINT
62   'Calculates and displays average team weight loss
63   If **intNumberOfEntries > 1** Then
64   lblAverageLoss.Visible = True

● **Calculate the Average Weight Loss** To calculate the average of the weight loss values the user entered, the value in the decTotalWeightLoss variable (accumulator) must be divided by the number of team

	HINT
65	decAverageLoss = decTotalWeightLoss / (intNumberOfEntries - 1)
66	lblAverageLoss.Text = "Average weight loss for the team is " &
67	decAverageLoss.ToString("F1") & " lbs"
68	Else
69	MsgBox("No weight loss value entered")
70	End If

members entered (counter). At the end of the loop shown in Figure 6-101, the value in the intNumberOfEntries variable always will be one greater than the actual number of team members entered, so the total weight loss must be divided by the value in intNumberOfEntries minus 1. This calculation should occur only if one or more team member weight loss values were entered, so an If statement must be used to check whether the value in the intNumberOfEntries variable is greater than 1. If so, the average weight loss is calculated; if not, the "No weight loss value entered" message should be displayed using a MsgBox. Using IntelliSense, write the code to perform this processing.

● **Change the Enter Weight Loss Button Enabled Property to False** After the average weight loss is calculated and displayed, the Enabled property of the

	HINT
71	
72	' Disables the Weight Loss button
73	btnWeightLoss.Enabled = False
74	

btnWeightLoss button is set to False to dim the button. Using IntelliSense, write the code to accomplish this processing.

The code for the btnWeightLoss button click event handler is completed (Figure 6-102).

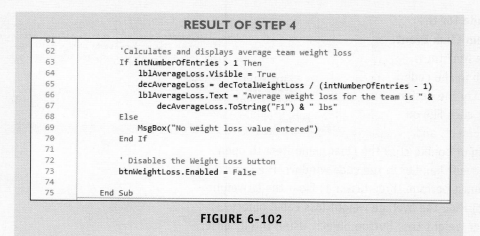

RESULT OF STEP 4

```
61
62          'Calculates and displays average team weight loss
63          If intNumberOfEntries > 1 Then
64              lblAverageLoss.Visible = True
65              decAverageLoss = decTotalWeightLoss / (intNumberOfEntries - 1)
66              lblAverageLoss.Text = "Average weight loss for the team is " &
67                  decAverageLoss.ToString("F1") & " lbs"
68          Else
69              MsgBox("No weight loss value entered")
70          End If
71
72          ' Disables the Weight Loss button
73          btnWeightLoss.Enabled = False
74
75      End Sub
```

FIGURE 6-102

(continues)

5

● **Run the Program** After coding a major section of the program, you should run the program to ensure it is working properly. Tap or click the Start Debugging button on the Standard toolbar to run the Fitness Challenge application. Tap or click the Enter Weight Loss button and then enter the weight loss of eight team members. Verify the weight losses are displayed properly and the average weight loss is correct. Close the program by tapping or clicking the Close button. Run the program again, tap or click the Enter Weight Loss button, enter the weight loss for four team members, enter a nonnumeric weight loss, enter a weight loss that is less than zero, and then tap or click the Cancel button in the input box. Ensure that the weight loss values are displayed properly, the average weight loss is correct, and the error messages are displayed properly in the input box. Close the program. Run the program again, tap or click the Enter Weight Loss button, and then tap or click the Cancel button in the input box. Ensure that the "No weight loss value entered" message is displayed. Close the program and then run it as many times as necessary to ensure the program is working properly. If the program does not run properly, consider setting a breakpoint and checking the values in the variables *(ref: Figure 6-78)*.

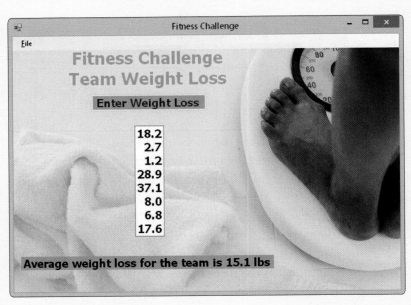

6

● **Enter the Code for the Clear Menu Item Click Event** Tap or click the frmFitness.vb[Design]* tab in the code window to display the design window. Tap or click File on the MenuStrip object, and then double-tap or double-click the Clear menu item to open the Clear click event handler in the code window. The Clear click event handler must perform three tasks: 1) Clear the lstWeight-Loss list box; 2) Hide the average weight loss Label object; 3) Enable the Enter Weight Loss Button object. Using IntelliSense, write the code for these three tasks.

```
                                    HINT
77    Private Sub mnuClear_Click(sender As Object, e As EventArgs) Handles mnuClear.Click
78        ' The mnuClear click event clears the ListBox object and hides
79        ' the average weight loss label. It also enables the Weight Loss button
80
81        lstWeightLoss.Items.Clear()
82        lblAverageLoss.Visible = False
83        btnWeightLoss.Enabled = True
84
85    End Sub
```

- **Enter the Code for the Exit Menu Item Click Event** Return to the design window. Double-tap or double-click the Exit menu item. In the code window, enter a Close procedure call that will close the window and terminate the program.

```
        HINT
                          0 references
87  ⊟    Private Sub mnuExit_Click(sender As Object, e As EventArgs) Handles mnuExit.Click
88              ' The mnuExit click event closes the window and exits the application
89
90           Close()
```

The code for the Clear menu item click event and the Exit menu item click event is completed (Figure 6-103). The code for the program is also completed.

RESULT OF STEP 6

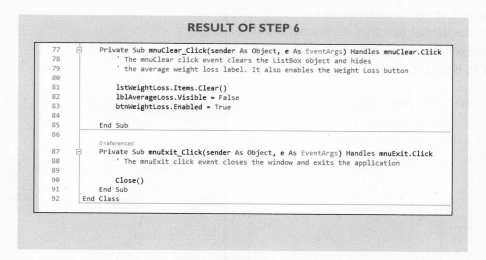

```
77  ⊟    Private Sub mnuClear_Click(sender As Object, e As EventArgs) Handles mnuClear.Click
78              ' The mnuClear click event clears the ListBox object and hides
79              ' the average weight loss label. It also enables the Weight Loss button
80
81           lstWeightLoss.Items.Clear()
82           lblAverageLoss.Visible = False
83           btnWeightLoss.Enabled = True
84
85       End Sub
86
             0 references
87  ⊟    Private Sub mnuExit_Click(sender As Object, e As EventArgs) Handles mnuExit.Click
88              ' The mnuExit click event closes the window and exits the application
89
90           Close()
91       End Sub
92  End Class
```

FIGURE 6-103

7

- **Publish the Fitness Challenge Application** After completing the program, you can publish it using ClickOnce deployment so it can be installed on multiple computers. To open the Publish Wizard and begin the deployment process, tap or click Build on the menu bar and then tap or click Publish Fitness Challenge on the Build menu *(ref: Figure 6-89)*.

- **Select the Publish File Location** The Publish Wizard dialog box asks where you want to publish the application. Change the default location to the same file location that you used to save your Windows application by tapping or clicking the Browse button and then selecting the drive. For example, select the E: drive, a USB drive. After selecting the drive, tap or click the Next button in the Publish Wizard dialog box *(ref: Figure 6-90)*.

(continues)

● **Select How Users Will Install the
Application** In the next Publish Wizard
dialog box, select the option that lets
users install the application from a
CD-ROM or DVD-ROM. Then, tap or click the
Next button *(ref: Figure 6-92)*.

HINT

◉ From a CD-ROM or DVD-ROM

● **Indicate the Application Will Not Check
for Updates** Tap or click the "The
application will not check for updates"
radio button to indicate no updates will be
checked. This is the normal selection when programs are placed
on CDs or DVDs. Then, tap or click the Next button in the Publish Wizard dialog box *(ref: Figure 6-93)*.

HINT

◉ The application will not check for updates

● **View the Summary Window** The Publish
Wizard summary is displayed. Tap or click the
Finish button to publish the application
(ref: Figure 6-94).

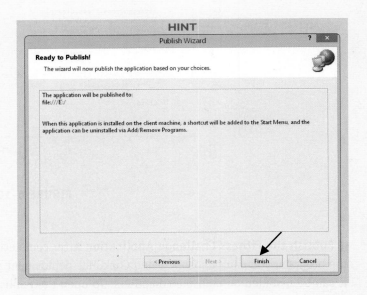

HINT

Publish Wizard   ? ☒

Ready to Publish!

The wizard will now publish the application based on your choices.

The application will be published to:
file:///E:/

When this application is installed on the client machine, a shortcut will be added to the Start Menu, and the
application can be uninstalled via Add/Remove Programs.

< Previous   Next >   Finish   Cancel

● **View the Installation Files** After the publishing succeeds, a
folder is created with the installation files that could be placed
on a CD, DVD, or other computer *(ref: Figure 6-96)*.

HINT

Removable Disk (E :)
☐ Name

　Application Files
☐ Fitness Challenge
　setup

Code Listing

The complete code for the sample program is shown in Figure 6-104.

```vbnet
1    ' Program Name: Fitness Challenge
2    ' Author:       Corinne Hoisington
3    ' Date:         September 30, 2017
4    ' Purpose:      The Fitness Challenge program enters the weight loss
5    '               loss from team members for a fitness challenge. It displays each
6    '               weight loss value. After all weight loss values have been entered,
7    '               it displays the average weight loss for the team.
8
9    Option Strict On
10
     2 references
11   Public Class frmFitness
         0 references
12       Private Sub btnWeightLoss_Click(sender As Object, e As EventArgs) Handles btnWeightLoss.Click
13           ' The btnWeightLoss_Click event accepts and displays up to 8 weight loss values
14           ' and then calculates and displays the average weight loss for the team
15
16           ' Declare and initialize variables
17
18           Dim strWeightLoss As String
19           Dim decWeightLoss As Decimal
20           Dim decAverageLoss As Decimal
21           Dim decTotalWeightLoss As Decimal = 0D
22           Dim strInputMessage As String = "Enter the weight loss for team member #"
23           Dim strInputHeading As String = "Weight Loss"
24           Dim strNormalMessage As String = "Enter the weight loss for team member #"
25           Dim strNonNumericError As String = "Error - Enter a number for the weight loss of team member #"
26           Dim strNegativeError As String = "Error - Enter a positive number for the weight loss of team member #"
27
28           'Declare and initialize loop variables
29
30           Dim strCancelClicked As String = ""
31           Dim intMaxNumberOfEntries As Integer = 8
32           Dim intNumberOfEntries As Integer = 1
33
34           ' This loop allows the user to enter the weight loss of up to 8 team members.
35           ' The loop terminates when the user has entered 8 weight loss vales or the user
36           ' taps or clicks the Cancel button or the Close button in the InputBox
37
38           strWeightLoss = InputBox(strInputMessage & intNumberOfEntries, strInputHeading, " ")
39
40           Do Until intNumberOfEntries > intMaxNumberOfEntries Or strWeightLoss = strCancelClicked
41
42               If IsNumeric(strWeightLoss) Then
43                   decWeightLoss = Convert.ToDecimal(strWeightLoss)
44                   If decWeightLoss > 0 Then
45                       lstWeightLoss.Items.Add(decWeightLoss)
46                       decTotalWeightLoss += decWeightLoss
47                       intNumberOfEntries += 1
48                       strInputMessage = strNormalMessage
49                   Else
50                       strInputMessage = strNegativeError
51                   End If
52               Else
53                   strInputMessage = strNonNumericError
54               End If
55
56               If intNumberOfEntries <= intMaxNumberOfEntries Then
57                   strWeightLoss = InputBox(strInputMessage & intNumberOfEntries, strInputHeading, " ")
58               End If
59
```

FIGURE 6-104 (continues)

```
60              Loop
61
62              'Calculates and displays average team weight loss
63              If intNumberOfEntries > 1 Then
64                  lblAverageLoss.Visible = True
65                  decAverageLoss = decTotalWeightLoss / (intNumberOfEntries - 1)
66                  lblAverageLoss.Text = "Average weight loss for the team is " &
67                      decAverageLoss.ToString("F1") & " lbs"
68              Else
69                  MsgBox("No weight loss value entered")
70              End If
71
72              ' Disables the Weight Loss button
73              btnWeightLoss.Enabled = False
74
75          End Sub
76
            0 references
77          Private Sub mnuClear_Click(sender As Object, e As EventArgs) Handles mnuClear.Click
78              ' The mnuClear click event clears the ListBox object and hides
79              ' the average weight loss label. It also enables the Weight Loss button
80
81              lstWeightLoss.Items.Clear()
82              lblAverageLoss.Visible = False
83              btnWeightLoss.Enabled = True
84
85          End Sub
86
            0 references
87          Private Sub mnuExit_Click(sender As Object, e As EventArgs) Handles mnuExit.Click
88              ' The mnuExit click event closes the window and exits the application
89
90              Close()
91          End Sub
92      End Class
```

FIGURE 6-104 (continued)

Summary

In this chapter you have learned to design and write code to implement loops and to create menus, list boxes, and an input box. The items listed in Figure 6-105 include all the new Visual Studio and Visual Basic skills you have learned in this chapter. Video 6-1 demonstrates the complete program execution.

Visual Basic Skills

Skill	Figure Number	Video Number
Run the Completed Program	Figure 6-1	Video 6-1
Place a MenuStrip Object on the Windows Form Object	Figure 6-5	Video 6-2
Code the Exit Menu Item Event	Figure 6-12	Video 6-3
Insert a Full Standard Menu	Figure 6-14	Video 6-4
Code the InputBox Function	Figure 6-17	
Add a ListBox Object	Figure 6-24	Video 6-5
Add an Item to a ListBox Object	Figure 6-27	
Add Items to a ListBox Object During Design	Figure 6-32	Video 6-6
Assign a Selected Item from a ListBox Object	Figure 6-36	
Add Background Image to Form Object	Figure 6-39	
Write Code using Compound Operators	Figure 6-41	
Write the Code for a For...Next Loop	Figure 6-42	
Use IntelliSense to Enter the Code for a For...Next Loop	Figure 6-52	Video 6-7
Write Code for a Top-controlled Do While Loop	Figure 6-58	
Use IntelliSense to Code a Do While Loop	Figure 6-61	Video 6-8
Write Code for a Bottom-Controlled Do While Loop	Figure 6-64	
Write Code for a Top-Controlled Do Until Loop	Figure 6-67	
Write Code for a Bottom-Controlled Do Until Loop	Figure 6-69	
Avoid Infinite Loops	Figure 6-70	
Prime a Loop	Figure 6-71	
Validate Data	Figure 6-72	
Create a Nested Loop	Figure 6-75	
Use a DataTip with a Breakpoint	Figure 6-77	Video 6-9
Publish an Application with ClickOnce Deployment	Figure 6-89	Video 6-10

FIGURE 6-105

Learn Online

Reinforcement activities and resources are available at no additional cost on www.CengageBrain.com. Visit http://solutions.cengage.com/ctdownloads/ for detailed instructions about accessing the available resources at the Student Companion Site.

Knowledge Check

1. Write a statement that displays the default value of 4.99 in the input box shown in Figure 6-106 and assigns the return value from the InputBox function to a variable named decHappyMeal with the message Cost of Happy Meal with the title Kids Meal.

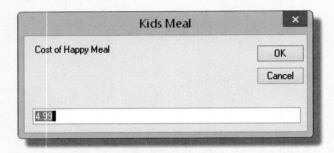

FIGURE 6-106

2. Write compound operators for the following equations:

    a. intFieldGoal = intFieldGoal+ 3

    b. dblCube = dblCube ^ 3

    c. strDog = strDog & "Treat"

3. Write For...Next loops that calculate the sum of the following ranges and assign their sum to a variable named intSum:

    a. The first 50 numbers starting with 1

    b. The even numbers beginning at 10 and ending with 100

    c. The numbers 20, 30, 40, 50, 60, and 70

4. Find the errors in the following For...Next header statements:

    a. For intCounter = "1" To "19"

    b. For intNumber = 98 To 71 Step 2

    c. For intValue = 12 To 52 Step −4

    d. For strCount = −15 To 5 Step 5

5. Explain the purpose of placing an ampersand before or within a MenuStrip item.

6. Write the command to clear a ListBox object named lstBaseballPlayers.

7. Write a command to add a list of cat breeds to a ListBox object named lstCatBreed.

8. What is the name of the property that displays an image as the background of a Form object?

9. Using a compound operator, write an assignment statement to decrease the value in intCounter by 3.7.

10. Using a compound operator, write an assignment statement to increment the value in intQuantity by 2.

11. Write a top-controlled Do Until loop with an empty body that would continue until intValue is less than 21.

12. Write a bottom-controlled Do While loop with an empty body that continues while the user enters "Yes" into the strContinue variable.

13. Write a Do While loop to validate that the user enters a nonzero integer into an input box for a variable named intDenominator.

14. Is the For...Next loop top-controlled or bottom-controlled?

15. Write the code for an infinite Do Until loop with the variable intRound.

16. Which loop should be used if you know the required number of times the loop will be executed?

17. What is the fewest number of times a top-controlled Do Until loop is executed?

18. Write a data validation Do loop to check that the variable intAge entered from an input box is between 1 and 117.

19. A loop inside another loop is called a _____ _____.

20. When you insert standard items in a MenuStrip object, what File menu items are automatically created by default?

Debugging Exercises

1. The loop shown in Figure 6-107 should repeat 10 times. If it will not repeat 10 times, change the code so it will.

```
7        For intRepeat = 20 To 10
8            MsgBox("The value is " & intRepeat.ToString("C0"))
9        Next
```

FIGURE 6-107

(continues)

2. What output does the code shown in Figure 6-108 produce? How would you change the code to produce a list box containing the values 12–20?

```
15          intRate = 12
16          Do While intRate <= 10
17              lstDisplay.Items.Add(intRate)
18              intRate += 1
19          Loop
```

FIGURE 6-108

3. What is the output of the code shown in Figure 6-109?

```
5           Dim intAdd As Integer
6           Dim intOuterLoop As Integer
7           Dim intInnerLoop As Integer
8
9           intAdd = 0
10          For intOuterLoop = 1 To 8
11              For intInnerLoop = 3 To 7
12                  intAdd += 1
13              Next
            Next
14          MsgBox.Show("The final value is " & intAdd.ToString())
```

FIGURE 6-109

4. What is the output of the code shown in Figure 6-110?

```
33          Dim intValue As Integer
34
35          intValue = 2
36          Do While intValue <= 9
37              lstDisplay.Items.Add(intValue & " " & intValue ^ 3)
38              intValue += 2
39          Loop
```

FIGURE 6-110

5. Fix the errors in the loop shown in Figure 6-111.

```
41          Dim intStart As Integer = 8
42
43          Loop
44          intStart = +4
45          Do While intStart < 24
```

FIGURE 6-111

6. What is the output of the code shown in Figure 6-112?

```
53          intCount = 40
54          Do Until intCount < 26
55              intCount -= 2
56              lstCount.Items.Add(intCount)
57          Loop
```

FIGURE 6-112

7. Fix the errors in the code shown in Figure 6-113.

```
 5          Dim decCost As Decimal = 3.5D
 6
 7          Do Until decCost > 10.5D
 8              MsgBox("The cost is now " & decCost.ToString("F1"))
 9              decCost -= 0.5
10          Loop
```

FIGURE 6-113

8. In the example shown in Figure 6-114, you want the code to count the odd numbers from 1 to 99. What is missing?

```
66          Dim intOddNumber As Integer = 1
67
68          Do While intOddNumber <= 99
69              lstDisplay.Items.Add("Odd Numbers: " & intOddNumber.ToString())
70          Loop
```

FIGURE 6-114

(continues)

Program Analysis

1. What is the value of lblResult after the code shown in Figure 6-115 is executed?

```
73            Dim intCounter As Integer = -20
74
75            Do While intCount < 25
76                intCount += 5
77                lblResult.Text &= intCount.ToString() & " "
78            Loop
```

FIGURE 6-115

2. What is the value of lblResult after the code shown in Figure 6-116 is executed?

```
80            Dim intCountIt As Integer
81
82            intCountIt = 6
83            Do
84                intCountIt += 3
85                lblResult.Text &= intCountIt.ToString() & " "
86            Loop Until intCountIt = 21
```

FIGURE 6-116

3. Rewrite the top-controlled Do While loop shown in Figure 6-117 as a top-controlled Do Until loop.

```
88            Dim intQuantity As Integer
89
90            intQuantity = -5
91            Do While intQuantity < 30
92                intQuantity += 5
93            Loop
```

FIGURE 6-117

4. Convert the Do loop shown in Figure 6-118 to a For...Next loop.

```
95            Dim intIncrease As Integer
96
97            intIncrease = 10
98            Do While intIncrease < 40
99                lstDisplay.Items.Add(intIncrease)
100               intIncrease += 2
101           Loop
```

FIGURE 6-118

5. How many times will the inner statement inside the nested loop in Figure 6-119 be executed?

```
103          For intOuterLoop = 3 To 5
104              For intInnerLoop = 6 To 10
105                  lstDays.Items.Add("Value: " & intOuterLoop.ToString() & _
106                      " Count: " & intInnerLoop.ToString())
107              Next
108          Next
```

FIGURE 6-119

6. How many times will the loop in Figure 6-120 be executed?

```
110          Dim intQuantitySold As Integer
111          Dim decTax As Decimal
112
113          intQuantitySold = 1
114          Do Until intQuantitySold = 5
115              decTax = intQuantitySold * 0.07
116              lstDisplay.Items.Add("Tax Amount: " & decTax.ToString())
117              intQuantitySold += 1
118          Loop
```

FIGURE 6-120

7. Write a For...Next loop that adds the odd numbers 1 through 49 and assigns their sum to the variable intSum. The program should start with the lines shown in Figure 6-121 (use the variables shown in lines 120–123 in your code).

```
120          Dim intLoopValue As Integer
121          Dim intStartvalue As Integer
122          Dim intEndvalue As Integer
123          Dim intSum As Integer
124
125          intStartvalue = 1
126          intEndvalue = 49
127          intSum = 0
```

FIGURE 6-121

(continues)

Case Programming Assignments

Complete one or more of the following case programming assignments. Submit the program and materials you create to your instructor. The level of difficulty is indicated for each case programming assignment.

● = Easiest
●● = Intermediate
●●● = Challenging

1 ●
CORN MAZE AVERAGE TIME

Design a Windows application and write the code that will execute according to the program requirements shown in Figure 6-122. Before writing the code, create an event planning document for each event in the program. The Use Case Definition document is shown in Figure 6-123 on the following page. The completed user interface is shown in Figure 6-124 on the following page.

REQUIREMENTS DOCUMENT

Date:	March 17, 2017
Date Submitted:	
Application Title:	Corn Maze Average Time
Purpose:	This Windows Desktop application is written for the corn maze of Dixon County to compute the average time in minutes needed to complete the entire corn maze.
Program Procedures:	In a Windows application, the user enters up to 10 values representing the number of minutes to complete the entire corn maze successfully to compute the average completion time.
Algorithms, Processing, and Conditions:	1. In an InputBox object, the user enters up to 10 corn maze completion times in minutes (nearest minute).
	2. Each number of minutes to complete the corn maze is displayed in the ListBox object.
	3. After 10 entries of maze completion times are entered, the average completion time is calculated and displayed.
	4. A File menu contains a Clear and an Exit option. The Clear menu item clears the average completion time and the 10 values representing the corn maze completion times. The Exit menu item closes the application.
	5. If the user taps or clicks the Cancel button in the input box before entering 10 values, compute the average of minutes entered.
	6. If the user taps or clicks the Cancel button before entering any completion time values, display a message indicating the user did not enter a value.
Notes and Restrictions:	1. Nonnumeric values should not be accepted.
	2. Negative values should not be accepted.
	3. The average completion time should be rounded to the nearest tenth of a minute.
Comments:	1. The application allows decimal entries.
	2. Obtain an image for this program from CengageBrain.com. The name of the image file is Maze.

FIGURE 6-122

Corn Maze Average Time (continued)

USE CASE DEFINITION

1. The Windows application opens with the heading "Race through the Corn Maze," a ListBox object that displays the maze completion times, an image, and a Button object that allows the user to begin entering their completion times.
2. A menu bar displays the File menu, which has two menu items: Clear and Exit.
3. The user enters up to 10 values in an InputBox object, with each value representing the number of minutes taken to complete the corn maze.
4. The program asks the user for the completion times again if the value is a negative number or the entry is a nonnumeric value.
5. The program displays the average of the completion times rounded to one decimal place.
6. The user can clear the input and the result by tapping or clicking the Clear menu item, and then can repeat Steps 3–5. If the user taps or clicks the Cancel button in the input box, the average for the values entered is calculated. If the user did not enter any values, the program displays an appropriate message.
7. The user taps or clicks the Exit menu item to close the application.

FIGURE 6-123

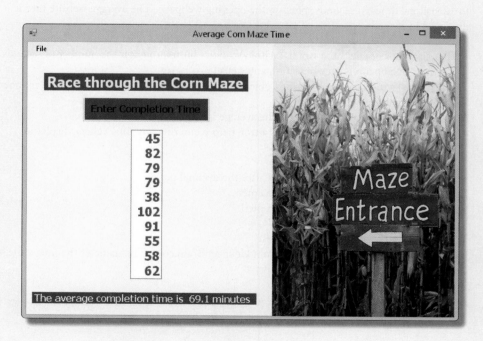

FIGURE 6-124

2

WEBSITE TRAFFIC METRIC

Design a Windows application and write the code that will execute according to the program requirements shown in Figure 6-125. Before writing the code, create an event planning document for each event in the program. The Use Case Definition document is shown in Figure 6-126 on the following page. The completed user interface is shown in Figure 6-127 on the following page.

REQUIREMENTS DOCUMENT

Date:	July 31, 2017
Date Submitted:	
Application Title:	Website Traffic Metric
Purpose:	This Windows Desktop application finds the average time in seconds spent on the opening page of a company's website, also called website traffic metrics or analytics. This market research is used to improve the effectiveness of the site.
Program Procedures:	A company wants to determine how much time is being spent on their opening page by computing the average in a Windows application. The application allows the user to enter up to 12 visitors' times in seconds spent on the opening webpage. The average website metric is displayed in seconds.
Algorithms, Processing, and Conditions:	1. The user taps or clicks the Enter Visitor Analytics button to enter the number of seconds spent on the opening page of a company website. 2. Each time is displayed in a ListBox object with a scroll bar that appears when the number of values exceeds the given space. 3. After 12 values have been entered, the average is displayed. 4. If the user taps or clicks the Cancel button before entering any time values, display an appropriate message.
Notes and Restrictions:	1. The result should include two places after the decimal point. 2. Nonnumeric values should not be accepted. 3. Negative numbers should not be accepted.
Comments:	1. The application allows integer entries. 2. Obtain an image for this program from CengageBrain.com. The name of the image file is Website.

FIGURE 6-125

Case Programming Assignments

Website Traffic Metric (continued)

USE CASE DEFINITION

1. The Windows application opens, displaying Website Traffic Estimate as the heading, a ListBox object that will display the seconds spent on the opening page of the website with a scroll bar as needed, and a Button object that allows the user to enter the number of seconds spent on the page.
2. In an InputBox object, the user enters up to 12 values representing the number of seconds spent on the opening page.
3. The program asks the user for the number of seconds again if the value is a negative or nonnumeric value.
4. The program displays the average time to two decimal places.
5. If the user taps or clicks the Cancel button in the input box before entering 12 time values, the program uses the number of seconds entered for calculations. If the user enters no time values, an appropriate message is displayed.

FIGURE 6-126

FIGURE 6-127

3 ● BOWLING SCOREBOARD

Design a Windows application and write the code that will execute according to the program requirements shown in Figure 6-128. Before writing the code, create an event planning document for each event in the program. The Use Case Definition document is shown in Figure 6-129 on the following page. The completed user interface is shown in Figure 6-130 on the following page.

REQUIREMENTS DOCUMENT

Date:	November 3, 2017
Date Submitted:	
Application Title:	Bowling Scoreboard
Purpose:	This application calculates the score of each frame during a bowling game for one person.
Program Procedures:	In a Windows Desktop application, the user enters the score of each frame to display the total on the scoreboard after 10 frames of bowling.
Algorithms, Processing, and Conditions:	1. The user taps or clicks the Enter Score button in an InputBox object to enter a score after each frame of bowling.
	2. The score for each frame and the running total is displayed in a ListBox.
	3. After the user taps or clicks the Cancel button in the InputBox object to end the scoring, the total final score is displayed.
	4. A File menu contains a Clear and an Exit option. The Clear menu item clears the result and the frame scores. The Exit menu item closes the application.
Notes and Restrictions:	1. Nonnumeric values should not be accepted.
	2. A negative value should not be accepted.
Comments:	Obtain an image for this program from CengageBrain.com. The name of the image file is Bowling. This image should be placed as a background image and stretched across the Form object.

FIGURE 6-128

Bowling Scoreboard (continued)

USE CASE DEFINITION

1. The Windows application opens with a heading, a Bowling Scoreboard subheading, a ListBox object that will display the frame scores throughout the game, and a Button object that allows the user to enter the scores.
2. A menu bar displays the File menu, which has two menu items: Clear and Exit.
3. In an InputBox object, the user enters points scored in each bowling frame.
4. The program asks the user for the score again if the value is a negative or nonnumeric number.
5. The program displays the running total score.
6. The program displays the final score when the user taps or clicks the Cancel button in the input box.
7. The user taps or clicks the Clear menu item to clear the input and the result.
8. The user taps or clicks the Exit menu item to close the application.

FIGURE 6-129

FIGURE 6-130

Mir-a/iStockphoto.com

Case Programming Assignments

4   ● ●
PENNY A DAY OR NICKEL A DAY

Design a Windows application and write the code that will execute according to the program requirements shown in Figure 6-131. Before writing the code, create an event planning document for each event in the program. Create a Use Case Definition document for the application.

REQUIREMENTS DOCUMENT

Date:	June 21, 2016
Date Submitted:	
Application Title:	Penny a Day or Nickel a Day
Purpose:	This Windows Desktop application finds the amount of your monthly pay if you are paid a penny or nickel for the first workday and the pay is doubled each subsequent workday. New employees are paid a penny for the first workday and experienced employees are paid a nickel for the first day.
Program Procedures:	The user enters the number of workdays in a monthly pay period and the pay for the first day. The program calculates and displays the amount of pay for the pay period.
Algorithms, Processing, and Conditions:	1. The user enters the number of days in the pay period. 2. The user selects a RadioButton object to indicate the pay amount for the first day: a penny or a nickel. 3. After the user enters the number of days and pay for the first day, the total amount earned is calculated and displayed. 4. A File menu contains a Clear and an Exit option. The Clear menu item clears the result and the RadioButton object. The Exit menu item closes the application.
Notes and Restrictions:	1. Nonnumeric values should not be accepted. 2. Negative values should not be accepted. 3. The minimum number of workdays in the pay period is 19 days for new employees and 16 days for experienced employees. The maximum number of workdays in a pay period is 22 days.
Comments:	n/a

FIGURE 6-131

5 ●●
LAKE EFFECT SNOWFALL

Design a Windows application and write the code that will execute according to the program requirements shown in Figure 6-132. Before writing the code, create an event planning document for each event in the program. Create a Use Case Definition document for the application.

REQUIREMENTS DOCUMENT

Date:	December 5, 2017
Date Submitted:	
Application Title:	Lake Effect Snowfall
Purpose:	This Windows Desktop application is written for the cities along the Great Lakes to compute the total snowfall for the months of October through April.
Program Procedures:	The user enters up to seven monthly snowfall amounts to compute the total snowfall for the cities that have lake effect snowfall.
Algorithms, Processing, and Conditions:	1. The user enters up to seven monthly snowfall totals in inches in an InputBox object. 2. Each month's total snowfall is displayed in a ListBox object. 3. After seven months of snowfall totals are entered, the total snowfall is calculated and displayed. 4. A File menu contains a Clear and an Exit option. The Clear menu item clears the total snowfall and the seven values representing the monthly snowfall totals. The Exit menu item closes the application. 5. If the user taps or clicks the Cancel button in the input box before entering seven values, compute the total for the number of months entered. 6. If the user taps or clicks the Cancel button before entering any snowfall values, display a message indicating the user did not enter a value.
Notes and Restrictions:	1. Nonnumeric values should not be accepted. 2. Negative values should not be accepted. 3. The average total snowfall should be rounded to the nearest tenth of an inch.
Comments:	The application allows decimal entries.

FIGURE 6-132

6 ●●
NEXT DECADE PAY CALCULATOR

Design a Windows application and write the code that will execute according to the program requirements shown in Figure 6-133. Before writing the code, create an event planning document for each event in the program. Create a Use Case Definition document for the application.

REQUIREMENTS DOCUMENT

Date:	August 23, 2016
Date Submitted:	
Application Title:	The Next Decade Pay Calculator
Purpose:	This Windows Desktop application computes the amount of money an employee will earn over the next decade based on a raise, which is a percentage amount.
Program Procedures:	In a Windows application, the user enters her present wage per hour and the raise percentage amount per year to compute her yearly pay over the next 10 years.
Algorithms, Processing, and Conditions:	1. The application opens, displaying a title and requesting the present amount of pay per hour and the expected raise percentage per year.
	2. When the Compute Future Pay button is tapped or clicked, the program calculates the yearly pay based on 40 hours per week and 52 weeks per year. The raise increases each amount after the first year.
	3. The yearly amount of pay earned is displayed for the next 10 years.
	4. A File menu contains a Clear and an Exit option. The Clear menu item clears the result. The Exit menu item closes the application.
Notes and Restrictions:	1. Nonnumeric values should not be accepted.
	2. Negative numbers should not be allowed.
Comments:	The application allows decimal entries.

FIGURE 6-133

7 ●●●
FACTORIAL MATH

Create a requirements document and a Use Case Definition document and design a Windows application based on the case project shown in Figure 6-134:

Most calculators have an operation called a "factorial," which is shown on a calculator key as an exclamation point. For example, 5! (5 factorial) multiplies 5 * 4 * 3 * 2 * 1 to calculate the result of 120. Using loops to compute the factorial, display the following factorials in a ListBox object:

1! 1
2! 2
3! 6
4! 24
5! 120
…
12! 479001600

FIGURE 6-134

8
●●●
COMET HOSTEL

Create a requirements document and a Use Case Definition document and design a Windows application based on the case project shown in Figure 6-135:

The Comet Hostel asks you to write a Windows application that computes the occupancy rate of the hostel. Occupancy rate is a percentage that is equal to the number of rooms sold divided by the total number of rooms available. The hostel has 13 floors. The user should use an InputBox function to respond to two questions about each floor: How many rooms are occupied on that floor? How many rooms on the floor are vacant? Display which floor you are asking about in each question. Display how many rooms are occupied and vacant on each floor in a ListBox object. After the user has entered all the information, display the following results: the total number of rooms at the hotel, the number of occupied rooms, and the number of vacant rooms. Also display the occupancy rate as a percentage, such as 61%. Nonnumeric values should not be accepted. Do not accept negative numbers. A menu should exit the program. Publish the application after testing it.

FIGURE 6-135

9 ●●●
START SAVING YOUR NEST EGG

Create a requirements document and a Use Case Definition document and design a Windows application based on the case project shown in Figure 6-136:

Your savings can be called a nest egg. Write a Windows application that allows you to enter the amount of money you would like in your nest egg to place a down payment on a home or for retirement, the interest rate, and a number of years. For example if you hope to buy a home in five years with a down payment, would the principal of $17,000 grow over five years at 4% interest to a down payment of $20,000? Display a ListBox object for each year and the amount of money in the account at the end of that year. Determine whether you have saved enough money for the home example. Nonnumeric and negative values should not be accepted. Debug and then publish the application. *Hint*: The formula for compound interest for one year is: Amount = Principal * (1 + Rate). For 5 years of compound interest, this formula should be executed 5 times with the principal increasing to the new amount each year.

FIGURE 6-136

CHAPTER 7

Using Procedures and Exception Handling

OBJECTIVES

You will have mastered the material in this chapter when you can:

- Create a splash screen

- Pause the splash screen

- Add a ComboBox object to a Windows form

- Write code for a SelectedIndexChanged event

- Understand procedures

- Code a Sub procedure

- Pass an argument to a procedure by value

- Pass an argument to a procedure by reference

- Code a Function procedure to return a value

- Create a class-level variable

- Catch an exception using a Try-Catch block

- Determine the order of exceptions in a Try-Catch block

Introduction

The programs you have written thus far in this course were relatively small applications. Most real-world software, however, solves more expansive problems. As an application grows, it is important to divide each facet of a problem into separate sections of code called **procedures**. By using the principle of divide and conquer to create procedures, the code becomes more manageable.

In previous programs you have learned about data verification to ensure the user enters valid data before the data is processed. To expand your knowledge of data verification, you need to understand exception handling using Try-Catch blocks, which can check for any error a user might commit. By managing exceptions using Try-Catch blocks, you build high-quality, robust applications.

Finally, one way to make your programs more professional is to display a splash screen while the full program loads. In this chapter, you will learn to design and write procedures, include Try-Catch blocks in your program, and create a splash screen.

Chapter Project

The sample program in this chapter displays two Windows forms and is more complex than previous applications. An international company has requested a Windows application that provides pricing information for escape-room puzzle games. The Mystery Escape is an interactive real-life suspense game with elements of a mystery game. Cities all over the world such as Dallas, Paris, and Singapore host escape games where you take a "time-travel" adventure into another century. The minute you step inside the room, you and the other players become experts, engrossed in a quest to solve the puzzles and mysteries within the time limit to escape. Each team can use their wits to find the key and unlock the door of the private room, holding two to six players. The purpose of the application is to display the pricing information for escape-room games at worldwide locations. The Mystery Escape game is located in Dallas, Paris, and Singapore. Each mystery specializes in a different type of escape game. Figure 7-1 shows the available escape game types, the challenge length of each game type, and the cost.

Location	Real Escape Game Type	Challenge Length	Price
Dallas	Spy in the Study	1 hour	$32 USD
	Hidden Cellar	1 hour	$39
	Team Building	2 hours	$55
Paris	The Encounter	1 hour	$38 USD
	Library Larceny	1 hour	$45
Singapore	Hidden Cellar	1 hour	$45 USD
	Team Building	2 hours	$65
	Amazing Race	4 hours	$75

FIGURE 7-1

The program begins with an opening screen called a splash screen. In Figure 7-2, the splash screen displays the company name and image logo for approximately five seconds.

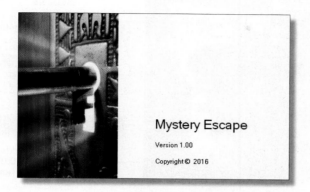

FIGURE 7-2

© iStock.com/DNY59

After the splash screen closes, the main form of the application opens and requests that the user select the mystery city location. When the user taps or clicks the ComboBox arrow, the three mystery city locations of Dallas, Paris, and Singapore appear in the drop-down list, as shown in Figure 7-3.

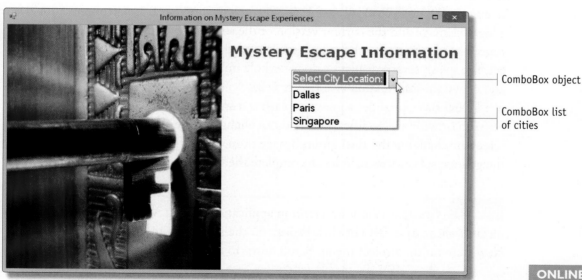

FIGURE 7-3

© iStock.com/DNY59

After the user selects the escape city location, the Windows form displays form controls that request the number of guests in the team and the type of game. The user enters the number of guests, selects the real escape game type she wants, and then taps or clicks the Find Team Cost button. As shown in Figure 7-4, the program displays the cost and length of the mystery escape game type.

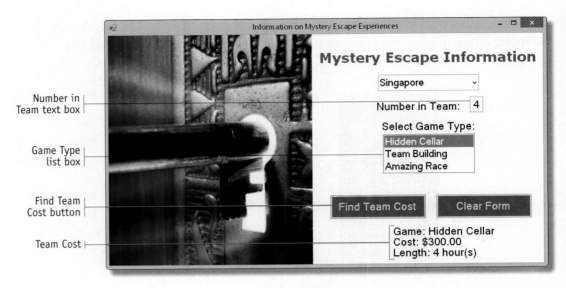

FIGURE 7-4

© iStock.com/DNY59

Create a Splash Screen

A **splash screen** is an opening screen that appears as an application is loading, signaling that the program is about to start and displaying an image and information to engage the user. Typically a splash screen on a computer or smartphone, provides a logo or image and the current version of the software product as an introduction page, disappearing after the main page is loaded. In the Mystery Escape chapter project, the splash screen displays a door keyhole image, a title, the application version, and copyright information (see Figure 7-2).

Visual Basic provides a generic splash screen template you can add to your project with or without modification. You can change the generic graphic on the splash screen by changing the BackgroundImage property on the Properties window. To use the generic splash screen, you can complete the following steps:

STEP 1   Create a Windows Desktop application named Mystery Escape. Name the form `frmEscape`. Tap or click Project on the menu bar and then tap or click Add New Item on the Project menu. Scroll down to view Splash Screen.

The Add New Item dialog box is displayed (Figure 7-5).

Add New Item dialog box

FIGURE 7-5

STEP 2   In the Add New Item dialog box, select Splash Screen in the center pane.

The Splash Screen template is selected (Figure 7-6).

FIGURE 7-6

STEP 3   Tap or click the Add button in the Add New Item dialog box.

A form preconfigured by Visual Studio as a splash screen opens as a new tab named SplashScreen1.vb[Design] in the Design window (Figure 7-7). The splash screen can be customized with different graphics and text to suit an application.

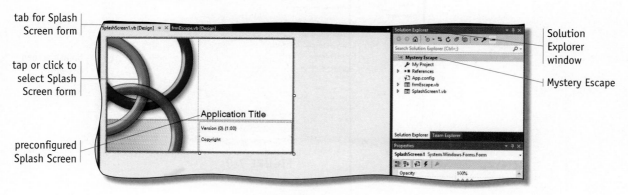

FIGURE 7-7

STEP 4   Tap or click the left side of the splash screen form to select it. To set the application to display the splash screen first, press and hold or right-click Mystery Escape in the Solution Explorer.

The splash screen form is selected (Figure 7-8). A shortcut menu opens.

FIGURE 7-8

STEP 5   Tap or click Properties on the shortcut menu. If necessary, scroll down until the Splash screen option is displayed.

The Project Designer opens and displays the Application tab (Figure 7-9). The Project Designer provides a central location for managing project properties, settings, and resources. The Project Designer appears as a single window in the Visual Studio IDE. It contains a number of pages that are accessed through tabs on the left.

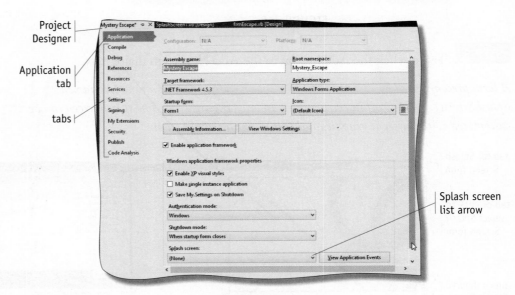

FIGURE 7-9

STEP 6   In the Windows application framework properties section, tap or click the Splash screen list arrow, and then tap or click SplashScreen1 to select it as the splash screen used for the project.

SplashScreen1 is selected in the Splash screen list (Figure 7-10).

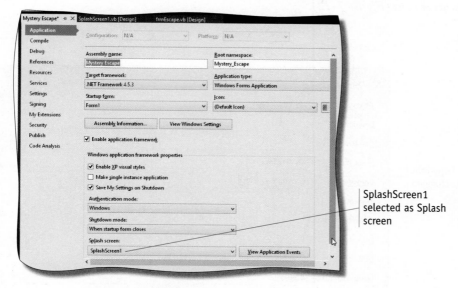

SplashScreen1
selected as Splash
screen

FIGURE 7-10

STEP 7   Scroll up and tap or click the Assembly Information button on the Project Designer to open the Assembly Information dialog box.

The Assembly Information dialog box opens (Figure 7-11).

Assembly Information
dialog box

Title

Copyright

Assembly Information	?	×

Title: Mystery Escape

Description:

Company:

Product: Mystery Escape

Copyright: Copyright © 2015

Trademark:

Assembly version: 1   0   0   0

File version: 1   0   0   0

GUID: 659e650c-87dc-4dcc-adf9-379671b2ef34

Neutral language: (None)

☐ Make assembly COM-Visible

OK   Cancel

FIGURE 7-11

STEP 8　To customize the splash screen, if necessary, change the copyright to the present year. The numbers in the File version boxes can be changed as you update the application.

The copyright year is changed. The text on the splash screen form will not change until the application runs (Figure 7-12).

Copyright changed

OK button

Assembly Information

Title: Mystery Escape

Description:

Company:

Product: Mystery Escape

Copyright: Copyright © 2016

Trademark:

Assembly version: 1　0　0　0

File version: 1　0　0　0

GUID: 659e650c-87dc-4dcc-adf9-379671b2ef34

Neutral language: (None)

☐ Make assembly COM-Visible

OK　Cancel

FIGURE 7-12

STEP 9　Tap or click the OK button on the Assembly Information dialog box. Close the Mystery Escape* Project Designer window. To change the predefined image, first make sure you have the Escape.jpg picture (available on CengageBrain.com) and that you stored the image in a location you remember. Then, tap or click the SplashScreen1.vb [Design] tab. Tap or click the left side of the splash screen, making sure to select the entire splash screen form. The Properties window should identify MainLayoutPanel if you have selected the entire splash screen form. Tap or click to the right of the BackgroundImage property in the Properties window, and then tap or click the ellipsis button. In the Select Resource dialog box, tap or click the Project resource file radio button, if necessary. Import the Escape.jpg picture by tapping or clicking the Import button in the Select Resource dialog box and selecting the Escape.jpg image from the location where you stored it. Tap or click the OK button in the Select Resource dialog box.

The splash screen background image changes from the predefined image to the Escape.jpg image (Figure 7-13).

SplashScreen1.vb [Design] tab

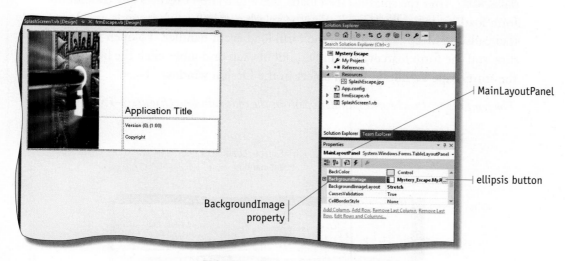

MainLayoutPanel

ellipsis button

BackgroundImage
property

FIGURE 7-13

© iStock.com/DNY59

STEP 10   Run the application by tapping or clicking the Start Debugging button on the Standard toolbar.

The application begins to run. The splash screen appears for a moment and immediately closes (Figure 7-14). The amount of time the splash screen is displayed is based on the time needed to open the main form.

FIGURE 7-14

© iStock.com/DNY59

Pause the Splash Screen

The user needs enough time to read the splash screen before it closes and the main form opens. To pause the splash screen for a specific time period, you can call the Sleep procedure. In fact, you can pause the execution of any application by calling the Thread.Sleep procedure. The Sleep procedure uses an integer value that determines how long the application should pause. To pause the splash screen, you can complete the following steps:

STEP 1   After the splash screen loads, the application executes any code in the form load event handler. To display the splash screen for five seconds, you insert code that calls the Sleep procedure in the form load event handler. To open the code window and the form load event handler, double-tap or double-click the background of the frmEscape Windows Form object in the Design window.

The frmEscape_Load event handler opens in the code window (Figure 7-15).

frmEscape_Load
event handler

FIGURE 7-15

STEP 2   Tap or click inside the frmEscape_Load event handler. Type `Threading.` (with an ending period) to have IntelliSense display a list of possible entries. If necessary, type `T` to select Thread from the IntelliSense list. Type `.S` to select Sleep from the IntelliSense list. Type `(5000)`.

The call for the Sleep procedure is entered (Figure 7-16). When the program runs and the frmEscape_Load event is executed, the Sleep procedure suspends the execution of the application for 5000 milliseconds (5 seconds). This means that while the splash screen is displayed, the form will not be loaded for five seconds. You can increase the number of milliseconds if you want a longer pause.

Sleep procedure call   5000 milliseconds

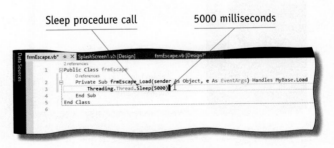

FIGURE 7-16

ONLINE REINFORCEMENT

To view a video of the process in the previous steps, visit CengageBrain.com and navigate to the resources for this title. Tap or click the link for Chapter 7 and then navigate to Video 7-3.

Add a ComboBox Object

The Mystery Escape sample program requires a new type of object, called a ComboBox object, to determine which mystery the user will select for their game type (Figure 7-17).

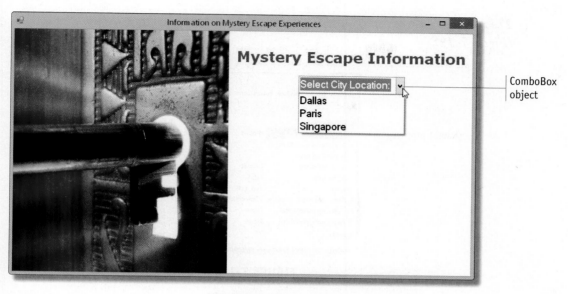

FIGURE 7-17

© iStock.com/DNY59

A ComboBox object consists of two parts. The top part is a text box that allows the user to enter text. The second part is a list box; when the user taps or clicks the arrow, the list box displays a list of items from which the user can select one item. To save space on a form, you can use a ComboBox object because the full list is not displayed until the user taps or clicks the list arrow. The prefix for the ComboBox object (Name) property is cbo. To place a ComboBox object on a Windows Form object, you can complete the following steps:

STEP 1   Drag the ComboBox .NET component from the Common Controls category of the Toolbox to the approximate location where you want to place the ComboBox object.

The ComboBox object is placed on the Windows Form object (Figure 7-18).

FIGURE 7-18

© iStock.com/DNY59

STEP 2   With the ComboBox object selected, scroll in the Properties window to the (Name) property. Double-tap or double-click in the right column of the (Name) property, and then enter the name cboCity.

The name you entered is displayed in the (Name) property in the Properties window (Figure 7-19).

FIGURE 7-19
© iStock.com/DNY59

STEP 3   In the Properties window, scroll to the Text property. Tap or click to the right of the Text property and enter `Select City Location:` to specify the text that appears in the combo box. Change the text size to 14. Resize the ComboBox object as needed to display the data in the box.

The Text property is changed to the instructions to select a mystery game location (Figure 7-20).

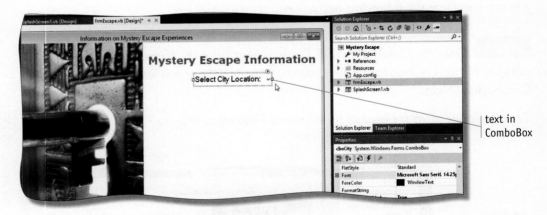

FIGURE 7-20

© iStock.com/DNY59

STEP 4   In the Properties window, scroll to the Items property, and then tap or click to the right of the Items property on the word (Collection). Tap or click the ellipsis button. The String Collection Editor dialog box opens. Enter the mystery game locations `Dallas` (press ENTER), `Paris` (press ENTER), and `Singapore`.

The three items for the ComboBox list are shown in the String Collection Editor dialog box (Figure 7-21).

String Collection
Editor dialog
box

FIGURE 7-21

STEP 5   In the String Collection Editor dialog box, tap or click the OK button. Tap or click the Start Debugging button on the Standard toolbar to run the application. Tap or click the list arrow on the right side of the ComboBox object to view the contents. You can select a choice from the list.

The list in the ComboBox object contains the names previously entered in the String Collection Editor dialog box (Figure 7-22). The user can select one of the items in the list.

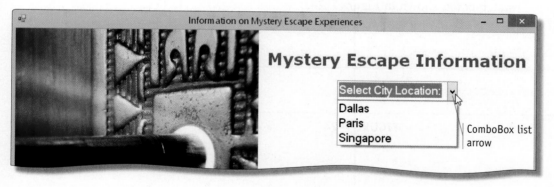

© iStock.com/DNY59

FIGURE 7-22

Determine the ComboBox Selected Index

To determine the cost of the game type selected in the Mystery Escape sample program, the user first selects the mystery game location from the ComboBox object list. Code for the program must determine both that a value was selected and which one was selected. When the user selects an item in the ComboBox object list, the **SelectedIndex** property of the ComboBox object is assigned a number that represents

ONLINE REINFORCEMENT

To view a video of the process in the previous steps, visit CengageBrain.com and navigate to the resources for this title. Tap or click the link for Chapter 7 and then navigate to Video 7-4.

Should I list the items in the ComboBox object in a certain order?

For ease of use, list items within a ComboBox should be listed in an order that best assists the user in finding their most likely option. For example, if you are listing states, alphabetical order makes sense. Many listings may have a predefined order such as freshman, sophomore, junior, and senior class levels.

the selected item. These numbers are a zero-based index, which means it begins with zero. For example, if the user selects Dallas, as shown in Figure 7-23, the index of 0 is the SelectedIndex for the ComboBox object. This index number can be assigned to an Integer data type variable.

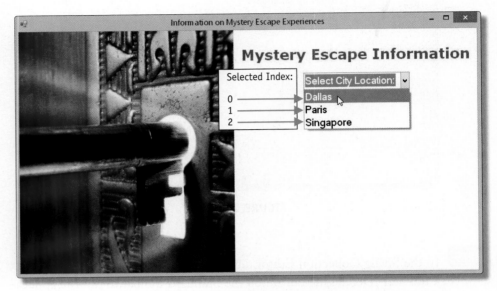

© iStock.com/DNY59

FIGURE 7-23

If the user has not made a selection, the SelectedIndex property is set to -1. To assign the item that the user selects using the SelectedIndex property, you can use a statement as shown in Figure 7-24.

```
32        intCityChoice =cboCity.SelectedIndex()
```

FIGURE 7-24

Handle SelectedIndexChanged Events

In the Mystery Escape application, the user's first action is to select the mystery game location. When the application opens, the user views the main title and a ComboBox object named cboCity, as shown in Figure 7-25.

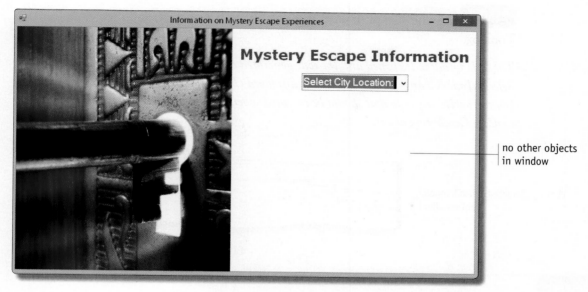

no other objects
in window

FIGURE 7-25

© iStock.com/DNY59

Notice that a Button object is not displayed in the window shown in Figure 7-25. When the user selects the mystery game location, the application displays other objects on the form that request the number of people in the team and the list of possible game type choices for the selected mystery. Instead of using a button click event to begin this process, another type of event handler called the **SelectedIndexChanged** event handler is executed when the user selects the mystery game location of the game type. The SelectedIndexChanged event is triggered by the user selecting an item in the ComboBox object because the selected index in the ComboBox object is changed when the user makes a selection. To create a SelectedIndexChanged event, you can complete the following steps:

STEP 1 Select the ComboBox object named cboCity on the Windows Form object.

The cboCity ComboBox object is selected on the form (Figure 7-26).

ComboBox
object selected

FIGURE 7-26
© iStock.com/DNY59

STEP 2 Double-tap or double-click the ComboBox object, and then close the Toolbox.

The code window is opened and the code generated by Visual Studio for the SelectedIndexChanged event handler is displayed (Figure 7-27). Within the event handler, you can write any code that should be executed when the user makes a selection in the cboCity ComboBox object.

cboCIty_SelectedIndexChanged
event handler

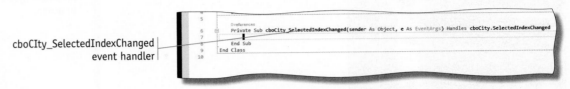

```
 5
 6        0 references
          Private Sub cboCity_SelectedIndexChanged(sender As Object, e As EventArgs) Handles cboCity.SelectedIndexChanged
 7
 8        End Sub
 9    End Class
10
```

FIGURE 7-27

By executing an event handler when the user selects a particular item in the cboCity ComboBox object, the program works efficiently without multiple user taps or clicks. Many objects, such as the ListBox and DropDownList objects, can be used in the same manner as the ComboBox object with a SelectedIndexChanged event handler.

Procedures

The Mystery Escape application is a larger and more complex program than those in previous chapters. Because the code for each event handler will be long, you should divide the code into smaller parts, each of which completes a specific task for the event handler. It is easier to deal with a larger program if you can focus on code that accomplishes a single task.

When a program is broken into manageable parts, each part is called a **procedure**. A procedure is a named set of code that performs a given task. In previous programs you have called procedures, such as the Clear procedure and the ToString procedure that have been written by the developers of Visual Studio. In the Mystery Escape program in this chapter, you will both write and call procedures.

Visual Basic provides two types of procedures: Sub procedures and Function procedures. The following sections explain these two types of procedures and how to code them.

CONSIDER THIS

How is breaking my programs into procedures like taking a detour on a highway?
A Sub procedure call is like a detour on the highway. After the Sub procedure is completed, control returns to the calling procedure. It is much easier to debug a smaller set of statements in a procedure than in a large program.

Code a Sub Procedure

A **Sub procedure** is a procedure that completes its task but does not return any data to the calling procedure. A Sub procedure in Visual Basic 2015 is defined by using the Sub keyword. A **Sub** procedure is the series of Visual Basic statements enclosed by the Sub and End Sub statements. Each time the Sub procedure is called, its statements are executed, starting with the first executable statement after the Sub statement and ending with the first End Sub statement. A Sub procedure is called with a statement consisting of the procedure name and a set of parentheses in the form of a **procedure call**, as shown in Figure 7-28.

General Format: Procedure Call

The procedure call is made:

```
ProcedureName()
```

The **procedure declaration** that begins the Sub procedure has the form:

```
Private Sub ProcedureName ()

    ' Line(s)of code

End Sub
```

FIGURE 7-28

In the Mystery Escape application, users can select the escape game type for each city. Based on the user's selection of a city, the ListBox object in Figure 7-29 is filled with the various game types that are available. For example, if the user selects Dallas, game types such as Spy in the Study, Hidden Cellar, and Team Building are displayed in the ListBox object.

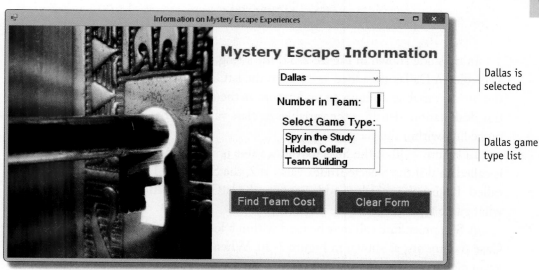

FIGURE 7-29

The items in the ListBox object are different based on the mystery escape location selected. Figure 7-30 shows the code in the SelectedIndexChanged event handler that calls a Sub procedure to fill in the items in the ListBox object based on the city location selected by the user.

FIGURE 7-30

In Figure 7-30, the selected index for the cboCity ComboBox is assigned to the Integer variable named intCityChoice. Then, in the Select Case statement, the appropriate Sub procedure is called based on the city the user selected. When the selected index is equal to zero, the user selected the first item in the ComboBox list, which is Dallas, so the DallasTeam Sub procedure is called. Notice that the name of the Sub procedure is specified with open and closed parentheses. As you learned previously, the Visual Basic compiler recognizes a procedure call by the parentheses.

The DallasTeam Sub procedure code is shown in Figure 7-31.

```
54     Private Sub DallasTeam()
55        ' This procedure fills in the possible game types offered in Dallas
56        lstGame.Items.Add(_strGame1)
57        lstGame.Items.Add(_strGame2)
58        lstGame.Items.Add(_strGame3)
59
60     End Sub
```

FIGURE 7-31

In the code shown in Figure 7-31, the string values for the types of game types available on Dallas are added as items in the lstGame ListBox object. Notice that the String variables contain an underscore as the first character. You will recall that this designation identifies the variables as class variables that can be referenced in any procedure within the class.

In Figure 7-30, if the SelectedIndex value is 1, the ParisTeam Sub procedure is called, and if the SelectedIndex value is 2, the SingaporeTeam Sub procedure is called. Each Sub procedure adds items to the lstGame ListBox object, depending on what game types are available for each city.

A Sub procedure call may be used within a loop, If statements, or even Select Case statements, as shown in Figure 7-30. When a Sub procedure is called, the program gives control to the called Sub procedure and executes the lines of code within it. After the Sub procedure has completed its execution, program control returns to the calling procedure and program execution resumes in the calling procedure.

Pass Arguments

Earlier chapters defined and used the term *scope* and explained that variables declared within a procedure are limited in scope to their procedure. Code outside a procedure cannot interact with the variables declared within another procedure.

When a procedure is called, however, the call statement can pass an argument to the called procedure. You have seen this in previous chapters when you passed a string value to the ToInt32 procedure to convert the string value to an integer value (Figure 7-32).

```
123        intTeamSize = Convert.ToInt32(txtTeam.Text)
```
procedure call　　argument

FIGURE 7-32

In Figure 7-32, the argument is contained within parentheses. In this example, the argument is the Text property of the txtTeam TextBox object.

In many applications, passing variables to another procedure is essential because the called procedure requires the value(s) in order to complete its processing. For example, in Figure 7-33, the btnDaysOfWeek_Click event determines whether a certain day of the week is part of the work week or the weekend. When the Weekday Sub procedure is called, a variable named intNumericDayOfWeek is passed to the Weekday Sub procedure because it must know the numeric day in order to perform its processing.

```
20      Private Sub btnDaysOfWeek_Click(ByVal sender As System.Object, ByVal e As System. ↙
        EventArgs) Handles btnDaysOfWeek.Click
21          Dim intNumericDayOfWeek As Integer
22
23          intNumericDayOfWeek = Convert.ToInt32(txtDay.Text)
24          Weekday(intNumericDayOfWeek)
25          MsgBox("Have a Great Week!", "Goodbye")
26      End Sub
27
28      Private Sub Weekday(ByVal intDay As Integer)
29          If intDay = 1 Or intDay = 7 Then
30              lblDisplayDay.Text = "Weekend"
31          End If
32          If intDay >= 2 And intDay <= 6 Then
33              lblDisplayDay.Text = "Weekday"
34          End If
35      End Sub
```

FIGURE 7-33

In Figure 7-33, the variable named intNumericDayOfWeek is passed to the Weekday Sub procedure by the calling statement on line 24. The value in the intNumericDayOfWeek variable should be 1 for Sunday, 2 for Monday, 3 for Tuesday, 4 for Wednesday, 5 for Thursday, 6 for Friday, and 7 for Saturday.

When a value is passed to a Sub procedure, its declaration, which identifies the name of the Sub procedure, must also contain an entry that defines the argument for use within the Sub procedure. In the Weekday Sub procedure in Figure 7-33, the parentheses following the Sub procedure name on line 28 contain the command ByVal intDay as Integer. This entry defines an Integer variable name (intDay) for use within the Sub procedure.

Visual Basic treats variables passed from a calling procedure to a called procedure in one of two ways: ByVal or ByRef. The following sections explain these two methods.

Pass Arguments by Value (ByVal)

When an argument is passed ByVal, it means the Sub procedure has access to the value of the passed argument but does not actually reference the variable declared in the calling procedure. Instead, the value is copied into a variable whose name is specified in the Sub procedure declaration statement. For example, in Figure 7-33 the argument is passed ByVal, so the value in intNumericDayOfWeek is copied to the variable defined in the procedure declaration of the called Sub procedure (intDay).

The intDay variable contains the value passed from the calling procedure only as long as the called Sub procedure has processing control. When the Sub procedure has completed processing and passes control back to the calling procedure, the variable is lost. If the Sub procedure is called again, the variable is created again as a new variable with no preexisting value. So, you can consider the variable defined in the Sub procedure declaration as a temporary variable that exists only during processing within the Sub procedure when the argument is passed ByVal.

The temporary variable can be given any name, including the name of the variable in the calling procedure, but most developers use different names to avoid confusion. Notice that the name used in the calling procedure is intNumericDayOfWeek and the name used in the Sub procedure for the temporary variable is intDay.

When the argument is passed ByVal, the Sub procedure code can change the value in the temporary variable and use it in any manner required. The original value of the variable in the calling procedure is not affected because the value is copied into the temporary Sub procedure variable and the variable in the calling procedure is never referenced in the Sub procedure.

ByVal is the default option for all passed arguments. The keyword ByVal is added automatically if you do not enter it when you code the Sub procedure declaration.

The code in Figure 7-34 illustrates the fact that the Sub procedure can change the passed value, but that value is not changed in the calling procedure when the value is passed ByVal.

```
22    Private Sub btnShowMessages Click(ByVal sender As System.Object, ByVal e As System.↵
      EventArgs) Handles btnShowMessages.Click
23        Dim strMessage As String
24
25        strMessage = "The Original Welcome Message"
26        MsgBox(strMessage, ,"First Message")
27        DisplayMessage(strMessage)
28        MsgBox(strMessage, ,"Fourth Message")
29    End Sub
30
31    Private Sub DisplayMessage(ByVal strShowMessage As String)
32        MsgBox(strShowMessage, ,"Second Message")
33        strShowMessage = "The Changed Welcome Message"
34        MsgBox(strShowMessage, ,"Third Message")
35    End Sub
36 End Class
```

FIGURE 7-34

The output for the code in Figure 7-34 is shown in Figure 7-35.

FIGURE 7-35

Figure 7-35 shows that the DisplayMessage Sub procedure in Figure 7-34 changed the message. The third message box displays this changed message: "The Changed Welcome Message." When the Sub procedure is finished and control is passed back to the calling procedure, however, the value in the strMessage variable is passed to the Sub procedure but is not changed, as shown in the Fourth Message window.

You can call the same Sub procedure repeatedly, as shown in Figure 7-36. The Sub procedure DisplayMessage is called once and the Square Sub procedure is called three times. Notice that either literals or variables can be passed to a Sub procedure.

```
23      Private Sub btnSquare_Click(ByVal sender As System.Object, ByVal e As System.    ↙
        EventArgs) Handles btnSquare.Click
24
25          Dim decNum As Decimal
26
27          decNum = 3.3
28          DisplayMessage()
29          Square(7.9)
30          Square(4.0)
31          Square(decNum)
32
33      End Sub
34
35      Private Sub Square(ByVal decValue As Decimal)
36          lstResult.Items.Add("The square of " & decValue & " is " & _
37            (decValue * decValue))
38
39      End Sub
40
41      Private Sub DisplayMessage()
42          lstResult.Items.Add("Squares:")
43      End Sub
```

FIGURE 7-36

After executing the code in Figure 7-36, the ListBox object would contain the values shown in Figure 7-37.

FIGURE 7-37

Pass Arguments by Reference (ByRef)

When an argument is passed ByVal, it means the Sub procedure has access to the value of the passed argument but does not actually reference the variable declared in the calling procedure. Instead, the value is copied into a variable whose name is specified in the Sub procedure declaration statement. As Figure 7-33 on page 467 shows, because the argument is passed ByVal, the value in intNumericDayOfWeek is copied to the variable defined in the procedure declaration of the called Sub procedure (intDay).

Passing a value by reference allows code in the Sub procedure to modify the contents of the variable that is being passed because when you use ByRef, you are passing a reference to the variable that holds the value instead of the value itself, as when you use ByVal. Thus, if a Sub procedure changes the value of a variable passed ByRef, the original variable in the calling procedure is changed. You should select the option to pass a variable by reference if you intend to change the original value when it is passed to the Sub procedure.

In the code example in Figure 7-38, the calling procedure assigns the value Vincent Van Gogh to the strFavoriteArtist variable (line 49) and then passes the variable ByRef (line 55).

```
46        Private Sub btnDisplayMessage_Click(ByVal sender As System.Object, ByVal e As          ↙
          System.EventArgs) Handles btnDisplayMessage.Click
47            Dim strFavoriteArtist As String
48
49            strFavoriteArtist = "Vincent Van Gogh"
50            MsgBox("Favorite Artist is " & strFavoriteArtist, , "First Message")
51            DisplayMessage(strFavoriteArtist)
52            MsgBox("Favorite Artist is now " & strFavoriteArtist, , "Fourth Message")
53        End Sub
54
55        Private Sub DisplayMessage(ByRef strshowArtist As String)
56            MsgBox("Favorite Artist is " & strshowArtist, , "Second Message")
57            ' The artist name is changed
58            strshowArtist = "Paul Cezanne "
59            MsgBox("Favorite Artist is " & strshowArtist, , "Third Message")
60        End Sub
61 End Class
```

FIGURE 7-38

The Sub procedure changes the value of the passed variable to Paul Cezanne (line 58). Because the variable is passed by reference (ByRef), the value in the variable that is passed from the calling procedure is changed to Paul Cezanne. In the output shown in Figure 7-39, the changed value is displayed in the fourth message box when the btnDisplayMessage_Click event displays the last message box (line 52).

WATCH OUT FOR

Passing ByVal means the Sub procedure *cannot* change the original value. Passing ByRef means the Sub procedure *can* change the original value.

FIGURE 7-39

Pass Multiple Arguments

You can pass as many arguments as needed to a Sub procedure. If you have more than one argument, the variables are passed in the same order in which they appear in the procedure call statement.

Function Procedures

A **Function procedure** is similar to a Sub procedure except that a Function procedure returns a single value to the calling procedure. Just like a Sub procedure, you can pass variables to the Function procedure using ByVal and ByRef. A Function procedure uses the keyword Function (instead of the keyword Sub) in the procedure declaration. You must also specify a return data type in the procedure declaration to define the type of variable that is being returned to the calling procedure by the Function procedure. The Function procedure call has the syntax shown in Figure 7-40.

General Format: Function Procedure Call

The procedure call is made:

```
VariableName = FunctionProcedureName ()
```

The **procedure declaration** that begins the Function procedure has the form:

```
Private Function FunctionProcedureName () as DataType

    ' Line(s) of code

    Return VariableName

End Function
```

FIGURE 7-40

The Private keyword is optional in the Function procedure declaration. If it is omitted, the default option is Public, which means any code in any class can reference the Function procedure. In many instances, Public access is not desirable, so the Private access modifier is used.

In the Function procedure call statement in Figure 7-40, the FunctionProcedureName on the right side of the assignment statement is replaced by the value that is returned from the Function procedure. That value then is assigned to the variable on the left side of the equal sign.

HEADS UP

You can exclude the receiving variable in the procedure call if you use the value immediately, as in lblResult.Text = "Price: " & FindPrice(intValue).ToString().

The Function procedure is different in appearance from a Sub procedure in the following ways:

- The Function procedure call has a receiving variable that is assigned the returned value from the Function procedure.
- The data type of the return value is listed in the procedure declaration.
- The keyword Return is used in the Function procedure to return a single value.

A Function procedure can pass only one value back to the calling procedure. The coding example in Figure 7-41 determines the gas mileage of a vehicle by dividing the number of miles driven by the number of gallons of gas used. The Compute-GasMileage Function procedure returns one value representing the gas mileage (Return statement on line 87). When the gas mileage value is returned, it is assigned to the receiving variable decMilesPerGallon (line 76 in the btnCompute_Click event).

```
69    Private Sub btnCompute_Click(ByVal sender As System.Object, ByVal e As System.   ↙
      EventArgs) Handles btnCompute.Click
70        Dim decMiles As Decimal
71        Dim decGallons As Decimal
72        Dim decMilesPerGallon As Decimal
73
74        decMiles = Convert.ToDecimal(txtMiles.Text)
75        decGallons = Convert.ToDecimal(txtGallons.Text)
76        decMilesPerGallon = ComputeGasMileage(decMiles, decGallons)
77        MsgBox("You are getting " & decMilesPerGallon.ToString("F1") & " miles per   ↙
      gallon", , "MPG")
78
79    End Sub
80
81    Function ComputeGasMileage(ByVal decMiles As Decimal, ByVal decGallons As Decimal)
      As Decimal
82        Dim decMileage As Decimal
83
84        decMileage = decMiles / decGallons
85        ' The following statement returns control to the calling
86        ' procedure and returns the value in the decMileage variable.
87        Return decMileage
88
89    End Function
```

FIGURE 7-41

When writing a Function procedure, do not place any lines of its code after the Return statement because control returns to the calling procedure when the Return statement is executed.

It is best to use a Function procedure when you plan to return a value from a called procedure. In the Mystery Escape chapter project, a Function procedure returns the final cost of the selected game type, as shown in Figure 7-42.

Calling Procedure

```
105               Select Case intCityChoice
106                   Case 0
107                       decTotalCost = DallasFindCost(intGameChoice, _
108                                                   intTeamSize, intLength)
```

Called Procedure

```
166      Private Function DallasFindCost(ByVal intGame As Integer, _
167       ByVal intTeam As Integer, ByRef intTime As Integer) As Decimal
168          ' This function calculates the cost of the team in Dallas
169
170          Dim decTeamCost As Decimal
171          Dim decFinalCost As Decimal
172          Dim decDallasGame1 As Decimal = 32D
173          Dim decDallasGame2 As Decimal = 39D
174          Dim decDallasGame3 As Decimal = 55D
175
176          Select Case intGame
177              Case 0
178                  decTeamCost = decDallasGame1
179                  intTime = _intOneHour
180              Case 1
181                  decTeamCost = decDallasGame2
182                  intTime = _intOneHour
183              Case 2
184                  decTeamCost = decDallasGame3
185                  intTime = _intTwoHour
186          End Select
187          decFinalCOst = decTeamCost * intTeam
189          Return decFinalCost
190
191      End Function
```

FIGURE 7-42

In Figure 7-42, the function call on line 107 calls the DallasFindCost Function procedure. The arguments include the integer value of the user's game choice in the list box (intGameChoice), the integer value of the number in the team (intTeamSize), and a variable to contain the length of the chosen game (intLength).

In the called Function procedure, the game type and team size are passed ByVal. The length of the game in hours is passed ByRef. Therefore, when the Function procedure changes a value in the length of a game, a change is made in the passed variable.

You can use Sub procedures and Function procedures in any Visual Basic application, including Windows Desktop applications, Web applications, and Windows Store applications.

Create a Private Class-Level Variable

In previous programs within this book, you have defined class-level variables for use in multiple procedures or event handlers within the class. In those programs, the variable was declared using the Dim statement. You will recall that a class-level variable is defined within the class but outside any procedure. When a class-level variable is declared using the Dim statement, it can be referenced by any code within any procedure within the class.

It cannot, however, be referenced by any code outside the class. (In larger projects, multiple classes can be created.) When a class-level variable cannot be referenced outside the class in which it is declared, the variable is said to have Private access. Generally, it is a good programming practice to limit the scope of a class-level variable to the class in which it is declared.

By default, a class-level variable declared using the Dim statement has Private access. You can also declare class-level variables by using the Private keyword instead of the Dim keyword. The class-level variables used in the Mystery Escape program in this chapter are shown in Figure 7-43.

```
8    Public Class frmEscape
9
10       ' Class variables
11       Private _intOneHour As Integer = 1
12       Private _intTwoHour As Integer = 2
13       Private _intFourHour As Integer = 4
14       Private _strGame1 As String = "Spy in the Study"
15       Private _strGame2 As String = "Hidden Cellar"
16       Private _strGame3 As String = "Team Building"
17       Private _strGame4 As String = "The Encounter"
18       Private _strGame5 As String = "Library Larceny"
19       Private _strGame6 As String = "Amazing Race"
20
```

FIGURE 7-43

As you can see in Figure 7-43, each of the variables is declared using the Private keyword. All of the variables will have Private access, which means code in any procedure within the class can reference the variables but code in another class cannot.

Exception Handling

In previous programs in this book, you have learned how to ensure that users enter valid data, which is an essential task. You have used loops and If statements to check the values entered by users to ensure that the data does not cause an exception within the program.

Visual Basic provides another tool you can use to detect exceptions and take corrective action. This tool is called the **Try-Catch** set of statements. The Try keyword means "Try to execute this code." The Catch keyword means "Catch errors here." A Try-Catch block includes a statement or statements that are executed in the Try block and the statements that are executed in the Catch block(s) when an exception occurs. The format of the Try-Catch block is shown in Figure 7-44.

General Format: Try-Catch block

```
Try
        'Try Block of Code – Executable statement(s) that may generate an exception.
Catch (filter for possible exceptions)
        'Catch Block of Code for handling the exception
[Optional: Additional Catch blocks]
[Optional Finally]
        'Optional statements that will always execute before finishing the Try block
End Try
```

FIGURE 7-44

To illustrate the use of a Try-Catch block, assume the value in one variable is being divided by the value in another variable. As you will recall, it is invalid to divide by zero. If a program tries to divide by zero, a DivideByZero exception will occur. Therefore, the division operation should be placed in a Try block and the Catch block should be set for a divide by zero exception. If the exception occurs, the code in Figure 7-45 will open a message box stating that an attempt was made to divide by zero.

```
91          Dim decNumerator As Decimal
92          Dim decDenominator As Decimal
93          Dim decDivision As Decimal
94
95          decNumerator = Convert.ToDecimal(txtNum.Text)
96          decDenominator = Convert.ToDecimal(txtDen.Text)
97          Try
98              decDivision = decNumerator / decDenominator
99          Catch Exception As DivideByZeroException
100             MsgBox("Attempt to divide by zero")
101         End Try
102
103     End Sub
104 End Class
```

FIGURE 7-45

In Figure 7-45, the division operation occurs in the statement on line 98. Note that the division operation is within the Try-Catch block, as defined by the Try keyword on line 97, the Catch keyword on line 99, and the End Try statement on line 101. You can define the particular class of exception in a Catch block by mentioning the name of the exception with the Catch keyword. In Figure 7-45, DivideByZeroException is included to catch the specific exception. If the value in decDenominator is zero when the division operation occurs, the code in the Catch block will display a message box with an error message. More importantly, the program will not be terminated. A Try-Catch block allows the program to handle exceptions elegantly so that the program does not abruptly terminate.

Different types of exceptions can occur. Figure 7-46 identifies some of the possible exceptions.

Exception Type	Condition when Exception Occurs	Code Example
ArgumentNullException	A variable that has no value is passed to a procedure	`Dim strTerm As String` `lstDisplay.Items.Add(strTerm)`
DivideByZeroException	A value is divided by zero	`intResult = intNum / 0`
FormatException	A variable is converted to another type that is not possible	`strTerm = "Code"` `intValue = Convert.ToInt32(strTerm)`
NullReferenceException	A procedure is called when the result is not possible	`Dim strTerm As String` `intValue = strTerm.Length`
OverflowException	A value exceeds its assigned data type	`Dim intCost As Integer` `intCost = 58 ^ 4000000000`
SystemException	Generic	`Catches all other exceptions`

FIGURE 7-46

Figure 7-47 shows another example of a Try-Catch block, in which a very large number assigned to the variable intBaseValue is squared within a Try-Catch block. Notice that when the value intBaseValue is squared, the result will exceed the range for an Integer data type, causing an OverflowException. When the exception occurs within the Try block, the Catch block is called to deal with the OverflowException.

```
105          Dim intBaseValue As Integer
106          Dim intSquaredValue As Integer
107
108          intBaseValue = 50000000
109          Try
110              intSquaredValue = intBaseValue ^ 2
111          Catch Exception As OverflowException
112              'This catch block detects an overflow of the range of the data type
113              MsgBox("The value exceeds the range of the data type", , "Error")
114          End Try
```

FIGURE 7-47

Multiple Catch blocks can be defined for a single Try block, in which each Catch block will catch a particular class of exception. This approach is useful when you want to state which type of error occurred and tell users the mistake they made. It is best to order exceptions in Catch blocks from the most specific to the least specific. In other words, the Catch block that is most likely to be needed for the most common exception should appear first in a series of Catch statements. If an exception occurs during the execution of the Try block, Visual Basic examines each Catch statement within the Try-Catch block until it finds one whose condition matches that error. If a match is found, control transfers to the first line of code in the Catch block. If no matching Catch statement is found, the search proceeds to the next Catch statement in the Try-Catch block. This process continues through the entire code block until a matching Catch block is found in the current procedure. If no match is found, an exception occurs that stops the program.

In the Mystery Escape application, you need to validate the variable that is assigned the value of the number in the team. You want to make sure that the user enters a number, not a letter or other symbol, and that the number is from 2 to 6 team players. The code in Figure 7-48 displays a Try-Catch block used within a Function procedure named ValidateNumberInTeam. It uses three Catch blocks.

```
114    Private Function ValidateNumberInTeam() As Boolean
115        ' This procedure validates the value entered for the team size
116
117        Dim intTeamSize As Integer
118        Dim blnValidityCheck As Boolean = False
119        Dim strNumberInTeamMessage As String = "Please enter the number of people in your team (2-6)"
120        Dim strMessageBoxTitle As String = "Error"
121
122        Try
123            intTeamSize = Convert.ToInt32(txtTeam.Text)
124            If intTeamSize >= 2 And intTeamSize <= 6 Then
125                blnValidityCheck = True
126            Else
127                MsgBox(strNumberInTeamMessage, , strMessageBoxTitle)
128                txtTeam.Focus()
129                txtTeam.Clear()
130            End If
131        Catch Exception As FormatException
132            MsgBox(strNumberInTeamMessage, , strMessageBoxTitle)
133            txtTeam.Focus()
134            txtTeam.Clear()
135        Catch Exception As OverflowException
136            MsgBox(strNumberInTeamMessage, , strMessageBoxTitle)
137            txtTeam.Focus()
138            txtTeam.Clear()
139        Catch Exception As SystemException
140            MsgBox(strNumberInTeamMessage, , strMessageBoxTitle)
141            txtTeam.Focus()
142            txtTeam.Clear()
143        End Try
144
145        Return blnValidityCheck
146
147    End Function
```

FIGURE 7-48

The Boolean variable blnValidityCheck (line 118 in the code in Figure 7-48) is initially set to false, but it is set to true if an exception is not thrown (line 125); in other words, the Catch block is not executed if an exception is not thrown. This Boolean variable set to True then is returned to the calling procedure (line 145), which can continue its processing.

If an exception is thrown when the value in the Text property of the txtTeam TextBox is converted to an integer (line 123), the statements below the Convert.ToInt32 statement will not be executed because control is passed to the appropriate Catch statement. The processing in each of the Catch blocks displays a message box with an error message, places the focus on the text box where the user enters the number in the team, and clears the text box.

When the processing in the Try-Catch block is complete, the Return statement on line 145 returns the value of the Boolean variable. If the data was valid, the Boolean variable contains the True value. If the data was not valid, the variable contains False because it initially was set to False (line 118) and its value was not changed by the Catch block processing.

An optional portion of the Try-Catch block is the Finally statement. The code in the Finally section always executes last, regardless of whether the code in the Catch blocks has been executed. Place cleanup code, such as code that closes files, in the Finally section. Code in the Finally section always is executed, no matter what happens in the Try-Catch blocks.

CRITICAL THINKING

Can Try-Catch statements be used for any other purpose than error checking?
Yes. Many developers code Try-Catch statements to alert a database administrator or trigger other actions when users do not enter an expected entry. For example, a call center taking sales orders may need to alert the warehouse if a large number of orders is getting "stuck" in high volume processing.

Program Design

As you have learned, the requirements document identifies the purpose of the program being developed, the application title, the procedures to be followed when using the program, any required equations and calculations, any conditions that must be tested, notes and restrictions that must be followed by the program, and any other comments that would be helpful to understanding the problem. The requirements document for the Mystery Escape application is shown in Figure 7-49.

REQUIREMENTS DOCUMENT

Date:	June 22, 2017
Date Submitted:	
Application Title:	Mystery Escape Application
Purpose:	This Windows Desktop application allows a customer to view Mystery Escape experiences available in various cities around the world.
Program Procedures:	The user can select a city location and game type and find out pricing information.

Algorithms, Processing, and Conditions:

1. The user first selects the mystery escape city with the title displayed. No other objects are displayed at this point.
2. When the user selects a city, the following items are displayed in the window: the Number in Team text box, a custom list of the available game types for the chosen city, a button to find the team cost of the game type selected, and a button to clear the form.
3. The user enters the number of the team size.
4. From the custom list of game types that are available for the chosen city, the user selects a game type.
5. The total team price of the game type is displayed.

Notes and Restrictions:

1. Validate numeric input with Try-Catch blocks.
2. Use multiple procedures to break the application into manageable sections.

Comments:

1. The picture shown in the window is available on CengageBrain.com. The name of the picture is Escape.
2. A splash screen is shown for approximately five seconds before the main window is displayed with a logo image and current year.

FIGURE 7-49

The Use Case Definition for the application is shown in Figure 7-50.

USE CASE DEFINITION

1. A splash screen welcomes the user for approximately five seconds.
2. The user selects a city.
3. The program displays a text box for the number of people in the team and a list of available game types for the selected city.
4. The user enters the number of people in the team, selects a game type, and taps or clicks the Find Team Cost button.
5. The program identifies the game type, calculates and displays the game type cost for the entire team, and specifies the length of the game type in hours.
6. The user can change any of the entries (city choice, number in team, and game type) and tap or click the Find Team Cost button to recalculate the game type cost.
7. The user can clear the form by tapping or clicking the Clear Form button.

FIGURE 7-50

Figure 7-51 contains information about available game types for each city, the game type lengths, and the game type costs.

Location	Real Escape Game Type	Challenge Length	Price
Dallas	Spy in the Study	1 hour	$32 USD
	Hidden Cellar	1 hour	$39
	Team Building	2 hours	$55
Paris	The Encounter	1 hour	$38 USD
	Library Larceny	1 hour	$45
Singapore	Hidden Cellar	1 hour	$45 USD
	Team Building	2 hours	$65
	Amazing Race	4 hours	$75

FIGURE 7-51

Program Design When Using Sub and Function Procedures

As noted previously, larger programs often should be divided into procedures that perform specific tasks within the program. The goal of using procedures is to make the program easier to read, understand, and debug. The final result is a program that is more reliable and easier to maintain.

The developer must determine what code should be placed in a procedure. Several rules are important to follow when creating procedures in a program; otherwise, the use of procedures might make the program more difficult and more confusing. These rules include the following:

- The Sub procedure or the Function procedure should perform a single, defined task, such as checking the validity of a specific user input or calculating the cost of a game type. Procedures that perform multiple tasks tend to become large and difficult to design and code.
- A Sub procedure or a Function procedure must perform reasonably substantial processing. It makes little sense to place a procedure call statement in a calling procedure and have the called procedure contain one or two program statements. In such cases, it would be easier and clearer just to place the statements in the calling procedure.
- When deciding whether a set of programming steps should be placed in a Sub procedure or a Function procedure, ask yourself the following questions: (1) Will the program be easier to read and understand if the code is placed in a separate procedure? (2) Does the proposed code perform a single task and does this task require more than three or four programming statements? (3) Can the Sub procedure or Function procedure perform its processing by receiving data as arguments and by returning data either using the Return statement or by using ByRef arguments?

If the answers to these questions are *yes*, then the code is a good candidate for a procedure within your program.

In the Mystery Escape application, four event handlers are required: (1) Selected Index Change: This event handler is executed when the user selects a mystery game type location from a combo box; (2) Find Cost Button: This event handler is executed when the user taps or clicks the btnFindCost Button object; (3) Clear Button: This event handler is executed when the user taps or clicks the btnClear Button object; (4) frmEscape Load Event: This event handler is executed when the Windows Form object is loaded.

Within each event handler, the event planning document is used to identify the tasks that must be accomplished. As each of the tasks is identified, you should ask the preceding questions. If it appears that the task should be accomplished in a procedure, the procedure must be included in the event planning document.

Event Planning Document

You will recall that the event planning document is a table that specifies which objects in the user interface will cause events, the action taken by the user to trigger each event, and the event processing that must occur. The event planning document for the program in this chapter must specify two forms and the events that occur for objects on each form. In addition, the tasks that must be accomplished for each event must be identified and decisions must be made for whether the tasks will be accomplished in a Sub or Function procedure. The event planning document for the Mystery Escape Trip Selection program is shown in Figure 7-52 and Figure 7-53.

EVENT PLANNING DOCUMENT

Program Name: Mystery Escape	Developer: Corinne Hoisington	Object: SplashScreen1	Date: June 22, 2017
OBJECT	**EVENT TRIGGER**	**EVENT PROCESSING**	
SplashScreen1_Load	Load	An opening splash screen appears with the company name, version number, and year of copyright	

FIGURE 7-52

EVENT PLANNING DOCUMENT

Program Name: Mystery Escape	Developer: Corinne Hoisington	Object: frmEscape	Date: June 22, 2017
OBJECT	**EVENT TRIGGER**	**EVENT PROCESSING**	
cboCity_ SelectedIndexChanged	Select Index	Assign mystery selection to an Integer SUB (DallasTeam(), ParisTeam(), SingaporeTeam()): Based on the game type, display a list of the available games in each city Change Visible property to True for all objects on the form Clear the labels that provide game information Set the focus on the Number in Team text box	
DallasTeam()	Sub procedure call	Display list of available game types (Spy in the Study, Hidden Cellar, and Team Building) in list box	
ParisTeam()	Sub procedure call	Display list of available game types (The Encounter and Library Larceny) in list box	
SingaporeTeam()	Sub procedure call	Display list of available game types (Hidden Cellar, Team Building, and Amazing Race) in list box	

FIGURE 7-53 (continues)

Program Name: Mystery Escape	Developer: Corinne Hoisington	Object: frmEscape	Date: June 22, 2017
OBJECT	EVENT TRIGGER	EVENT PROCESSING	

btnFindCost	Click	FUNCTION (ValidateNumberInTeam): Validate that the value in the Number in Team text box is valid
		FUNCTION (ValidateGameSelection): Ensure that the user has selected a game type in the list box
		If the number in the team is valid and a game type is selected:
		    Convert number in team to an integer
		    Change selected game typeindex to integer
		    FUNCTION(DallasFindCost,
		        ParisFindCost, SingaporeFindCost):
		        Calculate cost based on game type choice
		    Display game type, cost, and length
		Else display error message	

ValidateNumberInTeam()	Function procedure call	Set Boolean indicator to False
		Convert number in team to integer
		If conversion valid
		    If number >=2 and <=6
		        Set Boolean indicator to True for valid number
		If conversion not valid
		    Catch format, overflow, and system exceptions
		    Display error message boxes
		    Place focus in Number in Team text box
		    Clear Number in Team text box
		Return Boolean indicator	

ValidateGameSelection()	Function procedure call	Convert game type selection index to integer
		If conversion successful
		    Place selected item string in ByRef variable
		    Set Boolean validity indicator to True
		Else Display error message box
		    Set Boolean validity indicator to False
		Return game type selected index integer	

DallasFindCost()	Function procedure call	If game type selected is Spy in the Study
		    Set cost to Dallas Spy in the Study for one person
		    Set length to one hour
		If game type selected is Hidden Cellar
		    Set cost to Dallas Hidden Cellar for one person
		    Set length to one hour
		If game type selected is Team Building
		    Set cost to Dallas Team Building for one person
		    Set length to two hours
		Calculate cost of mystery escape: cost * number in team
		Return cost of mystery escape	

FIGURE 7-53 (continues)

Program Name: Mystery Escape	Developer: Corinne Hoisington	Object: frmEscape	Date: June 22, 2017
OBJECT	**EVENT TRIGGER**	**EVENT PROCESSING**	

ParisFindCost()	Function procedure call	If game type selected is The Encounter
		    Set cost to Paris - The Encounter game type for one person
		    Set length to one hour
		If game type selected is Library Larceny
		    Set cost to Paris Library Larceny for one person
		    Set length to one hour
		Calculate cost of mystery escape: cost * number in team
		Return cost of mystery escape	

SingaporeFindCost()	Function procedure call	If game type selected is Hidden Cellar
		    Set cost to Singapore Hidden Cellar for one person
		    Set length to one hour
		If game type selected is Team Building
		    Set cost to Singapore Team Building for one person
		    Set length to two hours
		If game type selected is Amazing Race
		    Set cost to Singapore Amazing Race for one person
		    Set length to four hours
		Calculate cost of mystery escape: cost * number in team
		Return cost of mystery escape	

btnClear	Click	Set Select City cboCity text to "Select City Location" Clear text box, list, and labels Hide all objects except Select City Listbox	
frmEscape_Load	Load	Set sleeping period to 5000 milliseconds	

FIGURE 7-53 (continued)

Design and Code the Program

After identifying the events and tasks within the events, the developer is ready to create the program. As you have learned, creating the program means designing the user interface and then entering Visual Basic statements to accomplish the tasks specified in the event planning document. As the developer enters the code, she will also implement the logic to carry out the required processing.

Guided Program Development

To design the user interface for the Mystery Escape application and enter the code required to process each event in the program, complete the steps on the following pages:

NOTE TO THE LEARNER

In the following activity, you should complete the tasks within the specified steps. Each of the tasks is accompanied by a Hint Screen. The purpose of the Hint Screen is to indicate where you should perform the activity in the Visual Studio window and to remind you which method to use. If you need further help completing a step, refer to the figure identified by *ref:*.

- **Create a New Windows Project** Open Visual Studio and then close the Start page. Tap or click the New Project button on the Standard toolbar. Begin a Windows Desktop Forms Application project and name the project `Mystery Escape`. Name the Form object `frmEscape.vb`.

- **Add a New Item to the Project** Tap or click Project on the menu bar and then tap or click Add New Item on the Project menu *(ref: Figure 7-5)*.

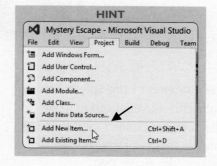

- **Select Splash Screen as the New Item** Select the Splash Screen template. Tap or click the Add button *(ref: Figure 7-6)*.

(continues)

● **Select the Generic Splash Screen**
When the generic splash screen opens,
tap or click the left side of the screen
to select it *(ref: Figure 7-7)*.

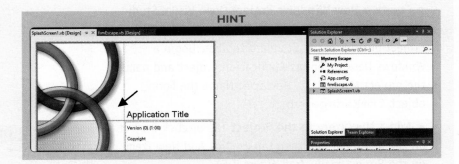

● **Prepare to Set the Contents of the Splash Screen**
Press and hold or right-click the application name
Mystery Escape in the Solution Explorer, and then tap
or click Properties on the shortcut menu to open the
Project Designer window *(ref: Figure 7-8)*.

● **Set the Splash Screen** On the Application tab,
scroll down and tap or click the Splash screen list arrow to change the setting of (None) to SplashScreen1
(ref: Figure 7-10).

● **Add Text to the Splash Screen** To change the text of the splash screen, tap or click the Assembly Information button in the Project Designer window *(ref: Figure 7-11)*.

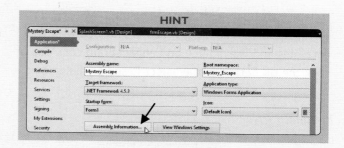

● **Set the Assembly Information** In the Assembly Information dialog box, change the title to Mystery Escape and change the copyright to the current year *(ref: Figure 7-12)*. Tap or click the OK button to close the dialog box. Close the Properties window. The information on the Splash Screen form does not change. The changes appear when the application is executed.

● **Change the Background Image** To customize the picture, tap or click the background on the left side of the splash screen and select the BackgroundImage property in the Properties window. Tap or click the ellipsis button *(ref: Figure 7-13)*.

● **Select the Project Resource File** The Select Resource dialog box opens. Tap or click the Project resource file option button, if necessary, and ensure that the Resources.resx file is selected.

(continues)

Guided Program Development   *continued*

• **Select an Image File** Tap or click Import and select the image file Escape.jpg, which is provided with your data files and is available on CengageBrain.com. Tap or click the OK button in the Select Resource dialog box.

The splash screen is designed (Figure 7-54).

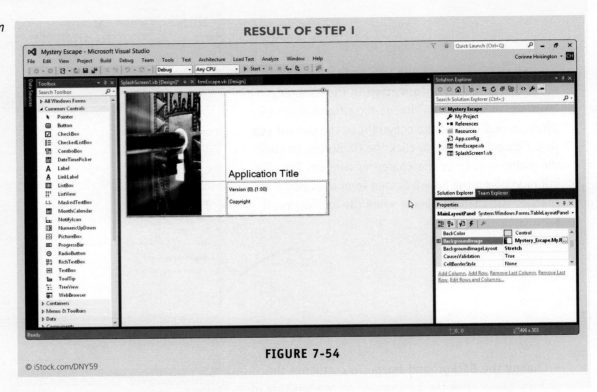

RESULT OF STEP 1

FIGURE 7-54

© iStock.com/DNY59

2

• **Resize the Windows Form Object** Resize the Windows Form object to (870,490) to view the entire image.

• **Assign a Title to the Form Object** With the Windows Form object selected, change its Text property to Information on Mystery Escape Experiences.

• **Add a Background Image** With the Windows Form object selected, tap or click the ellipsis button for the BackgroundImage property. Select the Escape image in the Select Resource dialog box. Tap or click the OK button in the Select Resource dialog box.

- **Add a Panel Object** Drag a Panel object from the Containers category of the Toolbox to the portion of the Windows Form object not covered by the image. Resize the Panel object so it covers the white space where no image is displayed.

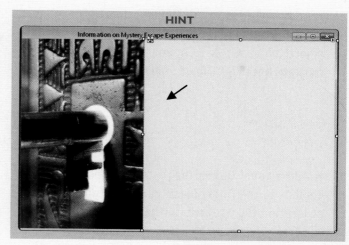

HINT

© iStock.com/DNY59

- **Change the Panel Object's BackColor to Transparent** In the BackColor property for the Panel object, tap or click the BackColor property arrow, tap or click the Web tab if necessary, and then tap or click Transparent on the Web palette. Making the panel transparent allows all the objects placed on the Windows Form object to be visible but allows you to center and align objects within the Panel object instead of the entire Windows Form object.

HINT

- **Add a Label and a ComboBox Object** Add a Label object on the right side of the Form object. Change the Text property to `Mystery Escape Information`. Name the Label object `lblTitle`. Change the font property to Verdana, Bold, 20 points. Change the FontColor property of the Label object to Sienna in the Web palette. The location of the Label object can be (8, 31). Add a ComboBox object below the Label object. The location is (130, 82). Name the ComboBox object `cboCity`. Change the Text property to `Select City Location:`. Change the font size to 14 points *(ref: Figure 7-20)*.

HINT

(continues)

- **Add the Terms in the Items Property** Enter the following terms in the Items property of the ComboBox object: `Dallas`, `Paris`, and `Singapore` on separate lines *(ref: Figure 7-21).*

- **Add a Label Object** Drag a Label object from the Toolbox to the Form object. Place the Label object at location (90,119) within the Panel object. Change the Text property to `Number in Team:`. Name the Label object `lblTeam`. Change the font size to 16 points.

- **Add a TextBox Object for the Number in Team** Drag a TextBox object from the Toolbox to the Panel object on the Windows Form object. Place the TextBox object at location (122,132). Resize the TextBox object to fit the length of approximately two numbers. Name the TextBox object `txtTeam`. Change the font size to 16 points.

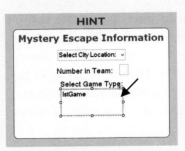

- **Add the Select Game Type Label Object** Drag a Label object from the Toolbox to the Windows Form object. The location is (132,171). Change the Text property to `Select Game Type:`. Name the Label object `lblSelect`. Change the font size to 14 points.

- **Add the Game ListBox Object** Drag a ListBox object from the Toolbox to the Windows Form object. The location is (139,199). Name the ListBox `lstGame`. Change the font size to 14 points.

- **Add the Find Team Cost Button Object** Drag a Button object from the Toolbox to the Windows Form object. The location is (34,316). Name the Button object `btnFindCost` and change the Text property to `Find Team Cost`. Resize the button until the text is visible. Change the BackColor property to Sienna and the ForeColor property to Khaki.

● **Add the Clear Button Object** Drag another Button object from the Toolbox to the Windows Form object. The location is (242, 316). Name the Button object `btnClear` and change the Text property to `Clear Form`. Change the BackColor property to Sienna and the ForeColor property to Khaki. Make the buttons the same size and centered in the Panel.

● **Add a Label Object for the Game Type** Drag a Label object from the Toolbox to the Windows Form object. The location is (139, 376). Name the Label object `lblGameType`. Enter 12 Xs for the Text property. Change the Font to size 16.

● **Add a Label Object for the Cost** Drag a Label object from the Toolbox to the Windows Form object. The location is (139, 397). Name this Label object `lblCost`. Enter 12 Xs for the Text property. Change the Font to size 16.

● **Add a Label Object for the Game Type Length** Drag a Label object from the Toolbox to the Windows Form object. The location is (139, 418). Name this Label object `lblLength`. Enter 12 Xs for the Text property. Change the Font to size 16.

● **Set the Visible Properties** Change the Visible property to False for the following objects: lblTeam, txtTeam, lblSelect, lstGame, btnFindCost, btnClear, lblGameType, lblCost, and lblLength. These objects are not displayed until the mystery is selected.

● **Set the Accept Button** Tap or click the background of the Windows Form object on its title bar and change the AcceptButton property of the Button object to btnFindCost.

(continues)

Guided Program Development *continued*

● **Set the Cancel Button** Tap or click the background of the Windows Form object on its title bar and change the CancelButton property of the Button object to btnClear. Close the Toolbox.

The Form object frmEscape is designed (Figure 7-55).

RESULT OF STEP 2

FIGURE 7-55

3

● **Code the Comments** Double-tap or double-click the cboCity ComboBox object on the frmEscape.vb [Design] tab to open the code window and create the cboCity_SelectedIndexChanged event handler. Close the Toolbox. Tap or click before the first word in Public Class frmEscape, and then press the ENTER key to create a blank line. Insert the first four standard comments. Insert the Option Strict On command following the comments to turn on strict type checking.

HINT

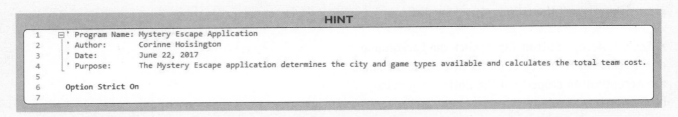

```
1   ' Program Name:  Mystery Escape Application
2   ' Author:        Corinne Hoisington
3   ' Date:          June 22, 2017
4   ' Purpose:       The Mystery Escape application determines the city and game types available and calculates the total team cost.
5
6   Option Strict On
7
```

● **Enter the Class Variables** Following the Public Class header line, enter the class variables required for the program. These class variables are (1) the hours for the length of each mystery game; (2) the types of games available (Spy in the Study, Hidden Cellar, Team Building, The Encounter, Library Larceny, and Amazing Race).

```
                2 references
8       ⊟Public Class frmEscape
9
10          ' Class variables
11          Private _intOneHour As Integer = 1
12          Private _intTwoHour As Integer = 2
13          Private _intFourHour As Integer = 4
14          Private _strGame1 As String = "Spy in the Study"
15          Private _strGame2 As String = "Hidden Cellar"
16          Private _strGame3 As String = "Team Building"
17          Private _strGame4 As String = "The Encounter"
18          Private _strGame5 As String = "Library Larceny"
19          Private _strGame6 As String = "Amazing Race"
```
HINT

● **Comment on the cboCity_SelectedIndexChanged Event Handler** Enter a comment to describe the purpose of the cboCity_SelectedIndexChanged event handler.

HINT
```
            0 references
21      ⊟   Private Sub cboCity_SelectedIndexChanged(ByVal sender As System.Object, ByVal e As System.EventArgs) Handles cboCity.SelectedIndexChanged, cboCity.SelectedIndexChanged
22              ' This event handler allows the user to enter the city choice and then calls subprocedures to place the game types in the list.
23              Dim intCityChoice As Integer
24
```

● **Code the Sub Procedure Calls to Place the Appropriate Game Types in the List Box** When the user selects a city in the cboCity ComboBox object, the SelectedIndexChanged event is triggered. In that event handler, the game type indicated by the selected index must be changed to an integer. Then, based on that integer, the appropriate Sub procedure is called to place the correct game types in the lstGame list box. Write the code to obtain the selected index integer, clear the lstGame ListBox object of any previous entries, and then call the appropriate Sub procedure *(ref: Figure 7-30)*.

HINT
```
21      ⊟   Private Sub cboCity_SelectedIndexChanged(ByVal sender As System.Object, ByVal e As System.EventArgs) Handles cboCity.SelectedIndexChanged,
22              ' This event handler allows the user to enter the city choice and then calls subprocedures to place the game types in the list.
23              Dim intCityChoice As Integer
24
25              intCityChoice = cboCity.SelectedIndex
26              lstGame.Items.Clear()
27              Select Case intCityChoice
28                  Case 0
29                      DallasTeam()
30                  Case 1
31                      ParisTeam()
32                  Case 2
33                      SingaporeTeam()
34              End Select
```

(continues)

● **Set the Visibility and Focus** After the user selects the mystery game city location from the ComboBox object and the event handler calls the Sub procedures to load the ListBox object with the correct game types, the objects on the Windows Form object must become visible. In addition, the Label objects for the game type, cost, and length must be cleared of the Xs placed in them during design. Finally, the focus should be set on the txtTeam TextBox object. Enter the code to complete this processing.

```
                              HINT
35            ' Make items visible in the window
36            lblTeam.Visible = True
37            txtTeam.Visible = True
38            lblSelect.Visible = True
39            lstGame.Visible = True
40            btnFindCost.Visible = True
41            btnClear.Visible = True
42            lblGameType.Visible = True
43            lblCost.Visible = True
44            lblLength.Visible = True
45            ' Clear the labels
46            lblGameType.Text = ""
47            lblCost.Text = ""
48            lblLength.Text = ""
49            ' Set focus on number in team text box
50            txtTeam.Focus()
51
52       End Sub
```

● **Code the Sub Procedures for Dallas Game Type Options** After the first event handler is completed, the Sub procedures called by the event handler should be written. The event handler that handles the cboCity_SelectedIndexChanged event calls three Sub procedures. Code the first referenced Sub procedure, which is called DallasTeam. To do so, tap or click below the End Sub statement for the event handler, press the ENTER key to insert a blank line, and then write the Sub procedure declaration. It begins with the word Private, followed by the word Sub and then the name of the Sub procedure. Press the ENTER key, write a comment that explains the purpose of the Sub procedure, and then write the statements that put the Dallas game types in the lstGame ListBox object (ref: Figure 7-31).

```
                              HINT
54       Private Sub DallasTeam()
55            ' This procedure fills in the possible game types offered in Dallas
56            lstGame.Items.Add(_strGame1)
57            lstGame.Items.Add(_strGame2)
58            lstGame.Items.Add(_strGame3)
59
60       End Sub
```

- **Code the Sub Procedures for the Paris and Singapore Game Type Options** In a similar manner, write the code for the Paris and Singapore Sub procedures that place the appropriate game type names in the lstGame ListBox object.

```
HINT
                    1 reference
62      Private Sub ParisTeam()
63          'This procedure fills in the possible game types offered in Paris
64          lstGame.Items.Add(_strGame4)
65          lstGame.Items.Add(_strGame5)
66
67      End Sub
68
                    1 reference
69      Private Sub SingaporeTeam()
70          'This procedure fills in the possible game types offered in Singapore
71          lstGame.Items.Add(_strGame2)
72          lstGame.Items.Add(_strGame3)
73          lstGame.Items.Add(_strGame6)
74
75      End Sub
76
```

- **Initialize the btnFindCost_Click Event and Write the Event Handler Variables** Tap or click the frmEscape.vb [Design] tab and then double-tap or double-click the Find Team Cost button to create the event handler for the button click event. The first step is to write a comment describing the purpose of the event handler. Then, code the variable declarations for the variables required in the event handler. These variables include (1) integer variables for the team size, game type choice, and length (duration in hours) of game type; (2) Boolean variables to indicate the validity of the number in the team and the game type selection; (3) a String variable to contain the name of the selected game type; (4) a Decimal variable to contain the total cost of the selected game type. Write the code to create and initialize these variables.

```
HINT
                    0 references
77      Private Sub btnFindCost_Click(ByVal sender As System.Object, ByVal e As System.EventArgs) Handles btnFindCost.Click
78          ' This button event handler determines the cost of mystery escape experience
79          ' and displays the size of the team, the cost, and the length
80
81          Dim intTeamSize As Integer
82          Dim blnNumberInTeamIsValid As Boolean = False
83          Dim blnGameIsSelected As Boolean = False
84          Dim intGameChoice As Integer
85          Dim strSelectedTeam As String = ""
86          Dim intCityChoice As Integer
87          Dim intLength As Integer = 0
88          Dim decTotalCost As Decimal
```

(continues)

● **Validate the User Input** The next steps are to call two Function procedures. The first procedure verifies that the value entered in the txtTeam TextBox object is valid, and the second verifies that a game type was selected. Write the two Function calls for these Function procedures. The ValidateNumberInTeam Function procedure returns a Boolean value indicating whether the number entered is valid (True) or not valid (False). The ValidateGameSelection Function procedure returns the number of the game type selected by the user. It also sets a Boolean value in the blnGame Boolean variable to indicate if a game type has been selected (true) or not selected (False). This value is set because the blnGame IsSelected variable is passed to the Function procedure ByRef.

	HINT
89	
90	' Call a function to ensure the number of people in the team is valid
91	blnNumberInTeamIsValid = ValidateNumberInTeam()
92	' Call a function to ensure a game type was selected
93	intGameChoice = ValidateGameSelection(blnGameIsSelected, strSelectedTeam)

● **Code the Rest of the btnFindCost_Click Event** Upon return from the procedure calls, the btnFindCost_Click event handler must determine whether the number of people in a team is valid and that a game type was selected. If both are true, the Text property of the txtTeam TextBox is converted to an integer value named intTeamSize. The Function procedures are passed three variables that are needed in the procedures. The variables intGameChoice and intTeamSize are passed by value because the values are not changed in the Function procedures. The variable intLength type is passed by reference because the value is changed in the Function procedures. The value returned from the Function procedures as the total cost of the game type is assigned to the variable decTotalCost. After the Function procedures are called, the event handler displays the selected game type, cost, and length. Write the code to implement this processing.

	HINT
95	If (blnNumberInTeamIsValid And blnGameIsSelected) Then
96	intTeamSize = Convert.ToInt32(txtTeam.Text)
97	intCityChoice = cboCity.SelectedIndex
98	Select Case intCityChoice
99	Case 0
100	decTotalCost = DallasFindCost(intGameChoice, intTeamSize, intLength)
101	Case 1
102	decTotalCost = ParisFindCost(intGameChoice, intTeamSize, intLength)
103	Case 2
104	decTotalCost = SingaporeFindCost(intGameChoice, intTeamSize, intLength)
105	End Select
106	' Display the cost of the ocean Team
107	lblGameType.Text = "Game: " & strSelectedTeam
108	lblCost.Text = "Cost: " & decTotalCost.ToString("C")
109	lblLength.Text = "Length: " & intLength.ToString() & " hour(s)"
110	End If
111	
112	End Sub

• **Code the ValidateNumberInTeam Function Procedure** The next step is to code the ValidateNumberInTeam Function procedure. Tap or click below the btnFindCost_Click event handler and enter the Function procedure declaration. The Function procedure returns a Boolean value that indicates whether the user entered a valid number. The value must be an integer that is greater than or equal to 2 and less than or equal to 6 because the Mystery Escape experience is limited to teams with two to six people. A Try-Catch block is used for the conversion to an integer operation to catch any invalid data the user entered. Multiple Catch blocks are used to catch specific exceptions. If an exception occurs, the error message is displayed in a message box, the focus is placed on the txtTeam TextBox object, and the value in the TextBox object is cleared. Write the code for this Function procedure *(ref: Figure 7-48).*

HINT

```
                    1 reference
114      Private Function ValidateNumberInTeam() As Boolean
115          ' This procedure validates the value entered for the team size
116
117          Dim intTeamSize As Integer
118          Dim blnValidityCheck As Boolean = False
119          Dim strNumberInTeamMessage As String = "Please enter the number of people in your team (2-6)"
120          Dim strMessageBoxTitle As String = "Error"
121
122          Try
123              intTeamSize = Convert.ToInt32(txtTeam.Text)
124              If intTeamSize >= 2 And intTeamSize <= 6 Then
125                  blnValidityCheck = True
126              Else
127                  MsgBox(strNumberInTeamMessage, , strMessageBoxTitle)
128                  txtTeam.Focus()
129                  txtTeam.Clear()
130              End If
131          Catch Exception As FormatException
132              MsgBox(strNumberInTeamMessage, , strMessageBoxTitle)
133              txtTeam.Focus()
134              txtTeam.Clear()
135          Catch Exception As OverflowException
136              MsgBox(strNumberInTeamMessage, , strMessageBoxTitle)
137              txtTeam.Focus()
138              txtTeam.Clear()
139          Catch Exception As SystemException
140              MsgBox(strNumberInTeamMessage, , strMessageBoxTitle)
141              txtTeam.Focus()
142              txtTeam.Clear()
143          End Try
144
145          Return blnValidityCheck
146
147      End Function
```

(continues)

● **Code the ValidateGameSelection Function Procedure** Tap or click below the ValidateNumberInTeam function and enter the ValidateGameSelection Function procedure declaration. This Function procedure ensures that the user selected a game type from the lstGame ListBox object and then returns an integer value for the list selection to the calling procedure. To determine if a game type was selected, the procedure uses a Try-Catch block to convert the selected index value to an integer. If the conversion is successful, a choice was made and the choice is returned. In addition, a Boolean variable in the calling procedure is set to True because the variable was passed ByRef. If the selected index is not converted, the user did not make a choice; an error message box is displayed and the Boolean variable is set to False. One Catch block is used because the only error that uses the ListBox object occurs if the user does not select a game type.

```
                                    HINT
         1 reference
149   ┌ Private Function ValidateGameSelection(ByRef blnGame As Boolean, ByRef strGame As String) As Integer
150          ' This function ensures the user selected a game type
151
152          Dim intGameTyoe As Integer
153          Try
154              intGameTyoe = Convert.ToInt32(lstGame.SelectedIndex)
155              strGame = lstGame.SelectedItem.ToString()
156              blnGame = True
157          Catch Exception As SystemException
158              ' Detects if a game type is not selected
159              MsgBox("Select a Game Type", , "Error")
160              blnGame = False
161          End Try
162          Return intGameTyoe
163
164      End Function
```

● **Code the DallasFindCost Function Procedure to Find the Cost of a Dallas Mystery Game Type** Tap or click below the ValidateGameSelection Function procedure and enter the DallasFindCost Function procedure declaration. The purpose of this Function procedure is to determine the cost of a Dallas game type. Three variables are passed to the function. Two are passed ByVal: the game type selection and the team size. Game type length is passed ByRef. The DallasFindCost Function procedure uses the game type selection and size to determine the cost of the game type based on published rates (*ref: Figure 7-51*). It also changes the values in the game type length field for use in the calling procedure. Write the code for the DallasFindCost Function procedure.

```
                               HINT
     1 reference
166  Private Function DallasFindCost(ByVal intGame As Integer, ByVal intTeam As Integer, ByRef intTime As Integer) As Decimal
167      ' This function calculates the cost of the team in Dallas
168
169      Dim decTeamCost As Decimal
170      Dim decFinalCost As Decimal
171      Dim decDallasGame1 As Decimal = 32D
172      Dim decDallasGame2 As Decimal = 39D
173      Dim decDallasGame3 As Decimal = 55D
174
175      Select Case intGame
176          Case 0
177              decTeamCost = decDallasGame1
178              intTime = _intOneHour
179          Case 1
180              decTeamCost = decDallasGame2
181              intTime = _intOneHour
182          Case 2
183              decTeamCost = decDallasGame3
184              intTime = _intTwoHour
185      End Select
186      decFinalCost = decTeamCost * intTeam
187      Return decFinalCost
188
189  End Function
```

● **Code the ParisFindCost Function Procedure to Find the Cost of a Paris Mystery Game Type** Tap or click below the DallasFindCost Function procedure and enter the ParisFindCost Function procedure declaration. The purpose of this Function procedure is to determine the cost of a Paris game type. It uses the same three passed variables as the DallasFindCost Function procedure. It also uses similar logic and returns the same values. Write the code for the ParisFindCost Function procedure.

```
                               HINT
     1 reference
191  Private Function ParisFindCost(ByVal intGame As Integer, ByVal intTeam As Integer, ByRef intTime As Integer) As Decimal
192      ' This function calculates the cost of the team in Paris
193
194      Dim decTeamCost As Decimal
195      Dim decFinalCost As Decimal
196      Dim decParisGame4 As Decimal = 38D
197      Dim decParisGame5 As Decimal = 45D
198
199      Select Case intGame
200          Case 0
201              decTeamCost = decParisGame4
202              intTime = _intOneHour
203          Case 1
204              decTeamCost = decParisGame5
205              intTime = _intOneHour
206      End Select
207      decFinalCost = decTeamCost * intTeam
208      Return decFinalCost
209
210  End Function
211
```

(continues)

● **Code the SingaporeFindCost Function Procedure to Find the Cost of a Singapore Mystery Game Type** Tap or click below the ParisFindCost Function procedure and enter the SingaporeFindCost Function procedure declaration. The purpose of this Function procedure is to determine the cost of a Singapore game type. It uses the same three passed variables as the ParisFindCost Function procedure. It also uses similar logic and returns the same values. Write the code for the SingaporeFindCost Function procedure.

HINT

```
        1 reference
212    Private Function SingaporeFindCost(ByVal intGame As Integer, ByVal intTeam As Integer, ByRef intTime As Integer) As Decimal
213         ' This function calculates the cost of the team in Singapore
214
215         Dim decTeamCost As Decimal
216         Dim decFinalCost As Decimal
217         Dim decSingaporeGame2 As Decimal = 45D
218         Dim decSingaporeGame3 As Decimal = 65D
219         Dim decSingaporeGame6 As Decimal = 75D
220
221         Select Case intGame
222             Case 0
223                 decTeamCost = decSingaporeGame2
224                 intTime = _intOneHour
225             Case 1
226                 decTeamCost = decSingaporeGame3
227                 intTime = _intTwoHour
228             Case 2
229                 decTeamCost = decSingaporeGame6
230                 intTime = _intFourHour
231         End Select
232         decFinalCost = decTeamCost * intTeam
233         Return decFinalCost
234
235    End Function
```

● **Code the Clear Button Click Event** After the Function procedures that are called from the btnFindCost_Click event handler have been coded, the next step is to write the code for the Clear Button click event handler. This event handler must reset the Windows Form object and objects on the form to look the same as when the program starts. This includes resetting the message in the cboCity ComboBox object, clearing the Number in Team text box and the game type list box, blanking the labels that display the results, and removing all the objects from view except the cboCity ComboBox object. Display the Design window and then double-tap or double-click the btnClear object to open the btnClear_Click event handler. Write the code for the event handler.

HINT

```
237    Private Sub btnClear_Click(ByVal sender As System.Object, ByVal e As System.EventArgs) Handles btnClear.Click
238         ' This event handler clears the form and resets the form for reuse when the user clicks the Clear button.
239
240         cboCity.Text = "Select City Location"
241         txtTeam.Clear()
242         lstGame.Items.Clear()
243         lblGameType.Text = ""
244         lblCost.Text = ""
245         lblLength.Text = ""
246         lblTeam.Visible = False
247         txtTeam.Visible = False
248         lblSelect.Visible = False
249         lstGame.Visible = False
250         btnFindCost.Visible = False
251         btnClear.Visible = False
252         lblGameType.Visible = False
253         lblCost.Visible = False
254         lblLength.Visible = False
255
256    End Sub
```

● **Code the frmEscape_Load Event** The last bit of code to write for the Mystery Escape program is the event handler for the frmEscape load event. You will recall that when the application begins, a splash screen opens first. To display the splash screen longer than the default time, you must add a sleep timer. Return to the frmEscape.vb [Design] window and double-tap or double-click the Windows Form object. Assuming that you want the splash screen to be displayed for 5 seconds, code the statement to delay program execution for 5000 milliseconds *(ref: Figure 7-16)*.

```
          HINT
          0 references
258   ⊟   Private Sub frmEscape_Load(sender As Object, e As EventArgs) Handles MyBase.Load
259             ' Hold the splash screen for 5 seconds
260
261             Threading.Thread.Sleep(5000)
262       End Sub
263   End Class
```

Code Listing

The complete code for the sample program is shown in Figure 7-56.

```vbnet
1   ' Program Name: Mystery Escape Application
2   ' Author:       Corinne Hoisington
3   ' Date:         June 22, 2017
4   ' Purpose:      The Mystery Escape application determines the city and game types available and calculates the total team cost.
5
6   Option Strict On
7
    2 references
8   Public Class frmEscape
9
10      ' Class variables
11      Private _intOneHour As Integer = 1
12      Private _intTwoHour As Integer = 2
13      Private _intFourHour As Integer = 4
14      Private _strGame1 As String = "Spy in the Study"
15      Private _strGame2 As String = "Hidden Cellar"
16      Private _strGame3 As String = "Team Building"
17      Private _strGame4 As String = "The Encounter"
18      Private _strGame5 As String = "Library Larceny"
19      Private _strGame6 As String = "Amazing Race"
20
        0 references
21      Private Sub cboCity_SelectedIndexChanged(ByVal sender As System.Object, ByVal e As System.EventArgs) Handles cboCity.SelectedIndexChanged, cboCity.SelectedIndexChanged
22          ' This event handler allows the user to enter the city choice and then calls subprocedures to place the game types in the list.
23          Dim intCityChoice As Integer
24
25          intCityChoice = cboCity.SelectedIndex
26          lstGame.Items.Clear()
27          Select Case intCityChoice
28              Case 0
29                  DallasTeam()
30              Case 1
31                  ParisTeam()
32              Case 2
33                  SingaporeTeam()
34          End Select
35          ' Make items visible in the window
36          lblTeam.Visible = True
37          txtTeam.Visible = True
38          lblSelect.Visible = True
39          lstGame.Visible = True
40          btnFindCost.Visible = True
41          btnClear.Visible = True
42          lblGameType.Visible = True
43          lblCost.Visible = True
44          lblLength.Visible = True
45          ' Clear the labels
46          lblGameType.Text = ""
47          lblCost.Text = ""
48          lblLength.Text = ""
49          ' Set focus on number in team text box
50          txtTeam.Focus()
51
52      End Sub
53
        1 reference
54      Private Sub DallasTeam()
55          ' This procedure fills in the possible game types offered in Dallas
56          lstGame.Items.Add(_strGame1)
57          lstGame.Items.Add(_strGame2)
58          lstGame.Items.Add(_strGame3)
59
60      End Sub
61
        1 reference
62      Private Sub ParisTeam()
63          'This procedure fills in the possible game types offered in Paris
64          lstGame.Items.Add(_strGame4)
65          lstGame.Items.Add(_strGame5)
66
67      End Sub
68
        1 reference
69      Private Sub SingaporeTeam()
70          'This procedure fills in the possible game types offered in Singapore
71          lstGame.Items.Add(_strGame2)
72          lstGame.Items.Add(_strGame3)
73          lstGame.Items.Add(_strGame6)
74
```

FIGURE 7-56 (continues)

```vbnet
75          End Sub
76
            0 references
77  ⊟   Private Sub btnFindCost_Click(ByVal sender As System.Object, ByVal e As System.EventArgs) Handles btnFindCost.Click
78          ' This button event handler determines the cost of mystery escape experience
79          ' and displays the size of the team, the cost, and the length
80
81          Dim intTeamSize As Integer
82          Dim blnNumberInTeamIsValid As Boolean = False
83          Dim blnGameIsSelected As Boolean = False
84          Dim intGameChoice As Integer
85          Dim strSelectedTeam As String = ""
86          Dim intCityChoice As Integer
87          Dim intLength As Integer = 0
88          Dim decTotalCost As Decimal
89
90          ' Call a function to ensure the number of people in the team is valid
91          blnNumberInTeamIsValid = ValidateNumberInTeam()
92          ' Call a function to ensure a game type was selected
93          intGameChoice = ValidateGameSelection(blnGameIsSelected, strSelectedTeam)
94          ' If number of people and the game type are valid, calculate the cost
95          If (blnNumberInTeamIsValid And blnGameIsSelected) Then
96              intTeamSize = Convert.ToInt32(txtTeam.Text)
97              intCityChoice = cboCity.SelectedIndex
98              Select Case intCityChoice
99                  Case 0
100                     decTotalCost = DallasFindCost(intGameChoice, intTeamSize, intLength)
101                 Case 1
102                     decTotalCost = ParisFindCost(intGameChoice, intTeamSize, intLength)
103                 Case 2
104                     decTotalCost = SingaporeFindCost(intGameChoice, intTeamSize, intLength)
105             End Select
106             ' Display the cost of the ocean Team
107             lblGameType.Text = "Game: " & strSelectedTeam
108             lblCost.Text = "Cost: " & decTotalCost.ToString("C")
109             lblLength.Text = "Length: " & intLength.ToString() & " hour(s)"
110         End If
111
112     End Sub
113
        1 reference
114 ⊟   Private Function ValidateNumberInTeam() As Boolean
115         ' This procedure validates the value entered for the team size
116
117         Dim intTeamSize As Integer
118         Dim blnValidityCheck As Boolean = False
119         Dim strNumberInTeamMessage As String = "Please enter the number of people in your team (2-6)"
120         Dim strMessageBoxTitle As String = "Error"
121
122         Try
123             intTeamSize = Convert.ToInt32(txtTeam.Text)
124             If intTeamSize >= 2 And intTeamSize <= 6 Then
125                 blnValidityCheck = True
126             Else
127                 MsgBox(strNumberInTeamMessage, , strMessageBoxTitle)
128                 txtTeam.Focus()
129                 txtTeam.Clear()
130             End If
131         Catch Exception As FormatException
132             MsgBox(strNumberInTeamMessage, , strMessageBoxTitle)
133             txtTeam.Focus()
134             txtTeam.Clear()
135         Catch Exception As OverflowException
136             MsgBox(strNumberInTeamMessage, , strMessageBoxTitle)
137             txtTeam.Focus()
138             txtTeam.Clear()
139         Catch Exception As SystemException
140             MsgBox(strNumberInTeamMessage, , strMessageBoxTitle)
141             txtTeam.Focus()
142             txtTeam.Clear()
143         End Try
144
145         Return blnValidityCheck
146
147     End Function
148
        1 reference
149 ⊟   Private Function ValidateGameSelection(ByRef blnGame As Boolean, ByRef strGame As String) As Integer
150         ' This function ensures the user selected a game type
151
```

FIGURE 7-56 (continues)

```vb
152            Dim intGameTyoe As Integer
153            Try
154                intGameTyoe = Convert.ToInt32(lstGame.SelectedIndex)
155                strGame = lstGame.SelectedItem.ToString()
156                blnGame = True
157            Catch Exception As SystemException
158                ' Detects if a game type is not selected
159                MsgBox("Select a Game Type", , "Error")
160                blnGame = False
161            End Try
162            Return intGameTyoe
163
164        End Function
165
           1 reference
166        Private Function DallasFindCost(ByVal intGame As Integer, ByVal intTeam As Integer, ByRef intTime As Integer) As Decimal
167            ' This function calculates the cost of the team in Dallas
168
169            Dim decTeamCost As Decimal
170            Dim decFinalCost As Decimal
171            Dim decDallasGame1 As Decimal = 32D
172            Dim decDallasGame2 As Decimal = 39D
173            Dim decDallasGame3 As Decimal = 55D
174
175            Select Case intGame
176                Case 0
177                    decTeamCost = decDallasGame1
178                    intTime = _intOneHour
179                Case 1
180                    decTeamCost = decDallasGame2
181                    intTime = _intOneHour
182                Case 2
183                    decTeamCost = decDallasGame3
184                    intTime = _intTwoHour
185            End Select
186            decFinalCost = decTeamCost * intTeam
187            Return decFinalCost
188
189        End Function
190
           1 reference
191        Private Function ParisFindCost(ByVal intGame As Integer, ByVal intTeam As Integer, ByRef intTime As Integer) As Decimal
192            ' This function calculates the cost of the team in Paris
193
194            Dim decTeamCost As Decimal
195            Dim decFinalCost As Decimal
196            Dim decParisGame4 As Decimal = 38D
197            Dim decParisGame5 As Decimal = 45D
198
199            Select Case intGame
200                Case 0
201                    decTeamCost = decParisGame4
202                    intTime = _intOneHour
203                Case 1
204                    decTeamCost = decParisGame5
205                    intTime = _intOneHour
206            End Select
207            decFinalCost = decTeamCost * intTeam
208            Return decFinalCost
209
210        End Function
211
           1 reference
212        Private Function SingaporeFindCost(ByVal intGame As Integer, ByVal intTeam As Integer, ByRef intTime As Integer) As Decimal
213            ' This function calculates the cost of the team in Singapore
214
215            Dim decTeamCost As Decimal
216            Dim decFinalCost As Decimal
217            Dim decSingaporeGame2 As Decimal = 45D
218            Dim decSingaporeGame3 As Decimal = 65D
219            Dim decSingaporeGame6 As Decimal = 75D
220
221            Select Case intGame
222                Case 0
223                    decTeamCost = decSingaporeGame2
224                    intTime = _intOneHour
225                Case 1
226                    decTeamCost = decSingaporeGame3
227                    intTime = _intTwoHour
228                Case 2
229                    decTeamCost = decSingaporeGame6
230                    intTime = _intFourHour
```

FIGURE 7-56 (continues)

```
230              intTime = _intFourHour
231          End Select
232          decFinalCost = decTeamCost * intTeam
233          Return decFinalCost
234
235      End Function
236
         0 references
237   ⊟ Private Sub btnClear_Click(ByVal sender As System.Object, ByVal e As System.EventArgs) Handles btnClear.Click
238          ' This event handler clears the form and resets the form for reuse when the user clicks the Clear button.
239
240          cboCity.Text = "Select City Location"
241          txtTeam.Clear()
242          lstGame.Items.Clear()
243          lblGameType.Text = ""
244          lblCost.Text = ""
245          lblLength.Text = ""
246          lblTeam.Visible = False
247          txtTeam.Visible = False
248          lblSelect.Visible = False
249          lstGame.Visible = False
250          btnFindCost.Visible = False
251          btnClear.Visible = False
252          lblGameType.Visible = False
253          lblCost.Visible = False
254          lblLength.Visible = False
255
256      End Sub
257
         0 references
258   ⊟ Private Sub frmEscape_Load(sender As Object, e As EventArgs) Handles MyBase.Load
259          ' Hold the splash screen for 5 seconds
260
261          Threading.Thread.Sleep(5000)
262      End Sub
263 End Class
```

FIGURE 7-56 (continued)

Summary

In this chapter you have learned to create applications using procedures. The items listed in the table in Figure 7-57 include all the new Visual Studio and Visual Basic skills you have learned in this chapter.

Visual Basic Skills		
Skill	Figure Number	Video Number
Examine the Mystery Escape Application	Figure 7-4	Video 7-1
Add the Generic Splash Screen	Figure 7-5	Video 7-2
Pause the Splash Screen	Figure 7-16	Video 7-3
Place a ComboBox Object on a Form	Figure 7-18	Video 7-4
Determine the ComboBox Selected Index	Page 461	
Create a SelectedIndexChanged Event	Figure 7-26	Video 7-5
Code a Procedure Call and a Sub Procedure	Figure 7-28	
Pass an Argument to a Called Procedure	Figure 7-33	
Pass an Argument by Value	Figure 7-34	
Pass an Argument by Reference	Figure 7-38	
Code a Function Procedure	Figure 7-40	

FIGURE 7-57

Learn Online

Reinforcement activities and resources are available at no additional cost on www.cengagebrain.com. Visit http://solutions.cengage.com/ctdownloads/ for detailed instructions about accessing the available resources at the Student Companion Site.

Knowledge Check

1. What is the name of the screen that displays a logo and version number of an application allowing the program to load?

2. Write the line of code that would display frmOpener for approximately seven seconds.

3. Name the two types of procedures.

4. What is the difference between passing by value and passing by reference?

5. What is the fewest number of arguments you can pass to a Sub procedure?

6. What section of code performs a specific task and does not return a value?

7. What section of code performs a specific task and returns a value?

8. What happens to the variables that were passed by value when you leave a Sub procedure?

9. How many values can a Function procedure return?

10. Write a Return statement that returns the variable intBirthYear.

11. Write the Visual Basic statements declaring a Sub procedure called PhotoBomb that receives one variable called intPhotos. The variable intPhotos will be changed in the procedure. Write only the first and last lines of the Sub procedure.

12. What is the name of a variable that is passed to a procedure?

13. If you want a copy of a variable passed to a procedure, which way should you pass it?

14. You must have a Return statement in a Sub procedure. True or false?

15. When multiple arguments are passed to a procedure, the order is not important. True or false?

16. You must have a Return statement in a Function procedure. True or false?

17. Which type of exception would be detected if you used the conversion command Convert.ToInt32 to convert a non-integer value?

18. Which type of exception would be detected if you used the conversion command Convert.ToDecimal to try to convert a letter of the alphabet?

19. If you enter a number that is too large for the data type, which type of exception would be detected?

20. When deciding whether a set of programming steps should be placed in a Sub procedure or a Function procedure, what are three questions you should ask?

1. Fix the code:

```
Private Sub btnCyberMonday_Click(ByVal sender As System.Object, ByVal e As
System.EventArgs) Handles btnCyberMonday.Click
    Dim decShop As Decimal
    Dim intCount As Decimal

        decShop = Convert.ToDecimal(txtCost.Text)
        Inventory(decShopt, intCount)
End Sub

Private Sub Inventory(ByVal shop, ByVal count)
        count +=3
        shop *= 0.7
End Sub
```

2. Fix the code:

```
Private Sub btnSoftball_Click(ByVal sender As System.Object, ByVal e As
System.EventArgs) Handles btnSoftball.Click
        Dim decHits As Decimal = 210
        Dim decTimesAtBat As Decimal = 428
        Dim decBattingAverage As Decimal

        decBattingAverage = BattingAverage(decHits, decTimesAtBat)
        lblHits.Text = "The batting average is " &
        decBattingAverage.ToString()
End Sub
Private Function BattingAverage(ByVal decHitsCount As Decimal, ByVal
decNumberAtBat)
        Dim decAverageAtBat As Decimal
        decAverageAtBat = decHitsCount / decNumberAtBat
End Function
```

3. Fix the code:

```
Private Sub btnMileage_Click(ByVal sender As System.Object, ByVal e As
System.EventArgs) Handles btnMileage.Click
        Dim decMiles As Decimal = 350D
        Dim decGallons As Decimal = 13.8D
        Dim decMilesPer As Decimal

        decMilesPer = Compute(decMiles, decGallons)
        lblDisplays.Text = "Your MPG is " & decMiles.ToString()
End Sub
```

(continues)

```
Private Sub Compute(ByVal decM As Decimal, ByVal decG) As Decimal
        Dim decMPG As Decimal
        decMPG = decM / decG
        Return MPG
End Function
```

Program Analysis

1. What is the output of the code in Figure 7-58?

```
Private Sub btnSevens_Click(ByVal sender As System.Object, ByVal e As
System.EventArgs) Handles btnSevens.Click
        Dim intCount As Integer
        For intCount = 1 To 8
            CalculateEights(intCount)
        Next
End Sub

Private Sub CalculateEights(ByVal intCountValue As Integer)
        Dim intResult As Integer
        intResult = intCountValue ^ 3
        lstAnswer.Items.Add(intResult.ToString())
End Sub
```

FIGURE 7-58

2. What is the output of the code in Figure 7-59?

```
Private Sub btnJoke_Click(ByVal sender As System.Object, ByVal e As System.
EventArgs) Handles btnJoke.Click
        DisplayRiddle()
        DisplayAnswer()
End Sub

Private Sub DisplayAnswer()
        lblAnswer.Text = "Because it has a spring in it"
End Sub

Private Sub DisplayRiddle()
        lblRiddle.Text = "Why should you carry a watch when crossing a
        desert?"
End Sub
```

FIGURE 7-59

(continues)

3. What is the output of the code in Figure 7-60?

```
Private Sub btnBedrock_Click(ByVal sender As System.Object, ByVal e As
System.EventArgs) Handles btnBedrock.Click
        Dim strFullName As String = "Fred Flintstone"
        Dim strSecondName As String = "Barney Rubble"

        CountLength(strFullName, strSecondName)
        lblEnd.Text = "My favorite was " & strSecondName
End Sub

Private Sub CountLength(ByVal strFullName As String, ByRef strSecondName
As String)
        lblFirst.Text = "The first name has " & strFullName.Length & "
        letters. "
        lblSecond.Text = "The second name has " & strSecondName.Length & "
        letters. "
        strSecondName = "Dino"
End Sub
```

FIGURE 7-60

4. What is the output of the code in Figure 7-61?

```
Private Sub btnStrangeFacts_Click(ByVal sender As System.Object, ByVal e As
System.EventArgs) Handles btnStrangeFacts.Click
        Dim intHangerLength As Integer = 44
        Dim intMen As Integer = 2000
        Dim intWomen As Integer = 8000
        Dim intValue As Integer

        intValue = Talk(intMen, intWomen)
        lblResponse.Text = "The couple would say " & intValue & " words a day"
        AverageHanger(intHangerLength)
End Sub

Private Sub AverageHanger(ByVal intHanger As Integer)
        lblPhrase.Text = "The average length of a coat hanger when
        straightened is " & intHanger & " inches."
End Sub

Private Function Talk(ByVal intM As Integer, ByVal intW As Integer) As Integer
        lblPhrase1.Text = "The average man says " & intM & " words a day"
        lblPhrase2.Text = "The average woman says " & intW & " words a day"
        Return intM + intW
End Function
```

FIGURE 7-61

Program Analysis *continued*

5. A program contains the procedure declaration shown in Figure 7-62. Write the Function call statement that assigns the returned value to intCubed and passes a variable named intValue.

```
Private Function Cube(ByVal intNum As Integer) As Integer
        Return intNum * intNum * intNum
End Function
```

FIGURE 7-62

6. A program converts and validates a value entered as the population of a city. Write a statement that passes the variable intBase to a procedure and assigns the return value to a variable named intSolution. Write the code that would declare a variable named intPopulation as an Integer. Allow the user to enter the population of her city in a TextBox object named txtCityPopulation. Convert the value to an integer within a Try block. Write a Try-Catch block with an overflow Catch block first, a format exception Catch block second, and a generic exception last. Each Catch block should display a message box that explains the problem with the user's input.

7. Write the code for a Sub procedure named FindHeight that will calculate a person's height in inches when given the feet and inches. For example, a person who is 5'10" is 70 inches tall. Display the result in a message box.

Complete one or more of the following case programming assignments. Submit the program and materials you create to your instructor. The level of difficulty is indicated for each case programming assignment.

● = Easiest
●● = Intermediate
●●● = Challenging

1
● SMARTPHONE PLANS

Design a Windows Desktop application and write the code that will execute according to the program requirements in Figure 7-63 and the Use Case Definition in Figure 7-64 on the next page. Before writing the code, create an event planning document for each event in the program. The completed Windows Form object and other objects for the user interface are shown in Figure 7-65.

REQUIREMENTS DOCUMENT

Date:	June 21, 2017
Date Submitted:	
Application Title:	Smartphone Plans
Purpose:	This Windows Desktop application computes the cost of two smartphone plan specials with varying base and data plans.
Program Procedures:	Allow the user to select from two smartphone specials plans, request the number of gigabytes used in the data plan, and compute the cost of the smartphone usage bill.
Algorithms, Processing, and Conditions:	1. The user is asked to select one of two smartphone plans from a ComboBox object (Basic Plan: $29 a month plus $4 per GB of data or Deluxe Plan: $39 a month plus $1 per GB of data). The other objects are not visible until the user selects this option.
	2. The user is asked to enter the number of gigabytes of data used over the past month.
	3. The value entered for data usage is sent to another procedure to be validated.
	4. One of two Function procedures will be called for the plan specials to compute and pass back the cost of the monthly bill.
Notes and Restrictions:	1. A Clear Form button should clear the form.
	2. A Try-Catch block in a separate procedure will validate the input.
Comments:	1. A splash screen begins this application for four seconds.
	2. Obtain an image for this program from CengageBrain.com. The name of the picture for the application is named Smartphone.

FIGURE 7-63

Case Programming Assignments

Smartphone Plans (continued)

USE CASE DEFINITION

1. The user views the opening splash screen for approximately four seconds.
2. The user selects the smartphone plan and enters the amount of data used. The user taps or clicks the Compute Total Bill button.
3. The user views the cost of this month's bill.

FIGURE 7-64

FIGURE 7-65a

FIGURE 7-65b

Case Programming Assignments

2 COUNTRY MUSIC EVENTS

Design a Windows Desktop application and write the code that will execute according to the program requirements in Figure 7-66 and the Use Case Definition in Figure 7-67 on page 516. Before writing the code, create an event planning document for each event in the program. The completed Windows Form object and other objects in the user interface are shown in Figure 7-68 on page 516.

REQUIREMENTS DOCUMENT

Date:	August 11, 2017
Date Submitted:	
Application Title:	Country Music Events
Purpose:	This Windows Desktop application computes either the cost of a four-day festival pass or a single-venue ticket.
Program Procedures:	The user can select country music festival four-day passes or individual venue tickets.

Algorithms, Processing, and Conditions:
1. The user first selects whether to compute the cost of country festival four-day passes or single-venue tickets.
2. After the user selects an option, display the necessary objects based on the selection. If the user selects festival passes, request the number of four-day festival passes. If the user chooses the single-venue ticket, request the number of single-venue tickets.
3. Based on the cost of $372.99 for a four-day pass or $89.00 for a single-venue ticket, calculate the cost of the number of passes or tickets. Use separate procedures to make the two calculations.
4. Display the result of the calculation on the form.

Notes and Restrictions:
1. A Clear Form button should clear the form.
2. The data the user enters should be validated in Try-Catch blocks in separate procedures as needed.

Comments:
1. The application should begin with a splash screen that holds for approximately three seconds.
2. Obtain images for this program from CengageBrain.com. The name of the picture for the Windows form is Country. The name of the picture on the splash screen is CountrySplash.

FIGURE 7-66

Country Music Events (continued)

USE CASE DEFINITION

1. The user views the opening splash screen for three seconds.
2. The user selects whether to purchase four-day pass or single-venue type tickets.
3. The user enters the number of tickets needed.
4. The user taps or clicks the Compute Cost button to display the final cost.
5. The user taps or clicks the Clear Form button to clear the responses.

FIGURE 7-67

FIGURE 7-68a

© iStock.com.com/DragonImages

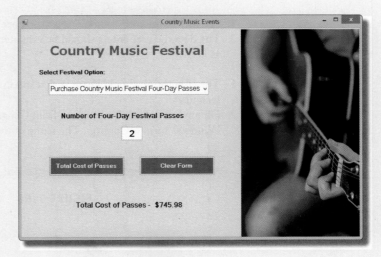

FIGURE 7-68b

3 ● ALAMO TOUR

Design a Windows application and write the code that will execute according to the program requirements in Figure 7-69 and the Use Case Definition in Figure 7-70 on page 518. Before writing the code, create an event planning document for each event in the program. The completed Windows Form object and other objects in the user interface are shown in Figure 7-71 on page 518.

REQUIREMENTS DOCUMENT

Date: September 24, 2017

Date Submitted:

Application Title: Alamo Tour

Purpose: This Windows Desktop application allows a user to select Alamo guided tours, weekend or weekday tours, and the number of tickets. The total cost with tax is computed.

Program Procedures: A user can select an Alamo tour, weekend or weekday, and the number of tickets, and then calculate the total cost of the tickets with tax.

Algorithms, Processing, and Conditions:
1. The user enters the Alamo tour (Alamo Story $19, Alamo Story with Battleground Tour $29, or the Mission Trail Deluxe Tour $49), weekend or weekday (10% discount), and the number of tickets needed. The type of Alamo Tour is selected from a ComboBox object. The other objects are not visible until the user selects this option.
2. A different Function procedure will be called for each tour to calculate the total cost of the tickets. Another Function will be called to compute the tax, regardless of which tour is selected.
3. Two types of day tours are available: weekend and weekday. The weekday tours receive a 10% discount before taxes.
4. Display the subtotal with applicable discount, city tax (12%), and final total of the tickets purchased.

Notes and Restrictions:
1. Validate input by using Try-Catch blocks in separate procedures as needed.
2. Use separate Sub and Functions for each portion of this program.

Comments:
1. The program opens with a splash screen that is displayed for approximately five seconds.
2. Obtain images for this program from CengageBrain.com. The name of the picture for the Windows form is Alamo.

FIGURE 7-69

Case Programming Assignments

Alamo Tour (continued)

USE CASE DEFINITION

1. The user views the opening splash screen for five seconds.
2. The user selects which type of tour tickets and whether they desire a weekend or weekday tour.
3. The user enters the number of tickets needed.
4. The user taps or clicks the Calculate Cost button or presses Enter to display the final cost.

FIGURE 7-70

FIGURE 7-71a

© iStock.com.com/robertcicchetti

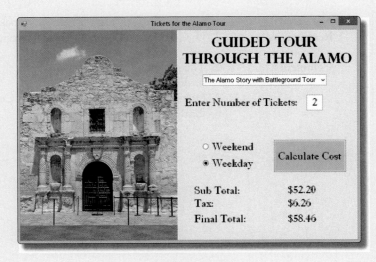

FIGURE 7-71b

Case Programming Assignments

4 •• BODY MASS INDEX (BMI) CALCULATOR

Design a Windows Desktop application and write the code that will execute according to the program requirements in Figure 7-72. Before designing the user interface, create a Use Case Definition. Before writing the code, create an event planning document for each event in the program.

REQUIREMENTS DOCUMENT

Date: October 19, 2017

Date Submitted:

Application Title: Body Mass Index (BMI) Calculator

Purpose: This Windows Desktop application allows the user to enter a height and weight and computes the user's body mass index.

Program Procedures: The user will enter a height and weight using either the imperial or metric system.

Algorithms, Processing, and Conditions:
1. The user first views a Windows application that displays a title, a BMI graphic, a ListBox object to select the imperial or metric system, and labels to enter information for the user's height and weight.
2. When the user selects imperial or metric and the height and weight, the Compute BMI button can be selected.
3. A Sub procedure should be called to handle the imperial and metric BMI calculations using the following formulas:
   BMI = (Weight in Pounds / (Height in Inches * Height in Inches)) * 703
   BMI = Weight in Kilograms / (Height in Meters * Height in Meters)
4. Two Function procedures should be called based on the system selected. Each Function procedure will calculate the BMI and return the Decimal value to the calling procedure. The original procedure will display the result.

Notes and Restrictions:
1. The result should be calculated to the hundredths place.
2. The input values should be validated by a Try-Catch block.

Comments:
1. An image from the web should be used for the BMI graphic.
2. An opening splash screen should be displayed for three seconds.

FIGURE 7-72

5

CASH FOR GOLD

Design a Windows application and write the code that will execute according to the program requirements in Figure 7-73. Before designing the user interface, create a Use Case Definition. Before writing the code, create an event planning document for each event in the program.

REQUIREMENTS DOCUMENT

Date:	July 1, 2017
Date Submitted:	
Application Title:	Cash for Gold
Purpose:	This Windows Desktop application calculates the amount of gold jewelry that can be sold to make a target amount of money or finds the amount of money earned based on the weight of gold jewelry collected at estate sales.
Program Procedures:	The user can select how many ounces of gold must be sold to earn a target amount of money or find the amount earned based on the weight of gold collected.
Algorithms, Processing, and Conditions:	1. The user first selects whether to compute a weight in ounces to reach a goal amount or to compute the amount earned by selling gold jewelry. 2. After the user selects an option, display the necessary objects based on the selection. If the user selects the goal amount, request the target amount the user hopes to earn. If the user chooses to find the amount earned based on the weight of her collected gold, request the weight in ounces. 3. Based on one ounce of gold selling for $1168.67, calculate the weight of gold the user needs to collect to make the goal or calculate the amount of money the collected gold jewelry is worth. Use separate procedures to make the two calculations. 4. Display the result of the calculation on the form.
Notes and Restrictions:	1. A Clear Form button should clear the form. 2. The data the user enters should be validated in Try-Catch blocks in separate procedures as needed.
Comments:	1. The application should begin with a splash screen that holds for approximately four seconds. 2. Obtain images for this program from the web.

FIGURE 7-73

6 •• COMMUTER COST CALCULATOR

Design a Windows Desktop application and write the code that will execute according to the program requirements in Figure 7-74. Before designing the user interface, create a Use Case Definition. Before writing the code, create an event planning document for each event in the program.

REQUIREMENTS DOCUMENT

Date:	March 12, 2017
Date Submitted:	
Application Title:	Commuter Cost Calculator
Purpose:	This Windows Desktop application computes the yearly cost of commuting to work via car, train, or bus.
Program Procedures:	The user selects how she commutes to work and then answers questions based on that response to compute the cost of traveling to and from work for one year.
Algorithms, Processing, and Conditions:	1. The user first views a Windows application with a title and a ComboBox object that asks how she commutes—car, train, or bus. The other objects on the form are not visible at this point.
	2. After the user selects the mode of travel, the questions related to that type of travel are displayed immediately.
	3. The following customized questions are displayed based on the user's choice:
	• Car: Daily round trip distance, days worked per month, car's mileage per gallon, cost per gallon of gas, monthly cost of maintenance and insurance, and monthly parking cost.
	• Train: Round trip transit fare and days worked per month.
	• Bus: Round trip transit fare and days worked per month.
	4. After the values have been validated, calculate the cost of commuting for one year for the selected choice.
Notes and Restrictions:	All values that the user enters should be validated.
Comments:	1. The picture shown should be selected from pictures available on the web.
	2. A splash screen should open the application.

FIGURE 7-74

Case Programming Assignments

7 ● ● ●
BALANCE AN ONLINE BANK STATEMENT

Create a requirements document and a Use Case Definition document and then design a Windows application based on the case project description in Figure 7-75. Before writing the code, create an event planning document for each event in the program.

Your college wants you to write a Windows application that students can use to balance their online bank accounts. This program will be installed on all computers in the student union. The application should allow the user to enter a starting balance and indicate whether the account has a monthly interest rate. Validate the beginning balance to verify that the number is possible. Allow the user to enter checks, ATM cash withdrawals, and deposits. Also, calculate the interest for one month and add the interest amount to the final balance. Users can make multiple debits and deposits and continue until indicating that they are finished making transactions. The interest will be added to the final balance after the transactions are completed. Data validation is needed for all input. An opening splash screen will be displayed as well.

FIGURE 7-75

8 ●●●
SALARIES FOR COMPUTER OCCUPATIONS

Create a requirements document and a Use Case Definition document and then design a Windows application based on the case project description in Figure 7-76. Before writing the code, create an event planning document for each event in the program.

Create a Windows application that analyzes four computer job titles from the information listed on the U.S. Department of Labor Statistics website at *www.bls.gov*. Search for the U.S. hourly mean wage and annual mean wage for the following occupations: Computer Developers, Computer System Analysts, Computer and Information Systems Managers, and Computer Software Engineers, Applications. Create a Windows form that has a drop-down list of the four occupations. Based on the user's selection, display the current median hourly pay and yearly pay. Also, project what the pay will be in five years based on a 4 percent raise per year for each of the present rates.

FIGURE 7-76

9 ●●●
SMARTPHONE GROWTH

Create a requirements document and a Use Case Definition document and then design a Windows application based on the case project description in Figure 7-77. Before writing the code, create an event planning document for each event in the program.

A national digital service provider would like you to create a Windows application that will display the global growth of smartphones. As of 2015, there were 2 billion smartphones worldwide. The smartphone market is growing at 22.5 percent per year. Based on this growth rate, create a Sub procedure that calculates and displays the next 10 years of growth in a ListBox object. Also, create a Function procedure that allows the user to enter a year from the next 10 years and then passes back that year's smartphone projection. Validate all entries. An opening splash screen will be displayed as well.

FIGURE 7-77

CHAPTER 8

Using Arrays and File Handling

OBJECTIVES

You will have mastered the material in this chapter when you can:

- Initialize an array

- Initialize an array with default values

- Access array elements using a loop

- Use ReDim to resize an array

- Determine the number of elements in an array using the Length command

- Use the For Each loop

- Initialize two-dimensional arrays

- Read a text file

- Write to a text file

- Calculate depreciation

- Use multiple Form objects

- Access variable objects on other forms

Introduction

You can use Visual Basic to create applications for small businesses or multinational corporations. As programming applications grow in size, the role of organizing, storing, and retrieving large amounts of data becomes vital. This chapter explains how to develop applications that can keep data for later processing, including sorting, calculating, and display.

Chapter Project

In the sample chapter project, a chain of men's retail stores named Trends Menswear requires a Windows application to compute the depreciation of its point of sale registers, sales racks, office computers, and store furniture. **Depreciation** is an accounting term that describes the decline in value of a physical asset over a certain period of time. Most assets lose value due to use, aging, obsolescence, and impairment. Depreciation is an estimate of this declining value and is used for determining taxes and other financial purposes.

Trends Menswear sells business and men's formal attire. The company cannot depreciate the cost of its clothing inventory, but it can claim the depreciated value of its physical assets, such as the point of sale registers and other store equipment. Each store item is assigned a four-character identifying code. A table that lists these items and associated codes is stored in a text file, which is kept on a storage medium such as a USB drive.

When the Windows application for Trends Menswear starts, it opens the text file and fills the Select Inventory Item ListBox object with the item numbers. Before calculating depreciation, the user selects an item and a depreciation method, as shown in Figure 8-1.

FIGURE 8-1

In Figure 8-1, the user taps or clicks the list box arrow to display the items in inventory. After selecting an item, the user can tap or click a radio button to select either the Straight-Line or the Double-Declining Balance depreciation method.

In straight-line depreciation, the asset is depreciated by the same amount each year for the life of the asset. In double-declining depreciation, the depreciation is accelerated.

After selecting an item number and a method of depreciation, the user taps or clicks the Calculate Depreciation button. The Windows form then displays the product name, the quantity in inventory, and the amount the item is worth over the next five years due to depreciation, as shown in Figure 8-2.

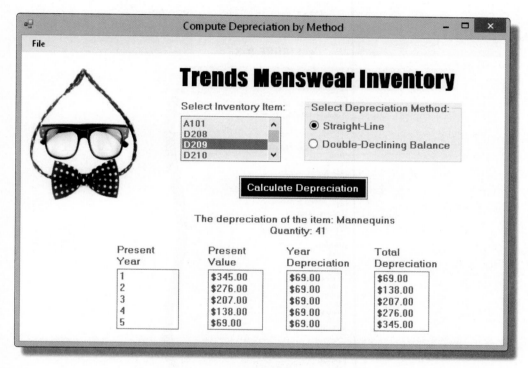

FIGURE 8-2

Trends Menswear purchased the items shown in Figure 8-3 in its first year of business.

Each item in Figure 8-3 is depreciated each year for tax reasons. The Internal Revenue Service allows depreciation deductions for five years because the average useful life of these types of items is five years. The items in Figure 8-3 are stored in a text file named inventory.txt. Figure 8-4 shows this file in Notepad. The Windows application opens the inventory.txt text file and reads the information for use in the program.

The Trends Menswear Depreciation application also contains a File menu that displays the following menu items: Display Inventory, Clear, and Exit (Figure 8-5).

Inventory Item	Item Number	Initial Cost	Quantity
Point of Sale Registers	A101	1599.99	12
Store Display Racks	D208	49.99	112
Mannequins	D209	345.00	41
End Cap Displays	D210	118.99	16
Hangers	D211	1.19	1200
Office Computers	E101	629.99	11
Chairs	F310	145.00	32
Sofas	F311	829.99	6

FIGURE 8-3

FIGURE 8-4

File menu

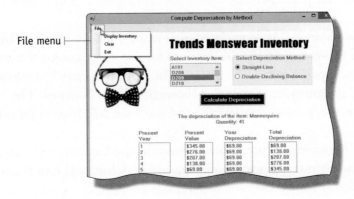

FIGURE 8-5

When the user taps or clicks the Display Inventory menu item, the application opens a second Windows Form object that shows the items in inventory in sorted alphabetical order (Figure 8-6).

FIGURE 8-6

© iStock.com/flyparade

Introduction to Arrays

After completing Chapters 1 through 7 in this book, you know how to create the user interface for the chapter project, which involves Button, ListBox, Label, and RadioButton objects. The challenge in this chapter is to write code that adds data to the form efficiently and accurately. To do so, you must understand arrays and file handling. The next section provides background on arrays.

Arrays

Every application you have developed thus far involved a limited number of variables and data, but in professional programming projects, applications deal with much larger sets of data that need numerous variables. You have learned that data type variables can store only one value at a time. Therefore, you have not used data types that contain more than one memory location to store more than one value at a time. If you changed a variable's value, the previous value was erased because a typical variable can store only one value at a time. For example, if you wanted to create an application that recorded dinner reservations at a restaurant for named groups with different numbers of people in the groups, you would need a unique variable name for each reservation, as shown in Figure 8-7.

```
5          Dim intBakerReservation As Integer = 4
6          Dim intLopezReservation As Integer = 5
7          Dim intBuckReservation As Integer = 12
8          Dim intChanReservation As Integer = 2
9          Dim intTirrellReservation As Integer = 8
```

FIGURE 8-7

For a large restaurant, you would need to create hundreds of variables to hold hundreds of reservations each night. Having hundreds of variables just to record each night's reservations is impractical and difficult to manage. As you can see, a different kind of variable that can hold more than one value is required.

The solution to developing applications with larger amounts of data is to use an array. An **array** variable is simply a variable that can store more than one value. In fact, an array in Visual Basic can hold more than a million values. Each individual item in an array that contains a value is called an **element**.

Arrays provide access to data by using a numeric **index**, or **subscript**, to identify each element in the array. Using an array, you can store a sequence of values of similar data type. For example, you can store six values of type Decimal without having to declare six different variables. Instead, each of the six values is stored in an individual element of the array, and you refer to each element according to its index within the array. Zero is the index used to reference a value in the first array element. Each subsequent element is referenced by an increasing index value, as shown in Figure 8-8.

decShoeSize(0)	decShoeSize(1)	decShoeSize(2)	decShoeSize(3)	decShoeSize(4)	decShoeSize(5)
9.0	11.5	6.0	7.5	13.0	8.0

FIGURE 8-8

CRITICAL THINKING

Can an array be used in a Visual Basic program to extract and display values from a database like Microsoft Access or Oracle?
Typically if you are storing a large amount of values, a database is the best option for organizing and retrieving information. Later in this text, values from a database will be retrieved and processed using a VB program.

In Figure 8-8, an array named decShoeSize holds six shoe sizes. Each shoe size is stored in an array element, and each element is assigned a unique index. The first value (9.0) is stored in the element with the index of 0. The element is identified by the term decShoeSize(0), which is pronounced "decShoeSize sub zero." The second shoe size (11.5) is stored in the second element of the array, which is referenced as decShoeSize(1). The same scheme is used for all elements in the array.

Initialize an Array

To declare an array in a program, you must include an array declaration statement, which states the name of the array, how many items it can store, and what sort of data it can store. To initialize or declare an array, just as in declaring any other variable, you must reserve the amount of memory that will be needed to store the array. The syntax for declaring an array begins with the word Dim (Figure 8-9).

General Format: Define an Array
Dim intReservations(300) as Integer

intReservations assigns the array name.

300 is the index or subscript reserving the amount of memory needed – it is the highest numbered index.

Integer determines the data type of the entire array.

FIGURE 8-9

The statement in Figure 8-9 declares intReservations as an array of integer variables that holds 301 elements. The first array element is intReservations(0), then intReservations(1), and so on to the last element in the array, intReservations(300). All arrays in Visual Basic 2015 are zero based, meaning that the index of the first element is zero and the indexes increase sequentially by 1. You must specify the number of array elements by indicating the upper-bound index of the array. The upper-bound number specifies the index of the last element of the array. Setting the size of an array is called dimensioning the array.

If you know the values to be placed in each element in the array, you can declare an array by assigning values to each element, as shown in Figure 8-10.

```
13        Dim strNames() As String = {"Baker", "Lopez", "Buck", "Chan", "Tirrell"}
14        Dim intReservations() As Integer = {4, 5, 12, 2, 8}
```

FIGURE 8-10

The data to be placed in each element is contained within curly brackets. An array can be any data type. In Figure 8-10, the first array is a String data type and the second array is an Integer data type. strNames() is an array of String variables that contains five names, with Baker stored in strNames(0), Lopez in strNames(1), and so on. intReservations() is an array of Integer variables that contains five values, with 4 stored in intReservations(0), 5 in intReservations(1), and so on.

These two arrays are **parallel arrays**. Parallel arrays store related data in two or more arrays. The information for one reservation includes strNames(0) for the Baker reservation and the number of people associated with it (4) in intReservations(0). The same subscript is used for the corresponding array elements, as shown in Figure 8-11 and Figure 8-12, which illustrate the arrays created by the code in Figure 8-10.

strNames(0)	strNames(1)	strNames(2)	strNames(3)	strNames(4)
Baker	Lopez	Buck	Chan	Tirrell

FIGURE 8-11

intReservations(0)	intReservations(1)	intReservations(2)	intReservations(3)	intReservations(4)
4	5	12	2	8

FIGURE 8-12

Visual Basic determines the size of the array by counting the number of items within the curly brackets. In this case, each array has five elements, and each element has an index number ranging from 0 to 4. The upper-bound index is 4, which specifies the last element of the array. When a number is not used in the declaration statement to state the size of the array, the array is **implicitly sized**, meaning that the number of values is determined at execution. Instead of stating the size, you list the values stored in the array.

Another way to declare an array is to specify its upper-bound index and assign each item of the array one by one, as shown in Figure 8-13. Each sport is assigned to a different element of the strAthlete() array.

HEADS UP

When declaring an implicitly sized array, do not place an upper-bound index in the parentheses following the array name in the declaration. If you do, an error will occur when the array is assigned elements.

```
17          Dim strAthlete(5) As String
18
19          strAthlete(0) = "Football"
20          strAthlete(1) = "Soccer"
21          strAthlete(2) = "Lacrosse"
22          strAthlete(3) = "Baseball"
23          strAthlete(4) = "Tennis"
24          strAthlete(5) = "Hockey"
```

FIGURE 8-13

Initialize an Array with Default Values

When you initialize an array but do not assign values immediately, each element is assigned a default value. The table in Figure 8-14 shows the default value assigned to each data type.

Data Type	Default Value
All numeric data types	0
String data type	Null
Boolean data type	False

FIGURE 8-14

After the array has been initialized, specific values can be assigned to each element, replacing the default value for each item. You can assign explicit values to the first few elements of the array and allow its remaining elements to be assigned to the default values automatically.

Access Array Elements Using a Loop

Because an array can contain multiple elements, in code you can use a loop to reference each element of an array. Loops can save valuable time when processing a large array because you don't have to write code for each array element. For example, if you were recording the lowest temperature for each day during the month of January to use in later calculations, the code in Figure 8-15 would allow the user to enter all 31 temperatures.

```
26        Dim intDailyTempJanuary(31) As Integer
27        Dim strTemp As String
28        Dim intDays As Integer
29
30        For intDays = 0 To 30
31            strTemp = InputBox("Enter the lowest temperature on January " _
32                & intDays + 1, "Obtain Temperatures")
33            intDailyTempJanuary(intDays) = Convert.ToInt32(strTemp)
34        Next
```

FIGURE 8-15

The array intDailyTempJanuary can hold the low temperature for each of the 31 days in January by using the elements referenced by the subscripts of 0 to 30. The loop counts from 0 to 30 using the variable intDays. The first time through the loop, the temperature obtained in an InputBox is assigned to a String named strTemp. Then, the value in strTemp is converted to an integer and assigned to the element intDailyTempJanuary(0). On each subsequent pass through the loop, the temperature obtained is placed in the next element, moving from intDailyTempJanuary(1) to intDailyTempJanuary(2) and so on until the final value for January 31 is assigned to the array element intDailyTempJanuary(30).

By using a loop in this manner, the program can process items in a large array with a few simple lines.

Array Boundaries

The Visual Basic compiler determines if each subscript is within the boundaries set when you initialized the array. For example, if you initialize an array to contain 31 elements but attempt to reference an element outside that boundary, as shown in Figure 8-16, an exception is produced when the code is executed.

```
37        Dim intDailyTempJanuary(30) As Integer
38        Dim strTemp As String
39        Dim intDays As Integer
40
41        For intDays = 0 To 31
42            strTemp = InputBox("Enter the lowest temperature on January " _
43                & intDays + 1, "Obtain Temperatures")
44            intDailyTempJanuary(intDays) = Convert.ToInt32(strTemp)
45        Next
```

FIGURE 8-16

The exception occurs when the loop tries to reference an element with the subscript 31. This element does not exist because the array contains 31 elements with an upper-bound index of 30. (Remember that an array's elements always are numbered beginning with zero.) The exception created by the code in Figure 8-16 is an IndexOutOfRangeException (Figure 8-17). A Try-Catch statement can catch this exception, but it is best to stay within the array boundaries of zero and the upper-bound array subscript.

FIGURE 8-17

Upper-Bound Index Constant

An array can use a constant value to represent its upper-bound index. By using a constant, the size of several arrays can be specified quickly; as you will learn in the next section, they also can be changed quickly. In Figure 8-18, the arrays strFirstNames() and strLastNames() are sized to hold 41 elements (the indexes are from 0 to 40).

```
47          Const intUpperBound As Integer = 40
48          Dim strFirstNames(intUpperBound) As String
49          Dim strLastNames(intUpperBound) As String
```

FIGURE 8-18

Reinitialize an Array

Although you usually set the number of elements in an array when you declare it, you can alter the size of the array later in the code. Every array in Visual Basic is considered **dynamic**, which means that you can resize it at run time. When you change the number of elements in an existing array, you redimension it. The **ReDim** statement assigns a new array size to the specified array variable. You use a ReDim statement to change the number of elements in an array. The code in Figure 8-19 reinitializes the strEmployees array.

```
51          Dim strEmployees(50) As String
52          ' Later in the code
53          ReDim strEmployees(65)
```

FIGURE 8-19

The strEmployees array originally is sized to hold 51 values, but is reinitialized later in the code to hold 66 values. When you use the ReDim statement to redimension the array, all the data contained in the array is lost. If you want to preserve the existing data, you can use the keyword **Preserve**, as shown in Figure 8-20. Preserve resizes the array and retains the data in the elements from 0 through 50.

```
55          Dim strEmployees(50) As String
56          ' Later in the code
57          ReDim Preserve strEmployees(65)
```

FIGURE 8-20

Use the Length Property

The Length property of an array contains the number of elements in an array. The code shown in Figure 8-21 displays 51 as the array size.

```
59        Dim strBranchOffices(50) As String
60
61        lblArraySize.Text = "The array size is " & (strBranchOffices.Length)
```

FIGURE 8-21

You can use the Length property in a loop to determine the exact number of iterations needed to cycle through each element in the array. Using the Length property can prevent the program from throwing the IndexOutOfRange exception. In the code in Figure 8-22, the For loop uses the Length property to determine the number of loop iterations.

```
63        Dim intYear(99) As Integer
64        Dim intCount As Integer
65
66        ' Assigns the years from 2001 to 2100 to the elements in the table
67        For intCount = 0 To (intYear.Length - 1)
68            intYear(intCount) = 2001 + intCount
69        Next
```

FIGURE 8-22

In the code in Figure 8-22, intYear.Length is equal to 100 (elements 0 through 99), one more than the array's upper-bound index number. In the For loop, the loop count will run from 0 through 99 (intYear.Length – 1), which means the loop will be executed 100 times, once for each element in the array.

Because an array can be resized anytime, the Length property is useful when you are unsure of an array's size.

Use Arrays

Arrays can be useful in many situations, such as when dealing with large amounts of data and finding totals and averages. For example, the code in Figure 8-23 computes the total yearly income and average yearly income for 10 employees in the warehouse department.

```
71          Dim intYearlySalary(9) As Integer
72          Dim intNumberOfEmployees As Integer
73          Dim intAdd As Integer
74          Dim intTotal As Integer
75
76          ' Allows the user to enter the 10 yearly salaries
77          For intNumberOfEmployees = 0 To (intYearlySalary.Length - 1)
78              intYearlySalary(intNumberOfEmployees) = _
79                  InputBox("Enter Salary #" & intNumberOfEmployees + 1, _
80                  "Warehouse Dept.")
81          Next
82
83          ' Finds the total amount of salaries entered
84          For intAdd = 0 To (intYearlySalary.Length - 1)
85              intTotal += intYearlySalary(intAdd)
86          Next
87
88          lblDisplayTotalSalary.Text = intTotal.ToString("C2")
89          lblDisplayAverageSalary.Text =_
90          (intTotal / intYearlySalary.Length).ToString("C2")
```

FIGURE 8-23

The reason the value accumulated in the intTotal variable is divided by the Length property is that the intYearlySalary array contains 10 elements. To find the average, you add all the numbers and divide by the number of elements. The line of code that finds the average (line 89) is outside of the loop because the average should be determined once, not repeatedly within the loop.

In the chapter project, the Items property of the lstInventoryId ListBox object must be filled with the inventory item numbers. The inventory item numbers are contained in the _strItemId array. The code in Figure 8-24 places the inventory item numbers in the Items property of the ListBox object. The Length property of the _strItemId array is used to determine the number of iterations in the For loop.

```
43          ' The ListBox object is filled with the Inventory IDs
44          For intFill = 0 To (_strItemId.Length - 1)
45              lstInventoryId.Items.Add(_strItemId(intFill))
46          Next
```

FIGURE 8-24

On line 44, the For loop begins with the intFill variable containing the value 0, which references the first element in the _strItemId array. On each pass through the loop, the value in intFill is incremented by 1 so it references the next element in the array. The loop terminates when the value in intFill is greater than the length of the array minus 1. Recall that the length of the array counts from 1 but the subscript counts from 0. Therefore, the length of the array minus 1 references the last element in the array.

The result of the code in Figure 8-24 is shown in Figure 8-25.

© iStock.com/flyparade

FIGURE 8-25

The For Each Loop

Recall from earlier chapters that a loop repeats a process. A special loop designed specifically for arrays is called a **For Each** loop. The loop syntax is shown in Figure 8-26.

General Format: For Each

For Each *Control Variable Name in Array Name*

```
' Lines of Code
```

Next

For Each — This type of loop iterates through an array until the array reaches the last element.

Control Variable Name — This variable will contain each individual element of the array without a subscript as the loop is processed. During the first iteration of the loop, the first element in the array is assigned to the control variable.

Array Name( ) — The name of the array that the loop cycles through. The array must be initialized first.

Next — This statement continues the loop to its next iteration.

FIGURE 8-26

A For Each loop cycles through each array element until the end of the array. In Figure 8-27, each element in the array is assigned to the variable strPioneer as the For Each loop is executed. The For Each loop does not require the program to keep track of the subscript for each element, and it stops when the loop has processed every element in the array.

Because each element in the array is assigned to the control variable, the elements and the variable must be the same data type. For example, in Figure 8-27, the array elements and the control variable are both Strings.

```
93      Private Sub btnHistory_Click(ByVal sender As System.Object, ByVal e As System.  ↙
        EventArgs) Handles btnHistory.Click
94
95          Dim strFamousComputerPioneers() As String = {"Pascal", _
96              "Babbage", "Ada", "Aiken", "Jobs"}
97          Dim strHeading As String = "Computer Pioneers:"
98          Dim strPioneer As String
99
100         lstPioneers.Items.Add(strHeading)
101         lstPioneers.Items.Add("")
102
103         For Each strPioneer In strFamousComputerPioneers
104             lstPioneers.Items.Add(strPioneer)
105         Next
106
107     End Sub
```

FIGURE 8-27

When the loop begins, the first element of the strFamousComputerPioneers array is placed in the strPioneer variable and the body of the loop is executed. In the body of the loop, the value in strPioneer is added to the Items property of the lstPioneers ListBox object. On the second iteration of the loop, the second element of the array is placed in the strPioneer variable and the body of the loop is executed again. This looping continues until all elements within the array have been processed.

After the loop processing is complete, the lstPioneers ListBox object displays the output shown in Figure 8-28.

FIGURE 8-28

Scope of Arrays

The scope of an array declared within a procedure is local to that procedure, but an array can be declared as a class-level variable. As with other variables, an array declared as a class-level variable is visible to all procedures within the class. For example, in the chapter project, multiple procedures will use the contents of the arrays that hold the inventory information for Trends Menswear. Therefore, these arrays should be declared as class-level arrays, as shown in Figure 8-29. Later in the chapter, the scope of these variables will be changed so that other classes can access the variables.

```
 9      Public Class frmDepreciation
10
11          ' Class Level Private variables
12          Private _intLifeOfItems As Integer = 5
13          Private _intSizeOfArray As Integer = 7
14          Private _strInventoryItem(_intSizeOfArray) As String
15          Private _strItemId(_intSizeOfArray) As String
16          Private _decInitialPrice(_intSizeOfArray) As Decimal
17          Private _intQuantity(_intSizeOfArray) As Integer
```

FIGURE 8-29

The arrays in Figure 8-29 can be referenced in any procedure following the declaration within the class. Notice that the size of the arrays is determined by the value in the _intSizeOfArray variable, which is declared on line 13.

Pass an Array

An array can be passed as an argument to a Sub procedure or a Function procedure. For example, if you need to find the sum of a salesperson's commissions, you can pass the array that holds the commission amounts to a Sub procedure. The Sub procedure named ComputeDisplayTotal in Figure 8-30 accepts a Decimal array. The For Each loop in this Sub procedure accumulates the sum of the commission amounts.

```
109     Private Sub btnCommission_Click(ByVal sender As System.Object, ByVal e As System. ↙
            EventArgs) Handles btnCommission.Click
110
111         Dim decCommissionAmounts() As Decimal = {1345.99, 7800.16, _
112             5699.99, 3928.09, 1829.45}
113
114         ComputeDisplayTotal(decCommissionAmounts)
115
116     End Sub
117
118     Private Sub ComputeDisplayTotal(ByVal decValueOfCommission() As Decimal)
119
120         Dim decAmount As Decimal
121         Dim decTotal As Decimal = 0
122
123         For Each decAmount In decValueOfCommission
124             decTotal += decAmount
125         Next
126
127         lblTotalCommission.Text = "The Total Commission is " _
128             & decTotal.ToString("C")
129     End Sub
```

FIGURE 8-30

Notice that the array is passed using the ByVal keyword, but with arrays ByVal has a different meaning. Arrays can be passed by value or by reference; however, the ByVal keyword does not restrict a Sub procedure or Function procedure from changing the array's elements. Whether you pass an array by value or by reference, the original array can be accessed and modified within the Sub or Function procedure. When passing arrays using ByVal, the array is not duplicated. If you change the value of any array element in a procedure, the original array is changed.

In Figure 8-31, the decCommissionAmounts array is defined on line 133. The third element is given the value 5699.99. On line 147 in the ChangeValue Sub procedure, the third element in the array, referenced as decValueOfCommission(2), is changed. When the array is displayed in the btnCommission_Click event (line 131), the third element has been changed (see Figure 8-32).

```
131     Private Sub btnCommission_Click(ByVal sender As System.Object, ByVal e As System. ↙
        EventArgs) Handles btnCommission.Click
132
133         Dim decCommissionAmounts() As Decimal = {1345.99, 7800.16, _
134             5699.99, 3928.09, 1829.45}
135         Dim decDisplay As Decimal
136
137         ChangeValue(decCommissionAmounts)
138
139         For Each decDisplay In decCommissionAmounts
140             lstDisplay.Items.Add(decDisplay.ToString("C"))
141         Next
142
143     End Sub
144
145     Private Sub ChangeValue(ByVal decValueOfCommission() As Decimal)
146
147         decValueOfCommission(2) = 4599.99
148
149     End Sub
```

FIGURE 8-31

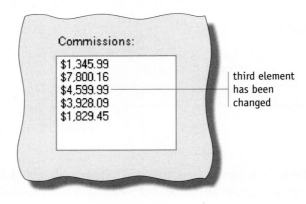

FIGURE 8-32

Sort an Array

The data in an array often is sorted for an organized display. For example, the telephone white pages are sorted by last name, which makes it easier to search for and locate friends and family members. To sort array contents in Visual Basic, you use a procedure named **Sort**. When the Sort procedure is applied to an array, the lowest value is placed in the first element in the array with an index of zero, the next lowest value is placed in the second element, and so on until the largest value is stored in the highest element of the array. The syntax for the Sort procedure is shown in Figure 8-33.

General Format: Sort Procedure

Array.Sort (ArrayName)

Coding Example:

Dim intAges() as Integer = {16, 64, 41, 8, 19, 81, 23}

Array.Sort(intAges)

After the sort executes, the values in the array are in the order 8, 16, 19, 23, 41, 64, and 81.

FIGURE 8-33

In the Trends Menswear Inventory Depreciation application, the array _strInventoryItem is declared as a class-level private variable that contains String data, as shown in Figure 8-34. Later the variable will be changed to public to be accessed by a second class. The size of the array is specified by the value in the _intSizeOfArray variable.

```
13      Private _intSizeOfArray As Integer = 7
14      Private _strInventoryItem(_intSizeOfArray) As String
```

FIGURE 8-34

The array is filled with data from a text file in another procedure. The inventory items in the text file are not sorted, but the items should be sorted before being displayed in a ListBox object. Therefore, the array is sorted using the Array.Sort procedure, as shown in Figure 8-35. After sorting, a For Each loop displays the elements in the array in ascending alphabetic (A to Z) order, as shown in Figure 8-36.

```
11          Dim strItem As String
12
13          ' Sorts the _strInventoryItem array
14          Array.Sort(frmDepreciation._strInventoryItem)
15
16          ' Displays the _strInventoryItem array
17          For Each strItem In frmDepreciation._strInventoryItem
18              lstDisplay.Items.Add(strItem)
19          Next
```

FIGURE 8-35

CRITICAL THINKING

Can I sort an array in reverse alphabetical order?
Yes. After you sort an array, the command Array. Reverse(ArrayName) reverses the order of the items in the array. A numerical array could be sorted in ascending order and then quickly changed to descending order with the Array. Reverse(ArrayName) command.

ascending alphabetical sequence

FIGURE 8-36

© iStock.com/flyparade

Search an Array

Arrays provide an excellent way to store and process information. Suppose an array holds 5,000 student names in alphabetical order. If you searched for one name in that array, the search could take some time. One search approach is to begin with the first name in index zero and evaluate each name until you find a match. Searching each element in an array is called a **sequential search.** Theoretically, you might have to search 5,000 names before you find a match or discover that the name is not even in the array. For these reasons, a sequential search is not the most efficient way of searching for an element.

If an array is large and requires many repeated searches, you need a more efficient search approach. The **BinarySearch** method searches a sorted array for a value using a binary search algorithm, which searches an array by repeatedly dividing the search interval in half. In an array with the contents shown in Figure 8-37, you could quickly find the value 405 using the BinarySearch method.

searching for this value

```
165          Dim intCalories() As Integer = {35, 45, 75, 110, 145, 160, 195, 405, 435}
```

FIGURE 8-37

The steps for the BinarySearch method are:

1. Determine the halfway point of the array, which is the number 145 in Figure 8-37. Compare that value first: 145 is less than 405.
2. If the first comparison is not equal to the number being searched, determine whether the value of the search number is less than the middle value. If the search value is less, narrow the search interval to the lower half of the array. Otherwise, narrow the search to the upper half of the array. The search value 405 is greater than the middle value 145, so the process narrows the search to the upper half of the array, which contains 160, 195, 405, and 435.
3. Repeatedly check each interval until the value is found or until the halving process evaluates the entire element list of the array.

The BinarySearch procedure returns the matching index value if the element is found. If the array does not contain the specified value, the method returns a negative integer. The BinarySearch procedure syntax is shown in Figure 8-38.

General Format: BinarySearch Procedure

```
intValue = Array.BinarySearch(arrayname, value)
```

If intValue returns a positive number or zero, a match was found at the subscript number equal to intValue.

If intValue returns a negative number, a match was not found.

FIGURE 8-38

As another example, a user enters the number of calories to consume, and the code in Figure 8-39 determines if the number of calories is found in the intCalories() array. The code also displays the food item index location if it finds a match with the number of calories entered. If the number of calories is not found, a message reports that the food item is not found.

```
165    Dim intCalories() As Integer = {35, 45, 75, 110, 145, 160, _
166        195, 405, 435}
167    Dim strFoods() As String = {"Carrots", "Kiwi", "Egg", "Orange", _
168        "Cola", "Taco", "Yogurt", "Apple Pie Slice", "Raisins"}
169    Dim intSelection As Integer
170    Dim intIndexLocation As Integer
171
172    intSelection = Convert.ToInt32(txtCalories.Text)
173    intIndexLocation = Array.BinarySearch(intCalories, intSelection)
174    If intIndexLocation >= 0 Then
175        lblLocation.Text = "The search item is found in subscript number " _
176            & intIndexLocation
177        lblFood.Text = strFoods(intIndexLocation)
178    Else
179        lblLocation.Text = "The food item not found"
180    End If
```

FIGURE 8-39

If the calorie value of 405 is entered into the txtCalories TextBox object, the message "The search item is found in subscript number 7" is displayed in lblLocation. The second Label object displays Apple Pie Slice.

Create a Two-Dimensional Array

An array that has a single index or subscript is called a one-dimensional array, but arrays can be multidimensional and hold complex information. An array that has two dimensions has two subscripts. A **two-dimensional array** holds data that is arranged in rows and columns, as shown in Figure 8-40. In other words, two-dimensional arrays store the elements of tables. The array intVal is initialized with three rows and four columns in Figure 8-41 (recall that the values in parentheses specify the highest numbered element).

```
           rows    columns

182    Dim intVal(2, 3) As Integer
```

FIGURE 8-40

	column 0	column 1	column 2	column 3
row 0	intVal(0,0)	intVal(0,1)	intVal(0,2)	intVal(0,3)
row 1	intVal(1,0)	intVal(1,1)	intVal(1,2)	intVal(1,3)
row 2	intVal(2,0)	intVal(2,1)	intVal(2,2)	intVal(2,3)

FIGURE 8-41

The table in Figure 8-42 shows the four busiest airports in the United States. The numbers are represented in millions, and identify the number of passengers traveling through each airport each year, according to the Bureau of Transportation Services. The table shows that Atlanta is the busiest airport in the United States, with over 34 million passengers flying through the airport each year. The table has four rows and two columns.

	column 0 2017	column I 2016	
Atlanta	35	34	row(0)
Chicago	28	27	row(1)
Dallas	24	23	row(2)
Los Angeles	20	19	row(3)

FIGURE 8-42

The array declared to hold the contents of the busiest airport table is the same as a one-dimensional array, except for the two subscripts that hold the row and column index values. The declaration statement in Figure 8-43 initializes an array with four rows (0, 1, 2, 3) and two columns (0, 1) named intPassengers.

```
184        Dim intPassengers(3, 1) As Integer
```

FIGURE 8-43

After the array has been initialized, users can enter the values into a TextBox object from the table information or the program can assign the values by using an implicitly sized array, such as the one shown in Figure 8-44.

```
192        Dim intPassengers(,) As Integer = {{35, 34}, {28, 27}, {24, 23}, _
193            {20, 19}}
```

FIGURE 8-44

In the code shown in Figure 8-45, the array representing the busiest U.S. airports is totaled by column to find the number of passengers who flew through the four airports in each of the two years. A nested loop is used to total the two columns of the two-dimensional array. The outer loop controls the column index and the inner loop controls the row index of the array.

```
192         Dim intPassengers(,) As Integer = {{35, 34}, {28, 27}, {24, 23}, _
193             {20, 19}}
194         Dim intTotalColumn As Integer = 0
195         Dim intCol As Integer
196         Dim intRow As Integer
197
198         For intCol = 0 To 1
199             'Resets the total to 0
200             intTotalColumn = 0
201             For intRow = 0 To 3
202                 intTotalColumn += intPassengers(intRow, intCol)
203             Next
204             MsgBox("The Sum of Column #" & intCol + 1 & " is " _
205                 & intTotalColumn.ToString & " million.")
206         Next
```

FIGURE 8-45

The output for the airport program is shown in Figure 8-46 and Figure 8-47.

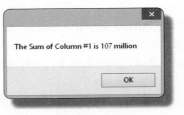

The Sum of Column #1 is 107 million

OK

FIGURE 8-46

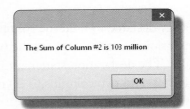

The Sum of Column #2 is 103 million

OK

FIGURE 8-47

File Handling

In the applications you created in this book so far, the information entered has originated from assigning data to variables or asking the user to enter data in objects on the form. In many business applications, entering information can be time consuming if you must enter data for thousands of items. To process data more efficiently, many developers use text files to store and access information for use within an application. Text files have a **.txt** extension. The Windows operating system provides a basic text editor called Notepad that allows you to save files with the .txt extension. A simple text file is called a **sequential file**.

For example, in the chapter project, Trends Menswear's inventory is stored in a text file. By gaining access to that information, the depreciation program can manipulate the data and compute the depreciation for items in the inventory. The text file is available at CengageBrain.com. Visual Basic can access many types of files, including text files, as discussed in this chapter, or various types of databases, which are covered in Chapter 10.

With Visual Basic 2015, the System.IO (input/output) namespace in the .NET Framework provides several classes for working with text files, binary files, directories, and byte streams. The System.IO namespace allows you to create, copy, move, and delete files. The file handler supports all types of data, including both string and numeric data types. The most commonly used classes are FileStream, BinaryReader, BinaryWriter, StreamReader, and StreamWriter.

Can I read other types of files besides a text file created in Notepad?
The code in this chapter deals specifically with text files created in a text editor such as Notepad, but the System.IO namespace in the .NET Framework provides several classes for working with text files, binary files, directories, and byte streams.

Read a Text File

To open a text file, you need an object available in the System.IO called a **StreamReader**. As its name suggests, this object reads streams of text. You create a StreamReader to provide access to standard input and output files.

To read a file, a variable object is first created for a data type called StreamReader. The prefix for an object is obj in the format used in Figure 8-48.

```
24          Dim objReader As IO.StreamReader
```

FIGURE 8-48

After the object variable is declared, an If statement in the form IO.File. Exists("*filename*") determines if the file is available, as shown in Figure 8-49. The command IO.File.OpenText("*filename*") opens the text file and assigns it to the object variable objReader.

```
31          If IO.File.Exists("e:\inventory.txt") = True Then
32              objReader = IO.File.OpenText("e:\inventory.txt")
33          Else
34              MsgBox("The file is not available. Restart the program when the  ↙
        file is available",,"Error")
35              Close()
36          End If
```

FIGURE 8-49

To read each line of the text file, you use a ReadLine procedure. The first line of data in the text file is assigned to the first element in the array _strInventoryItem (see Figure 8-50).

```
35          _strInventoryItem(intCount) = objReader.ReadLine()
```

FIGURE 8-50

To determine whether the end of the file has been reached, use the Peek procedure of the StreamReader object. The Peek procedure reads the next character in the file without changing position. If the end of the file is reached, the Peek procedure returns the value of −1. You can use a Do While loop to determine if all the lines in the file have been read. When the Peek procedure reaches the end of the file and returns a −1, the Do While loop ends, as shown in Figure 8-51.

```
34          Do While objReader.Peek <> -1
35              _strInventoryItem(intCount) = objReader.ReadLine()
36              _strItemId(intCount) = objReader.ReadLine()
37              _decInitialPrice(intCount) = Convert.ToDecimal(objReader.ReadLine())
38              _intQuantity(intCount) = Convert.ToInt32(objReader.ReadLine())
39              intCount += 1
40          Loop
```

FIGURE 8-51

```
40          objReader.Close()
```

FIGURE 8-52

CRITICAL THINKING

Before closing the application, be sure to close the file to terminate communications with it, as shown in Figure 8-52.

The Trends Menswear application opens and reads a file named inventory.txt. To read data from a text file, you can complete the following steps:

STEP 1 Open the code window by tapping or clicking the View Code button on the Solution Explorer toolbar. Tap or click inside the frmDepreciation_Load event.

The code window opens and the insertion point appears in the frmDepreciation_Load event handler (Figure 8-53).

insertion point

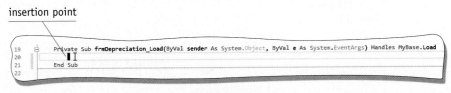

```
19    ⊟    Private Sub frmDepreciation_Load(ByVal sender As System.Object, ByVal e As System.EventArgs) Handles MyBase.Load
20
21         End Sub
22
```

FIGURE 8-53

STEP 2 Initialize the variables. Assign an object variable to the IO.StreamReader object. Initialize the StreamReader object by typing `Dim objReader As IO.` An IntelliSense window opens. Select StreamReader. Press ENTER. Finish declaring the rest of the variable names.

After the objReader object variable is initialized in the IO namespace, IntelliSense opens a listing of IO procedures. The variables are initialized (Figure 8-54).

```
19   Private Sub frmDepreciation_Load(ByVal sender As System.Object, ByVal e As System.EventArgs) Handles MyBase.Load
20       ' The frmDepreciation load event reads the inventory text file and
21       ' fills the Listbox object with the inventory items
22
23       ' Initialize an instance of the StreamReader object and declare variables
24       Dim objReader As IO.StreamReader
25       Dim intCount As Integer = 0
26       Dim intFill As Integer
27
28   End Sub
```

FIGURE 8-54

STEP 3 Verify that the inventory.txt data file is available by typing `If IO.` to open an IntelliSense window. Complete the rest of the line using IntelliSense, as shown in Figure 8-55. Assign the objReader variable by typing `objR` and then pressing CTRL+SPACEBAR to complete the variable name. Type `= IO.` to open an IntelliSense window. Type `F`.

The If statement confirms that the data file exists. The objReader is assigned to open the inventory.txt file (Figure 8-55).

IntelliSense list

```
22
23       ' Initialize an instance of the StreamReader object and declare variables
24       Dim objReader As IO.StreamReader
25       Dim intCount As Integer = 0
26       Dim intFill As Integer
27
28       If IO.File.Exists("e:\inventory.txt") Then
29           objReader = IO.F
30       End If
31   End Sub
32
     O references
     Private Sub btnCalculate...                    DriveType
33   ' The btnCalculateDe...                         EndOfStreamException
34                                                    ErrorEventArgs
35   ' Declare variables                             ErrorEventHandler
36       Dim intSelectedItem...                       File
37       Dim strMissingSelect...                      FileAccess
38       Dim strSelectDepreci...                      FileAttributes
39       Dim strSelectInvento...                      FileInfo
                                                       FileLoadException
```

FIGURE 8-55

STEP 4 Select File by typing a period and select OpenText from the IntelliSense list. Type `("e:\inventory.txt")` to access the inventory text file from the USB drive (drive E).

The inventory.txt file is opened on the USB drive (Figure 8-56).

```
28       If IO.File.Exists("e:\inventory.txt") Then
29           objReader = IO.File.OpenText("e:\inventory.txt")   ── open the
30                                                                   text file
31       End If
32   End Sub
```

FIGURE 8-56

STEP 5 To read each line of the text file, insert a Do While loop that continues until the Peek procedure returns the value of −1. Specify that the ReadLine() procedure reads each line of the text file. Use the variable intCount to determine the index of each array element.

The code is entered to read inventory item names, item IDs, initial price, and quantity from the text file and assign them to class module-level array variables until the last item of the file is read (Figure 8-57).

```
30      ' Verify the file exists
31      If IO.File.Exists(strLocationAndNameOfFile) Then
32          objReader = IO.File.OpenText(strLocationAndNameOfFile)
33          ' Read the file line by line until the file is completed
34          Do While objReader.Peek <> -1
35              _strInventoryItem(intCount) = objReader.ReadLine()
36              _strItemId(intCount) = objReader.ReadLine()
37              _decInitialPrice(intCount) = Convert.ToDecimal(objReader.ReadLine())
38              _intQuantity(intCount) = Convert.ToInt32(objReader.ReadLine())
39              intCount += 1
40          Loop
41
```

read each line of the text file into the appropriate array element

FIGURE 8-57

STEP 6 After the data file has been read, close the file. Insert an Else statement that informs the user if the file cannot be opened and then closes the application.

The object variable objReader file is closed and the Else statement informs the user if the file is not available (Figure 8-58).

if no file is available, inform the user and close the application window

if file was opened, close the file

```
40              Loop
41              objReader.Close()
42          Else
43              MsgBox(strFileError, , "Error")
44              Close()
45          End If
46
47      End Sub
```

FIGURE 8-58

ONLINE REINFORCEMENT

To view a video of the process in the previous steps, visit CengageBrain.com and navigate to the resources for this title. Tap or click the link for Chapter 8 and then navigate to Video 8-2.

CONSIDER THIS

Do I have to access a text file stored on a USB drive?
The text file can be stored on any local computer path or network path. When you select a file using File Explorer, Windows 8 has a feature called Copy path that allows you to copy the path where the file is stored. You can then paste that path into your code.

Write to a Text File

Writing to a text file is similar to reading a text file. The System.IO namespace also includes the **StreamWriter**, which is used to write a stream of text to a file. The following example writes a file of users with their names and logon passwords to a new text file named NewAccounts.txt. Each name and password is written to a separate line in the file. The btnCreateAccount_Click event creates a text file with the new customer information, as shown in Figure 8-59. The Notepad text file named NewAccounts.txt is displayed in Figure 8-60.

```vb
53    Private Sub btnCreateAccount_Click(ByVal sender As System.Object, ByVal e As System↙
      .EventArgs) Handles btnCreateAccount.Click
54        ' Initialize Variables
55        Dim strCustomerName(5) As String
56        Dim strPassword(5) As String
57        Dim objWriter As New IO.StreamWriter("e:\NewAccounts.txt")
58        Dim intCount As Integer
59
60        For intCount = 0 To (strCustomerName.Length - 1)
61            strCustomerName(intCount) = InputBox("Please enter your name:", "Login ↙
      Information")
62            strPassword(intCount) = InputBox("Please enter a password:", "Password ↙
      Information")
63            If IO.File.Exists("e:\NewAccounts.txt") Then
64                ' Write the file line by line until the file is completed
65                objWriter.WriteLine(strCustomerName(intCount))
66                objWriter.WriteLine(strPassword(intCount))
67            Else
68                MsgBox("The file is not available. Restart the program when ↙
      the file is available",,"Error")
69                Close()
70            End If
71        Next
72
73        ' The file is closed
74        objWriter.Close()
75
76    End Sub
```

FIGURE 8-59

FIGURE 8-60

Compute Depreciation

Depreciation is the decrease in property value and the reduction in the balance sheet value of a company asset to reflect its age and prolonged use. The U.S. Internal Revenue Service states that the life of office equipment is five years for depreciation purposes. The two common ways of computing depreciation are the straight-line method and the double-declining balance method.

The simplest and most common method, **straight-line depreciation**, is calculated by dividing the purchase or acquisition price of an asset by the total number of productive years it can reasonably be expected to benefit the company. This value is called the life of the asset. In the chapter project, each asset in the inventory file has a life of five years. Figure 8-61 shows the formula for computing straight-line depreciation.

```
95          decStraightDepreciation = _decInitialPrice(intItemId) / _intLifeOfItems
```

FIGURE 8-61

To calculate the depreciation for end cap displays in the Trends Menswear program, you can use the straight-line depreciation method shown in Figure 8-62.

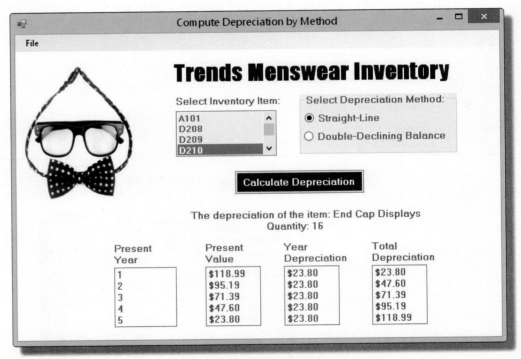

© iStock.com/flyparade

FIGURE 8-62

The double-declining balance depreciation method is like the straight-line method doubled. To use the double-declining balance method, first calculate depreciation using the formula in Figure 8-63. Notice that the price is doubled and divided by the item's life in years. After that asset is depreciated for the first year, subtract the depreciation amount from the initial price for the next year. The resulting value after subtracting the depreciation is used in the formula for each subsequent year.

```
127          ' The loop repeats for the life of the items
128          For intDoublePresentYear = 1 To  intLifeOfItems
129              ' The formula for double-declining depreciation inside the loop to repeat ↙
                 the process
130              decDoubleDepreciation = (decDoublePresentYearValue * 2D) / _intLifeOfItems
131              ' Accumulates the total of depreciation
132              decDoubleTotal+ = decDoubleDepreciation
133              ' Displays the depreciation amounts
134          Next
```

FIGURE 8-63

To calculate the depreciation for store display racks in the Trends Menswear program, you can use the double-declining balance depreciation method shown in Figure 8-64.

FIGURE 8-64

Use Multiple Form Objects

As program applications become larger, more than one Windows Form object often is needed to display information. Each Windows Form object in your program (Figure 8-65) is associated with a file displayed in the Solution Explorer. For example, the code stored in the frmDepreciation.vb file is displayed in the code window when you tap or click the frmDepreciation.vb tab in the design window.

FIGURE 8-65

Visual Basic 2015 allows you to add multiple Windows Form objects to an application. To add a second Windows Form object to an application, you can complete the following steps:

STEP 1   Tap or click Project on the menu bar, and then tap or click Add Windows Form.

The Add New Item dialog box opens (Figure 8-66).

FIGURE 8-66

STEP 2 In the Add New Item dialog box, tap or click Windows Form, and then type `frmDisplayInventory.vb` in the Name text box.

A Windows Form is selected to add as a new item to the Depreciation project. The form is named frmDisplayInventory.vb (Figure 8-67).

Windows Form selected

Windows Form name

Add button

FIGURE 8-67

STEP 3 Click the Add button in the Add New Item dialog box. A second Form object named frmDisplayInventory.vb opens in the Visual Basic 2015 window. In the Properties window, change the Text property of the frmDisplayInventory object to `Sorted Inventory Listing`.

The second Form object opens and its Text property is changed (Figure 8-68).

properties of new Windows Form object

new Windows Form object

Text property changed

FIGURE 8-68

ONLINE REINFORCEMENT

To view a video of the process in the previous steps, visit CengageBrain.com and navigate to the resources for this title. Tap or click the link for Chapter 8 and then navigate to Video 8-3.

Choose a Startup Object

Every application begins executing a project by displaying the object designated as the **Startup** object. For the depreciation application, the default Startup object is frmDepreciation.vb. However, you can change the Startup object if you want a different Form object to open first. To begin, press and hold or right-click the project name in Solution Explorer and then tap or click Properties on the shortcut menu. Tap or click the Application tab shown in Figure 8-69, tap or click the Startup form list arrow, and then tap or click the object you want to open when the application starts.

FIGURE 8-69

Create an Instance of a Windows Form Object

Now that you have multiple Windows Form objects in the application, you must write code that opens the Form objects as needed. As you create each Form object, code associated with the Form object creates a class declaration. Figure 8-70 displays the code.

```
96 Public Class frmDepreciation
97
98 End Class
```

FIGURE 8-70

The class frmDepreciation holds the object's properties and the procedures for that class. To display a second or subsequent form, the initial step is to create an **instance** of the Windows Form object. An instance is an object variable that references the second form's class name to access the object's procedures and properties. For example, in the code for the chapter project shown in Figure 8-71, the mnuDisplay_Click event opens when the user taps or clicks the Display Inventory menu item. The tap or click event declares an instance of the second form, which is named frmDisplayInventory. The object variable frmSecond references the instance of the Form object frmDisplayInventory.

```
163    Private Sub mnuDisplay_Click(ByVal sender As System.Object, ByVal e As System.
       EventArgs) Handles mnuDisplay.Click
164
165        ' The mnuDisplay click event creates an instance of the frmDisplayInventory
166        Dim frmSecond As New frmDisplayInventory
```

FIGURE 8-71

After the instance of the Form object is created, another statement must be written to display the instance of the second form. When creating multiple Windows Form objects, Visual Basic allows you to generate two types of forms: **modal** and **modeless**. A modal form retains the input focus while open, and the user cannot switch between Form objects until the first form is closed. You create a modal form with the ShowDialog procedure. In the code example in Figure 8-72, the second Form object, named frmSecond, is displayed using the ShowDialog procedure. The line preceding the ShowDialog() procedure hides the first form using the **Hide** procedure. The Hide procedure removes the first form from the user's screen so that it does not cover up the information it references.

HEADS UP

Command lines placed after the ShowDialog method call are not executed until the second Form object is closed.

```
167        'Hide this form and show the Display Inventory form
168        Hide()
169        frmSecond.ShowDialog()
```

FIGURE 8-72

The second method used when displaying multiple forms is referred to as a modeless Form object. A modeless form allows you to switch the input focus to another window. The first form stays open when you switch to another form, and lets you use the two forms at the same time. For example, a modeless form is useful for a help window that displays instructions. You create a modeless Form object with the Show procedure, as shown in Figure 8-73. A Hide method is not necessary because both Form objects are displayed at the same time.

```
91              frmSecond.Show()
```

FIGURE 8-73

Access Variables on Other Forms

When you create multiple Form objects, you might need to access the variable objects used in one form when you are working in another form. In the chapter project, the user can tap or click the Display Inventory menu item to open a second Form object that displays the sorted inventory items. The second form needs to reference the array initialized in the first form's code. You control the availability of a variable by specifying its access level, or **access specifier**. The access level determines what code has permission to read or write to a variable. To access a variable object on a different form, you can declare a class module-level variable with an access specifier other than Private. The access specifier Private determines that the variable can be used only with the class in which it is declared. For example, the variable _intLifeOfItems declared in Figure 8-74 can be accessed only within the class frmDepreciation because it has the access specifier Private.

```
11   Public Class frmDepreciation
12
13       ' Class Module-Level variable
14       Private _intLifeOfItems As Integer = 5
```

FIGURE 8-74

If you want to declare a variable object that can be used in the class where it is declared and in different classes within other Form objects, the variable can be declared using the access specifier Public Shared. A Public Shared variable is shared by all instances of a Form's class. In the chapter project, if you initialize the array of inventory items with the access specifier Public Shared in the frmDepreciation class, as shown in Figure 8-75, the Integer _intSizeOfArray and the array _strInventoryItem are now accessible in the second form. By using the Public Shared access specifier, the variable's values are shared across all objects in the depreciation application.

```
13     Public Shared _intSizeOfArray As Integer = 7
14     Public Shared _strInventoryItem(_intSizeOfArray) As String
```

FIGURE 8-75

After the variables are initialized with the access specifier Public Shared, they can be used within a different class on more than one form. To access the shared variable on another form, specify the name of the originating Form object followed by the name of the variable object. In the chapter project, a second Form object named frmDisplayInventory accesses the _strInventoryItem array. To access the array in the second form, the array name must begin with the originating form, frmDepreciation. The originating Form object and the variable name are separated by the dot operator, as shown in Figure 8-76. The array is sorted and displayed on the second Form object.

```
7   Private Sub frmDisplayInventory_Load(ByVal sender As System.Object, ByVal e As System. ↙
    EventArgs) Handles MyBase.Load
8       ' The frmDisplayInventory load event is a second form that
9       ' displays the sorted inventory items
10
11      Dim strItem As String                              originating
12                                                         form name
13      ' Sorts the _strInventoryItem array
14      Array.Sort(frmDepreciation._strInventoryItem)
15
16      ' Displays the _strInventoryItem array
17      For Each strItem In frmDepreciation._strInventoryItem
18          lstDisplay.Items.Add(strItem)
19      Next
20
21  End Sub                        dot operator          variable name
```

FIGURE 8-76

When you type frmDepreciation and the dot operator, IntelliSense displays the names of the shared variables from that Form object (see Figure 8-77).

FIGURE 8-77

After the second form opens, the user can tap or click the Return to Application button (Figure 8-78) to close the second Form object and return to the first Form object, frmDepreciation. The code in Figure 8-79 is executed when the Return to Application button is tapped or clicked. An instance of the first form, frmFirst, is created for frmDepreciation. The second form is hidden and the first form is opened again.

FIGURE 8-78

© iStock.com/flyparade

```
23      Private Sub btnReturn_Click(ByVal sender As System.Object, ByVal e As System.
        EventArgs) Handles btnReturn.Click
24          ' This Sub procedure opens the first form
25          Dim frmFirst As New frmDepreciation
26
27          Hide()
28          frmFirst.ShowDialog()
29
30      End Sub
```

FIGURE 8-79

Program Design

The requirements document for the Trends Menswear Inventory Depreciation application is shown in Figure 8-80, and the Use Case Definition document is shown in Figure 8-81.

REQUIREMENTS DOCUMENT

Date:	April 14, 2017
Date Submitted:	
Application Title:	Trends Menswear Inventory Depreciation Application
Purpose:	This Windows application opens an inventory data file and computes item depreciation based on the straight-line and double-declining balance methods.
Program Procedures:	A Windows application opens the inventory text file so that the user can select an item and the type of depreciation method. The depreciation is calculated for the five-year life of the inventory item.

Algorithms, Processing, and Conditions:

1. The user first views a Windows application that includes the following: a title; a File menu that includes Display Inventory, Clear, and Exit commands; a ListBox object that displays the inventory item IDs filled from the inventory text file; and a GroupBox object with two RadioButton objects that provide options for straight-line and double-declining balance depreciation methods. A Calculate Depreciation Button object is also available. The Trends Menswear logo is displayed on the left side of the Form object.

2. After the user selects an item ID and the depreciation method and then taps or clicks the Button object, the selected inventory item and quantity are displayed. ListBox objects display the present year, present value, year depreciation, and total depreciation.

3. If the user selects the Display Inventory menu item, a second Form object opens and displays the sorted inventory items list. The first Form object closes. The second Form object provides a Return to Application Button object to reopen the first Form object.

4. The user can select the Clear menu item to clear and reset the first Form object. The user can select the Exit menu item to close the application.

Notes and Restrictions:	The inventory.txt file is located on the USB drive (E:).
Comments:	The image shown in the window should be a picture available on the web.

FIGURE 8-80

USE CASE DEFINITION

1. The user selects the inventory item ID and the type of depreciation.
2. The user taps or clicks the Calculate Depreciation button to display the selected inventory item and quantity below the button.
3. The depreciation values are displayed for the present year, present value, year depreciation, and total depreciation.
4. The user taps or clicks the Display Inventory menu item to view the sorted inventory items.
5. The user taps or clicks the Clear menu item to clear and reset the form.
6. The user taps or clicks the Exit menu item to close the application.

FIGURE 5-81

Design the Program Processing Objects

The event planning documents for the Trends Menswear Inventory Depreciation application are shown in Figure 8-82 and Figure 8-83.

EVENT PLANNING DOCUMENT

Program Name: Depreciation	Developer: Corinne Hoisington	Object: frmDepreciation	Date: April 14, 2017
OBJECT	**EVENT TRIGGER**	**EVENT PROCESSING**	
frmDepreciation_Load	Load	Open the inventory.txt file from the USB drive; use If ... Else statements to handle possible errors when opening the file Assign each line of the text file to array variables Continue to read the text file until all items are assigned If the text file is not available, display a message Fill the ListBox object with the array of inventory item IDs	
btnCalculateDepreciation	Click	If the ListBox object and one RadioButton object are selected, call the appropriate Sub procedure based on the depreciation method selected If neither object is selected, display a message reminding the user to make a selection	

FIGURE 8-82 (continues)

EVENT PLANNING DOCUMENT

Program Name: Depreciation	Developer: Corinne Hoisington	Object: frmDepreciation	Date: April 14, 2017

OBJECT	EVENT TRIGGER	EVENT PROCESSING
StraightLineDepreciation	Called Sub procedure	Make objects visible to display results by calling the MakeObjectsVisible Sub procedure Display the inventory item selected and the quantity of that item Calculate the straight-line depreciation based on the following formula: initial price / life of the item in years Assign the initial price to the present year value In a loop that repeats five times due to the assigned life of the item, accumulate the total depreciation Display the present years in a ListBox object Display the present values in a ListBox object Display the year depreciation in a ListBox object Display the total depreciation in a ListBox object
DoubleDecliningDepreciation	Called Sub procedure	Show objects needed for results by calling the MakeObjectsVisible Sub procedure Display the inventory item selected and the quantity of that item Assign the initial price to the present year value In a loop that repeats five times due to the assigned life of the item, calculate the double-declining balance depreciation based on the following formula: initial price × 2 / life of the item in years Accumulate the total depreciation Display the present years in a ListBox object Display the present values in a ListBox object Display the year depreciation in a ListBox object Display the total depreciation in a ListBox object
MakeObjectsVisible	Called Sub procedure	Change the Visible property of the result objects to true Clear the ListBox objects
mnuDisplay	Click	Create an instance of the second Form object Hide the first Form object Show the second Form object
mnuClear	Click	Reset the ListBox SelectedIndex property to −1, clearing the user's selection Set the Checked property of the RadioButton objects to false, clearing the user's selection Change the Visible property of all the result objects to false Clear all the ListBox objects
mnuExit	Click	Close the application

FIGURE 8-82 (continued)

EVENT PLANNING DOCUMENT

Program Name:	Developer:	Object:		Date:
Trends Menswear Inventory Depreciation	Corinne Hoisington	frmDisplayInventory		April 14, 2017
Object	**Event Trigger**	**Event Processing**		
frmDisplayInventory_Load	Load	Sort the inventory item array Display the inventory item array in sorted order in a ListBox object		
btnReturn	Click	Hide the second Form object Open the first Form object		

FIGURE 8-83

Guided Program Development

To design the user interface for the Trends Menswear Inventory Depreciation application and enter the code required to process each event in the program, complete the steps in this section.

NOTE TO THE LEARNER

In the following activity, you should complete the tasks within the specified steps. Each of the tasks is accompanied by a Hint Screen. The purpose of the Hint Screen is to indicate where you should perform the activity in the Visual Studio window and to remind you which method to use. If you need further help completing a step, refer to the figure identified by *ref:*.

Phase I: Design the Form

1

• **Create a New Windows Project** Open Visual Studio and then close the Start page. Tap or click the New Project button on the Standard toolbar. Begin a Windows Forms Application project and name the project `Depreciation`.

• **Name the Form Object** Select the Form object. Change the (Name) property of the Form object to `frmDepreciation`.

• **Assign a Title to the Form Object** Open the main Form object. Select the Form object and change the Text property to `Compute Depreciation by Method`.

• **Create the User Interface** Using the skills you have acquired in this course, create the user interface for the frmDepreciation Windows Form object, as shown in Figure 8-84a and Figure 8-84b.

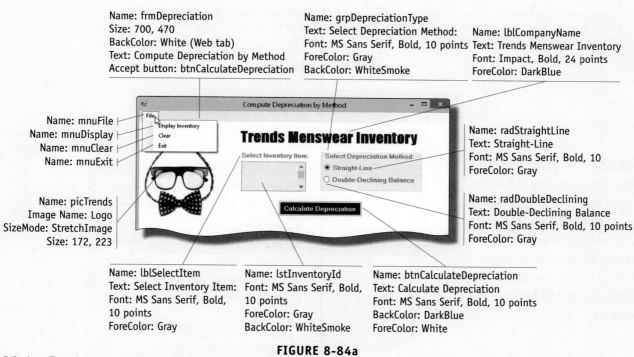

Name: frmDepreciation
Size: 700, 470
BackColor: White (Web tab)
Text: Compute Depreciation by Method
Accept button: btnCalculateDepreciation

Name: grpDepreciationType
Text: Select Depreciation Method:
Font: MS Sans Serif, Bold, 10 points
ForeColor: Gray
BackColor: WhiteSmoke

Name: lblCompanyName
Text: Trends Menswear Inventory
Font: Impact, Bold, 24 points
ForeColor: DarkBlue

Name: mnuFile
Name: mnuDisplay
Name: mnuClear
Name: mnuExit

Name: picTrends
Image Name: Logo
SizeMode: StretchImage
Size: 172, 223

Name: radStraightLine
Text: Straight-Line
Font: MS Sans Serif, Bold, 10
ForeColor: Gray

Name: radDoubleDeclining
Text: Double-Declining Balance
Font: MS Sans Serif, Bold, 10 points
ForeColor: Gray

Name: lblSelectItem
Text: Select Inventory Item:
Font: MS Sans Serif, Bold, 10 points
ForeColor: Gray

Name: lstInventoryId
Font: MS Sans Serif, Bold, 10 points
ForeColor: Gray
BackColor: WhiteSmoke

Name: btnCalculateDepreciation
Text: Calculate Depreciation
Font: MS Sans Serif, Bold, 10 points
BackColor: DarkBlue
ForeColor: White

FIGURE 8-84a

© iStock.omc/flyparade

(continues)

Guided Program Development *continued*

Name: lblPresentValue
Text: Present Value
Font: MS Sans Serif, Bold,
10 points
ForeColor: Gray
Visible: False

Name: lblItem
Text: 30 X's
Align: Form Horizontal Center
Font: MS Sans Serif, Bold, 10 points
ForeColor: Gray
Visible: False

Name: lblQuantity
Text: 9 X's
Align: Form Horizontal Center
Font: MS Sans Serif, Bold, 10 points
ForeColor: Gray
Visible: False

Name: lblYearDepreciation
Text: Year Depreciation
Font: MS Sans Serif, Bold, 10 points
ForeColor: Gray
Visible: False

Name: lblYear
Text: Present Year
Font: MS Sans Serif, Bold,
10 points
ForeColor: Gray
Visible: False

The depreciation of the item: Mannequins
Quantity: 41

Present Year	Present Value	Year Depreciation	Total Depreciation
1	$345.00	$69.00	$69.00
2	$276.00	$69.00	$138.00
3	$207.00	$69.00	$207.00
4	$138.00	$69.00	$276.00
5	$69.00	$69.00	$345.00

Name: lblTotalDepreciation
Text: Total Depreciation
Font: MS Sans Serif, Bold, 10 points
ForeColor: Gray
Visible: False

Name: lstYear
Visible: False
Size: 88,84
Align: All Form Horizontal
Center, Equal Spacing
ForeColor: Gray

Name: lstPresentValue
Visible: False
Size: 78,84
Align: All Form Horizontal
Center, Equal Spacing
ForeColor: Gray

Name: lstYearDepreciation
Visible: False
Size: 78,84
Align: All Form Horizontal
Center, Equal Spacing
ForeColor: Gray

Name: lstTotalDepreciation
Visible: False
Size: 78,84
Align: All Form Horizontal
Center, Equal Spacing
ForeColor: Gray

FIGURE 8-84b

2

• **Add a Second Form Object** Tap or click Project on the menu bar, and then tap or click Add Windows Form. In the Add New Item dialog box, tap or click Windows Form. Name the Windows Form object `frmDisplayInventory.vb`. Tap or click the Add button *(ref: Figure 8-67)*.

- **Assign a Title to the Form Object** Open the frmDisplayInventory.vb object. Select the Form object and change the Text property to Sorted Inventory Listing.

- **Create the User Interface for the Windows Form Object** Using the skills you have learned in this course, create the user interface for the frmDisplayInventory Windows Form object, as shown in Figure 8-85.

Name: frmDisplayInventory
Size: 387, 419
BackColor: White
AcceptButton: btnReturn
Text: Sorted Inventory Listing

Name: picMan2
Image: Logo.jpg
SizeMode: StretchImage
Size: 109,90

Name: lblSortedInventory
Text: Trends Menswear Inventory
Font: MS Sans Serif,
16 points
ForeColor: DarkBlue
Align: Form Horizontal Center

Name: lstDisplay
Font: MS Sans Serif, Bold, 12
points
ForeColor: Gray
Align: Form Horizontal
Center
BackColor: WhiteSmoke

Name: btnReturn
Text: Return to Application
Font: MS Sans Serif, Bold, 10
points
BackColor: WhiteSmoke
ForeColor: White
Align: Form Horizontal Center

© iStock.com/flyparade

FIGURE 8-85

(continues)

Phase 2: Code the Application

3

● **Code the Comments** Tap or click the View Code button to begin coding the application in frmDepreciation
.vb. Type the first four standard comments at the top of the code window. Insert the command Option Strict
On at the beginning of the code to turn on strict type checking.

```
                                    HINT
1   ⊟' Program Name: Trends Menswear Depreciation Windows Application
2    ' Author:       Corinne Hoisington
3    ' Date:         April 14, 2017
4    ' Purpose:      The Trends Menswear Inventory Windows Application determines
5    '               the depreciation based on a 5 year life of items in inventory
6    '               using the straight-line and double-declining balance methods.
7
8    Option Strict On
     5 references
9   ⊟Public Class frmDepreciation
```

● **Initialize the Variables** Enter the comment shown in the corresponding Hint Screen and
initialize the class module-level variables in the code window within the frmDepreciation class
(ref: Figure 8-29).

```
                                    HINT
9    ⊟Public Class frmDepreciation
10
11        ' Class Level Private variables
12        Private _intLifeOfItems As Integer = 5
13        Public Shared _intSizeOfArray As Integer = 7
14        Public Shared _strInventoryItem(_intSizeOfArray) As String
15        Private _strItemId(_intSizeOfArray) As String
16        Private _decInitialPrice(_intSizeOfArray) As Decimal
17        Private _intQuantity(_intSizeOfArray) As Integer
```

● **Code the frmDepreciation Load Event** To initialize the variables of this event, type the comments and
code shown in the corresponding Hint Screen.

```
                                    HINT
19   ⊟    Private Sub frmDepreciation_Load(ByVal sender As System.Object, ByVal e As System.EventArgs) Handles MyBase.Load
20            ' The frmDepreciation load event reads the inventory text file and
21            ' fills the Listbox object with the inventory items
22
23            ' Initialize an instance of the StreamReader object and declare variables
24            Dim objReader As IO.StreamReader
25            Dim strLocationAndNameOfFile As String = "d:\inventory.txt"
26            Dim intCount As Integer = 0
27            Dim intFill As Integer
28            Dim strFileError As String - "The file is not available. Restart when the file is available."
```

- **Code the If ... Else Statements** Inside the frmDepreciation_Load event, after the variables are initialized, insert an If statement that validates whether the inventory.txt file exists. The inventory file is opened from the USB drive and assigned to the instance of the StreamReader named objReader. The Do While loop continues to read each item in the file until the file is completed (Peek < > –1). Each line of the file is read and assigned to a unique array subscript by the ReadLine command. The counter intCount increments after each iteration of the loop to increase the subscript number *(ref: Figures 8-55, 8-56, 8-57)*.

```
                                        HINT
29
30              ' Verify the file exists
31              If IO.File.Exists(strLocationAndNameOfFile) Then
32                  objReader = IO.File.OpenText(strLocationAndNameOfFile)
33                  ' Read the file line by line until the file is completed
34                  Do While objReader.Peek <> -1
35                      _strInventoryItem(intCount) = objReader.ReadLine()
36                      _strItemId(intCount) = objReader.ReadLine()
37                      _decInitialPrice(intCount) = Convert.ToDecimal(objReader.ReadLine())
38                      _intQuantity(intCount) = Convert.ToInt32(objReader.ReadLine())
39                      intCount += 1
40                  Loop
```

- **Fill the ListBox Object** Inside the frmDepreciation load event, a For loop counts from the beginning of the array at the index of 0 until the end of the array is reached. The statement within the loop fills the inventory IDs in the lstInventoryId ListBox object. Because the file might not be found, include an Else statement to inform the user if the file is not available and close the application.

```
                                        HINT
41                  objReader.Close()
42
43                  ' The ListBox object is filled with the Inventory IDs
44                  For intFill = 0 To (_strItemId.Length - 1)
45                      lstInventoryId.Items.Add(_strItemId(intFill))
46                  Next
47              Else
48                  MsgBox(strFileError, , "Error")
49                  Close()
50              End If
51
52          End Sub
53
```

(continues)

Guided Program Development   *continued*

● **Code the btnCalculateDepreciation_Click Event** Tap or click the frmDepreciation.vb [Design] tab. Double-tap or double-click the Calculate Depreciation Button object. The btnCalculateDepreciation_Click event opens. If the lstInventoryId ListBox and one of the RadioButton objects have been selected by the user, one of the depreciation methods is called. A message box is displayed to remind the user to select one of the objects if they are left blank.

HINT

```
54    Private Sub btnCalculateDepreciation_Click(ByVal sender As System.Object, ByVal e As System.EventArgs) Handles btnCalculate
55        ' The btnCalculateDepreciation click event calls the depreciation Sub procedures
56        ' Declare variables
57        Dim intSelectedItemId As Integer
58        Dim strMissingSelection As String = "Missing Selection"
59        Dim strSelectDepreciationError As String = "Select a Depreciation Method"
60        Dim strSelectInventoryItemIDError As String = "Select an Inventory Item ID"
61
62        ' If the ListBox and a Depreciation RadioButton object are selected,
63        ' call the depreciation procedures
64        If lstInventoryId.SelectedIndex >= 0 Then
65            intSelectedItemId = lstInventoryId.SelectedIndex
66            If radStraightLine.Checked Then
67                StraightLineDepreciation(intSelectedItemId)
68            ElseIf radDoubleDeclining.Checked Then
69                DoubleDecliningDepreciation(intSelectedItemId)
70            Else
71                MsgBox(strSelectDepreciationError, , strMissingSelection)
72            End If
73        Else
74            MsgBox(strSelectInventoryItemIDError, , strMissingSelection)
75        End If
76
77    End Sub
```

• **Code the StraightLineDepreciation Sub Procedure** Begin a new Sub procedure that calculates the depreciation when the straight-line method is selected. The result objects are displayed in the MakeObjectsVisible Sub procedure. The cost of straight-line depreciation is calculated and displayed in the ListBox objects on the Form object *(ref: Figure 8-61)*.

```vbnet
                                        HINT
79   ⊟        Private Sub StraightLineDepreciation(ByVal intItemId As Integer)
80                  'This Sub procedure computes and displays the straight line depreciation for the item selected
81                  ' Declare variables
82                  Dim intStraightPresentYear As Integer
83                  Dim decStraightPresentYearValue As Decimal = 0
84                  Dim decStraightDepreciation As Decimal
85                  Dim decStraightTotal As Decimal
86                  Dim strDepreciationItem As String = "The depreciation of the item: "
87                  Dim strQuantityMessage As String = "Quantity: "
88
89                  ' The procedure MakeObjectsVisible is called to display the Form objects
90                  MakeObjectsVisible()
91                  ' Display the item and quantity of the selected item
92                  lblItem.Text = strDepreciationItem & _strInventoryItem(intItemId)
93                  lblQuantity.Text = strQuantityMessage & _intQuantity(intItemId).ToString()
94                  ' The formula for straight-line depreciation
95                  decStraightDepreciation = _decInitialPrice(intItemId) / _intLifeOfItems
96                  decStraightPresentYearValue = _decInitialPrice(intItemId)
97
98                  ' The loop repeats for the life of the items
99                  For intStraightPresentYear = 1 To _intLifeOfItems
100                     ' Accumulates the total of depreciation
101                     decStraightTotal += decStraightDepreciation
102                     ' Displays the depreciation amounts
103                     lstYear.Items.Add(intStraightPresentYear.ToString())
104                     lstPresentValue.Items.Add(decStraightPresentYearValue.ToString("C"))
105                     lstYearDepreciation.Items.Add(decStraightDepreciation.ToString("C"))
106                     lstTotalDepreciation.Items.Add(decStraightTotal.ToString("C"))
107                     decStraightPresentYearValue -= decStraightDepreciation
108                 Next
109
110           End Sub
```

(continues)

- **Code the DoubleDecliningDepreciation Sub Procedure** Begin a new Sub procedure that calculates the depreciation when the double-declining balance method is selected. The result objects are displayed in the MakeObjectsVisible Sub procedure. The cost of double-declining balance depreciation is calculated and displayed in the ListBox objects on the Form object *(ref: Figure 8-63)*.

HINT

```
112    Private Sub DoubleDecliningDepreciation(ByVal intItemId As Integer)
113        ' This Sub procedure computes and displays the double declining
114        ' balance depreciation for the item selected
115        Dim intDoublePresentYear As Integer
116        Dim decDoublePresentYearValue As Decimal = 0
117        Dim decDoubleDepreciation As Decimal
118        Dim decDoubleTotal As Decimal
119
120        ' The procedure MakeObjectsVisible is called to display the Form objects
121        MakeObjectsVisible()
122        ' Display the item and quantity of the selected item
123        lblItem.Text = "The depreciation of the item: " & _strInventoryItem(intItemId)
124        lblQuantity.Text = "Quantity: " & _intQuantity(intItemId).ToString()
125        decDoublePresentYearValue = _decInitialPrice(intItemId)
126
127        ' The loop repeats for the life of the items
128        For intDoublePresentYear = 1 To _intLifeOfItems
129            ' The formula for double-declining depreciation inside the loop to repeat the process
130            decDoubleDepreciation = (decDoublePresentYearValue * 2D) / _intLifeOfItems
131            ' Accumulates the total of depreciation
132            decDoubleTotal += decDoubleDepreciation
133            ' Displays the depreciation amounts
134            lstYear.Items.Add(intDoublePresentYear.ToString())
135            lstPresentValue.Items.Add(decDoublePresentYearValue.ToString("C"))
136            lstYearDepreciation.Items.Add(decDoubleDepreciation.ToString("C"))
137            lstTotalDepreciation.Items.Add(decDoubleTotal.ToString("C"))
138            decDoublePresentYearValue -= decDoubleDepreciation
139        Next
140
141    End Sub
```

• Code the MakeObjectsVisible Sub Procedure The Form objects that display the results are made visible. The ListBox objects are also cleared.

```
     2 references
143  ⊟   Private Sub MakeObjectsVisible()
144          ' This procedure displays the objects showing the results
145          lblItem.Visible = True
146          lblQuantity.Visible = True
147          lblYear.Visible = True
148          lstYear.Visible = True
149          lblPresentValue.Visible = True
150          lstPresentValue.Visible = True
151          lblYearDepreciation.Visible = True
152          lstYearDepreciation.Visible = True
153          lblTotalDepreciation.Visible = True
154          lstTotalDepreciation.Visible = True
155          ' The previous data is removed
156          lstYear.Items.Clear()
157          lstPresentValue.Items.Clear()
158          lstYearDepreciation.Items.Clear()
159          lstTotalDepreciation.Items.Clear()
160
161       End Sub
```

• Code the mnuDisplay_Click Event An instance of the second Form object, frmDisplayInventory, is named frmSecond. The first form is hidden and the second form is opened *(ref: Figure 8-71 and Figure 8-72)*.

```
163  ⊟   Private Sub mnuDisplay_Click(ByVal sender As System.Object, ByVal e As System.EventArgs) Handles mnuDisplay.Click
164          ' The mnuDisplay click event creates an instance of the frmDisplayInventory
165          Dim frmSecond As New frmDisplayInventory
166
167          'Hide this form and show the Display Inventory form
168          Hide()
169          frmSecond.ShowDialog()
170  .
171       End Sub
```

(continues)

● **Code the mnuClear_Click Event** The mnuClear_Click event clears the Form object for the next set of inputs.

HINT

```
        0 references
173  ⊟   Private Sub mnuClear_Click(ByVal sender As System.Object, ByVal e As System.EventArgs) Handles mnuClear.Click
174          ' The mnuClear click event clears and resets the form
175          lstInventoryId.SelectedIndex = -1
176          radStraightLine.Checked = False
177          radDoubleDeclining.Checked = False
178          lblItem.Visible = False
179          lblQuantity.Visible = False
180          lblYear.Visible = False
181          lstYear.Visible = False
182          lstYear.Items.Clear()
183          lblPresentValue.Visible = False
184          lstPresentValue.Visible = False
185          lstPresentValue.Items.Clear()
186          lblYearDepreciation.Visible = False
187          lstYearDepreciation.Visible = False
188          lstYearDepreciation.Items.Clear()
189          lblTotalDepreciation.Visible = False
190          lstTotalDepreciation.Visible = False
191          lstTotalDepreciation.Items.Clear()
192
193      End Sub
```

● **Code the mnuExit_Click Event** The mnuExit_Click event closes the application.

HINT

```
195  ⊟   Private Sub mnuExit_Click(ByVal sender As System.Object, ByVal e As System.EventArgs) Handles mnuExit.Click
196          ' The mnuExit click event closes the application
197          Application.Exit()
198
199      End Sub
200
201  End Class
```

The frmDepreciation code is completed (Figure 8-86).

RESULT OF STEP 3

```
1    ⊟' Program Name:  Trends Menswear Depreciation Windows Application
2     ' Author:        Corinne Hoisington
3     ' Date:          April 14, 2017
4     ' Purpose:       The Trends Menswear Inventory Windows Application determines
5     '                the depreciation based on a 5 year life of items in inventory
6     └                using the straight-line and double-declining balance methods.
7
8      Option Strict On
       5 references
9    ⊟Public Class frmDepreciation
10
11         ' Class Level Private variables
12       ─ Private _intLifeOfItems As Integer = 5
13         Public Shared _intSizeOfArray As Integer = 7
14         Public Shared _strInventoryItem(_intSizeOfArray) As String
15         Private _strItemId(_intSizeOfArray) As String
16         Private _decInitialPrice(_intSizeOfArray) As Decimal
17       ─ Private _intQuantity(_intSizeOfArray) As Integer ─
18
           0 references
19   ⊟     Private Sub frmDepreciation_Load(ByVal sender As System.Object, ByVal e As System.EventArgs) Handles MyBase.Load
20             ' The frmDepreciation load event reads the inventory text file and
21             ' fills the Listbox object with the inventory items
22
23             ' Initialize an instance of the StreamReader object and declare variables
24             Dim objReader As IO.StreamReader
25             Dim strLocationAndNameOfFile As String = "e:\inventory.txt"
26             Dim intCount As Integer = 0
27             Dim intFill As Integer
28           ─Dim strFileError As String = "The file is not available. Restart when the file is available."
29
30             ' Verify the file exists
31             If IO.File.Exists(strLocationAndNameOfFile) Then
32                 objReader = IO.File.OpenText(strLocationAndNameOfFile)
33                 ' Read the file line by line until the file is completed
34                 Do While objReader.Peek <> -1
35                     _strInventoryItem(intCount) = objReader.ReadLine()
36                     _strItemId(intCount) = objReader.ReadLine()
37                     _decInitialPrice(intCount) = Convert.ToDecimal(objReader.ReadLine())
38                     _intQuantity(intCount) = Convert.ToInt32(objReader.ReadLine())
39                     intCount += 1
40                 Loop
41                 objReader.Close()
42
43                 ' The ListBox object is filled with the Inventory IDs
44                 For intFill = 0 To (_strItemId.Length - 1)
45                     lstInventoryId.Items.Add(_strItemId(intFill))
46                 Next
47             Else
48                 MsgBox(strFileError, , "Error")
49                 Close()
50             End If
51
52         End Sub
53
```

FIGURE 8-86 (continues)

(continues)

Guided Program Development *continued*

```
54    Private Sub btnCalculateDepreciation_Click(ByVal sender As System.Object, ByVal e As System.EventArgs) Handles btnCalculateDepreciation.Click
55        ' The btnCalculateDepreciation click event calls the depreciation Sub procedures
56        ' Declare variables
57        Dim intSelectedItemId As Integer
58        Dim strMissingSelection As String = "Missing Selection"
59        Dim strSelectDepreciationError As String = "Select a Depreciation Method"
60        Dim strSelectInventoryItemIDError As String = "Select an Inventory Item ID"
61
62        ' If the ListBox and a Depreciation RadioButton object are selected,
63        ' call the depreciation procedures
64        If lstInventoryId.SelectedIndex >= 0 Then
65            intSelectedItemId = lstInventoryId.SelectedIndex
66            If radStraightLine.Checked Then
67                StraightLineDepreciation(intSelectedItemId)
68            ElseIf radDoubleDeclining.Checked Then
69                DoubleDecliningDepreciation(intSelectedItemId)
70            Else
71                MsgBox(strSelectDepreciationError, , strMissingSelection)
72            End If
73        Else
74            MsgBox(strSelectInventoryItemIDError, , strMissingSelection)
75        End If
76
77    End Sub
78
      1 reference
79    Private Sub StraightLineDepreciation(ByVal intItemId As Integer)
80        'This Sub procedure computes and displays the straight line depreciation for the item selected
81        ' Declare variables
82        Dim intStraightPresentYear As Integer
83        Dim decStraightPresentYearValue As Decimal = 0
84        Dim decStraightDepreciation As Decimal
85        Dim decStraightTotal As Decimal
86        Dim strDepreciationItem As String = "The depreciation of the item: "
87        Dim strQuantityMessage As String = "Quantity: "
88
89        ' The procedure MakeObjectsVisible is called to display the Form objects
90        MakeObjectsVisible()
91        ' Display the item and quantity of the selected item
92        lblItem.Text = strDepreciationItem & _strInventoryItem(intItemId)
93        lblQuantity.Text = strQuantityMessage & _intQuantity(intItemId).ToString()
94        ' The formula for straight-line depreciation
95        decStraightDepreciation = _decInitialPrice(intItemId) / _intLifeOfItems
96        decStraightPresentYearValue = _decInitialPrice(intItemId)
97
98        ' The loop repeats for the life of the items
99        For intStraightPresentYear = 1 To _intLifeOfItems
100           ' Accumulates the total of depreciation
101           decStraightTotal += decStraightDepreciation
102           ' Displays the depreciation amounts
103           lstYear.Items.Add(intStraightPresentYear.ToString())
104           lstPresentValue.Items.Add(decStraightPresentYearValue.ToString("C"))
```

FIGURE 8-86 (continues)

```
105            lstYearDepreciation.Items.Add(decStraightDepreciation.ToString("C"))
106            lstTotalDepreciation.Items.Add(decStraightTotal.ToString("C"))
107            decStraightPresentYearValue -= decStraightDepreciation
108        Next
109
110    End Sub
111

       1 reference
112  ⊟ Private Sub DoubleDecliningDepreciation(ByVal intItemId As Integer)
113        ' This Sub procedure computes and displays the double declining
114        ' balance depreciation for the item selected
115        Dim intDoublePresentYear As Integer
116        Dim decDoublePresentYearValue As Decimal = 0
117        Dim decDoubleDepreciation As Decimal
118        Dim decDoubleTotal As Decimal
119
120        ' The procedure MakeObjectsVisible is called to display the Form objects
121        MakeObjectsVisible()
122        ' Display the item and quantity of the selected item
123        lblItem.Text = "The depreciation of the item: " & _strInventoryItem(intItemId)
124        lblQuantity.Text = "Quantity: " & _intQuantity(intItemId).ToString()
125        decDoublePresentYearValue = _decInitialPrice(intItemId)
126
127        ' The loop repeats for the life of the items
128        For intDoublePresentYear = 1 To _intLifeOfItems
129            ' The formula for double-declining depreciation inside the loop to repeat the process
130            decDoubleDepreciation = (decDoublePresentYearValue * 2D) / _intLifeOfItems
131            ' Accumulates the total of depreciation
132            decDoubleTotal += decDoubleDepreciation
133            ' Displays the depreciation amounts
134            lstYear.Items.Add(intDoublePresentYear.ToString())
135            lstPresentValue.Items.Add(decDoublePresentYearValue.ToString("C"))
136            lstYearDepreciation.Items.Add(decDoubleDepreciation.ToString("C"))
137            lstTotalDepreciation.Items.Add(decDoubleTotal.ToString("C"))
138            decDoublePresentYearValue -= decDoubleDepreciation
139        Next
140
141    End Sub
142

       2 references
143  ⊟ Private Sub MakeObjectsVisible()
144        ' This procedure displays the objects showing the results
145        lblItem.Visible = True
146        lblQuantity.Visible = True
147        lblYear.Visible = True
148        lstYear.Visible = True
149        lblPresentValue.Visible = True
150        lstPresentValue.Visible = True
151        lblYearDepreciation.Visible = True
152        lstYearDepreciation.Visible = True
153        lblTotalDepreciation.Visible = True
154        lstTotalDepreciation.Visible = True
155        ' The previous data is removed
156        lstYear.Items.Clear()
```

FIGURE 8-86 (continues)

(continues)

```
157          lstPresentValue.Items.Clear()
158          lstYearDepreciation.Items.Clear()
159          lstTotalDepreciation.Items.Clear()
160
161      End Sub
162
         0 references
163 ⊟   Private Sub mnuDisplay_Click(ByVal sender As System.Object, ByVal e As System.EventArgs) Handles mnuDisplay.Click
164          ' The mnuDisplay click event creates an instance of the frmDisplayInventory
165          Dim frmSecond As New frmDisplayInventory
166
167          'Hide this form and show the Display Inventory form
168          Hide()
169          frmSecond.ShowDialog()
170
171      End Sub
172
         0 references
173 ⊟   Private Sub mnuClear_Click(ByVal sender As System.Object, ByVal e As System.EventArgs) Handles mnuClear.Click
174          ' The mnuClear click event clears and resets the form
175          lstInventoryId.SelectedIndex = -1
176          radStraightLine.Checked = False
177          radDoubleDeclining.Checked = False
178          lblItem.Visible = False
179          lblQuantity.Visible = False
180          lblYear.Visible = False
181          lstYear.Visible = False
182          lstYear.Items.Clear()
183          lblPresentValue.Visible = False
184          lstPresentValue.Visible = False
185          lstPresentValue.Items.Clear()
186          lblYearDepreciation.Visible = False
187          lstYearDepreciation.Visible = False
188          lstYearDepreciation.Items.Clear()
189          lblTotalDepreciation.Visible = False
190          lstTotalDepreciation.Visible = False
191          lstTotalDepreciation.Items.Clear()
192
193      End Sub
194
         0 references
195 ⊟   Private Sub mnuExit_Click(ByVal sender As System.Object, ByVal e As System.EventArgs) Handles mnuExit.Click
196          ' The mnuExit click event closes the application
197          Application.Exit()
198
199      End Sub
200
201  End Class
202
```

FIGURE 8-86 (continued)

● **Code the Comments for the Second Form, frmDisplayInventory** Tap or click the frmDisplayInventory tab to return to Design view. Double-click the Form object to open the code window. Code the comments for the form processing. Code the Option Strict On statement.

```
              HINT
1    ⊟' The frmDisplayInventory class is opened by frmDepreciation
2     | ' and displays the inventory file in sorted order
3
4      Option Strict On
       2 references
5    ⊟Public Class frmDisplayInventory
```

● **Code the frmDisplayInventory_Load Event** The _strInventoryItem array is sorted. The For Each loop starts at the beginning element and continues until the last item is displayed in the ListBox object *(ref: Figure 8-35).*

```
                                    HINT
5    ⊟Public Class frmDisplayInventory
6
       0 references
7    ⊟  Private Sub frmDisplayInventory_Load(ByVal sender As System.Object, ByVal e As System.EventArgs) Handles MyBase.Load
8          ' The frmDisplayInventory load event is a second forms that
9          ' displays the sorted inventory items
10
11         Dim strItem As String
12
13         ' Sorts the _strInventoryItem array
14         Array.Sort(frmDepreciation._strInventoryItem)
15
16         ' Displays the _strInventoryItem array
17         For Each strItem In frmDepreciation._strInventoryItem
18             lstDisplay.Items.Add(strItem)
19         Next
20
21     End Sub
```

(continues)

Guided Program Development   *continued*

● **Code the btnReturn_Click Event** Tap or click the frmDisplayInventory [Design]* tab. Double-click the
Return to Application button. Inside the btnReturn Click event, create an instance of the frmDepreciation
Form object named frmFirst. Hide the second form and open the first form.

HINT

```
23        Private Sub btnReturn_Click(ByVal sender As System.Object, ByVal e As System.EventArgs) Handles btnReturn.Click
24            ' This Sub procedure opens the first form
25            Dim frmFirst As New frmDepreciation
26
27            Hide()
28            frmFirst.ShowDialog()
29
30        End Sub
31    End Class
```

The frmDisplayInventory code is completed (Figure 8-87).

RESULT OF STEP 4

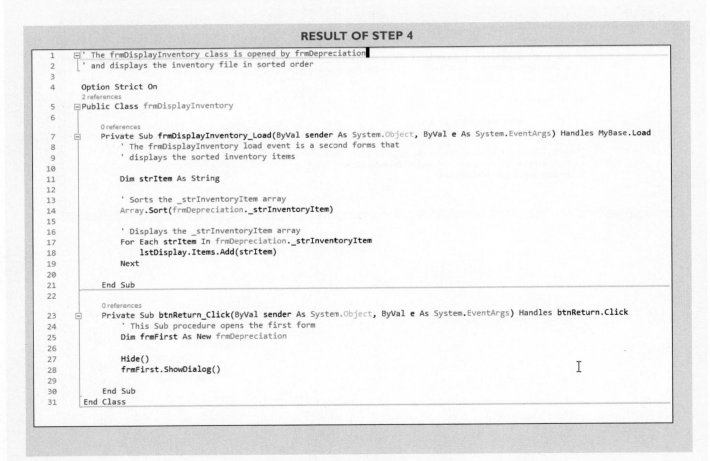

```
1     ' The frmDisplayInventory class is opened by frmDepreciation
2     ' and displays the inventory file in sorted order
3
4     Option Strict On
      2 references
5     Public Class frmDisplayInventory
6
          0 references
7         Private Sub frmDisplayInventory_Load(ByVal sender As System.Object, ByVal e As System.EventArgs) Handles MyBase.Load
8             ' The frmDisplayInventory load event is a second forms that
9             ' displays the sorted inventory items
10
11            Dim strItem As String
12
13            ' Sorts the _strInventoryItem array
14            Array.Sort(frmDepreciation._strInventoryItem)
15
16            ' Displays the _strInventoryItem array
17            For Each strItem In frmDepreciation._strInventoryItem
18                lstDisplay.Items.Add(strItem)
19            Next
20
21        End Sub
22
          0 references
23        Private Sub btnReturn_Click(ByVal sender As System.Object, ByVal e As System.EventArgs) Handles btnReturn.Click
24            ' This Sub procedure opens the first form
25            Dim frmFirst As New frmDepreciation
26
27            Hide()
28            frmFirst.ShowDialog()
29
30        End Sub
31    End Class
```

FIGURE 8-87

Summary

In this chapter you have learned to create a Windows application using arrays and data files. The items listed in the table in Figure 8-88 include all the new Visual Studio and Visual Basic skills you have learned in this chapter.

Visual Basic Skills		
Skill	**Figure Number**	**Video Number**
Examine the Trends Menswear Depreciation Application	Figure 8-1	Video 8-1
Read Data from a Text File	Figure 8-53	Video 8-2
Use Multiple Form Objects	Figure 8-66	Video 8-3

FIGURE 8-88

Learn Online

Reinforcement activities and resources are available at no additional cost on www.CengageBrain.com. Visit http://solutions.cengage.com/ctdownloads/ for detailed instructions about accessing the available resources at the Student Companion Site.

Knowledge Check

1. Using implicit sizing, assign the integers 29, 30, 31, 32, 34, and 36 to an array named intCommonPantSizes.

2. What is the upper-bound index of an array whose size is 99?

3. Write a statement that assigns the length of an array named strSongName to a variable named intLetterCount.

4. Write a line of code that initializes an array named intEven with the first five even numbers, starting with 0.

5. Answer the following questions about the following initialized array:
   Dim strCity(7) as String

   a. Assign Minneapolis to the first array location. What is the index number?

   b. Assign Los Angeles to the fourth location in the array. What would the assignment statement look like?

   c. What value does strCityNames.Length have?

   d. How many cities can this array hold?

   e. What would happen if you assigned strCityNames(8) = "Dallas"?

6. Can you have a Boolean data type array?

7. Write a line of code that assigns the values Jon Snow, Tyrion Lannister, and Cersei to the elements in the array strGameOfThrones().

8. Which of the three main characters in question 7 would be assigned to strGameOfThrones(1)?

9. What is the lower index of an array?

10. Write a statement that assigns the length of an array named intMovieTimes to intSpan.

11. Write a statement that assigns the elements shown in Figure 8-89 to a two-dimensional array with implicit sizing named intPinNumbers.

1659	2916	9876	3928
1117	9665	5397	4488
1211	0767	2956	2041

FIGURE 8-89

Debugging Exercises

12. How many elements can be stored in the array in Figure 8-90?

```
Dim decRoomSize(4, 6) As Decimal
```
FIGURE 8-90

13. Write a statement that assigns the value 17.3 to the last item in the array in question 12.

14. Write a statement that assigns the first line of an opened text file to the first element in an array named strHobbit.

15. Write a statement that opens a text file named E:\accesscodes.txt and assigns the instance of the StreamReader to objReader.

16. Write a Sort statement to sort an array named strStreetNames.

17. If a binary search returns a negative value, what does that mean?

18. What is the default value of the elements in an array called intTopSpeed()?

19. Write the statement that hides the Windows Form object that is currently open in an application.

20. Write the statement that would initialize the variable intFinalExam as a Public Shared class-level variable that can be accessed in other Windows Form objects.

Debugging Exercises

1. Correct the lines of code in Figure 8-91.

```
Dim intJellyBeans() As Integer = (23, 77, 89, 124, 25)
ReDim intJellyBeans(10) As Integer
```
FIGURE 8-91

2. Correct the line of code in Figure 8-92.

```
Dim strHighwayNumbers() As String = {95, 81, 605, 5}
```
FIGURE 8-92

(continues)

3. Rewrite the code shown in Figure 8-93 to fix any errors.

```
Dim strFriends(4) = {"Brea", "Eric", "Daniel", "Ryan", "Brittany"}
```

FIGURE 8-93

4. Rewrite the code shown in Figure 8-94 to fix any errors.

```
objReader = IO.File.OpenText{E:\testresults.txt}
```

FIGURE 8-94

5. Rewrite the code shown in Figure 8-95 to fix any errors.

```
For Each intPulseRate In intHeartRate()
        lstPulse.Items.Add(intHeartRate)

Next
```

FIGURE 8-95

6. What exception would be produced by the code shown in Figure 8-96?

```
Dim intPlaneType(300) As Integer
Dim intCount As Integer

For intCount = 0 To 301
        intPlaneType(intCount)=767

Next
```

FIGURE 8-96

7. Rewrite the code in Figure 8-97 to read each line of a text file into an array named strFordModel.

```
Do While objReader.Peek = -1
        strFordModel(intCount) = objReader.ReadLine()
        intCount += 1

Loop
```

FIGURE 8-97

8. Rewrite the statement in Figure 8-98 to fix the error.

```
Dim intEvenNumbers(4),(8) As Integer
```

FIGURE 8-98

Program Analysis

1. What is the output of the code shown in Figure 8-99?

```
Private Sub btnSuperHero_Click(ByVal sender As System.Object, ByVal e As
System.EventArgs) Handles btnSuperHero.Click

        Dim strName() As String = {"Wonder Woman", "Superman", "Spiderman",
"Green Lantern", "Batman"}

        Array.Sort(strName)
        lblFavorite.Text = "My favorite super hero is " & strName(3)

End Sub
```

FIGURE 8-99

2. What are the values for every element by subscript in the array when the code in Figure 8-100 has been executed?

```
Dim intJellyBeans() As Integer = {23, 77, 89, 124, 25}
intJellyBeans(3) = 59
ReDim intJellyBeans(6)
intJellyBeans(2) = 24
```

FIGURE 8-100

3. What are the values for every element by subscript in the array when the code in Figure 8-101 has been executed?

```
Dim intJellyBeans() As Integer = {23, 77, 89, 124, 25}
intJellyBeans(3) = 59
ReDim Preserve intJellyBeans(6)
intJellyBeans(2) = 24
```

FIGURE 8-101

4. In the array shown in Figure 8-102, what value would be displayed for these lines of code?

```
Dim intInsuranceQuotes() As Integer = {456, 398, 412, 508, 612}
lblResult.Text = "The Insurance Rate is " & _
        (intInsuranceQuotes(intInsuranceQuotes.Length - 1))
```

FIGURE 8-102

(continues)

5. What is the output of the code shown in Figure 8-103?

```
Private Sub frmCompute_Load(ByVal sender As System.Object, ByVal e As System.
EventArgs) Handles MyBase.Load
    Dim intQuantity() As Integer = {17, 22, 3, 7, 51, 27}
    lstResults.Items.Add(intQuantity(3))
    lstResults.Items.Add(intQuantity(1) + intQuantity(3))
    lstResults.Items.Add(intQuantity(2 + 3))

End Sub
```

FIGURE 8-103

6. Write a For Each loop that displays every element of an array named strSongNames in a ListBox named lstDisplay. The loop variable is named strPlay.

7. Write a section of code that declares an array named strStocksOwned initialized with the values in the table in Figure 8-104. Sort the array. Write the contents of the sorted array to a new file named e:\stockportfolio.txt. Close the file when the file has been created with the stock names.

Stocks Owned
Microsoft
Cisco
Coca-Cola
Disney
Exxon
Merck

FIGURE 8-104

8. Write a For Next loop using the Length command that computes the sum of an array named decMaySales. After the loop, display the average in a Label object named lblAverage with the currency format. Use Length in the formula that computes the average.

9. What is the output of the code shown in Figure 8-105?

```
Dim intDoubleArray(3, 2) As Integer
Dim strDisplay As String = " "
Dim intOuter As Integer
Dim intInner As Integer

For intOuter = 0 To 3
    For intInner = 0 To 2
        intDoubleArray(intOuter, intInner) = intOuter + intInner
        strDisplay &= intDoubleArray(intOuter, intInner) & " "
    Next
Next
txtValues.Text = strDisplay
```

FIGURE 8-105

10. Write the code to implicitly size an array named strDay and to determine the day of the week (such as Monday) if the user enters the number 1 into a TextBox object named txtDayOfWeek and the number is converted to an Integer variable named intDay. The day of the week is displayed in a Label object named lblFullDay.

11. An array is declared with the following Dim statement: Dim intSeniorGrades(12,8). After values have been assigned to this array, write a loop named intCount that computes the sum of the seventh row of the array. Assign the sum to intSeniorSum.

12. In the statement lblDisplay.Text = "The result is" & frmInitial.intBloodPressure, what was the name of the original Windows Form object that initialized intBloodPressure?

Complete one or more of the following case programming assignments. Submit the program and materials you create to your instructor. The level of difficulty is indicated for each case programming assignment.

●	= Easiest
●●	= Intermediate
●●●	= Challenging

1 ●
FRANCHISE INVESTMENT

Design a Windows Desktop application and write the code that will execute according to the program requirements in Figure 8-106 and the Use Case Definition in Figure 8-107. Before writing the code, create an event-planning document for each event in the program. The completed program is shown in Figure 8-108.

REQUIREMENTS DOCUMENT

Date:	January 24, 2017
Date Submitted:	
Application Title:	Franchise Investment
Purpose:	This Windows application determines the average cost for investing in a franchise restaurant.
Program Procedures:	In a Windows application, use data in a text file to compute the average investment cost for purchasing a restaurant franchise. The file contains the restaurant name and investment cost. (Source: www.entrepreneur.com/franchises)
Algorithms, Processing, and Conditions:	1. A Windows application displays a title and image. The application opens a text file named franchise.txt from a USB drive (E:). 2. The program assigns the text file contents to two arrays that hold the restaurant name and the investment cost. The array currently has 10 elements. 3. When the Compute Average Investment button is tapped or clicked, the program displays the average cost of investing in a franchise. 4. The program displays the franchise restaurant names in the first ListBox object and their corresponding investment cost in the second ListBox object. 5. A File menu is displayed with the menu items Clear and Exit; the Clear item clears the result from the Form object and the Exit item exits the application.
Notes and Restrictions:	Close the opened text file before the program exits.
Comments:	1. The franchise.txt file is available on CengageBrain.com. 2. Obtain an image for this program from CengageBrain.com. The name of the picture on the Windows form is Franchise.

FIGURE 8-106

(continues)

Franchise Investment (continued)

USE CASE DEFINITION

1. The user taps or clicks the Compute Average Investment button.
2. The user views the listing of franchise restaurant names and investment values.
3. The user taps or clicks the Clear menu item to clear the results on the Windows Form object.
4. The user taps or clicks the Exit menu item to exit the application.

FIGURE 8-107

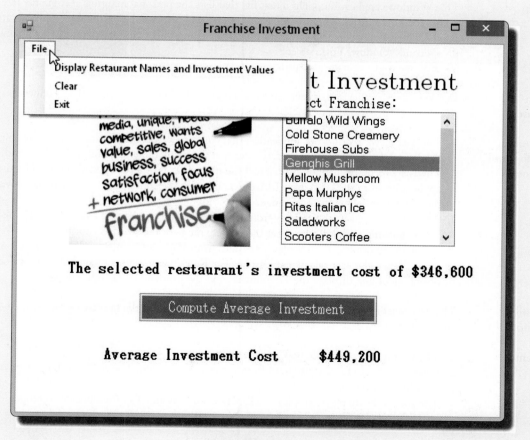

FIGURE 8-108

© iStock.com/Kaan Tanman

Case Programming Assignments

2   PERSONAL INCOME TAX COMPARISON BY COUNTRY

Design a Windows application and write the code that will execute according to the program requirements in Figure 8-109 and the Use Case Definition in Figure 8-110. Before writing the code, create an event planning document for each event in the program. The completed Windows application and other objects in the user interface are shown in Figure 8-111.

REQUIREMENTS DOCUMENT

Date:	April 2, 2017
Date Submitted:	
Application Title:	Personal Income Tax Comparison by Country
Purpose:	This Windows application opens a text file that lists the personal marginal income tax rate ranges for 17 countries. The user selects a country and displays the personal income tax rate range. A menu selection also can show the entire listing of the countries and the tax rate ranges on a second Windows Form object. (Source: www.gfmag.com/global-data/economic-data/personal-income-tax-rates)
Program Procedures:	In a Windows application, a user can view the individual income tax rate of 17 countries.
Algorithms, Processing, and Conditions:	1. The user views a Windows application that contains a title, graphic, and a ListBox object displaying the 17 individual tax rate ranges in the many modern countries in the world. The ListBox object is filled from a text file named tax.txt that is opened and read by the application from the USB drive (drive E:). The text file contains each country name with the current individual tax rate range.
	2. After the user selects the country from the ListBox object, and taps or clicks the Display Tax Range button, a label displays that the tax rate range in the selected country.
	3. A File menu displays the Display Tax Rates from Various Countries, Clear, and Exit menu items. When the user selects the Display Tax Rates menu item, a second Windows Form object opens and displays the 17 countries and their individual tax rate ranges.
Notes and Restrictions:	The user must select a country from the ListBox object before the tax rate of the selected country is displayed.
Comments:	1. The tax.txt file is available on CengageBrain.com.
	2. Obtain an image for this program from CengageBrain.com. The name of the picture on the Windows form is Tax.
	3. The second Form object displays a Display Countries and Tax Rate button to reopen the initial Form object.

FIGURE 8-109

(continues)

Case Programming Assignments

Personal Income Tax Comparison by Country (continued)

USE CASE DEFINITION

1. The user selects a city to display the individual tax rate range and taps or clicks the Display Tax Range button.
2. The user selects the Display Median Home Prices menu item to open a second form that displays the current median home prices in the 10 largest U.S. cities.
3. The user selects the Clear menu item to clear the form.
4. The user selects the Exit menu item to exit the application.

FIGURE 8-110

FIGURE 8-111

3

RAINFALL STATISTICS

Design a Windows application and write the code that will execute according to the program requirements in Figure 8-112 and the Use Case Definition in Figure 8-113. Before writing the code, create an event planning document for each event in the program. The completed Windows application and other objects in the user interface are shown in Figure 8-114.

REQUIREMENTS DOCUMENT

Date:	August 17, 2017
Date Submitted:	
Application Title:	Rainfall Statistics
Purpose:	This Windows application uses a text file of annual rainfall totals in Seattle for the years 2000 to 2017 to find the average rainfall and the rainiest year during the period. The user can also select a year within the range to display the total rainfall in inches that year.
Program Procedures:	A Windows application analyzes rainfall totals for the years 2000–2017. The user can select a year from the range and view the total rainfall in inches that year. The average rainfall for the range of years and the rainiest year are also displayed.
Algorithms, Processing, and Conditions:	1. The application first opens a text file of information from the National Weather Service. The file is named rain.txt, and it lists the total rainfall amounts in Seattle during the years 2000–2017. 2. The user can select a year in the range of data to view the total rainfall for that year. 3. When the user taps or clicks the Display Statistics button, the average rainfall for the years within the range and the rainiest year are displayed.
Notes and Restrictions:	Use two Sub methods to compute the average rainfall and the year with the most rainfall.
Comments:	1. The rain.txt file is available on CengageBrain.com. 2. Obtain an image for this program from CengageBrain.com. The name of the picture on the Windows form is Rain.

FIGURE 8-112

(continues)

Case Programming Assignments

Rainfall Statistics (continued)

USE CASE DEFINITION

1. From a list box, the user selects a year from the range of 2000–2017.
2. The program displays the inches of rainfall for that year.
3. The user taps or clicks the Display Statistics button to view the average rainfall for the years 2000–2017 and the rainiest year in the range.

FIGURE 8-113

FIGURE 8-114

4

FINAL AVERAGES FOR SEMESTER

Design a Windows application and write the code that will execute according to the program requirements in Figure 8-115. Before designing the user interface, create a Use Case Definition. Before writing the code, create an event planning document for each event in the program.

REQUIREMENTS DOCUMENT

Date:	May 17, 2017
Date Submitted:	
Application Title:	Final Averages for Semester
Purpose:	This Windows application allows an instructor to enter 13 project scores from a course and compute one student's grade for the semester. The application displays the student's final average for the semester when the two lowest scores are removed from the average. The 11 grades in sorted order and the final average are written to a text file named grades.txt, which is stored on a USB drive (drive E:).
Program Procedures:	In a Windows application, a student's grade is computed after the lowest two project scores are dropped. The results are written to a text file.
Algorithms, Processing, and Conditions:	1. The user views a Windows application that displays a title, a picture of a grade book, and an InputBox function that requests the 13 grades. 2. The program displays the final average for the semester with the two lowest scores dropped. 3. The program saves the sorted 11 grades and the final average to a text file named grades.txt, which is stored on the USB drive (drive E:).
Notes and Restrictions:	The project scores should be between 0 and 100.
Comments:	The image of a grade book should be selected from a picture available on the web.

FIGURE 8-115

5

••
PATIENT BLOOD PRESSURE REPORT

Design a Windows Desktop application and write the code that will execute according to the program requirements in Figure 5-116. Before designing the user interface, create a Use Case Definition. Before writing the code, create an event-planning document for each event in the program.

REQUIREMENTS DOCUMENT

Date:	February 14, 2016
Date Submitted:	
Application Title:	Patient Blood Pressure Report
Purpose:	This Windows application determines which patients have a systolic blood pressure reading that is considered too high.
Program Procedures:	In a Windows application, a text file of patient information named patient.txt is opened. The patients who have a systolic reading above 120 are written to a second text file named consult .txt for consultation. The systolic reading is the first number in blood pressure results.
Algorithms, Processing, and Conditions:	1. Each day, a text file named patient.txt is opened from the USB drive. The patient.txt file contains patient names, ID numbers, and systolic blood pressure results from a lab. 2. An opening graphic and title are displayed on the Windows Form object. 3. A File menu includes options to Display Patient Information, Clear, and Exit. Selecting the Display Patient Information option displays the contents of the patient.txt file on a second Windows Form object. 4. The patient names and systolic blood pressure levels are assigned to an array that holds 16 elements each. 5. Blood pressure systolic levels are tested to check whether the systolic number is above the value 120. 6. All patients who have a systolic level above 120 have their names and systolic results written to a text file named consult.txt on the USB drive. A nurse will contact these patients for further evaluation. 7. The program displays the number of patients who had a systolic level above 120 and the average systolic value of today's patients.
Notes and Restrictions:	n/a
Comments:	1. The patient.txt file is available on CengageBrain.com. 2. An appropriate image for this application should be selected from a picture available on the web.

FIGURE 8-116

6

WEDDING BAND

Design a Windows application and write the code that will execute according to the program requirements in Figure 8-117. Before designing the user interface, create a Use Case Definition. Before writing the code, create an event planning document for each event in the program.

REQUIREMENTS DOCUMENT

Date:	March 4, 2017
Date Submitted:	
Application Title:	Wedding Band
Purpose:	This Windows application opens a text file that contains song names ordered by popularity, their music genre, and the song length in minutes. The application determines how many songs from the playlist can be performed during the reception and displays the songs to be played. A list of songs in a particular genre can also be displayed.
Program Procedures:	In a Windows application, the user can enter the length of the reception and view the songs that will be performed from the playlist. The user can also select a type of music and have the appropriate songs on the playlist displayed in sorted order.
Algorithms, Processing, and Conditions:	1. The application opens and reads the values from a song list named songs.txt, which includes the title, genre, and length of each song. The length of each song is listed in the format *minutes. seconds*. For example, 3.16 represents 3 minutes and 16 seconds.
	2. The user can enter the length of the event and tap or click the Show Music List button to display the songs that will be performed from the playlist during the event.
	3. The user can tap or click a drop-down list of music genres, select a genre, and display the songs in the playlist from that genre.
	4. The user can select the Display Song Set menu item to open a second Form object that provides a choice of displaying the playlist in the current play order or as a sorted song list. The first Form object closes. The second Form object provides a button that the user can tap or click to return to the first Form object.
	5. The user can select the Clear menu item to clear and reset the first Form object. The user can also select the Exit menu item to close the application.
Notes and Restrictions:	n/a
Comments:	The songs.txt file is available on CengageBrain.com.

FIGURE 8-117

Case Programming Assignments

7 ●●●
SNOW CONE STAND

Create a requirements document and a Use Case Definition document and then design a Windows application based on the case project shown in Figure 8-118. Before writing the code, create an event planning document for each event in the program:

A local summer snow cone stand sells almost 5,000 snow cones per week in 10 flavors and saves this sales data in a text file. Create your own text file for your 10 favorite flavors of snow cones. Develop a Windows application that allows the manager of the stand to record how many snow cones were sold in each of the 10 flavors. The application will compute the total amount of snow cones sold for the week, the most popular flavor, the least popular flavor, and the average number of each flavor sold. Display the name of the snow cone stand within a logo on the Windows form. (Use two parallel arrays to hold the flavors and the amount sold of each flavor. You should use a different procedure for each of the results.)

FIGURE 8-118

8 ●●●
MOST POPULAR GAMES SOLD

Create a requirements document and a Use Case Definition document and then design a Windows application based on the case project shown in Figure 8-119. Before writing the code, create an event planning document for each event in the program:

If necessary, download the text file named games.txt from CengageBrain.com. The file contains the names of the nation's 10 top-selling video games and the domestic sales for each in millions of dollars. Open the text file and assign the contents to an array that identifies each game title. Allow the user to enter a title and determine if it is one of the 10 most popular video games. Display the domestic sales amount for the game if a match is made. Sort the array alphabetically by game title and display the sorted array on a second form. Compute the total amount of money made by the top 10 games and display the total on the second form.

FIGURE 8-119

9 ●●●
JOB GROWTH IN THE INFORMATION TECHNOLOGY FIELD

Create a requirements document and a Use Case Definition document and then design a Windows application based on the case project shown in Figure 8-120. Before writing the code, create an event planning document for each event in the program:

The U.S. Department of Labor has projected that the Information Technology job sector is growing. Enter the information from the following table into Notepad and save the text file.

Job Title	Jobs in 2015	Jobs Projected for 2020
Computer Developers	857,000	1,181,000
Computer Support	862,000	1,016,000
Systems Analysts	504,000	650,000
Database Administrators	119,000	154,000
Network Administrators	262,000	402,000
IT Managers	205,000	307,000

Calculate the changes in job numbers for each position and display the values. Compute the average number of positions that will be available in these fields each year during the period shown. Fill a ListBox object with the job titles so that the user can select a position and see the number of available jobs for the years 2015 and 2020 on a second form.

FIGURE 8-120

CHAPTER 9

Creating Web Applications

OBJECTIVES

You will have mastered the material in this chapter when you can:

- Create a web application

- Build a web form using ASP.NET 5

- Set web form properties

- Use the full screen view

- Add objects to a web form

- Add a DropDownList object

- Add a Calendar object

- Add a custom table for layout

- Validate data on web forms

- Use the <br> tag in Visual Basic code

- Use string manipulation methods in the String class

Introduction

Visual Studio allows you to create applications that can run on the web. Visual Basic 2015 includes ASP.NET 5 technology, with which you can create a user interface and a form for a web application. A **web form** is a page displayed in a web browser, such as Internet Explorer and Firefox, and requests data from the user. The Visual Basic tools and techniques you use will be familiar based on what you have learned thus far in this course.

A practical example of a web application developed using Visual Basic 2015 that can be delivered over the Internet is the project developed in this chapter — a cabin rental website that includes a Home page and Reservations page. This chapter project is based on a request from a resort called Big Bear Cabins to create a web application for guests who want to reserve cabins online. The application displays a webpage welcoming guests to the Big Bear Cabins, and then displays a web form that requests the guest's first and last names, email address, cabin selection(s), the number of nights the guest wants to stay, and the check-in date, as shown in Figure 9-1.

FIGURE 9-1

After the Home page is displayed in a browser, the user can tap or click the Reservations navigation button to complete the form by entering the requested information, and then tap or click the Submit button on the form. The application validates the information the user entered by confirming that the guest entered a name, provided an email address in the correct format, and selected a valid check-in date. If the user makes an error, a message identifies the error, as shown in Figure 9-2.

FIGURE 9-2

© 2015 - My ASP.NET Application

When the validation is complete, a reservation message is displayed that confirms the reservation information and calculates the total cost of the stay, as shown in Figure 9-3.

FIGURE 9-3

Create a Web Application

To develop a form such as the one shown in Figure 9-3 using Visual Basic, you create a web application, which is similar to creating a Windows application. When completed, a Visual Basic web application is displayed as one or more webpages in a browser.

A webpage that allows users to enter information on a web form, like the Big Bear Cabins page in this chapter, is considered a **dynamic** webpage because the user enters data and the webpage reacts to the data. In contrast, a webpage that displays information such as text and pictures with no interactivity is called a **static** webpage.

After a webpage is created, it is hosted (placed) on a web server. A **web server** is a computer that stores web documents and makes them available to people on the Internet. When you test your web application created using Visual Basic 2015, Visual Studio 2015 creates a temporary web server on your computer so you can view your webpage in a browser. When your webpage is ready for the world to see, it must be placed on an actual web server.

Active Server Page (ASP.NET 5) Platform

The ASP.NET 5 technology used with Visual Basic 2015 creates an **active server page (ASP)**. When describing an active server page, developers speak of the server-side computer and the client-side computer. The server-side computer is the web/cloud server that contains the actual active-server page and that will deliver the page to the client-side computer via the Internet. The client-side computer (often referred to as the client) runs the web browser that requests a webpage from the web server and displays the page. Visual Basic allows you to test the webpage using any installed browser such as Internet Explorer, Firefox, Google Chrome, Safari, and Windows Phone emulators. ASP.NET 5 optimizes the development of apps that are either deployed to the cloud or run on-premises on traditional computers, tablets, or mobile devices. Mobile devices can vary in size and form layout, and their screens are much smaller than desktop monitors. That means you may need to design completely different page layouts for them.

An active server page has two primary components: the generated code component that executes on the web server and the HTML component that is interpreted and executed by a web browser.

CONSIDER THIS

What is the purpose of HTML code?
Hypertext Markup Language (HTML) code is a standardized system for tagging text files to achieve font, color, graphic, and hyperlink effects on webpages displayed in browsers. You can view the HTML code on a webpage using the Internet Explorer browser by tapping or clicking View on the menu bar and then selecting Source.

When Visual Basic compiles an active server page using ASP.NET 5 technology, the page contains both the server-side code that will operate on data entered by the user, such as computing the total cost of a reservation in the Big Bear Cabins web application, and the HTML code that will display the page in a web browser on the client-side computer. When the page is requested by a browser, ASP sends the HTML code to the client requesting the webpage, where the page is displayed. The user can interact with the page by entering data or making selections, such as selecting the check-in date. When the user taps or clicks the Submit button, as in the Big

Bear Cabins application, the data is sent to the web server, where the coding within the application is executed. For example, the application code can calculate the total cabin cost and then display it on the web form.

When you develop an ASP page in Visual Basic, the work you do on the design page to create the user interface will generate the HTML code for the active server page. This code includes the HTML to format and display the page, and might include JavaScript code to perform certain processing, such as ensuring that a text box contains data.

The event handler code that you write in Visual Basic for an event, such as clicking the Submit button, is executed on the web server. When the user taps or clicks the Submit button on the Big Bear Cabins dynamic webpage, the control returns to the web server and the event handler code written by the developer is executed. This code can perform calculations and other processing as you have seen in previous chapters. When the event handler code changes an object displayed on the webpage, such as changing the Label object that contains the reservation message, that change immediately is displayed on the webpage.

Create a Dynamic Website Using Visual Basic

Using Visual Basic 2015 to create a dynamic website is similar to creating an interactive Windows application — you drag objects from the Toolbox and place them in a design window to build a form. Some of the web form objects are different from Windows objects because they are designed for online use. To create a Visual Basic web project for the Big Bear Cabins application, you can complete the following steps:

HEADS UP

To reopen a saved Visual Basic web application, open Visual Studio and then tap or click Open website on the File menu. Browse to the main project folder to open the website.

STEP 1 Start Visual Studio. Tap or click the File tab and then tap or click New Web Site.

The New Web Site dialog box opens (Figure 9-4).

New Web Site
dialog box

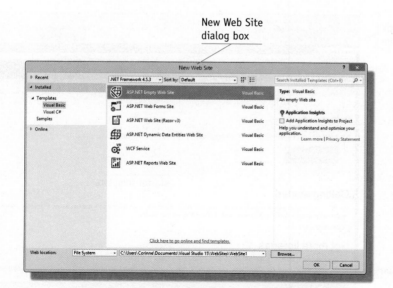

FIGURE 9-4

STEP 2 In the center pane, tap or click ASP.NET Web Forms Site. Use the Location text box to name the chapter project application `cabin`. As shown in Figure 9-5, the website is placed on the e: drive.

The ASP.NET website will be stored on the e: drive (Figure 9-5). The project name is lowercase because most website names use all lowercase letters.

ASP.NET Web Forms
Site selected

Cabin site
on drive e:

OK button

FIGURE 9-5

STEP 3 Tap or click the OK button in the New Web Site dialog box. If necessary, close the Toolbox.

The web application Design window opens (Figure 9-6). The Default.aspx page is displayed. On the scroll bar at the bottom of the page, the Design button is selected, showing that the Design window is displayed.

ScriptManager may show
Unnamed3 or another number

Default.aspx
page

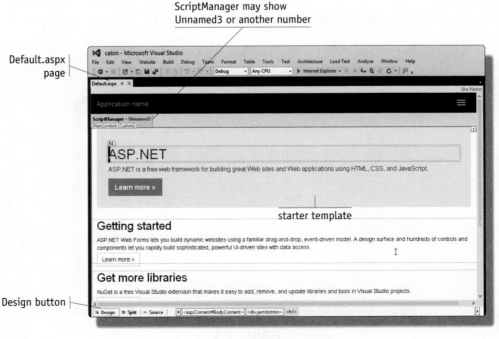

starter template

Design button

FIGURE 9-6

Use a Multipage Starter Template

Visual Basic 2015 provides a starter template to assist you in designing a webpage. The starter template allows you to create a new ASP.NET application with some layout and structure already implemented within it. When you first open the starter template, the Default.aspx page opens, but many other template pages are available with the starter template. Figure 9-7 shows the file named Site.master in the Solution Explorer. The **Site.master** file is a master page file that provides an overall layout for the site with headers, buttons, and footers. A **master page** is designed to create a consistent layout for the pages in your application. It defines the look and feel and standard behavior that you want for all of the pages in your website. If you change the color or title of the master page, all the pages in the site will reflect that same color and title. First design the master page and then customize the actual pages on the website. The website in this project has two pages. The default page (Default .aspx) serves as the Home page, which gives the traveler information about the Big Bear Cabins. The Reservations page (About.aspx) provides a reservation form that a traveler can use to make reservations.

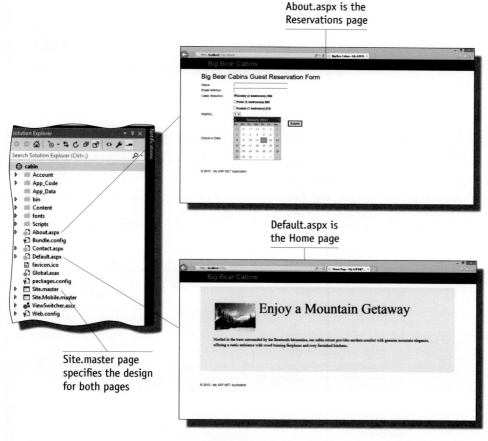

About.aspx is the
Reservations page

Default.aspx is
the Home page

Site.master page
specifies the design
for both pages

© iStock.com/gcoles

FIGURE 9-7

HEADS UP

If you prefer to design a webpage without using the starter templates, select ASP.NET Empty Web Site before you name the project when you create a new website project.

Customize the Master Page

The master page specifies the layout, color, and text that are repeated on the actual webpages that are displayed by the browser. A master page is basically defined as a nondisplaying page. It contains the information about the layout of the page, which will be used in the creation of body pages. It enables the user to create the layouts of the pages quickly and conveniently across the entire website. To change the text on the master page, you can complete the following steps:

STEP 1   In the Solution Explorer window, if necessary scroll down and then double-tap or double-click Site.master to open the page.

The Site.master page opens (Figure 9–8).

Application name
placeholder text

Site.master
page opened

FIGURE 9-8

STEP 2   Tap or click View on the menu bar, point to Toolbars, and then tap or click Formatting. Select the "Application name" placeholder text at the top of the Site .master page. Type Big Bear Cabins to replace the original title. On the Formatting toolbar, tap or click the Font Size box arrow, and then select xx-large (36 pt).

The title on the Master page changes to Big Bear Cabins. The font size is changed (Figure 9–9).

Formatting
toolbar

Font Size
box arrow

title text is
changed

FIGURE 9-9

ONLINE REINFORCEMENT

To view a video of the process in the previous steps, visit CengageBrain.com and navigate to the resources for this title. Tap or click the link for Chapter 9 and then navigate to Video 9-3.

Can I use the Formatting toolbar to change the color of the text or background?
Yes. When you select text within the webpage, you can change the foreground and background color using the Formatting toolbar.

Customize Navigation Links on the Master Template

The Master page has built-in navigation links that play an integral role in making your site easy to use and navigate. By default, the Master site has three links: Home, which connects to the Default.aspx page when tapped or clicked; About, which connects to the About.aspx page when tapped or clicked; and Contact, which connects to the Contact.aspx page (Figure 9-10). The chapter project has only two pages — Home and Reservations — so the Contact link should be deleted. It also would make more sense for the About link to be renamed Reservations. The site does not need a Register or Log in portion, so these default options will be deleted.

FIGURE 9-10

The easiest way to change the three navigational links and to delete the Register and Log in portion is to alter the HTML code. An ASP.NET 5 application consists of HTML and Visual Basic code. A traditional or mobile web browser can read HTML files and compose them into visible webpages. In Visual Basic, the Design tab is shown by default. To view the HTML code, tap or click the Source tab at the bottom left of the Site.master page. The highlighted lines in Figure 9-11 are responsible for displaying the three navigational links — Home, About, and Contact — as displayed on the webpage shown in Figure 9-10. The HTML code `li` stands for list item. The three list items are part of an unordered HTML list. The HTML code `<a runat="server" href="~/">Home</a>` represents the name of the hypertext reference link. The default navigation for every page in the application can be modified by changing the unordered navigation list element on the Site.Master page.

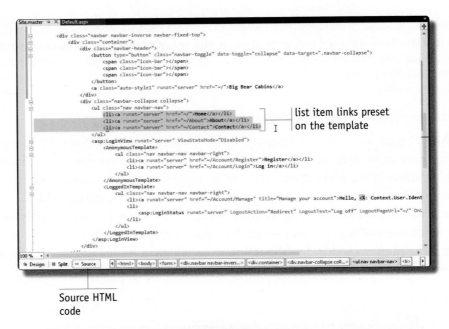

list item links preset
on the template

Source HTML
code

FIGURE 9-11

To delete the Contact navigational HTML link, rename the second navigational link to Reservations, and delete the Register and Log in tabs, follow these steps:

STEP 1 On the Site.master page, tap or click the Source tab at the bottom left. Select the HTML code `<li><a runat="server" href="~/Contact">Contact</a></li>`.

On the Source tab, the HTML list item is selected that creates a link to the Contact page (Figure 9–12).

Contact list item
link selected

FIGURE 9-12

STEP 2   Press the DELETE key to delete the Contact list item line of code. Select the black text "About" in the About list item link and type Reservations to rename the displayed text in the link.

The Contact list item link is deleted and the About text is renamed Reservations (Figure 9-13).

text changed to Reservations

FIGURE 9-13

STEP 3   Select the following HTML code that displays Register and Log in links on the Site.Master page:

```
<li><a runat="server" href="~/Account/Register">
Register</a></li>
<li><a runat="server" href="~/Account/Login">
Log in</a></li>
```

The Register and Log list item lines of code are selected (Figure 9-14).

Register and Log in list item links selected

FIGURE 9-14

STEP 4 Press the DELETE key to remove the Register and Log in links from the Site.master page.

The Register and Log in tabs are deleted (Figure 9-15).

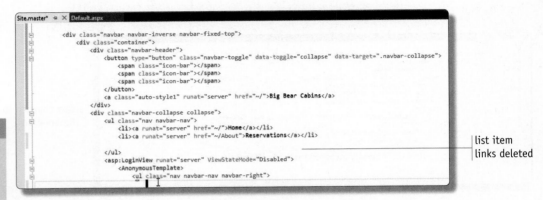

ONLINE REINFORCEMENT

To view a video of the process in the previous steps, visit CengageBrain.com and navigate to the resources for this title. Tap or click the link for Chapter 9 and then navigate to Video 9-4.

FIGURE 9-15

CRITICAL THINKING

Is it necessary to save the Site .master page to update the other customized page links?
Yes. As soon as you save the Site.master page, the title is updated on the Default, Home, and About webpages.

Customize the Default Page

After the Site.master page is designed, the content pages in this website automatically inherit the changes in the page style and navigation buttons. For example, the Default.aspx page, which serves as the Home page to the Big Bear Cabins site, inherits the font and link changes made when the Master page was customized. The customized links are changed on the Default, Home, and About webpages.

Add Objects to the Webpage

Using Visual Studio's ASP.NET 5 objects and code, you can create interactive web forms. You place objects on the webpage using a Toolbox similar to the one used for Windows applications, though the ASP.NET 5 categories of tools are different. The Big Bear Cabins application uses objects in the Standard and Validation categories of the Toolbox shown in Figure 9-16.

FIGURE 9-16

Toolbox objects unique to web applications include Login objects for allowing user access, Navigation objects for creating site maps, and Validation objects for checking web form input. Some Windows application objects work the same way, but have different object names in the web environment. For example, in a Windows application you use a PictureBox object to display a picture, but in an ASP.NET 5 webpage, you use an Image object. Both the PictureBox object and the Image object place an image into the application, but the Image object needs a URL to specify where the picture resides. The Big Bear Cabins Home page displays a picture, a description, and the address of the Big Bear Cabins.

Add an Image Object to the Default Page

On the Big Bear Cabins Home page (Default.aspx), an image of the Big Bear Cabins is displayed in an Image object on the left side of the page below the navigation buttons. The **Image** object is similar to the PictureBox object in a Windows application.

The major difference is where the Image object is stored. Most webpages reference a picture stored on a web server connected to the Internet. On an ASP.NET web form, you do this by specifying the entire URL (web address) in the ImageUrl property of an Image object. To add an Image object that displays an image stored on a web server, you can complete the following steps:

STEP 1 Close and save Site.master. Open the Toolbox. If necessary, in the Solution Explorer, double-tap or double-click Default.aspx. Notice that the Default.aspx page has inherited the title from the Site.master. Select the "ASP.NET" heading in the MainContent (Custom) area, and then press the DELETE key.

The Default.aspx page opens and the MainContent heading is cleared (Figure 9–17).

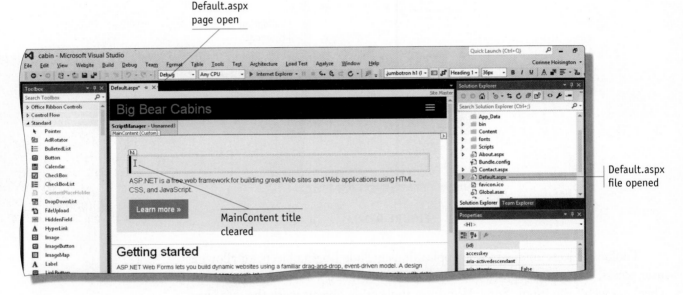

FIGURE 9-17

STEP 2 Double-tap or double-click the Image object in the Standard category of the Toolbox to display it on the webpage in the FeaturedContent area. Resize the object so that it is 175 pixels (Width property) by 150 pixels (Height property).

The Image object appears on the Default.aspx page and is resized (Figure 9–18).
A placeholder appears in the Image object until you specify a URL or path to an image file.

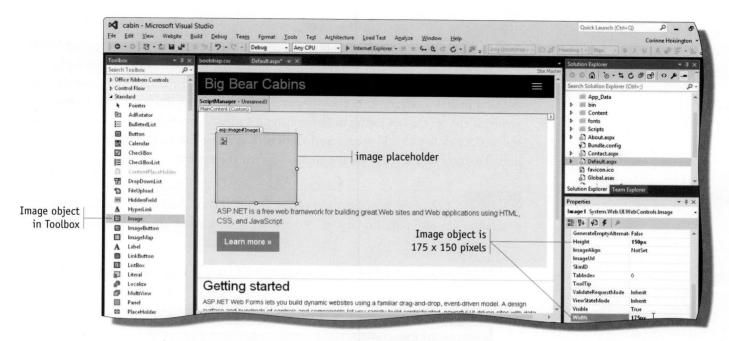

FIGURE 9-18

STEP 3   In the Properties window, name the Image object by entering `picCabins` in its (ID) property. Specify which image to display by entering the web address `http://delgraphics.delmarlearning.com/CourseTechnology/bearcabins.jpg` as the ImageUrl property. Press the ENTER key. You need Internet connectivity to view the image.

The bearcabins.jpg image appears in the Image object, replacing the placeholder (Figure 9-19).

ONLINE REINFORCEMENT

To view a video of the process in the previous steps, visit CengageBrain.com and navigate to the resources for this title. Tap or click the link for Chapter 9 and then navigate to Video 9-5.

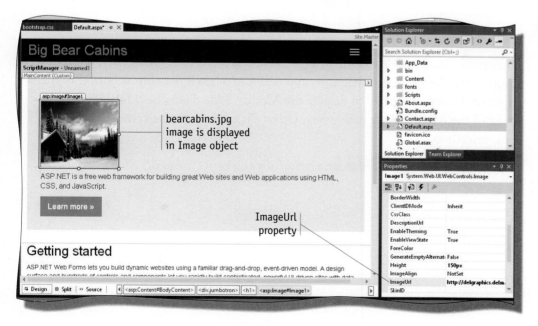

FIGURE 9-19

Enter Text Directly on the Webpage

ASP.NET 5 allows you to enter text directly on the webpage without creating labels. You should enter text directly on the page only if the text will not be changed by coded statements. Label objects are useful if you intend to change their contents after the user makes a selection on the webpage and the web application needs to display a result. If the text is not going to change, type it directly on the page. As you type, use the SPACEBAR key to add spaces and align text, and use the ENTER key to start a new line. To enter text directly on a webpage, follow these steps:

STEP 1 Tap or click to the right of the Image object. Add a space using the SPACEBAR key and type Enjoy a Mountain Getaway directly on the Default .aspx page.

The text Enjoy a Mountain Getaway appears to the right of the picture (Figure 9-20).

© iStock.com/gcoles

FIGURE 9-20

STEP 2 To change the vertical alignment, select the text, tap or click the style property in the Properties window, and then tap or click the ellipsis button to the right of the style property to display the Modify Style dialog box. In the Category pane of the Modify Style dialog box, tap or click Block. In the vertical-align drop box, select top.

The style property is changed to top vertical alignment in the Modify Style dialog box (Figure 9-21).

Block category and top
vertical-align are selected

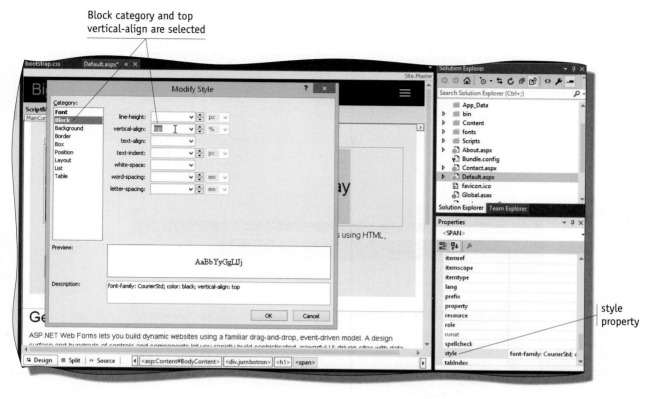

FIGURE 9-21

STEP 3 Tap or click the OK button, and then tap or click a blank spot to deselect
the text.

The typed text is vertically aligned to the top of the MainContent area (Figure 9–22).

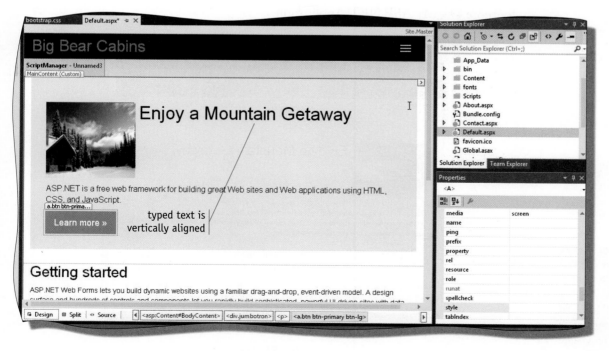

FIGURE 9-22

STEP 4 Select the text in the placeholder paragraph below the image and press the DELETE key. Change the font size to large using the Formatting toolbar. Enter the text `Nestled in the trees surrounded by the Beartooth Mountains, our cabin retreat provides modern comfort with genuine mountain elegance, offering a rustic ambiance with wood burning fireplaces and cozy furnished kitchens.`

The text describing the Big Bear Cabins is displayed on the page (Figure 9-23).

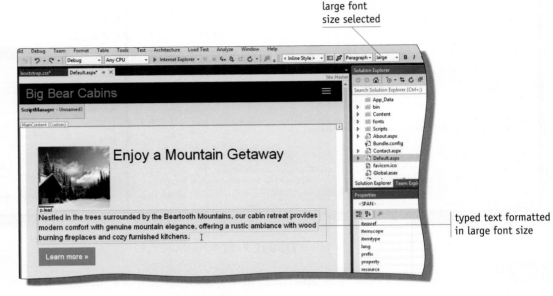

© iStock.com/gcoles

FIGURE 9-23

STEP 5 Delete the button and the rest of the text on the page. Do not delete the footnote © - My ASP.NET Application.

The remaining button and text on the default.aspx are deleted (Figure 9-24).

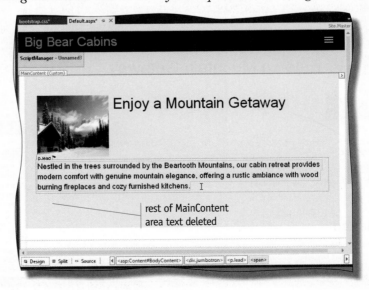

© iStock.com/gcoles

FIGURE 9-24

Create an ASP Web Form for the Reservations Page

Webpages are often interactive. For example, an online college application has text boxes that can be validated to be sure the information is correct. The Guest Reservation form in the chapter project will request each guest's name, email address, cabin type, the number of nights, and the date of arrival.

Add a Table for Alignment on a Web Form

A table is often used to organize website content into columns. On the Reservations page (About.aspx), a table is used to simplify object placement. The Guest Reservation form includes a table with seven rows and three columns filled with TextBox objects, CheckBox objects, a DropDownList object, and a Calendar object. To add a table to the Reservations page to organize form objects, follow these steps:

STEP 1 In the Solution Explorer window, double-tap or double-click About.aspx to create a web form for the Reservations page. Delete the text in the MainContent area. Tap or click in the MainContent area and type Guest Reservation Form. Press the ENTER key. Tap or click in the paragraph below the typed text and delete all the text below Guest Reservation Form. Tap or click Table on the menu bar, and then tap or click Insert Table. In the Size section of the Insert Table dialog box, change the number of Rows to 7 and the number of Columns to 3.

The Insert Table dialog box opens and the number of rows is changed to seven and the number of columns is changed to three in the About.aspx page (Figure 9-25).

FIGURE 9-25

STEP 2 Tap or click the OK button. To resize the columns, point to a column divider until a two-sided arrow appears. Drag the divider to change the column width. As you drag, a ScreenTip shows the width of the column in pixels. Resize the first column until it is 150 px wide. Resize the second column to 250 px wide.

The table is displayed in the About.aspx page. The column width of the first column is changed to 150 px and the second column is changed to 250 px (Figure 9-26).

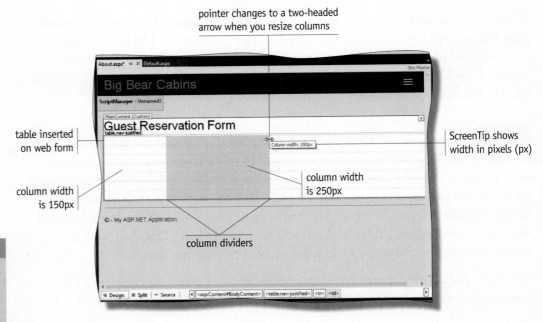

pointer changes to a two-headed arrow when you resize columns

table inserted on web form

column width is 150px

ScreenTip shows width in pixels (px)

column width is 250px

column dividers

FIGURE 9-26

ONLINE REINFORCEMENT

To view a video of the process in the previous steps, visit CengageBrain.com and navigate to the resources for this title. Tap or click the link for Chapter 9 and then navigate to Video 9-7.

Add TextBox and Button Objects

Like other web form objects, TextBox and Button objects are similar to their Windows counterparts apart from a few exceptions. A TextBox object on a webpage usually is provided for data entry, allowing a user to enter a name, an address, an email address, or a zip code, for example. The Text property of a TextBox object, therefore, is blank. A Button object on a web form serves the same purpose as it does in Windows applications. Because the user generally taps or clicks the Button object after completing the web form, the Text property for a Button object on a web form often is Submit. To name the TextBox and Button objects, you use the (ID) property. To add TextBox and Button objects, follow these steps:

STEP 1 On the About.aspx web form, tap or click in the first cell of the table and type Name: to enter text directly into the table. Open the Toolbox, drag a Text-Box object from the Toolbox to the form, and then position the TextBox object in the second cell in the first row of the table. Resize the TextBox object to a width of 250 px (Width property). Name this TextBox object txtName using the (ID) property.

Text is typed into the first cell and a TextBox object is placed inside the second cell on the top row of the table (Figure 9–27).

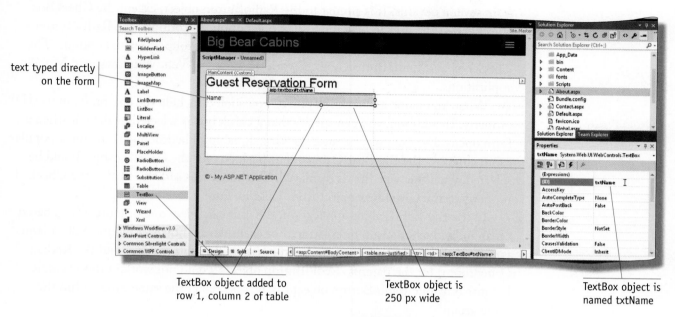

text typed directly
on the form

TextBox object added to
row 1, column 2 of table

TextBox object is
250 px wide

TextBox object is
named txtName

FIGURE 9-27

STEP 2   In the first cell in the second row of the table, type `Email Address:` to enter text directly into the table. Drag a TextBox object from the Toolbox to the form and then position the TextBox object in the second cell in the second row in the table. Resize the TextBox object to a width of 250 px (Width property). Name this TextBox object `txtEmail` using the (ID) property.

Text is typed into the first cell and a TextBox object is placed inside the second cell on the second row of the table (Figure 9–28).

ONLINE REINFORCEMENT

To view a video of the process in the previous steps, visit CengageBrain.com and navigate to the resources for this title. Tap or click the link for Chapter 9 and then navigate to Video 9-8.

text typed directly
on form

TextBox object added to
row 2, column 2 of table

TextBox object is
250 px wide

TextBox object is
named txtEmail

FIGURE 9-28

Add CheckBox Objects

Three CheckBox objects are used in the Guest Reservation form to determine which cabin(s) the guest wants to reserve. The **CheckBox** object allows the user to choose from several options. It is similar to the RadioButton object, except the CheckBox object allows the user to pick more than one option. In contrast, the RadioButton object allows a user to choose only one option from a group of related options. The CheckBox and RadioButton objects work the same in Web, Windows, and Mobile applications.

When you name a CheckBox object, you should include the chk prefix in its (ID) property. In addition, you can specify that a check box is selected by default when a form opens. For example, because the Grizzly cabin (3 bedrooms) is the most popular cabin choice at the Big Bear Cabins, the check box for the Grizzly cabin should be selected when the page first is displayed. To specify this setting, change the Checked property of the CheckBox object from False to True.

In the Big Bear Cabins application, the user can select one or more cabins based on an individual or group reservation. For example, as shown in Figure 9-29, a large family might select the Grizzly (3 bedrooms) for the teen children and the Kodiak (1 bedroom) for the parents. RadioButton objects would not work in this example because only one RadioButton object can be selected at the same time within the same group.

FIGURE 9-29

To place a CheckBox object on a web form, you can complete the following steps:

STEP 1   In the third row of the table, type `Cabin Selection:` in the first cell. Drag the CheckBox object from the Toolbox to the web form, and then position it in the third row, second cell.

The CheckBox object is placed on the web form (Figure 9-30). The placeholder text will remain until you change the Text property. It does not, however, appear on the webpage when the page is displayed in a web browser.

FIGURE 9-30

STEP 2 Name the CheckBox object by tapping or clicking to the right of its (ID) property in the Properties window and then entering chkGrizzly. Change the Text property of the CheckBox object to Grizzly (3 bedrooms) $99.

The CheckBox object is named chkGrizzly in the (ID) property. After changing the Text property of chkGrizzly, the CheckBox object on the form displays the new text (Figure 9–31).

FIGURE 9-31

STEP 3   At the Big Bear Cabins, the Grizzly is the most popular cabin. This cabin, therefore, should be checked when the form opens to save time for the user. To select the Grizzly check box, change the Checked property for the object from False to True.

The chkGrizzly CheckBox object appears with a check mark on the form, and the Checked property is set to True (Figure 9-32).

FIGURE 9-32

STEP 4   In the second column, fourth and fifth rows of the table, add two more CheckBox objects named `chkPolar` and `chkKodiak`, respectively. Change the Text property of the first CheckBox object to `Polar (2 bedrooms) $89` and the second CheckBox object to `Kodiak (1 bedroom) $79`.

Two CheckBox objects are added to the form (Figure 9-33).

FIGURE 9-33

Code for CheckBox Objects

After the user selects one or more CheckBox objects representing the cabin selections and taps or clicks the Submit button on the web form, control returns to the web server. On the web server, the event handler for the Submit button can evaluate which CheckBox objects are selected. The code shown in Figure 9-34 determines which CheckBox objects are selected by referring to the Checked property, in the same manner as when RadioButton objects are checked.

```
42        If chkGrizzly.Checked Then
43            decCabinCost += decGrizzlyCost
44        End If
45        If chkPolar.Checked Then
46            decCabinCost += decPolarCost
47        End If
48        If chkKodiak.Checked Then
49            decCabinCost += decKodiakCost
50        End If
```

FIGURE 9-34

In Figure 9-34, the statement on line 42 checks the Checked property for the chkGrizzly check box. If it is checked, the Grizzly cabin cost is added to the value in the decCabinCost variable. Similarly, if the chkPolar check box is checked, its cabin cost is added to the value in the decCabinCost variable. The same is true for the chkKodiak check box. If all three check boxes are checked, the value in the decCabinCost variable will be the sum of the individual cabin costs for all three cabins.

Add a DropDownList Object

On the Guest Reservation web form, guests can use a DropDownList object to specify the number of nights they plan to stay. The DropDownList object allows users to select one item from a predefined list. It is similar to the ListBox object used in Windows applications, except that for a DropDownList object, the list of items remains hidden until users tap or click the list arrow button.

After adding a DropDownList object to a form and naming it, you can specify the items you want to display in the list. You often want to order these items alphabetically or numerically for ease of use. The first item in this list appears in the DropDownList object by default. The DropDownList object will not display the items in the list until you run the application and display the web form in a browser. The user must tap or click the list arrow to view the complete list of items during execution. The prefix for the name (ID) of the DropDownList object in Visual Basic is ddl.

On the Guest Reservation form, a DropDownList object is used to determine the number of nights the guests plan to stay at the cabin. To add a DropDownList object to the web form, you can complete the following steps:

STEP 1 In the sixth row of the table, type `Night(s):` in the first column. Drag the DropDownList object to the second column of the sixth row. Name the DropDownList object by tapping or clicking to the right of the (ID) property in the object's Properties window and then typing `ddlNights`.

A DropDownList object appears on the web form and is named ddlNights (Figure 9-35).

DropDownList object

FIGURE 9-35

STEP 2 To fill the DropDownList object with list items, tap or click the Smart Tag on the upper-right corner of the object.

The DropDownList Tasks menu opens (Figure 9-36).

FIGURE 9-36

STEP 3   Tap or click Edit Items on the DropDownList Tasks menu.

The ListItem Collection Editor dialog box opens (Figure 9-37).

FIGURE 9-37

STEP 4   Tap or click the Add button. In the ListItem Properties pane on the right side of the dialog box, tap or click to the right of the Text property and enter 1.

The number 1 is entered as the first item in the DropDownList object (Figure 9-38).

FIGURE 9-38

STEP 5   Tap or click the Add button and enter 2 as its Text property. Repeat this step, entering the numbers 3 through 7 to specify the number of nights users can select in the DropDownList object. Tap or click the OK button in the ListItem Collection Editor dialog box. Resize the DropDownList object to the width of a single digit, if necessary. To view the completed DropDownList object, run the application by tapping or clicking the Start Debugging button on the Standard toolbar. If necessary, tap or click the Reservations navigation button to open the Reservations page in the browser. Tap or click the list arrow on the DropDownList object on the webpage.

HEADS UP

The first time the ASP.NET application is executed, a Debugging Not Enabled dialog box may open. Select the first option to modify the Web.config file to enable debugging, and tap or click the OK button.

After tapping or clicking the Start Debugging button, the browser opens. After tapping or clicking the list arrow on the DropDownList object, the list item contents appear (Figure 9-39).

FIGURE 9-39

Add a Calendar Object

The Guest Reservation form contains a calendar that allows guests to select their arrival date. Visual Basic provides an object to manipulate months, days, and years when specifying information such as reservations, anniversaries, or bill payments. The **Calendar** object is organized by month and displays the number of days in each month as appropriate for the year. For example, March has 31 days and February includes an extra day when the year is a leap year. By default, the Calendar object displays the current month according to the system date and selects the current day when the application is executed. You can use the Calendar object in any type of Visual Studio application, including Windows and web applications. When creating a Calendar object, use the prefix cld in the name. To place the Calendar object on a web form, you can complete the following steps:

STEP 1   Close the browser window. In the last row of the table, type `Check-in Date:`. Drag the Calendar object from the Toolbox to the web form, and then position it on the form. In the (ID) property, name the Calendar object `cldArrival`.

The Calendar object is placed on the Windows form (Figure 9-40).

FIGURE 9-40

Select the Calendar object, if necessary, and then tap or click the Smart Tag on the upper-right corner of the Calendar object.

The Calendar Tasks menu opens (Figure 9-41).

FIGURE 9-41

STEP 3 Tap or click Auto Format on the Calendar Tasks menu. When the Auto-Format dialog box opens, tap or click the Colorful 2 scheme in the Select a scheme list.

The AutoFormat dialog box previews the selected Colorful 2 scheme (Figure 9-42).

FIGURE 9-42

ONLINE REINFORCEMENT

To view a video of the process in the previous steps, visit CengageBrain.com and navigate to the resources for this title. Tap or click the link for Chapter 9 and then navigate to Video 9-11.

Specify a Web Form Title

A web form displays its title in the title bar of the browser used to view the form. Not all browsers have a title bar, but the title also appears as the title of the MainContent area and as the tab name in the browser. You specify the title bar text for a web form using the Title property. To change the browser Title property from its default of About Us on the Reservations page to the title, Big Bear Cabins Reservation Form, you can complete the following steps:

STEP 1   Tap or click the OK button to close the AutoFormat dialog box. In the Properties window of the Reservations web form, tap or click the drop-down box at the top and select DOCUMENT.

DOCUMENT is selected in the Properties window (Figure 9-43).

DOCUMENT selected in Properties window

FIGURE 9-43

STEP 2   In the Properties window, scroll until the Title property is visible, and then tap or click on the right column of the Title property. Enter the title `Big Bear Cabins` with a blank space following the text entry. When the webpage is displayed, the Title property appears before the MainContent title.

The title Big Bear Cabins is entered in the Title property of the Properties window. This title will be displayed in front of the MainContent title and on some browsers as the title bar or tab name of the Reservations page (Figure 9–44).

title appears before "Guest Reservation Form"

tab name changes in browser

FIGURE 9-44

Code for a Calendar Object

When using the Calendar object, two dates often are important: the selected date and the current date. In the Visual Basic code that you write in an event handler, you can include statements to reference both the selected date and the current date. The format of statements used to reference these two dates is shown in Figure 9-45.

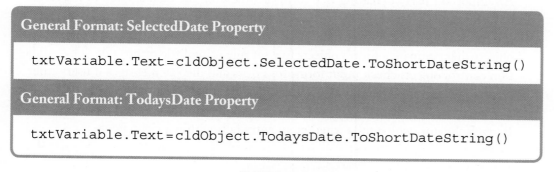

FIGURE 9-45

In Figure 9-45, the SelectedDate property references the date the user tapped or clicked in the Calendar object. In the general format, the ToShortDateString() procedure changes the date to a String format so it can be displayed in a TextBox object. If you are referencing only the selected date without the need to change it to a string value, the procedure is not required.

Similarly, the current date is referenced by the property TodaysDate.

In the Big Bear Cabins application, it is important to ensure that the date the user selects is equal to or greater than the current date. For a reservation date, a user cannot select a date that has already passed. One of the If statements used in the sample program to test this condition is shown in Figure 9-46.

```
32          If cldArrival.SelectedDate < cldArrival.TodaysDate Then
33              lblCalendarError.Visible = True
34          Else
35              lblCalendarError.Visible = False
36          End If
```

FIGURE 9-46

In Figure 9-46, the selected date for the cldArrival Calendar object is compared to the current date (TodaysDate) for the cldArrival Calendar object. If the selected date is less than the current date, an error message is displayed; otherwise the error message is not displayed.

If the user does not tap or click a date on the calendar prior to tapping or clicking the Submit button and running the event handler code, the Calendar object automatically returns a date that is less than the current date. Therefore, the If statement on line 32 will detect both the case when the user selects a date less than the current date and the case when the user does not select a date.

Add Validation Controls

An important part of creating web forms is validating the data entered in the form to make sure the user has entered reasonable values. Instead of using a series of If statements or other complex code, ASP.NET 5 provides built-in validation control objects that compare a form's objects to a set rule using little or no code. The validation control objects check input forms for errors and display messages if users enter incorrect or incomplete responses. Built-in validation control objects include RequiredFieldValidator, which verifies that a required field contains data, and RangeValidator, which tests whether an entry falls within a given range.

Apply a Required Field Validator

The simplest validation control is the **RequiredFieldValidator** object, which finds a specified object to validate and determines whether the object is empty. For example, in the Big Bear Cabins application, the user must enter her first and last name. Otherwise, a reservation cannot be made. The RequiredFieldValidator object reminds the user to complete all required fields. You can customize this reminder by changing the ErrorMessage property, which often is helpful to let users know what they have done incorrectly. If the user enters a value in a field, the RequiredField-Validator does not display an error message.

In the Big Bear Cabins Guest Reservation form, the first object to validate is the Name TextBox object, which is named txtName. You can add a RequiredFieldValidator object to the web form that tests txtName to determine if it is empty. If it is, an error message appears reminding the user to enter a first name. After adding the RequiredField-Validator object, you must specify that it validates the txtName TextBox object.

The prefix used for the RequiredFieldValidator is rfv. To validate a required TextBox object using a RequiredFieldValidator object, follow these steps:

STEP 1 In the Toolbox, hide the Standard tools by tapping or clicking the filled triangle icon next to Standard. Expand the Validation tools by tapping or clicking the open triangle icon next to Validation.

The seven Validation tools are displayed (Figure 9–47).

FIGURE 9-47

STEP 2 Drag the RequiredFieldValidator to the right of the Name TextBox object in the third column of the table.

The RequiredFieldValidator object is placed to the right of txtName (Figure 9–48).

FIGURE 9-48

STEP 3 Name the RequiredFieldValidator by typing `rfvName` in its (ID) property.

The RequiredFieldValidator object is named rfvName (Figure 9-49).

FIGURE 9-49

STEP 4 To specify that the rfvName RequiredFieldValidator object validates the txtName TextBox object, tap or click to the right of the ControlToValidate property in the Properties window, tap or click the list arrow, and then select txtName.

The ControlToValidate property is set to txtName (Figure 9-50).

FIGURE 9-50

STEP 5   In the Properties window for the RequiredFieldValidator, change the ErrorMessage property to * Enter Name.

*The ErrorMessage property is changed to * Enter Name (Figure 9-51).*

ErrorMessage property

ErrorMessage property value changed

FIGURE 9-51

When the application is run on a web browser with a Submit button, the error message will be displayed if the Submit button is tapped or clicked and no text has been entered in the txtName text box.

Apply the Range Validator

Another validation control built into ASP.NET 5 is the **RangeValidator** control, which tests whether an input value falls within a given range. If you were testing whether a number entered on a webpage was a valid day in a month, the RangeValidator control could test if the day number is between 1 and 31. The RangeValidator control uses the prefix rgv in its name, and the following five properties to complete its validation:

- The **ControlToValidate** property contains the name of the object you are validating.
- The **MinimumValue** property contains the smallest value in the range.
- The **MaximumValue** property contains the largest value in the range.
- The **Type** property matches the data type of the value, such as Integer or String.
- The **ErrorMessage** property explains to the user what value is requested.

CRITICAL THINKING

In addition to checking whether a number is between a minimum and a maximum value, can I use Range Validation to see if a character is in the first half of the alphabet (A through M)?
Yes. You can use a Range Validator with minimum and maximum character values.

Apply the Compare Validator

Another validation control is the **CompareValidator** object, which you use to compare an object's value with another object or a constant value. The CompareValidator control can also compare the value in one object to the value in another object. In the example shown in Figure 9-52, the user enters a password into a web form, and re-enters the password to confirm that the two passwords are the same. You can use the CompareValidator control to verify that the passwords match.

FIGURE 9-52

The CompareValidator uses three properties to complete its validation:

- The **ControlToValidate** property contains the name of the object that you are validating.
- The **ControlToCompare** property contains the name of the object that you are comparing to the ControlToValidate property.
- The **ErrorMessage** property contains a message stating that the value does not match.

In Figure 9-53, four properties are changed to apply the CompareValidator object to verify a password: (ID), ControlToCompare, ControlToValidate, and ErrorMessage. This figure also shows that the prefix for the CompareValidator object is cmv.

FIGURE 9-53

Apply the Regular Expression Validator

The **RegularExpressionValidator** control confirms whether the user entered data that matches standard formats such as a phone number, email address, URL, zip code, or Social Security number. If the user does not enter the data in the proper format, an error message is displayed. The prefix rev is used for the RegularExpression-Validator control. The RegularExpressionValidator uses three properties to complete its validation:

- The **ControlToValidate** property contains the name of the object that you are validating.
- The **ErrorMessage** property contains a message stating that the value does not match the valid format.
- The **ValidationExpression** property allows the user to select the format for the object.

In the Big Bear Cabins Guest Reservation form, the second TextBox object on the form requests the user's email address. To confirm that the information entered is a possible email address, a RegularExpressionValidator object can test the contents of the Text property of the txtEmail object and verify that it matches the format of a valid email address, which follows the format of *name@domain.com*. To incorporate a Regular-ExpressionValidator object in a webpage, you can complete the following steps:

STEP 1   Drag the RegularExpressionValidator object from the Toolbox to the right of the Email Address TextBox object in the table.

The RegularExpressionValidator object is placed in the table to the right of txtEmail (Figure 9-54).

FIGURE 9-54

STEP 2 Name the RegularExpressionValidator by typing `revEmail` in its (ID) property.

The RegularExpressionValidator object is named revEmail (Figure 9-55).

FIGURE 9-55

STEP 3 Tap or click to the right of the ControlToValidate property, tap or click the list arrow, and then tap or click txtEmail.

The ControlToValidate property is set to txtEmail (Figure 9-56).

FIGURE 9-56

STEP 4   Change the ErrorMessage property to * `Error Email Format`.

*The ErrorMessage property is changed to * Error Email Format (Figure 9-57).*

FIGURE 9-57

STEP 5   To set txtEmail to validate that it contains a standard email address, tap or click to the right of the ValidationExpression property, and then tap or click its ellipsis button. In the Regular Expression Editor dialog box, select Internet e-mail address in the Standard expressions list.

The Internet e-mail address is selected as the standard expression to validate (Figure 9-58).

FIGURE 9-58

STEP 6   Tap or click the OK button in the Regular Expression Editor dialog box. Run the application by tapping or clicking the Start Debugging button on the Standard toolbar. Enter a name and an email address without an @ symbol, such as lochlan.email.com, and then press the ENTER key.

An error message appears to the right of the Email Address TextBox object (Figure 9-59). When a valid email address is entered and the ENTER key is pressed again, the error message is removed.

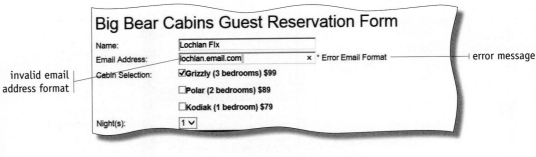

invalid email address format

error message

FIGURE 9-59

Apply Multiple Validations

You can apply more than one type of validation control on an object to validate more than one aspect of the data. Often you may want to make a certain control required using the RequiredFieldValidator object, and to check the range using the Range-Validator object. In Figure 9-60, a RequiredFieldValidator confirms that the number of hours worked is not left blank, and the RangeValidator verifies that the number entered is between 1 and 60. Each validation control displays an error message if the object does not meet the specified criteria.

RequiredFieldValidator error message

RangeValidator error message

FIGURE 9-60

Display a ValidationSummary Control

Instead of validating data, the **ValidationSummary** control lets you display validation error messages in a single location, creating a clean layout for the web form. By default, each validation control displays an error message next to the object it validates. On a large or complex form, however, the error messages might interfere with data or other objects. You can use the ValidationSummary object to display all of the error messages in a different place, listing them in a blank area at the top or bottom of the form, for example, where they will appear together when the validation criteria for any control are not met.

To use a ValidationSummary object, drag the object to the location on the webpage where you want the summary to appear. The prefix used for naming the ValidationSummary object is vsm.

Do I have to set the ControlToValidate property for a validation summary?
The validation summary displays the error messages for all the other validation objects, so you do not have to set the ControlToValidate property. The error message displayed in this control is specified by the ErrorMessage property of each validation control. If the ErrorMessage property of the validation control is not set, no error message is displayed for that validation control.

Use the
 Tag in Visual Basic Code

One HTML tag often used when creating webpages is the **
** tag, which stands for break; it breaks the text by starting a new line. When you are creating a web form in Visual Basic, you can use the <br> tag to skip a line before starting a new one in a Label object.

In the Big Bear Cabins chapter project, after the user enters reservation information, a confirmation message is displayed that includes details about the reservation such as the name, email address, cost of the cabins, date, and number of nights (Figure 9-61).

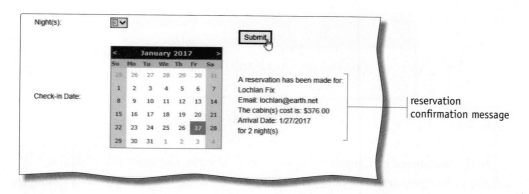

FIGURE 9-61

In Figure 9-61, the message consists of five lines. Based on your screen resolution, the text may wrap and you may have six lines. Each of the lines except the last line ends with the <br> tag so that the text that follows will be on the next line. The code to create the message is shown in Figure 9-62.

```
53          strMessage = "A reservation has been made for: " & "<br>" _
54              & strName & "<br>" & "Email: " & strEmail & "<br>"
55          strMessage &= "The cabin(s) cost is: " _
56              & decCabinCost.ToString("C") & "<br>"
57          strMessage &= "Arrival Date: " _
58              & cldArrival.SelectedDate.ToShortDateString() _
59              & "<br>" & " for " & intNumberOfNights & " night(s)"
60          lblReservation.Text = strMessage
61      Else
```

FIGURE 9-62

In Figure 9-62, the message to be displayed is built in the strMessage String variable. On line 53, the first line of the message is placed in the variable. The last item in the string is the <br> tag, which will cause the text that follows to be on the next line. Notice that the tag must be within double quotation marks because it is a string.

The statements on lines 54 and 56 also end with the <br> tag. As a result of the statements in Figure 9-62, a five-line message will be created.

Use String Manipulation Properties and Procedures in the String Class

The String class in Visual Basic has many properties and procedures that allow you to manipulate strings, which you often need to do when developing web forms. For example, you might want to find the length of the string that the user entered or convert lowercase text to uppercase. The commands discussed in this section work with ASP.NET 5 as well as in any Windows or mobile application.

Find String Length

You can use the **Length** property to determine the number of characters in a particular string. The syntax for determining string length is shown in Figure 9-63.

> **General Format: Determine String Length**
>
> ```
> intValue = strName.Length
> ```

FIGURE 9-63

In the statement intLength = "Visual Basic".Length, the value placed in the intLength Integer variable would be 12 because the Length property counts spaces as well as characters, and "Visual Basic" contains 11 characters and one space. The code shown in Figure 9-64 determines if the zip code entered in the txtZipCode TextBox object has a length of five characters.

```
8        Dim intCount As Integer
9
10       intCount = txtZipCode.Text.Length
11       If intCount <> 5 Then
12           lblError.Text = "You must enter 5 digits"
13       End If
14
```

FIGURE 9-64

If you enter only four digits in the zip code, as shown in Figure 9-65, a message appears reminding you to enter five digits.

FIGURE 9-65

Use the Trim Procedure

When entering information into a TextBox object, the user might accidentally add extra spaces before or after the input string. When that string is used later, the extra spaces might distort the format of the output. To prevent this, Visual Basic provides a procedure named **Trim** to remove spaces from the beginning and end of a string. The syntax for the Trim procedure is shown in Figure 9-66.

> **General Format: Trim Procedure**
>
> ```
> strName = strName.Trim()
> ```

FIGURE 9-66

In the Big Bear Cabins Guest Reservation form, the user enters a name and an email address. If the user includes spaces before or after the entries, the spaces will appear in the final output. The Trim procedure shown in Figure 9-67 removes extra spaces.

```
26        ' Trim additional spaces that are entered by the user
27        strName = txtName.Text.Trim
28        strEmail = txtEmail.Text.Trim
```

FIGURE 9-67

Convert Uppercase and Lowercase Text

The **ToUpper** and **ToLower** procedures convert a string to all uppercase or all lowercase, respectively. The syntax in Figure 9-68 shows how to use the ToUpper and ToLower procedures:

> **General Format: UpperCase and LowerCase Procedures**
>
> ```
> strName = strName.ToUpper()
>
> strName = strName.ToLower()
> ```

FIGURE 9-68

When you compare a string, Visual Basic checks if you entered the word as specified. For example, if you enter YES in response to a question, but the code accepts only yes, the If statement as shown in Figure 9-69 would convert the response of YES to yes. The ToUpper() and ToLower() methods save coding time because all the possible ways to enter a response do not have to be compared.

```
87        If strAnswer.ToLower() = "yes" Then
```

FIGURE 9-69

Program Design

As you have learned, the requirements document identifies the purpose of the program being developed, the application title, the procedures to be followed when using the program, any equations and calculations required in the program, any conditions within the program that must be tested, notes and restrictions that must be followed by the program, and any other comments that would be helpful to understanding the problem. The requirements document for the Big Bear Cabins web application is shown in Figure 9-70 and the Use Case Definition is shown in Figure 9-71.

REQUIREMENTS DOCUMENT

Date:	May 3, 2017
Date Submitted:	
Application Title:	Big Bear Cabins
Purpose:	This web application allows the user to book a reservation at the Big Bear Cabins using a web form.
Program Procedures:	From a web application, the user should complete an online reservation form to enter the guest's name, email address, cabin preference, number of nights, and starting date. The total cost of the stay should be calculated and displayed.

Algorithms, Processing, and Conditions:

1. The user must be able to enter the requested reservation information on a web form. The information should include the guest's name, email address, which cabins the guest prefers, number of nights, and starting date of the stay. The user can select one or more cabins from the following choices: Grizzly (3 bedrooms) $99, Polar (2 bedrooms) $89, and Kodiak (1 bedroom) $79.
2. After entering the reservation information, the user taps or clicks the Submit button.
3. The information entered is validated.
4. The application displays the final cost of the stay.

Notes and Restrictions:

1. Data in the Name TextBox object is required.
2. Data in the Email TextBox object is validated to confirm that it is in an email address format.
3. The Calendar object is checked to confirm that a date is selected and that the selected date is not before the current date. The maximum length of stay is seven nights.

Comments: Display a picture of the cabins on the web form.

FIGURE 9-70

USE CASE DEFINITION

1. The webpage opens, displaying the title Big Bear Cabins with a picture as well as TextBox objects to enter the guest's name and email address. A Calendar object is used to select the beginning date of the reservation. A DropDownList object is used to enter the number of nights. The cabin selections are entered with CheckBox objects.
2. User taps or clicks the Submit button.
3. The data entered is checked and validated.
4. If necessary, the user makes corrections and resubmits the data.
5. The application confirms the reservation and displays the final cost of the stay.

FIGURE 9-71

Event Planning Document

You will recall that the event planning document consists of a table that specifies an object in the user interface that will cause an event, the action taken by the user to trigger the event, and the event processing that must occur. The event planning document for the Big Bear Cabins web application is shown in Figure 9-72.

EVENT PLANNING DOCUMENT

Program Name: Big Bear Cabins	Developer: Corinne Hoisington	Object: Default.aspx	Date: May 3, 2017
OBJECT	**EVENT TRIGGER**	**EVENT PROCESSING**	
btnSubmit	Click	Validate the name to confirm it is not empty Validate email address to confirm it is in the email address format Trim extra spaces from name and email data Blank the reservation message If a cabin has not been selected 　Display a cabin error message 　If arrival date is not valid 　　Display a calendar error message 　Else 　Hide the calendar error message Else 　Hide cabin error message 　If arrival date is valid 　　Accumulate cabin costs 　　Convert number of nights to Integer 　　Calculate cost of cabin (total cabin costs * number of nights) 　　Create the reservation message 　　Display the reservation message 　Else 　　Display calendar error message	

FIGURE 9-72

Code the Program

After identifying the events and tasks within the events, you are ready to create the program. As you have learned, creating the program means designing the user interface and then entering Visual Basic statements to accomplish the tasks specified on the event planning document. As you enter the code, you also will implement the logic to carry out the required processing.

Guided Program Development

NOTE TO THE LEARNER

In the following activity, you should complete the tasks within the specified steps. Each of the tasks is accompanied by a Hint Screen. The purpose of the Hint Screen is to indicate where you should perform the activity in the Visual Studio window and to remind you which method to use. If you need further help completing a step, refer to the Figure identified by *ref:*.

Guided Program Development

Phase I: Customize the Master and Home Pages

1

- **Begin the Web Application** Start Visual Studio, and then create a Visual Basic Web Site Application project by tapping or clicking the New Web Site button on the Standard toolbar. In the center pane, tap or click ASP.NET Web Forms Site, if necessary. Enter the project name Cabin and store the program on the e: drive (or a network or USB drive of your choice). Tap or click the OK button *(ref: Figure 9-4).*

HINT

- **Display the Formatting Toolbar** Tap or click View on the menu bar, point to Toolbars, and then tap or click Formatting.

- **Change the Heading on the Site.master Page** In the Solution Explorer, double-tap or double-click the Site.master page. On the page, select the "Application name" placeholder text and type Big Bear Cabins. Select the typed title. On the Formatting toolbar, change the font size to xx-large *(ref: Figure 9-9).*

HINT

- **Change the Second Navigational Link Using HTML** On the Site.master page, tap or click the Source tab at the bottom left. Select the HTML code `<li><a runat="server" href="~/Contact">Contact</a></li>`. Press the DELETE key to delete the Contact list item line of code. Select the black text "About" in the About list item link and type Reservations to rename the displayed text in the link *(ref: Figures 9-12 and 9-13).*

HINT

- **Delete the Register and Log in Links** Select the HTML code that displays Register and Log in links on the Site .master page:

`<li><a runat="server" href="~/Account/Register">Register</a></li> <li><a runat="server" href="~/Account/Login">Log in</a></li>`

Press the DELETE key to remove the Register and Log in links from the Site.master page.

HINT

- **Add an Image Object** Close and save the Site.master and switch to the Default.aspx page. Delete the existing text in the title placeholder in the MainContent area. Double-tap or double-click the Image object in the Standard category of the Toolbox to display it within the webpage in the MainContent area. Resize the object so that it is 175 pixels (width) by 150 pixels (height). Change its ImageUrl property to `http://delgraphics.delmarlearning.com/CourseTech-nology/bearcabins.jpg` *(ref: Figure 9-19).*

- **Type Directly on the Page** Tap or click to the right of the Image object and type `Enjoy a Mountain Getaway`. Tap or click the ellipsis button of the style property in the Properties window. In the Modify Style dialog box, select the Block category and then select top in the vertical-align box. Tap or click the OK button *(ref: Figure 9-21)*.

HINT

- **Type the Paragraph** Select the text in the paragraph below the image and press the DELETE key. Change the font size to large using the Formatting toolbar. Enter the text `Nestled in the trees surrounded by the Beartooth Mountains, our cabin retreat provides modern comfort with genuine mountain elegance, offering a rustic ambiance with wood burning fireplaces and cozy furnished kitchens`. Delete the button and the rest of the text on the Default.aspx page. Do not delete the footnote © - My ASP.NET Application *(ref: Figure 9-23)*.

The Default.aspx webpage includes an image and typed text (Figure 9-73).

RESULT OF STEP 2

FIGURE 9-73

© iStock.com/gcoles

(continues)

Phase 2: Build the Guest Reservation Web Form

3

- **Insert a Table in the Web Form** In the Solution Explorer, double-tap or double-click the About.aspx file. Delete the text in the MainContent area. Type Guest Reservation Form in the MainContent area. Tap or click Table on the menu bar, and then tap or click Insert Table. In the Insert Table dialog box, enter 7 in the Rows text box and 3 in the Columns text box, and then tap or click the OK button to create a table with seven columns and three rows *(ref: Figure 9-25)*.

- **Change the Size of the Column Tables** Point to the divider between the first and second columns of the table, and then drag to resize the first column to 150 pixels. Resize the second column to 250 pixels *(ref: Figure 9-26)*.

Enter Text and Objects in the Table

- In the first column of the table, enter `Name:`, `Email Address:`, `Cabin Selection:`, `Night(s):`, and `Check-in Date:` in separate rows. In the second column, drag the first Text-Box object to the right of the Name title, and then name the Text-Box object `txtName` (*ref: Figure 9-27*).

- Drag the second TextBox object to the right of the Email Address title, and then name the TextBox object `txtEmail` (*ref: Figure 9-28*).

- Drag a CheckBox object to the right of the Cabin Selection text. Name the CheckBox object `chkGrizzly`. Change the Text property to `Grizzly (3 bedrooms) $99`. Change the Checked property to True (*ref: Figure 9-31*).

- Drag the second CheckBox object below the first CheckBox object, and then name the CheckBox object `chkPolar`. Change its Text property to `Polar (2 bedrooms) $89`. Drag the third Check-Box object below the second CheckBox object, and then name the third CheckBox object `chkKodiak`. Change its Text property to `Kodiak (1 bedroom) $79` (*ref: Figure 9-33*).

- Drag a DropDownList object to the right of the Night(s) title. Change the name of the DropDownList object to `ddlNights`. Tap or click the Smart Tag on the DropDownList object, and then tap or click Edit Items. The ListItem Collection Editor dialog box opens. Tap or click the Add button, and then enter the number 1 as the Text property. Tap or click the Add button as necessary to add the numbers 2 through 7. After adding number 7, tap or click the Remove button to remove the entry in the Members list, if necessary. Tap or click the OK button (*ref: Figure 9-38*).

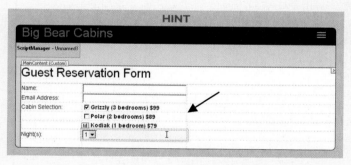

HINT

- Drag a Calendar object to the right of the Check-in Date text. Name the Calendar object cldArrival. Tap or click the Smart Tag on the Calendar object, and then tap or click Auto Format. Select Colorful 2, and then tap or click OK (*ref: Figure 9-42*).

(continues)

The Guest Reservation Form (About.aspx) includes typed text, text boxes, check boxes, a drop-down list, and a calendar (Figure 9-74).

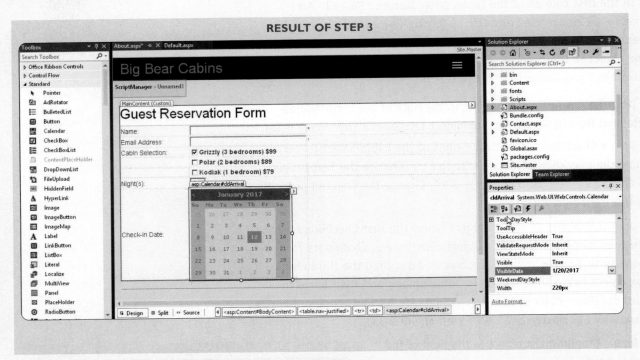

FIGURE 9-74

Phase 3: Add Validation Objects

4

- **Add the Required Validation Objects** In the Toolbox, expand the Validation controls by tapping or clicking the expand icon next to Validation (ref: Figure 9-47).

- **Validate the Name TextBox Object** Drag the RequiredFieldValidator object onto the web form to the first row in the third column. Name the Validator Object `rfvName`. Change its ErrorMessage property to `* Enter Name` (ref: Figure 9-51).

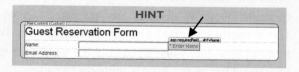

- **Select the TextBox Object to Validate** In the Properties window for the rfvName object, tap or click the list arrow in the ControlToValidate property and then tap or click `txtName` (ref: Figure 9-53).

- **Validate the Email TextBox Object** Drag the RegularExpressionValidator object onto the web form in the second row of the third column. Place the RequiredFieldValidator object to the right of the txtEmail TextBox object. Name the Validator object `revEmail`. Change its ErrorMessage property to `* Enter a Valid Email`. In the Properties window, tap or click the list arrow in the ControlToValidate property and then tap or click txtEmail.

- **Add Regular Expression Validator for Email** Drag the RegularExpressionValidator object below the Email Address field. Name the Validator object `revEmail`. Change its ErrorMessage property to `* Error Email Format`. Tap or click the list arrow in the ControlToValidate property, and then tap or click txtEmail. Tap or click the ellipsis button in the ValidationExpression property. When the Regular Expression Editor dialog box opens, select Internet e-mail address. Tap or click the OK button (ref: Figure 9-58).

- **Add the Missing Cabin Selection Message** Drag a Label object onto the web form to the third row in the third column. Place the label in the same row as the Grizzly check box. Name the label `lblCabinError`. Change the Text property to `* Select a Cabin`. Set the Visible property for the label to False.

(continues)

● **Add the Submit Button** Drag a Button object to the last row of the third column to the right of the Calendar object. Change the Button object (ID) property to `btnSubmit`. Change the Text property to `Submit`. Tap or click after the Submit button and press the ENTER key several times until the Submit button is at the top of the cell.

● **Add a Calendar Warning Label** Drag a Label object below the Submit button. Change the (ID) property of the Label object to `lblCalendarError`. Change the Text property to `* Select a valid date`. The warning message is displayed only if a valid date is not selected. Change the Visible property to False.

● **Add a Result Label** Drag a Label object below the Submit button and the calendar error Label object. Name the Label object `lblReservation`. Delete any value in the Text property. The lblReservation placeholder with the text [lblReservation] is displayed on the web form, but will not appear in the actual webpage.

● **Change the DOCUMENT Property** Tap or click the object arrow in the Properties window and then select DOCUMENT. Type `Big Bear Cabins` as the Title property.

The validation objects and messages are part of the web form (Figure 9-75).

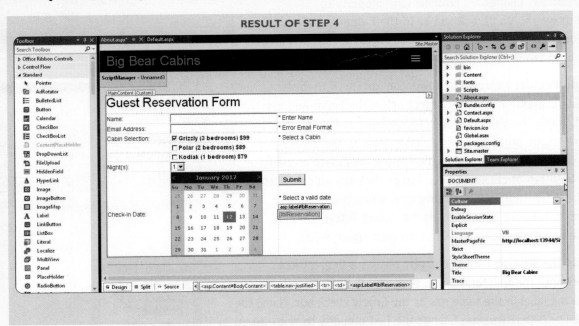

FIGURE 9-75

Phase 4: Code the Application

5

● **Code the Comments** Double-tap or double-click the Submit button on the form to begin coding the btnSubmit_Click event in the web application. Insert the first four standard comments at the top of the code window. Insert the command Option Strict On at the beginning of the code to turn on strict type checking.

HINT

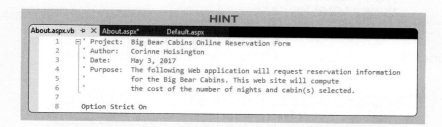

● **Comment on the btnSubmit Click Event** In the btnSubmit click event, enter a comment that explains the purpose of the click event.

HINT

```
 9   ⊟Partial Class About
10        Inherits System.Web.UI.Page
11
          -references
12   ⊟    Protected Sub btnSubmit_Click(ByVal sender As Object, ByVal e As System.EventArgs) Handles btnSubmit.Click
13            ' The btnSubmit Click Event will calculate the cost of the cost of the cabin
14            ' based on the type of cabin selected and the number of nights reserved.
```

● **Initialize Variables** Tap or click in the btnSubmit click event and enter the variables used in the application. These variables include String variables for the name and email address; Decimal variables that will contain the cabin costs for the three cabins and the result of the cabin cost calculation; an Integer value for the number of nights the user selects from the drop-down list; and a String variable in which to compose the reservation message.

HINT

Guided Program Development   *continued*

- **Trim the TextBox Object Data** Using the Trim procedure, write the code to remove excess spaces from the data the user entered. Place the trimmed Name from the TextBox object in the strName variable and the trimmed Email address in the strEmail variable *(ref: Figure 9-67)*.

```
           HINT
26          ' Trim additional spaces that are entered by the user
27          strName = txtName.Text.Trim
28          strEmail = txtEmail.Text.Trim
```

- **Clear the Reservation Message** Write a statement to clear the lblReservations label.

```
           HINT
29          lblReservation.Text = ""
```

- **Ensure a Cabin is Selected** Write an If statement that ensures a cabin has been selected. The Checked property of one or more of the CheckBox objects must be true. Use the Not operator to check for all three properties. If the cabin has not been selected, display the cabin error message.

```
           HINT
30          If Not (chkGrizzly.Checked Or chkPolar.Checked Or chkKodiak.Checked) Then
31              lblCabinError.Visible = True
```

- **Ensure a Valid Date Is Selected** Regardless of whether a valid cabin was selected, the program must ensure a valid date was selected. Therefore, if a cabin is not selected, write an If statement that ensures the date is valid (that is, the selected date is not less than the current date). If the date is invalid, display the calendar error message; otherwise, do not display the calendar error message.

HINT
30   If Not (chkGrizzly.Checked Or chkPolar.Checked Or chkKodiak.Checked) Then
31   lblCabinError.Visible = True
32   If cldArrival.SelectedDate < cldArrival.TodaysDate Then
33   lblCalendarError.Visible = True
34   Else
35   lblCalendarError.Visible = False
36   End If

- **Hide Cabin Message When Cabin Is Selected** If a cabin is selected, the cabin error message must be hidden; that is, the cabin error message Visible property must be set to False. Write the statement to set the Visible property to False.

HINT
37   Else
38   lblCabinError.Visible = False

- **Ensure a Valid Date Is Selected** When a cabin has been selected, the program must ensure a valid date was selected. If a cabin is selected and a valid date is selected, the data validity checking is complete and the cabin cost can be calculated. Write a statement to ensure that the selected date is greater than or equal to the current date, and if the date is valid, set the Visible property for the error message to False.

HINT
39   If cldArrival.SelectedDate >= cldArrival.TodaysDate Then
40   lblCalendarError.Visible = False

(continues)

● **Determine Total of Cabin Costs** The user can select more than one cabin. For example, one cabin might be for parents and another cabin might be for their children. Therefore, the program must determine if each check box is checked, and if so, the cabin cost per night is accumulated. Write the statements to determine if a cabin check box is checked and, if so, to accumulate the cabin costs in the decCabinCost variable.

	HINT
41	' Calculate the cost of the cabin(s) selected by the user
42	If **chkGrizzly.Checked** Then
43	**decCabinCost += decGrizzlyCost**
44	End If
45	If **chkPolar.Checked** Then
46	**decCabinCost += decPolarCost**
47	End If
48	If **chkKodiak.Checked** Then
49	**decCabinCost += decKodiakCost**
50	End If

● **Calculate Total Cabin Cost** To calculate the total cabin cost, the number of nights selected by the user from the drop-down list must be converted from a String to an Integer. Then, the total cabin costs (number of nights × cabin cost) must be calculated. Write the statements to perform these activities.

	HINT
51	**intNumberOfNights** = Convert.ToInt32(ddlNIghts.SelectedItem.Text)
52	**decCabinCost = intNumberOfNights * decCabinCost**

● **Create the Reservation Message** Write the code to create the reservation message and place it in the strMessage String variable. Then, place the message stored in the strMessage variable in the Text property of the lblReservation Label object *(ref: Figure 9-62)*.

	HINT
53	**strMessage** = "A reservation has been made for: " & "\<br\>" _
54	& strName & "\<br\>" & "Email: " & strEmail & "\<br\>"
55	**strMessage** &= "The cabin(s) cost is: " _
56	& decCabinCost.ToString("C") & "\<br\>"
57	**strMessage** &= "Arrival Date: " _
58	& cldArrival.SelectedDate.ToShortDateString() _
59	& "\<br\>" & " for " & intNumberOfNights & " night(s)"
60	**lblReservation.Text = strMessage**

● **Show Calendar Error Message** If the user did not select a valid date for the check-in date, display the calendar error message by changing the Visible property for the error message label to True.

	HINT
61	Else
62	**lblCalendarError.Visible** = True
63	End If
64	End If
65	End Sub
66	End Class
67	

Code Listing

The complete code for the sample program is shown in Figure 9-76.

```vbnet
1    ' Project:  Big Bear Cabins Online Reservation Form
2    ' Author:   Corinne Hoisington
3    ' Date:     May 3, 2017
4    ' Purpose:  The following Web application will request reservation information
5    '           for the Big Bear Cabins. This web site will compute
6    '           the cost of the number of nights and cabin(s) selected.
7
8    Option Strict On
     -references
9    Partial Class About
10       Inherits System.Web.UI.Page
11
        -references
12       Protected Sub btnSubmit_Click(ByVal sender As Object, ByVal e As System.EventArgs) Handles btnSubmit.Click
13           ' The btnSubmit Click Event will calculate the cost of the cost of the cabin
14           ' based on the type of cabin selected and the number of nights reserved.
15
16           ' Declare and initialize variables
17           Dim decGrizzlyCost As Decimal = 99D
18           Dim decPolarCost As Decimal = 89D
19           Dim decKodiakCost As Decimal = 79D
20           Dim strName As String
21           Dim strEmail As String
22           Dim decCabinCost As Decimal = 0D
23           Dim intNumberOfNights As Integer
24           Dim strMessage As String
25
26           ' Trim additional spaces that are entered by the user
27           strName = txtName.Text.Trim
28           strEmail = txtEmail.Text.Trim
29           lblReservation.Text = ""
30           If Not (chkGrizzly.Checked Or chkPolar.Checked Or chkKodiak.Checked) Then
31               lblCabinError.Visible = True
32               If cldArrival.SelectedDate < cldArrival.TodaysDate Then
33                   lblCalendarError.Visible = True
34               Else
35                   lblCalendarError.Visible = False
36               End If
37           Else
38               lblCabinError.Visible = False
39               If cldArrival.SelectedDate >= cldArrival.TodaysDate Then
40                   lblCalendarError.Visible = False
41                   ' Calculate the cost of the cabin(s) selected by the user
42                   If chkGrizzly.Checked Then
43                       decCabinCost += decGrizzlyCost
44                   End If
45                   If chkPolar.Checked Then
46                       decCabinCost += decPolarCost
47                   End If
48                   If chkKodiak.Checked Then
49                       decCabinCost += decKodiakCost
50                   End If
51                   intNumberOfNights = Convert.ToInt32(ddlNIghts.SelectedItem.Text)
52                   decCabinCost = intNumberOfNights * decCabinCost
53                   strMessage = "A reservation has been made for: " & "<br>" _
54                       & strName & "<br>" & "Email: " & strEmail & "<br>"
55                   strMessage &= "The cabin(s) cost is: " _
56                       & decCabinCost.ToString("C") & "<br>"
57                   strMessage &= "Arrival Date: " _
58                       & cldArrival.SelectedDate.ToShortDateString() _
59                       & "<br>" & " for " & intNumberOfNights & " night(s)"
60                   lblReservation.Text = strMessage
61               Else
62                   lblCalendarError.Visible = True
63               End If
64           End If
65       End Sub
66   End Class
67
```

FIGURE 9-76

Summary

In this chapter you have learned to create an online web application using ASP.NET 5. The items listed in the table shown in Figure 9-77 include all the new Visual Studio and Visual Basic skills you have learned in this chapter.

Visual Basic Skills		
Skill	**Figure Number**	**Video Number**
Examine the Big Bear Cabins Web Application	Figure 9-1	Video 9-1
Create a Visual Basic Web Project	Figure 9-4	Video 9-2
Change Text on the Master Page	Figure 9-8	Video 9-3
Rename Navigation Buttons	Figure 9-13	Video 9-4
Add an Image Object on the Webpage	Figure 9-17	Video 9-5
Enter Text Directly on the Webpage	Figure 9-20	Video 9-6
Add a Table for Alignment on a Web Form	Figure 9-25	Video 9-7
Add a TextBox Object	Figure 9-27	Video 9-8
Add a CheckBox Object	Figure 9-30	Video 9-9
Add a DropDownList Object	Figure 9-35	Video 9-10
Add a Calendar Object to a Web Form	Figure 9-40	Video 9-11
Specify a Web Form Title	Figure 9-43	Video 9-12
Write Code for Check Box Objects	Page 621	
Write Code for a Calendar Object	Page 627	
Validate TextBox Object Using a RequiredFieldValidator Object	Figure 9-48	Video 9-13
Validate the Range Using a RangeValidator Object	Page 631	
Validate Two Objects with the CompareValidator Object	Page 632	
Validate Data Using a RegularExpressionValidator Object	Figure 9-54	Video 9-14
Validate Data Using Multiple Validations	Page 636	
Display a ValidationSummary Control	Page 636	
Use the Tag in Visual Basic Code	Page 637	
Use the String Length Property	Page 638	
Use the Trim Procedure	Page 639	
Convert Uppercase and Lowercase Text	Page 640	

FIGURE 9-77

Learn Online

Reinforcement activities and resources are available at no additional cost on www.CengageBrain.com. Visit http://solutions.cengage.com/ctdownloads/ for detailed instructions about accessing the available resources at the Student Companion Site.

Knowledge Check

1. In an active server page, what type of computer executes the event handler code you write in Visual Basic 2015?

2. Name five locations where you can test and display a Visual Basic ASP.NET webpage.

3. Name five websites that incorporate web forms and state the purpose of each web form (such as to enter customer information for purchasing an item). Do not list any sites that were mentioned in this chapter.

4. What is the extension of an ASP webpage?

5. A webpage or website is hosted on a(n) _____ _____.

6. A website that allows you to enter information is considered a(n) _____ webpage.

7. In a Windows application, each object has a (Name) property. In a web application, each object has a(n) _____ property, which is similar to the (Name) property.

8. Write a line of code that would display the date selected by the user in the TextBox shown in Figure 9-78.

FIGURE 9-78

9. In the ListBox object shown in Figure 9-79, write the lines of code that would display in a Label named lblSizeDisplay "You have selected size: Large" if the user selects "L."

FIGURE 9-79

Knowledge Check *continued*

10. Explain the major difference between CheckBox and RadioButton objects.

11. What is the name of the property that assigns the object name to the validation control?

12. Which control validator checks if a value is between 7 and 21?

13. Which control validator confirms that the user enters the constant value of 13.2?

14. Which control validator confirms that a TextBox object is not left blank?

15. Write a line of code that would convert strGender to all lowercase letters.

16. Write a line of code that would assign the length of a string named strCourtFiling to the variable intSizeOfCourtFiling.

17. Write a line of code that would display in a Label object named lblDisplayBirthday the date a user selected from a Calendar object named cldBirthdate.

18. How does the Image object in ASP.NET differ from an image in a Windows application?

19. In the browser window shown in Figure 9-80, name the type of validation and list any changes that were made in the Properties window.

FIGURE 9-80

20. What is the name of the page that serves as a template for the pages that are actually displayed in the browser?

Debugging Exercises

1. What will be contained in the Text property of the lblResult Label object after executing the following code?

```
Dim strPhrase As String
strPhrase = " Start by doing what's necessary;"
strPhrase += " then do what's possible "
strPhrase+= "and suddenly you are doing the impossible."
strPhrase = strPhrase.Trim()
lblResult.Text=strPhrase
```

2. Fix the error(s) in the following line of code.

```
decRoyalTitle = strRoyalTitle(Text.Length)
```

3. Fix the error(s) in the following lines of code.

```
If (chkSpeedingTicket.Checked) = True Then
decSpeedingTicket += 210
End If
```

4. What is the output of the following code?

```
Dim strPhrase As String
strPhrase = "Shut the front door now"
lblResult.Text= "Count =" & strPhrase.Length
```

5. Write the output that would be displayed in the Info label after the following statements are executed.

```
lblInfo.Text = "Home Address: " & "<br>" & "356 Harvard Rd" & "<br>" &
"Lynchburg, VA 24502"
```

Program Analysis

1. Name each of the property changes that are required in the Properties window for a Range Validator in order to validate that a TextBox named txtDeductibleRange contains a value in the range 200.50 up to and including 400.00. Display an error message that states "Please enter an acceptable deductible between 200.50 and 400."

2. Write a Visual Basic statement that displays the length of a variable named strSentence in a Label object named lblStringLength.

3. Write the section of code that would display a list of services in a Label object named lblService if the user selects any of the corresponding CheckBoxes shown in Figure 9-81.

FIGURE 9-81

Complete one or more of the following case programming assignments. Submit the program and materials you create to your instructor. The level of difficulty is indicated for each case programming assignment.

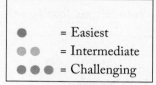

● = Easiest
●● = Intermediate
●●● = Challenging

1 ● YOUTH HOSTELS

Design a web application for a youth hostel booking application. Write the code that will execute according to the program requirements shown in Figure 9-82 and the Use Case Definition document shown in Figure 9-83. Before writing the code, create an event planning document for each event in the program. The completed webpage is shown in Figure 9-84 on page 667.

REQUIREMENTS DOCUMENT

Date:	August 11, 2017
Date Submitted:	
Application Title:	Youth Hostels
Purpose:	This web application allows the user to book hostels in Edinburgh, Florence, and Barcelona.
Program Procedures:	From a web application, the user completes an online reservation form to select the location of the hostel, the number of days for the stay, and the starting date.
Algorithms, Processing, and Conditions:	1. The user must be able to enter the requested reservation information on a web form. The information should include the user's name, the city location for the hostel (Edinburgh $17 a night, Florence $23 a night, or Barcelona $19 a night), the number of nights (maximum of 10 nights), and the start date. 2. After entering the reservation information, the user taps or clicks the Submit button. 3. The information entered is validated. 4. The application displays the final cost of staying at the selected hostel.
Notes and Restrictions:	1. Data validation controls should be used. The name is validated to confirm that it is not left blank. 2. The calendar object must have a date selected that is later than the current date. 3. Only one city can be selected. 4. The number of nights must be 1–10 nights. 5. A user may reserve only for one person.

FIGURE 9-82 (continues)

Case Programming Assignments

Youth Hostels (continued)

Comments:	1. Display a picture of a hostel on the web form. An image URL can be located with a search engine such as Bing or Google.
	2. Place the image and title on the Site.master page. Delete the navigational links to make a single page.

FIGURE 9-82 (continued)

USE CASE DEFINITION

1. The webpage opens, displaying a picture of a hostel, one TextBox object to request a name, three RadioButton objects to select a city location, a DropDownList object displaying the length of the stay (1–10 nights), a Calendar object to select the start date, and a Submit button.
2. The user enters the information, makes the appropriate selections, and taps or clicks the Submit button.
3. Validation controls check the data.
4. The application displays the final cost of the hostel stay.

FIGURE 9-83

Case Programming Assignments

Youth Hostels *(continued)*

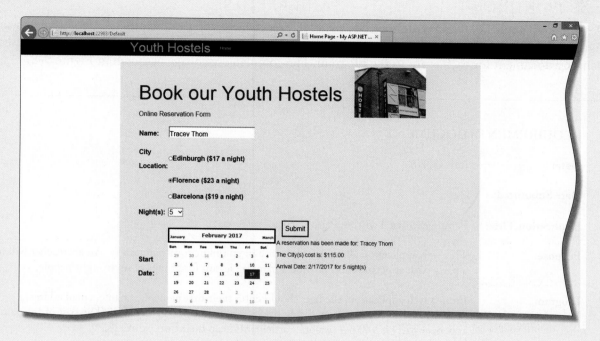

FIGURE 9-84

© iStock.com/JannHuizenga

2 ● PAINTING WITH A TWIST — PAINT PARTIES

Design a web application and write the code that will execute according to the program requirements shown in Figure 9-85 and the Use Case Definition document shown in Figure 9-86. Before writing the code, create an event planning document for each event in the program. The completed webpage is shown in Figure 9-87.

REQUIREMENTS DOCUMENT

Date:	July 31, 2017
Date Submitted:	
Application Title:	Painting with a Twist — Paint Parties
Purpose:	This web application allows an adult to sign up online for a paint party. An art teacher will hold a party with appetizers and provide a painting lesson for groups of up to eight people.
Program Procedures:	From a web application, the user should enter their first name, last name, email address, group size (1–8), and requested date to sign up for the paint party class. The cost of the paint/appetizer party is $40 per person. Participants keep their own paintings.
Algorithms, Processing, and Conditions:	1. The user must be able to enter their first and last name, email address, group size (1–8) using a DropDownList, and requested date to sign up for the paint party class. 2. The user taps or clicks the Submit button. 3. The information entered is validated. 4. The application displays the details about the painting party and the cost.
Notes and Restrictions:	Data validation tools should be used. The first and last names are validated to confirm that they are not left blank and the email address is valid.
Comments:	1. The email address will be displayed in lowercase letters. 2. Place the title and image on the Site.master page. Display a picture of paint party on the web form. An image URL can be located on a search engine such as Bing or Google. Delete the navigational links.

FIGURE 9-85

(continues)

Painting with a Twist — Paint Parties (continued)

USE CASE DEFINITION

1. The webpage opens, displaying the title, three TextBox objects to enter the user's name and email address, a DropDownList object for selecting the number of adults in the group, and a Submit button.
2. User enters their first name, last name, and email address.
3. User selects the size of the group and the date.
4. User taps or clicks the Submit button.
5. Validation controls check that the data was entered.
6. The application displays the details and cost of the paint party.

FIGURE 9-86

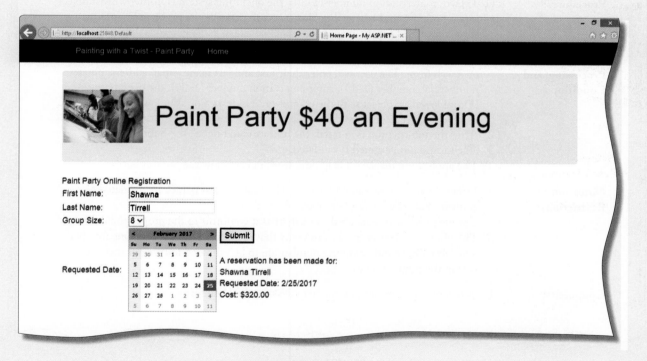

FIGURE 9-87

© iStock.com/monkeybusinessimages

3 • HELP DESK REQUEST

Design a web application and write the code that will execute according to the program requirements shown in Figure 9-88 and the Use Case Definition document in Figure 9-89. Before writing the code, create an event planning document for each event in the program. The completed webpage is shown in Figure 9-90.

REQUIREMENTS DOCUMENT

Date:	February 22, 2017
Date Submitted:	
Application Title:	Help Desk Request
Purpose:	This web application allows college staff to fill in a web form requesting help from a computer help desk.
Program Procedures:	From a web application, the user should enter their name, email address, lab number (1–15), computer station number (1–30), the operating system (DropDownList object with two options), and a large TextBox object to describe the problem in order to create a work ticket for the help desk.
Algorithms, Processing, and Conditions:	1. The user must be able to enter information about the requested computer repair on a web form. The user will enter their first and last name, email address, phone number, lab number (1–15), computer station number (1–30), the operating system (DropDownList object with the choices of Windows 8 or Windows 10), and a large TextBox object to describe the problem to create a work ticket for the help desk.
	2. After the information is entered, the user can tap or click the Submit button.
	3. The information entered is validated.
	4. The application displays a help desk work ticket below the Submit button.
Notes and Restrictions:	1. Data validation tools should be used. The first and last names are validated to confirm that they are not left blank.
	2. The email address is checked to verify that it conforms to the proper email format.
	3. The phone number is checked to verify that it conforms to a U.S. phone number.
	4. The lab number and computer number are to be validated to confirm they are within the proper ranges.
Comments:	Display a picture representing the help desk on the Web form.

FIGURE 9-88

(continues)

Help Desk Request (continued)

USE CASE DEFINITION

1. The webpage opens, displaying an information technology help desk request form with a picture representing the help desk, TextBox objects requesting the student's first and last names, email address, phone number, lab number, computer station, operating system DropDown List, a description of the issue, and a Submit button.
2. User taps or clicks the Submit button.
3. Validation controls check the data.
4. The application displays the information that was sent to the help desk.

FIGURE 9-89

FIGURE 9-90

4

●●
CLICK FOR TEE TIMES

Design a web application and write the code that will execute according to the program requirements shown in Figure 9-91. Before writing the code, create an event planning document for each event in the program. Create a Use Case Definition document for the application.

REQUIREMENTS DOCUMENT

Date:	January 4, 2017
Date Submitted:	
Application Title:	Click for Tee Times
Purpose:	This web application allows the user to sign up online for a golf tee time and date.
Program Procedures:	From a web application, the user should select a tee time and date.
Algorithms, Processing, and Conditions:	1. The website has two pages. The Home page provides information about the golf course. The second page allows users to sign up for a tee time. 2. The web form should include the name of the golfer requesting the tee time, the possible times, and a calendar to select a date. 3. After the selection is entered, the user taps or clicks the Submit button. 4. The information entered is validated.
Notes and Restrictions:	1. Data validation controls should be used. 2. No optional service is required. 3. A drop-down list control displays tee times on the half hour and hour from 8 am to 2 pm. 4. The golf date must be later than the current date.
Comments:	Display a golf picture representing the golf course on the web form.

FIGURE 9-91

5 ••
LA VILLA PIZZERIA

Design a web application that calculates the cost of pizza according to the prices listed in Figure 9-92. The Home page opens with a picture and information about the great homemade pizza pies at the pizzeria. The Order page provides an order form and displays the final price. Write the code that will execute according to the program requirements shown in Figure 9-93. Before writing the code, create an event planning document for each event in the program. Create a Use Case Definition document for the application.

Pizza Size	Cost
Small	$8.99
Medium	$12.99
Large	$15.99
Extra Large	$18.99
Each Extra Topping (Cheese Included)	$0.99

FIGURE 9-92

Case Programming Assignments

La Villa Pizzeria (continued)

REQUIREMENTS DOCUMENT

Date:	July 24, 2017
Date Submitted:	
Application Title:	La Villa Pizzeria
Purpose:	This web application allows a customer to fill out an online pizza order form.
Program Procedures:	From a web application, the user should enter their name, address, and phone number. They also should select the size of pizza they would like to order and the toppings. The final cost of the order will be displayed.
Algorithms, Processing, and Conditions:	1. The website has two pages. The Home page promotes the pizzeria and lists a phone number to call when ordering. The Order page displays an order form.
	2. The user must be able to enter information to order a pizza using a web form. The user will enter their first and last name, address, phone number, the size of the pizza from a DropDownList object and CheckBoxes displaying pizza topping choices (at least six kinds of toppings).
	3. After the information is entered, the user taps or clicks the Submit button.
	4. The information entered will be validated.
	5. The application displays the final cost of the pizza order and a message that the pizza will be delivered in under 45 minutes.
Notes and Restrictions:	1. Data validation tools should be used. The first and last names are validated to confirm that they are not left blank.
	2. The phone number is checked to ensure that it conforms to a U.S. phone number.
Comments:	A picture of a pizza will be displayed on the web form.

FIGURE 9-93

6 ●● PADDLE BOARD RENTALS

Design a web application and write the code that will execute according to the program requirements shown in Figure 9-94. Before writing the code, create an event planning document for each event in the program. Create a Use Case Definition document for the application.

REQUIREMENTS DOCUMENT

Date:	January 4, 2017
Date Submitted:	
Application Title:	Paddle Board Rentals
Purpose:	This web application allows the user to reserve paddle boards online. Paddle boards are stand-up surf boards that you paddle.
Program Procedures:	From a single-page web application, the user should enter their name, address, and phone number. They also should select the number of hours to rent the paddle board, the type of paddle board, and the number of paddle boards to rent. The final cost of the rental will be displayed.
Algorithms, Processing, and Conditions:	1. The user must be able to view a graphic of a paddle board, a DropDownList object with the number of hours (1–8), a calendar requesting the date the paddle board is being reserved, the type of paddle board (All Rounder, Hybrid, or Race), and a TextBox object indicating the quantity (check to make sure the number is between 1 and 12). 2. After the information is entered, the user taps or clicks the Submit button. 3. The information entered will be validated. 4. The application will display a summary of their reservation. All Rounder boards are $5 per hour, hybrid boards are $6 per hour, and race boards are $7.50 per hour per bike. The total cost will be displayed for the total reservation with the date.
Notes and Restrictions:	1. Data validation tools should be used. The range of the quantity ordered is 1–12. 2. The name, address, and phone number must be present. 3. The phone number must conform to a U.S. phone number.
Comments:	A picture of a paddle board will be shown on the web form.

FIGURE 9-94

7 ●●●
RE-CREATE AN ONLINE FORM

Create a requirements document and a Use Case Definition document, and then design a web application, based on the case project shown in Figure 9-95.

Find an online form on the Internet you would like to re-create that has varied objects such as a label, radio button, check box, text box, and drop down list objects. Use a similar layout of the existing website and at least eight objects on the form to display your own version of the website for practice. Validate the form using validation objects as needed.

FIGURE 9-95

Case Programming Assignments

8 •••
MOORE'S LAW

Create a requirements document and a Use Case Definition document, and then create a web application, based on the case project shown in Figure 9-96.

Create a web application that displays Moore's Law, which states that the computing power or the number of transistors within the same silicon processor doubles every 18 months. In other words, computing speed doubles every 18 months. As shown in the following table, allow the user to enter the current average speed in GHz and display the next 15 years of projected speed. Use the validation controls to make sure the entry is filled in and that the decimal value entered is between 1.0 and 10.0.

FIGURE 9-96

Case Programming Assignments

9 ●●●
JAVA SHOP

Create a requirements document and a Use Case Definition document, and then create a web application, based on the case project shown in Figure 9-97.

To speed up the ordering process, a local coffee shop will allow customers to order their coffee on a touch screen while standing in line. The web application will display the cost of the coffee. Allow the customer to enter their first name, display a DropDownList object with five coffee flavors, and allow the user to select the size of the coffee: Tall, Grande, and Vente. Prices for these sizes are shown in the table below. Use validation controls. The coffee shop also provides options such as a double shot, flavored syrups, whipped cream, and soy milk for 49 cents each. Display the person's name and order with the purchase price with a 6.5% sales tax.

Size	Price
Tall	$2.59
Grande	$3.09
Vente	$3.59

FIGURE 9-97

CHAPTER 10

Incorporating Databases with ADO.NET

OBJECTIVES

You will have mastered the material in this chapter when you can:

- Understand database files

- Connect to a database using ADO.NET 5

- Connect Form objects to the data source

- Bind database fields to the Windows Form object

- Access database information on a Windows Form object

- Add a record

- Delete a record

- Select records from a list

- Program beyond the Database Wizard

- Create the OleDbDataAdapter object

Introduction

As you have learned, information used in Visual Basic 2015 can originate from any source, including data entered into objects such as a TextBox, data assigned within the code, or data read from a text file. Large applications often need to connect to the data required in business today. Businesses store huge volumes of data in databases, and information technology (IT) must manage this data and perform database operations such as changes, additions, and deletions. IT must also retrieve database information for viewing and decision making. Increasingly, developers use Visual Basic 2015 to connect to databases and allow users to perform the aforementioned operations and more. Within the Visual Studio environment, applications can connect to a variety of database sources through the data access technology of ADO.NET.

Chapter Project

In the sample chapter project, the Creative Art Commission requires a Windows application to access its Art Prize Competition database, which documents local artists, the names of their submitted artwork, and the retail price of their artwork. Art from the community is displayed in galleries as well as in public and private collections. A prize will be awarded each year to the best artistic work submitted to the Creative Art Commission. The commission provides a platform for anyone to be an artist and for any space within the community to be a venue.

The information in the Art database is stored as a Microsoft Access database. By placing the information in a simple-to-use Windows application, the staff of the Creative Art Commission can easily view, update, and delete local artists' information. By accessing the Creative Art Windows application, the entire staff can identify local artists, their exhibition locations, and the sale price of their art.

The Creative Art Windows application loads information about local artists and their works from a Microsoft Access 2013 database named Art.accdb, which is stored on a USB drive. When the Windows form opens, it displays the first record, which indicates the first artist, as shown in Figure 10-1.

HEADS UP

The new LINQ database commands are featured in Appendix E. LINQ (Language Integrated Query, pronounced *link*) is one of the new features provided with Visual Basic 2015 and .NET Framework 5. LINQ makes it easy to query data using SQL (Structured Query Language) commands within the Visual Basic code window.

Move next button   Move last button

© iStock.com/dp_photo

FIGURE 10-1

The user can use the navigation toolbar at the top of the Windows form to continue through the other artists' information. The Windows form displays each of the 16 records that currently are saved in the Artist table, which was created using Microsoft Access 2013, as shown in Figure 10-2.

FIGURE 10-2

The Art.accdb database can also be updated to include new artists who are taking part in the Art Prize competition. The user can tap or click the Add new button on the navigation toolbar at the top of the Windows form to open a blank record. Figure 10-3 shows a new record entered into the Windows form to represent a new artist named Eric Matthews. After entering the record, the user can add the record to the database by tapping or clicking the Save Data button on the navigation toolbar. The original Access database is permanently updated.

© iStock.com/dp_photo

FIGURE 10-3

HEADS UP

A version of Microsoft Access that can open databases in the 2007–2010 format, such as Access 2013, must be installed on your computer before you can incorporate databases with ADO.NET.

A user can also change the Art.accdb Access database by deleting records using the Windows form interface. The user can delete a record by tapping or clicking the Delete button on the navigation toolbar. Tapping or clicking the Delete button removes the record currently displayed in the Windows form. For example, if William Stuart decides not to be part of the competition, the record of William's information needs to be removed from the Access database. The user taps or clicks the buttons on the navigation toolbar to access William's artist record and then taps or clicks the Delete button shown in Figure 10-4 to permanently remove any record of William's information.

Delete
button

FIGURE 10-4

© iStock.com/dp_photo

TextBox objects are not the only objects that can be used to display database data. In Figure 10-5, a ComboBox object is used to display the artist's name, which is stored in the Artist Name field. When a field such as Artist Name is displayed in a ComboBox object, the user can tap or click the ComboBox arrow to display a list of values in the field. The user then can tap or click a name in the Artist Name field list to navigate directly to the individual record for the selected artist. For example, the user can view information about artist Liam Fix by selecting his name from the ComboBox object for the Artist Name field, as shown in Figure 10-5.

FIGURE 10-5

© iStock.com/dp_photo

The Creative Art Commission intends to keep track of the retail price of all artwork because after the competition, several local art museums may be interested in purchasing the entire lot for their own collection. A Total Retail Value button allows the user to compute the total retail price of all art records within the database. Figure 10-6 shows the Creative Art form after the Total Retail Value button has been tapped or clicked. The artwork in the Art database currently has a total value of $22,743.78.

FIGURE 10-6

© iStock.com/dp_photo

Database Files

A **database** is a collection of related information stored in a structured format. Common examples of business databases include a customer list, product information, a mailing list, or a reservation system. A database organizes data in **tables**. A table is a collection of data about a specific topic, such as a listing of local artists vying for the prize sponsored by the Creative Art Commission. Using a separate table for each topic means that you store the data only once, which makes a database efficient and reduces data-entry errors.

The chapter project creates a user interface that accesses the data from the Creative Art Commission's database, which is named Art.accdb. The Art database contains a table shown in Figure 10-7 that displays each local artist's information and their submissions for the Art Prize competition. A table structures data into rows and columns. Each row is referred to as a **record**. A record in a table contains information about a person, product, item, or other entity.

Each record in the Artist table of the Art database contains information about a local artist and their submitted painting. In Figure 10-6, the selected record shows information about Liam Fix's art submission.

HEADS UP

ADO.NET 5 works with various types of databases such as Access 2013, Access 2010, SQL, and Oracle. This chapter is written specifically for an Access 2013/2010 database, but it will work with Access 2007/2003 as well.

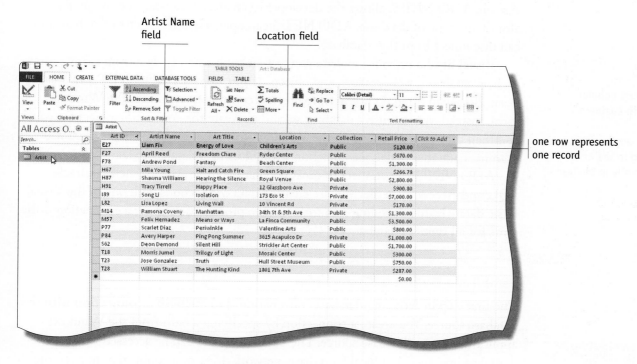

FIGURE 10-7

Each record begins with the Art ID, which is a unique number that identifies each submission in the Art Prize competition and can be used only once. The Art ID is contained in the Art ID field. Each column in a table is referred to as a **field**. A field contains a specific piece of data within a record. For example, in the Artist table, the column that lists the exhibition location of each artwork is the Location field. Each column in the table is a field and displays data such as the names of the artists, locations, whether the exhibition location is public or privately owned, and the retail price of the artwork.

Each table in a relational database must contain a unique value. Therefore, no two artists in the Art database are assigned the same Art ID. A unique field is an identifier that represents the **primary key** for the table. The Art ID is the primary key for the Artist table in the Art database. A primary key is used in relational databases to avoid problems such as duplicate records and conflicting values in fields.

Connect to a Database Using ADO.NET

To support databases that use Visual Basic 2015, a library called ActiveX Data Objects works within all Windows, Office, and Web applications. The current version, ADO.NET 5, allows the developer to create, administer, and manipulate almost any type of database. ADO.NET 5 can open a connection to a database and can disconnect from that database.

CRITICAL THINKING

Which is the most popular database used in business today?
Go to http://db-engines
.com/en/ranking to see which database is currently in the lead.

Visual Studio provides tools to connect an application to data from many sources, such as databases, web services, and objects. If you are using ADO.NET 5 in Visual Basic 2015, you often do not need to create a coded connection for the Windows form. Instead, you can use a database wizard to create the connection object for you and then drag data objects onto the Windows form. Later in the chapter, you will examine code that makes a connection without using a database wizard.

ADO.NET 5 can connect to most popular database systems such as Oracle, SQL, and Access. Whether you are creating data connections with one of the Visual Basic data wizards or coding a connection, the process of defining a connection is the same for all types of databases.

Establish a Database Connection

The first step in accessing database information is to establish a **connection** with the database source. You create a connection by specifying a path from the Windows application to the database source. The database source can be accessed from any digital source, such as a local hard drive, network drive, or a connection to a remote database through the Internet. To connect a Visual Basic 2015 application to data in a database, you can use the **Data Source Configuration Wizard**. After you complete the wizard, data is available in the **Data Sources window** for dragging onto a Windows form. A connection string contacts the data source and establishes a connection with the database using the Data Source Configuration Wizard. The wizard uses the Fill method to fill a DataSet object with table rows and columns from a selected table within a database. A **DataSet** object is a temporary cache storage for data retrieved from a data source. The DataSet object is a major component of the ADO.NET 5 architecture.

For the Creative Art chapter project, a Windows application must connect to the Access database table named Artist in the Art.accdb database. To connect to the database using the Data Source Configuration Wizard, you can complete the following steps:

STEP 1   Create a Windows application named Creative Art. Name the form `frmArtPrize`. Change the Text property to `Creative Art Commission - Art Prize Competition`. Resize the form to a size of `670, 450`. Change the BackColor property to White on the Web tab. An image representing one of the local artists, named Art.jpg, is available with your Data Files. Place a PictureBox object on the left side of the window. Name the PictureBox object `picArt`. Change the Size property to `293, 160`. Using the Image property, import the Art.jpg image for the PictureBox object. Change the SizeMode to StretchImage. On the right side of the form, place a Label object named `lblTitle`. Change the Text property to `Art Prize Finalists` on two lines. Make the Font property Script MT, Bold, size 40, and the ForeColor property OrangeRed on the Web tab. Center-align the text. Close the Toolbox, and then tap or click Project on the menu bar.

The Windows form is created and the Project menu is opened (Figure 10-8).

FIGURE 10-8

STEP 2   Tap or click Add New Data Source on the Project menu.

The Data Source Configuration Wizard opens and requests the Data Source Type (Figure 10–9).

Data Source
Configuration
Wizard

Database is
source of data

Next button

FIGURE 10-9

STEP 3 In the Choose a Data Source Type dialog box, tap or click Database, and then tap or click Next. In the Choose a Database Model dialog box, tap or click Dataset, and then tap or click Next.

After you select the Dataset option and tap or click the Next button, the Choose Your Data Connection dialog box opens (Figure 10-10).

FIGURE 10-10

STEP 4   Tap or click the New Connection button. In the Add Connection dialog box, tap or click the Change button to select the data source.

After the New Connection button is tapped or clicked, the Add Connection dialog box opens. After you tap or click the Change button, the Choose Data Source dialog box opens (Figure 10-11).

Choose Data Source dialog box

Microsoft Access Database File selected

FIGURE 10-11

STEP 5 In the Choose Data Source dialog box, select Microsoft Access Database
File because the Art database is an Access database. Tap or click the Continue button.

*The Add Connection dialog box reopens (Figure 10-12). The Data source appears as
Microsoft Access Database File.*

Add Connection
dialog box

Data source is
Microsoft Access
Database File

Browse button

FIGURE 10-12

STEP 6   Tap or click the Browse button to the right of the Database file name field. Select the USB device on the E drive and then select the file named Art.

The Access database file Art is selected on the USB E drive (Figure 10–13). The files and folders on your USB drive might be different from those shown here.

FIGURE 10-13

STEP 7 Tap or click the Open button.

The Add Connection dialog box reopens (Figure 10-14).

Add Connection
dialog box

Add Connection   ?   ×

Enter information to connect to the selected data source or click
"Change" to choose a different data source and/or provider.

Data source:

| Microsoft Access Database File (OLE DB) | Change... |

database
selected as
data source

Database file name:

| E:\Art.accdb | Browse... |

Log on to the database

User name: Admin

Password:

☐ Save my password

OK button   Advanced...

| Test Connection | OK | Cancel |

FIGURE 10-14

STEP 8 Tap or click the OK button in the Add Connection dialog box.

The Choose Your Data Connection dialog box opens to confirm the database file you are using (Figure 10-15).

data connection is an Access database file named Art.accdb

Next button

FIGURE 10-15

STEP 9 Tap or click the Next button.

A dialog box opens to remind you that the connection uses a local data file that is not in the current project (Figure 10-16). The dialog box also asks if you want to copy the file to your project. You do not want to add data and update the copied database. It is best to update the original database file.

FIGURE 10-16

STEP 10   Tap or click the No button and then tap or click the Next button. When the Choose Your Database Objects dialog box opens, select which database objects you want in the DataSet. Tap or click the expand icon next to the Tables option. Tap or click the Artist check box to select that table. A connection is made from the Visual Basic application to the Artist table within the Art.accdb database.

After the expand icon is tapped or clicked to display the available tables, the Artist check box is checked (Figure 10-17).

FIGURE 10-17

STEP 11 Tap or click the Finish button. Tap or click ArtDataSet.xsd to select the DataSet.

The dialog box closes, and a connection is made to the Artist table. The Solution Explorer displays the DataSet named ArtDataSet.xsd (Figure 10-18).

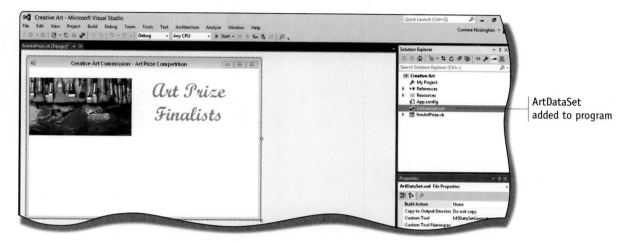

ArtDataSet added to program

FIGURE 10-18

© iStock.com/dp_photo

After a connection is established, you can design programs using the open connection and retrieve and manipulate the data accessed with the database file.

If I move my Access database file to a different path, how do I change that path within the Visual Basic application?
In the Solution Explorer, tap or click the App.config file to view the code for the database file path. In the line that begins with connectionString, you can view the path of the database file. You can change the path if you have moved the database to a different location—for example, from drive E: to drive C:.

CONSIDER THIS

View Data Available in the Source Database

After a connection is created to an existing data source, the DataSet can provide the application with the ability to interact with the database. The DataSet temporarily stores the data in the application while you work with it. After you have configured a DataSet with the Data Source Configuration Wizard, the next step is to load the DataSet with the data stored in the database. After the DataSet is filled with the table information, the data can be displayed on the Windows form. Loading the DataSet string is called **data binding**. Data binding allows you to display each field as an object on the form. You can complete data binding by dragging the fields on the form or by coding.

ONLINE REINFORCEMENT

To view a video of the process in the previous steps, visit CengageBrain.com and navigate to the resources for this title. Tap or click the link for Chapter 10 and then navigate to Video 10-2.

To view the data available in the source database, you can complete the following steps:

STEP 1 In the Art project window, point to the Data Sources tab on the left side. If the Data Sources tab is not visible, tap or click View on the menu bar, tap or click Other Windows, and then tap or click Data Sources.

The Data Sources tab is selected (Figure 10–19).

FIGURE 10-19

STEP 2 Tap or click Data Sources to view the database sources.

A DataSet named ArtDataSet is displayed along with a connection to the Artist table (Figure 10–20).

FIGURE 10-20

© iStock.com/dp_photo

STEP 3 Tap or click the expand icon for the Artist table to expand the list of field names within the table. Each bindable field item in the Data Sources window can be placed on the Windows Form object.

The fields of the Artist table are displayed (Figure 10-21). Each field is displayed by default with an icon that designates each database item as a TextBox object.

Data Sources
window

icon identifies a field
as a default
TextBox object

fields in the
Artist table

FIGURE 10-21

Bind Database Fields to the Windows Form

After a connection is created to link the database to the Windows application and the data source displays the existing field objects, you can drag the field objects to the Windows Form object. When you drag field objects from the Data Sources window, Visual Studio automatically creates a **databinding** to populate the form by binding the form object to the DataSet information.

After the first field item is placed on the Windows form, a navigation toolbar control called the **BindingNavigator** appears on the form, as shown in Figure 10-22. The BindingNavigator control consists of a ToolStrip with a series of ToolStripItem objects for most common data-related actions, such as navigating through data, adding data, and deleting data. By default, the BindingNavigator control contains the standard buttons shown in Figure 10-22.

© iStock.com/dp_photo

FIGURE 10-22

The first four arrow navigation buttons on the BindingNavigator control allow the user to move throughout the data in the associated table and to interact with the records. A user can also type a record number directly into the TextBox to navigate quickly to the associated record. The Add new button inserts a new row to add a new record to the original database table. The Delete button permanently deletes the current record displayed in the Windows form from the database table. The Save Data button saves any changes made on the current form, such as changing the spelling of a field item or updating a retail price. If a record is added or deleted, the Save Data button must be tapped or clicked to save the change to the original database table.

The BindingNavigator appears when the first table field is bound to the Windows form. To bind each database field to the Windows form object, follow these steps:

Select the Art ID field in the Data Sources window. Drag the Art ID field to the Windows Form object below the PictureBox object.

The Art ID field is placed on the Windows form (Figure 10-23). The Art ID TextBox object is now bound to the data in the table. A navigation toolbar called a Binding-Navigator control automatically is added to the top of the Windows Form object. An ArtDataSet, ArtistBindingSource, ArtistTableAdapter, TableAdapterManager, and BindingNavigator1 appear in the component tray and bind the database data to the Windows Form object.

FIGURE 10-23

© iStock.com/dp_photo

STEP 2 Drag the rest of the field objects from the Data Sources window to the Windows form. Select all the field labels and field TextBox objects and change their font size to 10 points and bold. Use the formatting tools on the Format menu to equally distribute the bound objects. You can select the Labels and the TextBox objects separately to move them independently of each other. Use the layout shown in Figure 10-24.

All of the field objects are placed on the Windows form and are formatted to align with one another (Figure 10-24).

© iStock.com/dp_photo

FIGURE 10-24

STEP 3 Run the application by tapping or clicking the Start Debugging button on the Standard toolbar to fill the Windows Form object with the data from the Artist table. Use the Move next button on the navigation toolbar to move through the records. Tap or click the Move last button to display the last record.

The Windows form opens and the data in the first record fills the TextBox objects. The Move next button on the navigation toolbar is tapped or clicked to view records. The last record is displayed (Figure 10–25).

last record
displayed

FIGURE 10-25

© iStock.com/dp_photo

ONLINE REINFORCEMENT

To view a video of the process in the previous steps, visit CengageBrain.com and navigate to the resources for this title. Tap or click the link for Chapter 10 and then navigate to Video 10-4.

Add Records

By running the application, the user can view every record within the database. In the Creative Art application, the Windows form allows the user to update the database by adding new artists. To add a new record to the database table, you can follow these steps:

STEP 1 If necessary, tap or click the Start button on the Standard toolbar to run the Creative Art application.

The Windows form opens, displaying the first record (Figure 10–26).

© iStock.com/dp_photo

FIGURE 10-26

STEP 2 Tap or click the Add new button to add a new record to the database table.

A blank record opens and displays 17 as the record number in the navigation toolbar (Figure 10–27).

17th record
displayed

Add new
button

© iStock.com/dp_photo

FIGURE 10-27

STEP 3   Add a new record by typing Y77 in the Art ID field. Type the rest of the information displayed in Figure 10-28. After the record is complete, tap or click the Save Data button on the BindingNavigator control to save the new record to the original database.

After the new record is typed into the Windows form, the Save Data button is tapped or clicked to add the record to the original database table (Figure 10–28).

17th record
displayed   Save Data
                 button   data entered for
                               new record

© iStock.com/dp_photo

FIGURE 10-28

Delete Records

Users might need to remove information for an artist who is no longer part of the Creative Art application. To delete an existing record from the database table, follow these steps:

___

STEP 1   If necessary, tap or click the Start button on the Standard toolbar to execute the Creative Art application.

The Windows form opens, displaying the first record (Figure 10-29).

FIGURE 10-29

STEP 2 Use the navigation buttons to move to Tracy Tirrell's record. Her artist record should be deleted because she has decided not to enter artwork in this year's competition. Tap or click the Delete button on the BindingNavigator control to delete her record from the database table. Tap or click the Save Data button to remove the record from the original database.

After the Delete button is tapped or clicked, Tracy Tirrell's record is deleted from the Windows form and William Stuart's record is displayed (Figure 10-30). Notice that the database now has 16 records instead of 17 records.

16 records in the database   one record has been deleted

© iStock.com/dp_photo

FIGURE 10-30

Select Records from a List

By default, the Data Sources window displays each table item as a TextBox object, but Visual Basic 2015 allows you to change the default TextBox object to another Toolbox object of your choice. In Figure 10-31, Art ID is selected in the Data Sources window, so a list arrow appears to the right of the field. When the list arrow is tapped or clicked, a listing of common Toolbox objects is displayed. The Customize option lets you select other Toolbox objects that are not already listed. For example, you can select Customize to add a MaskedTextBox instead of using the default Text-Box option if you are including a phone number or zip code.

FIGURE 10-31

In Figure 10-30, the only way to navigate through the records is to use the BindingNavigator control or enter a record number. A quicker way to move directly to a particular record is to select it from a ComboBox object. For example, in Figure 10-5 on page 683, the artist's name is displayed in a ComboBox object. The user taps or clicks the list arrow to view the items in the Artist Name list and then taps or clicks a name. The record matching the selected artist's name is displayed immediately.

To change the Toolbox object type, you can complete the following steps:

STEP 1 Select the Artist Name Label and TextBox objects on the Windows form. Press the DELETE key to delete the Artist Name objects from the Windows form. Select the Artist Name table field in the Data Sources window and then tap or click its list arrow.

The Artist Name objects are deleted from the Windows Form object (Figure 10-32). The Artist Name field in the Data Sources window displays a list of possible Toolbox object selections.

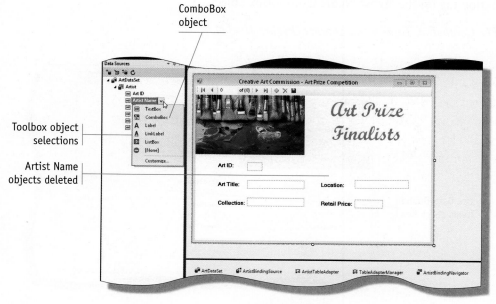

FIGURE 10-32

STEP 2   Tap or click the ComboBox object from the Toolbox object listing for the Artist Name field. Drag the Artist Name field ComboBox object to the original location of the Artist Name TextBox object on the Windows Form object. Change the font size to 10 and bold. Align the ComboBox with the other objects on the Windows form.

The Artist Name ComboBox object is placed on the Windows Form object (Figure 10-33).

Artist Name
ComboBox object

© iStock.com/dp_photo

FIGURE 10-33

STEP 3   To fill the ComboBox object with the names of the artists, the ComboBox object must be bound to the Artist Name field. To bind the items to the ComboBox object, select the Artist Name object on the Windows form and tap or click the Action tag on the Artist Name ComboBox object.

The ComboBox Tasks menu appears (Figure 10-34).

Action tag

Use Data Bound
Items check box

© iStock.com/dp_photo

FIGURE 10-34

STEP 4   Tap or click the Use Data Bound Items check box on the ComboBox Tasks menu. The Data Binding Mode list is displayed. Tap or click the Data Source list arrow under Data Binding Mode, and then select ArtistBindingSource to connect the table to the ComboBox object. Next, tap or click the Display Member list arrow and then select Artist Name. Tap or click the Value Member list arrow and then tap or click Artist Name in the list. Do not change the Selected Value entry.

The ComboBox object is now bound to the Artist Name field in the Artist table (Figure 10–35).

FIGURE 10-35

© iStock.com/dp_photo

STEP 5   Tap or click the Start Debugging button on the Standard toolbar to run the application. After the Windows form opens, tap or click the list arrow on the Artist Name ComboBox object.

The Artist Name ComboBox object displays the artists' names (Figure 10-36).

FIGURE 10-36

© iStock.com/dp_photo

STEP 6 Tap or click Song Li to move directly to the record containing the information for Song Li's artwork.

The application navigates directly to the selected record (Figure 10-37).

record for Song Li

© iStock.com/dp_photo

FIGURE 10-37

Program beyond the Database Wizard

Although the Database Wizard allows you to view, update, and delete records from a database, other operations, such as calculating an average or determining how many records meet certain criteria, often need to be programmed. For example, in the chapter project, the Creative Art Commission would like to use a Button object on the Creative Art Windows form to compute the total retail value of the Art Prize collection. The Creative Art Commission then can calculate and track the current worth of the entire Art Prize collection. Code must be written to handle that request.

Can I add a Try-Catch statement to confirm that the database is available?
In the Form Load event, you can add this code:

```
Try
     ArtistTableAdapter.Fill(ArtDataSet.Artist)
Catch
     MsgBox("The database is not on the USB")
End Try
```

CONSIDER THIS

Create the OleDbDataAdapter Object

The Database Wizard creates a bridge between the DataSet and the database that contains the data. The bridge that carries the database table information is called an **OleDbDataAdapter**.

The OleDbDataAdapter has two parts. The first part represents a set of data commands programmed using a SQL Select command. **SQL** stands for Structured Query Language, which is the language that communicates with databases. The second part of an OleDbDataAdapter is a path statement to connect to the database that fills the DataSet. The general format for the code that defines the two parts of the OleDbDataAdapter is shown in Figure 10-38.

General Format: OleDbDataAdapter

```
Dim odaName As New OleDb.OleDbDataAdapter(SQL Select command, Path statement)
```

Code:

```
'strSql is a SQL statement that selects all the fields from the Artists table
Dim strSql As String = "SELECT * FROM Artist"

' strPath provides the database type and path of the Art database
Dim strPath As String = "Provider=Microsoft.ACE.OLEDB.12.0 ;" - & "Data
Source=e:\Art.accdb"

Dim odaArtist As New OleDb.OleDbDataAdapter(strSql, strPath)
```

The SQL statement assigned to strSQL("SELECT * FROM Artist") is a query statement that requests that the entire table named Artist is opened for use by the application. The * symbol represents the wildcard symbol, which means all fields within the table are available.

The Path statement assigned to strPath("Provider=Microsoft.ACE.OLEDB.12.0 ;" & "Data Source=e:\Art.accdb") has two portions. The first portion represents the database source. Microsoft.ACE.OLEDB12.0 assigns the drivers needed to create a connection to an Access database. The second portion represents the path of where the database resides.

An instance of the OleDbDataAdapter is assigned to the variable odaArtist. The prefix oda is used for an OleDbDataAdapter.

FIGURE 10-38

Fill a DataTable Object

After the OleDbDataAdapter makes a connection to the database, a **DataTable** is needed to hold the data retrieved from that connection. The DataTable is a crucial object in the ADO.NET 5 library. The DataSet used in the Database Wizard is a collection of DataTable objects. The DataTable is initialized using the dat prefix.

After the DataTable is initialized, it must be filled using the **Fill** command with the data from the selected table. When the DataTable is filled, the appropriate tables and columns are created for the table data. As soon as you connect to the database and fill the DataTable object, the next statement should disconnect the application from the database. To keep the maximum number of connections available, you should keep connections open only as long as necessary. By using the database in disconnected form, the system resources of the computer and network are not overloaded. To disconnect from the database, use the **Dispose** command.

The code in Figure 10-39 can be executed in a program without using the Database Wizard, or you can run the wizard to access the data. The code opens a connection to the Artist table in the Art.accdb Access database on the USB drive. A DataTable named datValue is initialized. The DataTable datValue is then filled with the data from the Artist table. The Dispose procedure closes the connection for the datValue DataTable.

```vbnet
21
                    0 references
22          Private Sub btnValue_Click(sender As Object, e As EventArgs) Handles btnValue.Click
23              ' strSql is a SQL statement that selects all the fields from the
24              ' Artist table
25
26              Dim strSql As String = "SELECT * FROM Artist"
27
28              'strPath provides the database type and path of the Art database
29              Dim strPath As String = "Provider=Microsoft.ACE.OLEDB.12.0 ;" & "Data Source=e:\Art.accdb"
30              Dim odaArtist As New OleDb.OleDbDataAdapter(strSql, strPath)
31              Dim datValue As New DataTable
32              Dim intCount As Integer
33              Dim decTotalValue As Decimal = 0D
34
35              ' The DataTable name datValue is filled with the table data
36              odaArtist.Fill(datValue)
37              'The connection to the database is disconnected
38              odaArtist.Dispose()
39              For intCount = 0 To datValue.Rows.Count - 1
40                  decTotalValue += Convert.ToDecimal(datValue.Rows(intCount)("Retail Price"))
41              Next
42              lblTotalRetailValue.Visible = True
43              lblTotalRetailValue.Text = "The Total Retail Value is " & decTotalValue.ToString("C")
44          End Sub
45
46      End Class
```

FIGURE 10-39

After the DataTable is created, commands can access the data stored in its rows and columns. The number of rows or columns in the DataTable can be computed with the **Count** property. In the DataTable named datValue, the code entered with IntelliSense in Figure 10-40 determines the number of rows in the DataTable object. The Artist table contains 16 rows numbered 0 to 15.

```
46          Dim intNumberOfRows As Integer
47          intNumberOfRows = datValue.Rows.Count
```

FIGURE 10-40

The number of rows in the code in Figure 10-40 is equal to the number of records in the DataTable object. You can also compute the number of columns in a DataTable by entering the code in Figure 10-41.

```
49          Dim intNumberOfColumns As Integer
50          intNumberOfColumns = datValue.Columns.Count
```

FIGURE 10-41

The DataTable object can also be used with the Rows procedure to access individual fields within a database. For example, if you want to determine the first value in the Retail Price field for the first record, the field name "Retail Price" can be used with the DataTable Rows procedure. In Figure 10-42, the variable decFirstValue is assigned to the first record's retail price.

```
52          Dim decFirstValue As Decimal
53          decFirstValue = Convert.ToDecimal(datValue.Rows(0)("Retail Price"))
```

FIGURE 10-42

In Figure 10-42, the first argument for the Rows procedure (0) references the first row (row zero) in the data table, which is the first record in the table. The entry in the second parentheses ("Retail Price") identifies the field within the first row.

In the original database shown in Figure 10-2 on page 681, if datValue represents the DataTable for the Artist table, the first field value for the Retail Price field is assigned to decFirstValue. The value 120.00 is assigned to the variable decFirstValue in Figure 10-42.

Using the Rows method and the field name, you can also compute the total or average value of the Art Prize collection for all the records in the table. In the chapter project, when the user taps or clicks a button on the Windows Form object, the event handler for the button tap or click computes the retail price of the Art Prize collection.

To code a connection with a database and compute the total value of all artwork in the collection, you can complete the following steps:

STEP 1 Download the original Access database file Art.accdb again to overwrite any data you added or deleted from the database. Open the Creative Art Windows application. Add a Button object named `btnValue` to the Windows Form object and change the Text property to `Total Retail Value`. Change the font size to 12 and the ForeColor property to OrangeRed on the Web tab. Set the Size property for the button to `178, 28` and center the Button object horizontally across the form. Below the Button object, add a Label object named `lblTotalValue` with the Text property of 23 "Xs," and then center the text. Change the font size to 12 points. Set the Visible property to False for the lblTotalValue Label object because the Xs should not be displayed when the program begins.

A Button object and Label object are added to the Windows Form object (Figure 10-43).

Button object added

Label object added

FIGURE 10-43

STEP 2 Double-tap or double-click the Total Retail Value button to create the btnValue_Click event handler. To initialize the OleDbDataAdapter, enter the code shown in Figure 10-44 inside the click event. The first variable, strSql, is assigned the SQL statement that queries all the fields in the Artist table. The second variable, strPath, is assigned the database driver for Access and the path to the Art.accdb file. The third variable, odaArtist, is an instance of the OleDbDataAdapter.

Inside the btnValue_Click event, the variables are initialized for the OleDbDataAdapter (Figure 10-44).

```
22    Private Sub btnValue_Click(sender As Object, e As EventArgs) Handles btnValue.Click
23        ' strSql is a SQL statement that selects all the fields from the
24        ' Artist table
25
26        Dim strSql As String = "SELECT * FROM Artist"
27
28        'strPath provides the database type and path of the Art database
29        Dim strPath As String = "Provider=Microsoft.ACE.OLEDB.12.0 ;" & "Data Source=e:\Art.accdb"
30        Dim odaArtist As New OleDb.OleDbDataAdapter(strSql, strPath)
```

FIGURE 10-44

STEP 3 After the first three variables are initialized, initialize the rest of the variables needed for the Button object event handler. An instance named datValue is initialized to represent the DataTable object. The intCount variable is used to count through a For loop. The last variable, decTotalValue, will contain the total value of the Art Prize collection.

The rest of the variables are initialized (Figure 10-45).

```
31        Dim datValue As New DataTable
32        Dim intCount As Integer
33        Dim decTotalValue As Decimal = 0D
```

FIGURE 10-45

STEP 4 Continuing inside the btnValue_Click event handler, enter the code shown in Figure 10-46 to fill the DataTable with the contents of the Artist table. In the next line of code, use the Dispose method to close the connection.

The DataTable is filled and the connection is disconnected (Figure 10-46).

```
35          ' The DataTable name datValue is filled with the table data
36          odaArtist.Fill(datValue)
37          'The connection to the database is disconnected
38          odaArtist.Dispose()
```

FIGURE 10-46

STEP 5 Enter the code shown in Figure 10-47 to create a For loop to increment through each record in the Artist table. Because the rows are numbered 0 to 15, the upper range is one less than the number of rows in the table, making 16 records. The value in each Retail Price field is added to the value in the decTotalValue variable.

The total Art Prize collection value is computed in the For loop (Figure 10-47).

```
39          For intCount = 0 To datValue.Rows.Count - 1
40              decTotalValue += Convert.ToDecimal(datValue.Rows(intCount)("Retail Price"))
41          Next
```

FIGURE 10-47

STEP 6 Enter the code shown in Figure 10-48 to display the total value of the Art Prize collection.

The total value of the collection is displayed (Figure 10-48).

```
42          lblTotalRetailValue.Visible = True
43          lblTotalRetailValue.Text = "The Total Retail Value is " & decTotalValue.ToString("C")
44      End Sub
45
46  End Class
```

FIGURE 10-48

HEADS UP

You can use the process described beginning in Figure 10-43 with or without a database wizard.

CRITICAL THINKING

How could the code be changed to compute the average? Add a formula to the code to divide the sum of the values by the number of values.

ONLINE REINFORCEMENT

To view a video of the process in the previous steps, visit CengageBrain.com and navigate to the resources for this title. Tap or click the link for Chapter 10 and then navigate to Video 10-8.

Program Design

The requirements document for the Creative Art application is shown in Figure 10-49, and the Use Case Definition document is shown in Figure 10-50.

REQUIREMENTS DOCUMENT

Date Submitted:	February 22, 2017
Application Title:	Creative Art
Purpose:	This Windows application opens a Windows form that displays an Access database with data for local artwork. The data can be viewed, updated, and deleted. The application also computes the total value of the Art Prize collection.
Program Procedures:	In a Windows application, the Art Access database file is opened and the user can view, add, and delete records as needed. The user can calculate the total value of the Art Prize collection.
Algorithms, Processing, and Conditions:	1. The user first views a Windows application that loads an Access database table, which includes fields for the Art ID, Artist Name, Art Title, Location, Collection (public or private), and Retail Price. A navigation toolbar appears at the top of the Windows form, allowing the user to move from record to record. The Windows form also includes a title and artistic image.
	2. The user can tap or click the Add new button on the navigation toolbar to add a new artist. The record is saved when the user taps or clicks the Save Data button on the navigation toolbar.
	3. The user can tap or click the Delete button on the navigation toolbar to delete an artist's record. The record is permanently deleted when the user taps or clicks the Save Data button on the navigation toolbar.
	4. The user can tap or click the Total Retail Value button to compute the total value of the Art Prize collection.
Notes and Restrictions:	The Access database named Art.accdb is located on the USB drive (the E drive).
Comments:	1. The Art.accdb file is available on CengageBrain.com.
	2. Obtain an image for this program from CengageBrain.com. The name of the picture on the Windows form is Art.

FIGURE 10-49

USE CASE DEFINITION

1. The user views the Access database information about local artwork.
2. The user taps or clicks the Add new button to add an artist and taps or clicks the Save Data button to permanently save the new artist to the database.
3. The user taps or clicks the Delete button to delete an artist and taps or clicks the Save Data button to permanently delete the record from the database.
4. The user taps or clicks the Total Retail Value button to display the total value of the Art Prize collection.

FIGURE 10-50

Event Planning Document

The event planning document for the Creative Art Windows application is shown in Figure 10-51.

EVENT PLANNING DOCUMENT

Program Name:	Developer:	Object:	Date:
Creative Art Windows Application	Corinne Hoisington	frmArtPrize	February 22, 2015

OBJECT	EVENT TRIGGER	EVENT PROCESSING	
frmArtPrize	Load	Fill the DataSet object using the Data Source Configuration Wizard	
btnPrice	Click	Initialize the OleDbDataAdapter with the type of database and path statement Fill the data table Disconnect the database For each record in the database: Add each record's value to the total value of the collection Display the Total Retail Value of the collection	

FIGURE 10-51

Guided Program Development

Guided Program Development

Phase I: Design the Form

1

● **Create a New Windows Project** Open Visual Studio and then close the Start page. Tap or click the New Project button on the Standard toolbar. Begin a Windows Forms Application project and name the project Creative Art.

● **Name the Form Object** Select the Windows Form object. In the Solution Explorer, rename Form1.vb to `frmArtPrize.vb`.

● **Title the Form Object** Select the Windows Form object and change the Text property to `Creative Art Commission - Art Prize Competition`.

● **Build the Top Portion of the Windows Form Object** Using the skills you have learned in this course, complete the top portion of the Windows Form object. For detailed specifications, see Figure 10-8 on page 687.

The top portion of the form is completed (Figure 10-52).

RESULT OF STEP I

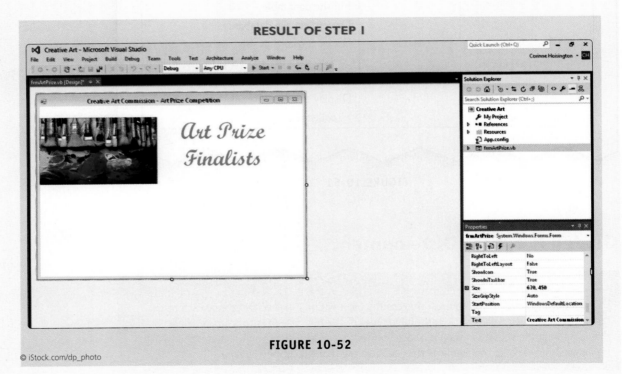

© iStock.com/dp_photo

FIGURE 10-52

2

● **Create a Connection Using the Data Source Configuration Wizard**
In the Creative Art project window, tap or click Project on the menu bar, and then tap or click Add New Data Source on the Project menu *(ref: Figure 10-8.)*

● **Choose the Data Source** If necessary, select Database in the "Where will the application get data from?" group in the Data Source Configuration Wizard. Tap or click the Next button.

(continues)

Guided Program Development   *continued*

● **Add a Connection** If necessary, tap or click
Dataset in the Choose a Database Model dialog
box and then tap or click the Next button.
Tap or click the New Connection button.
In the Add Connection dialog box, tap or click
the Change button to select the data source.

● **Change the Data Source** In the Choose
Data Source dialog box, select Microsoft
Access Database File because the Art database
was created in Microsoft Access.

● **Select the Database File** Tap or click
the Continue button. Tap or click the Browse
button to the right of the Database file name
field. Select the USB device on drive E: and
then select the Art file. Tap or click the Open
button. The Add Connection dialog box reopens.
Tap or click the OK button.

● **Respond to the Dialog Box Question** The
Choose Your Data Connection dialog box reopens.
Tap or click the Next button. A dialog box opens
to remind you that the connection uses a local
data file that is not in the current project.
Tap or click the No button.

- **Save the Connection String** The next dialog box opens and asks which connection your application should use. Tap or click the Next button.

- **Connect to the Artist Table** The Choose Your Database Objects dialog box opens. Tap or click the expand icon next to the Tables option. Tap or click the Artist check box to select the Artist table. Tap or click the Finish button. Tap or click ArtDataSet.xsd to select the DataSet.

The ArtDataSet is displayed in the Solution Explorer Figure 10-53.

FIGURE 10-53

(continues)

Guided Program Development   *continued*

3

- **Display the Data Sources Window** Tap or click the View menu, tap or click Other Windows, and then tap or click Data Sources to display the Data Sources window. If necessary, tap or click the Push Pin icon to pin the Data Sources window.

- **Display the Field Names** Tap or click the expand icon next to the Artist table to expand the listing of field names within the table.

- **Bind a Field to the Windows Form** Select the Art ID field in the Data Sources window. Drag the Art ID field to the Windows Form object *(ref: Figure 10-23)*.

- **Bind All the Fields to the Windows Form** Drag the remaining field objects from the Data Sources window to the Windows Form object. Select the field labels and TextBox objects and change the font size to 10 points and bold. Resize the Label and TextBox objects. Use the formatting tools on the Format menu to equally distribute the bound objects. Use the layout shown in Figure 10-54.

- **Add Button and Label Objects** Add a Button object named `btnPrice` to the Windows form with the Text property changed to `Total Retail Value`. Change the font size to 12 points and the ForeColor property to OrangeRed on the Web tab. Add a Label object named `lblTotalValue` with the Text property of 23 Xs. Change the font size to 12 points. Set the Visible property to False. Center the Label object on the form (see Figure 10-54 for layout).

The Windows Form object is designed (Figure 10-54).

FIGURE 10-54

4

- **Execute the Application to Load the Database Data** Tap or click the Start Debugging button on the Standard toolbar to run the application. The data fills the Windows form.

- **Use the Navigation Toolbar** With the application running, navigate through the database records. Add a record, and then delete a record.

The Windows form is designed and the database is connected to the application (Figure 10-55).

FIGURE 10-55

(continues)

Phase 2: Code the Application

5

- **Code the Comments** Tap or click the View Code button on the Solution Explorer toolbar to begin coding the application. Type the first four standard comments at the top of the code window.

```
1    ⊟ 'Title:      Creative Art Windows Application
2      'Author:     Corinne Hoisington
3      'Date:       February 22, 2017
4      'Purpose:    The application displays the artists who have entered the Art Prize competition as an interface for a Microsoft
5      '            Access database.
6
7

     3 references
```

- **Comment the Code Created by the Database Wizard** The Data Source Configuration Wizard creates two Sub methods. Enter the comments in the first line of the first Sub method, as shown in the adjacent Hint Screen.

```
1    ⊟ 'Title:      Creative Art Windows Application
2      'Author:     Corinne Hoisington
3      'Date:       February 22, 2017
4      'Purpose:    The application displays the artists who have entered the Art Prizes as an interface for a Microsoft
5      '            Access database.
6
7
     3 references
```

- **Code the OleDbDataAdapter for the btnValue_Click Event** Double-tap or double-click the Total Retail Value button in the Design window to create the btnValue_Click event handler. To initialize the OleDbDataAdapter, enter the code shown in the adjacent Hint Screen inside the click event. The first variable, strSql, is assigned the SQL statement that queries all the fields in the Artist table. The second variable, strPath, is assigned the database driver for Access and the path to the Art.accdb file. The third variable, odaArtist, is an instance of the OleDbDataAdapter (*ref: Figure 10-44*).

```
22   ⊟     Private Sub btnValue_Click(sender As Object, e As EventArgs) Handles btnValue.Click
23             ' strSql is a SQL statement that selects all the fields from the
24             ' Artist table
25
26             Dim strSql As String = "SELECT * FROM Artist"
27
28             'strPath provides the database type and path of the Art database
29             Dim strPath As String = "Provider=Microsoft.ACE.OLEDB.12.0 ;" & "Data Source=e:\Art.accdb"
30             Dim odaArtist As New OleDb.OleDbDataAdapter(strSql, strPath)
```

- **Fill the DataTable Object** Inside the btnValue_Click event, after initializing the OleDbDataAdapter, initialize an instance named datValue to represent the DataTable object. Declare the intCount variable for use in counting through a For loop. Initialize the last variable, decTotalValue, which will contain the total value of the Art Prize collection. Write the statement to fill the DataTable with the contents of the Artist table. Code the Dispose method to close the open connection.

```
31             Dim datValue As New DataTable
32             Dim intCount As Integer
33             Dim decTotalValue As Decimal = 0D
34
35             ' The DataTable name datValue is filled with the table data
36             odaArtist.Fill(datValue)
37             'The connection to the database is disconnected
38             odaArtist.Dispose()
```

● **Calculate and Display the Total Value of the Artwork** Write a For loop statement to increment the count for each record in the Artist table. Because the rows are numbered 0 to 15, the upper range is one less than the number of rows in the table, making 16 records. Write the code within the loop to add the value in each Retail Price field to the value in the decTotalValue variable. Write the code to display the total retail value of the Art Prize collection in the lblTotalRetailValue Label object, including the code that makes the Label object visible.

```
39          For intCount = 0 To datValue.Rows.Count - 1
40              decTotalValue += Convert.ToDecimal(datValue.Rows(intCount)("Retail Price"))
41          Next
42          lblTotalRetailValue.Visible = True
43          lblTotalRetailValue.Text = "The Total Retail Value is " & decTotalValue.ToString("C")
44      End Sub
45
46  End Class
```

The code is completed (Figure 10-56).

```
                                    RESULT OF STEP 5

1   ⊟'Title:      Creative Art Windows Application
2    'Author:     Corinne Hoisington
3    'Date:       February 22, 2017
4    'Purpose:    The application displays the artists who have entered the Art Prize competition as an interface for a Microsoft
5    '            Access database.
6
7
    3 references
8   ⊟Public Class frmArtPrize
      0 references
9   ⊟   Private Sub frmArtPrize_Load(sender As Object, e As EventArgs) Handles MyBase.Load
10          'TODO: This line of code loads data into the 'ArtDataSet.Artist' table. You can move, or remove it, as needed.
11          Me.ArtistTableAdapter.Fill(Me.ArtDataSet.Artist)
12
13      End Sub
14
      0 references
15  ⊟   Private Sub ArtistBindingNavigatorSaveItem_Click(sender As Object, e As EventArgs) Handles ArtistBindingNavigatorSaveItem.Click
16          Me.Validate()
17          Me.ArtistBindingSource.EndEdit()
18          Me.TableAdapterManager.UpdateAll(Me.ArtDataSet)
19
20      End Sub
21
      0 references
22  ⊟   Private Sub btnValue_Click(sender As Object, e As EventArgs) Handles btnValue.Click
23          ' strSql is a SQL statement that selects all the fields from the
24          ' Artist table
25
26          Dim strSql As String = "SELECT * FROM Artist"
27
28          'strPath provides the database type and path of the Art database
29          Dim strPath As String = "Provider=Microsoft.ACE.OLEDB.12.0 ;" & "Data Source=e:\Art.accdb"
30          Dim odaArtist As New OleDb.OleDbDataAdapter(strSql, strPath)
31          Dim datValue As New DataTable
32          Dim intCount As Integer
33          Dim decTotalValue As Decimal = 0D
34
35          ' The DataTable name datValue is filled with the table data
36          odaArtist.Fill(datValue)
37          'The connection to the database is disconnected
38          odaArtist.Dispose()
39          For intCount = 0 To datValue.Rows.Count - 1
40              decTotalValue += Convert.ToDecimal(datValue.Rows(intCount)("Retail Price"))
41          Next
42          lblTotalRetailValue.Visible = True
43          lblTotalRetailValue.Text = "The Total Retail Value is " & decTotalValue.ToString("C")
44      End Sub
45
46  End Class
47
```

FIGURE 10-56

Summary

In this chapter, you have learned to create a Windows application that uses database files and ADO.NET 5. The items listed in Figure 10-57 include all the new Visual Studio and Visual Basic skills you have learned in this chapter.

Visual Basic Skills		
Skill	**Figure Number**	**Video Number**
Examine the Creative Art Application	Figure 10-1	Video 10-1
Connect to the Database Using the Data Source	Figure 10-8	Video 10-2
View the Data Available in the Source Database	Figure 10-19	Video 10-3
Bind Each Database Field to the Windows Form Object	Figure 10-23	Video 10-4
Add a New Record to the Database Table	Figure 10-26	Video 10-5
Delete an Existing Record from the Database Table	Figure 10-29	Video 10-6
Change the Toolbox Object Type	Figure 10-32	Video 10-7
Code a Connection with a Database and Compute a Sum of Values	Figure 10-43	Video 10-8

FIGURE 10-57

Reinforcement activities and resources are available at no additional cost on www.CengageBrain.com. Visit http://solutions.cengage.com/ctdownloads/ for detailed instructions about accessing the available resources at the Student Companion Site.

Knowledge Check

1. ADO.NET 5 can work with Microsoft Access as well as many other databases, such as SQL or Oracle. True or False?

2. What is the name of a unique field that must be present in each relational database?

3. Define ADO.

4. Define SQL.

5. A database can only be stored on a local computer. True or False?

6. What is a DataSet object?

7. Does a row in a database table represent a record or a field?

8. Name five types of objects that can be dragged from a data field in the Data Sources window to the Windows Form object without using the Customize option.

9. What is the object name of the navigation toolbar?

10. When you add a record to a database using the Add new button on the navigation toolbar, the record is not added to the original database. What action is needed to add the record to the original data source?

11. How many records are contained in the database table named SouthernStates, as displayed in Figure 10-58?

APPROXIMATE POPULATION OF THE SOUTHERN STATES PROJECTED FOR 2025			
AutoNumber	**State Name**	**State Capital**	**Population**
1	Florida	Tallahassee	20,066,000
2	Georgia	Atlanta	10,962,000
3	South Carolina	Columbia	4,574,000
4	North Carolina	Raleigh	9,916,000
5	Virginia	Richmond	8,165,000
6	Alabama	Montgomery	5,224,000
7	Louisiana	Baton Rouge	5,111,000
8	Tennessee	Nashville	7,249,000
9	West Virginia	Charleston	1,864,000
10	Mississippi	Jackson	3,413,000
11	Kentucky	Frankfort	4,314,000
Source: http://www.census.gov/population/projections/state/stpjpop.txt			

FIGURE 10-58

Knowledge Check *continued*

12. In the table in Figure 10-58, name the field labels.

13. For the table in Figure 10-58, write a statement that references the capital of Virginia and assign the value to the strCapitalCity variable.

14. What properties under the Data Binding Mode must you set when you bind a ComboBox object to a Windows form?

15. What procedure places data in the DataTable?

16. What command disconnects a database connection?

17. Write a line of code to initialize a String variable named strOrder to a Select SQL statement that would select all the fields from a table named Tea.

18. Which wildcard symbol is used in a Select statement?

19. What does the wildcard symbol mean in the Select statement?

20. Write the statement that would fill a DataTable object named datRent if an instance of the OleDb DataAdapter is named odaCollection.

Debugging Exercises

1. The code shown in Figure 10-59 is designed to increment through each row in a database table. Correct the error in the code.

```
For intRecordCount = 0 To datPeople.Rows.Count
    ' Processing statements
Next
```
FIGURE 10-59

2. Correct the line of code shown in Figure 10-60:

```
strNumberOfRows = datCityName.Rows.Count
```
FIGURE 10-60

3. Rewrite the code shown in Figure 10-61 correctly:

```
strNumberOfRows = Convert.ToString(datBeachName.Rows(6)(Beach))
```
FIGURE 10-61

Program Analysis

1. Write a command that assigns an Access database named usedcarparts.accdb and a path located on the E drive to a string named strConnect for use later in an instance of an OleDbDataAdapter.

2. Consider the database table named BaseballStadiums shown in Figure 10-62. If the instance of the DataTable is named datStadium, what value would the statement in Figure 10-63 assign to the variable intCount?

Stadium Number	Stadium Name	Location	Team
203	Dodger Stadium	Los Angeles, CA	Dodgers
304	Petco Field	San Diego, CA	Padres
425	Wrigley Field	Chicago, IL	Cubs
509	Camden Yards	Baltimore, MD	Orioles
698	Fenway Park	Boston, MA	Red Sox
756	Citi Field	New York City, NY	Mets

FIGURE 10-62

```
intCount = datStadium.Rows.Count
```

FIGURE 10-63

3. Using the database table in Figure 10-62, what value would be assigned to strTeamName in the code in Figure 10-64?

```
strTeamName = Convert.ToString(datStadium.Rows(3)("Team"))
```

FIGURE 10-64

4. Using the database table in Figure 10-62, what value would be assigned to strLocation in the code in Figure 10-65?

```
strLocation = Convert.ToString(datStadium.Rows(1)("Location"))
```

FIGURE 10-65

5. Using the database table in Figure 10-62, what value would be assigned to intNumber in the code in Figure 10-66?

```
intNumber = (datStadium.Columns.Count) -1
```

FIGURE 10-66

Complete one or more of the following case programming assignments.
Submit the program and materials you create to your instructor. The level of
difficulty is indicated for each assignment.

●	= Easiest
●●	= Intermediate
●●●	= Challenging

Instructor's Note: If you open a student's project that was created with a different path to
the Access database, open the Solution Explorer of their program and then open the app.config file.
Change the following statement's path statement to the path of your local database: `<add name="Creative_`
`Art.My.MySettings.ArtConnectionString"connectionString="Provider=Microsoft.ACE.`
`OLEDB.12.0;Data Source=D:\Art.accdb"providerName="System.Data.OleDb"/`

1 ●

NATIONAL RODEO COMPETITION DATABASE

Design a Windows application and write the code that will execute according to the program requirements in Figure 10-67
and the Use Case Definition in Figure 10-68. Before writing the code, create an event planning document for each event in
the program. The completed Windows application and other objects in the user interface are shown in Figure 10-69.

REQUIREMENTS DOCUMENT

Date Submitted:	October 30, 2017
Application Title:	National Rodeo Competition Database
Purpose:	This Windows application opens an Access database that contains information about the top ten finalists competing in the National Rodeo this Saturday. The data in the database can be viewed, updated, and deleted.
Program Procedures:	In a Windows application, the Access database file is opened and the user can view, add, and delete records as needed.
Algorithms, Processing, and Conditions:	1. The user first views a Windows application that loads an Access database table named Rodeo, which includes the Contestant ID, Rider Name, Horse Name, Category, and Hometown. A navigation toolbar appears at the top of the Windows form, allowing the user to move from record to record. The Windows form also includes a title and an image.
	2. The user can tap or click the Add new button on the navigation toolbar to add a substitute rider or new rider. The record is saved when the user taps or clicks the Save Data button on the navigation toolbar.
	3. The user can tap or click the Delete button on the navigation toolbar to delete a rider. The record is permanently deleted when the user taps or clicks the Save Data button on the navigation toolbar.
Notes and Restrictions:	The Rodeo.accdb file is located on the USB drive (the E drive).
Comments:	1. The Rodeo.accdb file is available on CengageBrain.com.
	2. Obtain an image for this program from CengageBrain.com. The name of the picture on the Windows form is Rodeo.

FIGURE 10-67

(continues)

National Rodeo Competition Database (continued)

USE CASE DEFINITION

1. The user views the Access database, which displays the riders' names and their information.
2. The user taps or clicks the Add new button to add a new rider and taps or clicks the Save Data button to save the item to the database.
3. The user taps or clicks the Delete button to delete a rider and permanently deletes the record from the database by tapping or clicking the Save Data button.

FIGURE 10-68

FIGURE 6-69

© iStock.com/KeithBishop

2 ● TOP TEN TECHNOLOGY JOB DATABASE

Design a Windows application and write the code that will execute according to the program requirements in Figure 10-70 and the Use Case Definition in Figure 10-71. Before writing the code, create an event planning document for each event in the program. The completed Windows application and other objects in the user interface are shown in Figure 10-72.

REQUIREMENTS DOCUMENT

Date Submitted: April 22, 2017

Application Title: Top Ten Technology Job Database

Purpose: This Windows application opens an Access database that contains information about the current top ten technology jobs, their ranking placement, and the median salary. The data in the database can be viewed, updated, and deleted. The application can be used to help students make wise career decisions and go into fields that are hiring.

Program Procedures: In a Windows application, the Access database file is opened and the user can view, add, and delete records as needed.

Algorithms, Processing, and Conditions:
1. The user views a Windows application that loads an Access database table, which includes fields for job placement, job title, and median salary.
2. A navigation toolbar appears at the top of the Windows form, allowing the user to move from record to record. The Windows form also includes a title and a graphic image.
3. The user can tap or click the Add new button on the navigation toolbar to add a new job to the database. The record is saved when the user taps or clicks the Save Data button on the navigation toolbar.
4. The user can tap or click the Delete button on the navigation toolbar to delete a technology job. The record is permanently deleted when the user taps or clicks the Save Data button on the navigation toolbar.
5. The user can tap or click a list arrow to move directly to a particular job record.

Notes and Restrictions: The TechJobs.accdb file is located on the USB drive (the E drive).

Comments:
1. The TechJobs.accdb file is available on CengageBrain.com.
2. Obtain an image for this program from CengageBrain.com. The name of the picture on the Windows form is Jobs.

FIGURE 10-70

(continues)

Top Ten Technology Job Database (continued)

USE CASE DEFINITION

1. The user views the Access database information, which displays an image and the jobs that are currently considered the top ten technology jobs.
2. The user taps or clicks the Add new button to add a technology job and taps or clicks the Save Data button to save the position to the database.
3. The user taps or clicks the Delete button to delete a technology job and permanently deletes it from the database by tapping or clicking the Save Data button.
4. The user can tap or click a list arrow to display the jobs and move directly to a technology job's record.

FIGURE 10-71

© iStock.com/Erikona

FIGURE 10-72

3

PARADISE PLUMBING STAFFING DATABASE

Design a Windows application and write the code that will execute according to the program requirements in Figure 10-73 and the Use Case Definition in Figure 10-74. Before writing the code, create an event planning document for each event in the program. The completed Windows application and other objects in the user interface are shown in Figure 10-75.

REQUIREMENTS DOCUMENT

Date Submitted:	August 1, 2017
Application Title:	Paradise Plumbing Staffing Database
Purpose:	This Windows application opens an Access database in a Windows form that displays information about the 13 plumbers on staff at Paradise Plumbing. The data in the database can be viewed, updated, and deleted.
Program Procedures:	In a Windows application, the Access database file is opened and the user can view, add, and delete records as needed.
Algorithms, Processing, and Conditions:	1. The user first views a Windows application that loads an Access database table, which includes the plumber ID, plumber name, plumbing specialty, contact extension number, and whether the plumber prefers working days, nights, or both. A navigation toolbar appears at the top of the Windows form, allowing the user to move from record to record. The Windows form also includes a title and a graphic image.
	2. The user can tap or click the Add new button on the navigation toolbar to add a new plumber to the database. The record is saved when the user taps or clicks the Save Data button on the navigation toolbar.
	3. The user can tap or click the Delete button on the navigation toolbar to delete a plumber's record. The record is permanently deleted when the user taps or clicks the Save Data button on the navigation toolbar.
Notes and Restrictions:	1. The PlumberStaffing.accdb file is located on the USB drive (the E drive).
Comments:	1. The PlumberStaffing.accdb file is available on CengageBrain.com.
	2. Obtain an image for this program from CengageBrain.com. The name of the picture on the Windows form is Plumber.

FIGURE 10-73

(continues)

Paradise Plumbing Staffing Database (continued)

USE CASE DEFINITION

1. The user views the Access database information, which displays the plumbers on staff at Paradise Plumbing.
2. The user taps or clicks the Add new button to add a new plumber and taps or clicks the Save Data button to save the item to the database.
3. The user taps or clicks the Delete button to delete a plumber record and permanently deletes it from the database by tapping or clicking the Save Data button.

FIGURE 10-74

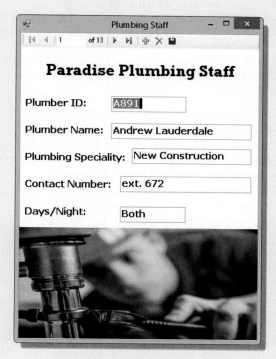

FIGURE 10-75

© iStock.com/AzmanL

Case Programming Assignments

4 ●●
LITTLE LEAGUE BASEBALL TEAM DATABASE

Design a Windows application and write the code that will execute according to the program requirements in Figure 10-76. Before designing the user interface, create a Use Case Definition. Before writing the code, create an event planning document for each event in the program.

REQUIREMENTS DOCUMENT

Date Submitted:	May 13, 2017
Application Title:	Little League Baseball Team Database
Purpose:	This Windows application opens an Access database that displays information about 22 boys and girls (ages 12–14) who are playing in the National Little League championship. The data in the database can be viewed, updated, and deleted in the Windows form. The application computes in three separate counts the number of team members who are 12, 13, or 14 years old and calculates the average age of the team.
Program Procedures:	In a Windows application, the Access database file is opened and the user can view, add, and delete records as needed. You can also display the total number of players of each age (12, 13, or 14) in the database.
Algorithms, Processing, and Conditions:	1. The user first views a Windows application that loads an Access database table, which includes the player's number, first name, last name, parent's name, address, city, state, zip, telephone, and age. A navigation toolbar appears at the top of the Windows form, allowing the user to move from record to record. The Windows form also includes a title and a graphic image.
	2. The user can tap or click the Add new button on the navigation toolbar to add a new player to the team. The record is saved when the user taps or clicks the Save Data button on the navigation toolbar.
	3. The user can tap or click the Delete button on the navigation toolbar to delete a player. The record is permanently deleted when the user taps or clicks the Save Data button on the navigation toolbar.
	4. The user can tap or click the Ages Button object to compute the total number of team members who are 12, 13, or 14 years old. The user can also compute the average age of the team.
Notes and Restrictions:	1. The LittleLeague.accdb file is located on the USB drive (the E drive).
	2. Use a Try-Catch statement to catch an exception if the file is not available.
Comments:	The LittleLeague.accdb file is available on CengageBrain.com.

FIGURE 10-76

5 ●●
COLLEGE MAJORS

Design a Windows application and write the code that will execute according to the program requirements in Figure 10-77. Before designing the user interface, create a Use Case Definition. Before writing the code, create an event planning document for each event in the program.

REQUIREMENTS DOCUMENT

Date Submitted:	March 9, 2017
Application Title:	College Majors

Purpose: This Windows application opens an Access database that displays information about 36 college majors in a Windows form. The data in the database can be viewed, updated, and deleted. The application also computes the total number of students attending the college. The user can select a major from a ComboBox list and the application will display the percentage of students participating in that major.

Program Procedures: In a Windows application, the Access database file is opened and the user can view, add, and delete records as needed. The total student population and percentage of students in a particular major can also be displayed.

Algorithms, Processing, and Conditions:

1. The user first views a Windows application that loads an Access database table, which includes fields for the department, college major, and number of students in that major. A navigation toolbar appears at the top of the Windows form, allowing the user to move from record to record. The Windows form also includes a title and a graphic image.
2. The user can tap or click the Add new button on the navigation toolbar to add a new major to the college. The record is saved when the user taps or clicks the Save Data button on the navigation toolbar.
3. The user can tap or click the Delete button on the navigation toolbar to delete a major. The record is permanently deleted when the user taps or clicks the Save Data button on the navigation toolbar.
4. The user can tap or click the Find Total button object to compute the total number of students enrolled in each major.
5. The user can select a major from a ComboBox list and the application will display the percentage of students at the college participating in that major.

Notes and Restrictions: The College.accdb file is located on the USB drive (the E drive).

Comments:

1. The College.accdb file is available on CengageBrain.com.
2. Use a graphic image you obtain from the web.

FIGURE 10-77

Case Programming Assignments

6 •• KID-FRIENDLY STOCKS

Design a Windows application and write the code that will execute according to the program requirements in Figure 10-78. Before designing the user interface, create a Use Case Definition. Before writing the code, create an event planning document for each event in the program.

REQUIREMENTS DOCUMENT

Date Submitted: August 17, 2017

Application Title: Kid-Friendly Stocks

Purpose: This Windows application opens an Access database in a Windows form that displays information about 16 child-centered stocks selected for an investment portfolio. The data in the database can be viewed, updated, and deleted. The application also computes the total investment made in the portfolio and lists the names of the stocks with their selected ratings.

Program Procedures: In a Windows application, the Access database file is opened and the user can view, add, and delete records as needed. The total portfolio investment is calculated.

Algorithms, Processing, and Conditions:
1. The user first views a Windows application that loads an Access database table, which includes fields for the stock symbol, the name of the stock, the price per share, number of shares, and the earning potential rating. A navigation toolbar appears at the top of the Windows form, allowing the user to move from record to record. The Windows form also includes a title and graphic image.
2. The user can tap or click the Add new button on the navigation toolbar to add a new stock purchase. The record is saved when the user taps or clicks the Save Data button on the navigation toolbar.
3. The user can tap or click the Delete button on the navigation toolbar to delete a stock purchase. The record is permanently deleted when the user taps or clicks the Save Data button on the navigation toolbar.
4. The user can select the stock symbol using the list arrow on a ComboBox object and move directly to the desired record.
5. The user can tap or click the Compute Total Investment Button object to compute the total worth of stock owned.
6. The stock ratings list includes Exceptional, High, Average, and Low; these ratings can be selected by the user. The application will display all the stock names in the selected rating in a ListBox object.

Notes and Restrictions:
1. The KidFriendlyStocks.accdb file is located on the USB drive (the E drive).
2. Update the stock values in the Access database to their current values.

Comments:
1. The KidFriendlyStocks.accdb file is available on CengageBrain.com.
2. Use a graphic image you obtain from the web.

FIGURE 10-78

7 ●●●
CALORIES CONSUMED

Create a requirements document and a Use Case Definition document, and then design a Windows application based on the case project shown in Figure 10-79. Before writing the code, create an event planning document for each event in the program.

A nutritionist often has patients create a food diary to see the amount of calories they consume each day. Create an Access database with the following fields: an item number as an AutoNumber field, food consumed, and number of calories. On the web, research the amount of calories each food contains. Enter calorie data into the database for all food and beverages consumed in one day (at least 12 items). Develop a Windows application that displays the Access database table of calories consumed in one day. The application will compute the total number of calories consumed. The U.S. Department of Health estimates that the average requirement for daily calorie intake is 1,940 for women and 2,550 for men. The application should ask whether the user is male or female. When the total number of calories is displayed, the percentage of calories consumed above or below the recommended daily intake should also be shown.

FIGURE 10-79

8 ●●●
GRADUATION PARTY EVENT

Create a requirements document and a Use Case Definition document, and then design a Windows application based on the case project shown in Figure 10-80. Before writing the code, create an event planning document for each event in the program.

Create an Access database that holds information for 15 people you would like to invite to a graduation party. The main table should have a primary key and include AutoNumber, first name, last name, address, city, state, zip code, and phone number fields for each person invited. Create a Windows form that will display the people who are invited to the graduation party. Also include a field in the database that requests the number of invitees who RSVP for the party. This number will accumulate in the Windows form as you receive RSVP responses. Compute the total amount of people who will attend the party.

FIGURE 10-80

Case Programming Assignments

9 ●●●
CREATE A VB INTERFACE FOR YOUR CLUB DATABASE

Create a requirements document and a Use Case Definition document, and then design a Windows application based on the case project shown in Figure 10-81. Before writing the code, create an event planning document for each event in the program.

Create an Access database with the following information about 12 or more of your fellow club members on campus or in the community: first name, last name, address, city, state, zip, and age. Create a database that uses a ComboBox object for last names. Compute and display the average age of your club members. Use an image and allow users to add and delete friends from the database.

FIGURE 10-81

CHAPTER 11

Multiple Classes and Inheritance

OBJECTIVES

You will have mastered the material in this chapter when you can:

- Use the TabIndex property

- Edit input, including MaskedTextBox, TextBox, and ComboBox objects

- Describe the three-tiered program structure

- Understand a class

- Create a class

- Instantiate an object

- Pass arguments when instantiating an object

- Write a class constructor

- Call a procedure in a separate class

- Code a base class and a subclass to incorporate inheritance

- Call procedures found in a base class and a subclass

- Write overridable and overrides procedures

- Create and write a comma-delimited text file

Introduction

In previous chapters, you have learned that a class is a named group of program code. Within a class such as Form1, you can define attributes, Sub procedures, and Function procedures. The classes you have used thus far have either been generated by the design feature of Visual Basic or were used from a library of classes supplied by Visual Studio 2015. In this chapter, you will define a class in code and will develop the code in the class to help complete the chapter project.

When you define classes, you have the option of using a feature called inheritance, which is common to object-oriented programming languages such as Visual Basic. Inheritance allows one class, called a subclass, to use attributes and procedures defined in another class, called a base class.

Finally, when you define your own classes, you have the opportunity to design a three-tiered structure for your program so it is more reliable, more robust, and more easily understood. The sample program in this chapter uses the three-tiered program structure.

Chapter Project

The sample chapter project features the College Registration Costs window displayed in Figure 11-1.

FIGURE 11-1

© iStock.com/roxanabalint

In the window shown in Figure 11-1, a student or a worker assisting the student enters the student ID number, the student name, and the number of units for which the student is registering. The user also identifies whether the student is living off campus or on campus, the housing and board an on-campus student is using, and the student's major.

Then, when the user taps or clicks the Calculate Costs button, the application calculates the total semester costs by multiplying the number of units times the cost per unit ($450.00). If the student is an on-campus resident, the cost for room and board is also calculated and placed in the final cost. The cost for Cooper Dorm is $2,900.00 per semester, the cost for Craig Hall is $3,400.00 per semester, and the cost for Julian Suites is $4,000.00 per semester. The total semester costs are shown below the buttons (Figure 11-2).

FIGURE 11-2

The user is required to enter valid values for each of the items on the registration form. If the user does not enter a value or enters an invalid value, such as a nonnumeric value in the Number of Units text box, a message box is displayed to prompt the user to enter a valid value (Figure 11-3).

Number Of
Units is blank

FIGURE 11-3

© iStock.com/roxanabalint

In Figure 11-3, the user failed to enter the number of units, so the message box directs the user to enter the number.

In addition to calculating the total semester costs, this program creates a log on disk for the students whose costs have been calculated. This log is kept as a text file. The program must write records in the text file as students use the program.

ONLINE REINFORCEMENT

To view a video of the program execution shown in Figure 11-1, visit CengageBrain .com and navigate to the resources for this title. Tap or click the link for Chapter 11 and then navigate to Video 11-1. Turn on your speakers to listen to the audio walkthrough of the steps.

Use the TabIndex Property in the User Interface

The user interface in the College Registration Costs program does not contain any objects that you have not seen in previous programs. However, the program does implement a new property that users often find useful.

When users enter data into a Windows Form object, they usually enter the data in sequence on the form. For example, in Figure 11-2, the user can enter the Student ID first, followed by the Student Name, then the Number of Units, and so on. Often, users prefer to press the TAB key to move the insertion point from one object on the Windows Form object to the next. To specify the sequence of objects that will be selected when the user presses the TAB key, you use the TabIndex property. To implement the TabIndex property for the Windows Form object in Figure 11-2, you can complete the steps on the next page:

STEP 1   Select the object that will be selected when program execution begins. In the example, the selected object will be the txtStudentID MaskedTextBox object. Scroll in the Properties window until the TabIndex property is visible and then double-tap or double-click the right column of the TabIndex property.

The TabIndex property for the MaskedTextBox object is selected (Figure 11–4).

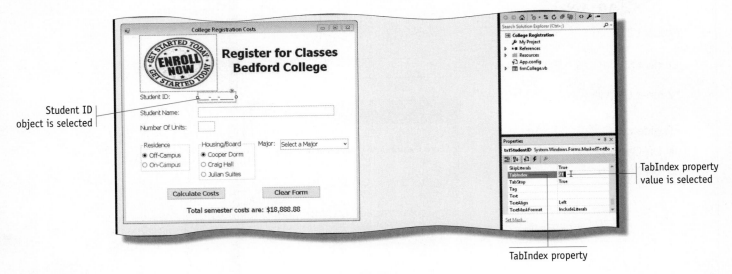

FIGURE 11-4

© iStock.com/roxanabalint

STEP 2   Type 1 and then press the ENTER key.

The value 1 in the TabIndex property of an object indicates that the object will be selected when the program begins execution (Figure 11–5). When program execution begins, the insertion point will be located in the txtStudentID MaskedTextBox object.

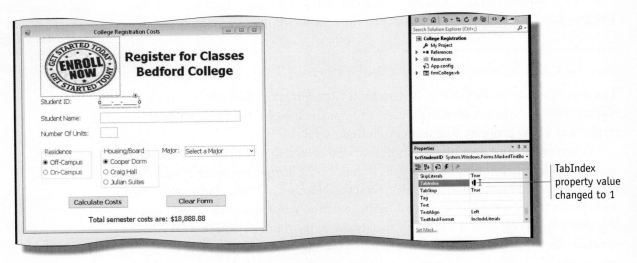

FIGURE 11-5

© iStock.com/roxanabalint

STEP 3   Select the object that should be selected when the user presses the TAB key. In the sample program, the txtStudentName TextBox object should be selected. Double-tap or double-click the right column of the TabIndex property for the txtStudentName TextBox object, type 2, and then press the ENTER key.

The TabIndex value for the txtStudentName object is set to 2 in the Properties window (Figure 11-6). When the user enters the Student ID value and presses the TAB key, the insertion point will be in the Student Name text box. Using these same techniques, you can continue to identify objects on the Windows Form object that will be selected when the user presses the TAB key.

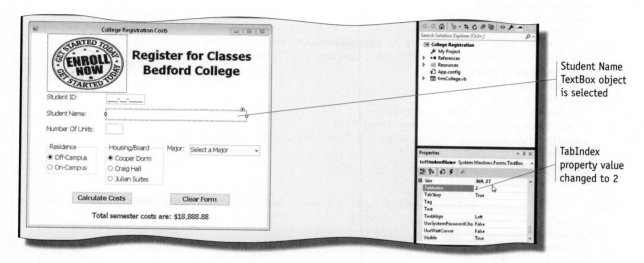

© iStock.com/roxanabalint

FIGURE 11-6

Edit Input Data

Like other applications in this book, the data that users enter in the College Registration Costs program must be checked to ensure its validity. When the user taps or clicks the Calculate Costs button, the following items must be checked:

1. Student ID: The Student ID object is a masked text box, and the mask is for the Social Security number in the same layout, so the mask ensures that the user can enter only numbers. However, the Social Security mask does not ensure that the user enters all nine numbers. Therefore, a check must be included in the program to require the user to enter all nine numeric digits.
2. Student Name: The program must ensure that the user enters characters in this TextBox object. In addition, spaces cannot be entered instead of actual alphabetic characters.
3. Number of Units: The user must enter a numeric value from 1 through 24 for the number of units the student is taking.
4. Major: The user must select a major from the list in the Major ComboBox object.

ONLINE REINFORCEMENT

To view a video of the process in the previous steps, visit CengageBrain.com and navigate to the resources for this title. Tap or click the link for Chapter 11 and then navigate to Video 11-2.

The code to implement these editing requirements is shown in Figure 11-7.

```
13
14      Dim objStudent As Student
15      Dim objOnCampusStudent As OnCampusStudent
16      Dim InputError As Boolean = False
17
18      ' Is student ID entered properly
19      If txtStudentID.MaskFull = False Then
20          MsgBox("Enter your Student ID in the Student ID box", , "Error")
21          txtStudentID.Clear()
22          txtStudentID.Focus()
23          InputError = True
24          ' Is student name entered properly
25      ElseIf txtStudentName.TextLength < 1 Or txtStudentName.Text < "A" Then
26          MsgBox("Enter your name in the Student Name box", , "Error")
27          txtStudentName.Clear()
28          txtStudentName.Focus()
29          InputError = True
30          ' Is number of units entered properly
31      ElseIf Not IsNumeric(txtNumberOfUnits.Text) Then
32          MsgBox("Enter the units in the Number of Units box", , "Error")
33          txtNumberOfUnits.Clear()
34          txtNumberOfUnits.Focus()
35          InputError = True
36          ' Has 1-24 units been entered
37      ElseIf Convert.ToInt32(txtNumberOfUnits.Text) < 1 Or Convert.ToInt32(txtNumberOfUnits.Text) > 24 Then
38          MsgBox("Units must be 1 - 24", , "Error")
39          txtNumberOfUnits.Clear()
40          txtNumberOfUnits.Focus()
41          InputError = True
42          ' Has a major been selected
43      ElseIf cboMajor.SelectedIndex < 0 Then
44          MsgBox("Please select a major", , "Error")
45          cboMajor.Focus()
46          InputError = True
47      End If
```

FIGURE 11-7

In Figure 11-7, on line 16, a Boolean variable named InputError is defined and given the value False. This variable will be set to a value of True if an error is found in the editing statements. If any input area contains an error, the registration costs will not be calculated.

The editing checks are completed within an If...Else If statement. Because of the checks in this statement, each of the fields must contain valid data before the next field is checked; for example, until the Student ID field contains valid data, the Student Name field is not checked. This approach ensures that each field will contain valid data before the registration costs are calculated.

To ensure that the Student ID masked text box contains all nine numeric digits, the MaskFull property is tested, as shown in Figure 11-8.

```
18              ' Is student ID entered properly
19          If txtStudentID.MaskFull = False Then
20              MsgBox("Enter your Student ID in the Student ID box", , "Error")
21              txtStudentID.Clear()
22              txtStudentID.Focus()
23              InputError = True
```

FIGURE 11-8

The MaskFull property identifies whether all digits have been entered into the mask. For the Student ID, if all nine numeric digits have been entered into the masked text box, the property will be true; otherwise, the property will be false. If the MaskFull property is false, a message box will be displayed that directs the user to enter the student ID in the Student ID box. In addition, the masked text box is cleared, the focus is placed in the masked text box, and the InputError Boolean variable is set to True, indicating an error occurred.

If the Student ID field is correct, the next check is to ensure that the Student Name text box contains data. The Else...If statement to check the Student Name text box is shown in Figure 11-9.

```
25          ElseIf txtStudentName.TextLength < 1 Or txtStudentName.Text < "A" Then
26              MsgBox("Enter your name in the Student Name box", , "Error")
27              txtStudentName.Clear()
28              txtStudentName.Focus()
29              InputError = True
```

FIGURE 11-9

The If statement tests whether the length of the data in the text box is less than 1 and whether the first character entered is less than the letter A. If the length is less than 1, no data was entered in the text box. If the first character is less than A, then either a space or a special character was entered as the first character, both of which are invalid. If either of these conditions is true, a message box appears and instructs the user to enter a student name, the text box is cleared, focus is placed back on the Student Name text box, and the InputError Boolean variable is set to True.

CRITICAL THINKING

If you compared txtStudentName.TextLength < "a", would that guarantee that the entry is a valid name? No. If the student entered a capital letter, the condition would be true because of the ASCII value chart (see Appendix A).

If the Student Name text box contains valid data, the Number of Units TextBox object is checked to ensure that it contains a numeric value from 1 through 24. To make this check, two If statements are required: one to check for numeric data (line 31 in Figure 11-10) and one to ensure that the value is 1 through 24 (lines 37–38 in Figure 11-10). If either of these tests finds an error, a message box is displayed again, the TextBox object is cleared, the focus is placed in the text box, and the InputError variable is set to True.

```
30              ' Is number of units entered properly
31          ElseIf Not IsNumeric(txtNumberOfUnits.Text) Then
32              MsgBox("Enter the units in the Number of Units box", , "Error")
33              txtNumberOfUnits.Clear()
34              txtNumberOfUnits.Focus()
35              InputError = True
36              ' Has 1-24 units been entered
37          ElseIf Convert.ToInt32(txtNumberOfUnits.Text) < 1 Or Convert.ToInt32(txtNumberOfUnits.Text) > 24 Then
38              MsgBox("Units must be 1 - 24", , "Error")
39              txtNumberOfUnits.Clear()
40              txtNumberOfUnits.Focus()
41              InputError = True
```

FIGURE 11-10

The last data-editing step is to ensure that the user selected a major in the Major ComboBox object (Figure 11-11).

```
42              ' Has a major been selected
43          ElseIf cboMajor.SelectedIndex < 0 Then
44              MsgBox("Please select a major", , "Error")
45              cboMajor.Focus()
46              InputError = True
47          End If
```

FIGURE 11-11

As you have learned, when testing for a selection in a ComboBox object, the SelectedIndex property will contain the value −1 if a selection has not been made and will contain the index value of the selected entry if a selection has been made. If the SelectedIndex property is less than zero, then a selection has not been made, so a message box displays an error message, the focus is placed on the ComboBox object, and the InputError Boolean variable is set to true.

If all tests are passed, the processing to compute the registration costs and other processing can occur.

Program Structure Using Classes

In previous programs, the Form class has been the basis of the program. It presented the user interface and has contained the Visual Basic statements that have processed data the user entered. In some programs, multiple procedures have been included in the class to complete the required processing.

When programs become larger and more complex, often you will divide the necessary processing into classes. This can have several benefits:

- The program is easier to read, understand, and maintain.
- A class can be used in more than one program for the same purpose. For example, the Button class that is used to create buttons in the user interface is used each time a Button object is placed on the Windows Form object.
- The processing accomplished in a class is separated from other classes, making the program easier to maintain and less prone to error.
- Variables defined in one class can be hidden from processing in other classes, so there is less likelihood of programming errors. Controlling the use of these variables (often called attributes or properties) by other classes reduces the inadvertent or purposeful inappropriate use of the attributes.

The concept of separating processing and hiding data within specific classes is called **encapsulation,** and is a major contributor to reliable and robust programs. Encapsulation is one of the fundamental principles of object-oriented programming. Encapsulation wraps related data and functions into a single entity.

Why should I use encapsulation?

- Encapsulation gives maintainability, flexibility, and extensibility to your code.
- Encapsulation provides a way to protect data from accidental corruption by keeping portions of the code in separate classes.
- Encapsulation hides information within an object.

CONSIDER THIS

When developing programs with multiple classes, a starting point for determining what classes should appear in a program is the three-tiered program structure. This structure specifies that a program is divided into three separate tiers: Presentation, Business, and Persistence (see Figure 11-12).

Presentation Tier	Business Tier	Persistence Tier
User Interface, Forms	Logic, Calculations	Data Storage (Files and Databases)

FIGURE 11-12

The **presentation tier** contains the classes that display information for the user and accept user input. In many programs, the presentation tier consists of one or more forms and the objects placed on the forms. In a Web application, the presentation tier is the web form and web page that appear to the user. In addition, the processing in the presentation tier ensures that valid data is entered into the program for processing in the business tier.

The **business tier** contains the logic and calculations that must occur to fulfill the requirements of the program. The class(es) in the business tier generally use data entered by users and data obtained from storage to perform the logic and calculations. The business tier is named for the fact that it implements the "business rules" required for the application.

The **persistence tier**, sometimes called the **data access tier**, contains the code required to read and write data from permanent storage. Data that is stored in a file or database on disk often is called persistent data because it remains after the program is terminated.

When designing a program using the three-tiered approach, a primary rule is that classes in the presentation tier can communicate only with classes in the business tier. They never can communicate with classes in the persistence tier. In the same manner, classes in the persistence tier cannot communicate with classes in the presentation tier.

By following this rule, a program is much easier to maintain if changes must be made. For example, if a program currently writes data to a text file, such as in the College Registration Costs program in this chapter, and a decision is made to write the data in a database instead, only the class(es) in the persistence tier must be examined and changed. The user interface classes should have nothing to do with how data is stored. Therefore, the developer can be confident that if the correct changes are made to the persistence classes, the program will run properly regardless of the processing in the presentation classes.

Similarly, the business classes need not be concerned with how the data is obtained or stored. While the business classes will decide what data is needed and what data should be written to storage, only the persistence classes will actually read or write data.

This same thinking holds true for the separation of the business and presentation tiers. The classes in the business tier, where the logic and calculations occur, should not have to be concerned with the functionality of the user interface, nor should the user interface classes be concerned with how the data is manipulated by the business classes.

By placing classes in one of the three tiers depending on each class's function, the program becomes much easier to design, develop, and maintain.

Sample Program Classes

The College Registration Costs program in this chapter uses the three-tiered approach. The classes in each of the tiers are as follows:

1. Presentation tier: The presentation tier contains the frmCollege class. This class displays the user interface in a Windows Form object and edits the user input data to ensure its validity.

2. Business tier: The business tier contains two classes: the Student class and the OnCampusStudent class. The Student class contains data for each registered student and calculates the registration costs for some students. The OnCampusStudent class is used for registered students who live in on-campus residence halls.

3. Persistence tier: The persistence tier consists of one class, StudentCostsFile, which creates and writes the Student Costs File.

Create a Class

The class in the presentation tier, the frmCollege class, is created when the new Windows application is started. The other classes are created using the technique shown in the following steps:

STEP 1   With Visual Studio open and a new Windows Application project started, press and hold or right-click the project name in the Solution Explorer window and then point to Add on the shortcut menu.

The shortcut menu is displayed (Figure 11-13). When you point to the Add menu item, the Add submenu is also displayed.

FIGURE 11-13

STEP 2 Tap or click Class on the Add submenu.

The Add New Item dialog box is displayed (Figure 11-14). Class is selected as an installed template in the middle pane.

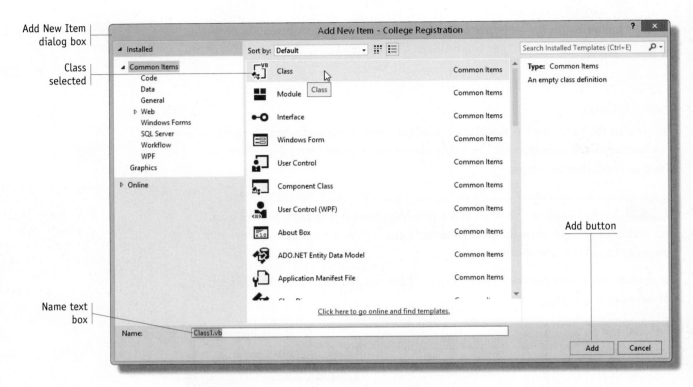

FIGURE 11-14

STEP 3 In the Name text box, type `Student` as the name of the class and then tap or click the Add button.

Visual Studio creates a new class called Student (Figure 11-15). The class is identified in the Solution Explorer window. The code window is opened for the class.

FIGURE 11-15

STEP 4 Using the same techniques, create the OnCampusStudent class and the StudentCostsFile class.

The Solution Explorer window now shows the four classes for the program: OnCampusStudent, frmCollege, Student, and StudentCostsFile (Figure 11-16). To select a class and display its code window, double-tap or double-click the class name in the Solution Explorer.

FIGURE 11-16

ONLINE REINFORCEMENT

To view a video of the process in the previous steps, visit CengageBrain.com and navigate to the resources for this title. Tap or click the link for Chapter 11 and then navigate to Video 11-3.

Code Classes

After the classes have been defined, you must write the code for each class. You can write code for each class using the same techniques you have used for previous programs. Before beginning, however, you must consider how classes communicate so you can write the correct code.

Instantiate a Class and Class Communication

As you have learned, the code in a class acts as a template for an object. For example, when you drag the Button .NET component from the Toolbox to the Windows Form object, the Button object is created, or instantiated, based on the code in the Button class. Properties of the Button object, such as the text shown in the button, are processed using the code in the Button class.

Similarly, whenever you define a class in your Visual Basic program, you must instantiate an object based on that class in order for the processing within the object to take place. To instantiate an object, you can use the New statement, as shown in Figure 11-17.

```
            name of object                name of class


21            Dim objStudent As Student
22
23            objStudent = New Student



                          New keyword
```

FIGURE 11-17

In Figure 11-17, the Dim statement on line 21 specifies a variable named objStudent that will contain the address of the Student object when it is created. The name of the class from which the object will be instantiated (Student) must follow the As keyword. As you have learned previously, an object name begins with the prefix obj.

The assignment statement on line 23 creates the new object from the Student class and places the address of the object in the variable called objStudent. The keyword New must follow the equal sign, followed by the name of the class. Once the object is created, public procedures, public variables or attributes, and properties of the object can be referenced by other objects within the project.

A single statement can also be used to create an object, as shown in Figure 11-18.

```
25            Dim objStudent As New Student
```

FIGURE 11-18

The Dim statement on line 25 in Figure 11-18 both creates a variable to hold the address of the object (objStudent) and instantiates the object by using the keyword New followed by the name of the class.

The technique shown in Figure 11-17 is more widely used because the variable can be defined in the variables section of the code and the object is not instantiated until it is needed.

Constructors in New Instantiated Classes

When a class is instantiated into an object using the New keyword, a special procedure called a constructor is executed in the class. The **constructor** prepares the object for use in the program. The code in the constructor executes before any other code in the object. In addition to processes that are automatically completed by the constructor, the user can choose to write code for the constructor as well.

If the developer writes no code for a class constructor, Visual Basic automatically generates any processing that must be accomplished to prepare the object for use. The developer can include a constructor with no executing code, as shown in Figure 11-19.

```
 1 Public Class Student
 2
 3     Sub New()
 4         'Constructor for Student class
 5
 6         'If required, initializing statements go here
 7
 8     End Sub
 9
10 End Class
```

FIGURE 11-19

Note in Figure 11-19 that the constructor begins with the statement Sub New(). No name is required for the constructor — the New keyword identifies the Sub procedure as the constructor.

Because the code in the constructor executes before any other code in the object, it is a good location to place initializing code statements that prepare the object for execution.

Pass Arguments When Instantiating an Object

When you instantiate an object, data often must be passed to the object. For example, in the College Registration Costs program, the user enters the Student ID, Student Name, and other data into the user interface form. The Student object requires this data to calculate the registration costs and cause the StudentCostsFile object to write the required text file. If an object requires data when it is instantiated, the data can be passed as part of the instantiation code. For example, to pass the Student ID, the Student Name, the Major, and the Number of Units from the Form object to the Student object when the Student object is instantiated in the Form object, the statement in Figure 11-20 can be used.

New keyword   arguments

```
51          objStudent = New Student(txtStudentID.Text, txtStudentName.Text,
              cboMajor.SelectedItem, txtNumberOfUnits.Text)
```

FIGURE 11-20

In Figure 11-20 on the previous page, the assignment statement that is specified in the Form class uses the New keyword in a manner similar to that shown in Figure 11-17 on page 760, except that arguments are included within the parentheses following the New keyword. Notice that the format of the arguments for the New statement is identical to the format used when passing arguments to a procedure, as you saw in Chapter 8. In Figure 11-20, the values in the txtStudentID Text property, the txtStudentName Text property, the cboMajor.SelectedItem property, and the txtNumberOfUnits Text property are passed to the instantiated object.

In the Student class, the New statement must be written with corresponding arguments; that is, the "signature" of the instantiating statement (Figure 11-20) must be the same as the constructor heading in the class. The New statement for the Student class is shown in Figure 11-21.

```
12    Sub New(ByVal strStudentID As String, ByVal strStudentName As String, ByVal
      strMajor As String, ByVal intUnits As String)
```

FIGURE 11-21

Note in Figure 11-21 that the arguments for the New statement in the Student class match up to the arguments in the instantiation statement in Figure 11-20. The arguments are passed ByVal, which you recall means a copy of the value is passed to the instantiated object but the original value is not used.

Once the object is instantiated and the arguments are passed, the constructor can use the values in the arguments to set the values in variables within the class. The code in Figure 11-22 illustrates the assignment statements in the constructor to set the value of the variables defined in the Student class to the values passed from the calling object by the statement in Figure 11-21.

```
9     Public Class Student
10
11        'Class variables
12        Protected _strStudentID As String
13        Protected _strStudentName As String
14        Protected _strMajor As String
15        Protected _intUnits As Integer
16        Protected _decCost As Decimal
17        Protected _decCostPerUnit As Decimal = 450D
18
19        Dim objStudentCostsFile As StudentCostsFile
20
          2 references
21        Sub New(ByVal strStudentID As String, ByVal strStudentName As String, ByVal strMajor As String, ByVal intUnits As String)
22            ' This subprocedure is a constructor for the Student class. It is called when the object is instantiated with arguments
23
24            'The following code assigns the arguments to class variables
25            _strStudentID = strStudentID
26            _strStudentName = strStudentName
27            _strMajor = strMajor
28            _intUnits = Convert.ToInt32(intUnits)
29
30        End Sub
```

FIGURE 11-22

In the constructor shown in Figure 11-22, the assignment statements on lines 25 through 27 place the values passed from the instantiation statement into the variables defined in the Student class (lines 12 through 17). When the object based on the Student class is instantiated, the constructor code ensures that the variables in the object contain data entered by the user.

Notice that the variables in the Student class are defined with Protected access. Generally, when using multiple classes within a program, variables (also called attributes) should not be available to code within other classes of the program. Classes can reference attributes within another class only if the class that contains the attributes allows it. You will learn techniques for such access later in this chapter, but attributes should usually be defined with Private access.

Call a Procedure in a Separate Class

Most of the time, separate classes in a program contain procedures that must be executed. For example, in the College Registration Costs program, the Student class must contain a procedure that calculates the registration costs. This procedure is shown in Figure 11-23.

```
15      Private _intUnits As Integer
16      Private _decCost As Decimal
17      Private _decCostPerUnit As Decimal = 450D
         .
         .
         .
32      Function ComputeCosts() As Decimal
33          ' This function computes the registration costs, and
34          ' returns the registration costs
35
36          _decCost = _intUnits * _decCostPerUnit
37
38          Return _decCost
39
40      End Function
```

FIGURE 11-23

In Figure 11-23, the ComputeCosts function in the Student class multiplies the number of units (_intUnits) times the cost per unit (_decCostPerUnit) to determine the cost (_decCost). The cost then is returned as a decimal value to the calling class by the Return statement on line 38.

You might ask why the statement on line 36 cannot be included in the Form class that calls the Student class instead of calling the ComputeCosts function in the Student class. The short answer is that it could be. However, when designing larger and more robust programs, it is important to keep the tasks of each class separate.

In this case, the presentation tier of the three-tiered structure, represented by the Form object, should have no knowledge of how student registration costs are calculated. In the sample program of this chapter, the calculation is a simple multiplication statement. In the future, the calculation of registration costs might involve multiple lookups in a database, complex calculations based on major, in-state or out-of-state residence, and so on. The presentation class(es) should have nothing to do with these processes; the Student class should be the class in the program that knows how to perform all student activities. Therefore, even when the calculation is simple, as in the sample program, these tasks should be contained within the correct class.

To call the ComputeCosts procedure in the Student object, a statement in the Form object must identify both the object and the procedure within the object. The statement on line 54 calls the ComputeCosts procedure, as shown in Figure 11-24.

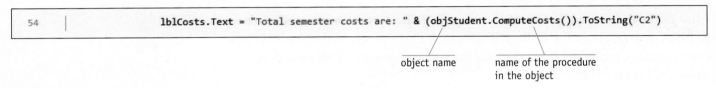

```
54          lblCosts.Text = "Total semester costs are: " & (objStudent.ComputeCosts()).ToString("C2")
```

                                                    object name   name of the procedure
                                                                        in the object

FIGURE 11-24

On line 54 in Figure 11-24, the statement objStudent.ComputeCosts() identifies the objStudent object from Figure 11-17 on page 760 and the ComputeCosts procedure from Figure 11-23 on page 763, separated by the dot operator (.). The dot operator specifies a member of a type or namespace. The statement says, "Pass control to the ComputeCosts procedure found in the objStudent object." The ComputeCosts procedure is a Function procedure, and the value returned from the procedure call is converted to a string and then assigned to the Text property of the lblCosts Label object so it can be displayed in the Windows Form object (see Figure 11-2 on page 748).

In this section, you have seen the entire process for creating a class, instantiating a class, and calling a procedure in a class. This process is fundamental when designing larger and more robust programs.

Inheritance

In the College Registration Costs program, the Student object contains student information from the Form object and performs calculations for the student. A student living on campus is a specialized student whose costs include housing and board. Therefore, the cost calculation for the on-campus student is different from that for an off-campus student. In addition, the On-Campus Student object must include Boolean indicators for the type of housing selected.

If the student lives off campus, a Student object will be instantiated, and if the student lives on campus, an On-Campus Student object will be instantiated. Because the Student and On-Campus Student objects contain some different attributes and their cost calculations are different, logically they could be separate objects. Visual Basic and other object-oriented programming languages offer an alternative, however. This alternative is inheritance.

Inheritance allows one class to inherit attributes and procedures from another class. For example, the Student object contains the Student ID, the Student Name, the Major, and the Number of Units. These same values are required for the on-campus student. In addition, the On-Campus Student object contains indicators for the housing selected. By using inheritance, the attributes of the Student object can be used by the On-Campus Student object as well. Inheritance is the ability to use all of the functionality of an existing class and extend those capabilities without rewriting the class (Figure 11-25).

FIGURE 11-25

In Figure 11-25, the Student class contains the Student ID, Student Name, Number of Units, and Major attributes. Because the OnCampusStudent class inherits from the Student class, the OnCampusStudent class can reference the Student ID variable in the Student class as if that variable were defined in the OnCampusStudent class. This is true of the other Student class variables as well. As you can see, the OnCampusStudent class inherits the attributes it can use from the Student class and then defines the unique attributes it requires as well.

In the example in Figure 11-25, the Student class is called the **base class**. The OnCampusStudent class is called the **subclass**. The subclass can use attributes from the base class as if those attributes were defined in the subclass.

The code for the attributes in the Student base class and the OnCampusStudent subclass is shown in Figure 11-26.

```vb
1    ' Class:        Student
2    ' Developer:    Corinne Hoisington
3    ' Date:         August 29, 2017
4    ' Purpose:      This business class for a registering college student calculates the semester costs for tuition. It also causes the
5    '               student costs file to be written.
6
7    Option Strict On
8
     3 references
9    Public Class Student
10
11       'Class variables
12       Protected _strStudentID As String
13       Protected _strStudentName As String
14       Protected _strMajor As String
15       Protected _intUnits As Integer
16       Protected _decCost As Decimal
17       Protected _decCostPerUnit As Decimal = 450D
18
19       Dim objStudentCostsFile As StudentCostsFile
```

FIGURE 11-26a

```vb
1    ' Class:        OnCampusStudent
2    ' Developer:    Corinne Hoisington
3    ' Date:         August 29, 2017
4    ' Purpose:      This business class for registering an on-campus college student calculates the semester costs, including tuition
5    '               and housing. It also causes the student costs file to be written.
6
7    Option Strict On
8
     2 references
9    Public Class OnCampusStudent
10       Inherits Student
11
12       ' Class variables
13       Private _Cooper As Boolean
14       Private _Craig As Boolean
15       Private _Julian As Boolean
16
17       Dim objStudentCostsFile As StudentCostsFile
```

FIGURE 11-26b

After the usual comment statements for the Student class, the variables required for the Student class are declared. You can see that the string variables for Student ID, Student Name, and Major are declared, together with an integer variable for the Number of Units. In addition, the _decCost Decimal variable will contain the result of the calculation, and _decCostPerUnit is a Decimal variable that contains the fixed cost per unit (450D) used in the calculation for semester costs.

Note that the variables in the Student class are declared with Protected access. Protected means statements in the subclasses of the base class can reference the variable as if the referencing statement were declared in the base class instead of the subclass. Statements outside the base class and the subclasses, however, cannot reference the variables.

In the OnCampusStudent subclass, the Class statement on line 9 includes the Inherits entry on line 10. This required entry indicates that the OnCampusStudent class inherits from the Student class. Any subclass must include the Inherits entry to indicate the class from which it inherits.

The three Boolean variables required in the subclass are declared, but no declarations are made for Student ID, Student Name, or the other variables declared in the Student base class. These variables can be used as if they are part of the OnCampusStudent subclass.

Why should I use inheritance?

- Inheritance provides a clear model structure that is easy to understand without much complexity.
- Inheritance enables you to create new classes that reuse, extend, and modify the behavior defined in other classes.
- Using inheritance manages code by dividing it into parent and child classes.

CONSIDER THIS

Constructors

Both the base class and the subclass must have constructors. The code for the base class constructor and the subclass constructor is shown in Figure 11-27 and Figure 11-28.

BASE CLASS CONSTUCTOR

```
20
        2 references
21      Sub New(ByVal strStudentID As String, ByVal strStudentName As String, ByVal strMajor As String, ByVal intUnits As String)
22          ' This subprocedure is a constructor for the Student class. It is called when the object is instantiated with arguments
23
24          'The following code assigns the arguments to class variables
25          _strStudentID = strStudentID
26          _strStudentName = strStudentName
27          _strMajor = strMajor
28          _intUnits = Convert.ToInt32(intUnits)
29
30      End Sub
```

FIGURE 11-27

SUBCLASS CONSTUCTOR

```
19      Sub New(ByVal StudentID As String, ByVal StudentName As String, ByVal Major As String, ByVal Units As String,
20              ByVal Cooper As Boolean, ByVal Craig As Boolean, ByVal Julian As Boolean)
21          ' This subprocedure is a constructor for the Student class. It is called when instantiated with arguments
22
23          MyBase.New(StudentID, StudentName, Major, Units)
24
25          'The following code assigns the arguments to class variables
26          _Cooper = Cooper
27          _Craig = Craig
28          _Julian = Julian
29
30      End Sub
```

FIGURE 11-28

In the constructor for the Student base class, the Student ID, Student Name, Major, and Number of Units are passed when the object is instantiated. The constructor places the Student ID, Student Name, and Major in string variables and converts the Number of Units to an integer.

In the constructor for the OnCampusStudent subclass, the Student ID, Student Name, Major, Number of Units, and the Boolean indicators for Cooper, Craig, and Julian are passed by the instantiating statement. The required first statement in the subclass constructor is the MyBase.New statement (line 23 in Figure 11-28 on the previous page). This statement calls the code in the base class (Student) constructor and executes it. Therefore, when the subclass is instantiated, both the base class and subclass constructors are executed.

In Figure 11-28, after the base class constructor is executed, the OnCampusStudent constructor places the Boolean indicators in variables so they can be tested in the class processing.

Again, it should be emphasized that the Student ID, Student Name, Major, and Number of Units variables are available to the OnCampusStudent subclass even though these variables are not declared within the class. They are available because of inheritance.

Inheritance and Procedures

When using inheritance, the subclass can use the procedures within the base class as well as its variables. Between the base class and the subclass, five different techniques can be used for referencing and calling a procedure from an outside class such as a Form class. After the base class and the subclass have been instantiated, the following techniques are available:

Base Class:
   1. Call a named procedure in the base class.
      Example: `objBaseClass.RegularBaseClassFunction()`

   2. Call an Overridable procedure in the base class.
      Example: `objBaseClass.OverridableBaseClassFunction()`

Subclass:
   1. Call an Overridable procedure in the subclass.
      Example: `objSubClass.OverridableBaseClassFunction()`

   2. Call a named procedure in the subclass.
      Example: `objSubClass.RegularSubClassFunction()`

   3. Call a base class procedure in the subclass.
      Example: `objSubClass.RegularBaseClassFunction()`

Each of these methods is explained in the following sections.

Call a Named Procedure in the Base Class

A Sub procedure or a Function procedure in the base class can be called from another class in the manner you have seen previously. Thus, if a base class contains a Function procedure called RegularBaseClassFunction, another class can call the function using the statement objBaseClass.RegularBaseClassFunction(), where objBaseClass is the instantiated base class object and RegularBaseClassFunction is the name of the Function procedure.

An example of the code for this process is shown in Figure 11-29.

FORM CLASS

```
 4          Dim objSubClass As SubClass
 5          Dim objBaseClass As BaseClass
 6
 7          objSubClass = New SubClass
 8          objBaseClass = New BaseClass
 9
10          MsgBox(objBaseClass.RegularBaseClassFunction())
```

FIGURE 11-29a

SUBCLASS CLASS

```
 3      Function RegularBaseClassFunction() As String
 4          Return "Regular base class function"
 5      End Function
```

FIGURE 11-29b

FIGURE 11-29c

In Figure 11-29a on the previous page, the objBaseClass object is instantiated on line 8 of the Form class. The statement on line 10 in Figure 11-29a calls the RegularBaseClassFunction in the objBaseClass object. When the function returns the text value, the value is displayed in the message box in Figure 11-29c. The process shown in Figure 11-29 is the normal process for calling a procedure in another class.

Call an Overridable Procedure in a Base Class

When a procedure is written in the base class, the procedure will perform its assigned processing. Sometimes, the subclass might require basically the same task to be completed but with some differences in how it is accomplished. For example, in the College Registration Costs sample program, the Student base class procedure determines the costs by multiplying the number of units times the cost per unit. In the OnCampusStudent subclass, the costs are calculated by multiplying the number of units times the cost per unit and then adding the housing/board costs.

Even though the process accomplishes the same task of computing costs, the calculations are different. When a task is accomplished in a different manner in a base class than in a subclass, the procedure can have the same name in both the base class and the subclass, but if the procedure in the subclass is called, it overrides the procedure in the base class. If the procedure in the base class is called, it is executed as a normal procedure call, as shown in Figure 11-30.

FORM CLASS

```
4       Dim objSubClass As SubClass
5       Dim objBaseClass As BaseClass
6
7       objSubClass = New SubClass
8       objBaseClass = New BaseClass
9
10      MsgBox(objBaseClass.OverridableBaseClassFunction())
```

FIGURE 11-30a

BASE CLASS

```
7    Overridable Function OverridableBaseClassFunction() As String
8        Return "Overridable base class function"
9    End Function
```

FIGURE 11-30b

FIGURE 11-30c

Notice in Figure 11-30b that the keyword Overridable precedes the Function keyword. Overridable means a subclass can contain a procedure with the same procedure name as that in the base class. If the procedure in the subclass is called (in other words, SubClassName.ProcedureName), then it is executed even though it has the same name as the procedure in the base class. In Figure 11-30a, however, the procedure named OverridableBaseClassFunction in the base class is called from the Form class, so that procedure is executed.

Call an Overridable Procedure in a Subclass

In Figure 11-31, a call is made to the OverridableBaseClassFunction that is defined in the subclass. Notice in Figure 11-31c that the Function name in the subclass is preceded by the Overrides keyword, which indicates the function in the base class will be overridden by the function in the subclass when the latter function is called.

FORM CLASS

```
4        Dim objSubClass As SubClass
5        Dim objBaseClass As BaseClass
6
7        objSubClass = New SubClass
8        objBaseClass = New BaseClass
9
10       MsgBox(objSubClass.OverridableBaseClassFunction())
```

FIGURE 11-31a

BASE CLASS

```
7    Overridable Function OverridableBaseClassFunction() As String
8        Return "Overridable base class function"
9    End Function
```

FIGURE 11-31b

SUB CLASS

```
8    Overrides Function OverridableBaseClassFunction() As String
9        Return "Overrode the base class overridable function"
10   End Function
```

FIGURE 11-31c

FIGURE 11-31d

In Figure 11-31b on the previous page, the function defined on line 7 of the base class is called OverridableBaseClassFunction, and the name is preceded by the Overridable keyword. In Figure 11-31c, the function with the same name on line 8 of the subclass overrides the function in the base class. As a result, when the subclass function is called (line 10 of the Form class in Figure 11-31a), the subclass message appears in the message box.

Call a Named Procedure in the Subclass

As with any other public procedure in a class, a named procedure in a subclass can be called (Figure 11-32).

FORM CLASS

```
4          Dim objSubClass As SubClass
5          Dim objBaseClass As BaseClass
6
7          objSubClass = New SubClass
8          objBaseClass = New BaseClass
9
10         MsgBox(objSubClass.RegularSubClassFunction())
```

FIGURE 11-32a

SUB CLASS

```
4      Function RegularSubClassFunction() As String
5          Return "Regular subclass function"
6      End Function
```

FIGURE 11-32b

FIGURE 11-32c

The example in Figure 11-32 is a straightforward procedure call to a procedure in another class.

Call a Base Class Procedure in the Subclass

The last common procedure call involving inheritance occurs when a procedure in the base class is called by referencing the subclass, as shown in Figure 11-33.

FORM CLASS

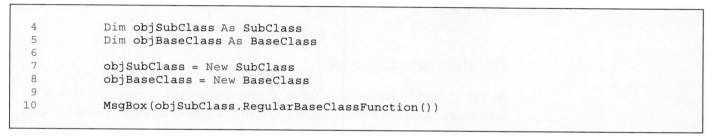

```
4          Dim objSubClass As SubClass
5          Dim objBaseClass As BaseClass
6
7          objSubClass = New SubClass
8          objBaseClass = New BaseClass
9
10         MsgBox(objSubClass.RegularBaseClassFunction())
```

FIGURE 11-33a

BASE CLASS

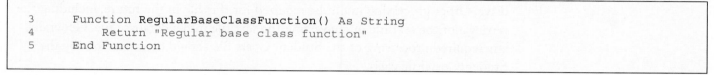

```
3      Function RegularBaseClassFunction() As String
4          Return "Regular base class function"
5      End Function
```

FIGURE 11-33b

Regular base class function

OK

FIGURE 11-33c

In Figure 11-33 on the previous page, the procedure call statement in the Form class (line 10 in Figure 11-33a) calls a procedure that is not even in the subclass. Nonetheless, the regular base class function is executed because when a procedure is called that is not in the class specified in the call statement, Visual Basic will move up to the base class to see if the procedure is located there. If so, the procedure in the base class is executed.

Inheritance can be a relatively complex subject that has more ramifications than you have learned in this chapter. Nonetheless, this beginning knowledge of inheritance will serve you well as you continue your education in programming and development.

Persistence Classes

As you learned earlier in this chapter, the persistence tier in an application is sometimes called the data access tier. It contains classes that are involved in saving and retrieving data stored on a permanent storage medium, such as a hard disk or a USB drive. A typical persistence class is the StudentCostsFile class in the College Registration Costs sample program in this chapter. This class is concerned with performing all tasks required for the Student Costs file. In the sample program, this processing consists of writing the file as a text file and saving it on a USB drive. Other processing might be required for this file in the future, including the retrieval of the text file or converting the text file into a database file. Generally, any required processing of the Student Costs file should be carried out by the StudentCostsFile class.

To define the StudentCostsFile class, you must write comments, variables, and a constructor, as you have seen earlier in this chapter. The code to define the StudentCostsFile class is shown in Figure 11-34.

```
1    ' Class:        Student Costs File
2    ' Developer:    Corinne Hoisington
3    ' Date:         August 29, 2017
4    ' Purpose:      This class represents the Student Costs File. The WriteRecord procedure writes a comma-delimited student costs file that
5    '               contains the Student ID, Student Name, Major, and Student Costs.
6
7    Option Strict On
8
     4 references
9    Public Class StudentCostsFile
10
11       ' Class variables
12       Private _strStudentID As String
13       Private _strStudentName As String
14       Private _strMajor As String
15       Private _decStudentCosts As Decimal
16
         2 references
17       Sub New(ByVal StudentID As String, ByVal StudentName As String, ByVal Major As String, ByVal Costs As Decimal)
18           ' This sub procedure is the constructor for the StudentCostsFile class.
19
20           ' The following code assigns the arguments to class variables
21           _strStudentID = StudentID
22           _strStudentName = StudentName
23           _strMajor = Major
24           _decStudentCosts = Costs
25
26       End Sub
```

FIGURE 11-34

In Figure 11-34, the typical comments are followed by the declaration of the variables used in the class. Notice that each of the variables is declared with Private access so they cannot be referenced by code in any other class within the program.

Following the variable declarations is the constructor procedure, as identified by the keyword New. Within the constructor, the code on lines 21–24 sets the values in the variables to the values passed to the StudentCostsFile class when it is instantiated.

Comma-Delimited Text Files

The StudentCosts file is a comma-delimited text file, which means a comma separates each field in a record in the file, as shown in Figure 11-35.

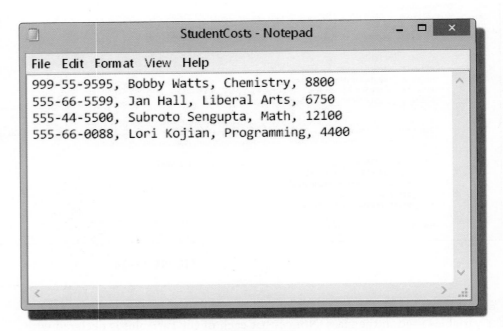

FIGURE 11-35

Notice in Figure 11-35 that a comma appears at the end of each field, but no comma is displayed at the end of the record. A comma-delimited text file is commonly used because it can be read into programs such as Microsoft Excel and Microsoft Access to import the data into the application.

In Chapter 8, you learned to use a StreamWriter to write a stream of text to a file. To create the file shown in Figure 11-35, a record that contains the Student ID, the Student Name, the Major, and the Costs must be added to the file each time new registration costs are calculated for a student. Because you do not know how many records will be placed in the file during the registration process, a StreamWriter must be created that can append, or add, records to the file. Because a record contains four fields, the first three of which are followed by a comma, a Write statement must be used so that a new line is not created in the file each time part of a record is written to the disk. The code to accomplish this processing is shown in the WriteRecord Sub procedure in Figure 11-36.

```
28      Sub WriteRecord()
29          ' This subprocedure opens the StudentCosts output text file and then writes a record in the comma-delimited file
30
31          Dim strNameandLocationOfFile As String = "e:\StudentCosts.txt"
32
33          Try
34              Dim objWriter As IO.StreamWriter = IO.File.AppendText(strNameandLocationOfFile)
35
36              objWriter.Write(_strStudentID & ",")
37              objWriter.Write(_strStudentName & ",")
38              objWriter.Write(_strMajor & ",")
39              objWriter.WriteLine(_decStudentCosts)
40              objWriter.Close()
41
42          Catch ex As Exception
43              MsgBox("No device available - program aborted", , "Error")
44              Application.Exit()
45
46          End Try
47
48      End Sub
49
50  End Class
```

FIGURE 11-36

In Figure 11-36, the Dim statement on line 34 declares a string that contains the name and location of the file to be written. A Try-Catch block is created on line 33 because if a USB drive is not located on drive E, an exception will be thrown. The Catch statement on line 42 catches the exception, displays a message box containing an error message, and exits the application.

Assuming no exception occurs, the Dim statement on line 34 declares the objWriter as an IO.StreamWriter. The identification of the IO.StreamWriter indicates that the writer will append text to the file. Appending the text means writing the next record in the file following the last record in the file; that is, the records accumulate in the file as it is written.

The Write procedure calls on lines 36–38 write the Student ID, the Student Name, and the Major in the record, each followed by a comma. The WriteLine procedure call on line 39 writes the Student Costs in the record and places a line return in the file so the next record can be written. Finally, the Close procedure call on line 40 closes the file.

Program Design

As you have learned, the requirements document identifies the purpose of the program being developed, the application title, the procedures to be followed when using the program, any required equations and calculations, any conditions that must be tested, notes and restrictions that must be followed by the program, and any other comments that would be helpful to understanding the problem. The requirements document for the College Registration Costs application is shown in Figure 11-37.

REQUIREMENTS DOCUMENT

Date Submitted:	August 29, 2017
Application Title:	College Registration Costs
Purpose:	This Windows application allows a user to enter student registration information for Bedford College and then calculates the student registration costs.
Program Procedures:	In a Windows application, the user enters the student ID, student name, and number of units (credits), selects an off-campus or on-campus resident status, selects housing and board if resident status is on-campus, and then selects a major. When the user taps or clicks a button, the application calculates the semester costs and records the information in a log file.
Algorithms, Processing, and Conditions:	1. The user first enters the student ID, student name, and number of units.
	2. The user selects either off-campus residence or on-campus residence. If on-campus residence is selected, the user indicates the housing/board selection (Cooper Dorm, Craig Hall, or Julian Suites). The user then selects the student's major from a list.
	3. When the user taps or clicks a button, the program calculates the semester costs and writes a log file.
	4. A Clear Form button should be available to clear the form and place the insertion point in the Student ID text box.
	5. The course cost is $450.00 per unit.

FIGURE 11-37 (continues)

6. The formula to calculate semester course costs is the number of units times the cost per unit.

7. If the student is an on-campus resident, the following housing/board costs must be added to the course costs: Cooper Dorm, $2,900.00 per semester; Craig Hall, $3,400.00 per semester; Julian Suites, $4,000.00 per semester.

8. The log file is a text file that contains the Student ID, the Student Name, the Major, and the semester costs. It should be a comma-delimited file.

Notes and Restrictions:

1. The student ID must be a complete Social Security number.

2. The student name cannot be left blank and must begin with an alphabetic character.

3. The number of units must be a numeric value of 1 through 24.

4. A major must be selected. The majors available are App Development, Biology, Business, Chemistry, Programming, Liberal Arts, Mathematics, Physics, Sociology, and Technology Education.

5. The housing/board selections should not be displayed in the window unless the user selects the on-campus resident status.

6. When the user taps or clicks the button to calculate costs and the program determines that an error occurred during data entry, a message box is displayed and the user must enter valid data before continuing.

7. Off-campus residency is the default selection; if a student is an on-campus resident, Cooper Dorm is the default selection.

Comments:

1. Obtain an image for this program from CengageBrain.com. The name of the picture is Enroll.

2. The program should use a three-tier structure with presentation, business, and persistence classes.

FIGURE 11-37 (continued)

The Use Case Definition for the application is shown in Figure 11-38.

USE CASE DEFINITION

1. The user enters the student ID, the student name, and the number of units.
2. If necessary, the user selects off-campus or on-campus resident status using radio buttons. If on-campus residency is selected, the housing/board choices are displayed. If necessary, the user selects the housing/board choice.
3. The user selects a major from a list.
4. The user taps or clicks the Calculate Costs button.
5. The program calculates and displays the semester costs, including the cost of housing/board if appropriate.
6. The program writes a log of the student registration costs.
7. If necessary, the user taps or clicks the Clear Form button to clear the form of data and place the insertion point in the Student ID text box.

FIGURE 11-38

Design the Program Processing Objects

You will recall that an event planning document is a table that specifies which objects in the user interface will cause events, the action taken by the user to trigger each event, and the event processing that must occur. In addition, an event planning document is required for each object in the program that is called from another object. The event planning documents for the College Registration Costs program are shown in Figure 11-39 through Figure 11-42 on page 783.

EVENT PLANNING DOCUMENT

Program Name: College Registration Costs	Developer: Corinne Hoisington	Object: frmCollege	Date: August 25, 2017
OBJECT	**EVENT TRIGGER**	**EVENT PROCESSING**	
btnCalculateCosts	Tap or click	Declare Student object Declare OnCampusStudent object Declare Boolean InputError indicator If student ID mask is not full 　　Display message box with error 　　　message 　　Clear student ID masked text box 　　Place focus on student ID masked 　　　text box	

FIGURE 11-39 (continues)

Object	Event Trigger	Event Processing
		Set input error indicator to true
		Else If student name text length < 1 or first character in text box less than "A"
		Display message box with error message
		Clear student name text box
		Place focus on student name text box
		Set input error indicator to true
		Else If number of units is not numeric
		Display message box with error message
		Clear number of units text box
		Place focus on number of units text box
		Set input error indicator to true
		Else If number of units is not 1–24
		Display message box with error message
		Clear number of units text box
		Place focus on number of units text box
		Set input error indicator to true
		Else If major selected index < 0
		Display message box with error message
		Place focus on major combo box
		Set input error indicator to true
		End If
		If no input error
		If off-campus radio button checked
		Instantiate student object with arguments
		Set costs label visible property to true
		Call student compute costs procedure
		Display student costs
		Else
		Instantiate on-campus student object with arguments
		Set costs label visible property to true
		Call on-campus student compute costs procedure
		Display student costs
		End If

FIGURE 11-39 (continues)

Object	Event Trigger	Event Processing
radOnCampus Radio Button	Selected	Make housing/board group visible
radOffCampus Radio Button	Selected	Make housing/board group not visible
btnClearForm	Tap or click	Clear student ID masked text box Clear student name text box Clear number of units text box Set major combo box selected index to −1 Set major combo box text property to "Select a Major" Set off-campus radio button checked property to true Set Cooper radio button checked property to true Set housing/board group visible property to false Set costs label visible property to false Place focus on student ID masked text box

FIGURE 11-39 (continued)

EVENT PLANNING DOCUMENT

Program Name: College Registration Costs	Developer: Corinne Hoisington	Object: objStudent (Student class)	Date: August 25, 2017
Object	**Event Trigger**	**Event Processing**	
New(student ID, student name, major, units)	Class constructor	Set student ID equal to passed student ID Set student name equal to passed student name Set major equal to passed major Convert number of units passed to Integer	
ComputeCosts	Function procedure call	Cost = units × cost per unit Instantiate objStudentCostsFile object Write the student record Return the cost	

FIGURE 11-40

EVENT PLANNING DOCUMENT

Program Name: College Registration Costs	Developer: Corinne Hoisington	Object: objOnCampusStudent (OnCampusStudent class)	Date: August 25, 2017
OBJECT	**EVENT TRIGGER**	**EVENT PROCESSING**	
New(student ID, student name, major, units, Cooper Boolean, Craig Boolean, Julian Boolean)	Class constructor	Call base class constructor (student ID, student name, major, units) Set Cooper Boolean to passed Cooper Boolean Set Craig Boolean to passed Craig Boolean Set Julian Boolean to passed Julian Boolean	
ComputeCosts	Function procedure call	If Cooper housing Set housing cost = Cooper cost Else If Craig housing Set housing cost = Craig cost Else If Julian housing Set housing cost = Julian cost End If Cost = (units * cost per unit) + housing cost Instantiate objStudentCostsFile object Write the student record Return the cost	

FIGURE 11-41

EVENT PLANNING DOCUMENT

Program Name: College Registration Costs	Developer: Corinne Hoisington	Object: objStudentCostsFile (StudentCostsFile class)	Date: August 25, 2017
OBJECT	**EVENT TRIGGER**	**EVENT PROCESSING**	
New(student ID, student name, major, costs)	Class constructor	Set student ID equal to passed student ID Set student name equal to passed student name Set major equal to passed major Set costs equal to passed costs	
WriteRecord	Function procedure call	Define stream writer for append text file Write student ID with comma Write student name with comma Write major with comma Write costs with line return Close text file	

FIGURE 11-42

Guided Program Development

To design the user interface for the College Registration Costs application and enter the code required to process each event in the program, complete the steps in this section.

NOTE TO THE LEARNER

In the following activity, you should complete the tasks within the specified steps. Each of the tasks is accompanied by a Hint Screen. The purpose of the Hint Screen is to indicate where you should perform the activity in the Visual Studio window and to remind you which method to use. If you need further help completing a step, refer to the figure identified by *ref:*.

Phase I: Design the Form

1

- **Create a New Windows Project** Open Visual Studio and then close the Start page. Tap or click the New Project button on the Standard toolbar. Begin a Windows Forms Application project and name the project `CollegeRegistrationCosts`.

- **Name the Form Object** Select the Form object. Change the (Name) property of the Form object to `frmCollege`.

- **Assign a Title to the Form Object** With the frmCollege object selected, change the Text property to `College Registration Costs`.

- **Change the Form Class Name** In the Solution Explorer window, press and hold or right-click Form1.vb, select Rename on the shortcut menu, and change the class name to `frmCollege.vb`.

(continues)

- **Create the User Interface** Using the skills you have acquired in this course and referencing the requirements document in Figure 11-37 on pages 778–779, create the user interface for the frmCollege object, as shown in Figure 11-43. The heading is Tahoma font, bold, 24 points. All other fonts are Tahoma, regular, 12 points.

FIGURE 11-43

© iStock.com/roxanabalint

Phase 2: Code the Application

2

● **Open the Calculate Costs Button Event Handler** On the Windows Form object in the Design window, double-tap or double-click the Calculate Costs Button object.

● **Enter Comments and Option Strict On** Enter the common comments for the frmCollege class. Include the Option Strict On statement.

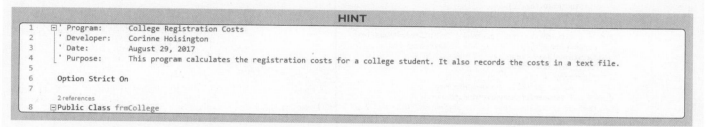

```
HINT
1      ⊟'  Program:      College Registration Costs
2       '  Developer:    Corinne Hoisington
3       '  Date:         August 29, 2017
4       '  Purpose:      This program calculates the registration costs for a college student. It also records the costs in a text file.
5
6        Option Strict On
7
         2 references
8      ⊟Public Class frmCollege
```

● **Enter Comments and Define the Variables for the Calculate Costs Button Event Handler** Below the event handler introductory code, write the comments and then define the variables required for the button event handler. The variables include the two object variables for the Student and OnCampusStudent objects and the Boolean input error indicator *(ref: Figure 11-7)*.

```
HINT
10     ⊟   Private Sub btnCalculateCosts_Click(ByVal sender As System.Object, ByVal e As System.EventArgs) Handles btnCalculateCosts.Click
11             ' This Calculate Costs button click event handler edits the  registration(costs) form to ensure it contains valid data.
12             ' Then, after passing control to the business class, it displays the cost.
13
14             Dim objStudent As Student
15             Dim objOnCampusStudent As OnCampusStudent
16             Dim InputError As Boolean = False
```

(continues)

● **Enter the If...ElseIf Statement to Check the Input Data** Enter the code to check the input data, as documented in the program requirements document *(ref: Figure 11-7)*.

HINT

```
17
18          ' Is student ID entered properly
19          If txtStudentID.MaskFull = False Then
20              MsgBox("Enter your Student ID in the Student ID box", , "Error")
21              txtStudentID.Clear()
22              txtStudentID.Focus()
23              InputError = True
24              ' Is student name entered properly
25          ElseIf txtStudentName.TextLength < 1 Or txtStudentName.Text < "A" Then
26              MsgBox("Enter your name in the Student Name box", , "Error")
27              txtStudentName.Clear()
28              txtStudentName.Focus()
29              InputError = True
30              ' Is number of units entered properly
31          ElseIf Not IsNumeric(txtNumberOfUnits.Text) Then
32              MsgBox("Enter the units in the Number of Units box", , "Error")
33              txtNumberOfUnits.Clear()
34              txtNumberOfUnits.Focus()
35              InputError = True
36              ' Has 1-24 units been entered
37          ElseIf Convert.ToInt32(txtNumberOfUnits.Text) < 1 Or Convert.ToInt32(txtNumberOfUnits.Text) > 24 Then
38              MsgBox("Units must be 1 - 24", , "Error")
39              txtNumberOfUnits.Clear()
40              txtNumberOfUnits.Focus()
41              InputError = True
42              ' Has a major been selected
43          ElseIf cboMajor.SelectedIndex < 0 Then
44              MsgBox("Please select a major", , "Error")
45              cboMajor.Focus()
46              InputError = True
47          End If
```

- **Enter the Code to Call the Appropriate Function Procedure in the Appropriate Object** If the input data is correct, enter the code to instantiate the Student class object or the OnCampusStudent class object and then call the ComputeCosts function in the appropriate object. Be sure to include the correct arguments for the New statement for each new object *(ref: Figure 11-20)*.

HINT

```
48              ' If no input error, process the registration costs
49          If Not InputError Then
50              If radOffCampus.Checked Then
51                  objStudent = New Student(txtStudentID.Text, txtStudentName.Text, Convert.ToString(cboMajor.SelectedItem),
52                      txtNumberOfUnits.Text)
53                  lblCosts.Visible = True
54                  lblCosts.Text = "Total semester costs are: " & (objStudent.ComputeCosts()).ToString("C2")
55              Else
56                  objOnCampusStudent = New OnCampusStudent(txtStudentID.Text, txtStudentName.Text, Convert.ToString(cboMajor.SelectedItem),
57                      txtNumberOfUnits.Text, radCooperDorm.Checked, radCraigHall.Checked, radJulianSuites.Checked)
58                  lblCosts.Visible = True
59                  lblCosts.Text = "Total semester costs are: " & (objOnCampusStudent.ComputeCosts()).ToString("C2")
60              End If
61          End If
62      End Sub
```

- **Write the Code for the Off-Campus Radio Button CheckedChanged Event** Write the code to hide the HousingBoard Group.

HINT

```
64      Private Sub radOffCampus_CheckedChanged(ByVal sender As System.Object, ByVal e As System.EventArgs) Handles radOffCampus.CheckedChanged
65          ' This event handler is executed when the Off Campus radio button is selected. It hides the Housing/Board radio buttons
66
67          grpHousingBoard.Visible = False
68
69      End Sub
```

- **Write the Code for the On-Campus Radio Button CheckedChanged Event** Write the code to make the HousingBoard Group visible.

HINT

```
71      Private Sub radOnCampus_CheckedChanged(ByVal sender As System.Object, ByVal e As System.EventArgs) Handles radOnCampus.CheckedChanged
72          ' This event handler is executed when the On Campus radio button is selected. It makes the Housing/Board radio buttons visible
73
74          grpHousingBoard.Visible = True
75
76      End Sub
```

(continues)

- **Write the Code for the Clear Form Button** Write the code to clear the form and place the focus on the Student ID text box, as defined in the event planning document *(ref: Figure 11-39)*.

The frmCollege code is completed (Figure 11-44).

```
1    □ ' Program:        College Registration Costs
2      ' Developer:      Corinne Hoisington
3      ' Date:           August 29, 2017
4      ' Purpose:        This program calculates the registration costs for a college student. It also records the costs in a text file.
5
6      Option Strict On
7
       2 references
8    □ Public Class frmCollege
9
         0 references
10   □     Private Sub btnCalculateCosts_Click(ByVal sender As System.Object, ByVal e As System.EventArgs) Handles btnCalculateCosts.Click
11           ' This Calculate Costs button click event handler edits the registration(costs) form to ensure it contains valid data.
12           ' Then, after passing control to the business class, it displays the cost.
13
14           Dim objStudent As Student
15           Dim objOnCampusStudent As OnCampusStudent
16           Dim InputError As Boolean = False
17
18           ' Is student ID entered properly
19           If txtStudentID.MaskFull = False Then
20               MsgBox("Enter your Student ID in the Student ID box", , "Error")
21               txtStudentID.Clear()
22               txtStudentID.Focus()
23               InputError = True
24               ' Is student name entered properly
25           ElseIf txtStudentName.TextLength < 1 Or txtStudentName.Text < "A" Then
26               MsgBox("Enter your name in the Student Name box", , "Error")
27               txtStudentName.Clear()
28               txtStudentName.Focus()
29               InputError = True
30               ' Is number of units entered properly
31           ElseIf Not IsNumeric(txtNumberOfUnits.Text) Then
32               MsgBox("Enter the units in the Number of Units box", , "Error")
33               txtNumberOfUnits.Clear()
34               txtNumberOfUnits.Focus()
35               InputError = True
36               ' Has 1-24 units been entered
37           ElseIf Convert.ToInt32(txtNumberOfUnits.Text) < 1 Or Convert.ToInt32(txtNumberOfUnits.Text) > 24 Then
38               MsgBox("Units must be 1 - 24", , "Error")
39               txtNumberOfUnits.Clear()
40               txtNumberOfUnits.Focus()
41               InputError = True
42               ' Has a major been selected
43           ElseIf cboMajor.SelectedIndex < 0 Then
44               MsgBox("Please select a major", , "Error")
45               cboMajor.Focus()
46               InputError = True
47           End If
48           ' If no input error, process the registration costs
49           If Not InputError Then
50               If radOffCampus.Checked Then
51                   objStudent = New Student(txtStudentID.Text, txtStudentName.Text, Convert.ToString(cboMajor.SelectedItem),
52                       txtNumberOfUnits.Text)
53                   lblCosts.Visible = True
54                   lblCosts.Text = "Total semester costs are: " & (objStudent.ComputeCosts()).ToString("C2")
55               Else
56                   objOnCampusStudent = New OnCampusStudent(txtStudentID.Text, txtStudentName.Text, Convert.ToString(cboMajor.SelectedItem),
57                       txtNumberOfUnits.Text, radCooperDorm.Checked, radCraigHall.Checked, radJulianSuites.Checked)
58                   lblCosts.Visible = True
59                   lblCosts.Text = "Total semester costs are: " & (objOnCampusStudent.ComputeCosts()).ToString("C2")
60               End If
61           End If
62       End Sub
63
         0 references
64   □     Private Sub radOffCampus_CheckedChanged(ByVal sender As System.Object, ByVal e As System.EventArgs) Handles radOffCampus.CheckedChanged
65           ' This event handler is executed when the Off Campus radio button is selected. It hides the Housing/Board radio buttons
66
67           grpHousingBoard.Visible = False
68
69       End Sub
```

FIGURE 11-44 (continues)

```
70
           0 references
71    ⊟    Private Sub radOnCampus_CheckedChanged(ByVal sender As System.Object, ByVal e As System.EventArgs) Handles radOnCampus.CheckedChanged
72              ' This event handler is executed when the On Campus radio button is selected. It makes the Housing/Board radio buttons visible
73
74              grpHousingBoard.Visible = True
75
76          End Sub
77
           0 references
78    ⊟    Private Sub btnClearForm_Click(ByVal sender As System.Object, ByVal e As System.EventArgs) Handles btnClearForm.Click
79              ' This event handler is executed when the user clicks the Clear Form button. It resets all objects on the user interface.
80
81              txtStudentID.Clear()
82              txtStudentName.Clear()
83              txtNumberOfUnits.Clear()
84              cboMajor.SelectedIndex = -1
85              cboMajor.Text = "Select a Major"
86              radOffCampus.Checked = True
87              radCooperDorm.Checked = True
88              grpHousingBoard.Visible = False
89              lblCosts.Visible = False
90              txtStudentID.Focus()
91
92          End Sub
93
94    End Class
95
```

FIGURE 11-44 (continued)

(continues)

3

- **Create the Classes Required for the Remainder of the Program** Press and hold or right-click the name of the project (CollegeRegistrationCosts) in the Solution Explorer, point to Add on the shortcut menu, and then tap or click Class on the shortcut menu. Add the Student.vb class. Use the same technique to add the OnCampusStudent.vb class and the StudentCostsFile.vb class *(ref: Figure 11-13)*.

HINT

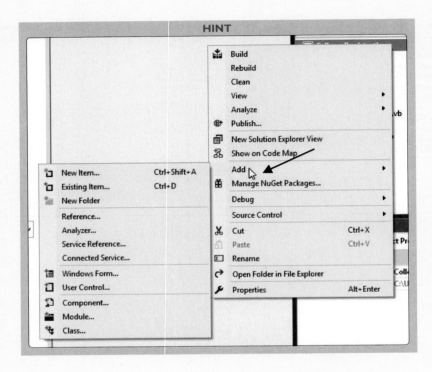

- **Enter Comments and Option Strict On for the Student Class** Display the Student class code window. Enter the common comments for the Student class. Include the Option Strict On statement.

HINT

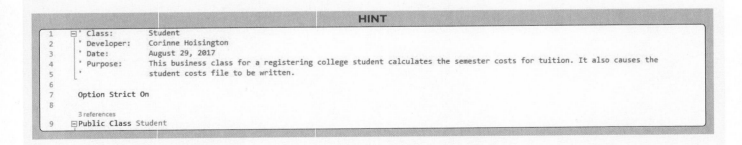

```
1   ' Class:       Student
2   ' Developer:   Corinne Hoisington
3   ' Date:        August 29, 2017
4   ' Purpose:     This business class for a registering college student calculates the semester costs for tuition. It also causes the
5   '              student costs file to be written.
6
7   Option Strict On
8
    3 references
9   Public Class Student
```

● **Define the Class Variables for the Student Class** Define the class variables for the Student class, including the declaration for the StudentCostsFile object. Remember that the variables should be declared with Protected access because they are used in the OnCampusStudent subclass.

HINT

```
11        'Class variables
12        Protected _strStudentID As String
13        Protected _strStudentName As String
14        Protected _strMajor As String
15        Protected _intUnits As Integer
16        Protected _decCost As Decimal
17        Protected _decCostPerUnit As Decimal = 450D
18
19        Dim objStudentCostsFile As StudentCostsFile
```

● **Write the Student Class Constructor** Write the code for the Student class constructor based on the requirements shown in the event planning document *(ref: Figure 11-21)*.

HINT

```
21    Sub New(ByVal strStudentID As String, ByVal strStudentName As String, ByVal strMajor As String, ByVal intUnits As String)
22        ' This subprocedure is a constructor for the Student class. It is called when the object is instantiated with arguments
23
24        'The following code assigns the arguments to class variables
25        _strStudentID = strStudentID
26        _strStudentName = strStudentName
27        _strMajor = strMajor
28        _intUnits = Convert.ToInt32(intUnits)
29
30    End Sub
```

● **Write the Code for the ComputeCosts Overridable Function Procedure** Write the code to calculate the cost, instantiate the object for the StudentCostsFile class, call the procedure to write the file, and return the cost.

HINT

```
32        Overridable Function ComputeCosts() As Decimal
33            ' This function computes the registration costs, writes a record in the student costs file, and returns the registration costs
34
35            'Calculate cost
36            _decCost = _intUnits * _decCostPerUnit
37
38            'Write the student record
39            objStudentCostsFile = New StudentCostsFile(_strStudentID, _strStudentName, _strMajor, _decCost)
40            objStudentCostsFile.WriteRecord()
41
42            'Return the calculated cost
43            Return _decCost
44
45        End Function
46
47    End Class
```

The Student class code is completed (Figure 11-45).

```vbnet
1    ⊟' Class:        Student
2    ' Developer:     Corinne Hoisington
3    ' Date:          August 29, 2017
4    ' Purpose:       This business class for a registering college student calculates the semester costs for tuition. It also causes the
5                     student costs file to be written.
6
7      Option Strict On
8
     3 references
9    ⊟Public Class Student
10
11        'Class variables
12        Protected _strStudentID As String
13        Protected _strStudentName As String
14        Protected _strMajor As String
15        Protected _intUnits As Integer
16        Protected _decCost As Decimal
17        Protected _decCostPerUnit As Decimal = 450D
18
19        Dim objStudentCostsFile As StudentCostsFile
20
     2 references
21    ⊟    Sub New(ByVal strStudentID As String, ByVal strStudentName As String, ByVal strMajor As String, ByVal intUnits As String)
22             ' This subprocedure is a constructor for the Student class. It is called when the object is instantiated with arguments
23
24             'The following code assigns the arguments to class variables
25             _strStudentID = strStudentID
26             _strStudentName = strStudentName
27             _strMajor = strMajor
28             _intUnits = Convert.ToInt32(intUnits)
29
30        End Sub
31
     1 reference
32    ⊟    Overridable Function ComputeCosts() As Decimal
33             ' This function computes the registration costs, writes a record in the student costs file, and returns the registration costs
34
35             'Calculate cost
36             _decCost = _intUnits * _decCostPerUnit
37
38             'Write the student record
39             objStudentCostsFile = New StudentCostsFile(_strStudentID, _strStudentName, _strMajor, _decCost)
40             objStudentCostsFile.WriteRecord()
41
42             'Return the calculated cost
43             Return _decCost
44
45        End Function
46
47    End Class
48
```

FIGURE 11-45

(continues)

4

- **Enter Comments and Option Strict On for the OnCampusStudent Class** Display the OnCampusStudent class code window. Enter the common comments for the OnCampusStudent class. Include the Option Strict On statement and the Inherits statement, which indicates that the OnCampusStudent class inherits from the Student class.

HINT

```
 1    ⊟ ' Class:        OnCampusStudent
 2      ' Developer:    Corinne Hoisington
 3      ' Date:         August 29, 2017
 4      ' Purpose:      This business class for registering an on-campus college student calculates the semester costs, including tuition
 5                      and housing. It also causes the student costs file to be written.
 6
 7      Option Strict On
 8
        2 references
 9    ⊟Public Class OnCampusStudent
10          Inherits Student
```

- **Define the Class Variables for the OnCampusStudent Class** Define the class variables for the OnCampusStudent class, including the declaration for the StudentCostsFile object. The variables should be declared with Private access.

HINT

```
12      ' Class variables
13      Private _Cooper As Boolean
14      Private _Craig As Boolean
15      Private _Julian As Boolean
16
17      Dim objStudentCostsFile As StudentCostsFile
18
```

- **Write the OnCampusStudent Class Constructor** Write the code for the OnCampusStudent class constructor based on the requirements shown in the event planning document *(ref: Figure 11-28)*.

HINT

```
19    ⊟    Sub New(ByVal StudentID As String, ByVal StudentName As String, ByVal Major As String, ByVal Units As String,
20                 ByVal Cooper As Boolean, ByVal Craig As Boolean, ByVal Julian As Boolean)
21              ' This subprocedure is a constructor for the Student class. It is called when instantiated with arguments
22
23              MyBase.New(StudentID, StudentName, Major, Units)
24
25              'The following code assigns the arguments to class variables
26              _Cooper = Cooper
27              _Craig = Craig
28              _Julian = Julian
29
30          End Sub
```

● **Write the Code for the ComputeCosts Overriding Function Procedure** Write the code to define
the variables, determine the housing/board cost, calculate the semester cost, instantiate the object for
the StudentCostsFile class, call the procedure to write the file, and return the semester cost.

HINT

```
                1 reference
32              Overrides Function ComputeCosts() As Decimal
33                  ' This function computes the registration costs, writes a record in the student costs file, and returns the registration costs
34
35                  'Define variables
36                  Dim HousingCost As Decimal
37                  Const cdecCooperHousingCost As Decimal = 2900D
38                  Const cdecCraigHousingCost As Decimal = 3400D
39                  Const cdecJulianHousingCost As Decimal = 4000D
40
41                  'Calculate the cost
42                  If _Cooper Then
43                      HousingCost = cdecCooperHousingCost
44                  ElseIf _Craig Then
45                      HousingCost = cdecCraigHousingCost
46                  ElseIf _Julian Then
47                      HousingCost = cdecJulianHousingCost
48                  End If
49
50                  _decCost = (_intUnits * _decCostPerUnit) + HousingCost
51
52                  'Write the student record
53                  objStudentCostsFile = New StudentCostsFile(_strStudentID, _strStudentName, _strMajor, _decCost)
54                  objStudentCostsFile.WriteRecord()
55
56                  'Return the calculated cost
57                  Return _decCost
58
59              End Function
60
61          End Class
```

The OnCampusStudent class code is completed (Figure 11-46).

```
1    ' Class:         OnCampusStudent
2    ' Developer:     Corinne Hoisington
3    ' Date:          August 29, 2017
4    ' Purpose:       This business class for registering an on-campus college student calculates the semester costs, including tuition
5    '                and housing. It also causes the student costs file to be written.
6
7    Option Strict On
8
     2 references
9    Public Class OnCampusStudent
10       Inherits Student
11
12       ' Class variables
13       Private _Cooper As Boolean
14       Private _Craig As Boolean
15       Private _Julian As Boolean
16
17       Dim objStudentCostsFile As StudentCostsFile
18
         1 reference
19       Sub New(ByVal StudentID As String, ByVal StudentName As String, ByVal Major As String, ByVal Units As String,
20              ByVal Cooper As Boolean, ByVal Craig As Boolean, ByVal Julian As Boolean)
21          ' This subprocedure is a constructor for the Student class. It is called when instantiated with arguments
22
23          MyBase.New(StudentID, StudentName, Major, Units)
24
25          'The following code assigns the arguments to class variables
26          _Cooper = Cooper
27          _Craig = Craig
28          _Julian = Julian
29
30       End Sub
31
         1 reference
32       Overrides Function ComputeCosts() As Decimal
33          ' This function computes the registration costs, writes a record in the student costs file, and returns the registration costs
34
35          'Define variables
36          Dim HousingCost As Decimal
37          Const cdecCooperHousingCost As Decimal = 2900D
38          Const cdecCraigHousingCost As Decimal = 3400D
39          Const cdecJulianHousingCost As Decimal = 4000D
40
41          'Calculate the cost
42          If _Cooper Then
43             HousingCost = cdecCooperHousingCost
44          ElseIf _Craig Then
45             HousingCost = cdecCraigHousingCost
46          ElseIf _Julian Then
47             HousingCost = cdecJulianHousingCost
48          End If
49
50          _decCost = (_intUnits * _decCostPerUnit) + HousingCost
51
52          'Write the student record
53          objStudentCostsFile = New StudentCostsFile(_strStudentID, _strStudentName, _strMajor, _decCost)
54          objStudentCostsFile.WriteRecord()
55
56          'Return the calculated cost
57          Return _decCost
58
59       End Function
60
61    End Class
62
```

FIGURE 11-46

5

- **Enter Comments and Option Strict On for the StudentCostsFile Class** Display the StudentCostsFile class code window. Enter the common comments for the StudentCostsFile class. Include the Option Strict On statement.

HINT

```
1    ⊟' Class:       Student Costs File
2     ' Developer:   Corinne Hoisington
3     ' Date:        August 29, 2017
4     ' Purpose:     This class represents the Student Costs File. The WriteRecord procedure writes a comma-delimited student costs file that
5     '              contains the Student ID, Student Name, Major, and Student Costs.
6
7      Option Strict On
8
       4 references
9    ⊟Public Class StudentCostsFile
```

- **Define the Class Variables for the StudentCostsFile Class** Define the class variables for the StudentCostsFile class. The variables should be declared with Private access.

HINT

```
11         ' Class variables
12         Private _strStudentID As String
13         Private _strStudentName As String
14         Private _strMajor As String
15         Private _decStudentCosts As Decimal
```

- **Write the StudentCostsFile Class Constructor** Write the code for the StudentCostsFile class constructor based on the requirements shown in the event planning document.

HINT

```
17    ⊟    Sub New(ByVal StudentID As String, ByVal StudentName As String, ByVal Major As String, ByVal Costs As Decimal)
18              ' This sub procedure is the constructor for the StudentCostsFile class.
19
20              ' The following code assigns the arguments to class variables
21              _strStudentID = StudentID
22              _strStudentName = StudentName
23              _strMajor = Major
24              _decStudentCosts = Costs
25
26         End Sub
```

(continues)

● **Write the Code for the WriteRecord Sub Procedure** Write the code to define the variable. Then, in a Try-Catch block, declare an IO StreamWriter, write the comma-delimited record in the file, and close the file (*ref: Figure 11-36*).

HINT

```
         2 references
28  ⊟    Sub WriteRecord()
29           ' This subprocedure opens the StudentCosts output text file and then writes a record in the comma-delimited file
30
31           Dim strNameandLocationOfFile As String = "e:\StudentCosts.txt"
32
33           Try
34               Dim objWriter As IO.StreamWriter = IO.File.AppendText(strNameandLocationOfFile)
35
36               objWriter.Write(_strStudentID & ",")
37               objWriter.Write(_strStudentName & ",")
38               objWriter.Write(_strMajor & ",")
39               objWriter.WriteLine(_decStudentCosts)
40               objWriter.Close()
41
42           Catch ex As Exception
43               MsgBox("No device available - program aborted", , "Error")
44               Application.Exit()
45
46           End Try
47
48       End Sub
49
50  End Class
```

The StudentCostsFile class code is completed (Figure 11-47).

```
1    ' Class:        OnCampusStudent
2    ' Developer:    Corinne Hoisington
3    ' Date:         August 29, 2017
4    ' Purpose:      This business class for registering an on-campus college student calculates the semester costs, including tuition
5    '               and housing. It also causes the student costs file to be written.
6
7    Option Strict On
8
     2 references
9    Public Class OnCampusStudent
10       Inherits Student
11
12       ' Class variables
13       Private _Cooper As Boolean
14       Private _Craig As Boolean
15       Private _Julian As Boolean
16
17       Dim objStudentCostsFile As StudentCostsFile
18
     1 reference
19       Sub New(ByVal StudentID As String, ByVal StudentName As String, ByVal Major As String, ByVal Units As String,
20              ByVal Cooper As Boolean, ByVal Craig As Boolean, ByVal Julian As Boolean)
21           ' This subprocedure is a constructor for the Student class. It is called when instantiated with arguments
22
23           MyBase.New(StudentID, StudentName, Major, Units)
24
25           'The following code assigns the arguments to class variables
26           _Cooper = Cooper
27           _Craig = Craig
28           _Julian = Julian
29
30       End Sub
31
     1 reference
32       Overrides Function ComputeCosts() As Decimal
33           ' This function computes the registration costs, writes a record in the student costs file, and returns the registration costs
34
35           'Define variables
36           Dim HousingCost As Decimal
37           Const cdecCooperHousingCost As Decimal = 2900D
38           Const cdecCraigHousingCost As Decimal = 3400D
39           Const cdecJulianHousingCost As Decimal = 4000D
40
41           'Calculate the cost
42           If _Cooper Then
43               HousingCost = cdecCooperHousingCost
44           ElseIf _Craig Then
45               HousingCost = cdecCraigHousingCost
46           ElseIf _Julian Then
47               HousingCost = cdecJulianHousingCost
48           End If
49
50           _decCost = (_intUnits * _decCostPerUnit) + HousingCost
51
52           'Write the student record
53           objStudentCostsFile = New StudentCostsFile(_strStudentID, _strStudentName, _strMajor, _decCost)
54           objStudentCostsFile.WriteRecord()
55
56           'Return the calculated cost
57           Return _decCost
58
59       End Function
60
61   End Class
62
```

FIGURE 11-47

(continues)

Summary

In this chapter, you have learned to create multiple classes using the three-tier program structure and to incorporate inheritance into your program. The items listed in the table in Figure 11-48 include all the new Visual Studio and Visual Basic skills you have learned in this chapter.

Visual Basic Skills		
Skill	**Figure Number**	**Video Number**
Examine the College Registration Costs Program	Figure 11-1	Video 11-1
Set the TabIndex Property	Figure 11-4	Video 11-2
Edit Input Data	Figure 11-7	
Code the MaskFull Property	Figure 11-8	
Code the TextBox TextLength Property	Figure 11-9	
Create a Class	Figure 11-13	Video 11-3
Instantiate a Class	Figure 11-17	
Code a Class Constructor	Figure 11-19	
Pass an Argument When Instantiating an Object	Figure 11-20	
Call a Procedure from Another Class	Figure 11-24	
Write Code for Inheritance	Figure 11-26	
Code Base Class and Subclass Constructors	Figure 11-27 and Figure 11-28	
Call and Code Procedures for Inheritance	Figure 11-29 through Figure 11-33	
Code a Persistence Class	Figure 11-34	
Write a Comma-Delimited Text File	Figure 11-36	

FIGURE 11-48

Learn Online

Reinforcement activities and resources are available at no additional cost on CengageBrain.com. Visit http://solutions.cengage.com/ctdownloads/ for detailed instructions about accessing the available resources at the Student Companion Site.

Knowledge Check

1. What are the names of the three tiers in a three-tiered program structure? What occurs in each of the three tiers?

2. What is the purpose of encapsulation within your application?

3. What property is used to ensure that the user has entered all digits in a MaskedTextBox object?

4. What property can you use to specify the sequence of objects that will be selected when the user presses the TAB key?

5. In a three-tiered program structure, which tiers are allowed to communicate with each other?

6. Identify the three steps to create a new class in a Visual Basic program.

7. Write the code to instantiate the objEmployee object based on the Employee class.

8. When is a class constructor executed?

9. Write the code to instantiate the objVehicle object based on the Vehicle class and to pass the following values to the object: Color, Model, Engine. Write the New statement in the Vehicle class.

10. Write a statement to call the ComputeDiscount procedure in the objDiscountItem object.

11. Explain the benefits of using separate classes in a program.

12. Complete the following sentence: Inheritance allows one class to inherit _____ and _____ from another class.

13. Describe the difference between a base class and a subclass when using inheritance.

14. What entry must be included in the Class statement of a subclass?

15. What is the first statement that must be coded in a subclass constructor?

16. What is an overridable procedure? Why is it used?

17. In a class, can an attribute be referenced that is not defined in the class? How is this attribute reference resolved?

18. Rewrite the following names in a comma-delimited text file format:

    Aragorn

    Bilbo Baggins

    Boromir

    Frodo

    Gandalf

    Pippin

19. When an IO.StreamWriter is created, what does the IO.File.AppendText entry mean?

20. What is the difference between the Write procedure and the WriteLine procedure in the IO.StreamWriter class?

1. The code in Figure 11-49 executes when a button is tapped or clicked on a Windows Form object. Identify what will happen when a single error occurs. What happens if two errors occur at the same time? What happens if three errors occur at the same time? How can this code be repaired?

```
16          Dim InputError As Boolean = False
17
18          ' Is student ID entered properly
19          If txtStudentID.MaskFull = False Then
20              MsgBox("Enter your Student ID in the Student ID box", , "Error")
21              txtStudentID.Clear()
22              txtStudentID.Focus()
23              InputError = True
24              ' Is student name entered properly
25          ElseIf txtStudentName.TextLength < 1 Or txtStudentName.Text < "A" Then
26              MsgBox("Enter your name in the Student Name box", , "Error")
27              txtStudentName.Clear()
28              txtStudentName.Focus()
29              InputError = True
30              ' Is number of units entered properly
31          ElseIf Not IsNumeric(txtNumberOfUnits.Text) Then
32              MsgBox("Enter the units in the Number of Units box", , "Error")
33              txtNumberOfUnits.Clear()
34              txtNumberOfUnits.Focus()
35              InputError = True
```

FIGURE 11-49

Debugging Exercises (continued)

2. Examine the following code and make any corrections required.

CALLING CLASS
```
62 Dim objSubClass As New SubClass(txtLastName, _
63     txtNumberOfDependents)
```

OBJSUBCLASS
```
4 Sub New(ByVal LastName)
```

3. Correct the following code.
```
4 Dim objWater As WaterName
5 WaterName = New WaterName
```

4. Referencing Exercise 3 above, correct the following statement:
```
22 lblWater = GetWater.objWater
```

Program Analysis

1. What is the output of the code in Figure 11-50?

```
        2 references
28   Sub WriteRecord()
29        ' This subprocedure opens the StudentCosts output text file and then writ
30
31        Dim strNameandLocationOfFile As String = "e:\StudentCosts.txt"
32
33        Try
34            Dim objWriter As IO.StreamWriter = IO.File.AppendText(strNameandLocat
35
36            objWriter.Write(_strStudentID & ",")
37            objWriter.Write(_strStudentName & ",")
38            objWriter.Write(_strMajor & ",")
39            objWriter.WriteLine(_decStudentCosts)
40            objWriter.Close()
41
42        Catch ex As Exception
43            MsgBox("No device available - program aborted", , "Error")
44            Application.Exit()
45
46        End Try
47
48   End Sub
```

FIGURE 11-50

2. Analyze the code in Figure 11-51a, Figure 11-51b, and Figure 11-51c. What is the output of the code?

```
17          Dim objCustomer As Customer
18          Dim objInternetCustomer As InternetCustomer
19
20          objCustomer = New Customer
21          objInternetCustomer = New InternetCustomer
22
23          MsgBox.Show(objInternetCustomer.CustomerFunction())
```

FIGURE 11-51a

```
1 Public Class Customer
2
3     Function CustomerFunction() As String
4         Return "Customer function"
5     End Function
6
7     Overridable Function OverridableCustomerFunction() As String
8         Return "Overridable customer function"
9     End Function
10
11
12 End Class
13
```

FIGURE 11-51b

```
1 Public Class InternetCustomer
2     Inherits Customer
3
4     Function InternetCustomerFunction() As String
5         Return "Internet customer function"
6     End Function
7
8     Overrides Function OverridableCustomerFunction() As String
9         Return "Overrode the customer overridable function"
10     End Function
11
12 End Class
13
```

FIGURE 11-51c

3. Analyze the code in Figure 11-52a, Figure 11-52b, and Figure 11-52c. What is the output of the code?

```
17          Dim objCustomer As Customer
18          Dim objInternetCustomer As InternetCustomer
19
20          objCustomer = New Customer
21          objInternetCustomer = New InternetCustomer
22
23          MsgBox.Show(objInternetCustomer.InternetCustomerFunction())
```

FIGURE 11-52a

```
1 Public Class Customer
2
3     Function CustomerFunction() As String
4         Return "Customer function"
5     End Function
6
7     Overridable Function OverridableCustomerFunction() As String
8         Return "Overridable customer function"
9     End Function
10
11
12 End Class
13
```

FIGURE 11-52b

```
1 Public Class InternetCustomer
2     Inherits Customer
3
4     Function InternetCustomerFunction() As String
5         Return "Internet customer function"
6     End Function
7
8     Overrides Function OverridableCustomerFunction() As String
9         Return "Overrode the customer overridable function"
10     End Function
11
12 End Class
13
```

FIGURE 11-52c

4. Analyze the code in Figure 11-53a, Figure 11-53b, and Figure 11-53c. What is the output of the code?

```
17        Dim objCustomer As Customer
18        Dim objInternetCustomer As InternetCustomer
19
20        objCustomer = New Customer
21        objInternetCustomer = New InternetCustomer
22
23        MsgBox.Show(objInternetCustomer.OverridableCustomerFunction())
```

FIGURE 11-53a

```
1 Public Class Customer
2
3     Function CustomerFunction() As String
4         Return "Customer function"
5     End Function
6
7     Overridable Function OverridableCustomerFunction() As String
8         Return "Overridable customer function"
9     End Function
10
11
12 End Class
13
```

FIGURE 11-53b

```
1 Public Class InternetCustomer
2     Inherits Customer
3
4     Function InternetCustomerFunction() As String
5         Return "Internet customer function"
6     End Function
7
8     Overrides Function OverridableCustomerFunction() As String
9         Return "Overrode the customer overridable function"
10    End Function
11
12 End Class
13
```

FIGURE 11-53c

5. Analyze the code in Figure 11-54a, Figure 11-54b, and Figure 11-54c. What is the output of the code?

```
17          Dim objCustomer As Customer
18          Dim objInternetCustomer As InternetCustomer
19
20          objCustomer = New Customer
21          objInternetCustomer = New InternetCustomer
22
23          MsgBox.Show(objCustomer.OverridableCustomerFunction())
```

FIGURE 11-54a

```
1  Public Class Customer
2
3      Function CustomerFunction() As String
4          Return "Customer function"
5      End Function
6
7      Overridable Function OverridableCustomerFunction() As String
8          Return "Overridable customer function"
9      End Function
10
11
12 End Class
13
```

FIGURE 11-54b

```
1  Public Class InternetCustomer
2      Inherits Customer
3
4      Function InternetCustomerFunction() As String
5          Return "Internet customer function"
6      End Function
7
8      Overrides Function OverridableCustomerFunction() As String
9          Return "Overrode the customer overridable function"
10     End Function
11
12 End Class
13
```

FIGURE 11-54c

Case Programming Assignments

Complete one or more of the following case programming assignments. Submit the program and materials you create to your instructor. The level of difficulty is indicated for each case programming assignment.

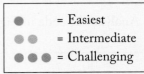

● = Easiest
●● = Intermediate
●●● = Challenging

1 ●
CHANNELS PLUS (TV/MOVIES ONLINE)

Design a Windows application and write the code that will execute according to the program requirements in Figure 11-55 and the Use Case Definition in Figure 11-56 on the next page. Before writing the code, create an event planning document for each event in the program. The completed Windows Form object and other objects in the user interface are shown in Figure 11-57 on page 812.

REQUIREMENTS DOCUMENT

Date Submitted:	July 18, 2017
Application Title:	Channels Plus Subscriptions
Purpose:	This Windows application allows the user to select a subscription plan called Channels Plus, which is similar to Hulu Plus.
Program Procedures:	From a Windows application, a user enters her name, home address, and zip code. The user also selects a monthly subscription plan for Channels Plus. These plans do not include multiple devices or HBO to Go. To add those features, users can select whether they have a single device or multiple devices, and whether they are interested in adding HBO to Go to their monthly subscription.
Algorithms, Processing, and Conditions:	1. The user enters her name, address, and zip code.
	2. The user selects a monthly subscription plan:
	• 25 Television Channels, $2.99 a month
	• Movies Only, $4.99 a month
	• Unlimited News and TV Stations, $3.99 a month
	• Unlimited TV, Movies, and News, $6.99 a month
	3. The user must select whether she plans to watch Channels Plus on a single device (no change in cost) or on multiple devices ($1.99 per month).
	4. The user must select whether she plans to add a feature called HBO to Go, which costs another $5 per month.
	5. After the user selects the HBO to Go option, the email address text box appears. The user must enter her email address.
	6. In a comma-delimited text file, the program keeps a log of the selected plan. The file should contain the user's name, zip code, plan, HBO to Go option, and final cost.

FIGURE 11-55 (continues)

(continues)

Case Programming Assignments

Notes and Restrictions: Validate data that the user enters using accepted standards. The zip code must have only five numbers.

Comments:
1. Obtain an image for this program from CengageBrain.com. The name of the picture is Stations.
2. The program should use a three-tiered structure with presentation, business, and persistence classes.

FIGURE 11-55 (continued)

USE CASE DEFINITION

1. The user views the opening screen, which displays an image.
2. The user enters her name, address, and zip code.
3. The user selects a desired monthly subscription plan from a drop-down list.
4. The user selects the radio button that corresponds to the number of devices she wants.
5. The user selects whether she wants to add HBO to Go from a drop-down list.
6. The user taps or clicks the Calculate Cost button to view the cost of the monthly subscription plan.
7. The program writes a record of the subscription plan and cost selection.
8. A Clear Form button is available to clear the form.

FIGURE 11-56

Channels Plus (TV/Movies online) (continued)

FIGURE 11-57

2   REAL ESTATE INVESTMENT BY CITY

Design a Windows application and write the code that will execute according to the program requirements in Figure 11-58 and the Use Case Definition in Figure 11-59. Before writing the code, create an event planning document for each event in the program. The completed Windows Form object and other objects in the user interface are shown in Figure 11-60 on the next page.

REQUIREMENTS DOCUMENT

Date Submitted:	July 18, 2017
Application Title:	Real Estate Investment by City

Purpose: This Windows application calculates the return on investment of buying a rental home in certain cities. For example, if you buy a home for $100,000 in Ocala, Florida, and the home earns an average of 10.23% in rental return per year, your return on investment after five years would be $51,500.00.

Program Procedures: From a Windows application, an investor sees which cities would be best for buying rental properties and determines the return on investment on the purchase of a rental home over a given number of years.

Algorithms, Processing, and Conditions:
1. The buyer enters his name, the number of rental years, the city, and home price.
2. The user can select a rental home location and rate of return from a list.
   - Memphis TN 10.38%
   - Ocala FL 10.23%
   - Atlanta GA 9.70%
   - Phoenix AZ 8.77%
   - Ogden UT 8.44%
3. Write a comma-delimited text file to record each sale. The text file should contain all the entered information.

Notes and Restrictions:
1. Validate data that the user enters using accepted standards.
2. The home price must be greater than $10,000.

Comments:
1. Obtain an image for this program from CengageBrain.com. The name of the picture is Investment.
2. The program should use a three-tiered structure with presentation, business, and persistence classes.

FIGURE 11-58

Real Estate Investment by City (continued)

USE CASE DEFINITION

1. The user views the opening screen.
2. The buyer enters his name, the number of rental years, and rental home price.
3. The user selects an option from the list of cities.
4. The user taps or clicks the Return on Investment button.
5. The program displays the return on investment amount.
6. The program writes a record of the investment in a text file.
7. A Clear Form button is available to clear the form.

FIGURE 11-59

FIGURE 11-60

3

APP DEVELOPERS BOOT CAMP

Design a Windows application and write the code that will execute according to the program requirements in Figure 11-61 and the Use Case Definition in Figure 11-62 on the next page. Before writing the code, create an event planning document for each event in the program. The completed Windows Form object and other objects in the user interface are shown in Figure 11-63 on the next page.

REQUIREMENTS DOCUMENT

Date Submitted:	February 28, 2017
Application Title:	App Developer's Boot Camp Training
Purpose:	This Windows application allows a person to register for an App Developer's Boot Camp, which presents the latest trends in the mobile application world.
Program Procedures:	In a Windows application, the user enters the visitor's corporation ID, first and last name, and the number of days the developer will be attending. The user selects whether a pre-conference course is being attended and selects the course if necessary. When the user taps or clicks a button, the application calculates and displays the costs of attending the conference and records the information in a log file.

Algorithms, Processing, and Conditions:

1. The user first enters the developer's corporation ID, first and last name, and number of days to attend.
2. The user selects whether the visitor will attend a pre-conference course (Pre-Conference Android Track or Windows Store Track) and then selects the course if necessary (for example, Mobile Security, Mobile Design, or Mobile Databases).
3. When the user taps or clicks a button, the program calculates the costs of attending the conference and writes a log file.
4. A Clear Form button should be available to clear the form and place the insertion point in the Corporation ID text box.
5. The conference cost is $299.00 per day. The minimum number of days is 1, and the maximum number of days is 4.
6. The formula to calculate conference costs is number of days times the cost per day.
7. If the visitor chooses to attend one of the pre-conference courses, it will cost $475.00. This cost should be added to the conference cost.
8. The log file is a text file that contains the Corporation ID, First Name, Last Name, pre-conference course taken, and total conference costs. If no pre-conference course is taken, the field should contain no data for it in the text file record. The file should be a comma-delimited file.

Notes and Restrictions:

1. The corporation ID must be five numeric digits.
2. The first name and last name cannot be left blank; all names must begin with an alphabetic character.
3. The number of days must be a numeric value of 1 through 4.
4. The pre-conference course selections should not be displayed in the window unless the user selects a type of pre-conference course.
5. When the user taps or clicks the button to calculate costs and the program determines that an error occurred during data entry, a message box should be displayed and the user must enter valid data before continuing.
6. No pre-conference course is the default value.

Comments:

1. Obtain an image for this program from CengageBrain.com. The name of the picture is Apps.
2. The program should use a three-tiered structure with presentation, business, and persistence classes.

FIGURE 11-61

(continued)

App Developers Boot Camp Training (continued)

USE CASE DEFINITION

1. The user enters the visitor's corporation ID, first name, last name, and the number of days the visitor will attend the conference.
2. If necessary, the user selects a type of pre-conference course and then selects a course.
3. The user taps or clicks the Calculate Costs button.
4. The program calculates and displays the conference costs, including the pre-conference course cost, if appropriate.
5. The program writes a log of the conference registration costs and other information.
6. If necessary, the user taps or clicks the Clear Form button to clear the form and place the insertion point in the Corporation ID text box.

FIGURE 11-62

FIGURE 11-63

© iStock.com/artishokcs

Case Programming Assignments

4 ●●
BANK ACCOUNT PROJECTION

Design a Windows application and write the code that will execute according to the program requirements in Figure 11-64. Before designing the user interface, create a Use Case Definition. Before writing the code, create an event planning document for each event in the program.

REQUIREMENTS DOCUMENT

Date Submitted:	July 12, 2017
Application Title:	Bank Account Projection
Purpose:	This Windows application calculates and displays the expected values of different types of bank accounts held for one year by current customers of Tenth Street Regional Bank.
Program Procedures:	In a Windows application, a user enters her name and current account number, selects one of five types of accounts, and then enters the amount to be placed in the account. The program calculates the projected value of the account after one year, assuming that the user makes no other deposits or withdrawals.
Algorithms, Processing, and Conditions:	1. The user enters her name and current account number.
	2. The user identifies the type of account being considered. The types of accounts are Regular Savings, Checking, 1-year CD, 2-year CD, and 5-year CD.
	3. The user enters the amount to be deposited. The minimum amount is greater than $1,000.00.
	4. When the user taps or clicks a button, the program calculates and displays the value of the account after one year.
	5. The value of the account is based on the following: Regular Savings, 1.75% interest; Checking, $25.00 per month service charge; 1-year CD, 1.85% interest; 2-year CD, 2.30% interest; 5-year CD, 2.37% interest.
	6. A comma-delimited text file is kept for each account inquiry. The text file contains the account number, the amount to be deposited, and the type of account selected.
	7. The user can tap or click a button to clear the form.
Notes and Restrictions:	Validate data that the user enters using accepted standards.
Comments:	1. Use the web to find an appropriate image for the user interface.
	2. The program should use a three-tiered structure with presentation, business, and persistence classes.

FIGURE 11-64

5 •• APP STORE PURCHASE

Design a Windows application and write the code that will execute according to the program requirements in Figure 11-65. Before designing the user interface, create a Use Case Definition. Before writing the code, create an event planning document for each event in the program.

REQUIREMENTS DOCUMENT

Date Submitted: August 12, 2017

Application Title: App Store Purchase

Purpose: This Windows application calculates the costs of apps from the App Store.

Program Procedures: In a Windows application, a user selects one of five apps to purchase from a list. The user enters the buyer's credit card number and expiration date and identifies whether the buyer is a student. The program calculates the cost of the app. It also keeps a log of purchases.

Algorithms, Processing, and Conditions:
1. The user enters the buyer's credit card number and expiration date.
2. The user identifies the app the buyer is purchasing.
3. The five software packages and their prices are: Speed Up the Internet, $1.99; A Writer's Writer, $0.99; Distance Personnel Management, $2.99; Email Photo Manager, $4.99; Keyboard SpeedLearner, $1.99.
4. For each package, a discount applies if the buyer is a student. The discounts are: Speed Up the Internet, 6%; A Writer's Writer, 8%; Distance Personnel Management, 8%; Email Photo Manager, 5%; Keyboard SpeedLearner, 2%.
5. After entering the information, the user can tap or click the Final Total button to determine the amount to be charged to the credit card.
6. The user can tap or click a button to clear the form.
7. The program writes a comma-delimited text file to keep track of all software purchases. The text file contains the credit card number, the name of the app purchased, the discount amount, and the total amount.
8. At any time, the user can tap or click the Daily Total button to have the program calculate and display the amount of sales that have been recorded in the text file.

Notes and Restrictions: Validate data that the user enters using accepted standards.

Comments:
1. Use the web to find an appropriate image for the user interface.
2. The program should use a three-tiered structure with presentation, business, and persistence classes.

FIGURE 11-65

Case Programming Assignments

6 ●●
USED CAR INVENTORY

Design a Windows application and write the code that will execute according to the program requirements in Figure 11-66. Before designing the user interface, create a Use Case Definition. Before writing the code, create an event planning document for each event in the program.

REQUIREMENTS DOCUMENT

Date Submitted: July 15, 2017

Application Title: Used Car Inventory

Purpose: This Windows application allows the user to add cars to the inventory of a used car dealer named Car Cruiser. The program displays the sticker price for each car based on discounts and allows the user to display the entire inventory.

Program Procedures: In a Windows application, a user enters the vehicle number, make, model, year, mileage, and standard price for a used car that is being placed in the inventory of the used car dealer. In addition, the user selects the car's color from a list of colors and indicates whether the vehicle is a convertible. The program creates the sticker price for the car and writes a record for the car in the inventory text file.

Algorithms, Processing, and Conditions:

1. The user enters the vehicle number, make, model, year, mileage, and standard price for a used car being placed in inventory.
2. The user selects the car color from a list of 17 common car colors, including black, dark gray, and red.
3. The user indicates whether the car is a convertible.
4. The program calculates the sticker price for the car on the used car lot.
5. If the car is black, a 15% discount is applied to the standard price to determine the sticker price. If the car is dark gray, a 21% surcharge is added to the standard price to determine the sticker price. If the car is red, a 9% surcharge is added to the standard price to determine the sticker price. For all other cars, the standard price and the sticker price are the same.
6. If the car is a convertible, a 26% surcharge is added to the sticker price calculated in step 5 to determine the total sticker price.
7. After the user enters all the data and taps or clicks a button, the sticker price is displayed.
8. When the button is tapped or clicked, the program also writes a comma-delimited text file that records the new entry into the inventory. The record includes the vehicle number, make, model, year, mileage, and sticker price.
9. At any time, the user can tap or click the Display Inventory menu item on the File menu to display the records in the inventory text file. In a separate window, the vehicle number, make, model, year, mileage, and sticker price should be displayed in a list for every car in the inventory.

Notes and Restrictions: Validate data that the user enters using accepted standards.

Comments:
1. Use the web to find an appropriate image for the user interface.
2. The program should use a three-tiered structure with presentation, business, and persistence classes.

FIGURE 11-66

7

● ● ●

NAIL SALON APPOINTMENTS

Create a requirements document and a Use Case Definition document and then design a Windows application based on the case project shown in Figure 11-67. Before writing the code, create an event planning document for each event in the program.

The Nirvana Nail Salon has asked you to create its new appointment system. The salon provides manicures and pedicures to customers. The salon needs to know the name of each customer and the date and time of each customer's appointment. (*Hint*: For the date, consider using the DateTimePicker object or the Calendar object.) Customers who are Nirvana members receive a 20% discount on a full manicure, which is normally $25.00. Pedicures are also available for $32.00; Nirvana members receive a 25% discount on a pedicure. All appointments should be made on the hour from 8 am to 7 pm. The following specials are available with manicures at an additional price: Gel Nails ($39.99); Paraffin Treatment ($15.00); French Manicure ($3.99); Spa Treatment ($19.99). For pedicures, the following specials can be added: Design Nail ($2.99); Spa Treatment ($19.99). When customers make an appointment, they should be told the total price of the services during the call. The owners of the nail salon would like to be able to view the list of appointments at any time.

FIGURE 11-67

8 •••
FISHING BOAT ORDERS

Create a requirements document and a Use Case Definition document and then design a Windows application based on the case project shown in Figure 11-68. Before writing the code, create an event planning document for each event in the program.

Your friend operates a charter fishing boat. She offers both full-day and half-day excursions. She receives a variety of requests for handling the fish that her customers catch and has determined prices for each type of request:

- Prepare individual filets and ship them to a given address. Filets are $9.25 per pound, and shipping charges are $3.89 per pound.
- Freeze the fish and ship the order to a given address. The fish is $8.75 per pound, and shipping charges are $5.95 per pound.
- Prepare filets and instruct a taxidermist to mount the fish. Ship the order to a given address. Filets are $9.25 per pound, and shipping charges are $3.89 per pound. The taxidermist charges a flat fee of $675.00 plus $85.00 per pound.
- Prepare the fish filets and donate them to a local charity. The charge for donation is $2.00 per pound.

Your friend has asked you to develop an application that can help her keep track of her orders. When she enters an order, she wants to be able to tell her customer the price at the same time. She would also like to be able to view all her orders and the dates they are due to ship.

FIGURE 11-68

9 ● ● ●

COMMUNITY APPLICATION

Create a requirements document and a Use Case Definition document and then design a Windows application based on the case project shown in Figure 11-69. Before writing the code, create an event planning document for each event in the program.

You have been asked to locate computer users on your campus or within your community, determine an application they need, and then write the application. Work with your users to develop and implement the application.

FIGURE 11-69

CHAPTER 12 (ONLINE CHAPTER)

Windows Store Apps

OBJECTIVES

You will have mastered the material in this chapter when you can:

- Describe a Windows Store app
- Describe a touch-first app
- Understand the Windows Store Application Life Cycle
- Get a free Windows developer license
- Create a Windows Store app
- Customize a splash screen
- Add image assets
- Customize a Split app and data model
- Code a Windows Store app
- Run a Windows Store app in a simulator
- Analyze the code
- Publish an app
- Monetize an app

This chapter describes Windows Store apps you can create for Windows 8.1 and Windows 10 devices using Visual Basic 2015. Because Windows 10 had not been released at the time of publication, this chapter is available free of charge online with the other resources for the book at CengageBrain.com.

APPENDIX A

Unicode

The 256 characters and symbols that are represented by ASCII and EBCDIC codes are sufficient for English and western European languages (see Figure A-1 on the next page), but do not provide enough characters for Asian and other languages that use different alphabets. Further compounding the problem is that many of these languages use symbols, called ideograms, to represent multiple words and ideas. One solution to the problem of accommodating universal alphabets is Unicode. Unicode is a 16-bit coding scheme that can represent all the world's current, classic, and historical languages in more than 65,000 characters and symbols. In Unicode, 30,000 codes are reserved for future use, such as ancient languages, and 6,000 codes are reserved for private use. Existing ASCII coded data is fully compatible with Unicode because the first 256 codes are the same. Unicode is implemented in several operating systems, including Windows 10, Windows 8, Windows 7, Mac OS X, and Linux. To view a complete Unicode chart, see www.unicode.org.

UNICODE KEYBOARD CHARACTERS				
Decimal	**Hexadecimal**	**Octal**	**Binary**	**Character**
32	20	040	00100000	
33	21	041	00100001	!
34	22	042	00100010	"
35	23	043	00100010	#
36	24	044	00100100	$
37	25	045	00100101	%
38	26	046	00100110	&
39	27	047	00100111	'
40	28	050	00101000	(
41	29	051	00101001	)
42	2A	052	00101010	*
43	2B	053	00101011	+
44	2C	054	00101100	,
45	2D	055	00101101	-
46	2E	056	00101110	.
47	2F	057	00101111	/
48	30	060	00110000	0
49	31	061	00110001	1
50	32	062	00110010	2
51	33	063	00110011	3
52	34	064	00110100	4
53	35	065	00110101	5
54	36	066	00110110	6
55	37	067	00110111	7
56	38	070	00111000	8
57	39	071	00111001	9
58	3A	072	00111010	:
59	3B	073	00111011	;
60	3C	074	00111100	<

FIGURE A-1 (continued)

Decimal	Hexadecimal	Octal	Binary	Character
61	3D	075	00111101	=
62	3E	076	00111110	>
63	3F	077	00111111	?
64	40	100	01000000	@
65	41	101	01000001	A
66	42	102	01000010	B
67	43	103	01000011	C
68	44	104	01000100	D
69	45	105	01000101	E
70	46	106	01000110	F
71	47	107	01000111	G
72	48	110	01001000	H
73	49	111	01001001	I
74	4A	112	01001010	J
75	4B	113	01001011	K
76	4C	114	01001100	L
77	4D	115	01001101	M
78	4E	116	01001110	N
79	4F	117	01001111	O
80	50	120	01010000	P
81	51	121	01010001	Q
82	52	122	01010010	R
83	53	123	01010011	S
84	54	124	01010100	T
85	55	125	01010101	U
86	56	126	01010110	V
87	57	127	01010111	W
88	58	130	01011000	X
89	59	131	01011001	Y
90	5A	132	01011010	Z

FIGURE A-1 (continued)

Decimal	Hexadecimal	Octal	Binary	Character
91	5B	133	01011011	[
92	5C	134	01011100	\
93	5D	135	01011101	]
94	5E	136	01011110	^
95	5F	137	01011111	]
96	60	140	01100000	,
97	61	141	01100001	a
98	62	142	01100010	b
99	63	143	01100011	c
100	64	144	01100100	d
101	65	145	01100101	e
102	66	146	01100110	f
103	67	147	01100111	g
104	68	150	01101000	h
105	69	151	01101001	i
106	6A	152	01101010	j
107	6B	153	01101011	k
108	6C	154	01101100	l
109	6D	155	01101101	m
110	6E	156	01101110	n
111	6F	157	01101111	o
112	70	160	01110000	p
113	71	161	01110001	q
114	72	162	01110010	r
115	73	163	01110011	s
116	74	164	01110100	t
117	75	165	01110101	u
118	76	166	01110110	v
119	77	167	01110111	w
120	78	170	01111000	x

FIGURE A-1 (continued)

Decimal	Hexadecimal	Octal	Binary	Character
121	79	171	01111001	y
122	7A	172	01111010	z
123	7B	173	01111011	{
124	7C	174	01111100	|
125	7D	175	01111101	}
126	7E	176	01111110	~
127	7F	177	01111111	DEL

FIGURE A-1

APPENDIX B

The My Namespace

Rapid application development (RAD) uses a number of tools to help build graphical user interfaces that would normally take a large development effort. One of the Visual Basic RAD tool innovations introduced in the 2005 version and continued with the 2015 version is the **My** namespace. The My namespace provides a shortcut to several categories of information and functionality and is organized so that you can use IntelliSense to find code elements you use often. Microsoft created the My namespace to make it easier to execute common code patterns that you use when developing .NET applications. By providing a shortcut to the most commonly used .NET Framework Class Library classes and methods, the My namespace helps you retrieve settings and resources that your application requires.

The My namespace feature provides rapid access to the classes and methods through the My classes shown in Figure B-1.

Object	Allows Access to
My.Application	The application information and its services such as name, version, log, and current directory.
My.Computer	The host computer and its resources and services. My.Computer provides access to a number of very important resources including My.Computer.Network, My.Computer.FileSystem, and My.Computer.Printers.
My.Forms	All the forms in the current project.
My.Request	The current web request.
My.Resources	The resource elements.
My.Response	The current web response.
My.Settings	The configuration settings of the user and application level. This object enables great personalization without writing many lines of code.

FIGURE B-1 (continued)

Object	Allows Access to
My.User	The security context of the current authenticated user. The My.User object analyzes the user at runtime, which assists security issues.
My.WebServices	The XML web services referenced by the current project. Consuming web services is a necessary ability for modern web applications.

FIGURE B-1

Coding Examples

My is a wrapper that makes accessing the advanced features of .NET easier. For example, you can use the class **My.Application** to determine the version of the current application by using the line of code shown in Figure B-2. Figure B-3 shows the dialog box that displays the version number. You often need to know the latest version of the application to determine whether the application is in final form.

```
MsgBox(My.Application.Info.Version.ToString())
```

FIGURE B-2

FIGURE B-3

The **My.Application** class can also be used to display the current setting of the culture of a computer. Figure B-4 shows the code you can use to display the culture, which is the language that the computer has been assigned in the language settings. In Figure B-5, the culture is set to English – United States.

```
MsgBox(My.Application.Culture.ToString())
```

FIGURE B-4

FIGURE B-5

Another class called **My.Computer** can return information about the computer on which the application is deployed, as determined at runtime. The My.Computer class provides properties for manipulating computer components such as audio, the clock, the keyboard, and the file system. The My.Computer class can play .wav files and system sounds using the Audio object. You can use the My.Computer.Audio.Play and My.Computer.Audio.PlaySystemSound methods to play .wav sound files and system sounds. The code shown in Figure B-6 plays a .wav file named beachmusic.wav.

```
My.Computer.Audio.Play("C:\beachmusic.wav")
```

FIGURE B-6

A .wav file can also be played in the background when a file named AudioPlayMode.Background is specified, as shown in Figure B-7.

```
My.Computer.Audio.Play("C:\blues.wav", _
            AudioPlayMode.Background)
```

FIGURE B-7

The My.Computer class can access the Clipboard and show what is temporarily stored in the system buffer. For example, if you copied the phrase, "Examples of the My.Computer Class", the phrase would be stored in the Clipboard system buffer of the computer. Use the code shown in Figure B-8 to display the contents of the Clipboard in a dialog box, as shown in Figure B-9.

```
MsgBox(My.Computer.Clipboard.GetText())
```

FIGURE B-8

FIGURE B-9

The My.Computer class can access an object that provides properties for displaying the current local date and time according to the system clock by entering the code shown in Figure B-10. Figure B-11 shows the dialog box that displays the system date and time.

```
MsgBox(My.Computer.Clock.LocalTime.ToString())
```

FIGURE B-10

FIGURE B-11

Another My.Computer class determines the current state of the keyboard, such as which keys are pressed, including the CAPS LOCK or NUM LOCK key. The code shown in Figure B-12 provides a true result if the CAPS LOCK key has been pressed. Figure B-13 shows the dialog box that displays the result.

```
MsgBox(My.Computer.Keyboard.CapsLock.ToString())
```

FIGURE B-12

FIGURE B-13

The My.Computer.Mouse class allows you to determine the state and hardware characteristics of the attached mouse, such as the number of buttons or whether the mouse has a wheel. The code shown in Figure B-14 determines if the mouse has a wheel, and Figure B-15 shows the dialog box that displays the result.

```
MsgBox(My.Computer.Mouse.WheelExists.ToString())
```

FIGURE B-14

FIGURE B-15

The My.Computer.Network class interacts with the network to which the computer is connected. For example, if the code in Figure B-16 is entered in the code window, the result would be true, as shown in Figure B-17, if the computer is connected to an intranet or Internet network.

```
MsgBox(My.Computer.Network.IsAvailable.ToString())
```

FIGURE B-16

FIGURE B-17

You can use the My.Computer.Network class to ping another computer. Ping is a basic network function that allows you to verify a particular IP address exists and can accept requests. Ping is used diagnostically to ensure that a host computer you are trying to reach is operating. The code shown in Figure B-18 determines if the IP address is active, and the dialog box shown in Figure B-19 displays the result.

```
MsgBox(My.Computer.Network.Ping("71.2.41.1"))
```

FIGURE B-18

FIGURE B-19

The My.Computer.Screen object can be used to determine many properties of the screen connected to the computer system. You can determine the properties of each monitor attached to the computer system, including the name, the brightness of the screen, and the working area size. The number of bits per pixel can be determined by the code shown in Figure B-20. In a digitized image, the number of bits used to represent the brightness contained in each pixel is called bits per pixel. *Bits per pixel* is a term that represents the brightness of the screen resolution. Figure B-21 shows the result of the code.

```
MsgBox(My.Computer.Screen.BitsPerPixel.ToString())
```

FIGURE B-20

FIGURE B-21

The My.Computer.Screen class can also display the current resolution of the user screen, as shown in Figures B-22 and B-23.

```
MsgBox(My.Computer.Screen.Bounds.Size.ToString())
```

FIGURE B-22

FIGURE B-23

Another class called **My.User** allows you to gather information about the current user. The code example in Figure B-24 shows how to use the **My.User.Name** property to view the user's log in name. An application uses Windows authentication by default, so **My.User** returns the Windows information about the user who started the application, as shown in Figure B-25.

```
MsgBox(My.User.Name)
```

FIGURE B-24

FIGURE B-25

The My namespace also provides a simpler way of opening multiple forms in the same project by using the My.Forms object. If the project includes more than one form, the code shown in Figure B-26 opens a second form named Form2.

```
My.Forms.Form2.Show()
```

FIGURE B-26

Naming Conventions

The table in Figure C-1 displays the common data types used in Visual Basic 2012 with the recommended naming convention for the three-character prefix preceding variable names of the data type.

Data Type	Sample Value	Memory	Range of Values	Prefix
Integer	48	4 bytes	$-2,147,483,648$ to $+2,147,483,647$	int
Double	5.3452307	8 bytes	$-1.79769313486232E308$ to $+1.79769313486232E308$	dbl
Decimal	3.14519	16 bytes	Decimal values that may have up to 29 significant digits	dec
Char	'?' or 'C'	2 bytes	Single character	chr
String	"The Dow is up .03%"	Depends on number of characters	Letters, numbers, symbols	str
Boolean	True or False	Typically 2 bytes; depends on implementing platform	True or False	bln

FIGURE C-1

The table in Figure C-2 displays the less common data types used in Visual Basic 2012 with the recommended naming convention for the three-character prefix preceding variable names of the data type.

Data Type	Sample Value	Memory	Range of Values	Prefix
Byte	7	1 byte	0 to 255	byt
Date	April 22, 2014	8 bytes	0:00:00 (midnight) on January 1, 0001 through 11:59:59 PM on December 31, 9999	dtm
Long	345,234,567	8 bytes	−9,223,372,036,854,775,808 to +9,223,372,036,854,775,807	lng
Object	Holds a reference	4 bytes (32-bit) 8 bytes (64-bit)	A memory address	obj
Short	16,567	2 bytes	−32,768 to 32,767	shr
Single	234,654.1246	4 bytes	−3.4028235E+38 to −1.401298E−45 for negative values and 1.401298E−45 to 3.4028235E+38 for positive values	sng

FIGURE C-2

Form Object Naming Conventions

The table in Figure C-3 displays the prefix naming conventions for Form objects. The three-letter prefixes used before variables names especially are helpful when you use IntelliSense.

Object Type	Prefix	Object Type	Prefix
Button	btn	ListBox	lst
Calendar	cld	MenuStrip	mnu
CheckBox	chk	NumericUpDown	nud
ComboBox	cbo	PictureBox	pic
CompareValidator	cmv	RadioButton	rad
DataGrid	dgd	RangeValidator	rgv
DateTimePicker	dtp	RegularExpressionValidator	rev
DropDownList	ddl	RequiredFieldValidator	rfv
Form	frm	TextBox	txt
GroupBox	grp	ValidationSummary	vsm
Label	lbl		

FIGURE C-3

INDEX